FORTRAN/77

An Introduction to Structured Problem Solving

FORTRAN/77

An Introduction to Structured Problem Solving

V. A. Dyck
J. D. Lawson
University of Waterloo

J. A. Smith
Dataproc Computer Consultants & Services Inc.

A RESTON BOOK
PRENTICE-HALL, INC., Englewood Cliffs, New Jersey 07632

Library of Congress Cataloging in Publication Data

Dyck, V. A.
  FORTRAN/77.

  Includes Index.
  1. FORTRAN (Computer program language) 2. Mathe-
matics—Computer programs. 3. Electronic digital
computers—Programming. I. Lawson, J. D. (John
Douglas) II. Smith, J. A. III. Title.
IV. Title: FORTRAN/seventy-seven.
QA76.73.F25D9 1983   001.64'24   83-13865
ISBN 0-8359-3163-3

© 1984 by Prentice-Hall, Inc.
A Division of Simon & Schuster
Englewood Cliffs, New Jersey 07632

10 9

Printed in the United States of America
from camera-ready pages supplied by the authors

To our parents:

Victor and Helen;
Gordon and Alice;

Gordon and Jean;
Jack and Sylvia;

James and Thelma.

Contents

Preface   *xix*

Part A   Problem Solving Techniques

1   Introduction to Problem Solving   *1*
   1.1   Computers in Perspective   *1*
   1.2   Transition: Computers and Problem Solving   *2*
   1.3   What is Problem Solving?   *2*
   1.4   The Mathematical Problem-Solving Process   *3*
   1.5   Problem-Solving Procedures   *4*
   1.6   Summary   *4*
   1.7   References   *4*
   1.8   Exercises   *5*

2   Problem Solving and Algorithms   *7*
   2.1   Introduction   *7*
   2.2   Pseudocode   *7*
   2.3   The Basics — A First Algorithm   *8*
      2.3.1   Variables   *9*
      2.3.2   Constants   *9*
      2.3.3   Assignment Operations   *10*
      2.3.4   The **put** Action   *10*
      2.3.5   The **stop** Action   *11*
   2.4   Repetition — A Second Algorithm   *11*
      2.4.1   The **while–do** Action   *14*
   2.5   Specifying Data — A Third Algorithm   *15*
      2.5.1   The **get** Action   *17*
   2.6   Selecting Alternatives — A Fourth Algorithm   *17*
      2.6.1   Conditions and Logical Operators   *19*
      2.6.2   The **if–then–else** Action   *20*

      2.6.3 The **if–then** Action *21*

  2.7 Another Approach to Repetition *22*
      2.7.1 The **for** Statement *23*

  2.8 Ups and Downs at the Indianapolis 500 *23*

  2.9 The Money Changing Problem *25*

  2.10 The Structure of Algorithms *26*

  2.11 Summary *29*

  2.12 Exercises *31*

3 Algorithms and FORTRAN/77 *37*

  3.1 Introduction *37*

  3.2 From Pseudocode to Programming Languages *38*
      3.2.1 Translation to BASIC *38*
      3.2.2 Translation to PASCAL *39*
      3.2.3 Translation to FORTRAN *41*
      3.2.4 Translation Summary *42*

  3.3 Processing a FORTRAN/77 Program *42*
      3.3.1 Handling Errors *44*

  3.4 FORTRAN/77 Features *48*
      3.4.1 Defining the Rules *48*
      3.4.2 Constants and Variables in FORTRAN/77 *48*
      3.4.3 Arithmetic Expressions and Assignment Statements *51*
      3.4.4 FORTRAN/77 Input—READ *52*
      3.4.5 FORTRAN/77 Output—PRINT *53*

  3.5 A Temperature Rating Algorithm in FORTRAN/77 *54*

  3.6 FORTRAN/77 Control Structures *55*
      3.6.1 Conditions *56*
      3.6.2 The **if–then–else** Statement *58*
      3.6.3 Control of Repetition in FORTRAN/77 *58*

  3.7 The STOP and END Statements *59*

  3.8 Summary *60*

  3.9 References *61*

  3.10 Exercises *61*

4 Elementary Algorithmic Techniques *67*

  4.1 Introduction *67*

  4.2 The Money Changing Problem Revisited *67*
      4.2.1 Integer Data Types in FORTRAN/77 *68*
      4.2.2 Built-in Functions *70*
      4.2.3 Basic Input and Output Techniques *70*
      4.2.4 End-of-Data Techniques—Counters and Flags *72*

  4.3 The Cashier's Problem *74*
      4.3.1 Developing the Algorithm *74*
      4.3.2 Translation into FORTRAN/77 *77*
      4.3.3 Conversion between REAL and INTEGER *82*

  4.4 A Prime Number Classification Problem *82*
      4.4.1 A First Algorithm *83*
      4.4.2 A More Efficient Algorithm *83*
      4.4.3 The LOGICAL Data Type *85*

  4.5 Correctness of Algorithms *87*
      4.5.1 Manual Testing of Algorithms *88*
      4.5.2 Testing of Programs *91*

  4.6 Summary *92*

  4.7 Exercises *92*

5   Modules and Subprograms   97
   5.1   Introduction to Modules   *97*
   5.2   Modules in Pseudocode   *98*
      5.2.1   Subroutine Modules   *99*
      5.2.2   A Prime Number Classification Algorithm as a Subroutine Module   *100*
      5.2.3   Using the Prime Number Classification Subroutine   *100*
      5.2.4   Function Modules   *101*
      5.2.5   Function Modules in the Prime Number Classification Problem   *102*
   5.3   Subroutines and Functions in FORTRAN/77   *103*
      5.3.1   FORTRAN/77 Subroutine Subprograms   *104*
      5.3.2   FORTRAN/77 Function Subprograms   *107*
   5.4   The Prime-Pairs Problem   *110*
   5.5   A Three Number Ordering Problem   *112*
      5.5.1   Developing the Algorithm   *113*
      5.5.2   Translation to FORTRAN/77   *114*
   5.6   Summary   *116*
   5.7   Exercises   *117*

Part B   Mathematical Functions and Applications

6   Characteristics of Mathematical Functions   125
   6.1   Introduction   *125*
   6.2   Functional Characteristics   *125*
   6.3   Function Tabulation   *127*
      6.3.1   Function Tabulation with Fractional Increments   *129*
   6.4   Evaluating Polynomials: Horner's Rule   *131*
   6.5   Trials and Tribulations of Function Evaluation   *132*
      6.5.1   Transcendental Functions   *132*
      6.5.2   Evaluating Rational Functions   *134*
      6.5.3   Functions in General   *136*
   6.6   Plotting a Single Function   *137*
   6.7   Plotting Several Functions   *140*
   6.8   Summary   *142*
   6.9   Exercises   *145*

7   Locating Zeros and Root Finding   151
   7.1   Introduction   *151*
   7.2   Graphical Search for a Zero   *152*
   7.3   Automatic Search for a Zero   *155*
   7.4   Systematic Refinement of the Zero Estimate   *155*
   7.5   Bisection   *159*
      7.5.1   Bisection as a Subroutine Module   *163*
   7.6   Faster Algorithms   *166*
      7.6.1   The Regula-Falsi Method   *167*
      7.6.2   The Secant Method   *168*
      7.6.3   Newton's Method   *171*
      7.6.4   Other Algorithms   *173*
   7.7   Summary   *173*
   7.8   References   *173*
   7.9   Exercises   *175*

8   Area Finding   *181*
   8.1   Introduction   *181*
   8.2   The Area Approximated by Sums   *182*
   8.3   Rectangle Rules   *182*
   8.4   Trapezoidal Rule   *184*
   8.5   Error Estimation for the Trapezoidal Rule   *187*
   8.6   Simpson's Rule   *188*
   8.7   Error Estimation for Simpson's Rule   *189*
   8.8   Summary   *191*
   8.9   References   *193*
   8.10 Exercises   *193*

Part C   Design and Efficiency of Algorithms

9   Algorithm Design   *199*
   9.1   Introduction   *199*
   9.2   Top-Down Design of Algorithms   *199*
   9.3   Step-Wise Refinement Using Pseudocode   *200*
   9.4   Techniques of Step-Wise Refinement   *200*
      9.4.1   The Prime Number Classification Problem   *203*
      9.4.2   The Cashier's Problem   *205*
   9.5   A Complete Algorithm Development   *206*
      9.5.1   The Quadratic Equation Problem   *206*
   9.6   Modularity as Part of Top-Down Design   *211*
      9.6.1   A Twin Primes Algorithm   *211*
   9.7   Summary   *213*
   9.8   References   *214*
   9.9   Exercises   *214*

10   Applications of Algorithm Design   *223*
   10.1   Introduction   *223*
   10.2   Computing the Area Between Two Curves   *223*
   10.3   The Depth Gauge Problem   *231*
   10.4   The Volume Gauge Problem   *237*
   10.5   Summary   *243*
   10.6   References   *244*
   10.7   Exercises   *244*

11   Efficiency of Algorithms   *251*
   11.1   Introduction   *251*
   11.2   Measures of Efficiency   *251*
   11.3   Determining Efficiency   *254*
      11.3.1   Efficiency of a Factoring Algorithm   *254*
      11.3.2   Efficiency of the Prime Number Classification Algorithms   *259*
      11.3.3   Efficiency of Algorithms for the Pythagorean Triples Problem   *261*
   11.4   Optimizations in General   *265*
   11.5   Summary   *265*
   11.6   References   *266*
   11.7   Exercises   *266*

Part D   Handling Large Masses of Data

12   Handling Large Masses of Data   *271*
   12.1   Introduction   *271*
   12.2   One-Dimensional Arrays in Pseudocode   *272*
      12.2.1   Representation   *272*
      12.2.2   Input and Output   *272*
      12.2.3   Processing   *273*
      12.2.4   Applications of Simple Arrays   *273*
   12.3   One-Dimensional Arrays in FORTRAN/77   *275*
      12.3.1   Representation   *275*
      12.3.2   Input and Output   *276*
      12.3.3   Applications of Simple Arrays   *278*
   12.4   Multidimensional Arrays   *279*
   12.5   Multidimensional Arrays in Pseudocode   *279*
      12.5.1   Representation   *280*
      12.5.2   Input and Output   *280*
      12.5.3   Processing   *281*
      12.5.4   Applications   *281*
   12.6   Multidimensional Arrays in FORTRAN/77   *283*
      12.6.1   Representation   *283*
      12.6.2   Input and Output   *285*
      12.6.3   Processing   *286*
      12.6.4   Applications   *286*
   12.7   Arrays and Modules   *286*
   12.8   Summary   *293*
   12.9   References   *293*
   12.10 Exercises   *294*

13   Searching and Sorting Techniques   *303*
   13.1   Introduction   *303*
   13.2   Searching Techniques   *304*
      13.2.1   Simple Linear Searches   *304*
      13.2.2   A Binary Search   *305*
      13.2.3   Efficiency of Linear Versus Binary Searches   *311*
   13.3   Sorting Techniques   *311*
      13.3.1   A Simple Selection Sort   *311*
      13.3.2   An Exchange Sort   *315*
      13.3.3   An Insertion Sort   *319*
      13.3.4   Quicksort   *321*
      13.3.5   Comparison of Sorting Methods   *336*
   13.4   Using Sorts in Applications   *336*
      13.4.1   Sorting With Added Information   *337*
      13.4.2   Sorting With a Compound Sort Key   *339*
      13.4.3   Application to a Specific Example   *339*
   13.5   Summary   *342*
   13.6   References   *342*
   13.7   Exercises   *343*

14   Statistics   *349*
   14.1   Introduction   *349*
   14.2   Tables and Graphs   *350*
      14.2.1   Frequency Tables   *351*
      14.2.2   Histograms   *353*
      14.2.3   Frequency Polygons and Curves   *359*
   14.3   Measures of Central Tendency   *363*

14.3.1   The Mean   *363*
14.3.2   The Median   *364*
14.3.3   The Mode   *364*
14.4   Measures of Dispersion   *365*
14.4.1   Mean Deviation   *365*
14.4.2   The Standard Deviation   *366*
14.4.3   The Variance   *368*
14.5   Computing the Statistical Measures   *368*
14.5.1   Analyzing Some Real-Life Data   *370*
14.6   The Normal Distribution   *372*
14.6.1   Standard Form of the Normal Distribution   *374*
14.7   Relationships Between Sets of Measurements   *376*
14.7.1   Scatter Plots and Correlation   *376*
14.7.2   Regression   *380*
14.8   Special Languages for Statistical Analysis   *385*
14.9   Summary   *386*
14.10   References   *386*
14.11   Exercises   *386*

15   Vectors, Matrices, and Linear Equations   *391*
15.1   Introduction   *391*
15.2   A Marketing Example   *391*
15.3   Matrix-Vector Multiplication   *392*
15.3.1   A Module for Matrix-Vector Multiplication   *393*
15.3.2   Applications of Matrix-Vector Multiplication   *395*
15.4   Multiplication of Matrices   *400*
15.4.1   A Matrix Multiplication Module   *401*
15.4.2   Applications of Matrix Multiplication   *402*
15.5   Undoing a Transformation or Solving Equations.   *406*
15.5.1   Solving Triangular Systems of Equations   *407*
15.5.2   A Module for Solving Triangular Systems of Equations   *408*
15.5.3   Solving General Systems of Linear Equations.   *409*
15.5.4   Using the Linear Equation Modules   *417*
15.6   Summary   *419*
15.7   References   *419*
15.8   Exercises   *420*

Part E   Simulation Techniques

16   Deterministic Simulation   *427*
16.1   Introduction   *427*
16.2   Simulation Models   *427*
16.3   Structure of Simulation Model Programs   *428*
16.4   An Investment Example   *429*
16.5   Pursuit Problems   *432*
16.5.1   The Bull-Hiker Pursuit Problem   *432*
16.6   Problems in Dynamics   *440*
16.6.1   The Bouncing Ball Problem   *440*
16.7   Population Dynamics   *444*
16.7.1   A Model for Single Species Populations   *444*
16.7.2   A Model for Single Species Populations with Competition   *444*
16.7.3   A Prey-Predator System   *446*
16.7.4   An Alternate Prey-Predator Model   *449*
16.8   Summary   *452*
16.9   References   *455*
16.10   Exercises   *456*

17 Probabilistic Simulation *463*
  17.1 Introduction *463*
  17.2 Simulating Stochastic Processes — Random Numbers *464*
  17.3 Uniformly Distributed Random Numbers *465*
    17.3.1 Generation of Uniformly Distributed Random Numbers *465*
    17.3.2 Uniformly Distributed Random Numbers in the Range [0,1) *466*
  17.4 Using Uniformly Distributed Random Numbers *468*
    17.4.1 Continuous Mappings of Standard Uniform Variates *468*
    17.4.2 Discrete Mappings of Standard Uniform Variates *469*
  17.5 The Investment Problem Revisited *471*
  17.6 Rolling a Die *472*
  17.7 Other Distributions *477*
    17.7.1 Generating Normally Distributed Variates *477*
    17.7.2 Generating Exponentially Distributed Variates *478*
    17.7.3 Generating Poisson Distributed Variates *479*
  17.8 Queuing Systems *481*
    17.8.1 Simulation of a Single-Pump Gas Station *482*
  17.9 Simulation of a Multiple-Pump Gas Station *489*
  17.10 Summary *493*
  17.11 References *493*
  17.12 Exercises *495*

Appendices

A A Summary of Pseudocode Algorithms *503*
  A.1 Constants *503*
  A.2 Variables *503*
  A.3 Arrays *504*
  A.4 Expressions *504*
  A.5 Assignment Statements *505*
  A.6 The **stop** Statement *506*
  A.7 Comment Statements *506*
  A.8 The **get** Statement *506*
  A.9 The **put** Statement *507*
  A.10 The **while–do** Statement *507*
  A.11 The **for** Statement *507*
  A.12 The **if–then–else** Statement *508*
  A.13 Modules *508*

B Algorithms Expressed in Flowcharts *511*
  B.1 Introduction *511*
  B.2 Basic Flowchart Symbols *511*
  B.3 Terminal Elements *512*
  B.4 Assignment Operations *512*
  B.5 The **get** Element *513*
  B.6 The **put** Element *513*
  B.7 The **while–do** Element *514*
  B.8 The **if–then–else** Element *515*
    B.8.1 The **if–then** Element *515*
  B.9 Drawing a Complete Flowchart *516*

C   Translation of Pseudocode to FORTRAN/77   *519*

   C.1 Constants   *520*
   C.2 Variables   *520*
   C.3 Arrays   *521*
   C.4 Expressions   *521*
   C.5 Assignment Statements   *522*
   C.6 The **stop** and STOP Statements   *523*
   C.7 Comment Statements   *523*
   C.8 The **get** and READ Statements   *523*
   C.9 The **put** and PRINT Statement   *524*
   C.10 The **if-then-else** and IF–THEN–ELSE Statements   *524*
   C.11 The **while-do** and FORTRAN/77 Equivalents   *525*
   C.12 The **for** and DO Statements   *525*
   C.13 Modules and Subprograms   *527*

D   Summary of FORTRAN/77 Statements and Rules   *529*

   D.1 Arithmetic Expressions   *530*
   D.2 Arithmetic IF   *531*
   D.3 Arrays   *532*
   D.4 ASSIGN Statement   *537*
   D.5 Assigned GOTO Statement   *538*
   D.6 Assignment Statements   *539*
   D.7 BACKSPACE Statement   *540*
   D.8 BLOCK DATA Subprogram   *540*
   D.9 Block IF Statement   *541*
   D.10 CALL Statement   *542*
   D.11 CHARACTER Expressions   *542*
   D.12 CHARACTER Statement   *543*
   D.13 CLOSE Statement   *543*
   D.14 COMMENT Line   *544*
   D.15 COMMON Statement   *544*
   D.16 Compile-time Initialization of Variables   *546*
   D.17 COMPLEX Statement   *547*
   D.18 Computed GOTO   *547*
   D.19 Constants   *548*
   D.20 CONTINUE Statement   *549*
   D.21 DATA Statement   *549*
   D.22 DIMENSION Statement   *551*
   D.23 DO Statement and DO Loop   *551*
   D.24 DOUBLE PRECISION Statement   *554*
   D.25 ELSEIF Statement   *554*
   D.26 END Statement   *555*
   D.27 ENDFILE Statement   *555*
   D.28 ENTRY Statement   *556*
   D.29 EQUIVALENCE Statement   *557*
   D.30 Executable and Non-Executable Statements   *559*
   D.31 Execution-Time Dimensioning of Arrays   *560*
   D.32 EXTERNAL Statement   *561*
   D.33 Files   *562*
   D.34 FORMAT Statement   *562*
   D.35 FUNCTION Subprograms   *563*
   D.36 GOTO Statement   *564*
   D.37 IMPLICIT Statement   *565*

D.38 Input/Output Statements *566*
D.39 Input/Output Statement Specifiers *566*
D.40 INQUIRE Statement *569*
D.41 INTEGER Statement *570*
D.42 Intrinsic (Built-in) Functions *571*
D.43 INTRINSIC Statement *572*
D.44 Logical Expressions *572*
D.45 Logical IF *573*
D.46 LOGICAL Statement *574*
D.47 OPEN Statement *574*
D.48 PARAMETER Statement *575*
D.49 PAUSE Statement *576*
D.50 PRINT Statement *576*
D.51 PROGRAM Statement *577*
D.52 Program Unit *577*
D.53 READ Statement *577*
D.54 REAL Statement *579*
D.55 Relational Expressions *579*
D.56 RETURN Statement *580*
D.57 REWIND Statement *580*
D.58 Statement Format *581*
D.59 Statement FUNCTIONS *582*
D.60 Statement Ordering *583*
D.61 STOP Statement *583*
D.62 SUBROUTINE Subprograms *584*
D.63 Variables *585*
D.64 WRITE Statement *586*

E Internal Representation of Data in FORTRAN/77 *587*
E.1 Number Systems *587*
E.2 Integer Numbers *590*
E.3 Real Numbers *590*
E.4 Character Information *591*
    E.4.1 EBCDIC *591*
    E.4.2 ASCII *592*

F Formatted Input and Output *595*
F.1 Introduction *595*
F.2 Alternate Input and Output Statements *596*
F.3 The FORMAT Statement *596*
F.4 FORMAT Codes and FORMAT Masks *596*
F.5 The A-Mask *597*
F.6 The BN and BZ Codes *598*
F.7 The D-Mask *599*
F.8 The E-Mask *599*
F.9 The F-Mask *601*
F.10 The G-Mask *602*
F.11 The H-Code *603*
F.12 The I-Mask *604*
F.13 The L-Mask *605*
F.14 The P-Mask *606*
F.15 The S-Code *607*
F.16 The T-Code *607*
F.17 The X-Code *608*
F.18 The /-Code *608*

F.19 The *'*-Code   *609*
F.20 The :-Code   *609*
F.21 Using FORMAT Codes and Masks   *610*
    F.21.1 Considerations for Printer Output   *610*
    F.21.2 Considerations for Input   *612*
    F.21.3 Field Counts   *613*
    F.21.4 Group Counts   *614*
    F.21.5 When the Number of Values and Masks Do Not Match   *614*
    F.21.6 General Considerations   *617*

G Character Manipulation   *619*
  G.1 Introduction   *619*
  G.2 Character Constants   *620*
  G.3 Character Manipulation in FORTRAN/77   *620*
    G.3.1 Character Variables and Arrays   *620*
    G.3.2 Compile Time Initialization of Character Variables   *621*
    G.3.3 Character Substrings   *621*
    G.3.4 Character Expressions, Operators and Assignment Statements   *622*
    G.3.5 Input and Output of Character Values   *623*
    G.3.6 Built-in Functions   *624*
    G.3.7 Function Subprograms   *624*
    G.3.8 Using Character Quantities   *625*
  G.4 Character Manipulation with Non-character Variables   *627*
    G.4.1 Character Storage   *627*
    G.4.2 Assignment of Character Values   *627*
    G.4.3 Input and Output of Character Values   *629*
    G.4.4 Using Character Quantities   *630*

H Manipulation of Logical Values   *631*
  H.1 Introduction   *631*
  H.2 Logical Constants   *631*
  H.3 Logical Variables   *631*
  H.4 Logical Operators   *632*
  H.5 Relational Operators   *633*
  H.6 Logical Expressions and Assignment Statements   *633*
  H.7 Input and Output of Logical Values   *634*
  H.8 Built-in Functions   *634*
  H.9 Function Subprograms and Statement Functions   *635*
  H.10 An Example Using Logical Variables   *635*

I Manipulation of Extended-Precision Values   *639*
  I.1 Introduction   *639*
  I.2 Extended-Precision Constants   *639*
  I.3 Extended-Precision Variables   *640*
  I.4 Arithmetic Expressions and Assignment Statements   *640*
  I.5 Input and Output of Extended-Precision Values   *641*
  I.6 Built-in Functions   *641*
  I.7 Function Subprograms   *642*
  I.8 Using Extended Precision in a Program   *642*

J Manipulation of Complex Values   *649*
  J.1 Introduction   *649*
  J.2 COMPLEX Constants   *649*
  J.3 COMPLEX Variables   *650*
  J.4 Arithmetic Expressions and Assignment Statements   *650*
  J.5 Input and Output of COMPLEX Values   *651*

J.6 Built-in Functions *651*
J.7 Function Subprograms and Statement Functions *652*
J.8 An Example Using COMPLEX Variables *652*

K The Plotting Package *657*
K.1 SETPLT *657*
K.2 STOPNT *658*
K.3 PLOT *658*

L Data Files *665*
L.1 Student Data File *665*
L.2 Physician Data File *667*
L.3 Indianapolis 500 Data *667*
L.4 Cigarette Tar and Nicotine Data *668*
L.5 National Hockey League Statistics *670*

M Areas Under the Standard Normal Curve *681*

N Built-in FORTRAN/77 Functions *683*

Index *687*

Preface

Computer use continues to grow explosively because of the indispensible role which computers play in daily life. This pervasive aspect of computation makes it critical that all educated people have some exposure to the serious use of computers. This text is intended as an introduction to computing for those students who will have occasion to make use of a computer in a mathematical or scientific context. That is to say, it is intended for future scientists, engineers, mathematicians, economists, and indeed any student for whom work with mathematical models will be of any importance. There is a need to provide students with basic mathematical skills and a knowledge of how these skills relate to the computer. Because the problems which justify computer solution are often large, it is very important that the student should also learn a formal organized approach to problem solving.

On most general purpose computing systems, efficient mathematical routines exist in program libraries to help problem solvers in their task. As a result, the intent in teaching such problem solving is not to create expert mathematical programmers, but rather to create intelligent users who are familiar with good programming practices. That is our aim in writing this text.

A common approach to teaching introductory computer courses has been to get the students on the computer immediately. Although this approach was valid when a prime objective was to teach a computer programming language (and this text certainly could be used in this way), the authors feel that this approach encourages poor programming practices. It has been our observation that students tend to neglect the design phase of program development and to rely instead on ad hoc incremental changes over many trial computer runs, which is wasteful of both human time and computer resources. We do agree that students should get some early exposure to the computer for motivation, excitement, and a sense of achievement. However, we would argue that some minimum level (say a few lectures) of instruction on algorithm design should be undertaken first.

As has been recognized in business and industry, the major effort in a programming exercise should be spent in the design process. Thus, it follows that the major effort in a programming course should be spent in teaching students techniques to facilitate this design process — techniques which are applicable regardless of which computer programming language is to be used. In programming, the major creative task is the algorithm design. Conversion to a computer program is then a routine, albeit painstaking matter.

In terms of the design process, a major step forward was the identification and development of the concepts which are referred to as *structured programming*. Many definitions for structured programming exist but all imply an organized approach to the design, implementation, and testing of computer software. For the purposes of this introductory text, we consider structured programming to be:

a) the use of *top-down design techniques*,
b) the use of *structured language constructions*, and
c) the use of *good coding style.*

It is not intended that this be a text on structured programming but rather a text that illustrates a structured approach to the development of solutions to problems of a mathematical nature.

The emphasis in this text is placed on the development of algorithms and the translation of these algorithms into computer programs. A simple *pseudocode* language is used for the systematic development of algorithms using step-wise refinement.

The use of pseudocode for algorithmic descriptions allows a student to concentrate on algorithm development at varying levels of abstraction without having to worry about the more complicated syntactic details of a particular programming language. The pseudocode language used in the text has a precise definition which makes for easy translation into a computer program. This preciseness is useful so that a beginning student may know what constitutes an acceptable algorithm. The pseudocode allows the control structures of sequence, **while-do** and **if-then-else**. Provision also exists for module definition and subscripted storage.

The language chosen for computer implementation of the pseudocode algorithms is FORTRAN/77. The details of the FORTRAN/77 language are introduced as they become necessary to solve the problems at hand. Complete descriptions of FORTRAN/77 constructs and syntax are supplied as easily referenced appendices.

This book is designed as the text for a first course in computing offered to students with good high-school mathematics backgrounds. There is more material than may reasonably be covered in a first course. However, many students have had some high-school computing experience and may then find the extra material worthwhile. Instructors may also find that very little supplementary material is needed for a two-semester introductory sequence.

Organization of the Text
This text is divided into five parts. The first two parts introduce the basic concepts of algorithms, their design, and their translation into FORTRAN/77. The other three parts deal with the development of mathematical tools and programming techniques for use in applications. As they become necessary for the applications, more advanced algorithmic techniques are introduced and discussed.

In the first part, Chapter 1 provides a perspective on problem solving and introduces the basic actions needed for describing algorithms. Chapter 2 describes how these basic actions may be written in pseudocode and gives examples of simple algorithms to illustrate these actions. Chapter 3 discusses conversion of pseudocode algorithms into several programming languages, with the emphasis on FORTRAN/77. Additional algorithmic techniques are given in Chapter 4 and the development of pseudocode modules and FORTRAN/77 subprograms are discussed in Chapter 5.

The second part is concerned with determining characteristics of mathematical functions and how to use and develop modules and subprograms to learn more about these characteristics. Chapter 6 looks at tabulation and plotting as initial ways of determining characteristics of functions. Chapters 7 and 8 describe methods for finding the zeros of functions and for the computation of areas.

The third part is devoted to the design and efficiency of algorithms. The intuitive design of algorithms used thus far is formalized in terms of top-down design and stepwise refinement in Chapter 9. It should be noted that the material of Chapter 9 has also been taught successfully at the end of part 1 of the text. Chapter 10 demonstrates how to use the modules of Chapters 7 and 8 in the development of solutions to several applied problems. This is followed by a discussion of efficiency in Chapter 11.

The theme of the fourth part is the problem of dealing with large masses of data. Chapter 12 discusses some general ideas concerned with storing and manipulating large quantities of data. Chapter 13 discusses internal sorting and searching algorithms. These aid in the organization of data and the extraction of information from it. Statistical techniques for summarizing the characteristics of masses of data are described in Chapter 14. Chapter 15 deals with vectors, matrices, and linear equations.

The fifth part is concerned with the use of simulation techniques to predict the behaviour of models of physical systems. Chapter 16 describes basic deterministic simulation techniques which are used for systems whose behaviour is predetermined by a set of fixed equations. Chapter 17 describes probabilistic simulation techniques which are used when the changes in a system are subject to some randomness.

Preparation of the Text

This text was developed at the University of Waterloo from the authors' previous texts, which used WATFIV-S and PASCAL.

Draft versions of the manuscript were prepared in machine-readable form and formatted for typesetting. All computer programs have been machine tested by executing them on the VAX VMS FORTRAN/77 compiler. The resulting computer output has been captured and is reproduced in the text with a minimal amount of editing, namely, the condensing of blank lines and spaces to conform to the size limitations of a textbook page. This final version of the book has been produced at the University of Waterloo from the machine-readable text files. The computing for the typesetting was performed at the Mathematics Faculty Computing Facility.

The authors have created a discipline for representing the three stages of problem solving: development of the mathematical model, creation of a pseudocode algorithm, and the translation to a programming language (FORTRAN/77). Unique type styles have been adopted for each of these stages to allow the reader to distinguish between them, and to emphasize references to the stages in the narrative description. For all pseudocode references, a distinctively simple typeface has been chosen.   Furthermore, different weights have been selected for comments and unrefined pseudocode, for pseudocode variables and constants, and for pseudocode keywords. Finally, the FORTRAN/77 programs, the output they produce, as well as references to FORTRAN/77 entities have been typeset in a monospace typeface simliar to that found on many computer line printers.

The authors trust that the presentation of accurate computer programs, virtually exact computer output, and the discipline in typesetting will enhance the reader's confidence and understanding of the material.

Acknowledgements

The authors would like to thank the many instructors, teaching assistants, and students who have assisted in debugging the text material.   We also thank our colleagues for their help and constructive comments over the course of development of this text.   We thank Professor A.K.C. Wong in the Department of Systems Design, for providing access to the VAX computer on which all sample programs were tested.

Finally, the authors gratefully acknowledge the efforts of Waterloo Computer Typography, especially Richard and Beth Beach, who supervised the preparation and phototypesetting of the manuscript.

V. A. Dyck
J. D. Lawson
J. A. Smith
March, 1983

Part A
Problem Solving Techniques

1 Introduction to Problem Solving *1*

2 Problem Solving and Algorithms *7*

3 Algorithms and FORTRAN/77 *37*

4 Elementary Algorithmic Techniques *67*

5 Modules and Subprograms *97*

1
Introduction to Problem Solving

1.1 Computers in Perspective

Computers are an important part of our everyday life. There is such a variety of computer applications that computers affect everyone either directly or indirectly. It is the assistance of computers, their speed, accuracy, and reliability that allows us to solve many problems that were previously difficult or even impossible.

In today's society computers are used in many areas. Business data processing applications include payroll, inventory, and billing systems. Scientists and engineers rely heavily on computers to assist in design and simulation studies. Computers also facilitate the use of the data "banks" found, for example, in medical information systems and airline reservation systems. Physical events, such as the changing of traffic lights and the movement of subway trains, are monitored and controlled by computer. The preparation of letters, reports, books, and newspapers is often accomplished with the aid of a computer. These are but a few of the many applications.

Although computers as we know them are a relatively recent invention, the use of devices to help solve numerical problems is far from new. Most of us have heard of the Chinese abacus, if not of its relative, the Japanese soroban, which were two of the earliest aids to calculations.

Later examples of computing aids included the mechanical adder built by Blaise Pascal in 1642 (to assist in adding long columns of numbers common in his father's tax accounting office) and the stepped-wheel machine of Gottfried Wilhelm Leibniz in 1694. This machine could be used to multiply and divide numbers as well as add them. The "difference" and "analytical" engine designs of Charles Babbage were noteworthy for their time, 1822, even though his ideas were ahead of the available technology, and the devices could never be actually constructed.

Punched card technology was first introduced in 1801 as a mechanism for controlling the complex weaving patterns in the Jacquard loom and later was used for numerical computation by Dr. Herman Hollerith of the United States. Dr. Hollerith, a statistician, was faced with the task of analyzing the 1890 census before it was time for the next census. Recording of information in this medium and performance of numerical calculations under control of punched cards were widely used aids to business data processing and indeed scientific calculations for the next several decades.

Much of the basic computer development took place in the 1930's and 1940's, in many cases in response to problems that arose in the war effort. Ballistic computations and code-breaking were two very important stimuli.

Many technological advances have led to improved versions of these early computers. The vacuum tubes that were important components of the "first generation" machines were bulky, very sensitive to temperature, and quite unreliable. The transistor based "second generation" computers of the 1960's were much more compact and reliable. Transistors in turn gave way to the integrated circuits of today's "third generation" computers. The current components are so small and inexpensive that they have been adapted for use in everyday pocket calculators. In fact whole computers (called microcomputers) may now be constructed on a single "chip," roughly the size of a small finger nail.

1.2   Transition: Computers and Problem Solving

Counting devices, mechanical and electrical calculators, and finally computers arose out of the need to solve problems. In fact, that is still the primary motivation today. Given a problem that is either too lengthy or too large to solve manually, one turns to a computer for assistance.

In order to make use of a computer, it is necessary to describe in an explicit manner exactly what operations are to be performed. These operations must be described to the computer in what is referred to as a *computer programming language*. The collection of operations is called a *computer program*. Many such languages exist for computers. In most cases these languages are best suited to one particular application area.

To use a computer then, it is necessary to learn something about that computer, specifically, to choose and to learn a language for one's application. Generally, these languages are well defined and not too difficult to master. The much more difficult process involves developing the problem to the point where it can easily be expressed in this computer language — this is where the problem solving takes place.

1.3   What is Problem Solving?

The term "problem solving" can be used in many different contexts and therefore can be defined in various ways. In this context, it will be taken to mean the provision of a quantitative answer to some question posed in physical terms. As an example, suppose the question were, "What will the weather be like next Friday?" A quantitative answer might be "With a probability of .4, it will be sunny; with a probability of .4, it will be overcast; and with a probability of .2, it will be raining;" whereas a response like "It likely won't rain" would be a nonquantitative answer.

Typically, the steps leading from the initial question to the quantitative answer require one to:

- analyze the information given in the question
- express the question in mathematical terms
- develop techniques to deal with this mathematics
- interpret the results.

It is impossible to solve a problem correctly until one understands exactly what information is given and what needs to be found.   Although this statement may seem obvious, too often a person begins to solve a problem without taking the time to arrive at an adequate definition of the problem.   As a result, the problem is rarely solved correctly on the first attempt, and much time and effort is wasted iterating toward a solution.

In order to quantify our problem definition, a mathematical statement of the problem is sought.   Solution of this mathematical problem, possibly aided by a computer, leads to quantitative answers to the original question.   At this stage, these answers may be found to be unsatisfactory, thus requiring a redefinition of the problem.

1.4   The Mathematical Problem-Solving Process

Obtaining a solution to a mathematical problem involves the two processes of *development* and *application.* The first process refers to the development of a procedure that describes how a problem or subproblem may be solved.   The second process refers to the application of the problem-solving procedure on a given set of data.

When describing such a procedure, the detail given must be sufficient for it to be followed, either manually or mechanically.   The more sophisticated the follower, the less detail is needed in the procedure.

If a problem is to be solved manually, the problem-solving procedure is generally *developed and applied* concurrently in a step-by-step manner.   Often the result of a given step determines the nature of the subsequent step.   This approach is possible since both the development and application of the problem-solving procedure are performed by the human problem-solver.

When a computer is introduced into problem solving, it assists in the application process.   However, the procedure must be more fully developed before it can be followed by the computer.   As a result, the procedure must allow for the occurrence of all possible outcomes.   Development of such a complete procedure is frequently far from trivial.

Hence, the loss involved in moving from the manual approach to the computer approach is a sacrifice of the versatility inherent in the concurrent development and application of a procedure.   The gain is in the speed, accuracy, and storage capabilities of the computer.   In addition, once a program has been written, it may be reused easily for different sets of data without further development.

1.5   Problem-Solving Procedures

A problem-solving *procedure,* often called an *algorithm,* specifies a set of operations that may be followed in order to solve the problem. Although there are many possible ways in which algorithms could be described, two common methods involve using a *pseudocode* description or a *flowchart* diagram.

A pseudocode description uses English, mathematical notations, and a limited set of special commands to describe the actions of an algorithm. A flowchart diagram provides exactly the same information graphically, using diagrams with a limited set of symbols in the place of the more elegant features of the pseudocode.

Unfortunately, neither pseudocode nor flowcharts are directly understood by a computer. However, the translation from either pseudocode or a flowchart to a computer programming language is relatively easy to learn.

In the description of an algorithm, there are a number of basic actions involved. Typically, it is necessary to find a means of expressing the following six basic activities:

1) specifying data values
2) recording results
3) performing calculations and assigning values
4) testing quantities and selecting alternate courses of actions
5) repeating actions
6) terminating the algorithm

In addition, it is sometimes desirable to have more sophisticated combinations or enhancements, but these activities will be introduced later as they become necessary.

1.6   Summary

The motivation for developing and using computing devices has been, and continues to be, providing assistance in the solution of problems. However, before a computer can be of such assistance, a problem must be formulated precisely. Then it is necessary to develop an algorithm that describes, in a step-by-step manner, precisely how the problem may be solved. Following this, the algorithm is translated into a computer programming language and the resulting program is prepared in machine readable form. Finally, the program is read by the computer and applied to a set of data values.

The above steps will be expanded upon in more detail in succeeding chapters.

1.7   References

Huskey, H.D. and Huskey, V.R. "Chronology of Computing Devices." *IEEE Transactions on Computers* 25(1976):1190-1199. (This article provides an excellent summary of the development of computing devices, beginning with the abacus, through desk calculators and analog computers, and finally, stored program automatic digital computers.)

Rosen, S.   "Electronic Computers: A Historical Survey." *Computing Surveys*
   1(1969):7-36.

Squires, E.   *The Computer – An Everyday Machine.* Reading, Mass.: Addison-Wesley
   Publishing Co., 1977.

Wilkes, M.V.   "Computers Then and Now." *Journal of the ACM* 15(1968):1-7.

1.8   Exercises

1.1   Name several other uses of computers that affect your life.

1.2   What are several future applications of computers that you can think of?

1.3   What are some examples of algorithms that you encounter in everyday life? These
      algorithms need not be mathematically oriented.

1.4   Describe an algorithm for an everyday task such as brushing your teeth, tying
      your shoes, or putting on a coat.   Have a friend follow your instructions *explicit-
      ly.*

1.5   In any group, there will be people of various shapes and sizes.   Describe how you
      would find the tallest person in a group.   How would you find the heaviest person
      in the group?   Describe how your above methods would change if you could look
      at only two people at any one time.

1.6   Describe an algorithm for finding the roots of the quadratic equation
      $ax^2 + bx + c = 0$ using only very simple mathematical operations.

2
Problem Solving and Algorithms

2.1 Introduction

Pseudocode is a language for describing algorithms. Many variations of pseudocode exist as people often develop their own version to suit their particular needs. A pseudocode algorithm consists of a series of statements or instructions which, when followed, will solve a particular problem. These instructions are the means of being precise about the required calculations and related activities so that the person or even an assistant could follow them. Eventually, of course, the "assistant" will be a computer for which instructions are called *code*. Thus, the term pseudocode is used for these instructions.

The pseudocode described in this chapter has been designed to parallel the features found in modern programming languages in order that the transition from a pseudocode algorithm to a computer program can be made easily.

2.2 Pseudocode

Pseudocode must be capable of describing the six basic actions of algorithms. The actions and corresponding pseudocode features follow.

	Action	*Pseudocode Feature*
1)	specifying data	**get**
2)	recording results	**put**
3)	performing calculations and assigning values	assignment operation
4)	testing quantities and selecting alternate courses of action	**if–then–else**
5)	repeating actions	**while–do**
6)	terminating an algorithm	**stop**

A pseudocode algorithm is composed of a set of actions or statements, specified in terms of the above features. The actions are performed sequentially, starting with the first action, and proceeding until termination. In order for a pseudocode algorithm to be correct, it must terminate after a finite number of steps. While exceptions to this idea do exist, that type of problem is beyond the scope of this discussion. Any group of actions listed sequentially will be referred to as an *action sequence.* Such a sequence may contain any combination of the above six actions.

2.3   The Basics — A First Algorithm

To introduce how the pseudocode actions may be used to describe an algorithm, a simple problem will be discussed. The problem is that of converting temperatures expressed in Fahrenheit degrees to temperatures in Celsius degrees. Mathematically, this conversion is expressed in terms of the following formula.

$$c = (f - 32)\frac{5}{9}$$

In algebra, the symbols c and f are called "unknowns" and are used to represent the unknown numeric values of temperature in degrees Celsius and Fahrenheit, respectively. Substitution of a Fahrenheit temperature value, f, into the formula will give the corresponding Celsius temperature for c.

The first algorithm will formalize the steps to be followed to perform a single temperature conversion using the above formula. This problem is stated below.

Example 2.1   Fahrenheit to Celsius Temperature Conversion
Develop an algorithm to take the single Fahrenheit temperature reading, 68°F, and convert the reading to degrees Celsius.

Since the formula for conversion is already known, the solution to this problem is straightforward. The pseudocode algorithm, appearing in Figure 2.1, gives the steps which may be followed or *executed* to perform the necessary conversion.

Figure 2.1   Pseudocode algorithm to convert from Fahrenheit to Celsius.

```
f ← 68
c ← (f − 32)*5/9
put f, c
stop
```

These steps are to be followed sequentially, from top to bottom. The first two statements are assignment operations and are used to express the necessary calculations. The first gives the constant value **68** to the symbol f while the second computes (f−32)*5/9 as (68−32)*5/9 = 36*5/9 = 180/9 = 20 which becomes the value of the symbol c. Notice the use of an asterisk for multiplication and a slash for division. The third statement directs that the results of the algorithm be recorded, that is, that the values of f and c, 68 and 20 respectively, are to be written on a separate sheet of paper. Finally, the **stop** statement indicates the conclusion of the algorithm.

Contained in this simple algorithm are many important concepts and features of pseudocode. These are described in the following subsections.

2.3.1 Variables

A fundamental idea in the algorithm is the use of the symbols c and f. In pseudocode such quantities are called *variables*. Unlike algebra, variables are used to represent known numeric values. In this algorithm the variable f is assigned the Fahrenheit temperature, **68**. Likewise the variable c is assigned the result of the expression which gives the equivalent Celsius temperature, **20**.

In general, variables in pseudocode may consist of any group of alphanumeric characters, that is, letters of the alphabet (a–z) or digits (0–9). The first symbol should be an alphabetic character to avoid confusion with numeric quantities. Listed below are examples of valid and invalid variables.

Valid Variables	*Invalid Variables*
f	2f
c	456
celsius	c+f
dollar	dollar−sign
r2d2	3peeoh

Variables are *undefined* until they have been assigned a value. An undefined variable may not be used in an arithmetic operation. Furthermore, a variable can only have one numeric value at any given time. Once a variable has been given a value, it retains that value until it is changed explicitly.

2.3.2 Constants

As well as variables, the algorithm uses numeric quantities called constants. Constants are simply numbers, such as:

68   32   5   9   −12.34   +3.14159   0. $2.99776*10^{10}$

Constants may be positive (with or without the + sign) or negative, and may be written in exponent form to save writing a long string of zeros.

2.3.3 Assignment Operations

The first two statements in the algorithm in Figure 2.1 are called assignments. The first line f ← 68 is read "f is assigned the value **68**." Similarly, line 2 means "c is assigned the numerical value of the expression (f−32)*5/9."

The assignment operation is the backbone of mathematical algorithms. It is used to express the evaluation of arithmetic expressions and the storage of intermediate results for future use. The general form of the assignment operation is:

variable ← expression

where variable is the name chosen to represent the result and expression indicates the arithmetic operations that are required in the calculation. The ← symbol is the assignment operator and indicates that the expression on the right-hand side (RHS) is to be calculated and *then* its value is to be assigned to the variable on the left-hand side (LHS).

An arithmetic expression can be a single constant; a single variable; or a combination of constants, variables, and the following arithmetic operators, used to express addition, subtraction, multiplication, and division.

+ − * /

Parentheses may also be used to order operations within an expression. Listed below are several arithmetic expressions and their evaluation. Notice that expressions are usually evaluated from left to right, but that given a choice between adjacent operations, exponentiation is completed first and multiplication or division precedes addition or subtraction. The → symbol is used informally to mean "evaluates to."

Expression	*Evaluation*
2 + 3*4	2 + 12 → 14
2.5 + 3^3/4	2.5 + 27/4 → 2.5 + 6.75 → 9.25
1.1 + 2.2 − 3.3	3.3 − 3.3 → 0
(4 + 5)*3	9*3 → 27

2.3.4 The put Action

When the actions of an algorithm are performed, many values may be calculated. In most cases these values will represent intermediate results which need not be recorded permanently as part of the solution to the problem. Therefore, an action is required to indicate those values that are important enough to be recorded. The **put** action is used for this purpose and its general form is:

put output list

where the output list contains messages and/or variables whose values are to be recorded. An output list may contain many such elements separated by commas.

In the previous algorithm, the statement **put** f, c states that the values of f and c are to be written on a separate sheet of paper. Since the numbers by themselves may be difficult to interpret, it is best to include a message to identify them. Thus, a modified **put** statement might be written as:

put f, 'degrees Fahrenheit is', c, 'degrees Celsius'

Note that messages are differentiated from variables by placing a single quote on either side.   Assuming that f and c have been assigned the values 68 and 20, the message written when this statement is performed is

68 degrees Fahrenheit is 20 degrees Celsius

2.3.5   The **stop** Action

Since all algorithms must halt, it is necessary to include a statement to indicate when this termination is to happen.   The pseudocode statement **stop** is used to terminate an algorithm and thus is always the last action performed.   Its general form is:

stop

Though the **stop** statement may appear many times and anywhere in an algorithm, good usage limits the number of occurrences to one, appearing as the last statement of the algorithm.   Such usage removes any doubt about where an algorithm terminates.

2.4   Repetition — A Second Algorithm

The example in the previous section investigated how a single temperature might be converted.   A more likely task requiring an algorithm is the production of a conversion table.   A formal statement of such a request follows.

Example 2.2   Temperature Conversion Table
   Develop an algorithm to produce a table of Fahrenheit and the equivalent Celsius
   temperatures for $0°F$, $1°F$, $2°F$, . . . , $212°F$.

Having accomplished the task of conversion for a single temperature, the solution to this problem would appear to be automatic.   The steps for each degree could be written out as:

```
f ← 0
c ← (f − 32)*5/9
put f, c

f ← 1
c ← (f − 32)*5/9
put f, c

  .
  .
  .

f ← 212
c ← (f − 32)*5/9
put f, c

stop
```

Several things quickly become apparent about this approach.   The task is tedious and there is a great deal of duplication.   In fact, it probably takes longer to *describe* the calculations than to do them by hand.   Since repetition in some form or other is necessary in a large number of calculations, a special pseudocode feature, called the **while–do**, exists.   Figure 2.2 illustrates its use in solving this problem.

Figure 2.2   Pseudocode algorithm to produce a Fahrenheit to Celsius conversion table.

```
* Generate a conversion table from Fahrenheit to Celsius
* for 0°F to 212°F in 1°F increments.

* Variables used:
* f - the Fahrenheit temperature
* c - the Celsius temperature

f ← 0
while f ≤ 212 do
    ⎡  c ← (f − 32)*5/9
    ⎢  put f, '°F is', c, '°C'
    ⎣  f ← f + 1
stop
```

The **while–do** statement specifies that the sequence of statements indicated by the indentation and the brace are to be repeated as long as f ≤ 212.   The variable f is assigned the value 0 prior to the **while** and is increased by 1 each time through the sequence.   These two steps are an integral part of the **while–do** feature.

In the discussion of the previous algorithm, it was mentioned that messages should be included to identify the output.   The **put** statement for this algorithm includes an abbreviation of the suggested messages for the previous example.

This algorithm also includes several lines that begin with an asterisk.   These lines are called *comment* statements and provide an English description of the algorithm to help the person reading the algorithm to understand the significance of the pseudocode statements.   In this example, the first two lines simply state the purpose of the algorithm.   Following the purpose is a list of variables and how they are used in the algorithm to follow.

Portions of the application of this algorithm are given in Figure 2.3.   A total of 855 statements are performed to complete the algorithm.

The process exhibited in this diagram is sometimes called *stepping through* the algorithm.   It is a worthwhile exercise to test an algorithm in this way for a few steps before converting it to a computer program.   The output that this process produces is illustrated as Figure 2.4.

The next subsection will explore the details of the **while–do** feature.

Figure 2.3   Step-by-step application of the Fahrenheit to Celsius conversion table algorithm of Figure 2.2.

Step	Statement Performed	Action Specified
1)	f ← 0	The variable f is assigned the value 0.
2)	**while** f ≤ 212 **do**	Since f is 0 and hence less than 212, perform the statements in the brace.
3)	c ← (f − 32)*5/9	compute (f−32)*5/9 → (0−32)*5/9 → (−32)*5/9 → (−160)/9 → −17.778 Assign −17.778 to the variable c.
4)	**put** f, '°F is', c, '°C'	Write the values of f and c, 0 and −17.778, and the messages on a separate piece of paper.
5)	f ← f + 1	Compute f+1 → 0+1 → 1 and assign 1 to f.
6)	**while** f ≤ 212 **do**	Since f is 1 and hence less than 212, perform the statements in the brace.
7)	c ← (f−32)*5/9	Compute (f−32)*5/9 → −17.222 Assign −17.222 to c.
8)	**put** f, '°F is', c, '°C'	Write the values of f and c, 1 and −17.222, and the messages on the piece of paper.
9)	f ← f + 1	Compute f+1 → 2 and assign 2 to f.
10)	**while** f ≤ 212 **do**	Since f is 2 and hence less than 212, perform the statements in the brace.
⋮	⋮	⋮
850)	**while** f ≤ 212 **do**	Since f is 212 and hence equal to 212, perform the statements in the brace.
851)	c ← (f−32)*5/9	Compute (f−32)*5/9 → 100 Assign 100 to c.
852)	**put** f, '°F is', c, '°C'	Write the values of f and c, 212 and 100, and the messages on the piece of paper.
853)	f ← f + 1	Compute f+1 → 213 and assign 213 to f.
854)	**while** f ≤ 212 **do**	Since f is 213 and hence greater than 212, continue with the first statement beyond the brace.
855)	**stop**	Terminate the application process.

Figure 2.4   Partial output from the Fahrenheit to Celsius conversion table algorithm from Figure 2.2.

0°F is −17.778°C
1°F is −17.222°C
⋮
⋮
212°F is 100°C

2.4.1 The while–do Action

In the previous example, the **while–do** feature was used to specify repetition of actions. Its general form follows:

while condition **do**
$$\left[\; \text{S} \right.$$

S is an action sequence, the set of statements to be repeated.   A brace or bracket as well as indentation is used to group the statements that form S.   This group of statements is called the _range_ of the **while** loop.   In the previous example, the action sequence consisted of the three statements:

c ← (f − 32)*5/9
put f, c
f ← f + 1

The condition is a _logical expression_ which tests the relationship between one or more pairs of arithmetic expressions and has a value of **true** or **false**.   The relationship between two arithmetic expressions may be tested using one of the following operators, called _relational operators_.

$$= \; \neq \; < \; \leq \; > \; \geq$$

The condition in the previous example was f ≤ 212.   Any variables contained in the condition are called _control variables_ of the **while–do** action.   In the example, f was the sole control variable.

The operation of the **while–do** feature may be understood by following the arrows in the picture in Figure 2.5.   Starting at the top of the picture, the arrow points to a diamond-shaped box containing the condition from the **while–do** statement.   Thus, the first step is to evaluate the condition.   If the condition is **true**, the exit arrow labeled **true** is taken from the diamond box to the rectangular box containing the action sequence S. Following the completion of the action sequence, the arrow points back to the condition in the diamond box.   The condition is reevaluated and the decision is made again.   As long as the condition is **true**, the action sequence is repeated.   If the value of the condition is **false**, either initially or following the completion of S, execution continues with the statements following the **while–do** action, that is, the first pseudocode statement following the brace.

In order to use **while–do** actions in an algorithm, however, more information must be specified.   In fact, each **while–do** has associated with it three important operations. Each operation is _essential_ for the **while–do** action to function correctly.   The operations are:

1) The initialization of the **while–do** control variables in actions preceding the **while–do** itself.   (The condition can not be evaluated unless its control variables have values.)
2) The condition evaluation, which controls termination of the **while–do** repetition.
3) The action sequence S which must change at least one **while–do** control variable. (If no control variable is ever changed by the action sequence, the **while–do** will never terminate.)

Figure 2.5 Operation of the **while–do** action.

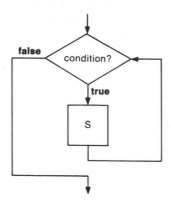

A careful analysis of the algorithm of Figure 2.2 reveals that all three of the above operations are present. The control variable, f, is assigned a value prior to the **while–do**. The condition involves evaluating f ≤ 212. Within the action sequence, the value of f is increased by 1. Thus, all three elements are accounted for.

2.5 Specifying Data — A Third Algorithm

The algorithm of Figure 2.1 was written to convert a single temperature reading from Fahrenheit to Celsius. The next algorithm in Figure 2.2 performed a similar conversion for the specific range 0°F to 212°F. Frequently, an algorithm is to be applied to a number of values that either are not known in advance or are difficult to generate in an assignment action. Thus, a mechanism is required to supply the algorithm with the necessary values, referred to as *data*. The next example illustrates such a situation.

Example 2.3   Converting 7 Temperatures
    Temperature readings from countries using the metric system are given in degrees Celsius. Develop an algorithm that will convert the Celsius temperature readings from 7 foreign locations to Fahrenheit degrees.

The formula for this conversion may be obtained by rearranging the previous formula as follows.

$$f = \frac{9}{5}c + 32$$

The definition of the problem implies that this conversion is to be applied repetitively to 7 unknown values. As was seen earlier, a convenient way to repeat such an operation is to make it part of a **while–do** action. Figure 2.6 illustrates this feature in solving Example 2.3. To accomplish the repetition 7 times, the variable count acts as a counter. It is assigned the initial value 1 and increased by 1 each time a conversion takes place.   To obtain the 7 values, the **get** action is used.   The statement **get** c is an instruction to find a value for c from a data list.   This data list is usually placed immediately following the **stop** statement.   In this case, the Celsius temperatures to be converted are 15, 18, 22, 25, 10, 8, and 15.

Figure 2.6   Pseudocode algorithm to convert 7 temperatures from Celsius to Fahrenheit.

* Convert 7 temperatures from Celsius to Fahrenheit.

* Variables used:
* c - the Celsius temperature
* f - the Fahrenheit temperature
* **count** - the counter for number of values processed

put 'Celsius', 'Fahrenheit'
count ← 1
while count ≤ 7 **do**

      get c
      f ← (9/5)*c + 32
      put c, f
      count ← count + 1

stop

15,18,22,25,10,8,15

Previous examples discussed the benefits of identifying numerical output from an algorithm with appropriate messages.   In this algorithm, a **put** statement to record the meaning of the numbers is located before the **while**–loop.   As a result, the words Fahrenheit and Celsius are recorded only once, before the numbers produced inside the **while**–loop.   Thus, these words will appear as column headings.

The table in Figure 2.7 indicates the action of the **get** statement on the data list and the values that the variables are given as the algorithm is performed.   The values of c are changed by the **get** statement; f is changed by the conversion formula.   The initial value of count is obtained through the statement count ← 1 and all remaining values from the statement count ← count + 1.   Note that before the algorithm is started, all variables are undefined.

Figure 2.7   Table of values for the Celsius to Fahrenheit conversion algorithm of Figure 2.6.

count	c	f	data list remaining
undefined	undefined	undefined	15,18,22,25,10,8,15
1	15	59	18,22,25,10,8,15
2	18	64.4	22,25,10,8,15
3	22	71.6	25,10,8,15
4	25	77	10,8,15
5	10	50	8,15
6	8	46.4	15
7	15	59	
8	→ exit from the **while** loop and perform the **stop**		

Finally, the output that would result from applying the algorithm is listed in Figure 2.8.   The next section will formalize the action of the **get** statement.

Figure 2.8   Output from the Celsius to Fahrenheit conversion algorithm of Figure 2.6.

Celsius	Fahrenheit
15	59
18	64.4
22	71.6
25	77
10	50
8	46.4
15	59

2.5.1   The get Action

The pseudocode feature designed for acquiring data values is called the **get** statement and has the following general form:

> **get** input list

where the input list consists of one or more variables for which values are required.   The variables in the list are separated from each other by commas.   The **get** action is, in fact, just another way of assigning values to variables.   The assigned values are selected sequentially from the *data list*. Naturally, for an algorithm to be considered correct, a **get** action cannot require more data values than are provided in the list.

By convention the list of data values for an algorithm is placed immediately after the **stop** statement.   Each time a **get** is performed, the next unused value on the data list is selected and assigned to the next variable in the input list.

2.6   Selecting Alternatives — A Fourth Algorithm

In learning to live with a new system of measurement, such as temperatures given in Celsius rather than Fahrenheit, the crux of the problem is to develop a feeling for the new system.   If the temperature for tomorrow is forecast to be 25°C, will that temperature be comfortable or not?   The next example will attach such a relative measure to several temperatures.   Since being comfortable is relative to the individual, the problem requires specification of both a lower and an upper temperature limit for comfort.   Temperatures outside these limits are rated uncomfortable while those within are rated comfortable.

Example 2.4   Comfortable Temperature Problem
Develop an algorithm that, given a lower and upper bound for temperatures that are comfortable (in °F) and given a specified number of Celsius temperature readings, will rate each temperature reading as comfortable or uncomfortable.

The solution to this problem, given in Figure 2.9, demonstrates the selection of alternatives using the **if–then–else** feature.

Figure 2.9   Pseudocode algorithm to rate several Celsius temperatures.

* Given limits for what temperatures are comfortable,
* produce a comfort rating for several temperatures.

* Variables used:
* **flo** - low comfortable temperature (°F)
* **clo** - low comfortable temperature (°C)
* **fhi** - high comfortable temperature (°F)
* **chi** - high comfortable temperature (°C)
* **num** - number of temperature readings to process
* **count** - count of readings
* **c** – given temperature reading (°C)

* Obtain the Fahrenheit comfort limits and convert to Celsius.

get flo, fhi
clo ← (flo − 32)*5/9
chi ← (fhi − 32)*5/9
put 'The low comfortable limit is', flo, '°F', clo, '°C'
put 'The high comfortable limit is', fhi, '°F', chi, '°C'

* Obtain the number of readings to evaluate.
* Process each reading by recording an appropriate message.

get num
put 'The number of temperatures to process is', num
count ← 1
while count ≤ num **do**
⎡ **get** c
⎢ **if** c ≥ clo **and** c ≤ chi **then**
⎢   ⎡ **put** c, 'is comfortable'
⎢ **else**
⎢   ⎡ **put** c, 'is uncomfortable'
⎣ count ← count + 1
stop
68, 86, 10, 22, 31, 17, 20, 22, 30, 34, 39, 25, 12

The algorithm begins by obtaining the comfort limits (in °F), converting them to °C, and recording both. Next, the specific number of temperatures in the data list is obtained, assigned to num, and recorded. Finally, the counting loop is designed to repeat the rating process num times. Within the loop a Celsius temperature is taken from the data list and assigned to c. The value of c is then compared with the values of clo and chi. If c is both greater than or equal to clo and less than or equal to chi, the message is comfortable is written beside the value of c. Otherwise, c must be either less than clo or greater than chi, in which case the message is not comfortable is written beside the value of c. In this way the **if–then–else** feature allows for the selection of the appropriate action to take.

Listed in Figure 2.10 is a portion of the results of applying the algorithm of Figure 2.9 to the data given. The complete output is given in Figure 2.11.

Figure 2.10   Step-by-step application of the Celsius rating algorithm of Figure 2.9.

Step	Statement Performed	Action Specified
1)	**get** flo, fhi	68 → flo
		86 → fhi
2)	clo ← (flo − 32)*5/9	20 → clo
3)	chi ← (fhi − 32)*5/9	30 → chi
4)	**put** 'The low . . .'	Write out the message
		The low . . . is 68°F, 20°C
5)	**put** 'The high . . .'	Write out the message
		The high . . . is 86°F, 30°C
6)	**get** num	10 → num
7)	**put** 'The number of . . .'	Write out the message
		The number of . . . is 10
8)	count ← 1	1 → count
9)	**while** count ≤ num **do**	1 ≤ 10, therefore perform loop.
10)	**get** c	22 → c
11)	**if** c ≥ clo & c ≤ chi **then**	22 ≥ 20 & 22 ≤ 30, therefore perform the statements in the range of the **then**.
12)	**put** c, 'is comfortable'	Write out: 22 is comfortable
13)	count ← count + 1	2 → count
14)	**while** count ≤ num **do**	2 ≤ 10, therefore perform loop.
15)	**get** c	31 → c
16)	**if** c ≥ clo & c ≤ chi **then**	31 ≥ 20 but 31 > 30, therefore perform the statements in the range of the **else**.
17)	**put** c, 'is uncomfortable'	Write out: 31 is uncomfortable
18)	count ← count + 1	3 → count
19)	**while** count ≤ num **do**	3 ≤ 10, therefore perform loop.
20)	**get** c	17 → c
21)	**if** c ≥ clo & c ≤ chi **then**	17 < 20, therefore perform the statements in the range of the **else**.
22)	**put** c, 'is uncomfortable'	Write out: 17 is uncomfortable
23)	count ← count + 1	4 → count
⋮ ⋮		⋮

2.6.1   Conditions and Logical Operators

There are three *logical operators* for manipulating logical quantities found in the conditions of the **while–do** and **if–then–else**. These logical quantities are normally the result of comparing arithmetic expressions using the relational operators, =, ≠, <, ≤, >, and ≥. The three logical operators are *not*, *and*, and *or* and are represented in pseudocode by the following symbols.

Figure 2.11 Output produced by applying the Celsius rating algorithm of Figure 2.9.

```
The low comfortable limit is 68°F 20°C
The high comfortable limit is 86°F 30°C
The number of temperatures to convert is 10
22 is comfortable
31 is uncomfortable
17 is uncomfortable
20 is comfortable
22 is comfortable
30 is comfortable
34 is uncomfortable
39 is uncomfortable
25 is comfortable
12 is uncomfortable
```

Logical Operation	Pseudocode Operator	Alternate Pseudocode Symbol
not	**not**	¬
and	**and**	&
or	**or**		

The **and** (&) and **or** (|) operators are called *binary* operators since they require a logical expression on either side. The **not** (¬) operator is a *unary* operator and the single operand is placed to the right. The result of an **and** operation is **true** if and only if the values of the logical expressions on both sides are **true**. If either or both is **false**, the result is **false**. The result of an **or** operation is **true** if either or both of its operands are **true**. Thus, the result is **false** only if both operands are **false**. Finally, the **not** operator negates its operand. If the operand is **true**, the result is **false**. If the operand is **false**, the result is **true**.

If several logical operators appear in the same expression, the highest priority is given to a **not** operator, the lowest priority is given to the **or** operator. In the general scheme of expression evaluation, logical operators are the last to be performed. Listed below are several examples and their evaluation.

Expression	Evaluation
not 2>3	**not false** → **true**
2>3 & 3>1	**false** & 3>1 → **false** & **true** → **false**
2>3 **or** 3>1	**false or** 3>1 → **false or true** → **true**
not 2>3 **and** 3>1	**not false and** 3>1 → **true and** 3>1
	→ **true and true** → **true**

2.6.2 The if–then–else Action

The selection of alternate courses of action based on the relationship between quantities is accomplished using the **if–then–else** feature.

if condition **then**

$\left[\begin{array}{c} S_1 \end{array}\right.$

else

$\left[\begin{array}{c} S_2 \end{array}\right.$

In its general form, the condition is a logical expression having a value of **true** or **false** and S_1 and S_2 signify *action sequences*. The action sequence S_1 may contain one or more actions while S_2 may contain zero or more actions. The first brace encloses the statements that form S_1, that is, the range of the **then**. The second brace encloses the statements that form S_2, that is, the range of the **else**.

The operation of the **if–then–else** action is described in Figure 2.12.

Figure 2.12   Operation of the **if–then–else** statement.

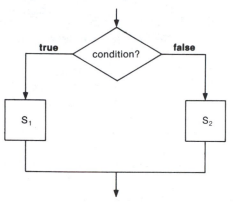

The first stage of the **if–then–else** statement is to evaluate the condition. If the value of the condition is **true**, the action sequence S_1 is performed. If the value of the condition is **false**, the action sequence S_2 is performed. After the completion of either S_1 or S_2, the action following the **if–then–else** is performed. It is important to note that the **if–then–else** does *not* perform any repetition by itself; only one of the action sequences, either S_1 or S_2, will be selected in one particular execution of the **if–then–else** action.

2.6.3   The if–then Action

There is a second form of the **if–then–else** which is used when the action sequence S_2 is null. This means that the **else** portion may be omitted, resulting in an **if–then** action. The general form of the **if–then** statement is given as follows,

if condition **then**

$\left[\begin{array}{c} S_1 \end{array}\right.$

where condition and S_1 are the same as for the **if–then–else** action. In the operation of an **if–then** statement, the condition is evaluated.   If the result is **true**, action sequence S_1 is executed, then the statements following the **if–then**.   However, if the result is **false**, execution continues immediately with the statements following the **if–then**.

2.7   Another Approach to Repetition

The last three algorithms have demonstrated the use of the **while–do** feature to describe the repetition of a sequence of activities.   An analysis of these algorithms reveals that each one uses a counting technique to control the number of repetitions.   In the Temperature Conversion Table algorithm of Figure 2.2, Fahrenheit temperatures from 0 to 212 are counted.   In Figure 2.6 the Converting 7 Temperatures algorithm uses a counter from 1 to 7.   The Comfortable Temperature Problem of Figure 2.9 uses the same counter but generalizes the upper limit to a variable num where the value of num is supplied as the first data item.

In each of these algorithms the control variable is a simple counter and is given an initial value prior to the loop.   The condition in the **while** statement involves comparing the counter variable to a final test value.   Finally, the last statement in the range of each **while** involves adding an increment to the counter variable.

Since the use of a counter to control the number of repetitions of a loop is such a common occurence in algorithms, it is convenient to incorporate the three elements just mentioned into a single pseudocode statement called the **for** statement.

As an illustration of the **for** statement consider the revised version of the Converting 7 Temperatures algorithm, presented in Figure 2.13.   Notice how the single **for** statement has replaced the lines count ← 1, **while** count ≤ 7 **do**, and count ← count + 1.   The actions of these three statements are implied in the wording of the **for** statement, allowing many algorithms to be stated more succinctly and elegantly.

Figure 2.13   Revised pseudocode algorithm to convert 7 temperatures from Celsius to Fahrenheit.

* Convert 7 temperatures from Celsius to Fahrenheit.

* Variables used:
* c - the Celsius temperature
* f - the Fahrenheit temperature
* count - the counter for number of values processed

put 'Celsius', 'Fahrenheit'
for count **from** 1 **to** 7 **by** 1
⎡ **get** c
⎢ f ← (9/5)*c + 32
⎣ **put** c, f
stop

15,18,22,25,10,8,15

2.7.1   The for Statement

The pseudocode **for** statement is an elegant construct for describing loops which are controlled by a single control variable (cv) which changes value from an initial value (iv) to a test value (tv) by a constant increment or stepping value (sv) for each repetition. Its general form is:

for cv **from** iv **to** tv **by** sv
$$\Big[\text{ S}$$

S is an action sequence, the set of statements to be repeated. As with the **while** construct, the brace and indentation are used to group the statements which form S, the *range* of the **for** loop. The iv, tv, and sv may be constants, variables for which values have been previously specified, or arithmetic expressions involving such constants or variables.

The picture in Figure 2.14 assists in understanding how the **for** statement is a specific type of **while–do** action. The three essential elements of the **while** loop are preserved: the control variable is assigned the initial value preceding the loop; the condition ensures repetition of the loop as long as the control variable is less than or equal to the test value; and the assignment following the range of the **for** ensures that the value of the control variable changes by the stepping value each time through the loop.

As further examples of the **for** statement, the three lines f ← 0, **while** f ≤ 212 **do**, and f ← f + 1 in Figure 2.2 could be replaced by **for** f **from** 0 **to** 212 **by** 1. Similarly, **for** count **from** 1 **to** num **by** 1 could be used in Figure 2.9.

2.8   Ups and Downs at the Indianapolis 500

The algorithms developed thus far in this chapter have been relatively straightforward. The formal topic of algorithm development is discussed in Chapter 4. In the meantime, it is useful to introduce several elementary techniques that are commonly used in solving problems. The next problem will introduce several new ideas. The problem makes use of the table of winning speeds at the Indianapolis 500 race, contained in Appendix L.

Example 2.5   Indianapolis 500 Problem
    Develop an algorithm to list the winning speeds at the Indianapolis 500 race and to
    indicate the amount that each speed is up or down from the previous race.

The basic idea of this problem appears to be similar to that of the previous problem. Several data values are to be obtained and processed. The solution to Example 2.4 assumed that the data values to be processed were preceded by a count of how many follow. Often it is a nuisance to count such values. Another technique involves the addition of a specific data value, called an *end-of-file sentinel* or *flag,* to the end of the list of values. Usually this value is chosen so that it could not possibly be a valid entry earlier in the data list. This technique is used in solving Example 2.5.

Figure 2.14 Operation of the **for** statement.

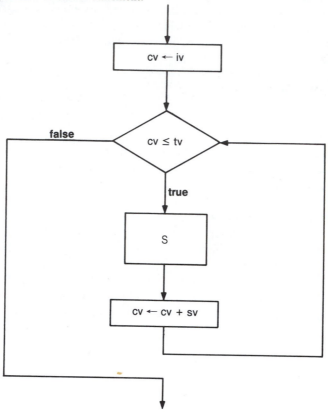

In order to decide whether a specific speed is up or down, it is necessary to retain the speed from the previous race.   Thus, the algorithm must always retain the winning speeds for two consecutive races.   This technique is also demonstrated in the solution presented in Figure 2.15.

Several points should be noted about the algorithm.   Only the previous winning speed needs to be retained; the year is not used subsequently.   If the winning speed decreased from the previous race, the sign of the change is made positive before the value is recorded.   This is done by replacing change by −change.   In this expression, the subtraction operator is used as a *unary* operator, requiring only a single operand to the right.   Normally, subtraction is a *binary* operator, requiring an operand on both sides.   Finally, the sentinel values chosen are −1 and −1.   Since the processing of race data is repeated until these sentinel values are obtained, it is not natural to control the loop repetitions using a **for** construct.   The application of the algorithm to the data is suggested as an exercise at the end of the chapter (see Exercise 2.3).

Figure 2.15   Pseudocode algorithm to list speeds and ratings for the Indianapolis 500 race.

* Given the winning speeds for the Indianapolis 500 race, list each winning speed
* and the amount by which it is up or down over the previous race.

* Variables used:
* **year** - the year of the current race
* **newspeed** - the winning speed for the current race
* **oldspeed** - the winning speed for the previous race
* **change** - the amount of change from the previous race

* Record titles for the output columns, then obtain and record the first winning speed.

put 'Year', 'Speed', 'Up or Down'
get year, oldspeed
put year, oldspeed

* Obtain the next year's race data and keep processing
* as long as the year and speed are positive.

get year, newspeed
while year > 0 **and** newspeed > 0 **do**

    change ← newspeed − oldspeed
    if change < 0 **then**

        change ← −change
        put year, newspeed, 'down', change

    else

        put year, newspeed, 'up', change

    * Remember the current speed and obtain the next.

    oldspeed ← newspeed
    get year, newspeed

stop
1911, 74.59, 1912, 78.72, 1913, 75.93, 1914, 82.47, 1915, 89.94, 1916, 84.00,
1919, 88.05, 1920, 88.62, 1921, 89.62, 1922, 94.48, 1923, 90.95, 1924, 98.23,
. . .
1977, 161.331, 1978, 161.363, 1979, 158.899, 1980, 142.862, −1, − 1

2.9   The Money Changing Problem

The intention of pseudocode is to provide an easy language for describing an algorithm, free of the restrictive details necessary in a programming language.   At the same time, it is useful to express algorithms in terms of the six features described in this chapter since this facilitates the eventual translation to a programming language.

Within the structure of these six features, it is quite legitimate to improvise and to define symbols or specific expressions to make the design of an algorithm easier. Several examples of such useful short-hand notation follow.   The letters **exp** are used to indicate an *arithmetic expression*.

Abbreviation	*Meaning*
$\sqrt{exp}$ or sqrt(exp)	the square root of the expression
|exp| or abs(exp)	the absolute value of the expression
int(exp)	the integral portion of the value of the expression
$\lfloor exp \rfloor$ or floor(exp)	the largest integer in magnitude less than the value of the expression
$\lceil exp \rceil$ or ceiling(exp)	the smallest integer in magnitude greater than the value of the expression
quotient(exp1,exp2)	the integer quotient resulting when the first expression is divided by the second
rem(exp1,exp2)	the remainder resulting when the first expression is divided by the second

Several of these abbreviations are used in solving the following money changing problem.

Example 2.6   Money Changing Problem

Given several amounts of money, each less than one dollar, determine the minimum number of coins (quarters, dimes, nickels, and pennies) that are necessary to make up each amount.

The amounts of money to be processed are assumed to be supplied in a data list.   Since no information is given about how many amounts there will be, it is again appropriate to use an end-of-file sentinel.   A value greater than 100 could be used since the problem definition indicates that such a value should not be processed.   Next, consider the problem of determining the number of coins needed.   The first step is to calculate the necessary number of quarters.   One possibility is to keep adding 25 to a sum until the sum is greater than the amount.   The number of 25's added, less one, would be the number of quarters needed.   A more elegant approach is to determine the quotient when the amount is divided by 25.   The amount left over is simply the remainder of this division.   This same technique, applied successively to the remaining amounts, can be used to calculate the number of dimes, nickels, and pennies.   This approach is used in the solution to this problem presented in Figure 2.16.   Notice that the variable left is used repeatedly to contain the amount left over after each computation.   Again, the application of this algorithm is left as an exercise (see Exercise 2.4).

2.10   The Structure of Algorithms

All algorithms and programming languages must have some method, either implicit or explicit, of controlling the order in which the statements are to be executed.   The term used to describe this feature is *control structures*.

In pseudocode, there are really only three control structures, sequence, **while–do**, and **if–then–else**.   The **for** statement is really just a special case of the **while–do** structure.   The diagrams for these control structures are repeated in Figure 2.17.

Figure 2.16 Pseudocode algorithm for the money changing problem.

* Determine the minimum number of coins needed
* to give change for a variable number of amounts.

* Variables used:
* **amount** - the given amount
* **quarters** - the number of quarters required
* **dimes** - the number of dimes required
* **nickels** - the number of nickels required
* **pennies** - the number of pennies required
* **total** - the total number of coins required
* **left** - the amount left at each stage

* Record titles for the output.

put 'Amount Quarters Dimes Nickels Pennies Total'

* Obtain the first amount, then keep processing
* as long as an amount < 100 is obtained.

get amount
while amount < 100 **do**

    quarters ← quotient(amount,25)
    left ← rem(amount,25)
    dimes ← quotient(left,10)
    left ← rem(left,10)
    nickels ← quotient(left,5)
    pennies ← rem(left,5)
    total ← quarters + dimes + nickels + pennies
    put amount, quarters, dimes, nickels, pennies, total
    get amount

stop

77, 89, 13, 67, 99, 100

Figure 2.17 Diagrams for the three control structures.

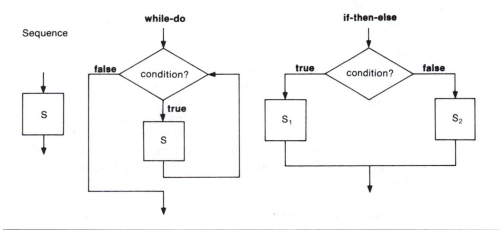

As implied by the diagram in Figure 2.17, a sequence structure is entered from the top and left from the bottom. The language features **get**, **put**, assignment, and **stop** obviously have this structure. The **while–do** and **if–then–else** control structures are somewhat more complicated as they control repetition and selection, respectively. These three control structures are all that are needed to describe algorithms.

As has been seen, the **while–do** and **if–then–else** structures provide much power in describing algorithms. Since these structures, taken as a whole, have only one entrance and one exit, they may also be regarded as sequences. This is illustrated in Figure 2.18.

Figure 2.18 The **while–do** and **if–then–else** as sequence structures.

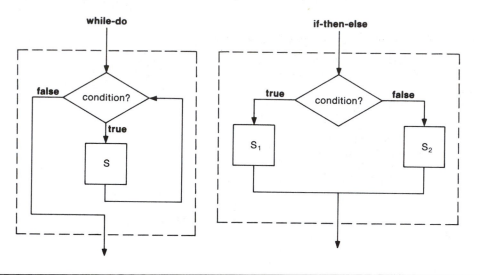

This observation makes it clear that the **while–do** and **if–then–else** may be placed anywhere that a sequence is legal. This means that it is possible to *nest* these structures to any level. That is, a **while–do** may appear in the sequence block of another **while–do**, or in the **then** and/or the **else** sequence block of an **if–then–else**. Examples of an **if–then–else** nested within a **while–do** were already seen in the examples earlier in the chapter.

Looking at this sequence concept from the point of the entire algorithm, an algorithm can be considered as just a series of sequence blocks with one starting point and one ending point. Or, taking the concept even further, an algorithm can be considered to be just one large block. This situation is illustrated in the diagrams or *flowcharts* of Figure 2.19. This point can be made even more strongly by drawing a flowchart of the structure of the algorithm of Figure 2.15 as shown in Figure 2.20.

The restriction that control structures have but one entrance and one exit permits all algorithms to be regarded as simple sequences. This observation suggests a possible approach to the development of algorithms. One begins with a simple description of the sequence of major tasks to be performed by the algorithm. At each stage of the development, such sequences may be broken into a series of subsequences, until each

Figure 2.19 Algorithms as sequence blocks.

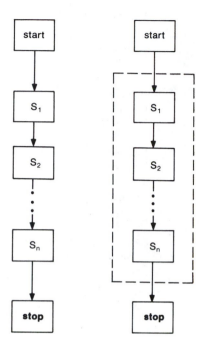

sequence contains a basic pseudocode structure.   This method of solving problems will be demonstrated in Chapter 9.

2.11   Summary

This chapter has introduced pseudocode as a means of describing mathematical algorithms.   Even though the number of pseudocode actions introduced so far is quite small, it is sufficient to allow algorithms of great complexity to be expressed.   An important consideration in the design of the pseudocode actions was the ability to translate them easily into a computer program.   That this objective was achieved will be demonstrated in Chapter 3.

Figure 2.20   The structure of the Indianapolis 500 algorithm of Figure 2.15.

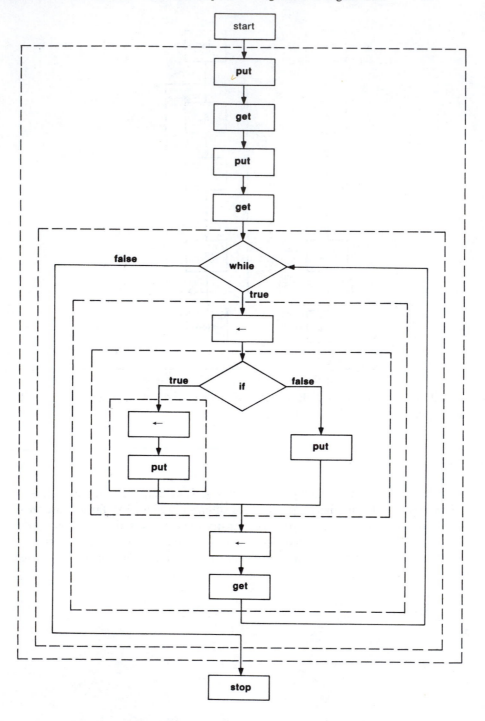

2.12   Exercises

2.1   Develop an algorithm to produce a table of Celsius and the equivalent Fahrenheit temperatures for 0°C, 1°C, 2°C, . . . , 100°C.

2.2   Modify the algorithm for Example 2.4 to be more explici. about temperatures that are uncomfortable, that is, to rate the temperatures less than the lower limit as too cool and those greater than the upper limit as too warm.

2.3   Manually apply the algorithm of Figure 2.15 for the first 10 years of the Indianapolis 500 race.   Your solution should be similar to the table in Figure 2.10 which illustrated the application of the algorithm of Figure 2.9.   Use a separate sheet of paper for the output.

2.4   Manually apply the algorithm of Figure 2.16 for the data values given.   Your solution should be similar to the table in Figure 2.10 which illustrated the application of the algorithm of Figure 2.9.   Use a separate sheet of paper for the output.

2.5   Develop a pseudocode algorithm to determine the minimum number of bills (ones, twos, fives, tens, or twenties) to give exact change for a given amount of money. Assume that the amount is an integral number of dollars.

2.6   a)   Develop a pseudocode algorithm to convert any given number of hours into an equivalent grouping of weeks, days, and hours.   In the grouping, the number of days should be ≤6 and the number of hours should be ≤23.
     b)   Develop a similar pseudocode algorithm to convert any given number of seconds into an equivalent grouping of days, hours, minutes, and seconds.   In this grouping, the number of hours should be ≤23, the number of minutes should be ≤59, and the number of seconds should be ≤59.

2.7   Modify the algorithm of Figure 2.16 to produce a table of the minimum number of coins necessary to give exact change for each amount from 1¢ to 99¢.   The table should list the required number of pennies, nickels, dimes, quarters, and total number of coins for each amount.

2.8   Modify the algorithm of Figure 2.15 to also record the year of the race that showed the most improvement over the previous race.

2.9   The following sequence of numbers, called the Fibonacci sequence,

     1, 1, 2, 3, 5, 8, 13, 21, . . .

has the property that each term after the first two is the sum of the two preceding terms.   Develop a pseudocode algorithm to generate the first 50 terms of this sequence.

2.10   Manually apply the following pseudocode algorithm.

```
whatisit ← 0
i ← 1
while i ≤ 15 do
    ┌ whatisit ← whatisit + i
    └ i ← i + 2
put 'The final answer is', whatisit

stop
```

What is the recorded output?   What would the output be if the 15 were changed to 100?   What is the algorithm designed to do?   Rewrite the algorithm to use a **for** loop.

2.11   Consider the following pseudocode algorithm, and answer the questions given following the algorithm.

```
a ← 0
b ← 0
c ← 0
get n
while n > 0 do
    ┌ get value
    │ if value < 0 then
    │     ┌ a ← a + 1
    │     └
    │ else
    │     ┌ if value = 0 then
    │     │     ┌ b ← b + 1
    │     │     └
    │     │ else
    │     │     ┌ c ← c + 1
    │     │     └
    │     └
    └ n ← n − 1
put a, b, c
stop
6, -1, 0, 0, 1, 2, 3
```

a)   What values are recorded by the algorithm?
b)   Suggest more meaningful variable names for a, b, and c.
c)   What three **if–then** statements, (with no **else** sequence) could be used instead of the nested **if–then–else** statements, to obtain the same result?
d)   Draw a flow diagram (or structured flowchart) for the given algorithm being careful to retain the structure and straight line effect of the logic.

2.12   State the output of the following pseudocode algorithm.

```
get num1, num2
value1 ← min(num1, num2)
value2 ← max(num1, num2)
k ← 1
answer ← 0
while answer = 0 and value1 ≥ k do
    [ if (value2 * k) mod value1 = 0 then
    [     [ answer ← value2 * k
    [ k ← k + 1
put 'The answer is ', answer
stop
6 8
```

The two abbreviations min(num1, num2) and max(num1, num2) compute the minimum and maximun of the two numbers.

2.13   Consider the following pseudocode algorithm and answer the questions relating to it that follow.

```
get m
c ← 1
while c ≤ m do
    [ get n
    [ t ← 1
    [ while t*t < n do
    [     [ t ← t + 1
    [ if t*t = n then
    [     [ put n, ' passes the test.'
    [ else
    [     [ put n, ' does not pass the test.'
    [ c ← c + 1
stop
5, 4, 5, 16, 10, 9, 25
```

a)   What are the control variable(s) for the outer **while**–loop?
b)   What are the control variable(s) for the inner **while**–loop?
c)   Suggest better names for the variables m, c, n, and t.
d)   Specify the output produced by the algorithm for the given data list.
e)   What is the *test* referred to in the output statements?
f)   Draw a flow diagram for the given algorithm. Be careful to retain the structure and straight line effect of the logic.

2.14   Consider the following pseudocode algorithm and answer the questions that follow.

```
lowest ← 999
highest ← 0
get avg, id
while avg > 0 do
    if avg < lowest then
        lowest ← avg
        lowid ← id
        put 'New low is: ', lowest
    else
        if avg ≤ highest then
            highest ← avg
            highid ← id
            put 'New high is: ', highest
    get avg, id
put 'Lowest average:', lowest, 'by', lowid
put 'Highest average:', highest, 'by', highid
stop
55, 80000011, 64, 80000022, 50, 80000033, 45, 80000044,
75, 80000055, 45, 80000066, 75, 80000077, 00, 00000000
```

    a)   Manually apply the algorithm to the data given, producing a table of values (such as the one in Figure 2.7 — minus the data list remaining) and the output produced (such as in Figure 2.8).

    b)   Draw a structured flow diagram (similar to the one in Figure 2.20) for *only* the **while–do** portion of the given algorithm.

2.15   Develop a pseudocode algorithm to arrange a set of 3 numbers in ascending order. Design your algorithm to handle several sets of input data.

2.16   Assume that you are given a set of positive data values that supposedly have been arranged in ascending order.   Develop and test a pseudocode algorithm which will check the ordering of these data values and record an appropriate message about the results.   Use a suitable technique to terminate your algorithm after all values have been tested.   Is it possible to also identify any values that are out of order?   Explain your answer.

2.17   It is often necessary to be able to determine the maximum and minimum values of an unordered set of data.   Develop a pseudocode algorithm that will perform this operation.

2.18   a)   The results of an election for one of three candidates have been entered in machine readable form, using a 1 for the first candidate, a 2 for the second, and a 3 for the third. Assuming there are no spoiled ballots, develop a pseudocode algorithm to tally the votes for each candidate.

    b)   Modify the algorithm of part a) to also determine the winner of the election. You may assume that there are no ties.

    c)   Modify the algorithm of part b) to remove the restriction of no ties.

d) Modify the algorithm of part a) to remove the assumption that there are no spoiled ballots.

e) Modify the algorithm of part a) to include the percentage of total votes for each candidate as well as spoiled ballots.

f) Modify the algorithm of part a) to handle an election for two of the three candidates and to determine the winners, including the possibility of ties.

g) Modify the algorithm of part a) to rank the three candidates in order of finish (first, second, third).

2.19 a) The game of golf traditionally has eighteen holes, with a number of strokes considered par for each hole. Assuming a simplified course where the par on each hole is 4, develop a pseudocode algorithm to obtain and record the number of strokes for each hole for a single golfer. For each hole, your algorithm should display a message specifying whether the number of strokes was below par, even par, or above par. A similar message should be displayed for the overall score.

b) Solve the same golf problem as in part a) but arrange to obtain the par score for each hole along with the number of strokes used by the golfer, since on a standard golf course, the par score varies from hole to hole. Furthermore, your algorithm should be more sophisticated in analyzing the score for each hole, identifying those scores that were holes-in-one, eagles, birdies, pars, bogies, and double bogies.

2.20 The linear equations

$$ax + by = c$$

$$dx + ey = f$$

have the solution $x = (ce - fb)/(ae - bd)$ and $y = -(af - dc)/(ae - bd)$ provided that the equations are not linearly dependent (that is, $ae \neq bd$). Develop a pseudocode algorithm which will solve the above equations. If a solution does not exist, the algorithm should record an appropriate message. Test your algorithm on the following coefficients:

a) $a = 5, b = 7, c = 31, d = 1, e = 2, f = 9$
b) $a = 3, b = 6, c = 42, d = 2, e = 4, f = 28$

2.21 It has been conjectured that for any positive integer n, $n^2 + 3n + 5$ is never divisible by 121. Develop a pseudocode algorithm which will test this conjecture for the integers from 1 to 10,000. Your algorithm should record an appropriate message as to whether the conjecture is true or false over the range of numbers.

2.22 A geometric progression is defined to consist of a sequence of terms in which each term is derived from the previous term by the multiplication of the same constant factor. The following is a geometric progression.

$$a, ar, ar^2, ar^3, \ldots$$

Develop a pseudocode algorithm which will compute and record the first n terms of the above progression. Test your algorithm for $a = 3, r = 2$ and $n = 1, 2, 5$.

2.23 The factorial of a number n, written as $n!$, is given by the following scheme:

$$0! = 1$$

$$1! = 1$$

$$2! = 2 \times 1$$

$$3! = 3 \times 2 \times 1$$

$$\vdots$$

$$n! = n \times (n-1) \times (n-2) \times (n-3) \times \cdots \times 3 \times 2 \times 1$$

Develop a pseudocode algorithm that will, for a given number n, compute its factorial. Test your algorithm on 4! and 7!.

2.24 Develop a pseudocode algorithm to tabulate the function:

$$\frac{1}{x!}$$

for $x = 0, 1, 2, \ldots, 10$. Note that each successive value of the function can be obtained from the previous value using a single multiplication, that is,

$$\frac{1}{x!} = \frac{1}{(x-1)!} \times \frac{1}{x}.$$

Incorporate this idea into the algorithm.

2.25 Suppose that a set of three numbers is to represent the lengths of three line segments. Develop a pseudocode algorithm that will determine if such a set of numbers:

- does not represent the sides of a triangle
- represents the sides of a triangle which is neither an isosceles nor equilateral triangle
- represents the sides of an isosceles triangle
- represents the sides of an equilateral triangle.

3
Algorithms and FORTRAN/77

3.1 Introduction

Pseudocode has been introduced as a means of expressing algorithms. Though it is suited to developing algorithms and applying them manually, pseudocode is not directly understood by a computer.

Before a computer may apply an algorithm, the algorithm must be described in a manner which the computer can understand. Thus, a pseudocode algorithm must be translated into a computer programming language. Following this translation, the statements in this language must be prepared in machine-readable form for processing by a computer.

There are many different programming languages. Some are especially well suited to expressing algorithms dealing with particular kinds of problems. The BASIC language, popular because of its simplicity, was developed for interactive computing and is now heavily used on microcomputers. A more recent and powerful language called PASCAL was developed in the early 1970's by N. Wirth and was designed to be applicable to a very broad spectrun of problems. The oldest and most widely used language for scientific applications is FORTRAN. Algorithms for mathematical and scientific problems are often expressed in some variant of FORTRAN, an acronym for FORmula TRANslation. This language has been extensively refined since its introduction in the 1950's. The most recent published standard is referred to as FORTRAN/77.

It should be mentioned that while BASIC, PASCAL, and FORTRAN are popular languages for solving mathematics and engineering problems, there are in fact many other programming languages. COBOL, a COmmon Business Oriented Language, is extensively used in the business world. PL/1, at one time heralded as the successor to all earlier languages, is suitable for both business and scientific problems. In fact, the proliferation of programming languages is sometimes characterized as the Biblical tower of Babel.

3.2 From Pseudocode to Programming Languages

The beauty of a pseudocode language such as that introduced in Chapter 2 is that algorithms expressed in pseudocode can be converted readily into any of a variety of programming languages. In most cases, there is a direct correspondence between each pseudocode construct and equivalent statements in each of these languages. The best way to illustrate the conversion and correspondence is to consider an example.

The simple pseudocode algorithm of Figure 3.1 was designed to convert a single temperature from Fahrenheit to Celsius. To be more specific, the algorithm obtains a single value from the data list, storing it in the variable f. It then converts the Fahrenheit reading in f to a Celsius reading in c. Next both values, f and c, are recorded with appropriate messages before the algorithm terminates.

Figure 3.1 A simple Fahrenheit to Celsius temperature conversion algorithm.

```
*  A pseudocode algorithm to read in a Fahrenheit temperature,
*  convert it to Celsius, and record both temperatures.

*  Variables used:
*   f - temperature in Fahrenheit degrees
*   c - temperature in Celsius degrees
get f
c ← (f - 32)*5/9
put f, 'degrees Fahrenheit is', c, 'degrees Celsius'

stop
68
```

As will be seen, the translation from pseudocode to a programming language is relatively straightforward for this simple algorithm. The observed variations among the languages will be relatively minor. Though these variations become more pronounced when control structures are considered, the translation of these control structures from pseudocode is still well defined for each language.

3.2.1 Translation to BASIC

In recent years the popularity of the BASIC language has increased tremendously with the advent of small, reasonably priced, microcomputers. BASIC is designed for use in an interactive manner. That is, the programmer has the freedom to make changes in the program easily and to interact with it by supplying input data as the computation proceeds. However, BASIC supports only a limited set of programming features in order to keep it easy to use and implement. This can become particularly awkward as programming problems become large and complex.

The translation from pseudocode is handled with ease, with the resulting program presented in Figure 3.2.

At first glance some differences between pseudocode and BASIC are immediately obvious. A major distinction is that each line in BASIC is identified by a number called a *line number*. Statements are usually separated from these line numbers by a single

```
00010 REM FIGURE 3.2 -- A BASIC PROGRAM TO READ IN A FAHRENHEIT
00020 REM                TEMPERATURE, CONVERT IT TO CELSIUS, AND
00030 REM                RECORD BOTH TEMPERATURES.
00040 REM
00050 REM VARIABLES USED:
00060 REM
00070 REM F - TEMPERATURE IN FAHRENHEIT DEGREES
00080 REM C - TEMPERATURE IN CELSIUS DEGREES
00090 REM
00100 INPUT F
00110 C = (F - 32)*5/9
00120 PRINT F, ' DEGREES FAHRENHEIT IS', C, ' DEGREES CELSIUS'
00130 STOP
```

blank and the statements may be upper and/or lower case depending upon the BASIC
system being used. Comments begin with the keyword REM, short for remark.

Consider the translation of the body of the algorithm. The **get** and **put** statements
of pseudocode are translated into INPUT and PRINT. The assignment operator of
pseudocode, ←, is translated to the = character in BASIC and the constants may have,
but do not need, any decimal points. The **stop** of pseudocode also becomes STOP in
BASIC.

A BASIC program is usually processed by a system program called an *interpreter*.
The function of the interpreter is to check each statement and to carry out its operation.
Since the statements are interpreted one at a time, making small changes to the program
is easy. Although such a process is very convenient for small programs, it can be very
inefficient for large ones.

Another aspect of BASIC is that it is designed to be an interactive language. Typically the programmer sits at a computer terminal and interacts with the program as it is
being interpreted. For example, in the given program, the interpreter will wait when
processing statement 100 until the programmer supplies the required data value 68.
Subsequently the answer from processing line 120 would be displayed at the terminal.

3.2.2   Translation to PASCAL

PASCAL is a recent language and, though designed as a teaching tool, it is also gaining
acceptance in production environments. As a newer language, it embodies many modern
concepts of a programming language. Furthermore, the rules of the language are clearly
defined.

Statement organization in PASCAL is very flexible. PASCAL statements may be
several lines in length, with one statement separated from the next by a semicolon.

A PASCAL translation of the temperature conversion algorithm appears in
Figure 3.3. Notice that a PASCAL program can be written in both upper and lower case
and this flexibility can be used to great advantage to make a PASCAL program easier to
read. Liberal use of extra spaces in a line as well as blank lines enhance the appearance
without affecting the execution of the program.

Comments in PASCAL are enclosed by braces { } and may be placed anywhere.
Thus, they may occupy lines by themselves or parts of lines, both of which are illustrated in the example.

```
{ Figure 3.3 -- A PASCAL program to read in a Fahrenheit
                 temperature, convert it to Celsius, and
                 record both temperatures.}
PROGRAM main(input,output);

VAR f: real;   { temperature in Fahrenheit degrees }
    c: real;   { temperature in Celsius degrees }

BEGIN {main}
    read(f);
    c := (f - 32)*5/9;
    writeln(f, ' degrees Fahrenheit is', c, ' degrees Celsius');
END {main}.
68
```

The start of the program must be identified by the declaration

> PROGRAM main(input,output);

where main is the name of the program. The words input and output instruct the PASCAL compiler that it must accommodate both input and output files for this program.

Following this introductory line is a section labelled VAR which describes to the compiler the variables to be used in the program. While a line such as:

> VAR f, c: real;

would have been sufficient, the demonstrated organization serves to describe the meaning of variables to the reader via comments as well as the type of variable to the compiler via the word real.

The body of the program is surrounded by the lines:

> BEGIN {main}
>   .
>   .
> END {main}.

While the commentary {main} is optional, it serves to specify what is begun and what is ended, namely the program main. As such, the program forms a *block* and the words BEGIN and END are used to surround such blocks in PASCAL. Note that the statements in the block are uniformly indented as a matter of style.

The body of the program thus has three statements to input, compute, and output. Like BASIC, the word **get** is read, but now the input list is surrounded by parentheses:

> read(input list);

Similarly, the word for **put** is writeln and the output list is enclosed in parentheses:

> writeln(output list);

As illustrated above, a semicolon follows most PASCAL statements. In the temperature conversion computation, the assignment operator has become :=, while the constants are the same as in pseudocode and BASIC. Note that the action of the **stop** statement in pseudocode is performed by the END. statement (with a period) in PASCAL.

A PASCAL program is processed by a computer somewhat differently than a BASIC program. In the case of PASCAL, a system program called a *compiler* converts the entire PASCAL program into another form which is easier for the computer to execute. Usually a compiler converts a high-level programming language into machine code which is the most elementary language for the computer. Once the program has been so compiled, the resulting machine code program can be executed interactively from a terminal as was the case with BASIC.

3.2.3 **Translation to** FORTRAN

FORTRAN continues to be a widely used language mainly in scientific applications. For many years this language was used as the vehicle for teaching programming. The language itself continues to evolve as more is learned about good programming techniques.

Figure 3.4 contains a FORTRAN/77 program which corresponds to the sample pseudocode algorithm in Figure 3.1. The translation is quite straightforward. Notice immediately that, except for comments, only capital letters have been used, a constraint dictated by early input devices (keypunches) and output devices (lineprinters).[1] Though similar in layout, this FORTRAN/77 equivalent includes some lines not found in the pseudocode algorithm. As with the other languages just considered, FORTRAN/77 has some simple rules regarding the translation process. To begin with, the positioning of statements in FORTRAN/77 is restrictive. The letter C to identify comment lines must be placed in column 1. Other statements begin in, or to the right of, column 7. Columns 1 to 5 are reserved for what are called *statement numbers* and column 6 is used to include a *continuation line indicator*.

Again the body of the program is similar to the pseudocode algorithm, but the specific words and the punctuation are different.

```
C Figure 3.4 -- A FORTRAN/77 program to read in a Fahrenheit temperature,
C                convert it to Celsius, and record both temperatures.
C Variables Used:
C F - temperature in Fahrenheit degrees
C C - temperature in Celsius degrees
      REAL F, C
      READ *, F
      C = (F - 32.0)*5.0/9.0
      PRINT *, F, 'DEGREES FAHRENHEIT IS', C, 'DEGREES CELSIUS'
      STOP
      END
```

Thus, in the FORTRAN/77 program, the word READ is used for input in place of **get** and

---

[1] This restriction has been removed in some of the more recent FORTRAN/77 compilers.

the word PRINT is used for output in place of **put**. In both cases a comma separates the *keyword* from the list of item(s) which follows. In the assignment statement, the operator ← has become an = character, and the constants are written consistently with a decimal point. The **stop** statement of pseudocode is replaced by a STOP in FORTRAN/77.

As with PASCAL, FORTRAN/77 is processed on a computer using a compiler and several of the language statements are directives to the compiler. The line REAL F, C is technically optional but serves to tell the compiler about the variables to be used in the program. The END statement is always the last in the program and is also an instruction to the compiler telling it to terminate the translation. By contrast, the compiler translates the STOP statement into a termination of execution.

3.2.4 Translation Summary

The pseudocode language introduced in Chapter 2 was designed to describe algorithms of an arithmetic nature. Pseudocode is a convenient way to describe and develop such algorithms. It is not as detailed as actual programming languages and thus allows the developer to concentrate on the algorithm without being burdened with precise language details. Also, a pseudocode algorithm may be translated easily into a number of different languages. In many cases this means that a decision with respect to language can be postponed until a design is complete.

3.3 Processing a FORTRAN/77 Program

The previous section discussed the manual translation of simple pseudocode algorithms into FORTRAN/77. Once this manual translation is complete, the resulting FORTRAN/77 program must be prepared in machine-readable form for processing on a computer.

Historically, the most common machine-readable medium has been the *punched card*. A punched card consists of 80 columns, each capable of representing a single character by a series of rectangular holes. The process of coding a character by punching the necessary holes is accomplished by a mechanical device called a *keypunch*. Normally, each line of the program and each line of data is keypunched on a separate card.

A more modern way of preparing programs in machine-readable form is to use a *text-preparation* or *text-editing* system. In such systems, programs are entered at special typewriters or TV-like devices called computer terminals. In these cases, the machine-readable copy of the program is stored within the computer itself.

Though programming languages such as FORTRAN/77 are relatively natural and easy for humans to use, these languages are not the language of the computer. The computer's language, called *machine language* is a purely numeric, binary-based language. In order for the computer to process a program written in FORTRAN/77, it must first convert the FORTRAN/77 program into machine language. Recall that this conversion step is done automatically by means of a special computer program called a *compiler*. Once this conversion is complete, the machine language version of the FORTRAN/77 program can be executed. Thus a program goes through two phases, a *compilation phase* which converts a FORTRAN/77 program into an equivalent machine language program and an *execution phase* in which the machine language program is actually executed by the computer.

As part of the compilation phase, a program is checked to make sure that the program conforms to the rules for FORTRAN/77 programs. A printer listing is usually generated which shows the entire program with compiler-generated line numbers on the left-hand side. Any errors which are found are pointed out with reference to the line number of the statement in which the error occurred. Recall that in BASIC, the programmer rather than the compiler supplied the line numbers.

The execution phase can also result in errors, such as an attempt to divide by zero. Such errors are also caught and a message is produced which refers to the line number of the offending statement.

High-level languages like FORTRAN/77 can be run on any computer which has a FORTRAN/77 compiler. Because different computers have different machine languages, each computer usually has a FORTRAN/77 compiler developed specifically for it. As a result of these separate development projects, different compilers have different features even though they all accept essentially the same FORTRAN/77 language. This text will assume the availability of a compiler which adheres to the 1977 FORTRAN standard. Note that two different compilers may even exist on the same computer.

As an example, the simple FORTRAN/77 program of Figure 3.4 has been processed on two different computers. Figure 3.5 shows a compiler listing from the VS FORTRAN compiler on an IBM 4341 computer.[2] Figure 3.6 shows a similar listing produced using a VAX–11 FORTRAN compiler on a DEC VAX–11/750. Both of these compilers are compatible with the 1977 FORTRAN standard. In both cases the FORTRAN/77 program was entered into machine readable form in a computer file using a text-editor and computer terminal. The actual commands required to process the programs vary from system to system. As well the information printed by the compilers varies considerably as demonstrated by these two examples.

Consider first the method of processing a program on the IBM VM/CMS system. To compile the program, a command of the form

```
FORTVS filename (options
```

is issued. The filename specifies the computer file where the prepared program resides. The programmer may also select specific compiler options but these are of minimal convern at this stage. The FORTVS command produces two more computer files, one containing a listing of the program and any associated messages (as shown in Figure 3.5) and a second containing the translated binary machine language program.

The listing depicted in Figure 3.5 has two pages. The first is used to display the program, the second to supply any diagnostic messages and program statistics. Each page has a title line listing among other things, the date and time when the program was processed. On page 1 this is followed by a list of the compiler options in effect and a line of column numbers to assist in displaying the program. Beside each non-comment line in the program is a compiler supplied number for future referencing if necessary. The summary is supplied at the bottom of the page. Since no errors were made in preparing the program page 2 contains only standard information. Normally the detection of errors would be reported here.

---

[2] Due to the width of a computer printer page, which exceeds the margins of this book, long lines have been broken by an ellipsis, ..., with the remainder right-justified on the following line.

This program is then executed by typing

```
LOAD filename (START
```

As the program is executed, input values are supplied by the programmer at the terminal and output is printed at the terminal. Users who prefer to place input data in a file and or send output to a file may do so by specifying additional commands.

The execution of the given program would produce output of the form

```
68.00000000000 DEGREES FAHRENHEIT IS 20.00000000000 DEGREES CELSIUS
```

The spacing and format of the numeric values are determined by the compiler.

Like the IBM system the VAX–11 requires that specific commands be entered at the computer terminal to cause the prepared program to be processed. A sequence of three commands is necessary on the VAX, namely:

```
FOR  file-specification-list
LINK file-specification-list
RUN  file-specification-list
```

The `file-specification-list` refers to the various computer files used for the program itself, the input for and output from the program, as well as intermediate files created in the compilation process. The `FOR` command causes the program file to be compiled, producing a partially translated program in another file. The `LINK` command completes the translation and the `RUN` command has the program executed.

The listing produced by the VAX–11 FORTRAN compiler, Figure 3.6, has both similarities and differences from the IBM compiler. Again there are two pages with similar information. Line numbers are printed to the left of each non-comment line in the program. The information printed following the program is of minimal concern to the beginning programmer but can be very useful in later stages in helping to diagnose problems in large programs.

When the VAX computer executes the given program the line of output is:

```
68.00000      DEGREES FAHRENHEIT IS    20.00000      DEGREES CELSIUS
```

Notice the differences in spacing from the IBM results.

3.3.1 Handling Errors

Both output listings in Figures 3.5 and 3.6 made provisions for handling errors in the FORTRAN/77 program. It is expected that programmers will make errors. The extent to which a compiler tries to diagnose errors can vary significantly from one compiler to another. Furthermore, there is considerable latitude with respect to handling various error conditions. At times the messages printed will be immediately helpful to the programmer, while at other times they will only provide some clues. And thus it is only with experience that a programmer learns to use the diagnostic capabilities of a compiler.

Figure 3.5   Results of processing the FORTRAN program in Figure 3.4 by an IBM VS compiler.

a) Page 1 of results:

```
LEVEL 1.2.0 (SEPT  82)          VS FORTRAN          DATE: JAN 30, ...
                 ... 1983    TIME: 21:38:02                   PAGE:    1
OPTIONS IN EFFECT:  NOLIST NOMAP NOXREF   GOSTMT NODECK   SOURCE    ...
                               ... TERM   OBJECT FIXED   NOTEST
                    OPTIMIZE(2)  LANGLVL(77) FIPS(F)  FLAG(I)       ...
                               ... NAME(MAIN   )  LINECOUNT(60)

              *....*...1.........2.........3.........4.........5.....
                                ....6.........7.*.......8

              C Figure 3.4 -- A FORTRAN/77 program to read in a ...
                                      ... Fahrenheit temperature
              C                 convert it to Celsius, and record ...
                                      ... both temperatures.

              C Variables used:

              C F - temperature in Fahrenheit degrees
              C C - temperature in Celsius degrees

ISN        1          REAL F, C

ISN        2          READ *, F
ISN        3          C = (F - 32.0)*5.0/9.0
ISN        4          PRINT *, F, 'DEGREES FAHRENHEIT IS', C, ...
                                      ...'DEGREES CELSIUS'

ISN        5          STOP

ISN        6          END

*STATISTICS*   SOURCE STATEMENTS = 6, PROGRAM SIZE = 360 BYTES, ...
                               ...PROGRAM NAME = MAIN    PAGE:    1.

*STATISTICS*     NO DIAGNOSTICS GENERATED.

****** END OF COMPILATION 1 ******
```

b) Page 2 of results:

```
LEVEL 1.2.0 (SEPT  82)          VS FORTRAN          DATE: JAN 30, ...
                 ...1983    TIME: 21:38:05    NAME: MAIN    PAGE:    2
SUMMARY OF MESSAGES AND STATISTICS FOR ALL COMPILATIONS
*STATISTICS*   SOURCE STATEMENTS = 6, PROGRAM SIZE = 360 BYTES, ...
                               ...PROGRAM NAME = MAIN    PAGE:    1.

*STATISTICS*     NO DIAGNOSTICS GENERATED.

****** END OF COMPILATION 1 ******

******* SUMMARY STATISTICS ******* 0 DIAGNOSTICS GENERATED. ...
                               ... HIGHEST SEVERITY CODE IS 0.
```

Programming errors are typically detected at three different times: compile time, execution time, and when the computed results of the program are being assessed or verified by the programmer.

Compile time errors are usually errors in program statements. Such errors are often caused by careless preparation of the program into machine-readable form or by a lack of knowledge or misinterpretation of the rules of the language. Consider a simple example such as forgetting the left parenthesis in the assignment statement in the line

Figure 3.6 Results of processing the FORTRAN program in Figure 3.4 by the VAX–11 FORTRAN compiler.

a) Page 1 of results:

```
... 22-Dec-1982 10:46:06     VAX-11 FORTRAN V2.3-53          Page    1
... 22-Dec-1982 10:42:56     _DRA0:[USR.JDLAWSON.CHAP3]FIG04.FOR;2

        C Figure 3.4 -- A FORTRAN/77 program to read in a ...
                                ... Fahrenheit temperature,
        C               convert it to Celsius, and record both ...
                                ... temperatures.

        C Variables Used:

        C F - temperature in Fahrenheit degrees
        C C - temperature in Celsius degrees
0001            REAL F, C

0002            READ *, F
0003            C = (F - 32.0)*5.0/9.0
0004            PRINT *, F, 'DEGREES FAHRENHEIT IS', C, 'DEGREES CELSIUS'
0005            STOP

0006            END
```

PROGRAM SECTIONS

	Name		Bytes	Attributes							
0	$CODE	...	101	PIC CON REL LCL		SHR	EXE		RD	NOWRT	LONG
1	$PDATA	...	36	PIC CON REL LCL		SHR	NOEXE		RD	NOWRT	LONG
2	$LOCAL	...	24	PIC CON REL LCL	NOSHR	NOEXE			RD	WRT	LONG

ENTRY POINTS

Address	Type	Name
0-00000000		FIG04$MAIN

VARIABLES

Address	Type	Name	Address	Type	Name
2-00000004	R*4	C	2-00000000	R*4	F

Total Space Allocated = 161 Bytes

b) Page 2 of results

```
... 22-Dec-1982 10:46:06     VAX-11 FORTRAN V2.3-53          Page    2
... 22-Dec-1982 10:42:56     _DRA0:[USR.JDLAWSON.CHAP3]FIG04.FOR;2
```

COMMAND QUALIFIERS

```
FORTRAN [.CHAP3]FIG04/LIST=[.CHAP3]FIG04.LIS/OBJECT=[.CHAP3]FIG04.OBJ

/CHECK=(NOBOUNDS,OVERFLOW)
/DEBUG=(NOSYMBOLS,TRACEBACK)
/F77  /NOG_FLOATING  /I4  /OPTIMIZE  /WARNINGS  /NOD_LINES ...
                        .../NOMACHINE_CODE   /CONTINUATIONS=19
```

COMPILATION STATISTICS

Run Time:	0.77 seconds
Elapsed Time:	3.23 seconds
Page Faults:	184
Dynamic Memory:	34 pages

```
C = F - 32.0)*5.0/9.0
```

The IBM VS FORTRAN compiler gives the following diagnosis after the program listing:

EXPRESSION HAS AN INCORRECT PAIRING OF PARENTHESIS. CHECK THAT
THERE IS A RIGHT PARENTHESIS FOR EVERY LEFT PARENTHESIS.

followed by a message to fix the errors and recompile the program. An attempt to execute the erroneous program will halt at the offending line.

For the same error, the VAX–11 FORTRAN compiler gives the rather cryptic message:

```
Extra characters following a valid statement [C = F - 32.0)]
```

immediately after the offending line in the program. The compiler ignores the remainder of the statement and then proceeds to complete the translation, warning that compilation diagnostics were issued.   An attempt to execute this program with the error results in the following erroneous output:

```
68.00000      DEGREES FAHRENHEIT IS    36.00000      DEGREES CELSIUS
```

Execution-time errors are errors in the meaning of program statements and therefore cannot be detected at translation time. Such errors are usually logic errors or things like division by zero or using variables before their values are defined. For example, if the temperature conversion had been written as:

```
C = (F - 32.0)*5.0/0.0
```

where the 9 was mistyped as a 0, VAX–11 FORTRAN would object with the words:

```
arithmetic fault, floating divide by zero
```

and then stop execution. The IBM compiler, on the other hand, also indicates a divide check but then continues executing to produce the result

```
68.00000000000 DEGREES FAHRENHEIT IS 0.723700515E+076 DEGREES CELSIUS
```

Finally, some errors cannot be detected until the programmer examines the computed results of a program. These errors may be relatively simple, such as dividing by 8 rather than 9 in the temperature conversion formula, or may be very significant yet difficult to discover. This represents one of the major challenges to a programmer. The task of finding errors or *bugs* in a program is called *debugging* and will be discussed in more detail at a later stage.

3.4   FORTRAN/77 **Features**

A cursory look at FORTRAN/77 has been presented using a simple temperature conversion program. To become more conversant with the language requires considerable attention to the rules of FORTRAN/77 and how they are defined. This section outlines some of the basic concepts in FORTRAN/77, while additional features will continue to be introduced throughout the text as required for various applications. A more complete definition of the FORTRAN/77 language appears in the appendices.

3.4.1   Defining the Rules

All programming languages have very specific rules about what constitutes a valid program. Such rules which govern what statements are valid are called *syntax rules*. In addition, there are rules which determine how statements in the language function or operate and these are called *semantic* rules. Both sets of rules are established by the language designer who relies somewhat on previous programming conventions. This is why many languages have common features. If a programming language becomes widely used, international standards are established to control the syntactic and semantic features of the language and to promote the sharing of programs.

The world of computing was in its infancy in the mid 1950's when the FORTRAN language was first conceived. The first versions contained many features now obsolete. As FORTRAN compilers became prevalent on a variety of makes of computers, the need for standards became apparent. The latest of these standards for FORTRAN was established in 1977/78 and hence the use of FORTRAN/77 as the FORTRAN dialect in this text.

The following subsections discuss the rules for individual statements in FORTRAN/77. These rules are described in an intuitive way with further details available in Appendix D.

3.4.2   Constants and Variables in FORTRAN/77

In pseudocode descriptions of algorithms, constants and variables were used to specify and remember numeric values respectively. In FORTRAN/77, the corresponding quantities are also called constants and variables, but must be expressed somewhat more formally since computers are capable of storing information other than numeric values. The initial distinction, due to the way in which computers perform arithmetic, is between numeric values called *integer* and *real*. Integers correspond to the notion of whole numbers, and reals to the real numbers in mathematics. As a result, there are both integer constants and variables and real constants and variables in most programming languages, including FORTRAN/77.

FORTRAN/77 *Constants*

An integer constant is a number written without a decimal point and thus may represent only whole number values which may be negative, zero, or positive. A real constant is a number written with a decimal point and thus may represent numbers with fractional values. Real constants may also be negative, zero, or positive. In addition, real constants may be written in an exponential form called E-notation or scientific notation. This E-notation, previously seen in the erroneous result from the zero division, is handy in a program for writing very large or very small values. Its general form is

$$\underbrace{\pm\, \texttt{xxxxx.xxxxx}}_{\texttt{mantissa}}\texttt{E}\underbrace{\pm\, \texttt{yy}}_{\texttt{exponent}}$$

where the x's and y's represent digits (0–9) and the letter E is read *times 10 to the power*. Thus, for example, 12.34 could be written as 12.34E 00 or 12.34E0 or 0.1234E 02 or 0.1234E2 or 1234.0E-02.   Below is a table illustrating examples of valid constants. It is followed by two lists of invalid constants.

Valid Integer Constants	*Valid Real Constants*
32	32.
-10	-10.0
0	0.0
5768	5768.0
	5.768E3
	0.005768E+6
	576800.0E-2

Invalid Integer Constants

123,456,789	(no commas allowed)
32.	(no decimal allowed)

Invalid Real Constants

5.768E3.0	(only integer exponent allowed)
32	(decimal missing)
123,456E789	(no commas allowed, exponent too large)

Depending on the compiler which is used, there are limits to the range of values that can be used. The following table indicates comparative values for three different computers.

Computer	IBM 4341	HIS Level 66	VAX–11
Compiler	VS FORTRAN	FORTRAN	FORTRAN
Binary Digits	32	36	32
greatest negative integer	-2147483648	-34359738368	-2147483648
greatest positive integer	+2147483647	+34359738367	+2147483647
real of least magnitude	0.5398605E-78	1.46936794E-39	~.29E-38
real of greatest magnitude	0.7237005E+76	1.70141182E+38	~.17E+38

The available accuracy or number of significant digits retained for real values is also a function of the computer being used and may vary from as few as 6 to as many as 18 significant digits.

FORTRAN/77 *Variables*

Variable names in FORTRAN/77 must be chosen in accordance with the following rules.   Variable names must:

1) be from 1 to 6 characters long
2) begin with a letter of the alphabet
3) consist of characters chosen from: letters A-Z, digits 0-9

Listed below are several examples of valid and invalid variables.

Valid Variables	*Invalid Variables*
C	2C
CLO	456
CELSIS	CELSIUS
DOLLAR	DOLLAR-SIGN
R2D2	2BY4

As in pseudocode, variables have undefined values until thay have been assigned a value, either via an assignment operation or a READ statement.   Both the IBM and the VAX FORTRAN compilers assume a value of zero for undefined variables. Consequently programmers must be alert to diagnose such errors since no error will be detected by the compiler.

Before a variable of either type can be used in a program, good practice dictates that its type be declared in a declaration statement as illustrated below.

```
INTEGER variable list
REAL variable list
```

Each declaration statement begins with the variable type (INTEGER or REAL) and is followed by a list of all names that are to be of that type.   Commas are used to separate the names in the variable list.   Normally, all such declarations are grouped at the beginning of the program as demonstrated in the sample program of Figure 3.7.   The statements:

```
INTEGER NUM, COUNT
REAL FLO, CLO, FHI, CHI, C
```

define NUM and COUNT to be variables of type INTEGER and FLO, CLO, FHI, CHI, and C to be REAL variables.

When assigning values to a variable or when using both constants and variables in arithmetic expressions, the numbers should be expressed consistently.   Thus, REAL constants should always include a decimal point whereas INTEGER constants should not. In the sample program, the conversion from Fahrenheit to Celsius involves only REAL variables and therefore the constants 32.0, 5.0, and 9.0 have been written with decimal points.   Conversely, statements involving the INTEGER variables should use constants without a decimal.

3.4.3   Arithmetic Expressions and Assignment Statements

The use of arithmetic expressions in programming languages is very natural and parallels their use in pseudocode.   In FORTRAN/77, the symbols used for the various arithmetic operations are summarized in the following table:

Symbol	*Operation*
**	exponentiation
*	multiplication
/	division
+	addition
–	subtraction

In addition, parentheses may be used to group subexpressions.   A valid arithmetic expression may consist of a single constant, a single variable, or a combination of constants and/or variables separated by any of the five arithmetic operators.

Listed below are several examples of valid arithmetic expressions.

```
(F - 32.0)*5.0/9.0
COUNT + 1
COUNT
1
```

Arithmetic expressions in FORTRAN/77 are evaluated much like pseudocode arithmetic expressions, according to the following scheme.

1) The expression is scanned from *left* to *right*.
2) Whenever an operand (constant or variable) has an operator on both sides, a priority scheme is applied.   Exponentiation has the highest priority, multiplication and division have the next priority, and addition and subtraction have the same, lowest priority.
3) Parentheses may be used to remove ambiguity or to change the normal pattern of evaluation.   Expressions within parentheses are evaluated as they occur in the scanning process.
4) Consecutive exponentiation operations are performed from *right* to *left*.
5) Consecutive multiplication and/or division operations are performed from *left* to *right*.
6) Consecutive addition and/or subtraction operations are performed from *left* to *right*.

The following examples illustrate the application of the above rules to evaluating several arithmetic expressions.

Expression	*Evaluation*
2 + 3*4	2 + 12 → 14
2*3 + 4	6 + 4 → 10
2 + 3**3/4	2 + 27/4 → 2 + 6 → 8
1.1 + 2.2 - 3.3	3.3 - 3.3 → 0.0
1 + 2 - 3	3 - 3 → 0
(4.1 + 5.2)*3.0	9.3*3.0 → 27.9
5*6*7	30*7 → 210
2**3**2	2**9 → 512
(212.0 - 32.0)*5.0/9.0	180.0*5.0/9.0 → 900.0/9.0 → 100.0

Notice that arithmetic involving REAL values always produces a REAL result and that arithmetic involving INTEGER constants always results in an integer, even if a fractional value must be dropped or *truncated,* as may occur with division. While FORTRAN/77 does allow a mixture of INTEGER and REAL values, such instances should usually be avoided. The rules for such expressions are described under "Arithmetic Expressions" in Appendix D.

In FORTRAN/77, the assignment operator, =, is used in place of the ← used in pseudocode to imply that the value of the arithmetic expression to the right is to be assigned to the variable on the left. The following example is taken from the sample program in Figure 3.4.

```
C = (F - 32.0)*5.0/9.0
```

3.4.4 FORTRAN/77 **Input**—READ
In FORTRAN/77, the simplest form of the **get** action is

```
READ *, input list
```

The word READ is followed by an asterisk, a comma, and a list of variable names requiring values. The asterisk is used to specify that the compiler defined default rules for the form and source of the input list are to be used.

The READ statement will acquire sufficient input values to assign a value to each of the listed variables. The method of supplying data values will depend on the compiler being used and the mode of operation. In some cases the values are included at the end of the program and are available to be used during the execution phase as required. In other cases the same lines of data values will be supplied in a separate computer file which is accessed at execution time. A third option consists of entering the data values at the computer terminal as the program is executed.

In pseudocode, the data was listed after the stop action, on one line, if possible. As each **get** statement was performed, the next numbers on the list were obtained and assigned to the variables in the list following the word **get**. While a similar operation takes place in FORTRAN/77, the numeric values are placed on successive punched cards, in separate lines of a computer file, or on separate lines at the computer terminal. However care must be used in determining how many values may be placed on each line.

Each READ statement causes the next line to be scanned.   Thus, the data for an individual READ statement must always begin on a new line.   When a line is read, it is scanned from left to right, looking for constants to assign to the variables in the input list.   As each constant is found, it is assigned to the corresponding variable.   The reading and scanning of lines continues until a value has been found for each variable.

Naturally, the type of each constant in the data must correspond to the type of the variable in the list.   Failure to do so may result in an error and termination of the program.   Similarly, if an insufficient number of values are given for a program, an error message may be issued and the program halted.   If several values are placed on the same data line, they must be separated by a single comma, or at least one blank, or a single comma and one or more blanks.

3.4.5   FORTRAN/77 **Output**—PRINT

In FORTRAN/77, the simplest form of the **put** action is:

```
PRINT *, output list
```

The word PRINT is followed by an asterisk, a comma, and the output list.   The * directs the compiler to use a simple predetermined layout or format and destination for the information to be displayed.   Messages as well as variable names may be included in the output list as illustrated in Figure 3.4.   As in pseudocode, messages must include a single quote on either side and successive messages and variables in the list are separated by commas.

Execution of a PRINT statement causes the messages and the values of each variable to be displayed and every PRINT statement always begins a new line of output.   Each FORTRAN/77 compiler uses a particular choice of the number of output columns and accuracy to express the value of each variable.   Different choices may be made by different compilers.   The default format used for output depends upon the actual value of the number and will be either a regular decimal format or an exponent notation.   The defaults for the IBM and VAX compilers are listed below. (The symbol ƀ represents a blank column.)

	IBM VS FORTRAN		VAX–11 FORTRAN	
	Number of Columns	*Example*	*Number of Columns*	*Example*
INTEGER	12	ƀƀƀƀƀƀƀƀƀ123	12	ƀƀƀƀƀƀƀƀƀ123
REAL (decimal)	17	ƀ123.0000000000ƀƀ	15	ƀƀƀ123.0000ƀƀƀƀ
REAL (exponent)	17	0.123450000E+028ƀ	15	ƀƀƀ1.23E+27ƀƀƀƀ

Though the facility exists for the programmer to control the output layout, that aspect of FORTRAN/77 is beyond the scope of this introduction.   A more complete discussion of this topic is given in Appendix F.

3.5   A Temperature Rating Algorithm in FORTRAN/77

In previous sections of this chapter, a simple FORTRAN/77 program was introduced and elementary concepts such as constants and variables were described. The statements discussed, namely assignment, input, and output, were all sequence actions. As with pseudocode, interesting programs in FORTRAN/77 involve possibly complex paths taken through an algorithm, depending upon results computed along the way. The two fundamental ways to program such paths are alternation and looping. In FORTRAN/77 as in pseudocode the **if–then–else** construction is used for alternation. However, the **while–do** construct is not explicitly available in the FORTRAN/77 standard. In spite of this some compilers do include a **while–do** as an extension to the language. To be consistent with the standard, this extension is not used in the FORTRAN/77 examples in this text. Instead, other FORTRAN/77 control structures will be used to simulate the **while–do**. These techniques are illustrated in Figure 3.7 in which a FORTRAN/77 version of the pseudocode algorithm for rating Celsius temperatures from Figure 2.9 in Chapter 2 is presented.

In many respects this program is similar to the pseudocode. One major difference is the use of the block IF with a GOTO statement to simulate the **while–do**. The FORTRAN/77 version of an **if–then–else** parallels the pseudocode. Additional details of both language features follow in the next section.

Another difference is the absence of square brackets to denote the limits of loop or **if–then–else** action sequences. Without these brackets, how does the FORTRAN/77 compiler *know* where the limits are? More importantly, how does the programmer *prescribe* such limits? The answer is that specific words such as ELSE and ENDIF are used to terminate the range of the **then** and the range of the **else** respectively. The indentation is very significant for the person reading the program in assisting to understand the ranges involved, particularly since the square brackets cannot be used. Technically the compiler does not require this indentation but to eliminate the spacing is poor programming practice.

Figure 3.8 a) displays an input file for the data values given in the pseudocode algorithm. The b) portion of Figure 3.8 lists the output that would result from processing the program with this input on the VAX–11. In fact, all succeeding output shown in this text will be from a VAX computer.

Listed below is a summary of the operation of the READ statements in the sample program on the given input data.

Next READ *Statement*	*Next Data Card*	*Resulting Assignments*
READ *, FLO, FHI	68.0, 86.0	68.0 → FLO
		86.0 → FHI
READ *, NUM	10	10 → NUM
READ *, C	22.0	22.0 → C
READ *, C	31.0	31.0 → C
.	.	.
.	.	.
.	.	.
READ *, C	12.0	12.0 → C

```
C Figure 3.7 -- A Temperature Rating Program.
C                A FORTRAN/77 program to take given limits for what
C                Fahrenheit temperatures are comfortable and to produce
C                a comfort rating for several Celsius temperatures.
C*******************************************************************************
C FLO     - low comfortable temperature (Fahrenheit)
C CLO     - low comfortable temperature (Celsius)
C FHI     - high comfortable temperature (Fahrenheit)
C CHI     - high comfortable temperature (Celsius)
C NUM     - number of temperature readings to process
C COUNT   - count of readings
C C       - given temperature reading (Celsius)
C*******************************************************************************
      INTEGER NUM, COUNT
      REAL FLO, CLO, FHI, CHI, C
C Obtain the Fahrenheit comfort limits and convert to Celsius.
      READ *, FLO, FHI
      CLO = (FLO - 32.0)*5.0/9.0
      CHI = (FHI - 32.0)*5.0/9.0
      PRINT *, 'THE LOW COMFORTABLE LIMIT IS', FLO, 'F', CLO, 'C'
      PRINT *, 'THE HIGH COMFORTABLE LIMIT IS', FHI, 'F', CHI, 'C'
      PRINT *, ' '
C Obtain the number of readings to evaluate.
C Process each reading by recording an appropriate message.
      READ *, NUM
      PRINT *, 'THE NUMBER OF TEMPERATURES TO PROCESS IS', NUM
      PRINT *, ' '
      COUNT = 1
  100 IF (COUNT .LE. NUM) THEN
         READ *, C
         IF (C .GE. CLO .AND. C .LE. CHI) THEN
            PRINT *, C, 'IS COMFORTABLE'
         ELSE
            PRINT *, C, 'IS UNCOMFORTABLE'
         ENDIF
         COUNT = COUNT + 1
         GOTO 100
      ENDIF
      STOP
      END
```

Note that the scanning always begins with the next line or card. Furthermore, the values given correspond in type to the variable in the list.

3.6   FORTRAN/77 **Control Structures**

As introduced in Chapter 2, the term control structure was used to describe the mechanism for controlling the order in which statements are executed. FORTRAN/77 has a variety of control structures. A number of these are supported to be compatible with earlier versions of FORTRAN but are somewhat inconsistent with modern structured

Figure 3.8   Input and output files for the temperature rating program in Figure 3.7.

a) Input file:

```
68.0, 86.0
10
22.0
31.0
17.0
20.0
22.0
30.0
34.0
39.0
25.0
12.0
```

b) Output file:

```
THE LOW COMFORTABLE LIMIT IS     68.00000     F    20.00000    C
THE HIGH COMFORTABLE LIMIT IS    86.00000     F    30.00000    C

THE NUMBER OF TEMPERATURES TO PROCESS IS           10

    22.00000    IS COMFORTABLE
    31.00000    IS UNCOMFORTABLE
    17.00000    IS UNCOMFORTABLE
    20.00000    IS COMFORTABLE
    22.00000    IS COMFORTABLE
    30.00000    IS COMFORTABLE
    34.00000    IS UNCOMFORTABLE
    39.00000    IS UNCOMFORTABLE
    25.00000    IS COMFORTABLE
    12.00000    IS UNCOMFORTABLE
```

programming practice. As a result the authors have chosen to emphasize some of the more modern structures.

The control structures other than simple sequences must test some condition in order to determine what is to be done. A discussion of how to handle conditions in FORTRAN/77 follows with the control structures described in detail thereafter.

3.6.1   Conditions

Conditions are expressions which provide the tests to control the operation of control structures. FORTRAN/77 conditions are similar to those in pseudocode. In FORTRAN/77, a condition is formally described as an expression which must have a true or false value, called a *logical* or *boolean result*. For example, a logical expression may compare two numeric values by a simple *relational expression* such as:

```
arithmetic expression    operator    arithmetic expression
```

In such relational expressions, each of the `arithmetic expressions` used may be a single variable or constant as well as combinations of variables and constants. The operators, called *relational operators*, must be chosen from the list of six given below. Notice that each pseudocode symbol is represented by a two-letter code surrounded by periods.

Pseudocode Symbol	FORTRAN/77 *Relational Operator*
=	.EQ.
≠	.NE.
>	.GT.
≥	.GE.
<	.LT.
≤	.LE.

It is also possible to express more complex logical conditions using *logical operators*. FORTRAN/77 provides the same three logical operators as pseudocode, using a very similar notation to express them.

Pseudocode Symbol	FORTRAN/77 *Logical Operator*
not	.NOT.
and	.AND.
or	.OR.

The operators are listed in order of priority, highest to lowest.

Several conditions were used in the comfort rating program in Figure 3.7, namely

```
(COUNT .LE. NUM)
(C .GE. CLO .AND. C .LE. CHI)
```

In the general scheme of expression evaluation, relational operators have a priority below that of the arithmetic operators while the logical operators have a lower priority still, in the order listed above.   This priority scheme is illustrated below for several simple expressions.

Expression	*Evaluation*
.NOT. 2 .GT. 3	.NOT. **false**
	→ **true**
2.0.GT.3.0 .AND. 3.LT.4	**false** .AND. 3.LT.4
	→ **false** .AND. **true**
	→ **false**
2.0.GT.3.0 .OR. 3.LT.4	**false** .OR. 3.LT.4
	→ **false** .OR. **true**
	→ **true**
.NOT. 2.GT.3 .AND. 3.LT.4	.NOT. **false** .AND. 3.LT.4
	→ **true** .AND. 3.LT.4
	→ **true** .AND. **true**
	→ **true**
.NOT.(2.GT.3 .AND. 3.LT.4)	→ .NOT.(**false** .AND. 2.LT.4)
	→ .NOT.(**false** .AND. **true**)
	→ .NOT. **false**
	→ **true**

3.6.2 The `if-then-else` Statement

The FORTRAN/77 version of the **if–then–else** appears much like the pseudocode construct. The statement ENDIF must be placed after the sequence of statements in the ELSE in order to compensate for the lack of square brackets.

```
IF condition THEN
    : statements in the range of the then
    .
ELSE
    : statements in the range of the else
    .
ENDIF
```

For emphasis and readability, the two ranges are indented to indicate their inclusion as part of the THEN or the ELSE. Naturally, the ELSE sequence may be omitted but the ENDIF statement must still be supplied.

In a similar fashion to the pseudocode, the IF-THEN-ELSE construct in the sample program was the following, used to select which of the two messages is to be printed:

```
IF (C .GE. CLO .AND. C .LE. CHI) THEN
    PRINT *, C, 'IS COMFORTABLE'
ELSE
    PRINT *, C, 'IS UNCOMFORTABLE'
ENDIF
```

As in pseudocode and as shown in the Temperature Rating Program, the IF-THEN-ELSE can be abbreviated to an IF-THEN when there is nothing to do if the condition is false.

3.6.3 Control of Repetition in FORTRAN/77

Two methods of controlling repetition will be discussed in this section, the simulation of a **while–do** using a block IF-THEN and a FORTRAN/77 version of the pseudocode **for** construct.

Simulating a **while–do**

As shown in Figure 3.7, it is possible to mimic the operation of the **while–do** via the use of the IF-THEN block with a statement label and an explicit return to this label. This achieves repetitive execution of the statements in the IF-THEN block as long as the condition remains true.

The general form of this simulated **while–do** is given below beside the corresponding pseudocode:

Pseudocode   FORTRAN/77

while (condition) **do**   label IF (condition) THEN

$\quad \left[\begin{array}{l} S \end{array} \right.$ $\quad$: S

$\qquad\qquad\qquad\qquad\qquad\qquad\qquad$ GOTO label
$\qquad\qquad\qquad\qquad\qquad\qquad$ ENDIF

The label, formally called a *statement number*, is a unique 1–5 digit number (between 1 and 99999) placed at the beginning of a line for identification purposes.   Most FORTRAN compilers demand that these statement numbers be placed anywhere in columns 1–5 of the line.   The GOTO statement, called an *unconditional branch* or *transfer*, is used to alter the sequential ordering of statement execution.   The use of the GOTO branch to the labelled beginning of the loop is an explicit representation of the implied return to the **while** condition at the completion of the sequence of statements S in pseudocode.   Though the GOTO statement and statement labels may be used in other instances, the authors recommend restricting their use to the simulation of the **while–do** construct.

Simulating a **for** *loop*

Section 2.7 in Chapter 2 motivated the used of a **for** loop as a succinct and elegant method of describing loops which are controlled by a single control variable (cv) which changes from an initial value (iv) to a test value (tv) by a constant increment or stepping value (sv) for each repetition.   The corresponding feature in FORTRAN/77 is the DO loop having the general form:

```
        DO label cv = iv,tv,sv
          : S
          .
  label   CONTINUE
```

Notice the use of a statement label on the CONTINUE statement as well as in the DO statement itself to explicitly indicate the end of the range of the DO loop.   The DO parameters, cv, iv, tv, sv, have the same function as in the pseudocode **for**.   cv must be an INTEGER or REAL variable.   However, iv, tv, and sv may be any valid INTEGER or REAL constants, variables, or expressions.   As a matter of style the statements in the range of the DO loop are indented three spaces with respect to the DO and CONTINUE statements to provide program clarity.

The Temperature Rating Program of Figure 3.7 satisfied the criterion for use of a DO loop.   Its implementation using a DO loop is shown in Figure 3.9.

3.7   The STOP and END Statements

The termination of a pseudocode algorithm was indicated by the **stop** action.   A FORTRAN/77 program must indicate where the two phases, compilation and execution, terminate.   The compilation phase is terminated by the END statement.   Naturally, the END statement must always be the last FORTRAN/77 statement in the program.   The completion of execution is indicated by the STOP statement which is optional if it occurs immediately before the END statement.   The STOP statement thus corresponds in function to the pseudocode **stop** statement.

```
C Figure 3.9 -- An Alternate Temperature Rating Program.
C                  A FORTRAN/77 program to take given limits for what
C                  Fahrenheit temperatures are comfortable and to produce
C                  a comfort rating for several Celsius temperatures.
C****************************************************************************
C FLO      - low comfortable temperature (Fahrenheit)
C CLO      - low comfortable temperature (Celsius)
C FHI      - high comfortable temperature (Fahrenheit)
C CHI      - high comfortable temperature (Celsius)
C NUM      - number of temperature readings to process
C COUNT    - count of readings
C C        - given temperature reading (Celsius)

C****************************************************************************
       INTEGER NUM, COUNT
       REAL FLO, CLO, FHI, CHI, C
C Obtain the Fahrenheit comfort limits and convert to Celsius.
       READ *, FLO, FHI
       CLO = (FLO - 32.0)*5.0/9.0
       CHI = (FHI - 32.0)*5.0/9.0
       PRINT *, 'THE LOW COMFORTABLE LIMIT IS', FLO, 'F', CLO, 'C'
       PRINT *, 'THE HIGH COMFORTABLE LIMIT IS', FHI, 'F', CHI, 'C'
       PRINT *, ' '
C Obtain the number of readings to evaluate.
C Process each reading by recording an appropriate message.
       READ *, NUM
       PRINT *, 'THE NUMBER OF TEMPERATURES TO PROCESS IS', NUM
       PRINT *, ' '
       DO 100 COUNT = 1, NUM, 1
           READ *, C
           IF (C .GE. CLO .AND. C .LE. CHI) THEN
               PRINT *, C, 'IS COMFORTABLE'
           ELSE
               PRINT *, C, 'IS UNCOMFORTABLE'
           ENDIF
   100 CONTINUE
       STOP
       END
```

3.8 Summary

Pseudocode algorithms are created by programmers to clarify their ideas about the precise organization of an algorithm. Thus, details such as punctuation, use of special words, and the precise form of input and output are rather unimportant.

The translation of such an algorithm into a machine-readable program written in a recognized programming language is necessary before a computer can process it. A compiler which *understands* FORTRAN/77 is most inflexible — **one must adhere strictly to the rules**. The programmer or a colleague may be able to interpret any reasonable description of an algorithm, but the compiler will insist that your program abide strictly by its rules.

This chapter has served to introduce the basic ideas from which to build a knowledge of programming with FORTRAN/77.

3.9   References

There are a large number of introductory texts for teaching programming languages. The texts in the following list present a few approaches.

American National Standard Programming Language FORTRAN.   New York, N.Y.: American National Standards Institute, 1978.

Boswell, F.D.; Grove, T.R.; and Welch, J.W.   *Waterloo microPascal: Tutorial and Reference Manual.*   Waterloo, Ont.: WATFAC Publications Ltd., 1981.

Dirksen, P.H.; Welch, J.W.   *Waterloo micro*FORTRAN*: Tutorial and Reference Manual.*   Waterloo, Ont.: WATFAC Publications Ltd., 1981.

Dyck, V.A.; Lawson, J.D.; Smith, J.A.; and Beach, R.J.   *Computing: An Introduction to Structured Problem Solving Using PASCAL.*   Reston, Va.: Reston Publishing Co., 1982.

Dyck, V.A.; Lawson, J.D.; and Smith, J.A.   *Introduction to Computing: Structured Problem Solving with* WATFIV-S.   Reston, Va.: Reston Publishing Co., 1979.

Graham, J.W.; McPhee, K.I.   *Waterloo microBasic: Tutorial and Reference Manual.*   Waterloo, Ont.: WATFAC Publications Ltd., 1981.

Graham, J.W; Welch, J.W.   *Waterloo BASIC: A Structured Programming Approach.*   Waterloo, Ont.: WATFAC Publications Ltd., 1979.

3.10   Exercises

In most of the following exercises a program is requested to solve a specific problem. For each problem it is recommended that a pseudocode algorithm be developed to solve the problem.   This algorithm should then be translated into FORTRAN/77 and run on the computer.   Where appropriate, the program should be tested with a variety of data sufficient to ensure that the program does what it is supposed to do.

3.1   Listed below are several short FORTRAN/77 programs.   Examine each carefully, identifying each error and stating whether it would be detected at compile time or execution time.   Then run the program as is to determine whether your diagnosis was correct.   Study the resulting computer listing and especially any error messages produced. Finally, correct the error(s) and run the program again to ensure the validity of your corrections.

```
C Exercise 3.1 a)
      REAL F, C
      F = 68.0
      C = (F - 32.0)*5.0/0.0
      PRINT *, F, 'DEGREES FAHRENHEIT IS', C, 'DEGREES CELSIUS'
      STOP
      END


C Exercise 3.1 b)
      REAL F, C
      F = 68.0
      C = (F - 32.0)*5.0/9.0
      PRINT *, F, DEGREES FAHRENHEIT IS', C, 'DEGREES CELSIUS'
      STOP
      END


C Exercise 3.1 c)
      REAL F, C
      F = 68.0
      C = (F - 32.0)5.0/9.0
      PRINT F, 'DEGREES FAHRENHEIT IS', C, 'DEGREES CELSIUS'
      STOP
      END


C Exercise 3.1 d)
      INTEGER COUNT
      COUNT = 1
12345 IF (COUNT .LE. 5) THEN
          PRINT *, COUNT
          GOTO 12345
      ENDIF
      STOP
      END


C Exercise 3.1 e)
      INTEGER COUNT
      COUNT = 1
12345 IF (COUNT .LE. 5) THEN
          PRINT *, COUNT
          COUNT = COUNT - 1
          GOTO 12345
      ENDIF
      STOP
      END
```

3.2   Correct the following FORTRAN/77 program by supplying the *minimal* corrections so that it operates as specified. For each correction, indicate if the corresponding error would be detected during compilation, execution or manual verification of output.

```
C Exercise 3.2 -- Print a table of numbers, their squares,
C                 and cubes for the numbers from 1 to 10.
      INTEGER I, ISQ, ICUBE,
      PRINT *, 'NUMBER SQUARE CUBE'
  100 IF (I .LT. 10) THEN
         ISQ = I*I
         ICUBE = I*ISQ
         PRINT *, I, ICUBE, ISQ
         I = I + 1
         GOTO 100
      ENDIF
      STOP
      END
```

3.3 The Indy 500 problem developed in Chapter 2 (see Figure 2.13) determined the amount by which each winning speed was up or down over the previous race. Modify the algorithm as indicated below. Then translate the resulting algorithm into FORTRAN/77 and test it on the computer using the Indy 500 data.

a) Modify the algorithm to record the year that showed the most improvement over the previous race, and the amount of the increase.

b) Modify the algorithm to compute and record the average of the magnitudes of the changes in speed.

c) Modify the algorithm to instead determine the amount by which each winning speed was up or down relative to the record winning speed. Each year that a new track record is set should be highlighted by several stars to the right of the output.

d) Modify the algorithm of part c) so that it will also determine the longest period over which no new record was established or, alternatively, the record that stood for the longest.

e) Modify the algorithm of part c) so that it will also determine the longest string of consecutive races in which a record was established each year.

3.4 a) Develop a pseudocode algorithm to tabulate the function

$$k = 2^n$$

for $n = 1, 2, 3, \ldots, 50$. Notice that each term can be obtained from the previous term using a single multiplication. Incorporate this feature into the algorithm.

b) Translate the algorithm of part a) into FORTRAN/77 and run the program on the computer. Study and explain the output.

c) Revise the algorithm of part a) and the program of part b) to tabulate the first 50 powers of 3. Run the resulting program and compare the results with part b).

3.5 S_n is defined as the sum of the first n terms of the following series.

$$\frac{1}{1^3} - \frac{1}{3^3} + \frac{1}{5^3} - \frac{1}{7^3} + \cdots$$

a)   Develop an expression for the nth term of the given series (call this term t_n).

b)   Devise a pseudocode algorithm and write the corresponding FORTRAN/77 program to tabulate t_n and S_n for $n = 1, 2, 3, \ldots, 50$.

c)   The algorithm in part b) was designed to compute S_{50} by adding the terms $t_1, t_2, \ldots, t_{50}$.   Alternatively, the algorithm could be designed to sum the series in reverse order.   Revise the algorithm of part b) to compute S_{50} by summing the terms in reverse order.   Translate this algorithm into FORTRAN/77 and run the program.

d)   Examine the output listings from the programs for part b) and c).   Are the answers for S_{50} identical?   Why?   Which answer would you expect to be more accurate?

3.6   The squares of the integers $1, 2, 3, \ldots$ can be generated by a method that involves adding successive odd numbers to the previous square, that is:

$1^2 = 0 + 1 = 1$

$2^2 = 1 + 3 = 4$

$3^2 = 4 + 5 = 9$

$\vdots$

[handwritten margin notes:]
integer i
i = 0
10 IF (K.ge.0) THEN
$(x^2+1)^2 = k^2 + (2k+1)$
i = i + 1
GOTO 10
STOP
END

or in general

$$(k + 1)^2 = k^2 + (2k + 1).$$

Develop a pseudocode algorithm which uses this technique to generate the squares of the integers from 1 to a given number n.   Translate the algorithm into a FORTRAN/77 program and run it on the computer.

3.7   The square root of a number may be found using an algorithm called Newton's method.   Successive values of x are produced by the following equations and will converge to the square root of a.

$$x_0 = \frac{a}{2}$$

$$x_{i+1} = \frac{1}{2}\left(x_i + \frac{a}{x_i}\right) \quad \text{for } i = 0, 1, 2, 3, \ldots$$

Develop a pseudocode algorithm that will repeat this calculation five times. Translate the algorithm into FORTRAN/77 and run the program on the computer.

3.8   The cube root of a number may also be found using Newton's method.   The successive values of x which are produced by the following equations will converge to the cube root of a.

$$x_0 = \frac{a}{3}$$

$$x_{i+1} = \frac{1}{3}\left(2x_i + \frac{a}{x_i^2}\right) \quad \text{for } i = 0, 1, 2, 3, \ldots$$

Develop a pseudocode algorithm that will perform this calculation until two successive values of x differ by less than 0.001. Translate the algorithm into FORTRAN/77 and run the program on the computer.

3.9　The value of a sum of money a, when invested at an interest rate of $p\%$ compounded annually, may be determined using $r = p/100$ as follows:

Number of Interest Periods	*Amount*
1	$a + (r \times a) = a(1 + r)$
2	$a(1 + r) \times (1 + r) = a(1 + r)^2$
3	$a(1 + r)^2 \times (1 + r) = a(1 + r)^3$
$\vdots$	$\vdots$
n	$a(1 + r)^{n-1} \times (1 + r) = a(1 + r)^n$

Develop a pseudocode algorithm that will perform the above tabulation. Test your algorithm on a $1000 investment at 10% interest over 5 years. Translate the algorithm into FORTRAN/77 and run the program on the computer.

3.10　Modify the pseudocode algorithm developed in Exercise 3.9 to perform the same tabulation when the interest is compounded semiannually. Test your algorithm with the same values and compare the results. Translate the algorithm into FORTRAN/77 and run the program on the computer.

3.11　A loan of x dollars with an interest rate of $r\%$ compounded monthly ($r/12\%$ per month on the outstanding balance) is to be repaid in monthly payments of y dollars. Develop a pseudocode algorithm that will generate a table of payments. Be sure to account for the fact that the last month's payment will be less than y dollars. Test your algorithm on a loan of $100 at 10% interest with monthly payments of $10. Translate the algorithm into FORTRAN/77 and run the program on the computer.

3.12　Develop a pseudocode algorithm that will perform the same tabulation as the previous question when the interest is compounded semiannually. Test your algorithm with the same values and compare the results. Translate the algorithm into FORTRAN/77 and run the program on the computer.

3.13　The monthly payments on a mortgage will change with the amortization period (time over which the loan is to be repaid). Develop a pseudocode algorithm which will determine the amount of the monthly payments if a mortgage of x dollars is to be repaid over a period of n years. Your algorithm should also compute and record the cost of the loan. Translate the algorithm into FORTRAN/77 and run the program on the computer. Test your algorithm by computing the monthly payments for a $60,000 mortgage at 15% interest compounded semiannually for amortization periods of 5, 10, 15, 20, and 25 years.

4
Elementary Algorithmic Techniques

4.1 Introduction

The previous two chapters have provided the foundation for solving quantitative (mathematical) problems using a computer. Chapter 2 presented a pseudocode language for developing the algorithms to solve such problems while Chapter 3 introduced the equivalent features in the programming language FORTRAN/77. Both aspects of problem solving, the development of algorithms and the resultant use of a programming language, will require practice. This chapter will serve to reinforce the points made earlier and to introduce new algorithmic and language features through the use of several examples.

4.2 The Money Changing Problem Revisited

In Section 2.8, a pseudocode algorithm was presented to calculate and list the minimum number of coins needed to make up a variable number of amounts of money. The algorithm dealt with integral quantities only and introduced the concept and use of quotients and remainders. Both of these calculations are available in a more formal way in FORTRAN/77. Figure 4.1 contains a FORTRAN/77 translation of the pseudocode algorithm from Figure 2.14, and Figure 4.2 contains the results of processing this FORTRAN/77 program.

As can be seen from the program, a number of FORTRAN/77 features have been illustrated. First, the variables used are all declared to be of type INTEGER rather than REAL. This implies that these variables may take on only integral values. In order to calculate quotients and remainders, special care must be taken in FORTRAN/77. While quotients are easy to calculate with INTEGER division, remainders are most easily found using a *built-in function* called MOD. Also of note is the statement to print the titles.

```
C Figure 4.1 -- The Money Changing Problem.
C                Determine the minimum number of coins needed
C                to represent several amounts of money,
C                each less than one dollar.
C**********************************************************************
C AMOUNT - the given amount
C QURTRS - the number of quarters required
C DIMES  - the number of dimes required
C NICKLS - the number of nickels required
C PENIES - the number of pennies required
C TOTAL  - the total number of coins required
C LEFT   - the amount left at each stage
C MOD    - the built-in modulus function
C**********************************************************************
       INTEGER AMOUNT, QURTRS, DIMES, NICKLS, PENIES, TOTAL, LEFT, MOD
C Record titles for the output.
       PRINT *, '     AMOUNT     QUARTERS        DIMES        NICKELS',
      +         '     PENNIES        TOTAL'
       PRINT *, ' '
C Obtain the first amount, then keep processing as long as an amount
C less than 100 is obtained.
       READ *, AMOUNT
  100  IF (AMOUNT .LT. 100) THEN
          QURTRS = AMOUNT/25
          LEFT = MOD(AMOUNT,25)
          DIMES = LEFT/10
          LEFT = MOD(LEFT,10)
          NICKLS = LEFT/5
          PENIES = MOD(LEFT,5)
          TOTAL = QURTRS + DIMES + NICKLS + PENIES
          PRINT *, AMOUNT, QURTRS, DIMES, NICKLS, PENIES, TOTAL
          READ *, AMOUNT
          GOTO 100
       ENDIF
       STOP
       END
```

Since the title message is too long to fit on one line, it is continued on a second line. In doing this, the message was broken into two parts, each in quotes and separated by a comma, to achieve the necessary spacing between headings. The symbol + was placed in column 6 of the second line to indicate to the compiler that the line is a continuation of the previous line. The next several sections will elaborate on these topics of integer data types, built-in functions and FORTRAN/77 output.

4.2.1   Integer Data Types in FORTRAN/77

Because computers are capable of performing arithmetic and storing numbers as either real numbers or integers, most languages including FORTRAN/77 provide a formal mechanism for differentiating between these types in a program. In FORTRAN/77, the REAL and INTEGER declaration statements have been shown as the way to declare the type of a variable to the compiler.

Figure 4.2 Input and output files for the money changing program of Figure 4.1.

a) Input file:

77
89
13
67
99
100

b) Output file:

AMOUNT	QUARTERS	DIMES	NICKELS	PENNIES	TOTAL
77	3	0	0	2	5
89	3	1	0	4	8
13	0	1	0	3	4
67	2	1	1	2	6
99	3	2	0	4	9

The topic of INTEGER and REAL data types appeared in Chapter 3 and arithmetic operations on them were discussed.   However there is more to be said.   When the arithmetic operations of addition, subtraction, and multiplication are applied to integers, the result is obviously integral. Division of integers, however, presents special problems. For example, does 3 divided by 2 give a result of 1, 1.5, or 2?   The answer in FORTRAN/77 is 1 since any operation with integer operands must produce an integral result and remainders are chopped off.   A built-in function MOD is provided to compute the remainder of such a division.   In the money changing problem, therefore, calculating the required number of quarters was written as:

    QURTRS = AMOUNT/25

to compute the integer quotient. The statement

    LEFT = MOD(AMOUNT,25)

assigns to the variable LEFT the integer remainder when the integer variable AMOUNT is divided by the integer 25.

The topic of mixing REAL and INTEGER quantities in the same arithmetic expression merits some discussion. Whenever possible such mixtures should be avoided. However, the rule is that any arithmetic operation on two constants or variables, one of which is REAL, produces a REAL result.

The following table will serve to give some numerical illustrations of these rules.

Expression	Evaluation
3 * 4	12
3.0 * 4	12.0
3 * 4.0	12.0
3.0 * 4.0	12.0
3/4	0
3.0/4	0.75
3/4.0	0.75
3.0/4.0	0.75
8/4	2
8.0/4.0	2.0
2.0 + 3 * 4	2.0 + 12 $\rightarrow$ 14.0
MOD(3,4)	3
MOD(9,4)	1

One final point regarding the mix of types concerns supplying values for variables in READ statements. While an integer constant may be supplied as input for a real variable with impunity, trying to supply a real value for an integer variable may cause undesirable consequences. For example, the VAX-11 compiler truncates the real value and continues with execution. No error indication is given. The IBM VS compiler on the other hand, displays an error message and the offending value, replaces the decimal with a zero, and continues with execution.

4.2.2 Built-in Functions
In Section 2.8 the notion of using abbreviations for computing common scientific and mathematical functions was introduced. In languages such as FORTRAN/77 designed specifically for solving scientific problems, it is also natural to facilitate such computations via a formal set of built-in functions. A complete list of the functions available is given in Appendix N.

4.2.3 Basic Input and Output Techniques
The organization and style of input and output statements in a program can vary depending on the program's intended use and on the computing environment in which it will be used. Presumably when small programs are written for a programmer's personal use, less attention needs to be given to how informative the input/output sequence is. However for large programs and for programs intended for others the input required and the output produced should be clearly specified. Furthermore how this is handled can depend on the source of the input data and the destination of the output results. One option is for the input data to be supplied interactively at the terminal during the execution of the program. Alternatively the complete set of data is first placed in a file and then accessed by the program at execution time. With respect to the output from a program, the results may be displayed at the terminal, sent to a file for later perusal, or directed to the printer for a paper copy.

The source of the input data for a program has a significant influence on the style of programming that may be used. If the data is accessed from a file, it is good practice to print the data values as part of the program output, accompanied by explanatory messages. This process is called *echo checking* since the input is echoed to allow the programmer to check its validity.   On the other hand if data is supplied at the terminal during execution, then it is good practice to *prompt* the user for the desired values by a PRINT statement preceding the READ statement.   It is also advisable to notify the user of how to terminate the processing of input values if appropriate.

The various destinations for program output also impact program design. In all cases printing words and messages as well as numbers is recommended. And while it may take additional effort to supply this information, the self-explanatory output produced is definitely worthwhile. The identification of output values can be done individually (for example, with a message as part of every PRINT statement) or may be done through titles (by including PRINT statements that output only messages near the beginning of an algorithmic segment). As a rule individual identification of output values is better for terminal output. In other cases printing of titles only may help to condense the display of output.

Aligning titles over columns of numbers requires some care. The number of output columns for constants of type real or integer typically varies from compiler to compiler but is consistent for a specific type for a given compiler. The VAX-11 compiler for example, uses 15 columns for reals and 12 columns for integers. Since integer values are placed right-justified in these *fields*, usually it is desirable to do likewise with the accompanying titles. Thus, in the program of Figure 4.1, the statement to print the title has the headings right-justified by

```
     PRINT *, '          AMOUNT     QUARTERS          DIMES       NICKELS',
     +                '          PENNIES        TOTAL'
```

rather than left-justified which would be given by

```
     PRINT *, 'AMOUNT           QUARTERS     DIMES          NICKELS          ',
     +              'PENNIES       TOTAL'
```

The same result could have been achieved using six individual messages, each 12 characters long, such as

```
     PRINT *, '          AMOUNT','     QUARTERS','          DIMES',
     +                '          NICKELS','        PENNIES','        TOTAL'
```

Although the information on the second line could have been typed anywhere on that line, positioning the messages underneath one another helps to insure the uniform lengths required.

The money changing problem in Figure 4.1 used the echo checking of its input in the AMOUNT column and supplied titles for the computed output.   The program was intended to be processed with file input and output, as shown in Figure 4.2. By comparison Figure 4.3 presents a revised version of the money changing program designed for terminal input and output.   The interaction between program and user during execution is displayed in Figure 4.4. Notice the conversational nature of the interaction.

```
C Figure 4.3 -- The Money Changing Problem for Interactive Use.
C                Determine the minimum number of coins needed
C                to represent several amounts of money,
C                each less than one dollar.
C*************************************************************************
C AMOUNT - the given amount
C QURTRS - the number of quarters required
C DIMES  - the number of dimes required
C NICKLS - the number of nickels required
C PENIES - the number of pennies required
C TOTAL  - the total number of coins required
C LEFT   - the amount left at each stage
C MOD    - the built-in modulus function
C*************************************************************************
      INTEGER AMOUNT, QURTRS, DIMES, NICKLS, PENIES, TOTAL, LEFT, MOD
C Obtain the first amount, then keep processing as long as an amount
C less than 100 is obtained.
      PRINT *, 'ENTER AN AMOUNT TO BE PROCESSED.',
      PRINT *, 'ENTER A VALUE GREATER THAN 99 TO TERMINATE.'
      READ *, AMOUNT
  100 IF (AMOUNT .LT. 100) THEN
         QURTRS = AMOUNT/25
         LEFT = MOD(AMOUNT,25)
         DIMES = LEFT/10
         LEFT = MOD(LEFT,10)
         NICKLS = LEFT/5
         PENIES = MOD(LEFT,5)
         TOTAL = QURTRS + DIMES + NICKLS + PENIES

         PRINT *, 'COINS REQUIRED:',QURTRS,'QUARTERS',DIMES,'DIMES'
         PRINT *, '                 ',NICKLS,'NICKELS ',PENIES,'PENNIES'
         PRINT *, ' '

         PRINT *, 'ENTER THE NEXT AMOUNT TO BE PROCESSED.'
         READ *, AMOUNT
         GOTO 100
      ENDIF

      STOP
      END
```

4.2.4   End-of-Data Techniques—Counters and Flags

Most algorithms involve repeating the same actions on each element of a set of data values, whether temperatures to rate, winning speeds to compare, or coinage to convert. In all cases, some technique is required to terminate the repetition.

One technique is to use a counter, as illustrated in the algorithm of Figure 2.9 and the program of Figure 3.8.   This technique involves reading in the count of items to be processed, counting as the items are input and processed, and terminating when the desired number of items have been processed.   An outline of this approach appears below.

Figure 4.4 Input and output from interactive processing of the money changing program of Figure 4.3.

```
ENTER AN AMOUNT TO BE PROCESSED.
ENTER A VALUE GREATER THAN 99 TO TERMINATE.
77
COINS REQUIRED:           3 QUARTERS        0 DIMES
                          0 NICKELS         2 PENNIES

ENTER THE NEXT AMOUNT TO BE PROCESSED.
89
COINS REQUIRED:           3 QUARTERS        1 DIMES
                          0 NICKELS         4 PENNIES

ENTER THE NEXT AMOUNT TO BE PROCESSED.
13
COINS REQUIRED:           0 QUARTERS        1 DIMES
                          0 NICKELS         3 PENNIES

ENTER THE NEXT AMOUNT TO BE PROCESSED.
67
COINS REQUIRED:           2 QUARTERS        1 DIMES
                          1 NICKELS         2 PENNIES

ENTER THE NEXT AMOUNT TO BE PROCESSED.
99
COINS REQUIRED:           3 QUARTERS        2 DIMES
                          0 NICKELS         4 PENNIES

ENTER THE NEXT AMOUNT TO BE PROCESSED.
100
```

* Acquire the number of items to process.

get number

* Process each of a number of items.

count ← 1
while count ≤ number **do**

    * Acquire and process a data item.

    count ← count + 1

Another option, called an *end-of-data flag* or *sentinel*, involves selecting an extra data item (or items) to signal the end of the data.   This approach is convenient when the number of data items is unknown or awkward to count accurately.   This technique was used in the money changing problem of Figures 2.14 and 4.1.   In these cases, it was understood that 99 cents is the maximum amount of money for which change was to be made.   Thus, as an alternative, one could examine the current amount of money read in from a data list and execute the statements contained within the **while**–loop only if amount<100.   Otherwise, execution would stop.   Inserting the number 100 (or any larger number) in the data list causes the algorithm to terminate.   The pseudocode structure to do this is as follows:

* Acquire the first data item.

get item

* Process items until the sentinel is encountered.

while item ≠ sentinel **do**

> * Process the current data item.
>
> * Acquire the next data item.
>
> **get** item

Note that in general, if different sections of an algorithm each require a set of data values to be read in, an end-of-data flag would be used at the end of each set. Furthermore, both organizations function properly in the special case of no data items to process.

4.3   The Cashier's Problem

To this point, little has been said about how to develop an algorithm for solving a problem. While a formal treatment of this topic is the subject of Chapter 9, it is appropriate here to gather and apply some informal observations about algorithms.

An algorithm typically includes acquiring some data, processing the data, and recording the results. Sometimes these steps are applied sequentially as, for example, in the problem to convert a single temperature from Fahrenheit to Celsius. At other times these steps are applied iteratively on sets of data as, for example, in the rating of several temperatures and the money changing problem.

These two algorithmic structures, sequential steps or iterative steps, provide a framework for the design of an algorithm. Consider applying these ideas to the following cashier's problem.

Example 4.1   Cashier's Problem

The cashier for a company which pays its employees in cash must make up individual pay envelopes for each employee. Each envelope shall contain the minimum number of bills and coins of each denomination. In addition, a statement is desired which lists the total number of bills and coins for the company payroll. Develop a FORTRAN program to perform such a task for a variable number of employees. For each employee, an identification number and an amount to be paid are supplied.

4.3.1   Developing the Algorithm

This is the largest problem encountered so far and thus requires some thought prior to writing out the FORTRAN statements involved. Since the cashier must use the minimum number of bills and coins, the experience gained from the money changing problem is helpful. Since there are a variable number of employees, some repetition will be involved so that an iterative algorithm structure is a good way to start. Finally, not only is information required for each employee, but a summary of total bill and coin requirements is necessary. Thus an informal first algorithm might imbed the repetitive processing within the following sequence:

1. Initialize counters for the total number of bills and coins required.
2. While there are more employees to process

   > Calculate the number of bills and coins required for this employee and record the resulting quantities.

3. Summarize the total bill and coin requirements.
4. **stop**

a) Refining the Initialization Steps   Initializing counters requires a knowledge of the denominations to be used. Despite inflation, many commercial establishments refuse to accept bills larger than twenty dollars, yet willingly take pennies. This suggests that bills of denomination $20, 10, 5, 2, and 1 be used (the authors are from Canada which has $2 bills in regular use) and that quarters, dimes, nickels, and pennies be used for coins. Counters will be required to total the quantity of bills and coins. The following pseudocode assignments suggest suitable names.

```
total20s ← 0
total10s ← 0
total5s  ← 0
total2s  ← 0
total1s  ← 0

total25c ← 0
total10c ← 0
total5c  ← 0
total1c  ← 0
```

In addition, it might be useful to have the algorithm compute the total amount of the payroll which must then also be initialized to 0.

```
totalamt ← 0
```

b) Refining the **while**–*loop*   The **while**–loop is, of course, the major component of the algorithm. As a first stage of development, consider only the looping mechanism to avoid being overwhelmed by the details of the calculations. The number of employees is variable. Therefore, an end-of-file flag approach to terminating the loop is in order. Since the amounts to be paid are presumably positive, it is appropriate to use an unlikely amount, say zero or negative, as such a sentinel. Now it is possible to restate the **while**–loop using this looping mechanism. The major steps involved in the calculations follow. Notice that this leaves four smaller subproblems to solve.

get employno, amount
while amount $\geq$ 0 **do**

> **2.1** Compute and total the number of bills required.
> **2.2** Compute and total the number of coins required.
> **2.3** Add the current amount to the payroll.
> **2.4** Record the bills and coins required.
> **get** employno, amount

c) Refining the Body of the Loop — Computing Quantities These steps are easy to write out using the computations in the money changing problem as a guide. However, it is first necessary to break the employee's amount into the dollar and cents portions which correspond to the integer and fractional parts of the pay amount. In pseudocode, this can be written as:

dollars $\leftarrow$ int(amount)
cents $\leftarrow$ 100 * (amount - dollars)

The technique for calculating the number of coins comes directly from the money changing program and with the statements to total the number of each type of coin, we get:

* Compute and total the number of coins required.
quarters $\leftarrow$ quotient(cents, 25)
left $\leftarrow$ rem(cents, 25)
dimes $\leftarrow$ quotient(left, 10)
left $\leftarrow$ rem(left, 10)
nickels $\leftarrow$ quotient(left, 5)
pennies $\leftarrow$ rem(left, 5)

total25c $\leftarrow$ total25c + quarters
total10c $\leftarrow$ total10c + dimes
total5c $\leftarrow$ total5c + nickels
total1c $\leftarrow$ total1c + pennies

Then the calculation and totaling of the number of bills becomes:

* Compute and total the number of bills required.
twenties $\leftarrow$ quotient(dollars, 20)
left $\leftarrow$ rem(dollars, 20)
tens $\leftarrow$ quotient(left, 10)
left $\leftarrow$ rem(left, 10)
fives $\leftarrow$ quotient(left, 5)
left $\leftarrow$ rem(left, 5)
twos $\leftarrow$ quotient(left, 2)
ones $\leftarrow$ rem(left, 2)

total20s $\leftarrow$ total20s + twenties
total10s $\leftarrow$ total10s + tens
total5s $\leftarrow$ total5s + fives
total2s $\leftarrow$ total2s + twos
total1s $\leftarrow$ total1s + ones

Note that it is not always necessary to follow the order of the algorithm's steps explicitly when expanding the pseudocode. In this case, the coin subproblem was familiar and led to a parallel solution for the bill subproblem.

d) Refining the Body of the Loop — Recording the Calculations   The remaining subproblems to complete the **while**–loop involve totaling the payroll and recording the number of bills and coins required for this pay envelope. In pseudocode, these steps are:

> totalamt ← totalamt + amount
> **put** employno, amount, twenties, tens, fives, twos, ones,
>   quarters, dimes, nickels, pennies.

e) Refining the Summary Step   This step simply involves a **put** statement to record the final totals.

> **put** totalamt, total20s, total10s, total5s, total2s,
>   total1s, total25c, total10c, total5c, total1c

f) Completing the Algorithm   These steps could now be collected into a complete algorithm for the cashier's problem. The complete algorithm would include a brief description of the purpose of the algorithm, a comprehensive list of all variables and their meanings, and the collection of pseudocode fragments, each preceded by appropriate comments. While this process may seem tedious, there are many potential benefits. Often errors are discovered when the sections are placed together, and the algorithm is reviewed. The complete algorithm serves as a record of the intended design of a project, and provides a second opinion when an error is discovered in the translated program (transcription error versus logic error). If the algorithm structure is complex or intricate, this assembly phase helps ensure that adequate attention has been paid to all possible situations. Since there is such a great similarity to the money changing problem, the complete pseudocode algorithm for this problem is omitted in the interests of brevity.

4.3.2   Translation into FORTRAN/77

The previous sections were devoted to introducing algorithm development and applying those thoughts to the cashier's problem. The result was a series of pseudocode steps to solve the problem. The complete pseudocode algorithm has been omitted, but Figure 4.3 shows the equivalent FORTRAN/77 program for the cashier's problem.

When the problem was developed as a series of smaller separate steps, the problem didn't appear to be as large or complicated as this final program. This is, of course, one of the advantages of using pseudocode and a development method which permits the programmer to deal with a number of small segments of the problem separately.

As a pseudocode algorithm is translated to a FORTRAN/77 program some consideration of the processing mode is necessary. The version in Figure 4.5 assumes that the program will be executed in a completely interactive mode and thus each request for input has been preceded by a prompting message. Had the program been intended for file input, these PRINT statements would be omitted and others to echo check the input values would be supplied instead.

```
C Figure 4.5 -- The Cashier's Problem.
C               A program to compute and total the minimum number of
C               bills and the minimum number of coins required for a
C               manual payroll envelope system.

C**********************************************************************
C EMPLNO - the current employee identification number
C AMOUNT - the amount the employee is to be paid
C DLLRS  - the dollar portion of the amount
C CENTS  - the cents portion of the amount
C TOTAMT - the total amount of the payroll

C NUM20S - the current number of twenties required
C NUM10S - the current number of tens required
C NUM5S  - the current number of fives required
C NUM2S  - the current number of twos required
C NUM1S  - the current number of ones required

C TOT20S - the total number of twenties required
C TOT10S - the total number of tens required
C TOT5S  - the total number of fives required
C TOT2S  - the total number of twos required
C TOT1S  - the total number of ones required

C NUM25C - the current number of quarters required
C NUM10C - the current number of dimes required
C NUM5C  - the current number of nickels required
C NUM1C  - the current number of pennies required

C TOT25C - the total number of quarters required
C TOT10C - the total number of dimes required
C TOT5C  - the total number of nickels required
C TOT1C  - the total number of pennies required

C LEFT   - the amount left at each stage

C**********************************************************************
C Declare the types of all variables.
        INTEGER EMPLNO, DLLRS, CENTS
        INTEGER NUM20S, NUM10S, NUM5S, NUM2S, NUM1S
        INTEGER TOT20S, TOT10S, TOT5S, TOT2S, TOT1S
        INTEGER NUM25C, NUM10C, NUM5C, NUM1C
        INTEGER TOT25C, TOT10C, TOT5C, TOT1C
        INTEGER IFIX, MOD
        REAL AMOUNT, TOTAMT

C Initialize the various counters at zero:
C  - the total amount of the payroll
C  - the number of each type of bill
C  - the number of each type of coin
        TOTAMT = 0

        TOT20S = 0
        TOT10S = 0
        TOT5S = 0
        TOT2S = 0
        TOT1S = 0

        TOT25C = 0
        TOT10C = 0
        TOT5C = 0
        TOT1C = 0
```

```
C Figure 4.5 (continued)
C Obtain the data for the first employee, then keep processing until a
C negative amount is encountered.
      PRINT *, 'ENTER THE EMPLOYEE''S ID NUMBER AND AMOUNT PAID.'
      PRINT *, 'ENTER A NEGATIVE AMOUNT TO TERMINATE PROCESSING.'
      READ *, EMPLNO, AMOUNT
  100 IF (AMOUNT .GE. 0.0) THEN
C         Divide the amount into the dollar and cents portions.
          DLLRS = IFIX(AMOUNT)
          CENTS = IFIX(100.0*(AMOUNT - DLLRS) + .5)
C         Compute and total the number of bills required.
          NUM20S = DLLRS / 20
          LEFT = MOD(DLLRS,20)
          NUM10S =   LEFT / 10
          LEFT = MOD(LEFT,10)
          NUM5S = LEFT / 5
          LEFT = MOD(LEFT,5)
          NUM2S = LEFT / 2
          NUM1S = MOD(LEFT,2)

          TOT20S = TOT20S + NUM20S
          TOT10S = TOT10S + NUM10S
          TOT5S = TOT5S + NUM5S
          TOT2S = TOT2S + NUM2S
          TOT1S = TOT1S + NUM1S
C         Compute and total the number of coins required.
          NUM25C = CENTS / 25
          LEFT = MOD(CENTS,25)
          NUM10C = LEFT / 10
          LEFT = MOD(LEFT,10)
          NUM5C = LEFT / 5
          NUM1C = MOD(LEFT,5)

          TOT25C = TOT25C + NUM25C
          TOT10C = TOT10C + NUM10C
          TOT5C = TOT5C + NUM5C
          TOT1C = TOT1C + NUM1C
C         Add the current amount to the payroll, record the bills and
C         coins required for the current employee, and acquire the data
C         for the next employee.
          TOTAMT = TOTAMT + AMOUNT
          PRINT *, ' '
          PRINT *, 'NUMBER OF 20''S REQUIRED:', NUM20S
          PRINT *, 'NUMBER OF 10''S REQUIRED:', NUM10S
          PRINT *, 'NUMBER OF  5''S REQUIRED:', NUM5S
          PRINT *, 'NUMBER OF  2''S REQUIRED:', NUM2S
          PRINT *, 'NUMBER OF  1''S REQUIRED:', NUM1S
          PRINT *, ' '
          PRINT *, 'NUMBER OF QUARTERS REQUIRED:', NUM25C
          PRINT *, 'NUMBER OF DIMES REQUIRED:   ', NUM10C
          PRINT *, 'NUMBER OF NICKELS REQUIRED: ', NUM5C
          PRINT *, 'NUMBER OF PENNIES REQUIRED: ', NUM1C
          PRINT *, ' '

          PRINT *, 'ENTER THE EMPLOYEE''S ID NUMBER AND AMOUNT PAID.'
          READ *, EMPLNO, AMOUNT

          GO TO 100
      ENDIF
```

```
C Figure 4.5 (continued)
C Record the total amount of the payroll as well as the number of bills
C and coins of each type.
      PRINT *, ' '
      PRINT *, 'TOTAL REQUIREMENTS'
      PRINT *, ' '
      PRINT *, 'TOTAL NUMBER OF 20''S REQUIRED:', TOT20S
      PRINT *, 'TOTAL NUMBER OF 10''S REQUIRED:', TOT10S
      PRINT *, 'TOTAL NUMBER OF  5''S REQUIRED:', TOT5S
      PRINT *, 'TOTAL NUMBER OF  2''S REQUIRED:', TOT2S
      PRINT *, 'TOTAL NUMBER OF  1''S REQUIRED:', TOT1S
      PRINT *, ' '
      PRINT *, 'TOTAL NUMBER OF QUARTERS REQUIRED:', TOT25C
      PRINT *, 'TOTAL NUMBER OF DIMES REQUIRED:   ', TOT10C
      PRINT *, 'TOTAL NUMBER OF NICKELS REQUIRED: ', TOT5C
      PRINT *, 'TOTAL NUMBER OF PENNIES REQUIRED: ', TOT1C
      PRINT *, ' '

      STOP
      END
```

Program Notes

- The amount each employee is paid and the total amount of the payroll are REAL amounts, all other variables are of type INTEGER.
- Prompt messages are introduced for processing in an interactive environment.
- In determining the number of dollars required advantage was taken of the automatic truncation of reals to integers.
- The pseudocode operations **quotient** and **rem** have been translated into FORTRAN/77 integer division and the MOD built-in function.
- The choice of variable names for the totals has been made consistently, using the suffix S for bills, and the suffix C for coins. A similar choice was made for the quantities for each individual employee.

Figure 4.6 A portion of the input and output for the cashier's problem in Figure 4.5.

```
ENTER THE EMPLOYEE'S ID NUMBER AND AMOUNT PAID.
ENTER A NEGATIVE AMOUNT TO TERMINATE PROCESSING.
1111,38.41

NUMBER OF 20'S REQUIRED:          1
NUMBER OF 10'S REQUIRED:          1
NUMBER OF  5'S REQUIRED:          1
NUMBER OF  2'S REQUIRED:          1
NUMBER OF  1'S REQUIRED:          1

NUMBER OF QUARTERS REQUIRED:           1
NUMBER OF DIMES REQUIRED:              1
NUMBER OF NICKELS REQUIRED:            1
NUMBER OF PENNIES REQUIRED:            1

ENTER THE EMPLOYEE'S ID NUMBER AND AMOUNT PAID.
2222,20.25

NUMBER OF 20'S REQUIRED:          1
NUMBER OF 10'S REQUIRED:          0
NUMBER OF  5'S REQUIRED:          0
     .          .                .
     .          .                .
     .          .                .
```

Figure 4.6   (continued)

```
 .              .                      .
 .              .                      .
 .              .                      .
ENTER THE EMPLOYEE'S ID NUMBER AND AMOUNT PAID.
5555, 2.01

NUMBER OF 20'S REQUIRED:              0
NUMBER OF 10'S REQUIRED:              0
NUMBER OF  5'S REQUIRED:              0
NUMBER OF  2'S REQUIRED:              1
NUMBER OF  1'S REQUIRED:              0

NUMBER OF QUARTERS REQUIRED:              0
NUMBER OF DIMES REQUIRED:                 0
NUMBER OF NICKELS REQUIRED:               0
NUMBER OF PENNIES REQUIRED:               1

ENTER THE EMPLOYEE'S ID NUMBER AND AMOUNT PAID.
6666, 1.00

NUMBER OF 20'S REQUIRED:              0
NUMBER OF 10'S REQUIRED:              0
NUMBER OF  5'S REQUIRED:              0
NUMBER OF  2'S REQUIRED:              0
NUMBER OF  1'S REQUIRED:              1

NUMBER OF QUARTERS REQUIRED:              0
NUMBER OF DIMES REQUIRED:                 0
NUMBER OF NICKELS REQUIRED:               0
NUMBER OF PENNIES REQUIRED:               0

ENTER THE EMPLOYEE'S ID NUMBER AND AMOUNT PAID.
7777,69.79

NUMBER OF 20'S REQUIRED:              3
NUMBER OF 10'S REQUIRED:              0
NUMBER OF  5'S REQUIRED:              1
NUMBER OF  2'S REQUIRED:              2
NUMBER OF  1'S REQUIRED:              0

NUMBER OF QUARTERS REQUIRED:              3
NUMBER OF DIMES REQUIRED:                 0
NUMBER OF NICKELS REQUIRED:               0
NUMBER OF PENNIES REQUIRED:               4

ENTER THE EMPLOYEE'S ID NUMBER AND AMOUNT PAID.
-1,-1

TOTAL REQUIREMENTS

TOTAL NUMBER OF 20'S REQUIRED:           5
TOTAL NUMBER OF 10'S REQUIRED:           2
TOTAL NUMBER OF  5'S REQUIRED:           3
TOTAL NUMBER OF  2'S REQUIRED:           4
TOTAL NUMBER OF  1'S REQUIRED:           2

TOTAL NUMBER OF QUARTERS REQUIRED:           5
TOTAL NUMBER OF DIMES REQUIRED:              2
TOTAL NUMBER OF NICKELS REQUIRED:            2
TOTAL NUMBER OF PENNIES REQUIRED:            6
```

4.3.3   **Conversion between** REAL **and** INTEGER

The conversion of integers to reals either within expressions or as an assignment occurs very naturally and informally in FORTRAN/77. Integer values may be read or assigned to real variables and arithmetic operations on two quantities, one of which is real and one integer produces real results. There is also a built-in function called FLOAT to convert a single integer argument to a real value. This might be used, for example, to find the square root of an integer variable I, such as SQRT(FLOAT(I)). The SQRT function expects to see a real argument. Converting the other way from a real to an integer requires more thought as some information may be lost in this process. There exist two standard techniques of representing a real by an integer: the integer part of the real, or the nearest integer, commonly referred to as truncation and rounding respectively. FORTRAN/77 truncates real values to produce integer results if a real value is assigned to an integer variable. Truncation of a real value means that the integer part of that value is retained. To complement the FLOAT built-in function there is also an IFIX function to truncate a real argument. In the following examples, I is assumed to be an integer variable and R is assumed to be a real variable.

Assignment	*Resulting Value*
I = 2.3	2
I = 2.9	2
I = -2.9	-2
I = IFIX(2.9)	2
R = 2	2.0
R = 2 + 2.9	4.9
R = SQRT(FLOAT(25))	5.0 (sometimes 4.999...)

4.4   A Prime Number Classification Problem

With most of the problems considered thus far, the solution has been reasonably straightforward with no obvious improvements possible to the complete algorithm. Frequently, however, the first version of a complete algorithm has several weaknesses which may be eliminated by making suitable changes to the algorithm. Consider the following example.

Example 4.2   Prime Number Classification Problem
     Given a single positive integer, determine whether the integer is prime or composite.

To solve this problem it is, of course, essential to understand the meanings of *prime* and *composite*. A positive integer *n* is said to be prime if it has no nontrivial divisors. A divisor of a number is simply an integer which divides the number evenly, producing an integer quotient and zero remainder. Trivial divisors of a number are 1 and the number *n* itself. Conversely, numbers which have nontrivial divisors are said to be composite. Numbers such as 2, 3, 5, 79 are prime, whereas 4, 6, 8, 9, 91 are composite.

4.4.1   A First Algorithm

Given this understanding of prime numbers, a first algorithm to determine whether a number n is prime or composite could be based on testing the number in question for divisibility by the integers 2, 3, 4, . . . , $n - 1$. That is, divide the number by all integers greater than 1 and less than the number itself. The algorithm involves the steps:

1. Acquire the number to be tested.
2. Determine whether the number is prime or composite.
3. Record whether the number is prime or composite.
4. **stop**

Notice that which answer to record in the third step depends on the results of the second step. An algorithmic tool for conveying such information is called a *flag* or *switch* and is often implemented in a programming language as a *logical* variable having a value of *true* or *false*. Expanding these steps in the algorithm is not too difficult. A complete algorithm for this problem is given in Figure 4.7. As can be seen, the first step becomes the statement **get** n. The second step is expanded into a **while**–loop which generates the divisors from 2 to n-1, performs the test divisions, and remembers if a divisor was found. A logical variable called prime is used for remembering this result. Step three tests the variable prime and prints out an appropriate message.

The descriptions of the variables in the algorithm have now become somewhat more precise and actually identify the types of the variables used, in this case Integer and Logical. While there is certainly no desire to be as formal about type declarations as in a programming language, nonetheless, since many languages insist on typing, it will be convenient to list the intended type of a variable in the comprehensive list of variables, as suggested by Figure 4.7.

4.4.2   A More Efficient Algorithm

Once an algorithm has been developed there remain two concerns. First, the algorithm should be correct, and second, the algorithm should be reasonably efficient. Both of these topics are important and deserve considerable discussion. The topic of correctness is the subject of Section 4.5 and the topic of efficiency is discussed in detail in Chapter 11.

It is possible, however, to give some brief glimpses into the efficiency topic using the current prime number classification problem. Examining the algorithm of Figure 4.5 allows the following observations to be made.

When a number is even (and not the only even prime, 2), there is no need to test any divisors other than 2, since the number is obviously composite. Thus the algorithm can check for evenness in just one step. For odd numbers test possible divisors 3, 5, 7, . . . , thereby reducing the number of tests by half.

Once any divisor is found, there is no need to continue searching for additional divisors. The **while**–loop may terminate at this early stage, when the logical flag prime is set **false**. The initialization of prime to **true** fits the assumption that the number is prime until a divisor is found.

Figure 4.7 A first algorithm for the prime number classification problem.

* An algorithm to determine if a given number is prime or composite.

* Integer variables used:
* n - the number to be tested
* divisor - possible divisors (2, 3, 4, . . . , n-1)

* Logical variables used:
* prime - indicates the truth of 'the number is prime'

* Acquire the number to be tested.

get n

* Assume the number is a prime.

prime ← **true**

* Test the numbers 2 to n-1 as possible divisors.

divisor ← 2
while (divisor ≤ n-1) **do**
> **if** rem(n,divisor)=0 **then**
>> prime ← **false**
>
> divisor ← divisor + 1

* Record whether the number is prime or not.

if prime **then**
> **put** n, 'is a prime number.'

else
> **put** n, 'is a composite number.'

stop

These two improvements are applied to the search portion of the algorithm as follows:

* Test whether the number is even and greater than 2.

if rem(n, 2) = 0 **and** (n > 2) **then**

⌈ prime ← **false**

else

⌈   * Otherwise, test odd values of the divisor from 3 to n-1.

     divisor ← 3
     while (divisor ≤ n-1) **and** prime **do**

        ⌈ **if** rem(n, divisor) = 0 **then**

            ⌈ prime ← **false**

        else

            ⌈ divisor ← divisor + 2

It is possible to make yet another substantial improvement in the efficiency of the algorithm. If p and q are two divisors of n such that $p \times q = n$, then it follows that one of the divisors must be less than or equal to $\sqrt{n}$. Otherwise, the product would be greater than n. Since all odd divisors are checked in order of increasing size from 3, 5, 7, . . . , there is no point in searching for an odd divisor larger than $\sqrt{n}$, if a smaller divisor has not yet been found. This improvement may be made by changing the **while** statement to:

    while (divisor ≤ $\sqrt{n}$) **and** prime **do**

However, since computation of the square root would be required to test each divisor and is also time-consuming, this statement may be improved by computing the square root only once as follows:

    rootn ← $\sqrt{n}$
    while (divisor ≤ rootn) **and** prime **do**

The final, improved version of the pseudocode algorithm is translated into FORTRAN/77 and appears in Figure 4.8.

4.4.3 The LOGICAL Data Type

The elementary programs given in Chapter 2 and 3 involved decisions to be made regarding the flow of control in the programs. In pseudocode, the constructions

    if (condition) **then**

and

    while (condition) **do**

```
C Figure 4.8 -- A Prime Number Classification Problem.
C              A program to determine whether a given number
C              is prime or composite.
C***********************************************************************
C N      - the number to be tested
C PRIME  - indicates the truth of "n is prime"
C DIVISR - possible divisors (3, 5, 7, 9, ... , IROOTN)
C IROOTN - largest integer less than the square root of the number N
C***********************************************************************
       INTEGER N, DIVISR, IROOTN, MOD
       REAL FLOAT, SQRT
       LOGICAL PRIME
C Acquire the number to be tested.
       PRINT *, 'ENTER THE NUMBER TO BE TESTED:'
       READ *, N
C Assume the number is a prime.
       PRIME = .TRUE.
C Test whether the number is even and greater than 2.
       IF (MOD(N,2) .EQ. 0 .AND. N .GT. 2) THEN
          PRIME = .FALSE.
       ELSE
C         Otherwise, test odd values of the divisor
C         from 3 to the square root of the number.
          DIVISR = 3
          IROOTN = SQRT(FLOAT(N)) + 1
  100     IF (DIVISR .LE. IROOTN .AND. PRIME) THEN
             IF (MOD(N,DIVISR) .EQ. 0) THEN
                PRIME = .FALSE.
             ELSE
                DIVISR = DIVISR + 2
             ENDIF
             GO TO 100
          ENDIF
       ENDIF
C Record whether the number is prime or not.
       IF (PRIME) THEN
          PRINT *, N, 'IS A PRIME NUMBER.'
       ELSE
          PRINT *, N, 'IS A COMPOSITE NUMBER.'
       ENDIF
       STOP
       END
```

Program Notes

- The LOGICAL data type in FORTRAN/77 is used for the first time in this program.
- Notice the use of FLOAT(N) in the calculation of the square root of an integer value.
- Since the result of the square root operation is real but may not be integral, it is necessary to convert it to an integer by truncating to the next lowest integer, and storing it in the integer variable IROOTN. Since the square root is only approximated, it is necessary to add 1 to this result. See a discussion in Section 4.5.2.

were introduced. The condition was a relationship involving one or more variables of the program and could be either true or false.

In FORTRAN/77, condition may be defined as a special data type, called LOGICAL, which assumes only the values .TRUE. and .FALSE.. Thus, a FORTRAN/77 program might contain statements to define logical variables, to assign them values of .TRUE. or .FALSE., and to evaluate WHILE or IF conditions. All three of these were demonstrated in the final FORTRAN/77 program for the prime number classification problem given in Figure 4.8.

Logical variables are often used in a program to indicate the occurrence of some event, such as "the number was found to be composite." Occurrence of the event may be verified at any point in the program by checking the true or false value of the associated logical variable, for instance, PRIME was .FALSE. when a divisor had been found.

Logical variables may be combined using the operators .AND. and .OR. and may be negated using the .NOT. operator as described in Chapter 3. It is also possible to compare logical quantities using the logical operators .EQV. and .NEQV. which abbreviate *equivalent* and *not equivalent*. Here equivalent is taken to mean that the logical values on either side are either both true or both false. The operator precedence rules are summarized below:

Highest Priority	* /
	+ -
	.EQ. , .NE. , .GT. , .GE. , .LT. , .LE.
	.AND.
	.OR.
Lowest Priority	.EQV. , .NEQV.

If in doubt about the order of evaluation, it is good practice to insert extra parentheses to clarify what is evaluated first. This may also make the statement easier to read and verify.

4.5   Correctness of Algorithms

In the previous sections and chapters, many examples of correct algorithms have been given. However, not all algorithms perform correctly the first time they are written and this subject should be addressed.

The topic of algorithm correctness is receiving much attention in the current computer science literature. People are beginning to realize that the time spent in assuring that an algorithm is correct is repaid many-fold in terms of both human and computer time when errors are corrected at the program level. For the relatively small problems encountered in this text, it is better to spend 5 to 10 minutes verifying an algorithm manually rather than an hour or more removing such errors as they are discovered in successive computer runs.

Formal algorithm verification methods are based upon mathematical proof techniques. Some assertions are made about how the algorithm should perform, and then it is proved whether or not the algorithm fulfils these assertions. An algorithm is considered correct if it performs properly according to these assertions and produces no undesirable side effects.

Even if the number of language constructs is minimized to aid in these mathematical proofs, the proofs are still quite involved. Furthermore, it is possible to make a mistake in stating the assertions. Thus, mathematical proofs of algorithm correctness are difficult and not routinely done in algorithm development. This situation may improve in the future as research progresses into automated verification techniques.

One way to achieve some confidence in the correctness is to use manual test techniques on the algorithm before it is translated into a computer program.

4.5.1   Manual Testing of Algorithms

Manual testing of algorithms may be done by taking the algorithm (or sections of it) and following the algorithm through step-by-step for some actual data. Simple examples of manual testing were demonstrated in Figures 2.3 and 2.10.

One of the first rules in the manual execution of an algorithm is to do exactly what the algorithm specifies at each stage. Do not assume that any section of the algorithm is working correctly until it has actually been tested.

The algorithm should be manually executed for the kind of data that the algorithm is designed to handle. Algorithms are not written in a vacuum. Algorithm designers should always know what problem they are trying to solve and thus have an idea of the expected outputs for at least several sets of input data. (If this is not true, then the algorithm design should not have been started. The designers should go back to the problem statement until they do understand it.)

Assuming then that something is known about the expected output of the algorithm for a given input, one may test the algorithm using this input data. If the algorithm is followed precisely and the output is incorrect, then the algorithm is in error. Unfortunately, even if this output is correct, there is no guarantee that the algorithm will be correct for all possible input data. The best one can say is that the output is correct for the given input. (There could be numerous other input data for which the algorithm would fail.)

Thus, the objective is to select several sets of input data which will test all aspects of the algorithm. For example, the money changing problem in Figure 4.1 should be tested originally with values that include 0 (no change), a number < 5 (only pennies in change), a number < 10 (only pennies and nickels in change), etc. The cashier's problem algorithm should be tested in a similar manner and the totalling calculations should also be verified. The prime number classification problem of Figure 4.6 should be tested with both prime numbers and even and odd composite numbers.

Testing one's own algorithm has a basic weakness; if bad assumptions were made in designing an algorithm, these assumptions will probably carry over into the testing phase and the error situations may not be discovered. One common, effective, and often humbling solution to this latter difficulty is to have someone else test the algorithm. This works quite well since it is unlikely that another person will make the same assumptions in testing it.

Further tests of an algorithm may involve breaking it apart into sections and examining these sections to convince oneself that the individual sections are working for all possible data values.   Then one may determine that the sections are working together correctly.   Conversely, one can even determine the circumstances under which a section of an algorithm will fail and then assure oneself that because of the way other sections are designed, those circumstances will not occur.

There are several common errors to check for.   Some of the most common errors involve **while**–loops which do not terminate, perform one iteration too few, or perform one iteration too many.   Another common mistake is the omission of statements to initialize variables.   One of the more convenient ways to detect these errors is to keep track of the state of the algorithm by using a table of variable values, such as in Figure 2.7.

To illustrate algorithm testing, the algorithm of Figure 4.7 will be used, which determines if an individual number is prime or composite.   This algorithm can be tested as a complete unit or broken up for testing in a number of ways.   The approach to be used here will break the algorithm into two sections.   The first section will be the statements to get the number and test it for primeness.   The second section will be the statements which print out the message that the number is prime or composite.

The statements which obtain the number and determine if the number is prime or composite are shown below.

```
get n
prime ← true
divisor ← 2
while (divisor ≤ n-1) do
      if rem(n, divisor) = 0 then
            prime ← false
      else
            divisor ← divisor + 1
```

This section of code has two possible outcomes. If the number is prime, then the variable prime should be **true**. If the number is composite, the variable prime should be **false**. Both of these possible outcomes should be tested.

Suppose that the number 5 is to be tested for primeness. Since this value is prime, the algorithmic section should end with prime having the value **true**. The table in Figure 4.9 shows the results as the algorithm is executed. The **get** statement sets n to 5 initially. When the **while**–loop is finished, the variable prime still has the value **true**. Thus, this algorithmic section correctly determined that 5 is a prime number.

To test the other possible outcome of this algorithmic section, the composite value 9 will be used. In this case, the variable prime should have the value **false** when this algorithmic section is finished. The table in Figure 4.10 gives the results of this test. When this algorithmic section ends, the value of prime is **false**. Thus, it correctly determined that 9 is a composite number.

Figure 4.9 Testing the prime number 5 in the body of the prime number classification algorithm of Figure 4.7.

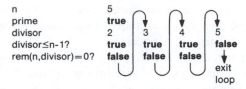

Figure 4.10 Testing the composite number 9 in the body of the prime number classification algorithm of Figure 4.7.

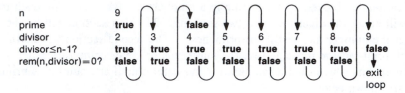

From the preceding two examples it seems that the prime number classification performs correctly.   It sets prime to **true** when the number is prime and prime to **false** when the number is composite.   Also, there is no way for prime to receive any value other than **false** or **true**.   Although other numbers could be tested, in this case there is no reason to believe that the results would be different.   The remaining section of the algorithm to be tested is the statements which print the message describing the outcome. These statements follow:

> **if** prime **then**
> > **put** n, 'is a prime number.'
>
> **else**
> > **put** n, 'is a composite number.'

This section of algorithm will record the message that the number is a prime when prime has the value **true** and that the number is composite when the value of prime is **false**. This is exactly what was wanted, and thus this section is correct.   The individual sections of the algorithm were tested and are correct for the cases tried.   The sections of the algorithm which interact were discussed, and the interactions are correct.

One final observation can be made.   The manual testing process often gives insight into the mechanics of an algorithm.   Redundant operations become tedious to perform by hand thereby motivating improvements to the efficiency of the algorithm. Consideration of Figure 4.10 leads to the modification of the prime number classification algorithm, which resulted in the more efficient FORTRAN/77 program in Figure 4.8.   A useful exercise for the reader would be to perform manual testing on the improved algorithm.

4.5.2   Testing of Programs

The fact that an algorithm has been manually tested and appears to be correct does not, unfortunately, guarantee that the corresponding program is correct.   There are many reasons for this.   Some errors may be introduced in translating the algorithm into a program or in transcribing the program into a machine-readable form.   Other errors result from intrinsic limitations of computers.   For instance, computers have a restriction on the number of significant digits they may store.   This limit on precision can cause arithmetic problems which may not have been anticipated at the algorithm design stage.   A direct translation of the algorithm in Figure 4.7 to FORTRAN/77 could produce a subtle error of this kind.   For example, if the number 49 is being tested in the program, then the built-in function SQRT may compute $\sqrt{49}$ as 6.99 . . . , giving a truncated value of 6.   Thus the testing of trial divisors would be terminated prematurely and thus 49 would be declared incorrectly as a prime number.   The error could remain undetected if the only test examples happened to produce computed square roots with values slightly larger than the true values.   Whether these computed square roots are larger or smaller than the true values is a function of the particular algorithms used for calculating square roots by the computer.   Examples of these arithmetic problems appear in Chapters 6, 7, and 8.   The process of detecting, isolating, and correcting the errors in a program is called *debugging*.

Debugging a program is greatly facilitated by a compiler which detects and identifies errors.   All compilers will diagnose syntax errors and some compilers will diagnose execution-time errors.   For instance, some compilers catch the use of variables with undefined values.   In addition, the compiler may detect divisions by zero or arithmetic operations which generate numbers too large or too small to be stored in the computer.   Compilers vary greatly in the quality of error diagnostics for execution-time errors.   Even though the reasons why these conditions exist may not be immediately obvious, one at least knows that something is wrong with the program.

Unfortunately, not all mistakes are detectable by a compiler.   The only effect some mistakes have is to produce erroneous results.   If these results are grossly incorrect, then the programmer can easily recognize the situation.   A more difficult case arises if some results are wrong but not blatantly so.   Subtle errors may require careful checking before they are discovered.   The usual procedure is to run the program first on at least one problem for which the *exact* solution is known.   When the program performs correctly on such a test problem, one may have more confidence in it for other problems.

Once it has been established that a program does contain an error, it is necessary to determine what caused the error.   Potentially the error may be caused anywhere in the calculations, perhaps by something as subtle as declaring a variable to be the wrong type.   Thus, isolation of the error may be difficult and frustrating.

A common isolation technique called *tracing* is to insert statements to output intermediate results for checking against manual calculations.   In large programs it is a good idea to leave these tracing statements in the program.   They may be part of an IF statement such that they may be turned on and off as desired.   For example, the following debugging statements allow the PRINT statement to be executed whenever the logical variable TRACE has the value .TRUE. and to be ignored when TRACE has the value .FALSE..

```
          .
          .
          .
     READ *, TRACE
          .
          .
          .
     IF (TRACE) THEN
          PRINT *, X, Y, I, J, 'AT LOCATION ...'
          .
          .
          .
```

Note that when an algorithm is translated into a computer program, the correctness issue expands to become one of *software reliability*. This phrase has been defined as including the concepts of *correctness* and *robustness*. The concept of program correctness is similar to that of algorithm correctness. Program robustness is concerned with the ability of a program to continue functioning in the presence of unforeseen events such as hardware failure or bad data. For example, when some compilers detect an undefined variable, a warning message is issued, the variable is set to 0, and the program continues execution. Other compilers (including the VAX-11 compiler) may not warn the user at all and thus it is up to the user to detect erroneous results.

4.6 Summary

The task of problem solving using a computer is often called *programming* and has many facets. It includes developing the algorithm, testing the algorithm for correctness, translating the algorithm into a program, and then debugging the program.

Learning effective programming requires much practice. There are many rules and techniques which must be added to each programmer's repertoire and this takes time.

This chapter has touched on some of these basic *tools of the trade*. These tools will be used and developed in subsequent chapters when more problems are encountered which require new problem solving techniques.

4.7 Exercises

In most of the following exercises a program is requested to solve a specific problem. For each problem it is recommended that a pseudocode algorithm be developed to solve the problem. This algorithm should then be translated into FORTRAN/77 and run on the computer. Where appropriate, the program should be tested with a variety of data sufficient to ensure that the program does what it is supposed to do.

4.1   Consider the following FORTRAN/77 program and answer the questions which follow.

```
      INTEGER NUM1, NUM2, RESULT
      READ *, NUM1, NUM2
      RESULT = 0
  100 IF (NUM1 .NE. 0) THEN
          IF (MOD(NUM1,2) .EQ. 1) THEN
              RESULT = RESULT + NUM2
          ENDIF
          NUM1 = NUM1/2
          NUM2 = NUM2*2
          GOTO 100
      ENDIF
      PRINT *, RESULT
      STOP
      END
```

a)   What output would be produced for input values 37 and 41?

b)   What output would be produced for input values 31 and 17?

c)   What does RESULT represent in terms of NUM1 and NUM2?

d)   Modify the program to print the values of NUM1 and NUM2 on the same line as the value of RESULT.

4.2   Correct the following FORTRAN/77 program by supplying the *minimal* corrections so that it operates as specified.   For each correction, indicate if the corresponding error would be detected during compilation, execution, or manual verification of the output.

```
C Exercise 4.2 -- Categorize several numbers as even or odd.
      REAL NO
      READ *, NUM
  420 IF (NUM .NE. 0) THEN
          IF (NUM/2*2 = NUM) THEN
              PRINT *, NUM, 'IS ODD'
          ELSE
              PRINT *, NUM, 'IS EVEN'
          ENDIF
          READ *, NUM
          GOTO 420
      ENDIF
      STOP
      END
```

4.3   A formula for computing the day of the week for any given day of the Gregorian calendar was developed by a Reverend Zeller.   The input to the algorithm is specified in the following manner:

- let m be the month of the year, starting with March as $m = 1$.   January and February are months 11 and 12 of the previous year.
- let d be the day of the month.
- let y be the year of the century.
- let c be the previous century.

For example, to convert April 1, 1979, $m = 2$, $d = 1$, $y = 79$, and $c = 19$. To compute the day of the week on which this date falls,

a) Take the integer part of the ratio $(13m - 1)/5$. Call this A.

b) Take the integer part of the ratio $y/4$. Call this B.

c) Take the integer part of the ratio $c/4$. Call this C.

d) Compute $D = A + B + C + d + y - 2c$.

e) Divide the resulting D by 7 and keep the remainder, R.

f) If R is 0, the day is Sunday, if R is 1, the day is Monday, . . . , and if R is 6, the day is Saturday.

Describe this algorithm in pseudocode, then translate it to FORTRAN/77 and run it on the computer.

4.4   An algorithm for computing the date of Easter for any given year is given below:

a) Call the year y. Subtract 1900 from y and call the difference n.

b) Divide n by 19. Call the remainder a.

c) Divide $(7a + 1)$ by 19. Ignore the remainder and call the quotient b.

d) Divide $(11a + 4 - b)$ by 29. Call the remainder m.

e) Divide n by 4. Ignore the remainder and call the quotient q.

f) Divide $(n + q + 31 - m)$ by 7. Call the remainder w.

g) The date of Easter is $25 - m - w$. If the result is positive, then the month is April. If the result is nonpositive, then the month is March, interpreting 0 as March 31, -1 as March 30, -2 as March 29, and so on up to -9 as March 22.

Describe this algorithm in pseudocode, then translate it into a FORTRAN/77 program and run it on the computer.

4.5   a) For each of 7 employees, the rate per hour and the number of hours worked on each of Monday, Tuesday, Wednesday, Thursday, and Friday is given. Ignoring any deductions, develop a pseudocode algorithm to calculate the gross pay for each of the 7 employees. Translate the program to FORTRAN/77 and run it on the computer.

b) Modify the program in part a) to handle a variable number of employees rather than the fixed number 7.

c) Modify the program in part b) to pay time and a half for any overtime hours worked. The standard work week is 37-1/2 hours.

d) Modify the program in part c) to deduct 20% of the gross pay for income tax purposes.

4.6   Develop a pseudocode algorithm which will determine all distinct, nontrivial factors of a number. If no factors exist for a given number, the algorithm should put out an appropriate message. Translate your algorithm into a FORTRAN/77 program and test it on the computer.

4.7   Develop a pseudocode algorithm which will test each number in a set to determine if it is prime or composite. The algorithm should handle negative numbers as well as positive numbers. Negative numbers are not prime. Translate your algorithm into a FORTRAN/77 program and test it on the computer.

4.8   Develop a pseudocode algorithm which will determine the prime factors of a number *n*.   Translate your algorithm into FORTRAN/77 and test it on the computer.

4.9   Develop a pseudocode algorithm which will identify all three digit numbers (numbers between 100 and 999) whose digits when cubed, sum to the number itself.   For example, the number 153 has this property since $1^3 + 5^3 + 3^3 = 153$.   Translate your algorithm into a FORTRAN/77 program and test it on the computer.

4.10   Develop a pseudocode algorithm to find all positive integers less than 1000 which do not end in zero and have the property that if the rightmost digit is deleted, the integer obtained divides into the original evenly.   For example, 39 is such an integer since 3 remains after deleting the rightmost digit, and 3 divides 39 evenly.   Translate the algorithm into a FORTRAN/77 program and run it on the computer.

4.11   The four-digit number 3025 has the following property: if the number formed by considering only the first two digits (30) is added to the number formed by considering only the last two digits (25), (the total will be 55), and if this number (55) is squared, the result will be the original number.   Develop a pseudocode algorithm to find all four-digit numbers having this property, then translate the algorithm into a FORTRAN/77 program and run it on the computer.

4.12   The greatest common divisor (GCD) of two numbers is the largest factor of both numbers.   For example, the GCD of 54 and 63 is 9.   Develop a pseudocode algorithm which will compute the GCD of any two given numbers.   Translate your algorithm into a FORTRAN/77 program and test it on the computer.

4.13   The least common multiple (LCM) of two numbers is the smallest integer evenly divisible by both numbers.   For example, the LCM of 9 and 12 is 36.   Develop a pseudocode algorithm which will find the LCM of any two given numbers.   Translate your algorithm into a FORTRAN/77 program and test it on the computer.

4.14   Two numbers are said to be relatively prime if they do not have any common, nontrivial factors.   For example, 9 and 16 are relatively prime whereas 15 and 21 are not since they have a common factor of 3.   Develop a pseudocode algorithm which will determine if any two given numbers are relatively prime.   Translate your algorithm into a FORTRAN/77 program and test it on the computer.

4.15   A number is said to be a perfect number if it is equal to the sum of its factors other than itself.   For instance, the number 28 is a perfect number since 1+2+4+7+14 = 28.   Develop a pseudocode algorithm which will test a given number to determine if it is a perfect number.   Translate your algorithm into a FORTRAN/77 program and run it on the computer.

4.16   Extend the algorithm of Exercise 4.15 such that the algorithm will test all numbers in the range 25 to 300 for perfectness.   Translate your algorithm into a FORTRAN/77 program and run it on the computer.

4.17   Two positive integers are said to be friendly if each one is equal to the sum of the divisors (including 1, excluding the number itself) of the other.   For example the numbers 220 and 284 are friendly since:

divisors of 220: 1+2+4+5+10+11+20+22+44+55+110 = 284
divisors of 284: 1+2+4+71+142 = 220.

Develop a pseudocode algorithm which will find all pairs of friendly numbers such that both numbers are less than 1500. Translate your algorithm into a FORTRAN/77 program and test it on the computer.

4.18 It has been conjectured that the product of two consecutive numbers lies between two odd numbers of which at least one is prime. Develop a pseudocode algorithm which will test this conjecture for all pairs of consecutive positive integers such that both are in the range from 1 to 100 inclusive. Translate your algorithm into a FORTRAN/77 program and test it on the computer.

4.19 Twin primes are defined to be two consecutive odd numbers which are both primes. For example, 11 and 13 are twin primes. Develop a pseudocode algorithm which will generate all of the twin primes in the set of numbers less than 200. Translate your algorithm into a FORTRAN/77 program and test it on the computer.

4.20 Pairs of prime numbers exist such that the larger prime is just 1 more than twice the smaller prime. For example, 3 and 7 form such a pair. Develop a pseudocode algorithm which will find all such pairs of prime numbers from the set of numbers less than 200. Translate your algorithm into a FORTRAN/77 program and test it on the computer.

4.21 In the following number problems, the letters take the place of digits and each distinct letter represents a different digit.

```
     I            IS
   +AM          +IT
  -------       -------
    OK            OK
```

Develop a separate pseudocode algorithm for each of the above puzzles, which will determine all possible combinations of digits for the letters such that the arithmetic holds. Translate your algorithms into FORTRAN/77 programs and test them on the computer.

5
Modules and Subprograms

5.1   Introduction to Modules

Many algorithms which solve computing problems contain repeated or complex sections. Programmers often want a way to use these repeated pieces of code without recopying them each time. Copying complex sections of algorithms by hand is prone to error, and programmers should avoid this hazard. These pieces of an algorithm which form parts of larger algorithms are called *modules* when organized appropriately.

A program module is a *small*, relatively *self-contained* section of an algorithm. The module must have a specific purpose and requires an *interface* to its environment of other modules. The module interface must clearly specify the values needed by the module and the results produced by the module. A module interface is *well-defined* if *all* such input values and results are specified for a module.

A modular algorithm may contain many modules and a typical structure is illustrated by Figure 5.1. The boxes indicate the modules and the lines between modules imply intermodule references, with the arrow indicating the direction of the reference. For example, module 1 is the *main* module and it references or *invokes* modules 2, 3 and 6; modules 2 and 3 in turn invoke the modules as shown. A module performs some specific task for the module that invokes it and usually returns some result to that referencing module.

Many benefits accrue from the use of modular design of algorithms and programs. All of them result from the fact that the modules are small, perform a readily identifiable task and have a well-defined interface. Individual modules may be written independently of other modules. They may be proven correct, tested, or modified separately. Algorithms are much easier to understand in modular form because the level of detail in each module is so much reduced. In fact, some modules may consist primarily of invocations of other modules.

Figure 5.1   A typically structured modular algorithm.

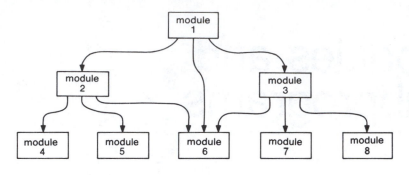

Usually a modular algorithm will be shorter than a *monolithic* (nonmodular) one. For example, if a sequence of operations is to be performed in many different places within the same algorithm, then this set may be referenced when needed, rather than rewritten. By having only one *instance* of that algorithmic segment, one is assured that exactly the same operations are being performed each time the module is referenced.

One of the best ways of creating modules is to assign modules on the basis of functionality, such that the amount of data they require and the number of results they produce is relatively small. That is, each module should perform a single, logically distinct algorithmic function. As a further guide, a rule of thumb suggests that a module should be one page or so in length. That is, if the module requires more than one page, it may be too large and could be broken down further.

Programmers use two kinds of modules: *subroutines* and *functions*. A subroutine module represents a sequence of computations and appears as one step in an algorithm. A function module computes a single result and appears within an expression.

5.2   Modules in Pseudocode

The main objective in choosing the pseudocode form for a module is to obtain a form which is simple and precise and which lends itself naturally to writing correct algorithms.

There are two basic attributes that a module must have: a *unique name* and a *well-defined interface*. The unique name distinguishes one module from other modules. The interface specifies the values, called *imports*, which the module needs for its operation, as well as the results, called *exports*, which it produces. Once a module is defined, it may be used or *invoked* by simply giving its name, together with values for its imports and variable names for its exports. In the algorithms developed thus far, it is expedient to think of them as special modules which are exceptions to this format and are called *main* modules. Each algorithm must have one, but only one, such main module.

5.2.1   Subroutine Modules

A subroutine module is defined as indicated by the general form of Figure 5.2.

Figure 5.2   Defining a subroutine module in pseudocode.

smodule name (**imports**: import parameter list;
            exports: export parameter list)

  ⋮

pseudocode to perform the required computations

  ⋮

end module

In the *module header*, the actual name of the module is inserted following the keyword **smodule** and the interface specifies the **imports** and **exports**. The import and export lists consist of pseudocode variables which are separated by commas and referred to simply as *parameters*. The import parameters receive values from, and the export parameters return values to, the invoking module.

A subroutine module is invoked by simply calling the name of the module and its two argument lists. The general form of the **call** statement for subroutine modules is shown in Figure 5.3. The individual items of the invoking argument lists are referred to as *arguments* and are separated by commas.

Figure 5.3   Invoking a subroutine module in pseudocode.

call name(import argument list; export argument list)

The import arguments may be variables, constants, or expressions, the values of which are to be used by the subroutine module. The export arguments may only be variables since they will be assigned values by the subroutine module. The number of import and export arguments must agree exactly with the corresponding number of import and export parameters of the module. When a subroutine module is called, the values of the import arguments are copied into the corresponding import parameters. Then the body of the referenced module is performed starting at the first statement following the **smodule** header. When the **end module** is reached, the values of the export parameters are copied into the corresponding export arguments and a return is made to the calling module to resume execution from the point of invocation.

The relationships between module parameters and arguments are illustrated by the sequence of events in Figure 5.4. The numbered events occur in order. This diagram represents only a single call of a subroutine. When several calls are made by the calling module, each invocation would follow the sequence of actions in Figure 5.4 with each set of import and export arguments copied into and out of the corresponding module parameters. This facility of associating different values with a module provides the generality needed to perform the module in different contexts without recopying all the statements involved.

Figure 5.4   The relationships of import and export arguments to module parameters during a subroutine invocation.

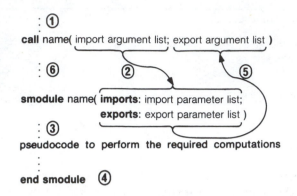

1 prepare import argument values
2 transfer import values
3 perform **smodule** actions
4 complete **smodule**
5 transfer export values
6 resume calling module
   after module invocation

Since these modules are completely self-contained, all pseudocode variables are *local* to each module. Thus, the only way for modules to communicate is through the arguments and parameters. The variable names used as arguments need bear no relationship to the variable names chosen for the parameters. Indeed, the actual names of the parameters need not be known to the users of a module. Note that it is possible for a subroutine module to be defined without any import parameters, without any export parameters, or even without any parameters at all.

5.2.2   A Prime Number Classification Algorithm as a Subroutine Module

As an example of subroutine module definition and use, the more efficient prime number classification algorithm developed in Section 4.4 will be used. In this case, the pseudocode which performs the test for a prime number will be placed in a module.

This module is quite simple to define since most of it has already been written. It is only necessary to decide upon a module name, its parameters, and to replace the **stop** statement with an **end module** statement. Figure 5.5 defines such a subroutine module named primetest which has one import parameter, n, the number to be tested, and one export parameter, prime, which indicates whether the assertion that the number is prime is **true** or **false**.

5.2.3   Using the Prime Number Classification Subroutine

The main module which calls the primetest module is given in Figure 5.6. This algorithm obtains the number to be tested, calls the module primetest, and then determines its response. When primetest is called, the value of number is copied into n and the module is executed from the beginning. When the **end module** is reached, the value of prime is copied into aprime and a return is made to the main module. Execution resumes in the main module with the statement following the reference to primetest.

Figure 5.5   A pseudocode subroutine module to test a number for primeness.

smodule primetest(**imports**: n;   **exports**: prime)

* Subroutine module to determine whether a given number n is a prime number
* (return prime as **true**) or is a composite number (return prime as **false**).

* Integer variables used:
* **divisor** - possible divisor of n (3, 5, 7, 9, . . . , rootn)
* **rootn** - square root of n

* Logical variables used:
* **prime** - indicates the truth of "the number is a prime"

* Assume the number n is a prime.

prime ← **true**

* Test whether the number is even and greater than 2.

if rem(n, 2) = 0 **and** n > 2 **then**

⎡ prime ← **false**

else

⎢   * Otherwise, test odd values of the divisor from 3 to the square root of n.

⎢   divisor ← 3
⎢   rootn ← $\sqrt{n}$
⎢   **while** divisor ≤ rootn **and** prime **do**

⎢   ⎡ **if** rem(n, divisor) = 0 **then**

⎢   ⎢   ⎡ prime ← **false**

⎢   ⎢ **else**

⎢   ⎢   ⎡ divisor ← divisor + 2

end module

5.2.4   Function Modules

The action of testing for prime numbers represents a special case of a module in which a single export is produced. In mathematics, it is natural to define functions which produce a single result, perhaps from one or more inputs. In algorithms, it is also convenient to define functions which compute a single result, and to use those functions within expressions.

The pseudocode function header requires the keyword **fmodule**, a unique function name, and an import parameter list, as shown in Figure 5.7.   Conventionally, function modules do not have an export list, and the single result computed will be assigned to the name of the function as one of the calculations within the function module. This resembles the practice in mathematics of defining functions by their names, such as the absolute value function

$$abs(x) = \begin{cases} x & \text{if } x \geq 0 \\ -x & \text{if } x < 0 \end{cases}$$

Figure 5.6 Using the prime number classification subroutine module primetest.

* Determine if a number is prime or composite by using the
* prime number classification subroutine module **primetest**.

* Integer variables used:
* **number** - number obtained from input to be tested

* Logical variables used:
* **aprime** - indicates the truth of "the number is a prime"

* Acquire the number to be tested from the input data.

get number

* Perform the test for a prime number.

call primetest(number; aprime);

* Use the logical flag to select the appropriate message.

if aprime **then**

    ⎡ **put** number, ' is a prime number'

else

    ⎡ **put** number, ' is a composite number'

stop

Figure 5.7 Defining a function module in pseudocode.

fmodule name (**imports**: import parameter list)

   ⋮

pseudocode to perform the required computations

   ⋮

name ← the computed result
end module

Invoking a pseudocode function is natural and straightforward. Within an expression, the function name with an appropriate set of import arguments set off by parentheses is used as if it were a variable. Thus, wherever an expression is permitted, a function invocation is legitimate, such as on the right-hand side of an assignment, within an output list, within a set of import arguments, or in a condition for an **if** or **while** statement. Some sample invocations are presented in Figure 5.8.

5.2.5 Function Modules in the Prime Number Classification Problem
Since the prime number classification subroutine module primetest developed earlier meets the constraints for function modules, it is instructive to pursue its definition as a function module, shown in Figure 5.9.

Figure 5.8   Sample invocations of functions in a variety of expressions.

* Using a function in an assignment.

x ← name(import argument list)

* Using a function in an output list.

put 'The result of computing the function is', name(import argument list)

* Using a function as an import to another module.

call primetest(name(import argument list); aprime)

* Note that the import argument list is for the function **name**, rather than the module **primetest**.
* The grouping of the parentheses will determine which module gets the imports.

The subroutine module had only one import, the number to be tested, and computed only the necessary single export, the truth of "the number is prime." Therefore the function module must produce this export as its result and assign it to the function name **aprime**. Choosing the function name to naturally sound like the question "is this number a prime?" will help make the calling modules more readable. The changes from a subroutine module to a function module are mainly in the **fmodule** header, in the commentary describing the variables used, and of course, in the assignment of the computed result to the function name.

The use of the function module **aprime** by a main module which checks a given input number for primeness is given in Figure 5.10. The algorithm is quite similar to Figure 5.6 which used the subroutine module **primetest**. However, the use of a logical function module leads to a simple and more elegant algorithm. Therefore, function modules are excellent tools for building algorithms when only a single result is computed by the module. If more, or possibly fewer, results are produced, or if the action performed is more logically considered as a complete algorithm step, then a subroutine module would be used.

5.3   Subroutines and Functions in FORTRAN/77

In FORTRAN/77 modules are referred to as *subprograms*. As with pseudocode, there are two types of subprograms, called *subroutine* subprograms and *function* subprograms respectively. Although the similarities are great, one important difference between pseudocode modules and FORTRAN/77 subprograms is that FORTRAN/77 does not distinguish explicitly between import and export parameters. Nonetheless, distinguishing between the two roles for these parameters is an important consideration in developing good algorithms. In FORTRAN/77 the value of each argument is copied into the corresponding parameter on invocation and on return the value of every parameter is copied into its corresponding argument.[1] Furthermore, since in FORTRAN/77 all variables have a type (so far REAL, INTEGER, or LOGICAL) associated with them, the type of

---

[1] Exceptions to this rule will be discussed at a later stage.

Figure 5.9   A function module for the prime number classification problem.

fmodule aprime(**imports**: n)

* Function module to determine whether a given number n is a prime number
* (return function result as **true**) or is a composite number (return function result as **false**).

* Integer variables used:
* **divisor** - possible divisor of n (3, 5, 7, 9, . . . , rootn)
* **rootn** - square root of n

* Logical variables used:
* **prime** - temporary variable for the function result

* Assume the number n is a prime.

prime ← **true**

* Test whether the number is even and greater than 2.

if rem(n, 2) = 0 **and** n > 2 **then**

$\quad$ [prime ← **false**

else

$\qquad$ [* Otherwise, test odd values of the divisor from 3 to the square root of n.

$\qquad$ divisor ← 3
$\qquad$ rootn ← $\sqrt{n}$
$\qquad$ **while** divisor ≤ rootn **and** prime **do**

$\qquad\quad$ [**if** rem(n, divisor) = 0 **then**

$\qquad\qquad$ [prime ← **false**

$\qquad\quad$ **else**

$\qquad\qquad$ [divisor ← divisor + 2

* Assign the computed result of the prime number classification to the function result.

aprime ← prime
end module

---

an argument must agree with the type of its corresponding parameter.   The method for declaring the type of variables in subprograms is the same as for a main program.   At compilation time, each subprogram is compiled in isolation from both the main program and other subprograms.

To illustrate how FORTRAN/77 subprograms are defined and used the following sections will first show how to convert modular pseudocode algorithms into subprograms in general and then will use the prime number algorithms as more concrete examples.

5.3.1   FORTRAN/77 **Subroutine Subprograms**

A pseudocode subroutine module is converted into a FORTRAN/77 subroutine subprogram as shown in Figure 5.11.   A module named **sample** and a reference to it are converted into FORTRAN/77.

Figure 5.10 Using a function module for the prime number classification problem.

* Determine if a number is prime or composite by using
* the prime number classification function module **aprime**.

* Integer variables used:
* **number** - number obtained from input to be tested

* Acquire the number to be tested from the input data.

get number

* Classify the number by the result of the boolean function **aprime**.

if aprime(number) **then**

$\quad\Big[$ **put** number, ' is a prime number'

else

$\quad\Big[$ **put** number, ' is a composite number'

stop

Figure 5.11 Translation of pseudocode subroutine modules into FORTRAN/77 subroutines.

a) Reference

```
                                    REAL  A,B,C
                                    INTEGER  D
  .                                 .
  .                                 .
call sample (a,b; c,d)              CALL  SAMPLE(A,B,C,D)
  .                                 .
  .                                 .
```

b) Definition

```
smodule sample (imports: r,s; exports: x,y)   SUBROUTINE  SAMPLE  (R,S,X,Y)
                                              REAL  R,S,X
                                              INTEGER  Y
  .                                           .
  .                                           .
body of sample                                body  of  SAMPLE
  .                                           .
  .                                           .
end module                                    RETURN
                                              END
```

In this case, the conversion actually needs only slight changes. The word SUBROUTINE replaces the word **smodule** in the first line and the parameter list specifies all of the parameters, both import and export. The distinction between import and export parameters is not explicit but is implied by the action of the program. Although this means that a single FORTRAN/77 parameter can assume both roles, parameters should be restricted to a single role, if at all possible. The second line of the subroutine subprogram declares the types of the parameters. Here the assumption is made that variables R, S, and X are to be of type REAL and Y of type INTEGER. The other change in converting the module is that the FORTRAN/77 statements RETURN and END are used to specify a return to the calling program and to indicate the end of the subprogram respectively.

The module reference is converted almost directly with the change being the replacement of the argument list semicolon with a comma. Also, the types of the arguments must be the same as the corresponding parameters, so the variables A, B, and C are declared REAL and D is declared INTEGER.

Using the above transformations as a guide, the complete prime number algorithm (Figures 5.5 and 5.6) would be converted into a FORTRAN/77 subroutine subprogram and a main program as shown in Figure 5.12. Other than the fact that the subroutine name has been shortened to the FORTRAN/77 limit of six characters the translation follows the example given previously. The statements of a subroutine subprogram are usually placed immediately following the END statement of the main program. If many subprograms are used, they are simply placed one after the other.

```
C Figure 5.12 -- A Prime Number Classification Program.
C                 Determine if a given number is prime or composite using
C                 the prime number classification subroutine PRIMET.
C**********************************************************************
C NUMBER - the number to be tested
C APRIME - indicates the truth of "NUMBER is prime"
C**********************************************************************
      INTEGER NUMBER
      LOGICAL APRIME
C Acquire the number to be tested.
      PRINT *, 'ENTER THE NUMBER TO BE TESTED:'
      READ *, NUMBER
C Perform the test for a prime number.
      CALL PRIMET(NUMBER,APRIME)
C Use the logical flag APRIME to select the appropriate message.
      IF (APRIME) THEN
          PRINT *, NUMBER, 'IS A PRIME NUMBER.'
      ELSE
          PRINT *, NUMBER, 'IS A COMPOSITE NUMBER.'
      ENDIF
      STOP
      END
```

```
C Figure 5.12 (continued)
C Subroutine PRIMET -- Determine whether a given number N is a prime
C                      number (return PRIME as .TRUE.) or is a composite
C                      number (return PRIME as .FALSE.).

C*********************************************************************
C N      - the number to be tested
C PRIME  - indicates the truth of "n is prime"
C DIVISR - possible divisors (3, 5, 7, 9, ... , IROOTN)
C IROOTN - largest integer less than the square root of the number N

C*********************************************************************
       SUBROUTINE PRIMET(N,PRIME)

       INTEGER N, DIVISR, IROOTN, MOD
       REAL FLOAT, SQRT
       LOGICAL PRIME
C Assume the number is a prime.
       PRIME = .TRUE.
C Test whether the number is even and greater than 2.
       IF (MOD(N,2) .EQ. 0 .AND. N .GT. 2) THEN
           PRIME = .FALSE.
       ELSE
C          Otherwise, test odd values of the divisor
C          from 3 to the square root of the number.
           DIVISR = 3
           IROOTN = SQRT(FLOAT(N)) + 1
   100     IF (DIVISR .LE. IROOTN .AND. PRIME) THEN
               IF (MOD(N,DIVISR) .EQ. 0) THEN
                   PRIME = .FALSE.
               ELSE
                   DIVISR = DIVISR + 2
               ENDIF
               GOTO 100
           ENDIF
       ENDIF

       RETURN
       END
```

When the call to the subroutine PRIMET is executed, the value of the INTEGER argument NUM is copied to the INTEGER parameter N and the (undefined) value of the LOGICAL argument ANSWER is copied to the LOGICAL parameter PRIME. The fact that ANSWER is undefined in the main program has no side effects in the subroutine since PRIME is treated as an export parameter. The subroutine will assign PRIME a value of .TRUE. or .FALSE.. At the completion of the subroutine, when the RETURN statement is executed, the values of the parameters N and PRIME are copied to the arguments NUM and ANSWER. Execution then resumes with the IF statement in the main program.

5.3.2 FORTRAN/77 **Function Subprograms**
A FORTRAN/77 function subprogram is also very similar to the pseudocode function module definition. However, since FORTRAN/77 distinguishes between real, integer, and logical values, the type of value that the function subprogram returns must be specified.

Thus, a function subprogram also has a type of REAL, INTEGER, or LOGICAL. This type should be declared in both the definition of the subprogram and the referencing program.

To illustrate this conversion the pseudocode module named **test** shown in Figure 5.13 will be used.

Figure 5.13 Translation of pseudocode function modules into FORTRAN/77 functions.

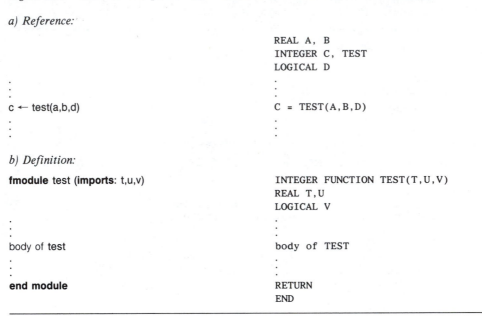

a) Reference:

```
                                    REAL A, B
                                    INTEGER C, TEST
                                    LOGICAL D
 .                                  .
 .                                  .
 .                                  .
c ← test(a,b,d)                     C = TEST(A,B,D)
 .                                  .
 .                                  .
```

b) Definition:

fmodule test (imports: t,u,v)

```
                                    INTEGER FUNCTION TEST(T,U,V)
                                    REAL T,U
                                    LOGICAL V
 .                                  .
 .                                  .
body of test                        body of TEST
 .                                  .
 .                                  .
end module                          RETURN
                                    END
```

This module has three import parameters (two of type REAL and one of type LOGICAL) and returns one result (assumed to be INTEGER) in the function name. Because of the type of the result, the function should be converted into an INTEGER-valued function program. Such a function subprogram begins with the words INTEGER FUNCTION followed by only the import parameters. The second statement of the program declares the type of each parameter. At the end of the function subprogram is the standard RETURN, END sequence and somewhere in the body of **test** there must be a statement which assigns to the function name the value to be returned. The pseudocode reference to the module is converted into FORTRAN/77 directly. Declarations for the import arguments *and* the function name are provided at the start of the referencing program.

Using the above techniques on the prime number algorithm (Figures 5.9 and 5.10) gives the program of Figure 5.14. Function subprograms are also placed following the END statement of the main program. If many function and subroutine subprograms exist, they may be placed in any order.

```
C Figure 5.14 -- A Prime Number Classification Program.
C                 Determine if a given number is prime or composite using
C                 the prime number classification function APRIME.

C***********************************************************************

C NUMBER - the number to be tested
C APRIME - indicates the truth of "NUMBER is prime"

C***********************************************************************

      INTEGER NUMBER
      LOGICAL APRIME

C Acquire the number to be tested.

      PRINT *, 'ENTER THE NUMBER TO BE TESTED:'
      READ *, NUMBER

C Classify the number by the result of the logical function APRIME.

      IF (APRIME(NUMBER)) THEN
         PRINT *, NUMBER, 'IS A PRIME NUMBER.'
      ELSE
         PRINT *, NUMBER, 'IS A COMPOSITE NUMBER.'
      ENDIF

      STOP
      END

C***********************************************************************

C Function APRIME -- Determine whether a given number N is a prime
C                    number (return function result as .TRUE.) or is
C                    a composite number (return function result as
C                    .FALSE.).

C***********************************************************************

C N      - the number to be tested
C PRIME  - indicates the truth of "n is prime"
C DIVISR - possible divisors (3, 5, 7, 9, ... , IROOTN)
C IROOTN - largest integer less than the square root of the number N

C***********************************************************************

      LOGICAL FUNCTION APRIME(N)

      INTEGER N, DIVISR, IROOTN, MOD
      REAL FLOAT, SQRT
      LOGICAL PRIME
C FUNCTION APRIME continued on page 110.
```
C FUNCTION APRIME continued on page 110.

```
C Figure 5.14 (continued)
C Assume the number is a prime.
      PRIME = .TRUE.
C Test whether the number is even and greater than 2.
      IF (MOD(N,2) .EQ. 0 .AND. N .GT. 2) THEN
         PRIME = .FALSE.
      ELSE
C         Otherwise, test odd values of the divisor
C         from 3 to the square root of the number.
         DIVISR = 3
         IROOTN = SQRT(FLOAT(N)) + 1
  100    IF (DIVISR .LE. IROOTN .AND. PRIME) THEN
            IF (MOD(N,DIVISR) .EQ. 0) THEN
               PRIME = .FALSE.
            ELSE
               DIVISR = DIVISR + 2
            ENDIF
            GOTO 100
         ENDIF
      ENDIF
      APRIME = PRIME
      RETURN
      END
```

5.4   The Prime-Pairs Problem

In the previous sections, the topics concentrated on the definitions of modules. There is very little need to reorganize an algorithm as a main module and a subroutine or function module when the module is to be performed only once. This section deals with another prime number problem which does require more applications of a module to complete the task.

Example 5.1   Prime Pairs Problem
   Pairs of prime numbers exist such that the larger prime is just 1 more than twice the smaller prime. For example, 3 and 7 form such a prime pair. Find all such pairs from the set of numbers between 3 and 200.

a) Problem Analysis   Since the prime pairs are limited to numbers between 3 and 200, it will be necessary to check only odd numbers in the range 3 to 99. For each such prime p, its possible prime pair $2p + 1$ must also be checked for primality.

b) Outline of the Algorithm   The pseudocode algorithm will have the following general form:

```
* Search for prime pairs of the form p, 2p+1
* in the range (3,200).

p ← 3
while  p ≤ 99  do
        ⎡  * Check if first number p is a prime.
        ⎢
        ⎢  if p is a prime then
        ⎢          ⎡  * Check if its pair 2p+1 is a prime.
        ⎢          ⎢
        ⎢          ⎢  if 2p+1 is a prime then
        ⎢          ⎢          ⎡ put p, 2p+1, 'are a prime pair.'
        ⎢          ⎣
        ⎣  p ← p + 2
stop
```

If the **fmodule** aprime of Figure 5.9 is used to accomplish the tests for primality, this algorithm may be expanded immediately to give the final pseudocode version in Figure 5.15.

Figure 5.15   A pseudocode algorithm for the prime pairs problem.

```
* Search for prime pairs of numbers of the form p, 2p+1
* in the range (3,200).

* Integer variables used:
* p - search values 3, 5, 7, . . . , 99

* Search from first number 3 until last number 99.

p ← 3
while  p ≤ 99  do
        ⎡  * If p is prime, then check its pair, 2p+1.
        ⎢
        ⎢  if  aprime(p)  then
        ⎢          ⎡  if  aprime(2*p + 1)  then
        ⎢          ⎢          ⎡ put p, 2*p + 1, ' form a prime pair.'
        ⎢          ⎣
        ⎣  p ← p + 2
stop
```

The reader should note that this form of the algorithm is quite simple and elegant, given an understanding of what the function module aprime does. If the algorithm were to incorporate two copies of the code contained in the module, the resulting algorithm would be longer and more difficult to comprehend.

Finally, a FORTRAN/77 version of this algorithm is presented as Figure 5.16, followed by its output in Figure 5.17.

```
C Figure 5.16 -- A Prime Pairs Program.
C                 A program to search for prime pairs of numbers of the
C                 form p, 2p+1 in the range (3,200).
C***********************************************************************
C P       - search values 3, 5, 7, ... , 99
C***********************************************************************
        INTEGER P
        LOGICAL APRIME
C Search from the first number 3 until last number 99.
        DO 100 P = 3, 99, 2
C         If P is prime then check its pair, 2P + 1.
          IF(APRIME(P)) THEN
              IF(APRIME(2*P + 1)) THEN
                  PRINT *, P, 2*P + 1, 'ARE A PRIME PAIR'
              ENDIF
          ENDIF
  100 CONTINUE
        STOP
        END
C Append the function APRIME here.
```

Figure 5.17 Output from the prime pairs program of Figure 5.16.

```
        3          7 ARE A PRIME PAIR
        5         11 ARE A PRIME PAIR
       11         23 ARE A PRIME PAIR
       23         47 ARE A PRIME PAIR
       29         59 ARE A PRIME PAIR
       41         83 ARE A PRIME PAIR
       53        107 ARE A PRIME PAIR
       83        167 ARE A PRIME PAIR
       89        179 ARE A PRIME PAIR
```

5.5   A Three Number Ordering Problem

This section introduces a small ordering problem which can be found as part of larger sorting algorithms or algorithms that must select the largest or smallest element of a set. The three number ordering problem serves to illustrate the use of modules to build other modules.

Example 5.2   *Three Number Ordering Problem*
Develop a module which will accept three arbitrary numbers, a, b, c, and will interchange their values, if necessary, so that the variables are ordered $a \leq b \leq c$.

An immediately obvious solution might be to select the largest value of the three numbers a, b, and c, then the next largest, and finally the smallest value, but some extra storage would be necessary. (Why?) Another solution to this problem which leads to an elegant algorithm is based on performing exchanges among pairs of variables to achieve the desired arrangement from smallest to largest.   Consider the sequence of actions:

1.   Interchange a and b, if necessary, so that $a \leq b$.
2.   Interchange b and c, if necessary, so that $b \leq c$.

At this point, c will contain the largest value. However, a and b may not be in the right order, thus a third step is needed:

3.   Interchange a and b, if necessary, so that $a \leq b$.

Now it should be clear that $a \leq b \leq c$.

5.5.1   Developing the Algorithm
a) Module Suggestion   This previous discussion suggests that a more basic problem has emerged, namely the arrangement of two numbers in order. This might be achieved by the use of a subroutine module, since the same interchange operation occurs three times in the suggested algorithm. The subroutine module sort2 is designed to do this ordering for an arbitrary pair of numbers x and y.

```
smodule sort2(imports: x,y; exports: x,y)

* Arrange 2 arbitrary numbers, x, y,
* by interchanging the variables so that x ≤ y.

* Integer variables used:
* temp - temporary variable used during an exchange

* If the variables are out of order, then exchange them.
if (y < x) then
  ┌ temp ← y
  │ y ← x
  └ x ← temp
end module
```

Note that if the interchange of x and y had been written simply as two assignment statements:

```
y ← x
x ← y
```

then x and y would have the same values.   Thus, the variable temp is needed to retain the old value of y while y is updated and then x can be updated from temp. This sequence is depicted in Figure 5.18.   Such a three-statement interchange using a temporary variable occurs frequently in other algorithms.

Figure 5.18   Schematic representation of an interchange between two variables.

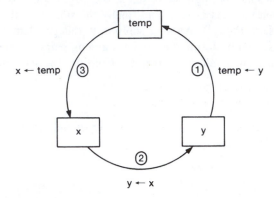

b) Algorithm Completion   The solution to the original ordering problem may now be achieved by the use of subroutine module sort2 in the three-step exchange outlined earlier.

```
smodule sort3(imports: a,b,c; exports: a,b,c)

* Arrange 3 arbitrary numbers, a, b, c,
* by interchanging the variables so that a ≤ b ≤ c.

call sort2(a, b; a, b)
call sort2(b, c; b, c)
call sort2(a, b; a, b)
end module
```

c) Testing the Module   Testing the sort3 module requires a strategy for exercising all possible outcomes. Since three numbers are required for the sort3 module, the input data should include all permutations of three numbers, say 1, 2, 3. This gives 6 test cases, and the output should always be the same: 1, 2, 3. Another set of tests should include data which are negative or which contain duplicates. Again all permutations can be checked.

5.5.2   Translation to FORTRAN/77

There are now two modules developed to solve the three number ordering problem, and they must be translated into FORTRAN/77 and used in a main program. The required main program and accompanying subroutines appear in Figure 5.19.

```
C Figure 5.19 -- The Three Number Ordering Program.
C                  A program to test the subroutine SORT3.

C***********************************************************************

C I, J, K - numbers to be arranged in order.

C***********************************************************************

      INTEGER I, J, K

C Acquire numbers to be ordered, terminating when all three are zero.

      PRINT *, 'ENTER THREE NUMBERS TO BE ORDERED.'
      PRINT *, 'TERMINATE WITH ALL THREE NUMBERS ZERO.'
      READ *, I, J, K

  100 IF (.NOT.(I.EQ.0 .AND. J.EQ.0 .AND. K.EQ.0)) THEN
         CALL SORT3(I,J,K)
         PRINT *, 'THE ORDERED NUMBERS ARE', I, J, K
         PRINT *, ' '
         PRINT *, 'ENTER THREE MORE NUMBERS TO BE ORDERED:'
         READ *, I, J, K
         GOTO 100
      ENDIF
      STOP
      END

C***********************************************************************

C Subroutine SORT3 -- Arrange 3 arbitrary numbers, A, B, C by inter-
C                     changing the variables so that A <= B <= C.

C***********************************************************************

      SUBROUTINE SORT3(A,B,C)
      INTEGER A, B, C

      CALL SORT2(A,B)
      CALL SORT2(B,C)
      CALL SORT2(A,B)

      RETURN
      END

C***********************************************************************

C Subroutine SORT2 -- Arrange 2 arbitrary numbers, X, Y by inter-
C                     changing the variables so that X <= Y.

C***********************************************************************

      SUBROUTINE SORT2(X,Y)
      INTEGER X, Y, TEMP

C If the variables are out of order, then exchange them.

      IF (Y.LT.X) THEN
         TEMP = Y
         Y = X
         X = TEMP
      ENDIF

      RETURN
      END
```

The FORTRAN/77 subroutines defined for sort2 and sort3 have parameters which were both **imports** and **exports** in pseudocode. Since this is a special case where variables appear in a module header as both an **import** and an **export**, the FORTRAN/77 subroutine header lists the variables only once since in effect all variables are copied in and out and are thus essentially imports and exports in FORTRAN/77.

The FORTRAN/77 program for testing the three number ordering module given in Figure 5.19 was executed with a selection of test data as suggested above. The test data input and the output produced are presented in Figure 5.20.

Figure 5.20   Input test data and output produced by the test program for the three number ordering problem of Figure 5.19.

a) Input file:

```
1  2  3
4  10  5
2  2  1
4  3  2
0  0  0
```

b) Output file:

```
ENTER THREE NUMBERS TO BE ORDERED.
TERMINATE WITH ALL THREE NUMBERS ZERO.
1 2 3
THE ORDERED NUMBERS ARE            1         2          3

ENTER THREE MORE NUMBERS TO BE ORDERED:
4 10 5
THE ORDERED NUMBERS ARE            4         5          10

ENTER THREE MORE NUMBERS TO BE ORDERED:
2 2 1
THE ORDERED NUMBERS ARE            1         2          2

ENTER THREE MORE NUMBERS TO BE ORDERED:
4 3 2
THE ORDERED NUMBERS ARE            2         3          4

ENTER THREE MORE NUMBERS TO BE ORDERED:
0 0 0
```

5.6   Summary

Problem solving can be made easier through the use of modules in the design of algorithms. Repeated or complex sections of algorithms can be organized into subroutine or function modules. The module interface defines how calling modules must pass and receive values to the module. The FORTRAN/77 language provides several features for defining and using modules, both subroutines and functions.

Examples of using modules demonstrate how algorithms can be more simple and elegant when they rely on modules. These modules may be created to solve this particular problem, or they may be retained from some previous problem and reused.

The use of modules in algorithms will be discussed in many places in the following chapters: to define mathematical functions, to create plots of interesting data, to implement useful techniques for zero-finding, area-finding, searching data, sorting data, matrix operations, and so on. Modules play an important role in simplifying algorithms which use these techniques, in reducing the time and cost of developing algorithms, and in eliminating many errors by using tested and correct modules.

5.7   Exercises

In most of the following exercises a program is requested to solve a specific problem. For each problem it is recommended that a pseudocode algorithm be developed to solve the problem. This algorithm should then be translated into FORTRAN/77 and run on the computer. Where appropriate, the program should be tested with a variety of data sufficient to ensure that the program does what it is supposed to do.

5.1   Consider the following FORTRAN/77 program.

```
C Exercise 5.1
      INTEGER NUM1, NUM2, ANSWER, RESULT
      READ *, NUM1, NUM2
   52 IF (NUM1*NUM2 .NE. 0) THEN
         ANSWER = RESULT(NUM1,NUM2)
         PRINT *, NUM1, NUM2, ANSWER
         READ *, NUM1, NUM2
         GOTO 52
      ENDIF
      STOP
      END

      INTEGER FUNCTION RESULT(NO1,NO2)
      INTEGER NO1, NO2, COPY1, COPY2, DUMMY, MOD
      COPY1 = NO1
      COPY2 = NO2
      DUMMY = 0
   52 IF (COPY1 .NE. 0) THEN
         IF (MOD(COPY1,2) .EQ. 1) THEN
            DUMMY = DUMMY + COPY2
         ENDIF
         COPY1 = COPY1/2
         COPY2 = COPY2*2
         GOTO 52
      ENDIF
      RESULT = DUMMY
      RETURN
      END
```

a)   Follow the program manually and specify the output it produces for the following input data:

$$
\begin{array}{rr}
37 & 41 \\
41 & 37 \\
37 & -41 \\
-37 & 41 \\
0 & 0
\end{array}
$$

Explain the results. What does the answer represent?

b)   What changes would be necessary to convert from a function to a subroutine? Test your answer by running it on the computer.

5.2   Consider the following pseudocode algorithm:

```
get q
while q > 0 do
      get n1, n2, n3
      call name(n1, n2; answer)
      call name(answer, n3; answer)
      put n1, n2, n3, answer
      q ← q - 1
stop
smodule name(imports: x,y; exports: z)
if x < y then
      z ← x
else
      z ← y
end module
3, 1, 2, 3, 1, 3, 2, 3, 2, 1
```

a)   Follow the algorithm manually and specify the output it produces.

b)   What does answer represent in terms of n1, n2, and n3?

c)   Translate the algorithm to FORTRAN/77 and test it on the computer.

d)   Rewrite the algorithm to use a function module.

e)   Translate the resulting algorithm in part d) to FORTRAN/77 and run it on the computer.

5.3   Given below is a mainline program to solve any 2×2 system of linear equations of the following form:

$$ax + by = c$$

$$dx + ey = f$$

```
C Exercise 5.3 -- Solve any 2 x 2 system of equations.
      REAL A, B, C, D, E, F, X, Y, DENOM
C Acquire and record the coefficients for the two equations.
      READ *, A, B, C
      READ *, D, E, F
      PRINT *, A, 'X +', B, 'Y =', C
      PRINT *, D, 'X +', E, 'Y ='. F
C Solve for the two unknowns.
      DENOM = A*E - D*B
      X = (C*E - F*B) / DENOM
      Y = (A*F - D*C) / DENOM
C Record the resulting solutions.
      PRINT *, 'X =', X, 'Y =', Y
      STOP
      END
```

a) What changes would be necessary to convert this mainline program into a FORTRAN/77 subroutine module to solve any 2×2 system of equations?

b) What changes would be necessary to convert this mainline program into one that uses the FORTRAN/77 subroutine of part a)?

c) What changes would be necessary to convert this mainline program into a FORTRAN/77 function module to solve any 2×2 system of equations?

5.4 It has been conjectured that the product of two consecutive numbers lies between two odd numbers of which at least one is prime. Develop a pseudocode algorithm that will test this conjecture for all pairs of consecutive positive integers such that both are in the range from 1 to 100 inclusive. Translate your algorithm into a FORTRAN/77 program and test it on the computer.

5.5 Twin primes are defined to be two consecutive odd numbers which are both primes. For example, 11 and 13 are twin primes. Develop a pseudocode algorithm which will generate all of the twin primes in the set of numbers less than 200. Translate your algorithm into a FORTRAN/77 program and test it on the computer.

5.6 a) Develop a pseudocode module to arrange four numbers in descending order.

b) Translate the module of part a) into FORTRAN/77 and test it on the computer with a suitable main program.

5.7 Assume that you are given a data list which contains experimental measurements in the form of $[a,b]$ pairs. Within each number pair $a \neq b$, thus there is one larger number and one smaller number per pair. Develop a pseudocode algorithm that will process these number pairs and determine the range of numbers for the smaller values in the pairs and the range of numbers for the larger number in the pairs. Assume that the data list is preceded by a data count which gives the number of pairs in the list. For example, the data 3, 5, 3, 1, 4, 4, 2, would lead to the following output:

pairs	largest # in pair	smallest # in pair
5 3	5	3
1 4	4	1
4 2	4	2
	range 5-4	range 3-1

5.8   In a particular course, three projects are assigned and three tests are given. All are marked out of 25 (no fractional marks). A student's mark in the course is determined by excluding the lowest project mark and excluding the lowest test mark. The information for each student is keypunched one student per card, with an ID number followed by the three project marks followed by the three test marks. Assuming that the number of students is known, develop a FORTRAN/77 program to compute each student's final mark.

5.9   The Fibonacci numbers may be defined as

$$f_1 = 1, \quad f_2 = 1, \quad f_3 = f_2 + f_1, \quad f_4 = f_3 + f_2, \ldots, \quad f_i = f_{i-1} + f_{i-2}$$

where i is the index of the Fibonacci number.

a)   Develop a pseudocode module, named f i b1, that when given an index will return the value of the corresponding Fibonacci number.

b)   An *approximation* to the i-th Fibonacci number is given by the formula

$$f_i = 0.447264 \times (1.61803)^i.$$

Develop a pseudocode module, named f i b2, that when given an index will return an approximation to the corresponding Fibonacci number.

c)   Develop a pseudocode main module that will tabulate the percentage error

(difference $\times$ 100/exact value)

between the values calculated by f i b1 and f i b2 for indices of $i = 1, 5, 10, 15, \ldots, 50$.

d)   Translate the complete algorithm into a FORTRAN/77 program and test it on the computer.

5.10   The following series

$$-\frac{x^1}{1^1} + \frac{x^2}{2^2} - \frac{x^3}{3^3} + \frac{x^4}{4^4} - \cdots$$

has the property that each term is of the form

$$\left[-\frac{x}{i} \right]^i.$$

One way to evaluate this series (although not an efficient way) is to use two function modules as requested in the following problem.

a)   Develop a function module named term which has two parameters x and i. When referenced, this module will calculate the value of the i-th term of the series and return this value for the function name.

b) Develop a function module named **series** which has one parameter x. When referenced, this module will use the function module **term** (part a) in computing the value of 5 terms of the series for the given value of x. The value of the series should be returned as the value of the function.

c) Develop a main program which will use the function module **series** (part b) in calculating the value of the above series for the range of
x = 0.0, 0.5, 1.0, . . . , 10.0. Output the value of x and the value of the series with appropriate identification.

5.11 A particular series is defined by:

$$p_1(x) = x$$

$$p_2(x) = \frac{3x^2 - 1}{2}$$

$$\vdots$$

$$p_i(x) = \frac{(2i - 1) \times x \times p_{i-1}(x) - (i - 1) \times p_{i-2}(x)}{i}, \text{ for } i \geq 3.$$

Develop a FORTRAN/77 program that will evaluate the first 10 terms of the series. Since all terms for $i \geq 3$ have the same formula use a function module
term(p1,p2,i,x) which, when referenced in the main module, will calculate the general formula for the given parameters and return its value as the value of the function. Run your program for x = 1.0 and print out the value of each term with suitable identification.

5.12 The Euclidean Algorithm is commonly used to determine the greatest common divisor of any two positive integers. The algorithm begins by dividing the first number by the second and retaining the remainder. At each successive stage the previous divisor is divided by the previous remainder. The algorithm continues until the remainder is zero. The greatest common divisor is the last nonzero remainder (or the last divisor). Consider a numerical example.

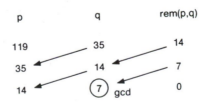

a) Show by example that the algorithm still works if the second number is larger than the first.

b) Develop a module to use the Euclidean Algorithm to determine the greatest common divisor of any two positive integers.

c) Develop a main program to find the greatest common divisor for each of several pairs of numbers. · Pairs that are relatively prime (that is, their GCD is 1) should be highlighted by an appropriate message.

5.13 a) Develop a module which accepts a three-digit integer and produces a second three-digit integer with the digits of the first integer in reverse order.

b) Develop a module which accepts any integer and produces a second integer with the digits of the first integer in reverse order.

c) A series of digits is said to be a palindrome if the digits read the same backwards and forwards.   Develop a main program to use the module of part b) to determine if each of a series of integers is a palindrome.   Each integer should have an appropriate message printed beside it.

5.14 The factorial of a positive integer n is defined as:

$$n! = n[(n-1)!] \quad \text{where} \quad 0! = 1$$

(that is, the product of the integers from 1 to n)

or $n! = n(n-1)(n-2) \cdots (3)(2)(1)$

(for example, $5! = 5(4!) = 5(4)(3!) = \cdots = 5(4)(3)(2)(1) = 120$).
$_nP_r$ is the number of permutations (arrangements) of n objects taken r at a time and is given by:

$$_nP_r = \frac{n!}{(n-r)!}.$$

For example, consider the number of permutations of the 3 letters A, B, and C taken 2 at a time, AB, BA, AC, CA, BC, and CB.   The number of these permutations can be calculated by:

$$_3P_2 = \frac{3!}{(3-2)!} = \frac{6}{1} = 6.$$

$_nC_r$ is the number of combinations of n distinct objects taken r at a time without repetition and can be evaluated using the following formula.

$$_nC_r = \frac{_nP_r}{r!} = \frac{n!}{r!(n-r)!}$$

For example, consider the number of combinations of the 3 letters A, B, and C taken 2 at a time without repetitions.   These combinations are AB, AC, and BC and their number can be predicted by the following calculation.

$$_3C_2 = \frac{3!}{2!(3-2)!} = \frac{6}{(2)(1)} = 3$$

a) Develop a module to compute $n!$ for any integer greater than zero.

b) Develop a module to use the module of part a) to calculate $_nP_r$ for given n and r.

c) Develop a module to use the modules of parts a) and b) to compute $_nC_r$ for given n and r.

d) Develop a main module to produce a table of combinations $_nC_1$, $_nC_2$, $_nC_3$, . . . , $_nC_n$ for any given n.   Translate the resulting complete algorithm into FORTRAN/77 and test it on the computer.

Part B
Mathematical Functions and Applications

6 Characteristics of Mathematical Functions   *125*

7 Locating Zeros and Root Finding   *151*

8 Area Finding   *181*

6
Characteristics of Mathematical Functions

6.1   Introduction

Mathematics is playing an increasingly important role in helping to study complex phenomena in today's society.   Mathematical models are used to describe relationships in a variety of fields including not only traditional areas such as physics, chemistry, and engineering, but also in other fields such as economics, sociology, biology, and ecology.

In many of these studies, physical relationships are expressed in terms of mathematical formulas or equations.   A very basic notion is that of the dependence of one quantity upon another, referred to mathematically as a functional relationship.   The task of understanding these physical phenomena is facilitated by using a computer to manipulate the mathematical functions.

This chapter discusses several common characteristics of functions and examines tabulation and plotting as means of studying them.

6.2   Functional Characteristics

There are a number of characteristics of these mathematical relationships or functions which are of interest.   Some of the questions often asked are listed below.

- What does the function look like for a given range of arguments?   Figure 6.1 illustrates two common functions graphically, a hyperbola and a polynomial.
- Does the function have more than one value for a particular argument?   The illustrated polynomial is single-valued for all values of x.   The hyperbola has two values for $|x| \geq b$.

Figure 6.1   Graphs illustrating characteristics of functions.

a) *Graph of the hyperbola* $x^2 - y^2 = b^2$

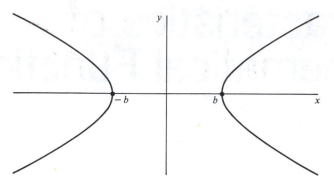

b) *Graph of the polynomial* $a_n x^n + a_{n-1} x^{n-1} + \cdots + a_1 x + a_0 = 0$

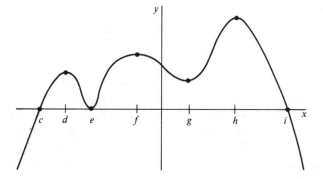

- Is the function defined over a given range or do arguments exist for which the function is undefined?   The hyperbola, for example, is undefined for values of x between $-b$ and $+b$.
- Is the function continuous?   The polynomial is continuous for all values of x.
- Are there arguments for which the function is zero?   The hyperbola is zero for $x = -b$ and $x = +b$ while the polynomial function is zero for $x = c$, $x = e$, and $x = i$. In fact the polynomial has a double zero at $x = e$.
- Does the function have a maximum or minimum?   If so, what and where are the maximum and minimum values?   For example, the polynomial has two relative maxima at $x = d$ and $x = f$ and an absolute maximum at $x = h$, as well as two relative minima at $x = e$ and $x = g$.
- For what values of x is the function increasing or decreasing?

The answers to the above questions are often necessary in mathematical problem solving. In many cases it is relatively easy to develop algorithms and write computer programs to assist in answering these questions.   A selection of these problems will be discussed in sections of this and subsequent chapters.

6.3   Function Tabulation

Perhaps the simplest technique used to study the characteristics of a function is to evaluate that function at a given set of values of the independent variable.   Normally this evaluation begins with one specific value and proceeds to a final value using a constant step-size or increment.   Consider a specific example.

Example 6.1   Function Tabulation Problem
      Tabulate $y = x^3 + x^2 - 37x + 35$ from -10 to $+10$ in steps of 1.

The pseudocode algorithm for this example, shown in Figure 6.2, is straightforward and similar to several examples presented in Chapter 2.

Figure 6.2   Pseudocode algorithm to tabulate a polynomial function.

* Tabulate the polynomial $y = x^3 + x^2 - 37x + 35$ from -10 to $+10$ in steps of 1.

* Real variables used:
* x - current x value
* y - current y value

* Record column titles.

put ' x ', ' y '

* Tabulate the polynomial varying x from -10 to $+10$ in steps of 1.

for x **from** -10 **to** $+10$ **by** 1

$\quad \begin{bmatrix} y \leftarrow x^3 + x^2 - 37x + 35 \\ \textbf{put } x, y \end{bmatrix}$

stop

       A FORTRAN/77 program for this algorithm is given in Figure 6.3, and several points regarding the conversion are made in the notes section following the program.
       The output produced by this program is given in Figure 6.4.   By scanning this table of values several points of special interest may be observed.   The value of Y changes sign between X = -8 and X = -6, and a zero of the function occurs at X = -7.   Additional zeros can be found at X = 1 and X = 5.   A relative maximum can be detected near X = -4 since at that point Y = 135 while points on either side yield smaller functional values.   Similarly, there is a relative minimum near X = 3.

```
C Figure 6.3 -- Polynomial Tabulation Problem.
C               Tabulate the polynomial x**3 + x**2 - 37x + 35
C               from -10 to +10 in steps of 1.
C*******************************************************************
C X - current x value
C Y - current y value
C*******************************************************************
      REAL X, Y
C Record column titles.
      PRINT *, '     X                  Y'
      PRINT *, ' '
C Tabulate the polynomial varying x from -10 to +10 in steps of 1.
      DO 100 X = -10.0, 10.0, 1.0
         Y = X**3 + X**2 - 37.0*X + 35.0
         PRINT *, X, Y
  100 CONTINUE
      STOP
      END
```

Program Notes

- Though all values in the program will be integers, it is desirable to be able to change the program to use fractional limits or increments.   Thus, both X and Y are declared as REAL variables.

Figure 6.4   Tabulation of the polynomial $x^3 + x^2 - 37x + 35$, output from the program of Figure 6.3.

X	Y
-10.00000	-495.0000
-9.000000	-280.0000
-8.000000	-117.0000
-7.000000	0.0000000E+00
-6.000000	77.00000
-5.000000	120.0000
-4.000000	135.0000
-3.000000	128.0000
-2.000000	105.0000
-1.000000	72.00000
0.0000000E+00	35.00000
1.000000	0.0000000E+00
2.000000	-27.00000
3.000000	-40.00000
4.000000	-33.00000
5.000000	0.0000000E+00
6.000000	65.00000
7.000000	168.0000
8.000000	315.0000
9.000000	512.0000
10.00000	765.0000

6.3.1   Function Tabulation with Fractional Increments

Often it may be necessary to repeat the tabulation of a function over a short interval with a small increment in x values to examine the details of function behavior at some critical point. The following example illustrates some difficulties that might occur.

Example 6.2   Function Subtabulation Problem
  Tabulate $y = x^3 + x^2 - 37x + 35$ from -2 to $+2$ in steps of 0.2.

This problem involves no new program but merely a change in the range of the DO loop in the program of Figure 6.3. The revised loop required would be:

```
        DO 100 X = -2.0, 2.0, 0.2
          Y = X**3 + X**2 - 37.0*X + 35.0
          PRINT *, X, Y
    100   CONTINUE
```

The results of executing the modified program are given in Figure 6.5.

Figure 6.5   Subtabulation of the polynomial $x^3 + x^2 - 37x + 35$, output from the modified program of Figure 6.3.

X	Y
-2.000000	105.0000
-1.800000	99.00800
-1.600000	92.66400
-1.400000	86.01600
-1.200000	79.11200
-0.9999998	71.99999
-0.7999998	64.72800
-0.5999998	57.34399
-0.3999999	49.89600
-0.1999999	42.43200
1.4901161E-07	35.00000
0.2000002	27.64799
0.4000002	20.42399
0.6000001	13.37600
0.8000001	6.551996
1.000000	-3.8146973E-06
1.200000	-6.232006
1.400000	-12.09600
1.600000	-17.54401
1.800000	-22.52801

Unfortunately, these results contain some unpleasant surprises. First, the values of X are not quite what one might expect. For example, -0.6 is represented as -5.999998 and 0.4 as 0.4000002, whereas 1.4 remains as 1.400000. Why should these deviations occur? Also, for the value X = 1.0, there seems to be no error in representing X, but this version of the program calculates Y as -3.8146973E-06, while the previous version gave Y as 0.0. Should we abandon our faith in the consistency of the machine? Finally, the program was supposed to produce a value for X = 2.0, but stopped at X = 1.8. Can we tolerate this kind of disobedience?

The explanation for all three of these problems lies in the *approximate nature* of machine arithmetic. All numbers used by the computer must fit within the fixed and limited number of digits established for that particular machine and FORTRAN compiler. If a number representation is too large, some least significant digits are deleted by rounding-off or simply chopping off the excess. For example, we know that the number 1/3 should be represented as an infinite string of the form 0.333 · · · in base 10 arithmetic, but will often use 0.33333 in a calculation for which 5 digits seem to be sufficient.

Virtually all current generation computers use arithmetic to base 2 or base 16. In both systems, an innocent number such as 0.2 is a non-terminating binary number and there is some rounding error associated with even storing this number in the computer. Subsequent operations, such as adding 0.2 several times to the starting value of -2.0 in this subtabulation, may increase this error. The error may or may not be discerned, because computers often compensate when they convert back to base 10 for the output display. This explains the first two questions — irregularities in the values of x and the fact that the computer displays X = 1.0 for an internal value which is just slightly different.

The other disturbing aspect of the output was the failure of the program to do what was intended. Values of the function were requested at the 21 points -2.0, -1.8, . . . , 1.8, 2.0, but only the first 20 appeared, ignoring the value for X = 2.0. Why did this occur? The answer lies in the way the DO loop operates for REAL values of the control variable. The loop terminates and the statements within the range of the DO are not executed *when the control variable exceeds the upper limit*. In this case, the round-off error in *computing* 2.0 creates a value slightly greater than 2.0, so the evaluation of the function for this value of x is skipped.

A very undesirable consequence of the above problems is that the same program may not run the same way on two different computers! A program which will run on different machines is said to be *portable*. When this program is run on an IBM 4341 with FORTRAN VS, for example, the value for X = 2.0 is generated, even though both the VAX machines and IBM 4341 machines use the same word-size in their number representations.

The problems just discussed may often be avoided by dealing with numbers, particularly increments, which have exact internal representations. Integers or negative powers of 2, such as 0.25 $(1/2^2)$ or 0.125 $(1/2^3)$, or sums of these powers, such as 0.1875 $(3/2^4)$, all have this exact property, provided the integer or power are not too large. In the above example, changing the problem to require the tabulation at steps of 1/4 rather than 1/5 eliminates the difficulties. Thus changing the DO statement in Figure 6.3 to DO 100 X = -2.0, 2.0, 0.25 will generate the output shown in Figure 6.6. Notice that now all values of X are displayed exactly as expected.

In summary, to avoid difficulties with portability of programs and uncertainty about what output a program will create, the authors recommend that DO loops have increments restricted to numbers which will have an exact representation on any machine on which the program will be run.

Figure 6.6 Subtabulation of the polynomial $x^3 + x^2 - 37x + 35$, output from the modified program of Figure 6.3.

X	Y
-2.000000	105.0000
-1.750000	97.45313
-1.500000	89.37500
-1.250000	80.85938
-1.000000	72.00000
-0.7500000	62.89063
-0.5000000	53.62500
-0.2500000	44.29688
0.0000000E+00	35.00000
0.2500000	25.82813
0.5000000	16.87500
0.7500000	8.234375
1.000000	0.0000000E+00
1.250000	-7.734375
1.500000	-14.87500
1.750000	-21.32813
2.000000	-27.00000

6.4 Evaluating Polynomials: Horner's Rule

In the previous example, the evaluation of the polynomial

$$x^3 + x^2 - 37x + 35$$

involved two multiplications to get x^3, one to compute x^2, and a fourth to calculate $37x$. To reduce this amount of arithmetic, computer scientists often evaluate polynomials in a slightly different manner using a technique called Horner's Rule. For the current example, the polynomial would be rewritten as

$$((x + 1)x - 37)x + 35$$

Figure 6.7 compares the steps involved to evaluate the function at $x = 2$.

Figure 6.7 Example comparing evaluation of polynomials.

Step	$x^3 + x^2 - 37x + 35$	$((x + 1)x - 37)x + 35$
1	$4x + x^2 - 37x + 35$	$((3)x - 37)x + 35$
2	$8 + x^2 - 37x + 35$	$(6 - 37)x + 35$
3	$8 + 4 - 37x + 35$	$(-31)x + 35$
4	$8 + 4 - 74 + 35$	$-62 + 35$
5	$12 - 74 + 35$	-27
6	$-62 + 35$	
7	-27	

Seven steps are required to evaluate the polynomial the standard way, whereas Horner's Rule involves only five steps. Horner's Rule is recommended as a useful device for improving efficiency of polynomial evaluation.

6.5   Trials and Tribulations of Function Evaluation

In the previous section, a polynomial function was tabulated and studied. Unfortunately, not all function evaluations are as straightforward. A variety of problems may arise as functions become more complicated. This section will deal with difficulties in two specific areas, the evaluation of transcendental functions and rational functions.

6.5.1   Transcendental Functions

Many physical relationships are expressed using more complicated mathematical tools such as the trigonometric or exponential functions, which are classified as *transcendental* functions. In addition to problems in obtaining values for such functions, complications arise due to the limitations and peculiarities of computer arithmetic. Consider the following example.

Example 6.3   Transcendental Function Tabulation
      Tabulate $\sqrt{x}\ \sin(\pi x)$ for x from 1 to 3 in steps of 0.125.

The pseudocode algorithm for this example, given in Figure 6.8. It is a slightly more general form of the algorithm presented for Example 6.1.

Figure 6.8   Pseudocode algorithm to tabulate a transcendental function.

* Tabulate the transcendental function $\sqrt{x}\sin(\pi x)$ from **1** to **3** in steps of **0.125**.

* Real variables used:
* **x** - current x value
* **xfirst** - initial x value
* **xincr** - increment in x value
* **xlast** - terminal x value
* **y** - current y value

* Obtain the tabulation parameters.

put 'Enter the initial value of x:'
get xfirst
put 'Enter the increment in x values:'
get xincr
put 'Enter the terminal value of x:'
get xlast

* Record column titles.

put ' x ',' y '

* Tabulate points varying **x** from **xfirst** to **xlast** in steps of **xincr**.

for x **from** xfirst **to** xlast **by** xincr
$$\left[\begin{array}{l} y \leftarrow \sqrt{x}\sin(\pi x) \\ \textbf{put}\ x,\ y \end{array}\right.$$
stop

1, 0.125, 3

In this case, the initial value of x, the increment in x, and the final value of x are obtained via the **get** action, thus allowing for more flexibility.   Should the first range of x not provide sufficient information about the function, it is only necessary to change the input list and try the algorithm again for a different range.

To follow this algorithm manually would require considerable effort.   For each value of x, it would be necessary to search a table of values for the appropriate sine and square root values.   Not only would this process be time consuming and prone to error, but the values of these functions are likely to be expressed to 4 or 5 decimal places and higher accuracy would tend to be cumbersome.   Of course, use of a scientific calculator would make this problem fairly easy to handle.   FORTRAN/77 also has features designed to facilitate scientific calculations.   Functions such as SIN and SQRT were built into the language and can be used simply by specifying the correct name for the function together with a value in parentheses as the *argument.* A large number of such *built-in functions* are provided by FORTRAN/77.   A complete list is presented in Appendix N.   The resulting FORTRAN/77 implementation is shown in Figure 6.9.

```
C Figure 6.9 -- Transcendental Function Tabulation Problem.
C                   Tabulate the function sqrt(x)*sin(pi*x).
C************************************************************************
C X      - current x value
C XFIRST - initial x value
C XINCR  - increment in x value
C XLAST  - terminal x value
C Y      - current y value
C PI     - the mathematical constant 3.141593
C************************************************************************
      REAL X, XFIRST, XINCR, XLAST, Y, PI, SQRT, SIN
      PI = 3.141593
C Obtain the tabulation parameters.
      PRINT *, 'ENTER THE INITIAL VALUE OF X:'
      READ *, XFIRST
      PRINT *, 'ENTER THE INCREMENT IN X VALUES:'
      READ *, XINCR
      PRINT *, 'ENTER THE TERMINAL VALUE OF X:'
      READ *, XLAST
C Record column titles.
      PRINT *, ' '
      PRINT *, '    X                  Y'
      PRINT *, ' '
C Tabulate points varying x from XFIRST to XLAST in steps of XINCR.
      DO 100 X = XFIRST, XLAST, XINCR
         Y = SQRT(X) * SIN(PI*X)
         PRINT *, X, Y
  100 CONTINUE
      STOP
      END
```

Program Notes

- The built-in functions SIN and SQRT are used in evaluating the mathematical function.   Notice that an arithmetic expression may be provided as the argument to the sine function.

The output for the program is listed in Figure 6.10.

Figure 6.10 Tabulation of the function $\sqrt{x}\,\sin(\pi x)$, output from the program of Figure 6.9.

```
ENTER THE INITIAL VALUE OF X:
1.0
ENTER THE INCREMENT IN X VALUES:
0.125
ENTER THE TERMINAL VALUE OF X:
3.0
```

X	Y
1.000000	-3.2584137E-07
1.125000	-0.4058975
1.250000	-0.7905697
1.375000	-1.083345
1.500000	-1.224745
1.625000	-1.177720
1.750000	-0.9354136
1.875000	-0.5240102
2.000000	9.2161855E-07
2.125000	0.5578532
2.250000	1.060661
2.375000	1.423794
2.500000	1.581139
2.625000	1.496855
2.750000	1.172603
2.875000	0.6488701
3.000000	-1.6931214E-06

The values of X are now exact since the increment is $1/8$ and thus, the values of the function at X = 1, 2, and 3 should be zero. However, they are computed to be very small numbers, both positive and negative, close to zero. This is partly a result of the approximation used for defining the constant π and the roundoff error inherent in the routines which compute the sine of πx and $\sqrt{x}$.

6.5.2 Evaluating Rational Functions
In the previous example the limitations of computer representation of numbers was only an inconvenience. Sometimes, however, the problems created are more serious. Consider an example involving two polynomials.

Example 6.4   Rational Function Tabulation
Tabulate the following function for a given set of values.

$$\frac{x^3 + 2x^2 - 7x - 10}{x^2 - x - 2}$$

Evaluating this function requires a little more care than the previous examples. Values of x which cause the denominator to be zero must be avoided since the function is undefined at these points. Attempts by a computer to evaluate such a function value will result in either a divide by zero error, or an overflow error when attempting to represent a number too large to store as a REAL. Avoiding these errors can be accomplished in several ways, either by checking for known x values or by checking for a zero denominator. For generality, the latter technique is usually preferred. The pseudocode algorithm incorporating such a check is given in Figure 6.11.

Figure 6.11 Pseudocode algorithm for Example 6.4.

* Tabulate the rational function $\dfrac{x^3 + 2x^2 - 7x - 10}{x^2 - x - 2}$

* Real variables used:
* x - current x value
* xfirst - initial x value
* xincr - increment in x value
* xlast - terminal x value
* y - current y value

* Obtain the tabulation parameters.

put 'Enter the initial value of x:'
get xfirst
put 'Enter the increment in x values:'
get xincr
put 'Enter the terminal value of x:'
get xlast

* Record column titles.

put ' x ', ' y '

* Tabulate points varying x from **xfirst** to **xlast** in steps of **xincr**.

for x **from** xfirst **to** xlast **by** xincr

    denom ← $x^2 - x - 2$
    if denom = 0 **then**

        put x, 'y is undefined'

    else

        y ← $(x^3 + 2x^2 - 7x - 10)$/denom
        put x, y

stop

−4, .25, 3

Converting this algorithm to a FORTRAN/77 program presents some practical problems. Specifically, how does one check for a zero denominator? Because of roundoff error, the exact values of x which cause a zero denominator may or may not be encountered. Even if this x value is computed exactly, the corresponding denominator may not be computed to be exactly zero due to roundoff error. Again, because a computer only retains a fixed number of digits in its arithmetic and its representations, the result of a computation such as $(2.000005)^2 - 4.0$ could be zero. The safest check, therefore, involves looking for denominator values which are very close to zero, both positive and negative.   The use of the absolute value function abs to perform this check is illustrated in the program of Figure 6.12.   All denominators between -0.00005 and +0.00005 are avoided.

```
C Figure 6.12 -- Rational Function Tabulation Problem.
C               Tabulate x**3+2x**2-7x-10 / x**2-x-2.
C************************************************************************
C X      - current x value
C XFIRST - initial x value
C XINCR  - increment in x value
C XLAST  - terminal x value
C Y      - current y value
C DENOM  - denominator of the function
C************************************************************************
      REAL X, XFIRST, XINCR, XLAST, Y, DENOM, ABS
C Obtain the tabulation parameters.
      PRINT *, 'ENTER THE INITIAL VALUE OF X:'
      READ *, XFIRST
      PRINT *, 'ENTER THE INCREMENT IN X VALUES:'
      READ *, XINCR
      PRINT *, 'ENTER THE TERMINAL VALUE OF X:'
      READ *, XLAST
C Record column titles.
      PRINT *, ' '
      PRINT *, '    X               Y'
      PRINT *, ' '
C Tabulate points varying X from XFIRST to XLAST in steps of XINCR.
      DO 100 X = XFIRST, XLAST, XINCR
C         Avoid division by zero when the denominator is almost zero.
          DENOM = (X - 1)*X - 2.0
          IF (ABS(DENOM) .LE. 0.00005) THEN
              PRINT *, X, '   Y MAY BE UNDEFINED'
          ELSE
              Y = (((X + 2.0)*X - 7.0)*X - 10.0) / DENOM
              PRINT *, X, Y
          ENDIF
  100 CONTINUE
      STOP
      END
```

The corresponding output appears in Figure 6.13.   The rational function is undefined in the neighbourhood of X = -1 and also X = 2.   Zeros of the function can be detected between -3.25 and -3.0, -1.5 and -1.25, and 2.25 and 2.5.

6.5.3   Functions in General

The preceding two subsections have dealt specifically with transcendental and rational functions.   The difficulties exhibited by the examples are also evident in evaluating functions in general.   Though a detailed study of pitfalls in numerical computation is

Figure 6.13 Tabulation of a rational function, output from the program of Figure 6.12.

```
ENTER THE INITIAL VALUE OF X:
-4.0
ENTER THE INCREMENT IN X VALUES:
0.25
ENTER THE TERMINAL VALUE OF X:
3.0
```

X	Y
-4.000000	-0.7777778
-3.750000	-0.5286561
-3.500000	-0.2818182
-3.250000	-3.8359787E-02
-3.000000	0.2000000
-2.750000	0.4304511
-2.500000	0.6481481
-2.250000	0.8441176
-2.000000	1.000000
-1.750000	1.072222
-1.500000	0.9285714
-1.250000	-9.6153848E-02
-1.000000	Y MAY BE UNDEFINED
-0.7500000	5.886364
-0.5000000	4.900000
-0.2500000	4.824074
0.0000000E+00	5.000000
0.2500000	5.307143
0.5000000	5.722222
0.7500000	6.264286
1.000000	7.000000
1.250000	8.101851
1.500000	10.10000
1.750000	15.65909
2.000000	Y MAY BE UNDEFINED
2.250000	-5.211538
2.500000	0.3571429
2.750000	2.372222
3.000000	3.500000

beyond the scope of this introduction, references are given at the end of the chapter for those interested in pursuing this topic further.

6.6 Plotting a Single Function

The discussion in the previous sections of this chapter has been concerned with tabulating functions of various complexities and then studying the tables of values.   There is an old adage which states that a picture is worth a thousand words.   In a similar vein, a graph would be worth a thousand(?) tabulated points.   Is there some method of having the computer generate a graph for a function?

To answer this question, consider how a graph might be drawn manually for a sample cubic polynomial.

Example 6.5   Plotting a Cubic Polynomial
   Plot a graph for the cubic polynomial $x^3 - 2x^2 - 5x + 6$ from -2.5 to $+3.5$ with points plotted at intervals of 0.25.

The general structure of the algorithm would be very similar to the algorithm for tabulating the function.   Some initial decisions would be necessary about the overall size of the graph and how the points should be kept.   As the function is evaluated repetitively, each x value and corresponding functional value must be retained for future plotting.   After the points have been tabulated, it is necessary to scan the table to determine the range of functional values.   This range would be used to determine the scale factors necessary to produce a graph of the correct size.   Next, each pair of values must be scaled to size and positioned on the graph.   These steps are crudely incorporated into the general algorithm in Figure 6.14.

Figure 6.14 Pseudocode algorithm to plot a graph of a function.

* Plot a graph for the cubic polynomial $x^3 - 2x^2 - 5x + 6$

* Real variables used:
* **x** - current x value
* **xfirst** - initial x value
* **xincr** - increment in x value
* **xlast** - terminal x value
* **y** - current y value

* Obtain the plotting parameters.

put 'Enter the initial value of x:'
get xfirst
put 'Enter the increment in x values:'
get xincr
put 'Enter the terminal value of x:'
get xlast

''Prepare to record (x,y) pairs''
''Choose the graph size''

* Plot points varying **x** from **xfirst** to **xlast** in steps of xincr.

for x **from** xfirst **to** xlast **by** xincr

$\quad\Big[\quad$ y ← $x^3 - 2x^2 - 5x + 6$

$\quad\Big[\quad$ ''Retain the (x,y) pair for plotting''

''Determine the range of values''
''Compute the scale factors''
''Scale and plot each (x,y) pair''

stop

−2.5, 0.25, 3.5

Though this algorithm may provide sufficient detail if applied manually, some big questions exist if the algorithm were to be applied by a computer. And although it would be possible to refine this algorithm to make it specific enough for translation into a computer program, fortunately this is not necessary. Since plotting is a commonly desired activity, the graph plotting algorithm can be developed by taking advantage of subprograms already implemented by other programmers.

Such commonly used modules as plotting subprograms are typically maintained by each individual computing facility. By properly referring to the appropriate module, it may be possible to solve problems more easily.

The FORTRAN/77 program in Figure 6.15 illustrates the use of a package of three such modules developed for plotting elementary graphs on an ordinary line printer. Appendix K contains a complete description of the SETPLT, STOPNT, and PLOT modules.

```
C Figure 6.15 -- Polynomial Plotting Problem.
C                 Plot a graph for the cubic polynomial x**3-2x**2-5x+6
C***********************************************************************
C X      - current x value
C XFIRST - initial x value
C XINCR  - increment in x value
C XLAST  - terminal x value
C Y      - current y value
C***********************************************************************
      REAL X, XFIRST, XINCR, XLAST, Y
C Obtain the plotting parameters.
      PRINT *, 'ENTER THE INITIAL VALUE OF X:'
      READ *, XFIRST
      PRINT *, 'ENTER THE INCREMENT IN X VALUES:'
      READ *, XINCR
      PRINT *, 'ENTER THE TERMINAL VALUE OF X:'
      READ *, XLAST
C Initialize the plotting routines.
      CALL SETPLT(51,31)
C Plot points varying X from XFIRST to XLAST in steps of XINCR.
      DO 100 X = XFIRST, XLAST, XINCR
         Y = ((X - 2.0)*X - 5.0)*X + 6.0
         CALL STOPNT(X,Y,'C')
  100 CONTINUE
C Plot the graph.
      CALL PLOT(1)
      STOP
      END
```

The preparation for plotting and recording (x,y) pairs is performed by the SETPLT subroutine module. Naturally, it must be the first of these routines to be executed and should only be executed once for each graph. It is possible to choose the size of the plotting surface of the graph by specifying values for the arguments of SETPLT. The package will plot a graph with *x* coordinates spread across the printed page and with *y* coordinates down the page. By default, the limits are set to 81 characters in the *x* direction and 51 characters in the *y* direction, if the program does not invoke the SETPLT subroutine. For the sample program, these values are 51 characters and 31 lines respectively. Valid sizes in the *x* direction are 11, 21, 31, . . . , or 81, while in the *y* direction valid sizes are 11, 21, 31, 41, . . . , or 51.

The STOPNT routine is used to retain or store points for future plotting. Some installations may have to limit the number of points plotted because of storage requirements. Execution of the statement:

```
CALL STOPNT(X, Y, 'Q')
```

causes the values of X and Y and the letter Q to be remembered for plotting later. Notice that the desired character to be plotted at the specified position is written between single quotes.

After all points to be plotted have been collected, several major steps in the plotting process remain. It is necessary to determine the range of values and compute the scale factors. Finally, each point must be scaled and plotted. All of these actions are accomplished by the PLOT subroutine. The single parameter for this module determines the type of graph, a value of 0 implying that no axes should be printed while a value of 1 causes axes to be superimposed on the plotted points.

The output produced by the sample plotting program is included in Figure 6.16. The message above the graph states that all 25 of the points submitted were plotted. The graph itself includes the scale of *y* values at regular intervals in a column to the left. The scale in the *x* direction is printed in a line at the bottom of the graph. For reference, the scale factors for the ordinate or *y* coordinates and for the abscissa or *x* coordinates are printed following the graph.

Though limited by the accuracy of character positions on a printer, the graph does give a reasonable characterization of the function. The function appears to be continuous. It increases from X = -2.4 to about X = -1.2, then decreases to a relative minimum near X = +2 before increasing until at least the edge of the graph at X = +3.5. Approximating by eye, the maximum value near X = -1.2 appears to be about 9 while the minimum value near X = 2 is about -4.

As indicated above, the package of printer-plot routines offers a more convenient way to study mathematical functions than simple tabulation. As with many routines written by other programmers, these subroutines may not offer all of the flexibility a user might desire. In some cases it is necessary to rewrite the modules; in others, it is more desirable to find a way to mold the routines to the task at hand.

6.7 Plotting Several Functions

In the previous section, a program was developed to plot a single function. It is often desirable to plot two functions on the same graph, perhaps to determine their points of intersection. Consider such an example.

Figure 6.16 Graph of the polynomial $x^3 - 2x^2 - 5x + 6$, output from the program of Figure 6.15.

```
ENTER THE INITIAL VALUE OF X:
-2.5
ENTER THE INCREMENT IN X VALUES:
0.25
ENTER THE TERMINAL VALUE OF X:
3.5
   NUMBER OF POINTS : SUBMITTED          25  PLOTTED              25


                          C C       :
                              C      :
                    C          C     :                          C
    5.94271         C               C:
                                     :  C
                                     :
                 C                   :
    2.97135                          +   C                       C
                                     :
                                     :     C
    0.00000-+--C------+--------------+-------C-+----------+----C----
                                     :
                                     :        C
                                     :               C
                                     :           C
   -2.97135                          +                      C
                                     :                  C
                C                    :              C C
                                     :
   -5.94271                          +
                                     :
                                     :
                                     :
   -8.91406                          +
             C                       :
          -2.4000    -1.2000    0.0000    1.2000    2.4000

   THE Y - AXIS SCALE FACTOR IS 10**              0
          THE X - AXIS SCALE FACTOR IS 10**              0
```

Example 6.6   Plotting a Line and Polynomial
  Plot a single graph for the polynomial $y = x^3 - 2x^2 - 5x + 6$ and the straight line $2y = 8 - 5x$ from -2.5 to $+3.5$.

Since the plotting routines merely remember points to be plotted, incorporating a second function on the same graph simply involves computing and storing values of the points on the straight line as well as values of the cubic polynomial for each step of the DO loop. The statements

```
Y = 4.0 - 2.5*X
CALL  STOPNT(X,Y,'S')
```

may be inserted after the CALL STOPNT(X,Y,'C') of the previous program to accomplish this.

A somewhat better program design would avoid the DO loop with REAL values of the control variable. If the program is given the starting and ending value of *x* along with the *number of steps* to take between these values, then this integer number of steps (called NSTEPS in the program) may be used to control the DO loop.

The necessary changes have been incorporated in the program of Figure 6.17. This version eliminates the frustration of discovering that the final point desired has been omitted from one's graphical output (recall section 6.3.1). Notice that the letter C was used for the cubic polynomial, and the letter S was used for points on the straight line. The plotting package places an asterisk wherever the two curves intersect.

From this graph, the points of intersection are easy to see. Estimating by eye (using the axes tick marks which are placed every 10 characters on the *x* axis and every 5 characters on the *y* axis), the three points of intersection are near (-1.4,7.4), (0.6,2.4), and (2.5,-2.4). Notice that the graph did not show any asterisks for the intersections due to the way that points are scaled to printer positions. In addition, it is possible to approximate the zeros of the cubic as -2.0, 1.0, and 3.0, a fact which in this case can be checked analytically by factoring the polynomial as $(x + 2)(x - 1)(x - 3)$.

6.8   Summary

This chapter has provided an introduction to the study of several characteristics of mathematical functions. Examples have been demonstrated for tabulating and plotting elementary functions. It is possible to design many other algorithms to assist in understanding the functions being studied. Some of these are suggested in the exercises to follow. Other specific problems such as determining zeros of a function and finding areas between a curve and the *x* axis will be discussed in succeeding chapters.

```
C Figure 6.17 -- Several Function Plotting Problem.
C               Plot a graph for x**3-2x**2-5x+6 and 2y=8-5x.
C***********************************************************************
C X      - current x value
C XFIRST - initial x value
C NSTEPS - number of steps from XFIRST to XLAST
C XLAST  - terminal x value
C XINCR  - increment in x value
C YCUBIC - current y value for the cubic polynomial
C YLINE  - current y value for the straight line
C I      - loop counter
C***********************************************************************
       REAL X, XFIRST, XINCR, XLAST, YCUBIC, YLINE
       INTEGER NSTEPS, I
C Obtain the plotting parameters.
       PRINT *, 'ENTER THE INITIAL VALUE OF X:'
       READ *, XFIRST
       PRINT *, 'ENTER THE TERMINAL VALUE OF X:'
       READ *, XLAST
       PRINT *, 'ENTER THE NUMBER OF STEPS:'
       READ *, NSTEPS
C Initialize the plotting routines.
       CALL SETPLT(61,41)
C Compute the increment in X values between plotted points.
       XINCR = (XLAST - XFIRST)/NSTEPS
C Plot points varying X from XFIRST to XLAST in steps of XINCR.
       X = XFIRST
       DO 100 I = 0, NSTEPS
          YCUBIC = ((X - 2.0)*X - 5.0)*X + 6.0
          CALL STOPNT(X,YCUBIC,'C')
          YLINE = 4.0 - 2.5*X
          CALL STOPNT(X,YLINE,'S')
          X = X + XINCR
  100 CONTINUE
C Plot the graph.
       CALL PLOT(1)
       STOP
       END
```

Figure 6.18 Final graph of the polynomial and straight line, output from the program in
Figure 6.17.

```
ENTER THE INITIAL VALUE OF X:
-2.5
ENTER THE TERMINAL VALUE OF X:
3.5
ENTER THE NUMBER OF STEPS:
30
```

NUMBER OF POINTS : SUBMITTED   62 PLOTTED   62

```
            S
  0.99375   S
              S
                S
                  S       C C
                    S   C     C
  0.74531         S         C   +                                        C
                  C S             C
                    S         C
              C         S        :C
  0.49687             S      +
                       S:   C                                        C
                  C     :S
                          S C
                          S
  0.24844             +      S
                            C S
          C                       S                        C
                            C   S
                              S
  0.00000-----+---------+---------+---------+------S--+---------+-----
                            :      C     S
            C                     C        S       C
                                       C        S   S C
 -0.24844             +           C       C       S
                                      C       C   S
                                       C   C C      S
                                                      S
 -0.49688   C         +
                      :
 -0.74531             +
                      :
          C
            -2.0000   -1.0000   0.0000   1.0000   2.0000   3.0000
```

THE Y - AXIS SCALE FACTOR IS 10**   1
    THE X - AXIS SCALE FACTOR IS 10**   0

6.9   Exercises

In most of the following exercises a program is requested to solve a specific problem.   It is recommended that an algorithm be developed in pseudocode to solve the problem. Modules introduced in the text should be used wherever applicable.   This algorithm should then be translated into FORTRAN/77 and run on the computer.   Where appropriate, the program should be tested with a variety of data sufficient to ensure that the program does what it is supposed to do.

6.1   Tabulate each of the following functions over a suitable range of values.   Use the resulting table of values to discuss properties of the function.

a) $x^4 - 6x^3 - 6x^2 - 70x + 9$
b) $x^4 + 3x^3 - 3x^2 - 6x + 2$
c) $x^4 + 3x^3 - 3x^2 - 6x + 4$
d) $x^4 + 3x^3 - 3x^2 - 6x + 6$
e) $x^4 - x^3 - 85x^2 - 403x + 200$
f) $(\sqrt{\sin x + 3} + \sqrt[4]{|\cos x|}) / (2x^2 - 2x - 3)$
g) $(|\sin x| + 12)^{1/12} / (\tan [x + 4\sqrt{x} + 2])$

h) $\dfrac{e^{-m} m^k}{k!}$ for given values of m and $k = 0, 1, 2, \ldots, 12$.

6.2   Plot each of the following functions over a suitable range of values.   On the graph, indicate the noticeable properties of the function.   Estimate each zero and relative maxima or minima.

a) $2x^3 - 15x^2 + 26x + 7$
b) $x^4 - 5x^3 - 8x^2 - 7x + 55$
c) $x^4 - x^3 - 3x^2 + 5x - 2$
d) $x^4 - 2x^3 - x - 2$
e) $x^4 - 10x^2 + 25$
f) $x^5 + x^4 + 2x^3 + 2x^2 - 8x - 8$
g) $2x^4 - 14x^3 - 2x^2 + 68x + 56$
h) $(\sin x / \cos x) - x$
i) $\sqrt{x - 1} + (x + e^{-x}) / \sqrt{x}$

6.3   Develop a program to study each of the following limits.

a) $\lim\limits_{t \to 0} [\cos 2t] \dfrac{1}{t^2}$

b) $\lim\limits_{t \to 0} \left[\dfrac{1 + t}{t} - \dfrac{1}{\log (1 + t)} \right]$

c) $\lim\limits_{t \to \infty} \left[\dfrac{3x^3 - 2x + 4}{2 - 3x^2 - 2x^3} \right]$

d) $\lim\limits_{n \to \infty} \left[\dfrac{\left(1 + \dfrac{1}{n^2}\right)^{1/2}}{1 + \dfrac{1}{n}} \right]$

6.4 Series expansions are often used to generate values for commonly used mathematical functions. In many cases, a term in the series can be derived from the previous term by several simple arithmetic operations rather than by evaluating a general form of the term. Develop programs to evaluate each of the following series for a given range of x.

a) $\dfrac{1}{1+x} = 1 - x + x^2 - x^3 + \cdots$

b) $\sqrt{1+x} = 1 + \dfrac{1}{2}x - \dfrac{1}{8}x^2 + \dfrac{1}{16}x^3 - \cdots$

c) $\ln(1+x) = x - \dfrac{x^2}{2} + \dfrac{x^3}{3} - \dfrac{x^4}{4} + \cdots$

d) $e^x = 1 + x + \dfrac{x^2}{2!} + \dfrac{x^3}{3!} + \cdots$

e) $\sin x = \dfrac{x^1}{1!} - \dfrac{x^3}{3!} + \dfrac{x^5}{5!} - \dfrac{x^7}{7!} + \cdots$

f) $\cos x = 1 - \dfrac{x^2}{2!} + \dfrac{x^4}{4!} - \dfrac{x^6}{6!} + \cdots$

6.5 Polar coordinates are a useful tool for studying a variety of mathematical functions.

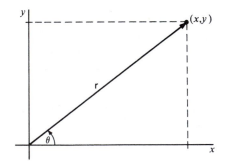

For any point (x,y) on the coordinate plane, $x = r \cos \theta$ and $y = r \sin \theta$. Make use of polar coordinates to plot the following functions. The letters a and b are given constants.

Hint: Vary the angle θ to calculate successive values for r and subsequently x and y.

a) A parabolic arc, $x^{1/2} + y^{1/2} = a^{1/2}$.
b) The folium of Descartes, $x^3 + y^3 - 3axy = 0$.
c) The cissoid of Diocles, $y^2 = x^3/(2a - x)$.
d) An astroid, $x^{2/3} + y^{2/3} = a^{2/3}$.
e) The witch of Agnesi, $x^2 y = 4a^2(2a - y)$.
f) A strophoid, $y^2 = x^2(a + x)/(a - x)$.
g) A cardioid, $r = a(1 - \cos \theta)$.
h) A limaçon, $r = b - a \cos \theta$, $(b < a)$.
i) The spiral of Archimedes, $r = a\theta$.
j) A hyperbolic spiral, $r\theta = a$.
k) The lemniscate of Bernoulli, $r^2 = a^2 \cos 2\theta$.
l) A three-leaved rose, $r = a \sin 3\theta$.
m) A four-leaved rose, $r = a \sin 2\theta$.
n) A cycloid, $x = a(\theta - \sin \theta)$, $y = a(1 - \cos \theta)$.
o) A trochoid, $x = a\theta - b \sin \theta$, $y = a - b \cos \theta$, for values of $a < b$.

6.6 The following two functions intersect in two places.

$$f_1(x) = \sqrt{4 - x^2}$$

$$f_2(x) = 1 + x^2$$

Plot a graph of the functions which clearly illustrates the points of intersection and approximate their coordinates.

6.7 Develop a program to draw a straight line between any two points, (x_1, y_1) and (x_2, y_2). The resulting graph should include both an x axis and a y axis.

6.8 Develop a program to draw a circle of given radius and given center. The resulting graph should include both an x axis and a y axis.

6.9 Under ideal conditions, a bullet fired into the air will travel a horizontal distance d in a time t as described by the following equations.

$$d = \frac{v^2 \sin 2\theta}{g}$$

$$t = \frac{2v \sin \theta}{g}$$

where v is the initial velocity, θ is the angle of inclination and g, the force due to gravity, is 9.8 meters/second^2. Develop a program to produce a single graph of both d and t as a function of θ as θ ranges from $0°$ to $90°$. Arrange to input a value for v.

6.10 A law of optics states that:

$$\frac{1}{a} + \frac{1}{b} = \frac{1}{f}$$

where f is the focal length of the lens, a is the distance from the lens to the object, and b is the distance from the lens to the image. If b is positive, then the image is a real image. If b is negative, then the image is said to be virtual.

However, if $1/b = 0$, then there is no image. Develop a program which tabulates the image distance, b, for all values of $a = 1, 2, 3, \ldots, 10$ and $f = 1, 2, 3, \ldots, 10$. The program should record an appropriate message beside each value of b.

6.11   Consider the diagram in Figure 6.19.

Figure 6.19 Banded area for Exercise 6.11.

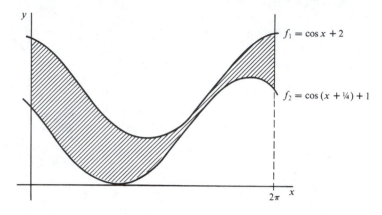

Develop a program to plot the pictured band. The area between the two curves should be filled with slashes.

6.12   Through the use of attached plotters and cathode-ray tube terminals, computers have the ability to provide graphical output in addition to the regular alphanumeric printouts. For some applications, the information to be drawn does not always fit in the limited drawing or viewing area. Thus, a method of trimming the drawing information must be used.

Figure 6.20 illustrates a situation for which the drawing information (straight lines) does not fit completely within the drawing area. The lines A and B are within the area, the lines C and D are partially within the area and must be trimmed, and the lines E and F lie outside the area and may be discarded. Develop a program which will take a specified viewing area, and for each of a series of lines with given endpoints, (x_1, y_1) and (x_2, y_2), determine if the line

a)   is within the drawing area
b)   is outside the drawing area
c)   pierces the drawing area (one end in, one end out)
d)   cuts the drawing area (similar to D in the diagram).

The program should record an appropriate message in each case.

6.13   The problem of finding a maximum point of a function can sometimes be solved analytically but must, in many cases, be solved numerically with the aid of a computer. Consider the following numerical technique. The continuous function $f(x)$ is known to have a single relative maximum in the interval $[a, b]$.

Figure 6.20 Drawing information doesn't always fit (Exercise 6.12).

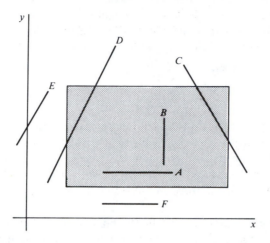

Figure 6.21 Finding a maximum of a function (Exercise 6.13).

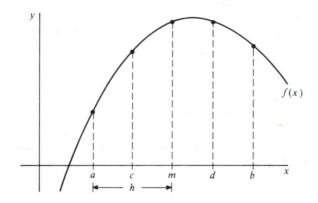

Divide the interval $[a,b]$ into four equal subintervals as shown in Figure 6.21.   If $f(c)>f(m)$, then the maximum must be in the subinterval $[a,m]$.   If $f(d)>f(m)$, then the maximum must be in the subinterval $[m,b]$.   Otherwise, the maximum must lie in the subinterval $[c,d]$.   In any case, the search is refined to the new subinterval and the procedure is repeated, this time with a smaller value of h.   The algorithm continues until h, half the interval size, is sufficiently small, that is, $h \leq \epsilon$.   Develop a program to use this method to find the maximum value of $f(x) = 2.25x - x^3$ in the interval $[0,1]$ with ϵ equal to 0.5×10^{-8}. Compare the resulting approximation with that obtained by applying analytical methods.

6.14   Biorhythm theory originated in Europe toward the end of the last century. According to this theory, each person has a set of life rhythms or life cycles which begin on the day a person is born. There are three such rhythms known as the physical, emotional, and intellectual cycles. Each of these cycles takes the form of a sine wave with the following periods.

- physical cycle (23 days)
- emotional cycle (28 days)
- intellectual cycle (33 days)

In the case of the physical cycle, the theory proposes that in the first half, or positive portion, of the cycle, one's physical well-being is enhanced as opposed to the second half, or negative portion, of the physical cycle. Similar reasoning is applied to the emotional and intellectual cycles. The worst days are the critical days when any one of the three rhythms switch from negative to positive or vice versa.

The calculation of a person's biorhythm requires knowing the number of days since they were born. This may be determined by calculating the Julian Day number of the date of birth and the Julian Day number of the required day and subtracting them. The Julian Day number for a given day may be calculated by the following formula (valid for all dates A.D.).

$$\text{Julian Day} = 1721060 + 365y + 31(m - 1) + d + \lfloor y'/4 \rfloor - \lfloor y'/100 \rfloor + \lfloor y'/400 \rfloor - x$$

where $\lfloor z \rfloor$ = the largest integer $\leq z$, y = the year, m = the month, d = the day, and for $m \leq 2$, $x = 0$ and $y' = y - 1$, for $m > 2$, $x = \lfloor .4m + 2.3 \rfloor$ and $y' = y$. Once the number of days is known, it may be divided by the length of each cycle to determine the status of the cycles on the required day.

Develop a program which will generate a plot of the biorhythm cycles for a given person over a specified period of time. The input for the program should be the person's birthdate, the date the plot is to start, and the date the plot is to end. The dates may be given in the form YYYY MM DD. The output from the program should be a plot containing the three biorhythm curves, using the characters P, E, and I for the respective curves, versus the Julian Day number. To the diagram add markings by hand to indicate the days of the month.

7
Locating Zeros and Root Finding

7.1 Introduction

In a number of examples in the previous chapter, it was noted that the value of a function could become zero for a certain specific value of its argument. Such a value of x, for which $f(x)$ is 0, is called a *zero* of $f(x)$. Similarly, one refers to the solution of an equation $f(x) = 0$ as a *root* of the equation. In this case the root of the equation and the zero of the function coincide and this leads to some confusion between the two terms. For example, a root of the equation $f(x) = a$ is not a zero of the function $f(x)$, unless $a = 0$.

Historically, mathematicians sought ways of solving for the roots of equations by explicit formulas, such as the quadratic formula:

$$\frac{-b \pm \sqrt{b^2 - 4ac}}{2a}$$

for the roots of the equation $ax^2 + bx + c = 0$. Later on, it was shown that such formulas are impossible to obtain for polynomial equations of degree greater than four and for virtually all transcendental equations. The need to have *approximate* methods for finding the roots of equations was recognized and studied over three centuries ago, and aspects of such methods still attract the attention of eminent scientists. In this chapter, various techniques for approximating the location of zeros are discussed and several algorithms are developed.

7.2   Graphical Search for a Zero

A sound way to approach the problem of locating a zero of $f(x)$ is to start with a *graph* of the function.   From such a graph, one may be able to identify the location of a zero well enough for the purpose at hand.   At the very least one can conclude that a zero lies in some rough interval, say $a \leq x \leq b$.   Here a and b are two points between which it is certain that the values of $f(x)$ have changed sign.   (This implies the presence of a zero between them if $f(x)$ is continuous.)

   The ability to draw a graph requires only values of the function for specific values of the independent variable.   These are easy to obtain automatically by a function tabulation program as was illustrated in Chapter 6.   The values may be plotted by hand but most computer systems have provision for automatic plotting, such as the modules introduced in the previous chapter.   In fact one may use plotting as the basis of an *algorithm* for the solution of the zero-finding problem to *any* accuracy required.   The steps involved would be:

1)   graph $f(x)$ for $a \leq x \leq b$;
2)   estimate a better interval $[a',b']$ by eye;
3)   graph $f(x)$ for $a' \leq x \leq b'$;
4)   repeat 2) and 3) until the interval is small enough.

This algorithm may actually be quite useful to the scientist who needs a "quick and dirty" estimate of a zero for planning purposes, particularly if there is immediate access to interactive computing facilities.

   As an illustration of how to apply this algorithm, consider the function

$$f(x) = x^3 - 4x^2 - 4x + 15.$$

Figure 7.1 shows an initial printer-plot graph of this function in the range -2.5 to $+5$. This graph illustrates the rough location of all three zeros.   Each of these zeros could be refined using the above algorithm.   For example, consider applying this algorithm to the leftmost zero.   The curve crosses the x axis between 3 and 4 printer positions to the left of -1.5.   Since each print position represents 0.15, the zero in question must lie in the interval $[-2.1, -1.95]$.   These better limits may be used in the next graph which appears as the top graph in Figure 7.2.   From this second graph, each printer position represents 0.003 and this leads to the interval $[-1.962, -1.953]$.   A third attempt plots the function between these points to produce the bottom graph in Figure 7.2.   From this graph, the zero would appear to be close to -1.9575.   Of course, this procedure could be continued to approximate the zero more accurately if desired.

   As demonstrated above, this method provides one way to determine a zero of a function.   It may be performed entirely by hand or with the assistance of the computer. However, even with the aid of a computer, the necessity for human involvement makes this algorithm tedious to implement, particularly if a high degree of accuracy is desired.

Figure 7.1 Initial graph of the function $f(x) = x^3 - 4x^2 - 4x + 15$.

```
ENTER THE INITIAL VALUE OF X:
-2.5
ENTER THE TERMINAL VALUE OF X:
5.0
ENTER THE NUMBER OF STEPS:
50
 NUMBER OF POINTS : SUBMITTED           51  PLOTTED           51
                         :                                C
                         :
 1.78125                 +
                         :
                         :
                    CCCCC:                               C
                   C     C
 1.33594          C      +C
                 C       : C
                         :  C                           C
                C        :   C
                         :
 0.89063       C         +    C
                         :     C                       C
                         :      C
              C          :
                         :       C
 0.44531                 +                            C
             C           :        C
                         :         C
                         :                           C
            C            :          C
 0.00000-------+---------+---------+-C-------+------C--+---
                         :
                         :            C            C
           C             :             C
                         :              C         C
-0.44531                 +               C       C
                         :                C     C
          C              :                 CCCCC
                         :
                         :
                         :
-0.89063                 +
                         :
         C               :
                         :
                         :
-1.33594                 +
                         :
                         :
        C                :
             -1.5000    0.0000    1.5000    3.0000    4.5000
  THE Y - AXIS SCALE FACTOR IS 10**           1
          THE X - AXIS SCALE FACTOR IS 10**          0
```

Figure 7.2   Second and third graphs of the function $f(x) = x^3 - 4x^2 - 4x + 15$.

a) Graph of $f(x)$ from -2.1 *to* -1.95:

```
NUMBER OF POINTS : SUBMITTED           51   PLOTTED              51
                                                             CC
  0.00000+---------+---------+---------+---------+------CC-+
                                                    CCC    !
                                                 CCC       !
                                                CC         !
                                             CCC           !
 -0.91904                                   CC             +
                                         CCC               !
                                      CCC                  !
                                    CC                     !
                                 CCC                       !
 -1.83807                        CC                        +
                               CC                          !
                            CCC                            !
                          CC                               !
                        CCC                                !
 -2.75711             CC                                   +
                   CCC                                     !
                  CC                                       !
                CC                                         !
              CC                                           !
          -2.1000    -2.0700    -2.0400    -2.0100    -1.9800    -1.9500

     THE Y - AXIS SCALE FACTOR IS 10**              0
            THE X - AXIS SCALE FACTOR IS 10**            0
```

b) Graph of $f(x)$ from -1.962 *to* -1.953:

```
NUMBER OF POINTS : SUBMITTED           51   PLOTTED              51
                                                             CC
  1.04203                                                  CC !
                                                        CCC   !
                                                      CC      !
                                                   CCC        !
  0.52102                                          CC         +
                                                CCC           !
                                              CC              !
                                           CCC                !
                                         CC                   !
  0.00000+---------+---------+---CCC---+---------+---------+
                                  CC                          !
                               CCC                            !
                             CC                               !
                          CCC                                 !
 -0.52102              CC                                     +
                    CCC                                       !
                   CC                                         !
                CCC                                           !
              CC                                              !
 -1.04203CC                                                   +
          -1.9620    -1.9602    -1.9584    -1.9566    -1.9548    -1.9530

     THE Y - AXIS SCALE FACTOR IS 10**              -1
            THE X - AXIS SCALE FACTOR IS 10**            0
```

7.3   Automatic Search for a Zero

A simple-minded approach to an automatic search for a zero might be to evaluate the function over a set of points, checking for a point at which the function is exactly zero. The difficulty with such a technique is that the zeros of functions studied in real applications rarely have integer or simple fractional values such as those sometimes encountered in classroom and textbook examples. Thus, choosing appropriate points to "hit" a zero exactly is virtually impossible. In addition, when using a computer, round-off errors in the computation of $f(x)$ would probably cause nonzero values for $f(x)$ even if one did hit the theoretical zero of the function.

The best result which one should expect to achieve, therefore, is the identification of an *interval* containing a zero. That is, one should be able to find two successive values of x such that the corresponding values of $f(x)$ differ in sign. Such an algorithm, given in Figure 7.3, breaks the original interval [xfirst,xlast] into nsteps smaller intervals of length xstep, which are scanned from left to right. In each small interval, the algorithm checks for a change in the sign of $f(x)$ and writes out the values of the endpoints of the first small interval in which a sign change is detected. Note that although a change in sign could be detected by:

if f(xl) $\leq$ 0 **and** f(xr) $\geq$ 0 **or** f(xl) $\geq$ 0 **and** f(xr) $\leq$ 0 **then**

$\lceil$ **put** 'There is a sign change'

it is more elegant and efficient to observe that there will be a sign change whenever

f(xl)*f(xr) $\leq$ 0

This simpler test is used in the algorithm.

Since this algorithm determines an interval of width xstep which contains a zero, *either endpoint* of the interval is an approximation to the zero within a tolerance of xstep. Thus, arbitrarily high accuracy could be achieved by taking a small enough xstep (that is, a large enough nsteps). However, this would be very inefficient in that three digit accuracy, for example, would require several thousand function evaluations, many more than the 150 or so required to achieve the same accuracy by plotting 3 or 4 graphs, each of 50 or so points.

7.4   Systematic Refinement of the Zero Estimate

It was observed that three-digit accuracy in a zero estimate could be achieved graphically in about 150 function evaluations by repeatedly "blowing up" the graph at the point of interest. If a similar strategy were adopted in an automatic approach, then perhaps a similar saving might result. Such a scheme is possible by simply applying successively the search algorithm of Figure 7.3. The recorded output from one application of the algorithm would become the input to the next.

Figure 7.3   Scan for the first subinterval containing a sign change.

* Algorithm to look for the first sign change in f(x).

* Real variables used:
* **xfirst,xlast** - initial interval
* **xstep** - size of each step
* **xl,xr** - endpoints of successive subintervals

* Integer variables used:
* **nsteps** - number of steps

* Initialize the parameters.

get xfirst, xlast, nsteps
put 'The initial interval is', xfirst, xlast
put 'The number of steps to be used is', nsteps

* Verify that the initial interval contains a zero.

if f(xfirst)*f(xlast) > 0 **then**

    ⎡ **put** 'No sign change in this interval'

else

    ⎡ * Scan successive small intervals for a sign change,
      * and reset the endpoints if there is none.

      xstep ← (xlast − xfirst)/nsteps
      xl ← xfirst
      xr ← xl + xstep
      while f(xl)*f(xr) > 0 **do**

          ⎡ xl ← xr
          ⎣ xr ← xr + xstep

      * Record the endpoints of the subinterval containing a zero.

      put 'There is a zero between', xl, 'and', xr

stop

The algorithm in Figure 7.4 automatically performs this repetition until the desired tolerance is achieved. For each successive application of the algorithm, the initial interval is arbitrarily subdivided into 25 subintervals. At the end of each application, the resulting subinterval becomes the new interval to be divided and scanned.

The equivalent FORTRAN/77 program, presented in Figure 7.5, applies this algorithm to the polynomial

$$x^3 - 4x^2 - 4x + 15 \ .$$

Several improvements have been made to the algorithm in the process of translation. In moving from one small interval to the next, the previous right endpoint becomes the left endpoint of the new interval, and the value of $f(x)$ does not need to be recomputed. For efficiency, variables FL and FR, are introduced so that the information may be saved.

Figure 7.4   Algorithm for a systematic refinement of a zero estimate.

```
* An algorithm to systematically refine a zero estimate
* of a given function, by successively reducing the length of
* the interval bounding the zero estimate.

* Real variables used:
* xfirst - left end of initial interval
* xlast - right end of initial interval
* xstep - computed size of step between subintervals
* xl, xr - left, right endpoints of subinterval
* eps - desired tolerance in zero estimate

* Obtain the initial interval and desired tolerance.

get xfirst, xlast, eps
put 'The initial interval is', xfirst, 'to', xlast
put 'The desired tolerance is', eps

* Verify that the initial interval contains a zero.

if f(xfirst)*f(xlast) > 0 then
    [ put 'No sign change in this interval'
else
    [ * Refine the interval until its width is within the tolerance.

      while |xlast − xfirst| > eps do
          [ * Search for the first subinterval containing a sign change.

            xstep ← (xlast − xfirst)/25
            xl ← xfirst
            xr ← xl + xstep
            while f(xl)*f(xr) > 0 do
                [ xl ← xr
                  xr ← xr + xstep
            * Reset the endpoints for the next refinement of the interval.

            xfirst ← xl
            xlast ← xr
      put 'There is a zero between', xfirst, 'and', xlast
stop
```

The output from this program is given in Figure 7.6.   Compare the successive intervals with the graphs used earlier.   The first subinterval chosen by the program is about $[-1.98, -1.94]$, which is somewhat better than the one chosen graphically.   Of course, the program continues to refine the interval to a greater tolerance. The guess of -1.9576 made from the graph is relatively close to the zero estimate of -1.9575865, which is the midpoint of the last interval.

In the example above, the algorithm required four refinements to achieve the desired tolerance.   If it should be necessary for the entire interval to be scanned before finding the subinterval containing the zero, a total of 26 function evaluations would be

```
C Figure 7.5 -- Systematic Refinement of a Zero Estimate.
C                A program to systematically refine a zero estimate
C                of a given function, by successively reducing the
C                length of the interval bounding the zero estimate.
C*********************************************************************
C XFIRST - left end of initial interval
C XLAST  - right end of initial interval
C XSTEP  - computed size of step between subintervals
C XL,XR  - left, right endpoints of subinterval
C FL,FR  - function values corresponding to XL, XR
C EPS    - desired tolerance in zero estimate
C F      - function to be evaluated
C*********************************************************************
      REAL XFIRST, XLAST, XSTEP, XL, XR, FL, FR, F, EPS, ABS
C Define the polynomial using an arithmetic statement function.
      F(X) = ((X - 4.0)*X - 4.0)*X + 15.0
C Obtain the initial interval and desired tolerance.
      PRINT *, 'ENTER THE LEFT ENDPOINT OF THE INITIAL INTERVAL:'
      READ *, XFIRST
      PRINT *, 'ENTER THE RIGHT ENDPOINT OF THE INITIAL INTERVAL:'
      READ *, XLAST
      PRINT *, 'ENTER THE DESIRED TOLERANCE:'
      READ *, EPS
      PRINT *, ' '
C Verify that the initial interval contains a zero.
      IF (F(XFIRST)*F(XLAST) .GT. 0.0) THEN
          PRINT *, 'NO SIGN CHANGE IN THIS INTERVAL'
      ELSE
C         Refine the interval until its width is
C         within the desired tolerance.
  100     IF (ABS(XLAST - XFIRST) .GT. EPS) THEN
C             Search for the first subinterval
C             containing a sign change.
              XSTEP = (XLAST - XFIRST)/25.0
              FL = F(XFIRST)
              XR = XFIRST + XSTEP
              FR = F(XR)
  200         IF (FL*FR.GT.0.0) THEN
                  XR = XR + XSTEP
                  FL = FR
                  FR = F(XR)
                  GOTO 200
              ENDIF
C             Reset endpoints for the next refinement
C             of the interval.
              XFIRST = XR - XSTEP
              XLAST = XR
              PRINT *, 'THERE IS A ZERO BETWEEN', XFIRST, XLAST
              PRINT *, ' '
              GOTO 100
          ENDIF
      ENDIF
      STOP
      END
```

Program Notes

- The variables FL and FR are used to retain the function values at each end of the interval.   Each time the interval is advanced, the current value of FR is moved to FL and a new FR is computed.
- The variable XL, while documented, is redundant because of this shift technique.
- The PRINT statement has been moved inside the while–loop to demonstrate how successive intervals approach the zero.   The original position is better for a production program.

Figure 7.6   Output from the systematic refinement program of Figure 7.5.

```
ENTER THE LEFT ENDPOINT OF THE INITIAL INTERVAL:
-2.5
ENTER THE RIGHT ENDPOINT OF THE INITIAL INTERVAL:
-1.5
ENTER THE DESIRED TOLERANCE:
1.0E-05
THERE IS A ZERO BETWEEN   -1.980000      -1.940001

THERE IS A ZERO BETWEEN   -1.957600      -1.956000

THERE IS A ZERO BETWEEN   -1.957600      -1.957536

THERE IS A ZERO BETWEEN   -1.957588      -1.957585
```

required per pass.   On the average, one would expect to scan only about half of the interval, thus necessitating 26/2 or 13 evaluations per refinement step.   Therefore, a total of about 52 (13 × 4) evaluations might be expected.   The actual count in this case is 42, which was determined by using a counter in the program and adding one to it each time the function was evaluated.

7.5   Bisection

In the previous section an algorithm was created for refining the estimate of a zero of a function given an initial estimate in the form of an interval containing the zero.   The search scheme involved a subtabulation of function values in a given interval such that the new interval of tabulation was 1/25th the size of the original.   Thus, after one such search, the uncertainty in the location of a zero is reduced by the factor 1/25.   As observed in the last section, it is very easy to alter the search program to use a number of subintervals other than 25, say 10 or 100.   This naturally suggests the question as to what would be the *best* number of subintervals to choose.   If several experiments with different values of this constant were conducted, it would be apparent that the total number of function evaluations would tend to decrease as fewer intervals were chosen. The fewest possible intervals is, of course, two.

A search scheme to use only two steps has the further advantage that it is logically very simple.   The function is computed at the midpoint of the interval, and either the left half or right half of the interval is retained, depending upon which half proves to have a sign change of $f(x)$ within it.   This is called the *bisection algorithm*.   It is illustrated graphically in Figure 7.7 and is given in pseudocode form in Figure 7.8.   The algorithm successively bisects the interval [xl,xr] with midpoint xmid until the condition |xl−xmid| ≤ epsilon.   This test guarantees that xmid is an approximation to the zero with error less than the chosen tolerance.   The algorithm also contains an initial test on fl*fr. If fl*fr≤0, the algorithm assumes that the interval has a single zero (in fact, there could be an odd number of zeros, but bisection will still find one of them).   If fl*fr>0, the algorithm considers the interval to have no zeros.   In fact, there could be an even number of zeros in the interval, but bisection can not be guaranteed to find one of them.

Figure 7.7   Geometry for bisection.

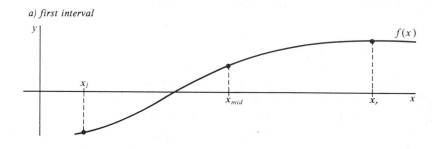

a) first interval

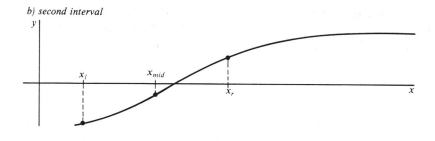

b) second interval

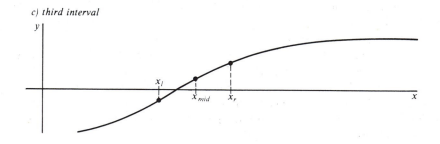

c) third interval

Figure 7.8   The bisection zero-finding algorithm.

* The bisection algorithm for estimating a zero of a given function.

* Real variables used:
* xl,xr - endpoints of successive intervals
* fl,fr - function values at the endpoints
* xmid - midpoint of the interval, xl, xr
* fmid - function value at the midpoint
* eps - desired tolerance in the zero estimate

* Obtain the initial interval and tolerance.

get xl, xr, eps
put 'Initial interval is', xl, 'to', xr
put 'The desired tolerance is', eps

* Compute f(x) at the interval endpoints.

fl ← f(xl)
fr ← f(xr)

* Provided a zero exists in the given interval, bisect the
* interval and choose the subinterval with a sign
* change, until the interval width is within tolerance.

if fl*fr > 0 **then**

    put 'No sign change in this interval'

else

    xmid ← (xl + xr)/2
    while |xl − xmid| > eps **do**

        fmid ← f(xmid)
        if fl*fmid ≤ 0 **then**

            * Choose the left subinterval.

            xr ← xmid

        else

            * Choose the right subinterval.

            xl ← xmid
            fl ← fmid

        xmid ← (xl + xr)/2

    put 'The zero in the interval is', xmid
    put 'The function value there is', f(xmid)

stop

The FORTRAN/77 program in Figure 7.9 applies the bisection algorithm to find the leftmost zero of the same cubic polynomial example used earlier in this chapter.

The resulting output in Figure 7.10 demonstrates how 16 iterations or steps (and their 16 iterative plus 2 original function evaluations) were required to achieve a tolerance of less than 10^{-5}. This compares quite favorably with the previous refinement process when 42 function evaluations were required to achieve the same accuracy.

```
C Figure 7.9 -- The Bisection Zero-Finding Algorithm.
C                 A program to implement the bisection technique
C                 for estimating a zero of a given function.

C**********************************************************************
C XL,XR    - endpoints of successive intervals
C FL,FR    - function values at the endpoints
C XMID     - midpoint of the interval XL, XR
C FMID     - function value at the midpoint
C EPS      - desired tolerance in the zero estimate
C F        - function to be evaluated

C**********************************************************************
      REAL XL, FL, XR, FR, XMID, FMID, F, EPS, ABS
C Define the function to be evaluated.

      F(X) = ((X - 4.0)*X - 4.0)*X + 15.0

C Obtain the initial interval and tolerance.

      PRINT *, 'ENTER THE LEFT ENDPOINT OF THE INITIAL INTERVAL:'
      READ *, XL
      PRINT *, 'ENTER THE RIGHT ENDPOINT OF THE INITIAL INTERVAL:'
      READ *, XR
      PRINT *, 'ENTER THE DESIRED TOLERANCE:'
      READ *, EPS
      PRINT *, ' '

C Compute F(X) at the interval endpoints.

      FL = F(XL)
      FR = F(XR)

C Provided a zero exists in the given interval, bisect
C the interval and choose the subinterval with a sign
C change, until the interval width is within tolerance.

      IF (FL*FR .GT. 0.0) THEN
         PRINT *, 'NO SIGN CHANGE IN THIS INTERVAL'
      ELSE
         XMID = (XL + XR)/2.0
  100    IF (ABS(XL - XMID) .GT. EPS) THEN
            FMID = F(XMID)
            IF (FL*FMID .LE. 0.0) THEN
C              Choose the left subinterval.

               XR = XMID
            ELSE
C              Choose the right subinterval.

               XL = XMID
               FL = FMID
            ENDIF
            PRINT *, 'CURRENT INTERVAL IS',XL,' TO',XR
            XMID = (XL + XR)/2.0
            GOTO 100
         ENDIF

         PRINT *, ' '
         PRINT *, 'THE ZERO IN THE INTERVAL IS', XMID
         PRINT *, 'THE FUNCTION VALUE THERE IS', F(XMID)
      ENDIF
      STOP
      END
```

Program Notes

- A PRINT statement has been added to output the successive intervals obtained in the bisection process. This statement could be deleted in further uses of the program, when only the final approximation to the zero is desired.

Figure 7.10   Output from the bisection program of Figure 7.9.

```
ENTER THE LEFT ENDPOINT OF THE INITIAL INTERVAL:
-2.5
ENTER THE RIGHT ENDPOINT OF THE INITIAL INTERVAL:
-1.5
ENTER THE DESIRED TOLERANCE:
0.00001
CURRENT INTERVAL IS  -2.000000    TO  -1.500000
CURRENT INTERVAL IS  -2.000000    TO  -1.750000
CURRENT INTERVAL IS  -2.000000    TO  -1.875000
CURRENT INTERVAL IS  -2.000000    TO  -1.937500
CURRENT INTERVAL IS  -1.968750    TO  -1.937500
CURRENT INTERVAL IS  -1.968750    TO  -1.953125
CURRENT INTERVAL IS  -1.960938    TO  -1.953125
CURRENT INTERVAL IS  -1.960938    TO  -1.957031
CURRENT INTERVAL IS  -1.958984    TO  -1.957031
CURRENT INTERVAL IS  -1.958008    TO  -1.957031
CURRENT INTERVAL IS  -1.958008    TO  -1.957520
CURRENT INTERVAL IS  -1.957764    TO  -1.957520
CURRENT INTERVAL IS  -1.957642    TO  -1.957520
CURRENT INTERVAL IS  -1.957642    TO  -1.957581
CURRENT INTERVAL IS  -1.957611    TO  -1.957581
CURRENT INTERVAL IS  -1.957596    TO  -1.957581

THE ZERO IN THE INTERVAL IS  -1.957588
THE FUNCTION VALUE THERE IS -2.7656555E-05
```

7.5.1   Bisection as a Subroutine Module

Since the bisection algorithm is used frequently as one major task in the solution of a larger problem, it is useful to consider the expression of the algorithm as a module. The exports from the module would be a zero of the function (if found successfully) and also an error status indication, to indicate success or failure of the algorithm. Therefore, an **smodule** is required rather than an **fmodule**. The latter could be used if one were certain that the algorithm would always succeed in finding a zero, but would be a poor design choice for general use.

The information which is supplied to the bisection algorithm consists of four items. It needs an initial interval $[x_1, x_r]$, the tolerance epsilon, and the function $f(x)$ for which the zero is sought. These four items would comprise the import parameter list of the **smodule** bisect. Including the export parameters zero and error gives the following form for the bisect module interface:

smodule bisect(**imports**: xl,xr,tolerance,f(x); **exports**: error,zero)

Fairly obvious changes to the bisection algorithm in Figure 7.8 would complete the definition of this module, and a discussion of these details is omitted for brevity.

The production of a FORTRAN/77 subroutine also involves small changes to the program of Figure 7.9. The imports PL, PR, and EPS will be parameters of type REAL, and ERROR and ZERO will be parameters of types LOGICAL and REAL, respectively. Figure 7.11 shows a FORTRAN/77 subroutine BISECT which incorporates this parameter list.

When the subroutine BISECT is called, the parameters PL and PR receive the values of the interval endpoints, EPS receives the value of the tolerance, and F receives the name of the function. The parameter ERROR is set to .FALSE. if the initial interval contains a sign change, indicating success of the algorithm and is set to .TRUE. when there is no sign change and indicating that the algorithm was not successful. The parameter ZERO sends back the zero approximation. Of course, this approximation is valid only when the value of ERROR is .FALSE..

The body of the subroutine BISECT is quite similar to the previous bisection program. The major difference is that instead of printing a message when FL*FR > 0 (considered to mean no zero in the interval), the program merely sets ERROR to .TRUE. and returns. This eliminates the need for printing a message from within BISECT. It is now up to the calling program to check the argument corresponding to ERROR and to take the appropriate action.

Figure 7.12 shows a program which uses the subroutine BISECT to look for a zero of the function $x^3 - 4x^2 - 4x + 15$. The main program reads in the interval to be tested, calls subroutine BISECT, and then, after checking the error flag, prints out an appropriate message regarding the zero. In order for both the main program and BISECT to be able to reference F(X), it must be defined as a function subprogram. If it were defined as a statement function within the subroutine BISECT, the definition would not be accessible to the main program. Futhermore, such a definition would be awkward in the sense that the subroutine BISECT would have to be altered each time it is used. It is preferable that the subroutine BISECT be suitable for use at the appropriate point of any main program, *without alteration*.

When a function name is used in the argument list of a call to a subroutine, that function name (here FUNC) must be declared EXTERNAL to ensure that the compiler does not confuse the name of the function with a variable name.

```
C Figure 7.11 -- The Bisection Zero-Finding Subroutine.
C                   A subprogram to implement the bisection technique
C                   for estimating a zero of a given function.

C********************************************************************
C PL,PR   - endpoints of the initial interval
C XL,XR   - endpoints of successive intervals
C FL,FR   - function values at the endpoints
C XMID    - midpoint of the interval XL, XR
C FMID    - function value at the midpoint
C EPS     - given tolerance in the zero estimate
C F       - function containing a zero
C ERROR   - error flag: true if no sign change

C********************************************************************
      SUBROUTINE BISECT(PL,PR,EPS,F,ERROR,XMID)

      REAL PL, PR, XL, XR, FL, FR, XMID, FMID, F, EPS, ABS
      LOGICAL ERROR
C Set up the initial interval.
C Compute F(X) at the initial endpoints.
      XL = PL
      XR = PR
      FL = F(XL)
      FR = F(XR)

C Provided a zero exists in the given interval, bisect
C the interval and choose the subinterval with a sign
C change, until the interval width is within tolerance.
      IF (FL*FR .GT. 0.0) THEN
         ERROR = .TRUE.
      ELSE
         ERROR = .FALSE.
         XMID = (XL + XR)/2.0
  100    IF (ABS(XL - XMID) .GT. EPS) THEN
            FMID = F(XMID)
            IF (FL*FMID .LE. 0.0) THEN
C              Choose the left subinterval.
               XR = XMID
            ELSE
C              Choose the right subinterval.
               XL = XMID
               FL = FMID
            ENDIF
            XMID = (XL + XR)/2.0
            GOTO 100
         ENDIF
      ENDIF
      RETURN
      END
```

Program Notes

- Since the values of XL and XR are changed in the course of bisecting the interval, variables PL and PR are provided to prevent the corresponding import arguments from being changed on return to the calling program.

```
C Figure 7.12 -- The Bisection Zero-Finding Technique.
C                A main program to demonstrate the use of
C                subroutine bisect to estimate the zero
C                of a given function within a given range.
C****************************************************************************
C A,B    - endpoints of the initial interval
C EPS    - desired tolerance
C ZERO   - computed approximation to the zero
C ERROR  - exception ERROR from subroutine BISECT
C****************************************************************************
      EXTERNAL FUNC
      REAL A, B, EPS, ZERO, FUNC
      LOGICAL ERROR
C Obtain the initial interval and tolerance.
      PRINT *, 'ENTER THE LEFT ENDPOINT OF THE INITIAL INTERVAL:'
      READ *, A
      PRINT *, 'ENTER THE RIGHT ENDPOINT OF THE INITIAL INTERVAL:'
      READ *, B
      PRINT *, 'ENTER THE DESIRED TOLERANCE:'
      READ *, EPS
      PRINT *, ' '
C Find a zero if possible and output an appropriate message.
      CALL BISECT(A,B,EPS,FUNC,ERROR,ZERO)

      IF (ERROR) THEN
         PRINT *, 'BISECT FOUND NO ZERO IN THE INTERVAL.'
      ELSE
         PRINT *, 'THE ZERO IN THE INTERVAL IS', ZERO
         PRINT *, 'THE FUNCTION VALUE THERE IS', FUNC(ZERO)
      ENDIF

      STOP
      END
C****************************************************************************
C Function FUNC -- Given a value for X, evaluate the function
C                       x**3 - 4x**2 - 4x + 15
C****************************************************************************
      REAL FUNCTION FUNC(X)
      REAL X
      FUNC = ((X - 4.0)*X - 4.0)*X + 15.0
      RETURN
      END
C Subroutine BISECT would be placed here.
```

7.6   Faster Algorithms

Some zero-finding problems involve functions which are very costly to compute. In other cases, the zero-finding process may be only a portion of some complex algorithm and may have to be performed thousands of times in one program. In such situations, it becomes important to reduce the number of function evaluations as much as possible. This is accomplished by the use of algorithms more sophisticated than bisection.

7.6.1   The Regula-Falsi Method

Historically, the regula-falsi method was proposed as an alternative to bisection. Like bisection, it retains an interval surrounding the zero. The function between the two endpoints of the interval is approximated by a straight line. The intersection of this line with the x axis rather than the midpoint is used as one of the endpoints of an improved interval. This is shown graphically in Figure 7.13.

Figure 7.13   Geometry for the regula-falsi method.

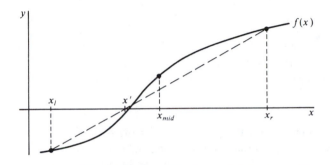

In this figure, $f(x)$ is shown, together with the straight line joining $(x_l, f(x_l))$ to $(x_r, f(x_r))$. This line intersects the x axis at x'. In general, the equation of the line passing through any two points (x_l, y_l) and (x_r, y_r) is given by

$$\frac{y - y_l}{x - x_l} = \frac{y_r - y_l}{x_r - x_l} \ .$$

Notice that the right-hand side of this equation represents the slope of the line. By using this equation and solving for its intersection with the x axis ($y = 0$), it is seen that

$$x' = x_l - f(x_l) \times \frac{x_r - x_l}{f(x_r) - f(x_l)} \ .$$

Although the point x', found by the regula-falsi method, is closer to the actual zero of $f(x)$ than is the point x_{mid}, found by bisection, the interval which brackets the zero, namely $[x', x_r]$, is clearly longer than the interval $[x_l, x_{mid}]$. Therefore, in practice it is unwise to use the regula-falsi method as an interval shrinking algorithm. One end point of the interval may converge to a zero while the other end point remains fixed, even for very simple functions. For this reason, no discussion of algorithm development is appropriate for the regula-falsi method.

7.6.2 The Secant Method

The secant method is similar in principle to the regula-falsi method except that it does not maintain a bracketing of the zero; rather the points are used in the order in which they are generated. The initial points are labeled x_1 and x_2 with corresponding function values $f_1 = f(x_1)$ and $f_2 = f(x_2)$. A new point can be computed as

$$x_3 = x_2 - f_2 \times \frac{x_1 - x_2}{f_1 - f_2} .$$

The geometry calculation here is similar to the regula-falsi method. In this case x_3 is a zero of the straight line through (x_1, f_1), (x_2, f_2). Regardless of whether or not they bracket a zero, the points x_2 and x_3, together with f_2 and f_3, are used to generate x_4, and so forth. The general formula for a new point is

$$x_{n+1} = x_n - f_n \times \frac{x_{n-1} - x_n}{f_{n-1} - f_n} .$$

Note that in this case, the slope of the secant is

$$\frac{f_{n-1} - f_n}{x_{n-1} - x_n} .$$

The geometrical motivation for this method is that the secant to a curve *ought* to cross the x axis somewhere close to the point at which the curve crosses the axis, namely, at a zero of the function. Figure 7.14 illustrates a possible sequence of points produced by the secant method.

Figure 7.14 Geometry for the secant method.

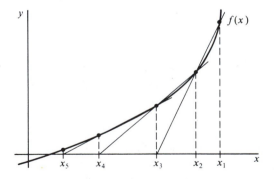

Since the idea of retaining a zero-containing interval at each stage has been abandoned in the secant method, there is no longer any guarantee that the process will converge to a zero. It is possible to find that at some stage of the scheme, f_{n-1} and f_n may be nearly equal, which would obviously produce a nonsensical value for x_{n+1}. This may happen if the two points lie close to a zero of the *derivative* of $f(x)$, for example.

A FORTRAN/77 implementation of the secant method is given in Figure 7.15. The algorithm is implemented as a FORTRAN/77 subroutine which may be used in a manner similar to the bisection subroutine. The algorithm itself is straightforward. The WHILE–loop proceeds to pass a secant line through successive pairs of points until the desired tolerance is achieved. In this case, however, there is no inference that the zero is located between the last two estimates. (It usually is not.) The algorithm is terminated successfully, with ERROR = .FALSE. when these two estimates differ by less than the specified tolerance, and the last estimate is taken as the zero. The program detects the error condition whenever the slope of the secant line becomes very small and sets ERROR = .TRUE. to terminate the WHILE–loop. Also, see Exercise 7.17 for further discussion of error checks in the secant subroutine.

The subroutine can be tested by imbedding it in a main program similar in style to that given in Figure 7.12, supplying the same function and starting points as were used for the bisection scheme. An additional output statement can be inserted in the subroutine to show the successive values of the intercepts. These are tabulated in Figure 7.16. Only six iterations are necessary to achieve the desired tolerance (a total of 8 function evaluations).

```
C Figure 7.15 -- The Secant Zero-Finding Subroutine.
C                 The secant method is used to estimate the zero
C                 of a given function within a given range.

C*********************************************************************
C P1,P2  - initial estimates of the zero
C X1,X2  - successive zero estimates
C XNEW   - new estimate closer to the zero
C EPS    - tolerance of desired answer
C F      - function to be evaluated
C F1     - function evaluated at X1
C F2     - function evaluated at X2
C SMALL  - an arbitrary small value

C*********************************************************************
        SUBROUTINE SECANT(P1,P2,EPS,F,ERROR,ZERO)

        REAL P1, P2, X1, X2, XNEW, F, EPS, F1, F2, ZERO, ABS
        LOGICAL ERROR

C Set up the initial interval and error flag.

        X1 = P1
        X2 = P2
        SMALL = 1.0E-4
        ERROR = .FALSE.

        F1 = F(X1)
        F2 = F(X2)

C Pass a secant line through the points (X1,F(X1)) and
C (X2,F(X2)).  Use the x intercept to improve the estimate
C of the zero, until the desired tolerance is achieved.

   100 IF (ABS(F1 - F2).GT.EPS .AND. .NOT.ERROR) THEN

C           Check if the slope is sufficiently horizontal
C           to cause an erroneous x-intercept.

            IF (ABS(F1 - F2) .LT. SMALL) THEN
               ERROR = .TRUE.
            ELSE
               XNEW = X2 - F2*(X1 - X2)/(F1 - F2)
               X1 = X2
               F1 = F2
               X2 = XNEW
               F2 = F(X2)
               PRINT *, 'THE CURRENT APPROXIMATION IS', XNEW
            ENDIF
            GOTO 100
         ENDIF
         ZERO = XNEW
         RETURN
         END
```

Program Notes

- Since the values of X1 and X2 are changed in the course of refining the interval, variables P1 and P2 are provided to prevent the corresponding import arguments from being changed on return to the calling program.
- A variable SMALL is given an arbitrary small value to guard against starting near a zero of the derivative of the function.
- Since only the most recent two points are needed at any one time, it is not necessary to retain all values of X.   Thus, the program uses the variables X1 and X2 to label the current two points of interest. Each time a new secant is to be formed, X1 and F1 take on the old values of X2 and F2 while X2 takes on the value at XNEW.

Figure 7.16 Output from the secant method subroutine of Figure 7.15.

```
ENTER THE TWO ZERO ESTIMATES:
-2.5 -1.5
ENTER THE DESIRED TOLERANCE:
0.00001
THE CURRENT APPROXIMATION IS   -1.855670
THE CURRENT APPROXIMATION IS   -1.981852
THE CURRENT APPROXIMATION IS   -1.956506
THE CURRENT APPROXIMATION IS   -1.957576
THE CURRENT APPROXIMATION IS   -1.957587
THE CURRENT APPROXIMATION IS   -1.957587

THE ZERO IN THE INTERVAL IS    -1.957587
THE FUNCTION VALUE THERE IS     2.8610229E-06
```

7.6.3 Newton's Method

Newton's method has an ancient and honored place in the history of zero-finding methods. Geometrically, it is motivated by the same consideration as the secant method. The tangent to the graph of $f(x)$ ought to cross the x axis at a point close to the zero of $f(x)$. The slope of the tangent to $f(x)$ at x_n is $f'(x_n)$, so Newton's method becomes

$$x_{n+1} = x_n - \frac{f(x_n)}{f'(x_n)} .$$

Notice that only one starting value is needed, but that a formula is required for the derivative as well as the function. As with the secant method, convergence cannot be guaranteed if a starting value or subsequent estimate lies near a point where $f'(x)$ vanishes. Figure 7.17 illustrates a sequence of estimates of a zero produced by Newton's method.

Figure 7.17 Geometry for Newton's method.

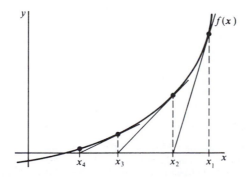

In Figure 7.18 a FORTRAN/77 subroutine is presented for Newton's method. The great similarity to the program for the secant method should be noted, but there is now only one initial estimate rather than two, and there is now a second function parameter to define the derivative.

```
C Figure 7.18 -- Newton's Method for Zero-Finding Subroutine.
C               Subroutine NEWTON to use Newton's method
C               to find a zero of a given function.

C**********************************************************************
C P1     - initial estimate of the zero
C X1     - successive zero estimates
C CORR   - correction to the current zero estimate (F(X1)/F'(X1))
C EPS    - tolerance of zero estimate
C F      - function to be evaluated
C DF     - derivative of the function
C SMALL  - an arbitrary small value

C**********************************************************************
        SUBROUTINE NEWTON(P1,EPS,ERROR,ZERO,F,DF)

        REAL P1, X1, EPS, ZERO, F, DF, ABS
        REAL SMALL, CORR
        LOGICAL ERROR

C Pass a line through (X1,F(X1)) with slope F'(X1) using the
C x intercept to improve the estimate of the zero until the
C correction to the zero estimate is less than the tolerance.

        X1 = P1
        SMALL = 1.0E-4
        CORR = 2*EPS
        ERROR = .FALSE.
  100 IF (ABS(CORR).GT.EPS .AND. .NOT.ERROR) THEN

C           Check if the slope is sufficiently horizontal
C           to cause an erroneous x intercept.

            IF (ABS(DF(X1)) .LT. SMALL) THEN
                ERROR = .TRUE.
            ELSE
                CORR = F(X1)/DF(X1)
                X1 = X1 - CORR
                PRINT *, 'THE CURRENT APPROXIMATION IS', X1
            END IF
            GOTO 100
        ENDIF
        ZERO = X1
        RETURN
        END
```

Program Notes

- The derivative function must also be specified and this, too, is made a formal parameter of the subroutine.
- In order to enter the WHILE-loop, the correction to the zero estimate is initialized at double the tolerance. Similarly, no error condition is assumed until one is found.
- Once the previous value of X1 has been used to evaluate the function and its derivative, it is no longer needed. Thus, the new value is assigned. To prevent damage to the import argument, its name has been changed to P1.

A complete program to incorporate the Newton's method subroutine is given as Figure 7.19. Note how this program handles the details of the specific problem, while leaving the details of the Newton iteration to the subroutine. The output from this program as given in Figure 7.20 is very similar to that of the secant method given in Figure 7.16. An additional output line was imbedded in the subroutine to show the sequence, as before. As a general observation, one should expect to see very little difference in the performance of the secant and Newton's method. For this application of Newton's Method, the four iterations involve four evaluations of the function plus four evaluations of its derivative.

The authors have a small preference for the secant method in that one does not need to have an explicit formula for the derivative of the function whose zero is sought. It is somewhat difficult to compare the numbers of function evaluations. Although Newton's method converges in fewer steps than the secant method, it requires evaluations of both $f(x)$ and its derivative for each approximation.

7.6.4   Other Algorithms

Over the years, many zero-finding algorithms of great mathematical sophistication have been developed and used. Some are adapted to solve particular problems very well. A number of such methods are discussed in Ralston (1965).

For general use in finding a single real zero experts now recommend a variation of the simple methods which have been examined in this chapter. A particularly effective combination is the secant method and bisection method, which are the important components of Dekker's algorithm. A variation of this is given in Forsythe et al. (1977).

7.7   Summary

In this chapter, several simple methods have been developed to find a single zero of a given function. The bisection algorithm is very reliable, but may be somewhat slow to converge to a zero. Newton's method or the secant method are faster when they do work, but either method may fail completely.

The authors recommend the bisection algorithm for simple general purpose use unless speed is crucial. Then the choice would be the secant method or, better still, the use of a library program which implements a combination of these methods.

7.8   References

Barrodale, I.; Roberts, F.D.K.; and Ehle, B.L. *Elementary Computer Applications.* New York: John Wiley and Sons, 1971.

Forsythe, G.E.; Malcolm, M.A.; and Moler, C.B. *Computer Methods for Mathematical Computations.* Englewood Cliffs, N.J.: Prentice-Hall, 1977.

Ralston, A.; and Rabinowitz, P. *A First Course in Numerical Analysis.* New York: Mcgraw-Hill Book Co., 1978.

```
C Figure 7.19 -- The Newton Zero-Finding Technique.
C                 A main program to demonstrate the use of
C                 subroutine NEWTON to estimate the zero
C                 of a given function within a given range.

C**********************************************************************
C A      - initial approximation of the zero
C EPS    - desired tolerance in the zero
C ZERO   - computed approximation to the zero
C ERROR  - exception flag from subroutine NEWTON

C**********************************************************************
      EXTERNAL FUNC, DFUNC
      REAL A, EPS, ZERO, FUNC, DFUNC
      LOGICAL ERROR

C Obtain the initial approximation and tolerance.
      PRINT *, 'ENTER THE INITIAL APPROXIMATION:'
      READ *, A
      PRINT *, 'ENTER THE DESIRED TOLERANCE:'
      READ *, EPS
      PRINT *, ' '

C Find a zero if possible and output an appropriate message.
      CALL NEWTON(A,EPS,ERROR,ZERO,FUNC,DFUNC)

      PRINT *, ' '
      IF (ERROR) THEN
         PRINT *, 'NEWTON FOUND NO ZERO WITH THE INITIAL APPROXIMATION'
      ELSE
         PRINT *, 'THE ZERO FOUND BY NEWTON IS', ZERO
         PRINT *, 'THE FUNCTION VALUE THERE IS', FUNC(ZERO)
      ENDIF

      STOP
      END

C**********************************************************************
C Function FUNC -- Given a value for X, evaluate the function
C                  x**3 - 4x**2 - 4x + 15

C**********************************************************************
      REAL FUNCTION FUNC(X)
      REAL X
      FUNC = ((X - 4.0)*X - 4.0)*X + 15.0
      RETURN
      END

C**********************************************************************
C Function DFUNC -- Given a value for X, evaluate the derivative
C                   function 3x**2 - 8x - 4

C**********************************************************************
      REAL FUNCTION DFUNC(X)
      REAL X
      DFUNC = (3*X - 8.0)*X - 4.0
      RETURN
      END

C Subroutine NEWTON would be placed here.
```

Figure 7.20 Output from the Newton's method program of Figure 7.19.

```
ENTER THE INITIAL APPROXIMATION:
-2.5
ENTER THE DESIRED TOLERANCE:
0.00001
THE CURRENT APPROXIMATION IS  -2.050360
THE CURRENT APPROXIMATION IS  -1.961048
THE CURRENT APPROXIMATION IS  -1.957592
THE CURRENT APPROXIMATION IS  -1.957587

THE ZERO FOUND BY NEWTON IS  -1.957587
THE FUNCTION VALUE THERE IS -1.9073486E-06
```

7.9 Exercises

In most of the following exercises a program is requested to solve a specific problem.   It is recommended that an algorithm be developed in pseudocode to solve the problem. Modules introduced in the text should be used wherever applicable.   This algorithm should then be translated into FORTRAN/77 and run on the computer.   Where appropriate, the program should be tested with a variety of data sufficient to ensure that the program does what it is supposed to do.

7.1   In Figure 7.3, the algorithm to scan for a sign change was designed to find the first such interval.

a)   What modifications would be necessary to find only the last such interval?
b)   What modifications would be necessary to find all subintervals containing sign changes?

7.2   The two curves $f(x) = 10 - x^2$ and $g(x) = 5 - (x - 5)^2$ each have a zero in the interval [2,4].   Develop a program to determine the distance between these zeros.

7.3   Consider the following polynomial.

$$f(x) = x^4 + 9.75x^3 + 17.75x^2 - 17.75x - 26.25$$

a)   Plot a graph of $f(x)$ exhibiting its 4 zeros.
b)   Using graphical techniques, estimate the smallest zero (in magnitude) of $f(x)$, correctly rounded to three decimal places.
c)   Prove that the estimate from b) is correct.
d)   Use systematic refinement to estimate the remaining zeros of $f(x)$, correctly rounded to four decimal places.

7.4   The following function has three real zeros.

$$f(x) = 8x^3 + 2x^2 - 5x + 1$$

Plot a graph of the function which clearly shows all three zeros.   From this graph obtain an interval around each zero, and use these as input to a single program which uses the bisection subroutine to find the zeros more exactly.

7.5 For *each* value of $k = -1, -0.95, -0.9, -0.85, \ldots, 0.95, 1$, the equation $\tan x - kx = 0$ has one root $g(k)$ which lies between $\pi/2 + \epsilon$ and $3\pi/2 - \epsilon$ (where ϵ is an arbitrary small number). Write a program to use the bisection subroutine to find each root, $g(k)$, over the given range of k and plot a graph of $g(k)$ versus k.

7.6 Consider the following function:

$$f(x) = .05x + \sin x$$

Develop a program to find all zeros of the function between $x = 0$ and $x = 12$. Beginning with the obvious solution at $x = 0$, there is at most one additional zero in each successive interval of length $\pi/2$ ($f(x)$ has a sinusoidal term). Generate the end points of intervals of length $\pi/2$ starting with $x = 0$ and determine if another zero lies within the interval. If it does not, generate the next interval. If it does, use bisection to find the zero. The recorded output should include the intervals as well as the zeros contained within them.

7.7 Find the two zeros with the largest magnitude for the following function:

$$f(x) = x^5 + x^4 + 2x^3 + 2x^2 - 8x - 8$$

Use both the systematic refinement program of Figure 7.5, and the bisection program of Figure 7.9. In each case, record the exact number of function evaluations; be certain to specify the same intervals to each program to ensure comparable results. Present these results in tabular form.

7.8 Modify the bisection subroutine in Figure 7.11 to implement trisection of the interval. Test the resulting TRSECT module using a main program similar to that in Figure 7.12.

7.9 Develop a program based on the search algorithm in Exercise 7.1b) to isolate all subintervals containing sign changes in a given interval [xfirst,xlast] and to use bisection to accurately approximate the zero in each subinterval containing a sign change.

7.10 It would frequently be useful to visualize a zero-finding algorithm as it converges to a zero. For the bisection algorithm, a composite graph like that in Figure 7.21 could be produced using the plotting package of Chapter 6 to draw vertical lines from the x axis to the function value at each successive midpoint.

a) Develop a FORTRAN/77 subroutine module to *draw* a vertical line at a given x value from the axis to a given y value.

b) Develop a revised BISECT subroutine to draw vertical lines as demonstrated in Figure 7.21.

c) Run the FORTRAN/77 main program in Figure 7.12 with a relatively large value of the tolerance to demonstrate the revised BISECT subroutine in part b).

Figure 7.21   Visualizing the convergence of bisection.

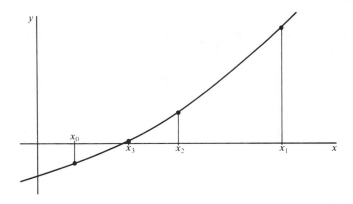

7.11   Develop a subroutine for the regula-falsi method and use it to approximate the zeros of the following funcions:

a) $f(x) = x^4 - 10x^3 + 31x^2 + 312x + 370$
b) $f(x) = e^{x^2 \cos x}(-2x^2 + 7x - 3) + 0.01$

7.12   Use the secant method subroutine to approximate the zeros of each of the following functions.

a) $f(x) = x^4 - x^3 - 3x^2 + 5x - 2$
b) $f(x) = x^4 - 10x^2 + 20$
c) $f(x) = x^4 - 10x^2 + 25$
d) $f(x) = x^5 + x^4 + 2x^3 + 2x^2 - 8x - 8$
e) $f(x) = 2x^4 - 14x^3 - 2x^2 + 68x + 56$

7.13   Repeat Exercise 7.12 using the Newton's method subroutine.

7.14   Consider the following function:

$$f(x) = x^4 + 3x^3 - 3x^2 - 6x + 1$$

Changing the constant term by 1 has the effect of shifting the graph by 1 in the y direction.   Modify the program which uses the Newton's method subroutine to determine the change in each zero as the constant term changes from 1 to 2, 2 to 3, and 3 to 4.

7.15   If a function is continuous and well behaved, the zero-finding method of successive substitution may converge to a zero faster than bisection.   The use of this technique to find a solution of an equation, $f(x) = 0$, involves rearranging a given equation to define x in terms of itself.   As an example, consider the following equation:

$$f(x) = x^3 - x^2 - x - 1 = 0$$

One simple rearrangement involves moving x across the equals sign.

$$x = x^3 - x^2 - 1$$

By starting with an initial estimate, say x_1, for the solution x and substituting into the right-hand side of the above expression, a new estimate of x, say x_2, is obtained. This subroutine can be continued as follows:

$$x_2 = x_1^3 - x_1^2 - 1$$

$$x_3 = x_2^3 - x_2^2 - 1$$

$$x_4 = x_3^3 - x_3^2 - 1$$

.

.

.

$$x_{n+1} = x_n^3 - x_n^2 - 1$$

This process may be continued until two consecutive estimates of the solution, x_{n+1} and x_n, differ by less than some epsilon.

a) Develop a program to apply successive substitution to the sample equation with a starting value of 2.0.

b) Modify the program to use the following rearrangement and to use the starting value 2.0.

$$x = 1 + \frac{1}{x} + \frac{1}{x^2}$$

c) Modify the program to approximate a zero of $f(x) = x^2 - 2x - 1$ using the following rearrangement and using 2.0 as the starting value.

$$x = x^2 - x - 1$$

7.16 Successive approximations to the solution of the equation $x = f(x)$ in a given interval $[a,b]$ can be found using the Steffensen's method in an extension of the method of the preceding exercise. It has the form:

$$x_{n+1} = \frac{x_n f(f(x_n)) - f(x_n)f(x_n)}{f(f(x_n))} - 2f(x_n) + x_n$$

for $n = 0, 1, 2, \ldots$, where x_0 is an initial approximation or starting value. The formula is applied repeatedly until successive approximations differ by less than some tolerance ϵ or until a given maximum number of iterations have been performed.

a) Develop a FORTRAN/77 subroutine to implement Steffensen's method, then develop a main program to test the subroutine.

b) Test the method on the three examples of the previous exercise.

c) Test the method on the problem $x - e^{-0.5x} = 0$.

7.17   The polynomial $x^2 - 1/4 + 1 - 0.145898(x^2 - 1/4)^2$ has two real zeros.

   a)   Try to use the secant subroutine to find one of them with starting values
        2.118035, -0.5. Include an output statement in the subroutine so that you
        may follow the sequence of iterations. Repeat with starting values -0.5,
        2.118035. Repeat with values 2.13, -0.5 and 2.11, -0.5 as starting values
        and comment on the results.

   b)   Produce a printer-plot of the polynomial and sketch the first four successive
        secant lines for the first case.

   c)   Both the secant method and Newton's method may fail by getting trapped in
        a *cycle* as illustrated here. Design a change for either the Newton or Secant
        subroutine which terminates the algorithm if more than say 20 iterations are
        attempted.

8
Area Finding

8.1   Introduction

In this chapter another elementary problem related to the graph of a function $f(x)$ is examined. The area bounded by the graph of the function, the x axis, and two ordinates at $x = a$ and $x = b$ is sought, as shown in Figure 8.1.

Figure 8.1   Area under a curve f(x).

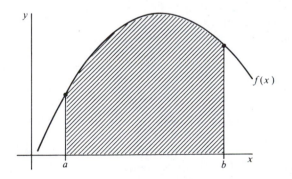

To the reader familiar with calculus, this is a *definite integral,* represented by

$$\int_a^b f(x)\, dx$$

Such problems arise in applications in a wide variety of contexts.   One would need to solve this integration problem to calculate the strength of an aircraft wing, to compute the amount of earth to be moved in leveling out a hill during construction, to construct a fuel gauge for an irregularly shaped tank, or to decide whether a particular re-entry path will cause intolerable heat build-up in a space shuttle. The list is really endless since this is probably the most basic and frequently posed mathematical problem arising from the construction of mathematical models of the real world.

Historically, the mathematical treatment of this problem is old and well-developed, as is the development of computational tools for its approximate solution.

Simple mechanical devices called planimeters can be used to give a crude approximation to the area of a plotted curve. Of course, for a rough solution to the problem, one can always do the plot on squared graph paper and count the squares enclosed.

It is the intent of this chapter to give some tools which will enable most of the work in such integration problems to be passed over to the computer. Some elementary algorithms will be developed together with some methods for assuring that the answers produced are correct.

8.2   The Area Approximated by Sums

The symbol for the definite integral originated with the relationship of the integral to the sum of the areas of small rectangles of width $x_{i+1} - x_i$ and height $f(x'_i)$, where x'_i is any point between x_i and x_{i+1}. This sum is denoted as S_n.

$$S_n = \sum_{i=1}^{n} f(x'_i) \times (x_{i+1} - x_i)$$

Such a sum is illustrated in Figure 8.2. The integral is, in fact, defined as the *limiting value* of S_n as n, the number of rectangles, becomes large, but in such a fashion that the width of the largest rectangle shrinks to zero as n increases.

It should be observed that negative values of $f(x)$ subtract from the sum. Therefore, the integral will be interpreted as the difference between areas above and below the x axis should $f(x)$ have one or more zeros between a and b.

8.3   Rectangle Rules

One of the simplest methods of approximating the desired area is derived from the definition of S_n. In fact, the diagram of Figure 8.2 suggests that there will always be one or more values, x', such that $S_1 = (b - a) \times f(x')$ will be precisely the area desired. Dressed up a bit, this is called the *mean-value theorem* of calculus. It assures that it is not necessary to take the limit of S_n to get the area if a clever choice is made for the point(s) at which $f(x)$ is computed. This is illustrated in Figure 8.3, where the area is seen to be $(b - a) \times f(x')$, assuming that the two shaded areas are equal.

To compensate for the fact that the appropriate point is not known, a weighted average of values of $f(x)$ at a number of different points is computed, to give a formula of the form

Figure 8.2   Area approximated by a sum of rectangles.

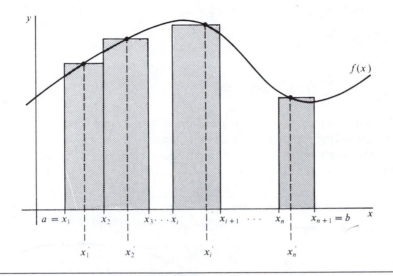

Figure 8.3   Area calculation using one rectangle based on x'.

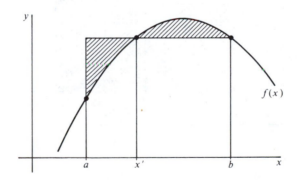

$$S = (b - a) \times \sum_{i=1}^{n} w_i \times f(x_i), \text{ where } \sum_{i=1}^{n} w_i = 1 .$$

One of the simplest such formulas involves choosing all weights to be equal, that is, $w_i = 1/n$, and choosing the x_i's to be the left (or right) endpoints of the i-th rectangle of width $(b - a)/n$.   That is,

$$x_i = a + \frac{i \times (b - a)}{n}, i = 0, 1, 2, \ldots , n - 1, \text{ or}$$

$$x_i = a + \frac{i \times (b - a)}{n}, \ i = 1, 2, \ldots, \ n.$$

Thus, the two rectangle formulas are:

$$R' = \frac{(b - a)}{n} \times \sum_{i=0}^{n-1} f(x_i), \text{ and}$$

$$R'' = \frac{(b - a)}{n} \times \sum_{i=1}^{n} f(x_i), \text{ respectively.}$$

For a function which increases as x increases from a to b, it may be seen that R' is always less than the actual area, and R'' is always greater. This is illustrated in Figure 8.4 for the case $n = 2$. R' is the darker shaded area, and R'' is the sum of the light and dark areas.

Figure 8.4 Geometry for the rectangle rules.

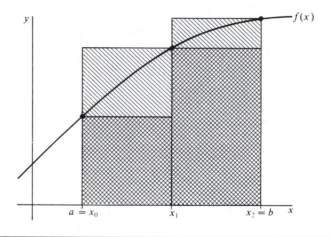

8.4 Trapezoidal Rule

From Figure 8.4, it is seen that the two Rectangle Rules respectively underestimate and overestimate the actual area, and by similar amounts. Averaging the two rules should have the effect of canceling the errors, and lead to a better formula. This averaging is indicated below.

$$T = \frac{R' + R''}{2}$$

$$= \frac{1}{2} \left[\frac{(b - a)}{n} \times \sum_{i=0}^{n-1} f(x_i) + \frac{(b - a)}{n} \times \sum_{i=1}^{n} f(x_i) \right]$$

$$= \frac{(b-a)}{2 \times n} \times \left[f(x_0) + 2 \times \sum_{i=1}^{n-1} f(x_i) + f(x_n) \right]$$

$$= \frac{h}{2} \times \left[f(a) + 2 \times \sum_{i=1}^{n-1} f(a + i \times h) + f(b) \right] \quad \text{where } h = \frac{b-a}{n}.$$

This is called the *Trapezoidal Rule* since the area under the curve is approximated by the area of a number of trapezoids, rather than rectangles.   This is shown in Figure 8.5 for $n = 1$ and $n = 2$.   The dark shading shows the area for one trapezoid. The light plus the dark shading is the area for two trapezoids.

Figure 8.5   Geometry for the Trapezoidal Rule with $n = 1$ and $n = 2$.

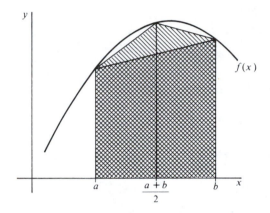

It is clear that this formula gives the exact value of the area if the graph of the function is a straight line between endpoints, since the actual figure is then a trapezoid.   The area found by the Trapezoidal Rule will not be precisely right if $f(x)$ is curved, but it will be a *better approximation* than is provided by the Rectangle Rules.

It should also be observed from Figure 8.5 that the approximation using 2 trapezoids is substantially better than the result using 1. Just how much better is a question which will be examined after considering Figure 8.6 which gives a FORTRAN/77 program for the Trapezoidal Rule.   This program tests the algorithm on a function $f(x) = 7 - 7x^6$, for which the area between $x = 0$ and $x = 1$ is known to be 6.0.

The output of this program is given in Figure 8.7 for the particular data presented. Such a single numerical output may be quite useless as an area estimate, since there is no assurance of its validity.   Such assurance could come from a mathematical analysis or it could come from a better algorithm which incorporates an error estimation.

```
C Figure 8.6 -- The Trapezoidal Rule Area-Finding Technique.
C               A program to compute the area under the function
C               7 - 7X**6 using the Trapezoidal Rule.

C**********************************************************************
C A,B     - endpoints of the integration interval
C N       - number of subintervals to use
C I       - current subinterval index
C H       - subinterval width
C SUM     - sum of values of F(X)
C AREA    - computed area under curve
C F       - function to be integrated

C**********************************************************************
      REAL A, B, F, H, SUM , AREA, X
      INTEGER N, I

C Define the specific problem.

      F(X) = 7.0 - 7.0*X**6

C Obtain the endpoints and the number of intervals N,
C which controls the accuracy of the area computed.

      PRINT *, 'ENTER THE ENDPOINTS OF THE INTEGRATION INTERVAL:'
      READ *, A, B

      PRINT *, 'ENTER THE NUMBER OF SUBINTERVALS:'
      READ *, N

C Calculate the subinterval width.

      H = (B - A)/N

C Evaluate the trapezoidal area formula.

      SUM =  0.0
      DO 100 I = 1, N-1
         X = A + I*H
         SUM = SUM + F(X)
  100 CONTINUE

C Assemble the terms and record the computed area.

      AREA = H*((F(A) + F(B))/2.0 + SUM)
      PRINT *, 'THE AREA UNDER THE CURVE IS', AREA

      STOP
      END
```

Program Notes

- An integer I is used to count the proper number of terms in the sum, rather than comparing the current argument X to the endpoint B.   A comparison such as X .LE. B will be unreliable due to roundoff errors for some values of A, B, and N.

Figure 8.7   Output from the Trapezoidal Rule program of Figure 8.6.

```
ENTER THE ENDPOINTS OF THE INTEGRATION INTERVAL:
0.0, 1.0
ENTER THE NUMBER OF SUBINTERVALS:
16
THE AREA UNDER THE CURVE IS    5.986347
```

8.5   Error Estimation for the Trapezoidal Rule

The simplest way to increase confidence in the area estimate is to repeat the calculation with a larger number of intervals (say twice as many) and compare the results.
Figure 8.5 should convince us that, for small intervals and a smoothly varying function, the difference between the results for $2n$ and for n intervals (light shading) is larger than the difference between the true area and the result for $2n$ intervals (unshaded area). This difference provides an error *estimate* which is quite reliable.   To illustrate this, the previous program was modified to tabulate results for several values of n.   The results are given together with the actual errors and the error estimates in Figure 8.8.

Figure 8.8   Trapezoidal Rule with errors tabulated.

n	T_n	*Actual Error*	*Estimated Error* $(T_n - T_{n/2})$
2	5.195313	0.804687	----------
4	5.785767	0.214233	0.590454
8	5.945597	0.054403	0.159828
16	5.986347	0.013653	0.040750
32	5.996584	0.003416	0.010237

There are several observations which may be made from this table. The difference which was suggested as an error estimate grossly overestimates the actual error.   Closer inspection shows that the estimate is about three times the error, particularly for large values of n.

The table also suggests the hypothesis that the size of the error decreases by a factor of four when n is doubled. That is, the error is very well described by the formula

$$\text{Error} \simeq \frac{c}{n^2},$$

where, in this case, c is about 3.5 but would assume other values for different functions. It may be shown by a mathematical analysis that this will always be the *form* of the error for large n and smooth $f(x)$.

More analysis would also establish that the relationship suggested in the table, namely,

$$\text{Error} \simeq \frac{T_n - T_{n/2}}{3},$$

follows from the above formula for the error, and is quite easy to compute by an additional application of the Trapezoidal Rule. In Figure 8.9, this estimate is compared to the actual error, for the previous example.

Figure 8.9 Comparison of error and error estimates for Trapezoidal Rule.

n	*Actual Error*	$\dfrac{T_n - T_{n/2}}{3}$
2	0.804687	----------
4	0.214233	0.196818
8	0.054403	0.053276
16	0.013653	0.013583
32	0.003416	0.003412

8.6 Simpson's Rule

Just as the Trapezoidal Rule could be obtained as an average of Rectangle Rules, the Trapezoidal Rule may also be manipulated to produce an improved formula. In the last section it was observed that the Trapezoidal Rule could be applied with n intervals and with $2n$ intervals to provide an error estimate $(T_{2n} - T_n)/3$. This error estimate may be visualized as an approximation to the area which lies between the graph of the function and the shaded area of the trapezoids (see Figure 8.5). An improved formula must surely result if this area is added to the area of the trapezoids. For the case of one and two trapezoids of Figure 8.5, the formula becomes:

$$S = T_2 + \frac{T_2 - T_1}{3}$$

$$= \frac{4}{3} T_2 - \frac{1}{3} T_1$$

$$= \frac{4}{3} \left[\frac{(b-a)}{4} \times \left[f(a) + 2f\left(\frac{a+b}{2}\right) + f(b) \right] \right] - \frac{1}{3} \left(\frac{(b-a)}{2} \times [f(a) + f(b)] \right)$$

$$= \frac{b-a}{6} \left(f(a) + 4 \times f\left(\frac{a+b}{2}\right) + f(b) \right).$$

This is known as a single application of *Simpson's Rule* for approximating the value of an integral.

In assessing the error involved in using Simpson's Rule, an important observation may be made. There is *no error* if the function $f(x)$ is a *polynomial* of degree three or less (see Exercise 8.6). Phrased in another way, this method gives the actual area under the polynomial function which has the same value as $f(x)$ at $x = a$, $x = (a + b)/2$, and $x = b$.

For functions which are not polynomials of degree three or less, one may expect to incur some error in applying this formula. Again, to reduce this error, the formula may be applied many times to narrow strips, referred to as panels, and the results added. One panel corresponds to a single application of Simpson's Rule, but is based on two applications of the Trapezoidal Rule. The result for n panels is referred to as the *Compound Simpson's Rule* and may be obtained by expanding the expression

$$S_{2n} = \frac{4}{3} T_{2n} - \frac{1}{3} T_n \ .$$

Letting $h = (b - a)/2n$, which represents half the width of one panel, and expanding gives the following formula:

$$S_{2n} = \frac{h}{3} [f(a) + 4f(a + h) + 2f(a + 2h) + 4f(a + 3h) + 2f(a + 4h) + \cdots$$
$$+ 2f(b - 2h) + 4f(b - h) + f(b)] \ .$$

The formula can be grouped into function values for even intervals and for odd intervals. This grouping is used in writing the FORTRAN/77 function for Simpson's Rule presented in Figure 8.10. Since this area-finding module produces only one export, the computed approximation to the area, a function module is a natural choice. The import parameters to the SIMP module are the interval endpoints, A and B, the number of integration panels PANEL, and the function to be integrated F. This latter parameter provides the means to apply the area-finding module to any problem by supplying the name of a FORTRAN/77 function module to evaluate the integrated function.

```
C Figure 8.10 -- The Simpson's Rule Area-Finding Function.
C                 Function subprogram to find the AREA under
C                 the curve F between the endpoints A and B
C                 using PANEL integration panels.

C*********************************************************************
C A,B     - endpoints of integration interval
C PANEL   - number of integration panels
C F       - function to integrate
C H       - subinterval width
C SUMEVN  - sum of F(X) values at even subintervals
C SUMODD  - sum of F(X) values at odd subintervals

C*********************************************************************
      REAL FUNCTION SIMP(A,B,PANEL,F)
         REAL A, B, F, H, SUMEVN, SUMODD, X
         INTEGER PANEL, I
C Calculate the subinterval width and initialize summations.
         H = (B - A)/(2*PANEL)
         SUMEVN = 0.0
         SUMODD = F(A+H)
C Sum function values at each subinterval.
         DO 100 I = 1, PANEL-1, 1
            X = A + 2.0*I*H
            SUMEVN = SUMEVN + F(X)
            SUMODD = SUMODD + F(X+H)
  100    CONTINUE
C Assemble the Simpson's Rule integration formula.
         SIMP = (H/3.0) * (F(A) + 4.0*SUMODD + 2.0*SUMEVN + F(B))

         RETURN
         END
```

The main program of Figure 8.11 which invokes the area-finding module SIMP to compute an area approximation for several different numbers of panels. The output of this program is tabulated in Figure 8.12, giving the number of panels computed and the area approximation. The effect of the number of panels on the error of Simpson's Rule will be discussed in the next section.

```
C Figure 8.11 -- The Simpson's Rule Area-Finding Technique.
C                 Main program to use function SIMP to find the area
C                 under 7 - 7X**6 between 0 and 1, for 2, 4, 8, ...,
C                 128 subintervals.
C******************************************************************
C A,B    - endpoints of the integration interval
C PANEL  - current number of integration panels
C MAXPAN - maximum number of panels to compute
C AREA   - computed approximation to the area
C******************************************************************
      EXTERNAL FUNC
      REAL A, B, AREA, FUNC, SIMP
      INTEGER PANELS, MAXPAN
C Obtain the interval and maximum number of panels.
      PRINT *, 'ENTER THE INTEGRATION INTERVAL:'
      READ *, A, B
      PRINT *, 'ENTER THE MAXIMUM NUMBER OF PANELS:'
      READ *, MAXPAN
C Compute the area for each number of panels up to the maximum.
      PRINT *, ' '
      PRINT *, '     PANELS    AREA ESTIMATE'
      PRINT *, ' '
      PANELS = 2
  100 IF (PANELS .LE. MAXPAN) THEN
         AREA = SIMP(A,B,PANELS,FUNC)
         PRINT *, PANELS, AREA
         PANELS = PANELS * 2      <- counter statement
         GOTO 100
      ENDIF
      STOP
      END
C******************************************************************
C Function FUNC -- Given a value for X, evaluate the function
C                    7 - 7X**6
C******************************************************************
      REAL FUNCTION FUNC(X)
      REAL X
      FUNC = 7.0 - 7.0*X**6
      RETURN
      END
C Function SIMP would be placed here.
```

Figure 8.12 Output from the Compound Simpson's Rule program of Figure 8.11.

```
ENTER THE INTEGRATION INTERVAL:
0.0, 1.0
ENTER THE MAXIMUM NUMBER OF PANELS:
128
        PANELS    AREA ESTIMATE
             2    5.982585
             4    5.998874
             8    5.999929
            16    5.999996
            32    6.000001
            64    6.000000
           128    6.000001
```

8.7 Error Estimation for Simpson's Rule

When applying the Compound Simpson's Rule, one would expect to see rapid improvement in the quality of the results as n is increased; this is easily seen to be the case for the output of the example program since the actual answer is 6.0. However, if this program were run on a FORTRAN/77 system which used a small number of digits to represent real numbers, then roundoff error would eventually lead to an *increase* rather than a *decrease* in the error as n is increased.

A study of the errors tabulated in Figure 8.13 shows that their behavior is governed by the formula:

$$\text{Error} \simeq \frac{c}{n^4}$$

where c is about 0.29. Since this c would not be known for a problem whose answer is sought, it is more useful to observe that the following estimate for the error follows from this formula:

$$\text{Error} \simeq \frac{S_n - S_{n/2}}{15}$$

The validity of this estimate is checked in Figure 8.14. There is a good prediction of the error for all values of n.

Figure 8.13 Simpson's Rule with errors tabulated.

n	S_{2n}	*Actual Error*	$S_{2n} - S_{2n/2}$
2	5.982585	+0.017415	----------
4	5.998874	+0.001126	+0.016289
8	5.999929	+0.000071	+0.001055
16	5.999996	+0.000004	+0.000067
32	6.000001	−0.000001	+0.000005
64	6.000000	+0.000000	−0.000001
128	6.000001	−0.000001	+0.000001

Figure 8.14 Comparison of error and error estimates for Simpson's Rule.

n	*Actual Error*	$\dfrac{S_{2n} - S_{2n/2}}{15}$
2	0.017415	----------
4	0.001126	0.001086
8	0.000071	0.000070
16	0.000004	0.000004
32	0.000001	0.000000

Roundoff error can complicate the use of sophisticated formulas for error estimation. If S_n and $S_{n/2}$ agree to k digits, then S_n is probably correct to $k + 1$ digits, unless roundoff error has contaminated the result. If so, the computation should be repeated with more precision.

A detailed analysis of the effects of roundoff error is difficult to do before a calculation. It depends upon the characteristics of the computer arithmetic, primarily the number of digits used in number representation and the rules regarding the truncation of a longer number to fit into such a representation.

The FORTRAN/77 programs in this section were run on a VAX-11 computer, which uses a binary number system in its representation of numbers. The standard word size is equivalent to between 6 and 7 decimal digits.

8.8 Summary

Many books have been written which are wholly or largely devoted to the development of approximate methods for solution of this area finding problem, and research continues on better ways to solve it.

With rare exceptions, Simpson's Rule is a remarkably effective method for solving integration problems, and the suggested method of error appraisal is quite reliable. The authors recommend its general use without reservation.

Some recent work develops the ideas presented here to create an algorithm which enables the computer to "learn" how to best use the Compound Simpson's Rule or a similar integration formula. Such *Adaptive Quadrature* algorithms automatically solve an integration problem to some preassigned error tolerance in the most efficient possible way. Although beyond the scope of this text, some readers might like to investigate these ideas in Forsythe, et al., (1977).

8.9   References

Barrodale, I.; Roberts, F.D.K.; and Ehle, B.L.   *Elementary Computer Applications.*
   New York: John Wiley and Sons, 1971.

Conte, S.D. and DeBoor, C.   *Elementary Numerical Analysis.* New York: McGraw-Hill
   Book Co., Third Edition 1980.

Forsythe, G.E.; Malcolm, M.A.; and Moler, C.B.   *Computer Methods for Mathematical
   Computations.* Englewood Cliffs, N.J.: Prentice-Hall, 1977.

8.10   Exercises

In most of the following exercises a program is requested to solve a specific problem.   It
is recommended that an algorithm be developed in pseudocode to solve the problem.
Modules introduced in the text should be used wherever applicable.   This algorithm
should then be translated into FORTRAN/77 and run on the computer.   Where
appropriate, the program should be tested with a variety of data sufficient to ensure that
the program does what it is supposed to do.

8.1   a)   Develop a program to approximate the area under a given function for
         specified endpoints and number of intervals using the left rectangle rule.
         Test the program on a simple example with known area.
     b)   Develop a program to approximate the area under a given function for
         specified endpoints and number of intervals using the right rectangle rule.
         Test the program on a simple example with known area.
     c)   Combine the programs of parts a) and b) into a single program.   Use this
         program to produce a table comparing the values produced by both rectangle
         rules for 2, 4, 8, . . . , 64 intervals.   Test the program on each of the follow-
         ing functions.

$$f(x) = x, \ x^2, \ x^3, \ x^4, \ x^5$$

8.2   Develop a program to use the Trapezoidal Rule to approximate the area enclosed
     by the sine curve and the x axis between $-\pi$ and $+\pi$.

8.3   Find $\int_0^\pi x \sin x \, dx$ for 2, 4, 8, . . . , 32 intervals, for both Trapezoidal and
     Simpson's Rule using a single program.   Tabulate the actual error for both.   The
     output from your program should be a table of 5 columns including the number of
     intervals, the Trapezoidal area, the Trapezoidal error, the Simpson's area, and the
     Simpson's error.

8.4   Develop a program which will find the area under the following curves between
     the limits $x = 1$ and $x = 2$ using Simpson's Rule.
     a) $f(x) = \sqrt{2 - \sin x^2}$
     b) $f(x) = x \cos \dfrac{x}{2}$
     c) $f(x) = (x^3 - 2x^2 + x + 5)^{1/3}$

8.5 An approximation to the area under a curve $f(x)$ may be calculated using what could be called a midpoint-rectangle rule. It is similar to the rectangle rules of this chapter in that it sums the areas of n rectangles in the given interval. However, for this rule, the height of a rectangle with sides $x = a$ and $x = b$ is calculated using the height of the midpoint of the rectangle, that is, $f\left(\dfrac{a+b}{2}\right)$.

a) Develop a general formula which when evaluated will give an approximation to an area using the midpoint-rectangle rule with a general number of intervals, n.
b) Develop a function subprogram which will use the above formula.
c) Use this function subprogram in a program to calculate the area under $f(x) = x \cos \dfrac{x}{2}$ in the interval [1,2], with the number of intervals $n = 4$, 8, 16, 32.

8.6 a) Show that Simpson's Rule with a single interval is exact for the functions $f(x) = 1$, x, x^2, x^3 on the interval $[-1,1]$.
Hint: The areas are 2, 0, 2/3, 0 respectively.
b) Deduce that Simpson's Rule with a single interval is exact for any polynomial $f(x) = a_3x^3 + a_2x^2 + a_1x + a_0$ on any interval $[a,b]$.
Hint: This question requires some calculus.

8.7 In the development of area finding methods in Section 8.3, two rectangle rules were discussed. One rectangle rule always used the function evaluated at the left end-point of the interval while the other always used the function evaluated at the right end-point of the interval.

For a function which increases in a subinterval (see the picture on the left as follows), the left end-point rule would underestimate the desired area while the right end-point rule would overestimate the area. For a function which decreases in a subinterval (see the picture on the right below), the reverse would be true.

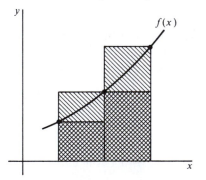 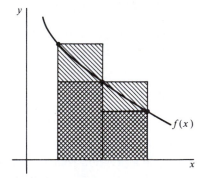

In some applications it might be desirable to use rectangle rules which would give both an *upper* bound and a *lower* bound for the area under a function $f(x)$ in the interval $[a,b]$. Such bounds could be found by selecting the end-point used depending on its functional value rather than its position (left or right), as illustrated below.

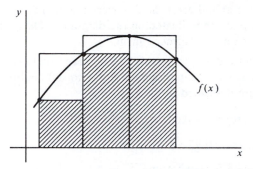

Develop a FORTRAN/77 program similar to the Trapezoidal Rule program in Figure 8.6 to use modified rectangle rules to determine both an upper bound and a lower bound for the area under the function $x^3 - 3x^2 + 5$ in the interval $[1,3]$ using 25 subintervals. Write the program in a general fashion. You may assume that there are no zeros in the given interval.

8.8   A farmer has a very irregularly shaped farm bounded on one side by a winding brook, on a second side by a winding river, and on the third side by a curved road as illustrated in Figure 8.15.

Figure 8.15   A farmer's irregularly shaped field (Exercise 8.8).

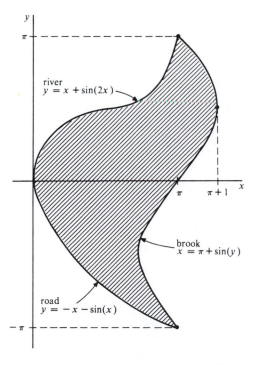

After considerable trial and error, he discovers the boundaries of his farm can be described by the equations indicated on the diagram. Develop a program to approximate the area of the farmer's farm.

8.9   On the farm of Exercise 8.8, the owner has observed that crop yields vary with location in direction x, but not in direction y, due to soil quality. For crops c_1 and c_2, the variations are described by

yield c_1 (per acre) $= 1 + 0.02x$

yield c_2 (per acre) $= 0.95 + 0.015x^2$

What is the total yield for each crop?

Part C
Design and Efficiency of Algorithms

9 Algorithm Design *199*

10 Applications of Algorithm Design *223*

11 Efficiency of Algorithms *251*

9
Algorithm Design

9.1   Introduction

To date, many examples of algorithms have been presented. The algorithms of the first three chapters were relatively straightforward and could be developed without any formal techniques. As the algorithms progressed in difficulty in Chapter 4, some notions about algorithm design were introduced to help the reader develop and organize these algorithms. However, real-life problems can be much more complex. Thus, it is now appropriate to discuss in detail a method of algorithm design such that correct algorithms may be developed in a reasonable amount of time. There are several ways of approaching algorithm development. The technique to be discussed here is called *top-down design* using *step-wise refinement*.

9.2   Top-Down Design of Algorithms

Algorithm development for large problems is difficult because of the vast amount of detail which must be managed. Top-down design is a constructive approach to algorithm development which establishes a hierarchy of algorithmic operations, describing the relationship of these operations to each other. Thus, one is forced to resolve major design issues early in the design process. This allows the designer to concentrate on the problem at various levels of abstraction and keep to a minimum the number of details which must be considered at any one time. Hopefully, this technique allows the whole design process to become *intellectually manageable*.

The top-down design process is a divide-and-conquer approach, which involves decomposing the original problem into several subproblems, each of which is easier to deal with. Since the relationships between these subproblems are also established at this time, each subproblem may be considered independently. As the decomposition proceeds, the algorithm becomes a more and more detailed description of how to solve the problem.

Problem decomposition is probably the most important aspect of the design process since the form of the final algorithm depends upon the choices made in the decomposition. Fortunately, this task becomes easier with experience as one acquires knowledge of algorithm development techniques.

There are many vehicles which may be used to implement the top-down design process. Step-wise refinement using pseudocode is one which has become widely accepted and is the one to be used here.

9.3   Step-Wise Refinement Using Pseudocode

The basic notion of step-wise refinement is to start with a simple English language description of an algorithm which is known to be correct, and expand it through several stages until a detailed pseudocode version of the algorithm is produced. At each stage, one step or action of the algorithm is chosen for expansion. This step is decomposed into several more detailed substeps. Any step which is too vague for the algorithm follower is a candidate for expansion. Expansion terminates when all steps are sufficiently detailed. For this discussion it will always be assumed that the computer will eventually be the algorithm follower. Thus, the final version of the algorithm should be in terms of the basic pseudocode actions, all of which can easily be translated into a programming language. The restriction of pseudocode, in Chapter 2, to three control structures, sequence, repetition, and alternation, helps reduce the complexity of the step-wise refinement.

If the original statement of the problem is correct and if the expansions at each stage of the step-wise refinement are correct, then the final algorithm will also be correct. Thus, it is important to keep these expansions small enough that their correctness is easily maintained. This is not meant to imply that maintaining correctness at each stage is an easy task. It requires attention to detail and a careful investigation of the mathematical principles which are being used. If an incorrect decomposition is made at any stage and is not discovered until much later in the refinement, it is necessary either to backtrack and try a different decomposition or to change some part of the algorithm which was assumed to be complete.

Step-wise refinement is an organized approach to algorithm development, which by its nature aids in producing correct algorithms. This does not imply that the resulting algorithm will be the most efficient. Algorithm efficiency is discussed in Chapter 11.

9.4   Techniques of Step-Wise Refinement

The main power of step-wise refinement is that a very small number of problems are dealt with at any one time and attention is usually focused on refinement of only one problem. Each such refinement has one of the following results:

1) the problem is decomposed into subproblems
2) the problem is translated directly into pseudocode
3) the problem is decomposed into some pseudocode and some subproblems.

The process is then repeated in turn on each of the subproblems.

During the refinement process it is usually convenient to isolate a problem and concentrate on it.   After all refinements are finished, the generated pseudocode may be collected to form the final algorithm.   To facilitate refinement and the subsequent recombination, a label will be associated with each subproblem.   The relative positions of the subproblems will be recorded through the use of index levels in the label.

The following diagram illustrates the labeling scheme.   Each number signifies a problem still to be refined and the arrows indicate the result of a decomposition or refinement.   As each problem is decomposed, another numeric index level is added to the original label as illustrated in Figure 9.1.   In this diagram, the original problem is decomposed into four subproblems, labeled **1.**, **2.**, **3.**, and **4.**.   When problem **1.** is decomposed, two subproblems labeled **1.1** and **1.2** result.   This labeling indicates that these subproblems are the first and second subproblems respectively of problem **1.**. Subsequent refinement of problem **1.1** results in subproblems **1.1.1**, **1.1.2**, and **1.1.3**, each of which is refined further into pseudocode.   Unlike problem **1.1**, problem **1.2** needs no further decomposition and is refined directly into pseudocode.

Figure 9.1   An example of the step-wise refinement labeling scheme.

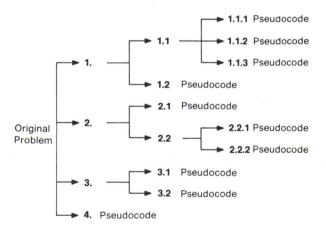

When a problem is decomposed, it may be possible to make use of an algorithm or module which was developed earlier.   Then, those previous results may be used without repeating a formal development of this segment of the algorithm.

Although it may seem that the first decomposition should be difficult, in fact the opposite is usually true.   Almost all mathematical algorithms will, in one way or another, perform:

- the acquisition of parameters for a computation,
- some computations on these parameters,
- recording of some results, and
- termination of the algorithm.

Thus, an initial decomposition which performs these operations is always a good first try.

When a problem has a single set of input parameters, the resulting algorithm will, at the first level, consist of just a sequence of statements. For situations such as these, the steps in Figure 9.2 are appropriate as an initial decomposition.

Figure 9.2 Version 1 of an algorithm using a sequence decomposition.

1. Acquire values for the parameters.
2. Perform the required computations and record the intermediate results.
3. Summarize the results.
4. Terminate the algorithm.

For some problems which process more than one set of data, some form of iteration is needed in the algorithm. For situations which fall in this category, the initial decomposition shown in Figure 9.3 can be used successfully. Notice that this second decomposition does not explicitly specify the acquisition of values for the parameters but assumes this action is implicit in the **while–do** condition. The reason for this is to maintain as much generality as possible since parameter acquisition and termination of the **while**–loop are interrelated and may be accomplished in many different ways. Thus, the label **2.** is associated with the entire **while**–loop and implicitly includes any initialization statements and termination statements which will be generated upon subsequent refinements.

Figure 9.3 Version 1 of an algorithm using an iterative decomposition.

1. Initialize the computation.
2. While the computation should continue

   $\lceil$ perform the required computations and record the intermediate results.

3. Summarize the results.
4. Terminate the algorithm.

Both of the above decompositions refer to intermediate and summary results. In many problems, one or the other of these may be omitted, depending on the problem requirements. The following examples will illustrate both situations.

The labels are used as a reminder that steps **1.** to **4.** of both the sequence decomposition and the iteration decomposition require further refinement. Of course, when dealing with an actual problem, these steps would be more specific as to the actual computation which is to be performed. Although the foregoing discussion was phrased in terms of an initial decomposition, any decomposition which arises during algorithm development will be refined into either a sequence of statements or into an iterative structure.

The use of pseudocode comments is important to document the purpose and behaviour of an algorithm. Many of these comments can be generated quite naturally as part of the step-wise refinement by merely converting the step descriptions into an initial comment when the step is refined into pseudocode. These descriptions are usually the most appropriate comments possible because they describe exactly what the generated pseudocode is supposed to do. This technique will be demonstrated in the examples which follow.

9.4.1 The Prime Number Classification Problem

Since the prime number problem is already familiar to readers of this text, it will be used to introduce the formal techniques of step-wise refinement. An algorithm for the prime number classification problem was discussed informally and then optimized in Chapter 4. This same algorithm was also converted into a pseudocode module in Chapter 5.

Example 9.1   Prime Number Classification Problem
Develop a prime number classification algorithm which will test a given number to determine if it is prime or composite.

Before starting the formal development process, it is a good practice to state or restate the problem in one's own words, primarily to reinforce the exact purpose of the algorithm to be developed. Such restatements can be labeled version 0 of an algorithm and are useful at a later stage as the initial documentation for the complete algorithm. Such a version 0 for the prime number classification problem is shown in Figure 9.4.

Figure 9.4   Version 0 of the prime number classification algorithm for a single number.

Determine if a given number is prime or composite.

The next step in the refinement of an algorithm is to gain a complete understanding of what the problem requires. Much time and effort will be lost if either the wrong problem is solved or if the right problem is not solved correctly. To emphasize this phase of algorithm development, it will be given the formal title of *problem analysis*. This analysis and the subsequent refinements are described below.

a) Problem Analysis   In this section the mathematical background regarding prime numbers would be examined and discussed. For the prime number classification problem, the discussion would encompass a definition of prime and composite numbers along with elaboration upon the calculation method as was given in Sections 4.4 and 4.4.2.

b) Selecting an Initial Decomposition   This step provides the initial unrefined steps of the algorithm. Since the prime number calculation is to be applied to only one number, the sequence decomposition can be applied to version 0 to give the initial decomposition shown in Figure 9.5. Note that the version 0 statement of the problem has been incorporated as a pseudocode comment.

Figure 9.5 Version 1 of a prime number classification algorithm.

* An algorithm to determine if a given number is prime or composite.

1. Acquire the number to be tested.
2. Determine whether the number is prime or composite.
3. Record whether the number is prime or composite.
4. Terminate the algorithm.

---

c) Refining Step **1.**   Each numbered step of the algorithm will be refined. In Step **1.**, the number can be represented by the variable n, and either a value assigned or a value obtained by a **get** action. The latter method is preferred since it is more general. Usually a **put** statement should be included to record the number being tested. This refinement follows, with the previous description of the step included as a comment:

> * Acquire the number to be tested.
>
> **get** n
> **put** 'The number being tested is ', n

d) Refining Step **2.**   This step is the one which does all the work and could have several levels of refinement. During these refinements there will usually be several ways in which the expansion can be done; some will lead to successful solutions, others will not. The successful solutions may not always be identical in form, as there is rarely a unique solution to a problem.

For the problem at hand, it is necessary to refine Step **2.** to test several divisors to determine if the number is composite. A refinement which assumes the number is a prime, and attempts to prove a contradiction follows:

> * Determine whether the number is a prime or composite.
>
> **2.1** Assume the number is prime.
> **2.2** Test possible divisors for a contradiction.

Using a logical variable **prime** to indicate the truth of *the number is prime*, Step **2.1** can be refined immediately by assigning the value **true** to prime. Step **2.2**, however, requires a decomposition to process several divisors, which means using an iterative decomposition, such as the **while**–loop in Figure 4.5:

> * Test the numbers 2 to n-1 as possible divisors
>
> **2.2.1** divisor ← 2
> **2.2.2 while** (divisor ≤ n-1) **do**
> > **2.2.3** Test if divisor divides n evenly
> > **2.2.4** divisor ← divisor + 1

The refinement of iterative decompositions should start by attacking the loop control mechanism. This involves a first step to initialize the control variables, a second step to properly phrase the termination condition of the **while** statement, and a fourth step to modify the control variables. The sequence of steps inside the loop to perform the computations and record intermediate results is the third substep and the details left for subsequent refinement. While this process may appear unnecessarily tedious on this simple problem, it provides a reliable way to decompose a large or complex problem.

e) The Final Algorithm After Step **3.** has been refined as a straightforward **put** statement and Step **4.** has been refined as a **stop** statement, all the pieces of the algorithm can be collected together. The refinements may not have been done in order, so the step numbers serve to collect the pieces into the right sequence.

This collection phase can be important to ensure that all steps have been refined, and that when collected together, all steps will work in sequence.

9.4.2 The Cashier's Problem

The cashier's problem was first introduced in Chapter 4 and an algorithm was developed for it using techniques which we now recognize as those of step-wise refinement.

This problem required processing the pay envelope amounts for many employees. The development technique involves stating a version 0 of the algorithm such as that shown in Figure 9.6.

Figure 9.6 Version 0 of an algorithm for the cashier's problem.

Determine the number of bills and coins of each denomination which are required for each employee on a payroll. Calculate the total bill and coin requirements as well.

A problem analysis would follow which outlines the calculation technique. Then one of the decompositions would be used to give a version 1 of the algorithm. Since many employees are to be processed through the same calculation, the iterative decomposition should be used. This is where Section 4.3.1 began its discussion. That iterative decomposition is repeated in Figure 9.7.

Figure 9.7 Version 1 of an algorithm for the cashier's problem.

1. Record titles for the columns of bills and coins and initialize counters for the quantities of these items required.
2. While there are more employees to process

   > calculate the number of bills and coins required for this employee and record the resulting quantities.

3. Summarize the total bill and coin requirements.
4. Terminate the algorithm.

The subsequent refinements of the algorithm are also shown in Section 4.3.1. However, the refinement of the **while**–loop is worth discussing further. The label **2.** was placed on the entire **while**–loop since this represents the step of the algorithm refined thus far. The refinement of the loop will usually generate pseudocode statements to control the looping, and unrefined statements inside the loop as follows:

```
* Obtain the data for the first employee, then keep processing
* until a negative amount is encountered.
2.1 get employno, amount
2.2 while amount ≥ 0 do
    ⌈ 2.3 Calculate the number of bills and coins required for this employee and record
    |     the resulting quantities.
    ⌊ 2.4 get employno, amount
```

Subsequent refinement of Step **2.3** would lead to the four substeps presented in Section 4.3.1.

9.5   A Complete Algorithm Development

Now that the concepts of step-wise refinement have been applied to problems that have been discussed previously, consider applying them to a new problem.

9.5.1   The Quadratic Equation Problem

The quadratic equation $ax^2 + bx + c = 0$ is familiar to most students and the general form of the solution of the equation is also well known. However, if one wishes to have an algorithm for solving such equations, the details of the many possibilities in the algorithm are complicated enough that step-wise refinement is a handy tool to organize these details.

Example 9.2   Quadratic Equation Problem
   Develop an algorithm to solve the equation $ax^2 + bx + c = 0$ for several sets of coefficient values *a*, *b*, and *c*.

Version 0 of the algorithm is shown in Figure 9.8.

Figure 9.8   Version 0 of the quadratic equation solving algorithm.

Solve the equation $ax^2 + bx + c = 0$ for several sets of coefficient values.

---

a) Problem Analysis   The equation $ax^2 + bx + c = 0$ is a quadratic equation which has two roots of the form

$$root\ 1 = \frac{-b + \sqrt{b^2 - 4ac}}{2a}; \quad root\ 2 = \frac{-b - \sqrt{b^2 - 4ac}}{2a}.$$

If the algorithm simply computed these roots given arbitrary values for *a*, *b*, and *c*, the computer would object to the square root of a negative number, or to a divide by zero if the denominator was zero, for certain coefficient values. To treat these cases properly, the algorithm must recognize them and determine the correct roots.

When $a \neq 0$, there will be two roots. If the discriminant $b^2 - 4ac$ is negative, then there will be two complex roots. When $a = 0$, then the equation simplifies to the linear form $bx + c = 0$, which has a single root $-c/b$, assuming $b \neq 0$. If both $a = 0$ and $b = 0$, then there is no equation, and no roots are possible.

b) Selecting an Initial Decomposition   This problem requires the solution of the equation for several sets of coefficient values a, b, c.   Thus, the iteration decomposition may be used as demonstrated in Figure 9.9.

Figure 9.9   Version 1 of the quadratic equation solving algorithm.

* Solve the equation $ax^2+bx+c=0$ for several sets of coefficient values.

1.   While coefficient values remain

⎡   solve $ax^2+bx+c=0$ for the current coefficient values and record the results.

2.   stop

---

c) Refining Step **1.**   Each set of input parameters will contain three coefficient values, one each for a, b, and c.   In this problem assume that an end-of-data flag, consisting of three zero values, follows the data list.   These special values are used to terminate the processing.   These refinements of the loop control mechanism are listed below with the **while–do** body broken up and numbered for subsequent refinement.

> **1.1 get** a, b, c
> **1.2 while not** ((a=0) **and** (b=0) **and** (c=0)) **do**
> > ⎡   **1.3** Solve $ax^2 + bx + c = 0$ for the current a, b, c values and record the results.
> > ⎣   **1.4 get** a, b, c

This decomposition should include statements to echo the coefficients of the quadratic equation being solved.   Such echoing **put** statements could be placed after each **get**, but this would include printing the end-of-data flag.   The coefficients could be recorded when the results are known, but this might result in an error message being created before any results are produced, leaving the programmer to guess what had happened.   A better placement of the **put** statement is immediately after the **while** statement.   Only equation coefficients pass the **while**–condition, and they would be printed before an error in the computations could occur.

As the next part of the refinement process, Step **1.3** would be expanded.   Often in algorithm designs, it is natural to split a "solve and record" step into two substeps, such as

> **1.3.1** Solve $ax^2 + bx + c = 0$.
> **1.3.2** Record the results.

However, in this problem, there are several different results which can be computed: two real roots, two complex roots, one real root, or no roots.   Separating Step **1.3** into substeps requires that the solution step pass along to the record step extra information about the kind of result to be recorded.   In this case, it would include the number of roots, the type of roots, and the values of the roots.   If no other use was to be made of this information, a simpler decomposition of Step **1.3** would be to record each result as it is computed.

The attempt at one refinement, the discovery that it creates difficulties and the trying of another refinement is called the process of *backtracking*.   Learning to observe the potential difficulties of a decomposition or refinement at an early stage comes with experience.   The use of pseudocode rather than a detailed programming language during this design process lessens the cost of backing up and trying again.

d) Refining Step **1.3**   There are four possible outcomes and it is necessary to determine the algorithm structure for selecting the correct outcome. The outcomes and their selection criteria are listed below:

- two real roots, if $a \neq 0$ and $b^2 - 4ac \geq 0$
- two complex roots, if $a \neq 0$ and $b^2 - 4ac < 0$
- one real root, if $a = 0$ and $b \neq 0$
- no roots, if $a = 0$ and $b = 0$.

Care must be taken to make the criteria complete because any missing conditions in the program may create an error during execution, an error which may be difficult to debug.

Since the list of criteria contains several opposite conditions, such as $a \neq 0$ and $a = 0$, the algorithm can use a sequence of **if–then–else** actions. Thus, Step **1.3** could be refined as follows:

```
* Solve the equation ax² + bx + c = 0 for the current coefficient values a, b, c
* and record the results.

if a=0 then
        if b=0 then
                1.3.1 Record that this is not an equation.
        else
                1.3.2 Solve bx + c = 0 and record the root.
else
        if b² – 4ac ≥ 0 then
                1.3.3 Solve for two real roots and record them.
        else
                1.3.4 Solve for two complex roots and record them.
```

e) Refining Step **1.3.1**   This step can be refined immediately into pseudocode:

put 'Not an equation'

f) Refining Step **1.3.2**   Solving a linear equation produces a single real root, and the refinement is given below:

> * Solve bx + c = 0 and record the root.
>
> root ← − (c/b)
> **put** 'Single root ', root

g) Refining Step **1.3.3**   Solving the quadratic equation for two real roots can be refined directly as follows:

> * Solve for two real roots and record them.
>
> root1 ← (− b + $\sqrt{b^2 - 4ac}$)/2a
> root2 ← (− b − $\sqrt{b^2 - 4ac}$)/2a
> **put** 'Two real roots ', root1, root2

h) Refining Step **1.3.4**   Solving for the two complex roots requires computing the real and imaginary parts of the roots. Since the square root function can only accept positive values, the expression has been rearranged to compute the imaginary part of the complex root.

> * Solve for two complex roots and record them.
>
> real1 ← −(b/2a)
> imag1 ← + $\sqrt{4ac - b^2}$/2a
> real2 ← −(b/2a)
> imag2 ← − $\sqrt{4ac - b^2}$/2a
> **put** 'Complex roots', real1, imag1, real2, imag2

i) The Final Algorithm   All of the refined steps have been combined to form the final version of the algorithm given in Figure 9.10.   This algorithm, which in total turns out to be reasonably complicated, evolved from a simple statement of the problem.   The algorithm determines, records, and identifies the roots of any equation of the form $ax^2 + bx + c = 0$.   If the coefficients do not form an equation, then this fact is noted by the algorithm.   A data list for three sets of a, b, c values is included following the algorithm.

Figure 9.10   Final version of an algorithm for the quadratic equation problem.

* An algorithm to solve quadratic equations of the form $ax^2+bx+c=0$
* for several sets of coefficient values a, b, c

* Real variables used:
* root - root of bx+c=0
* root1,root2 - two real roots
* real1,real2 - real part of complex roots
* imag1,imag2 - imaginary part of complex roots

* Process equations until a=b=c=0.

get a, b, c
while not(a=0 **and** b=0 **and** c=0) **do**

> **put** 'The coefficients of the equation are', a, b, c
> **if** a=0 **then**
>
>> * Solve bx+c=0 and record the results.
>>
>> **if** b=0 **then**
>>> **put** 'Not an equation'
>> **else**
>>> root ← −(c/b)
>>> **put** 'Single root', root
>
> **else**
>
>> * Solve for 2 roots and record the results.
>>
>> **if** $b^2-4ac \geq 0$ **then**
>>> * Solve for real roots and record them.
>>> root1 ← $(-b+\sqrt{b^2-4ac})/2a$
>>> root2 ← $(-b-\sqrt{b^2-4ac})/2a$
>>> **put** 'Two roots', root1, root2
>> **else**
>>> * Solve for complex roots and record them.
>>> real1 ← −(b/2a)
>>> imag1 ← $+\sqrt{4ac-b^2}/2a$
>>> real2 ← −(b/2a)
>>> imag2 ← $-\sqrt{4ac-b^2}/2a$
>>> **put** 'Complex roots', real1, imag1, real2, imag2
>
> **get** a, b, c

stop

1, −5, 6,   0, 5, −15,   1, 3, 4,   0, 0, 0

9.6   Modularity as Part of Top-Down Design

As the reader may have already recognized, the concept of modularity is a natural extension of the step-wise refinement process. Recall that in step-wise refinement the idea is to decompose problems into smaller and simpler subproblems. At each stage of the decomposition an attempt is made to make each subproblem as independent of others as possible. Furthermore, every subproblem is represented as an action sequence with one entrance and one exit. Thus, in order to introduce modularity into the step-wise refinement process, it is only necessary to select a *suitable* (sub)problem and designate it as a module.

Once it has been decided that a problem is to be refined as a module, then that module may either already exist, or it will need further decomposition. If further decomposition is performed, it could result in the definition of even more modules. The extent to which each module is dependent on other modules determines its interface parameters.

9.6.1   A Twin Primes Algorithm

As an example of a step-wise refinement which involves the use of modules, the twin primes problem will be discussed. This problem requires repeated prime/composite calculations and thus a module to determine primeness is useful.

Example 9.3   Twin Primes Problem
    Develop an algorithm to generate twin primes.

From the example statement, version 0 of the algorithm can be stated as shown in Figure 9.11. To make the problem statement more precise, a range will be required for the twin prime generation.

Figure 9.11   Version 0 of the twin primes algorithm.

Generate all twin primes less than a given limit.

---

a) Problem Analysis   Twin primes are defined to be two consecutive odd numbers which are both primes. Any generation or testing for twin primes would consider only the consecutive odd numbers beginning at 3 and up to some limit.

b) Selecting an Initial Decomposition   The problem requires that all twin primes up to a certain limit be generated. There is just a single input value required for the limit and thus the sequence decomposition can be used as shown in Figure 9.12.

Figure 9.12   Version 1 of the twin primes algorithm.

* An algorithm to generate all twin primes less than a given limit.

1.   Acquire the limit on the range to be tested.
2.   Test all candidate numbers within the range for twin primeness and record the results.
3.   **stop**

---

c) Refining Step **1.**   This step can be refined completely into pseudocode with statements which obtain and echo the limit to be tested.

> * Acquire the limit on the range to be tested.
>
> **get** limit
> **put** 'Generate twin primes up to the limit ', limit

d) Refining Step **2.**   In order to generate all twin primes in the given range, the algorithm must test each pair of consecutive odd numbers for primeness. This means that the first potential prime of the pair may be chosen from all odd numbers from 3 to limit−2 which must be generated in a loop. The loop to generate the test numbers can be written as follows:

> * Test all candidate numbers within the range for twin primeness
> *   and record the results.
>
> $n \leftarrow 3$
> **while** $n \leq$ limit−2 **do**
> > **2.3** Test n and n+2 for twin primeness.
> > $n \leftarrow n+2$

This illustrates again how an iterative structure can result from the refinement of a sequence step.   Notice that the labels for the Steps **2.1**, **2.2**, and **2.4** are implied.

e) Refining Step **2.3**   The numbers n and n+2 will be twin primes only if both of them are prime. Thus, as an intermediate stage, Step **2.3** can be rephrased as:

> **2.3** If n is a prime and n+2 is a prime
> > Record that n and n+2 are twin primes.

A primeness test is a well-defined operation and as such is a prime candidate (pun intended) for representation by a module. Since a prime testing function module called aprime was developed in Chapter 5 and given in Figure 5.9, that module will be used here.

If such a module did not exist, then a digression to develop the module would be appropriate at this point. Then, with the module interface defined, the interrupted refinement could proceed. Examples of such digressions will be given in later examples.

The tests for primeness are incorporated easily using the function aprime. It is very tempting and indeed would be acceptable to write:

> **if** aprime(n) **and** aprime(n+2) **then**

However, this would result in checking n+2 for primeness even if n is not a prime. To avoid this potential inefficiency, it is better to rephrase Step **2.3** once more, this time as:

2.3 If n is a prime

$\quad\lceil$ If n+2 is a prime

$\quad\quad\lceil$ Record that n and n+2 are twin primes.

Thus the final refinement is:

if aprime(n) **then**

$\quad\lceil$ **if** aprime(n+2) **then**

$\quad\quad\lceil$ **put** 'The numbers ', n, ' and ', n+2, ' are twin primes'

f) The Final Algorithm   Since there are no more steps to be refined, the pseudocode segments may be collected together to form the final algorithm shown in Figure 9.13.

Figure 9.13   Final version of the twin primes algorithm.

* An algorithm to generate all twin primes less than a given limit.

* Integer variables used:
*   limit - limit of numbers to be tested for twin primes
*   n - the first number of the pair to be checked for twin primes
* Acquire the limit on the range to be tested

get limit
put 'Generate twin primes up to the limit ', limit

* Test all candidate numbers within the range for twin primeness
* and record the results.

n ← 3
while n ≤ limit−2 **do**

$\quad\lceil$ **if** aprime(n) **then**

$\quad\quad\lceil$ **if** aprime(n+2) **then**

$\quad\quad\quad\lceil$ **put** 'The numbers ', n, ' and ', n+2, ' are twin primes'

$\quad\lfloor$ n ← n+2

stop

9.7   Summary

The development of large algorithms is a difficult task because of the vast amount of detail that must be maintained. The method of top-down design using step-wise refinement provides an orderly way to approach the development of both small and large algorithms. It establishes a hierarchy of algorithmic operations by performing successive decompositions of problems into subproblems.

Although a top-down design approach aids in producing correct algorithms, it is still possible for an incorrect algorithm to result. Manual testing of the algorithm is a good way to detect many of these incorrect situations.

9.8   References

Brown, A.R. and Sampson, W.A.   *Program Debugging.* Computer Monograph Series, New York: Elsevier-North Holland Pub. Co., 1973.

Dahl, O.J.; Dijkstra, E.W.; and Hoare, C.A.R.   *Structured Programming.* New York: Academic Press, 1972.

Freeman, P.   "Software Reliability and Design: A Survey." *13th Design Automation Conference,* New York: IEEE Computer Society and Association for Computing Machinery, 1976.   (An excellent and very readable survey on the state of software reliability.)

Hughes, J.K and Michton, J.I.   *A Structured Approach to Programming.* Englewood Cliffs, N.J.: Prentice-Hall, 1977.

McGowan, C.L. and Kelly, J.R.   *Top-Down Structured Programming Techniques.* New York: Petrocelli Charter, 1975.

Wirth, N.   *Systematic Programming: An Introduction.* Englewood Cliffs, N.J.: Prentice-Hall, 1973.

9.9   Exercises

In most of the following exercises a program is requested to solve a specific problem. For each problem it is recommended that step-wise refinement be used in developing a pseudocode algorithm to solve the problem.   This algorithm should then be translated into FORTRAN/77 and run on the computer.   Where appropriate, the program should be tested with a variety of data sufficient to ensure that the program does what it is supposed to do.

9.1   For each of the following problems, state whether a sequence or iterative initial decomposition should be used, then write out the resulting first version of each algorithm.

    a)   Develop an algorithm to convert any given number of hours into an equivalent grouping of weeks, days, and hours.   In the grouping, the number of days should be ≤ 6 and the number of hours should be ≤ 23.

    b)   Develop an algorithm to arrange a set of 3 numbers in ascending order. Design your algorithm to handle several sets of input data.

    c)   It is often necessary to be able to determine the maximum and minimum values of an unordered set of data.   Develop an algorithm which will perform this operation.

    d)   A number is said to be a perfect number if it is equal to the sum of its factors other than itself.   For instance, the number 28 is a perfect number since

$1 + 2 + 4 + 7 + 14 = 28$. Develop an algorithm using the step-wise refinement technique, which will test a given number to determine if it is a perfect number.

e) Extend the algorithm of Exercise 9.1d) such that the algorithm will test all numbers in the range 25 to 300 for perfectness.

f) Suppose that a set of three numbers is to represent the lengths of three line segments. Develop an algorithm which will determine if such a set of numbers:

- does not represent the sides of a triangle
- represents the sides of a triangle which is neither an isosceles nor equilateral triangle
- represents the sides of an isosceles triangle
- represents the sides of an equilateral triangle.

g) The greatest common divisor (GCD) of two numbers is the largest factor of both numbers. For example, the GCD of 54 and 63 is 9. Develop an algorithm which will compute the GCD of any two given numbers.

9.2 Given below is a partial step-wise refinement to solve the following problem:

Find the lowest common multiple (LCM) for each pair of several pairs of numbers.

Mathematical Background The LCM of any two numbers is the smallest integer evenly divisible by both numbers.

Examples The LCM of 6 and 9 is 18; the LCM of 5 and 10 is 10; the LCM of 7 and 13 is 91.

Initial Decomposition Since there are several pairs of numbers to work with, select an iterative decomposition as a starting point.

1. While pairs of numbers remain to process

    ⌈ Determine and record the LCM of the current pair of numbers.

2. **stop**

Provide *only* the next refinement of step 1. Do not complete the refinement of the entire algorithm.

9.3 Given below is a partial step-wise refinement to solve the following problem:

Determine whether the numbers in each of several pairs of integers are twin primes.

Initial Decomposition Since a set of numbers is to be examined, select an iterative decomposition as a starting point. Version 1 follows:

1. While pairs of numbers remain to process

    ⌐ Determine whether the current pair of numbers are twin primes and record
    ⌊ them if they are.

2. **stop**

a) How would you refine Step **1.** if you knew in advance how many pairs there
    were to process?

b) How would you refine Step **1.** if the number of pairs was not known in
    advance?

9.4   Complete the step-wise refinement from the partially refined algorithm presented
below. Show all steps leading to the complete algorithm, but you do not need to
write out the final algorithm.

In an algorithm to score the game of golf, each hole must be classified as being above or below par. Special names are given to certain scores, such as *hole-
in-one* for a score of 1, *par* for a score equal to what was expected on that hole,
birdie for one shot less than par, *eagle* for two shots less than par, *bogey* for one
shot more than par, *double bogey* for two shots more than par. Note that this
does not completely describe all scores on a hole (for instance, on a par-5 hole, the
score of 2 is not given a special name, nor is 8, 9, 10, . . .). The following refinement has been developed for a program to score such a golf game:

    * Obtain scores for one player over 18-holes of golf.

    1.1 hole ← 1
    1.2 while hole ≤ 18 **do**

        ⌐ **1.3 get** score, par
        │ **1.4** Classify the score on this hole.
        │ **1.5** Total the score and the par for the game.
        ⌊ **1.6** hole ← hole + 1

    2.   Record the total score and the par total for the game.
    3.   **stop**

Complete the refinement of the algorithm.

9.5   A partial step-wise refinement is provided below for an algorithm which will
determine the Fibonacci numbers which exist above and below a specific given
number. The Fibonacci sequence is the following sequence of numbers:
1, 1, 2, 3, 5, 8, 13, 21, . . . where each number after the first is found by adding
the two previous numbers in the sequence. For example, the 13 is found by adding 5 and 8; the 21 is found by adding 8 and 13. In the following algorithm, if
the specific given number is 15, then the Fibonacci numbers found should be 13
and 21. On the other hand, if the specific number was 8, one of the Fibonacci
numbers, then the numbers found should be 5 and 13.
Version 1.

1. Acquire the given number.
2. Determine and record the Fibonacci number above and below the given number.
3. **stop**

Version 2.

* Acquire and record the given number.

get x
put 'The given number is ', x
2.1 Initialize the first 2 Fibonacci numbers.
2.2 While some condition

$\left[\vphantom{X} \right.$ Determine the next Fibonacci number.

2.3 Record Fibonacci numbers below and above x.
3. **stop**

Complete the refinement of each step of the algorithm.

9.6 Provide only the next level of step-wise refinement in the following algorithm. This will involve completing the control structure, and not the detailed actions in the algorithm.

In a simulation of the behaviour of an air conditioning system, an algorithm is required to decide how to change the temperature and humidity. The system has four devices that the algorithm can turn on or off: a heater to raise the temperature, an air conditioner to cool the temperature, a humidifier to raise the humidity, and a dehumidifier to lower the humidity. The heater and air conditioner can operate alone, but the humidifier only works if the heater is also turned on, and the dehumidifier only works if the air conditioner is turned on. This implies that when it is too hot and too low humidity, that both the air conditioner and heater will be on with the humidifier.

The algorithm will be provided with a temperature reading and a humidity reading, and 4 range limits: lowtemp, hitemp, lowhumid, hihumid. Upon entry to the algorithm, any of the devices may be either on or off randomly, so they must be explicitly turned on or off as appropriate. Complete only the next level in the step-wise refinement of this algorithm:

* Obtain the range of temperature and humidity limits.

1. **get** lowtemp, hitemp, lowhumid, hihumid

* Control devices for a variety of temperature and humidity situations.

2.1 **get** temp, humid
2.2 **while** temp $>$ 0 **and** humid $>$ 0 **do**

$\left[\vphantom{X} \right.$ 2.3 Categorize the temperature and humidity situation and control the appropriate devices.
2.4 **get** temp, humid

3. **stop**

9.7   The Faculty of Mathematics at the University of Waterloo has the following
       policy regarding the repetition of a course:

      A single course may be repeated as often as desired with the highest mark
      obtained being used for the course, *provided* the course has not been passed
      more than twice. Once the course has been passed twice, all succeeding
      marks are ignored.

    Listed below are several numerical examples:

```
Successive Marks            Mark Used  Comments

45                              45
45, 40                          45
40, 45                          45
40, 50                          50
40, 50, 45                      50
50, 51                          51
51, 50                          51
50, 45, 51                      51
50, 51, 52                      51       The 52 is ignored.
40, 50, 51, 45, 52              51       The 45 and 52 are ignored.
50, 40, 51, 45, 52              51       The 45 and 52 are ignored.
```

Suppose an algorithm is required to process several sets of students' attempts to
pass a single course and assume that the data is organized as:

```
id number,
number of tries for the course,
mark on try 1,
mark on try 2,
   .
   .
mark on try n,
```

for each student and that a zero id number is used to terminate the algorithm.
Part of such an algorithm has been refined and is listed below. Study the algorithm and then complete the refinement of step **1.1.2**.

* Acquire the ID number for the first student,
* then keep processing as long as the ID number is nonzero.

get idno
while idno ≠ 0 **do**

> * Record the ID number for the current student.
>
> **put** 'The current student is: ', idno
>
> * Obtain and record the number of marks for the current student.
>
> **get** notries
> **put** 'The number of tries for the course is: ', notries
>
> * Obtain and process the marks for the current student.
>
> cctries ← 1
> **while** cctries ≤ notries **do**
>
> > **get** mark
> > **put** mark
> > **1.1.2** Determine and record the mark used for the course.
> > cctries ← cctries + 1
>
> * Acquire the ID number for the next student.
>
> **get** idno

stop

Provide the successive step-wise refinements you would use to *complete* the algorithm.

9.8 Write out Version 1. and the first refinement of Version 1. of a step-wise design of the following problem. You should present the algorithm at the stage when you have steps **1.1**, **1.2**, . . . , **2.1**, **2.2**, . . . , etc. Do not present the complete refinement.

   This algorithm will produce a payment schedule for a loan, which is to be repaid in equal monthly payments. The loan is described by the amount of the loan, the annual interest rate, and the monthly payment. Interest on the loan is accumulated monthly on the balance outstanding at the end of the month. The payment is made at the beginning of each month. The payment schedule table will show the month, the monthly payment, the interest from the previous month, the amount that the principal was reduced by whatever was left of the payment, and the outstanding balance of the loan.

9.9 A bank wishes to process monthly statements for its chequing accounts. The transactions for each account are collected and entered in machine readable form. Each transaction is entered on a separate line and consists of two numbers, the day of the month and the amount of the transaction with deposits entered as positive numbers and cheques entered as negative numbers. Two zeros are used to terminate the set of transactions for each account. Furthermore, the transactions are already sorted by day of the month. Each set of transactions is preceded by the account number for the account as well as the balance brought forward from the previous month. The monthly statement is to include four columns, one for the date of the transaction, one for deposits, one for cheques, and one for the balance.

Using top-down design and step-wise refinement, develop a FORTRAN/77 program to process these account transactions.

9.10 Using step-wise refinement develop a pseudocode algorithm to solve the following problem. A given amount of money is to be invested at the beginning of *each* month at a given interest rate (stated as an annual rate but in fact compounded monthly) for a given number of months. You may assume that interest is paid at the end of each month based on the minimum monthly balance. At the end of each month, tabulate the month, the amount which was invested for that month, the interest earned on the investment that month, the new deposit to be added to the investment, and the total amount that will be invested for the next month. Your algorithm should also record the final value of the investment scheme.

In addition to submitting the step-wise refinement and the final algorithm for this problem work through your algorithm for the following problem. Submit your answer in the form suggested by Figures 2.7 and 2.8.

Invest $250 at the beginning of each month for 10 months at an interest rate of 12% annually.

9.11 From your collection of books, gather the following information: the number of pages in each chapter for at least 3 or 4 books. The number of books isn't important and you might like to choose books which don't have very many chapters in them.

Using step-wise refinement, develop a pseudocode algorithm to solve the following problem. Determine the average number of pages per chapter for each book as well as the length of the shortest and longest chapters in the entire collection of books. Design your algorithm to be general so that only the data list needs to be changed for a different set of books. Include the data list with the final algorithm.

9.12 Develop a pseudocode algorithm, using the step-wise refinement technique, which will find and record the first 50 positive integers which have no prime factors other than 2, and/or 3, and/or 5. (Numbers in this category include: 2 (factor is 2), 3 (factor is 3), 5 (factor is 5), 6 (factors are 2 and 3), 10 (factors are 2 and 5), . . . , 120 (factors are 2, 3, and 5), ...) Translate your algorithm into a FORTRAN/77 program and test it on the computer.

9.13 Two positive integers are said to be friendly if each one is equal to the sum of the divisors (including 1, excluding the number itself) of the other. For example the numbers 220 and 284 are friendly since:

divisors of 220: $1+2+4+5+10+11+20+22+44+55+110 = 284$
divisors of 284: $1+2+4+71+142 = 220$.

Develop a pseudocode algorithm, using the step-wise refinement technique, which will find all pairs of friendly numbers such that both numbers are less than 1500. Translate your algorithm into a FORTRAN/77 program and test it on the computer.

9.14 Every integer has the property that it is divisible by 9 if and only if the sum of its digits is divisible by 9. For example, 4520 is not divisible by 9 since 4+5+2+0=11 is not divisible by 9; 4527 is divisible by 9 since 4+5+2+7=18 is divisible by 9. Develop a pseudocode algorithm, using the step-wise refinement technique, to test a variable number of integers for divisibility by 9 using this test. The algorithm should output an appropriate message for each integer. Translate your algorithm into a FORTRAN/77 program and test it on the computer.

9.15 If the sides of a right-angled triangle are restricted to be of integral lengths, then only certain triplets of integers will form such a triangle. Develop separate pseudocode algorithms, using the step-wise refinement technique, which will produce all triplets of integers which represent the sides of a right-angled triangle:

a)   whose hypotenuse is < 100,
b)   whose perimeter is < 100.

Recall that for a right-angled triangle, the hypotenuse squared is equal to the sum of the squares of the other two sides (Pythagorean Identity). Translate your algorithms into FORTRAN/77 programs and test them on the computer.

9.16 Using step-wise refinement, develop a pseudocode algorithm to keep score for a single game of ten-pin bowling. The input for the algorithm should be the number of pins knocked down by each successive ball thrown. Your algorithm should be able to detect errors (such as 6 and 7 on the first two balls thrown) and take appropriate action. If you are not familiar with the game of ten-pin bowling, it is your responsibility to find out, since researching a problem is an integral part of the problem solving process.

Translate your final algorithm to FORTRAN/77 and test the resulting program with several sets of data to demonstrate that it works properly.

10
Applications of Algorithm Design

10.1 Introduction

The problems solved in the previous chapter were well-defined mathematical problems, and their analyses were straightforward. When more complicated problems are encountered, the problem analysis becomes much more involved. It is important to emphasize that the problem analysis investigates perhaps several solution techniques to select a problem solution. The step-wise refinement structures the algorithm to describe the steps in the solution in an orderly way. The following examples of more involved problems demonstrate the benefits of problem analysis and step-wise refinement.

10.2 Computing the Area Between Two Curves

In Chapters 7 and 8, the algorithms for finding zeros of functions and areas under curves were discussed without much regard to their application. As an extension of these ideas, Example 10.1 introduces the more challenging problem of finding an area bounded by intersecting curves.

Example 10.1   Area Between Two Curves Problem
Develop an algorithm to find the area between two arbitrary intersecting curves $f(x)$ and $g(x)$ as illustrated by the shaded area in Figure 10.1.

a) Problem Discussion   From previous chapters it is known that numerical integration may be used to calculate areas.   However, the previous examples involved finding only the area between one curve and the x axis.   A useful technique in problem analysis is to

Figure 10.1   Graph of two intersecting curves.

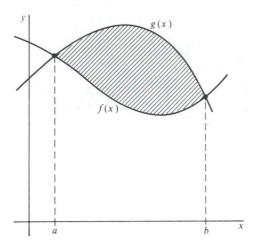

reduce a problem to a familiar one whose solution has already been worked out.   In this problem, it can be observed that the shaded area is really just the area under *g* minus the area under *f* between the points of intersection.   Thus, a promising start has been made on this solution.

To complete the solution along these lines, the remaining task is to determine the limits [*a,b*] for the integration, which means the intersection points of the two curves must be found.   Finding such intersections is also something which has not been discussed previously.   The closest related problem is that of finding the intersection of a curve with the *x* axis, that is, finding a zero of the function.   Again, a way is sought to reduce this latest problem to a known one.   The question is, how can the intersection of two arbitrary curves be formulated as a zero-finding problem?   Or stated another way, can an equation be derived which would have zeros corresponding to the intersection points of the two curves?   A little reflection indicates that the intersections of *f* and *g* correspond to zeros of the function $h = g - f$.   That is, *h* is zero at the intersection points.   Thus, by performing a zero-finding operation on *h*, it is possible to find an intersection point.   Illustrating this graphically, Figure 10.2 shows this *difference curve* *h* in relation to *f* and *g*.

Looking at this diagram, an added benefit can be seen.   Since the *y* value of each point on the difference curve corresponds to the separation between *f* and *g*, the area under *h* between its zeros will be exactly the same as the required area.   Thus, as a final bonus to this discussion, the area between two curves may be found by simply integrating *h* between the points of intersection, a fact that can be verified by calculus:

$$\int_a^b g \, dx - \int_a^b f \, dx = \int_a^b (g - f) \, dx = \int_a^b h \, dx$$

Figure 10.2   The difference curve for two arbitrary curves.

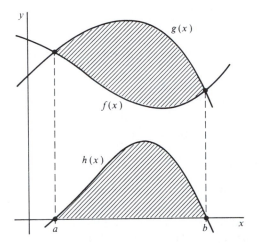

b) *Selection of an Initial Decomposition*   Since this problem requires the computation of only one area, the sequence decomposition should be used.   Assuming that the functions *f*, *g*, and thus *h* are defined, the algorithm will involve calculation of the intersection points *a* and *b*, followed by integration of $h(x)$ from *a* to *b*. A first version of the algorithm follows as Figure 10.3.

Figure 10.3   First version of a pseudocode algorithm for calculating the area between two curves.

1. Find the curve intersection points as the zeros of h(x).
2. Compute the area and record the results.
3. **stop**

c) *Refining Step* **1.**   Before this refinement may proceed, a decision must be made about the zero-finding technique to be used.   Since a bisection module for zero-finding was developed in Chapter 7, it is convenient to use it here.   For this discussion it is assumed that an **smodule** bisect is available with a module interface of the form

smodule bisect(**imports**: xl, xr, eps, f(x); **exports**: error, zero)

To use this module, initial intervals are needed for both intersection points (zeros) and an error tolerance is required.   The zero-finding computations may then proceed.

* Find the intersection points, if possible.

1.1 Obtain initial approximations for the intersections and the error tolerance.
1.2 Find and record the intersection points.

d) Refining Step **1.1**   Initial approximations to the intervals would probably be determined from a plot of the functions and provided as input data. This leads to the following refinement:

* Obtain initial approximations for the intersections and the error tolerance.

get x1, x2, x3, x4, eps
put 'The initial interval on the left is', x1, x2
put 'The initial interval on the right is', x3 , x4
put 'The error tolerance for intersection points is', eps

e) Refining Step **1.2**   This step consists of several distinct operations which are to be performed sequentially.   However, the computation of either intersection point may result in an error from the bisect module if a bad interval is supplied. The intersection calculations are independent of each other, and thus it is reasonable to attempt both calculations even if one is in error.   If both intervals are in error, both errors will be caught on the initial run of the program instead of requiring two runs.   To find the points of intersection requires the application of bisect to the intervals [x1,x2] and [x3,x4] on the function h.   This gives the following steps:

* Find and record intersection points, if possible.
* If not, record an error message.

call bisect(x1, x2, eps, h; lerror, a)
if lerror **then**

    ⌈ **put** 'There was no intersection found in the left interval.'

else

    ⌈ **put** 'The left intersection point is', a

call bisect(x3, x4, eps, h; rerror, b)
if rerror **then**

    ⌈ **put** 'There was no intersection found in the right interval.'

else

    ⌈ **put** 'The right intersection point is', b

f) Refining Step **2.**   The flags lerror and rerror indicate the presence of errors in the computation of the intersection points.   Thus, these flags should be checked before performing the area calculation.

* Provided that there was no error on the intersection calculations,
* compute and record the area between the two intersections.

2.1 if lerror **or** rerror **then**

[**2.2 put** 'No area calculated.'

else

[**2.3** Compute and record the area.

g) Refining Step **2.3**   To find the area requires an integration which can be performed using the Simpson's Rule module of Chapter 8. However, this module requires the number of panels to use. Since this parameter affects the cost of computing the area, it is preferable that it be supplied as an input to the algorithm. Therefore, while refining Step **2.3**, an additional input and **put** action are needed in Step **1.1**. Changes like these occur frequently in algorithm development as new information is learned during a step-wise refinement. When they do occur, it is necessary to review the affected steps to ensure that the algorithm structure is still straightforward and correct.

The pseudocode refinement of Step **2.3** can now be presented as follows:

area ← simp(a, b, n, h)
put 'The area between the two curves is ', area

h) Final Version of Algorithm   Combining all the refinement steps gives the final version of the algorithm shown in Figure 10.4.

i) Program for the Final Version of the Algorithm   The final algorithm was developed in a general way without reference to any specific mathematical functions.   Consider applying the algorithm to finding the area between the parabola $y = 16 - x^2$ and the straight line $7x + 4y = 36$.   Figure 10.5 illustrates two graphs, the top graph giving a plot of both the parabola and the straight line and the bottom graph plotting the difference curve.   These graphs are used to supply the input values for the program of Figure 10.6.   It is assumed that the subprograms BISECT and SIMP are available and can be inserted at the indicated points or supplied from an on-line subprogram library. The difference function H(X) is written without explicitly defining the functions F(X) and G(X).   If for some reason the main program needed these two functions, then they could be defined and the difference function changed accordingly.   Note that two panels suffice to compute this area exactly, as discussed in Chapter 8.   The output from this program is given in Figure 10.7.

Figure 10.4   Final version of the pseudocode algorithm for computing the area between curves.

* Compute the area between two intersecting curves using modules **bisect** and **simp**.

* Real variables used:
* x1,x2 - starting interval end points for left intersection
* x3,x4 - starting interval end points for right intersection
* eps - error tolerance for intersection points
* a,b - intersection points
* **area** - computed area between two curves

* Integer variables used:
* n - number of panels for **simp** area calculation

* Logical variables used:
* lerror,rerror - error flags for left and right intersections

* Obtain and record initial approximations for intersections,
* the error tolerance, and the number of integration panels.

get x1, x2, x3, x4, eps, n
put 'The initial interval on the left is', x1, x2
put 'The initial interval on the right is', x3 , x4
put 'The error tolerance for intersection points is', eps
put 'The number of integration panels is', n

* Find and record intersection points, if possible.
* If not, record an error message.

call bisect(x1, x2, eps, h; lerror, a)
if lerror **then**

    ⌈ **put** 'There was no intersection found in the left interval.'

else

    ⌈ put 'The left intersection point is', a

call bisect(x3, x4, eps, h; rerror, b)
if rerror **then**

    ⌈ **put** 'There was no intersection found in the right interval.'

else

    ⌈ **put** 'The right intersection point is', b

* Provided that there were no errors in the intersection calculations,
* compute and record the area between the two intersections.

if lerror **or** rerror **then**

    ⌈ **put** 'No area calculated.'

else

    ⌈ area ← simp(a, b, n, h)
      put 'The area between the two curves is', area

stop

Figure 10.5 The graphs for the parabola $y = 16 - x^2$ and the straight line $7x + 4y = 36$, plotted from -5 to $+5$ in 20 steps.

a) *The two curves on one graph.*

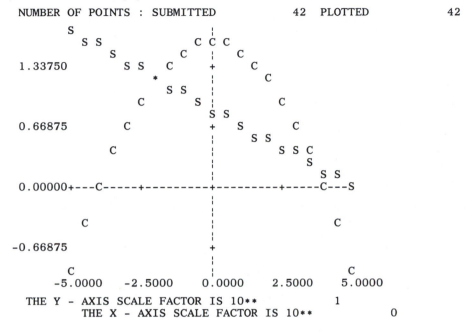

b) *The difference curve.*

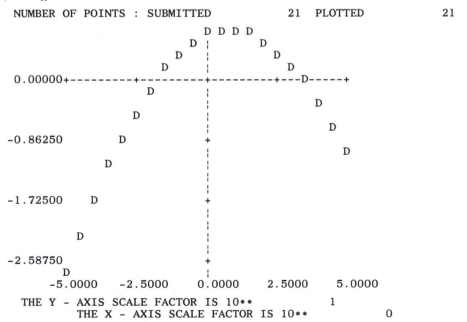

```
C Figure 10.6 -- Compute the Area Between Two Curves.
C                A program to find the area between the parabola
C                y=16-x**2 and the line 7x+4y=36.

C************************************************************************
C H      - difference function g(x) - f(x)
C X1,X2  - starting interval to find left intersection
C X3,X4  - starting interval to find right intersection
C EPS    - error tolerance for intersection points
C A,B    - left, right intersection points
C N      - number of panels for Simpson's Rule
C LERROR - error flag for left intersection
C RERROR - error flag for right intersection
C AREA   - computed area between two curves

C************************************************************************
      REAL X1, X2, X3, X4, A, B, H, EPS, AREA
      INTEGER N
      LOGICAL LERROR, RERROR
      EXTERNAL H

C Obtain initial approximations for the intersections, the
C error tolerance, and the number of integration panels.
      PRINT *, 'ENTER THE INTERVAL ON THE LEFT (X1, X2):'
      READ *, X1, X2
      PRINT *, 'ENTER THE INTERVAL ON THE RIGHT (X3, X4):'
      READ *, X3, X4
      PRINT *, 'ENTER THE DESIRED TOLERANCE:'
      READ *, EPS
      PRINT *, 'ENTER THE DESIRED NUMBER OF INTEGRATION PANELS:'
      READ *, N
      PRINT *, ' '

C Find and record intersection points, if possible.
C Otherwise record an error message.
      CALL BISECT(X1,X2,EPS,H,LERROR,A)
      IF (LERROR) THEN
         PRINT *, 'THERE WAS NO INTERSECTION FOUND IN LEFT INTERVAL'
      ELSE
         PRINT *, 'THE LEFT INTERSECTION POINT IS', A
      ENDIF
      CALL BISECT(X3,X4,EPS,H,RERROR,B)
      IF (RERROR) THEN
         PRINT *, 'THERE WAS NO INTERSECTION FOUND IN RIGHT INTERVAL'
      ELSE
         PRINT *, 'THE RIGHT INTERSECTION POINT IS', B
      ENDIF

C Provided that there were no errors in the intersection
C calculations, compute and record the area between the
C two intersections.
      IF (LERROR .OR. RERROR) THEN
         PRINT *, 'NO AREA CALCULATED'
      ELSE
         AREA = SIMP(A,B,N,H)
         PRINT *, 'THE AREA BETWEEN THE TWO CURVES IS', AREA
      ENDIF
      STOP
      END
```

```
C Figure 10.6 (continued)
C Function H -- Given a value for X, evaluate the difference
C               function G(X) - F(X), where
C               F(X) = (36.0 - 7.0*X)/4.0
C               G(X) = 16.0 - X*X
C***********************************************************************
      REAL FUNCTION H(X)
      REAL X
      H = 16.0 - X*X  -  (36.0 - 7.0*X)/4.0
      RETURN
      END
```

Figure 10.7 Output from the area between two curves program of Figure 10.6.

```
ENTER THE INTERVAL ON THE LEFT (X1, X2):
-2.0 -1.0
ENTER THE INTERVAL ON THE RIGHT (X3, X4):
3.0 4.0
ENTER THE DESIRED TOLERANCE:
0.00005
ENTER THE DESIRED NUMBER OF INTEGRATION PANELS:
2

THE LEFT INTERSECTION POINT IS  -1.911713
THE RIGHT INTERSECTION POINT IS   3.661713
THE AREA BETWEEN THE TWO CURVES IS   28.85383
```

10.3   The Depth Gauge Problem

As another example of algorithm development on more applied problems, consider measuring the volume of oil at various depths in a storage tank. The volume is measured by inserting a ruled stick through the top opening. Assume that the stick is marked every 10 centimeters and that one wishes to know the volume of the tank at each mark. The oil tank has an elliptical cross section 8 meters wide, 4 meters high and is 7 meters in length. The situation is illustrated in Figure 10.8. The problem can now be posed as follows:

Example 10.2   Depth Gauge Problem
   Generate a table that gives the volume of oil stored in an elliptical tank for each depth mark on a ruled stick.

a) Problem Analysis Since the volume of the oil at any level is just the length times the cross-sectional area of the oil at that stage, this problem also reduces to one of finding an area.   In this case, the area is bounded by the tank sides and the surface of the oil, both of which may be represented by simple equations in an appropriate coordinate

Figure 10.8   Geometry for the elliptical tank.

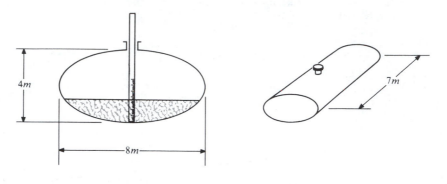

system.   The diagrams in Figure 10.9 indicate the equations and the two level conditions which must be considered.   The equation of the ellipse is $x^2/160000 + y^2/40000 = 1$.   All values have been converted to centimeters and the origin is taken to be at the center of the tank.

Figure 10.9   Two different level conditions for the elliptical tank.

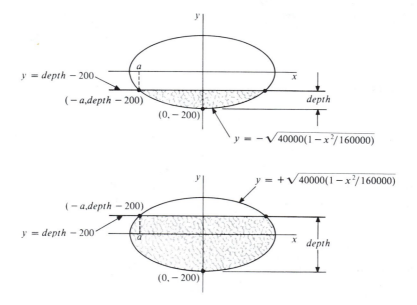

The two diagrams illustrate that different equations are needed when the oil level is above or below the *x* axis. Because of symmetry, the area for only half the tank on one side of the *x* axis needs to be computed, and then doubled. This problem now seems very similar to the problem of Section 10.2.   The area to be found is bounded by two curves in the y direction and by $[a,0]$ in the x direction.   Again, an intersection point of two curves must be found.   Applying these calculations to the area computation when the oil is below the x axis, diagram a) in Figure 10.9 is straightforward.

However, when the oil surface is above the x axis, as in diagram b), the area is more involved.   In this case, the shaded area is given by:

$2 \times$ (area below x axis) $-$ (area between the two curves) .

On the basis of the above discussion the area could be calculated, but it would be necessary to calculate the areas under both curves and subtract them instead of using the difference function approach.   This restriction is caused by the fact that the curve $y = depth - 200$ changes with $depth$ and the function modules as used in the zero-finding and numerical integration modules allow only the one argument x.   Therefore this area would have to be calculated in the main program.   Thus, a complicated but feasible approach has now been found.   Is there possibly a simpler way?

If one steps back for a moment and takes a closer look at the above diagrams, it seems that the proposed solution is really just a crude way of performing a numerical integration along the y axis.   By turning the diagram on its side this fact is made clearer, as shown in Figure 10.10.   From this diagram it can be seen that the area may actually be found by performing a regular numerical integration as a function of y instead of x.   The equation for x is found by rearranging the equation for the ellipse.

Figure 10.10   Transforming the elliptical tank.

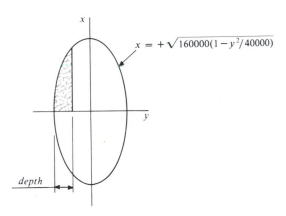

$$x = +\sqrt{160000(1 - y^2/40000)}$$

The limits for this integration are $[-200, -200 + depth]$, and there is no problem crossing the x axis.   This latter approach will be developed below.

b) *Selection of an Initial Decomposition*   This problem requires the calculation of many volumes, one for each marking on the stick.   Thus, the iterative decomposition should be used.   A first version of the algorithm is given in Figure 10.11.

Figure 10.11   First version of a pseudocode algorithm for the depth gauge problem.

1.   While oil levels remain

⌈ calculate the volume for the current oil level and record it.

2.   stop

---

c) Refining Step **1.**   The volume of oil in the tank is to be calculated at intervals of 10 centimeters between − 200 and + 200 centimeters. This means that the depth of oil in the tank will vary from 10 to 400 centimeters in steps of 10 centimeters.

　　* Calibrate volumes of oil corresponding to depth gauge
　　* levels from 10 cm. to 400 cm. in steps of 10 cm.

1.1 for depth **from 10 to 400 by** 10

⌈ **1.2** Calculate the volume for the current oil level and record it.

d) Refining Step **1.2**   The current volume expressed in cubic meters is simply seven meters times the cross-sectional area in square centimeters divided by 10,000. The area is calculated by integrating the curve

$$f(y) = \sqrt{160000(1 - y^2/40000)}$$

between $[-200, -200 + depth]$ and doubling the result. This gives the formula for the volume of $2 \times 7 \times area/10000$ which reduces to $7 \times area/5000$. The resulting refinement is given below.

　　* Calculate the volume for the current oil level and record it.

　　area ← simp(−200, −200+depth, n, tank)
　　volume ← 7*area/5000
　　put 'The volume at level', depth, 'is', volume

Note that the Simpson's Rule module requires a number of panels as an integration parameter. The value for this parameter must be obtained earlier in the program and therefore a **get** n should be inserted at the beginning of the program.

e) Final Version   Combining the refinements gives the algorithm shown in Figure 10.12.

　　As a further refinement, one may increase the efficiency of the program by computing only the *change* in volume as the depth is increased by 10 centimeters. This change in volume would then be added to the previous volume. The increased efficiency results since a smaller number of integration panels may be used on the change in volume. The previous version must allow for the worst case interval which involves the integration over an interval 40 times longer than each of the intervals of the improved algorithm.   In the more efficient version, Simpson's Rule is invoked to compute the area between depth−210 and depth−200 with 8 panels rather than 32. The changes to the pseudocode algorithm of Figure 10.12 are shown in Figure 10.13.

Figure 10.12 Final version of the pseudocode algorithm for the depth gauge problem.

```
* An algorithm to find the volume of oil in an elliptical tank
* at depth intervals of 10 centimetres.

* Real variables used:
* depth - current marking on the depth gauge
* area - half cross-sectional area of oil in tank
* volume - the oil volume at the current depth

* Integer variables used:
* n - number of integration panels for Simpson's Rule

* Obtain the number of integration panels for Simpson's Rule.

get n
put 'The number of integration panels for simp is', n

* Calibrate volumes of oil corresponding to depth gauge
* levels from 10 cm. to 400 cm. in steps of 10 cm.

for depth from 10 to 400 by 10
        * Calculate the volume for the current oil level and record it.

        area ← simp(-200,-200+depth,n,tank)
        volume ← 7*area/5000
        put 'The volume at level', depth, 'is', volume

stop
32
```

Figure 10.13 Changes to the algorithm in Figure 10.12 to compute the volume of oil more efficiently.

```
* Calibrate volumes of oil corresponding to depth gauge
* levels from 10 cm. to 400 cm. in steps of 10 cm.

volume ← 0
for depth from 10 to 400 by 10
        * Calculate the change in volume at this depth.

        area ← simp(depth-210,depth-200,n,tank)
        volume ← volume + 7*area/5000
        put 'The volume at level', depth, 'is', volume

stop
8
```

f) Program for Final Version of Algorithm   The program given in Figure 10.14 is an implementation of the more efficient algorithm.   The output from this program is shown in Figure 10.15.

```
C Figure 10.14 -- The Depth Gauge Problem.
C                 Find the volume of oil in an elliptical tank
C                 at depth intervals of 10 centimeters.

C*********************************************************************

C DEPTH  - current marking on the depth gauge
C AREA   - half cross-sectional area of oil in tank
C VOLUME - the oil volume at the current depth
C N      - number of integration panels for SIMP

C*********************************************************************

      REAL DEPTH, AREA, VOLUME, TANK, SIMP
      INTEGER N
      EXTERNAL TANK

C Read the number of intervals for SIMP.

      PRINT *, 'ENTER THE NUMBER OF INTEGRATION PANELS FOR SIMP'
      READ *, N
      PRINT *, ' '
      VOLUME = 0.0

C Calibrate volumes of oil corresponding to depth gauge
C levels from 10cm. to 400cm. in steps of 10cm.

      DO 100 DEPTH = 10.0, 400.0, 10.0

C         Calculate the volume for the current oil level and record it.

          AREA = SIMP(DEPTH-210.0,DEPTH-200.0,N,TANK)
          VOLUME = VOLUME + 7.0*AREA/5000.0
          PRINT *, 'THE VOLUME AT LEVEL', DEPTH, ' IS', VOLUME
  100 CONTINUE

      STOP
      END


C*********************************************************************

C Function TANK -- Given a value for X, evaluate elliptical tank
C                  function.

C*********************************************************************

      REAL FUNCTION TANK(X)
      REAL X, SQRT
      TANK = SQRT(160000.0*(1.0 - X*X/40000.0))
      RETURN
      END
```

Figure 10.15 Output from the depth gauge program of Figure 10.14.

```
ENTER THE NUMBER OF INTEGRATION PANELS FOR SIMP
8
```

THE VOLUME AT LEVEL	10.00000	IS	1.169443
THE VOLUME AT LEVEL	20.00000	IS	3.286404
THE VOLUME AT LEVEL	30.00000	IS	5.992315
THE VOLUME AT LEVEL	40.00000	IS	9.153815
THE VOLUME AT LEVEL	50.00000	IS	12.69048
THE VOLUME AT LEVEL	60.00000	IS	16.54569
THE VOLUME AT LEVEL	70.00000	IS	20.67602
THE VOLUME AT LEVEL	80.00000	IS	25.04629
THE VOLUME AT LEVEL	90.00000	IS	29.62688
THE VOLUME AT LEVEL	100.0000	IS	34.39211
THE VOLUME AT LEVEL	110.0000	IS	39.31917
THE VOLUME AT LEVEL	120.0000	IS	44.38747
THE VOLUME AT LEVEL	130.0000	IS	49.57808
THE VOLUME AT LEVEL	140.0000	IS	54.87339
THE VOLUME AT LEVEL	150.0000	IS	60.25682
THE VOLUME AT LEVEL	160.0000	IS	65.71260
THE VOLUME AT LEVEL	170.0000	IS	71.22557
THE VOLUME AT LEVEL	180.0000	IS	76.78105
THE VOLUME AT LEVEL	190.0000	IS	82.36469
THE VOLUME AT LEVEL	200.0000	IS	87.96236
THE VOLUME AT LEVEL	210.0000	IS	93.56002
THE VOLUME AT LEVEL	220.0000	IS	99.14366
THE VOLUME AT LEVEL	230.0000	IS	104.6991
THE VOLUME AT LEVEL	240.0000	IS	110.2121
THE VOLUME AT LEVEL	250.0000	IS	115.6679
THE VOLUME AT LEVEL	260.0000	IS	121.0513
THE VOLUME AT LEVEL	270.0000	IS	126.3466
THE VOLUME AT LEVEL	280.0000	IS	131.5372
THE VOLUME AT LEVEL	290.0000	IS	136.6055
THE VOLUME AT LEVEL	300.0000	IS	141.5326
THE VOLUME AT LEVEL	310.0000	IS	146.2978
THE VOLUME AT LEVEL	320.0000	IS	150.8784
THE VOLUME AT LEVEL	330.0000	IS	155.2487
THE VOLUME AT LEVEL	340.0000	IS	159.3790
THE VOLUME AT LEVEL	350.0000	IS	163.2342
THE VOLUME AT LEVEL	360.0000	IS	166.7709
THE VOLUME AT LEVEL	370.0000	IS	169.9324
THE VOLUME AT LEVEL	380.0000	IS	172.6383
THE VOLUME AT LEVEL	390.0000	IS	174.7553
THE VOLUME AT LEVEL	400.0000	IS	175.9247

10.4   The Volume Gauge Problem

As a final example, consider what appears to be a simple change to the previous problem. The depth gauge problem required the volume at uniform levels on the ruled stick. Now change the problem to marking the stick according to predetermined volume levels. This change may appear somewhat minor but, in fact, the ramifications on the calculation techniques are significant.

Example 10.3   Volume Gauge Problem

For the elliptical tank of the previous discussion, locate the markings on a depth gauge (to the nearest millimeter) corresponding to volumes of 5, 10, 15, . . . , 175 cubic meters, the approximate total volume of the tank.

a) Problem Analysis   Again, it will be expedient to imagine that the tank is turned on its side as shown in Figure 10.10. Using the same coordinate system, the first problem to be solved is: Find *depth* so that the volume of the tank to the left of $y = -200 + depth$ is 5 cubic meters. Subsequently, values of *depth* corresponding to volumes of 10, 15, . . . , 175 cubic meters should also be found.

If the volume corresponding to position y on the *depth* axis is denoted $V(y)$, then the level of oil y must be found to satisfy the equation $V(y) = 5$, or rearranged as $V(y) - 5 = 0$. Subsequent values of y should be found to correspond to solutions of $V(y) - 10 = 0$, $V(y) - 15 = 0$, and so on, as illustrated in Figure 10.16.

Figure 10.16 Graph of the volume of an elliptical tank at various depths.

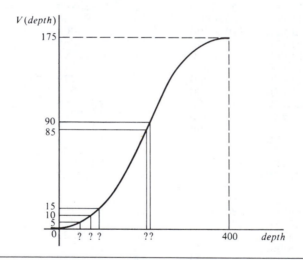

The awkward thing about this formulation is that the function $V(y)$ is not given by a simple formula. However, the last section demonstrated that $V(y)$ could be calculated for any given y although it required substantial computation through use of area finding. This volume function replaces the simple polynomial functions used in the zero-finding programs. With this formulation, the problem reduces to a zero-finding problem and the bisection algorithm can be used[1].

---

[1] Other zero-finding techniques could be used provided that they do not require the derivative function. Therefore, Newton's method could not be used, although the secant method might be.

b) Selection of an Initial Decomposition   This problem is naturally expressed as an iteration algorithm, involving computation of the calibration mark position for 35 successive volumes. A first version of the algorithm is given in Figure 10.17.

Figure 10.17   First version of the volume gauge algorithm.

1.   While volumes remain

⌈ Calculate the level for the current oil volume and record it.

2.   **stop**

---

c) Refining Step **1.**   The levels to be calculated start with a volume of 5 cubic meters and proceed in steps of 5 cubic meters to 175 cubic meters.

> * Calibrate depth levels corresponding to volumes of oil from
> * 5 cubic meters to 175 cubic meters in steps of 5 cubic meters.

1.1 volume ← 5
1.2 while volume ≤ 175 **do**

⌈ **1.3** Calculate the level for the current oil volume and record it.
⌊ **1.4** volume ← volume + 5

d) Refining Step **1.3**   The calibration mark corresponding to the current volume of oil must be a zero of the function $V(y) - volume$. The bisection zero-finding algorithm can be used to compute the coordinate of the new calibration mark corresponding to such a y. However, suitable interval end-points are needed to conduct a zero-finding search. From the volume computations tabulated in Figure 10.15 of the previous section, the range of depths of 5 cubic meters of oil can be determined. For instance, near the top or bottom of the tank, 5 cubic meters is always less than 30 cm. deep, while at the middle of the tank, it is always more than about 7 cm. deep. These upper and lower bounds on the distances between 5 cubic meter calibration marks provide suitable initial-interval end-points for the bisection algorithm to ensure its success in finding a zero of $V(y) - volume$.

The coordinate systems for the depth of oil and the tank function do not share the same origin. This difference must be overcome by translating from one system to the other and back again when using the bisection zero-finding algorithm. The y coordinate of the tank volume function corresponds to $-200 + depth$, so the interval end-points for bisection will have to be computed from the previous oil level. Variables olddepth and newdepth will be used to remember the previous and next calibration markings, while newy will be used to remember the new y coordinate of the next marking found by bisection. The previous depth level for olddepth must be initialized to 0 cm. outside the iteration. Therefore this will have to be added to Step **1.1**.

The refinement of Step **1.3** may now be completed.

* Calculate the level for the current oil volume and record it.

yl ← −200 + olddepth + 7
yr ← −200 + olddepth + 30
call bisect(yl, yr, 0.05, tankvol; error, newy)
if error **then**

> ⌈ **1.3.2** Error detected in bisect; terminate the algorithm.

else

> ⌈ **1.3.3** Record new calibration point.

Note that the function module tankvol has been referenced in the bisection module invocation, but has not yet been refined.   This will be done shortly.

e) Refining Step **1.3.2**   This step reflects an error condition which should not arise if the bisection intervals are well chosen.   In the event that something is wrong or the function tankvol computes erroneous values, it is wise to detect this condition and stop further processing.   Previous experience with early termination of loops involved logical variables, such as prime in the prime number classification problem, which were used in the **while**–loop condition.   Since the variable error is used for the bisection error condition, it could also be used to terminate the algorithm prematurely.   The revised **while**–condition would look like

> **while** volume ≤ 175 **and not** error **do**

with an appropriate initialization of error to **false** added to Step **1.1**.

f) Refining Step **1.3.3**   The recording of the new calibration mark requires converting the new *y* coordinate saved in newy into a depth level.   After recording the oil level mark, it is necessary to shift the new depth level into the previous depth level variable, olddepth.   This step can be refined as follows:

* Record the current level and prepare for next one.

newdepth ← newy + 200
put volume, newdepth
olddepth ← newdepth

g) Development of the tankvol *function module*   This module will compute the function $V(y)$−volume, where $V(y)$ is the total volume up to coordinate y. Assume that the previous calibration mark was at olddepth on the calibration stick.   Let this correspond to coordinate *oldy* and total volume $V(oldy)$.   The simplest and most efficient way to calculate the tank volume tankvol is to observe that volume = $V(oldy) + 5$.   Thus, tankvol = $V(y)$−volume = $V(y) - V(oldy) - 5$.   The increment in volume $V(y) - V(oldy)$ may be computed by the simp module in the same way as in the previous section.   Appropriate integration limits are *oldy* and *y*, which correspond to −200+olddepth and y.

fmodule tankvol(**imports**: olddepth, y)

* Compute the volume of oil in the elliptical tank from the
* previous calibration mark **olddepth** to **y**.
* The cross-sectional area is computed using the **simp** module
* and this area is converted to a volume increment −**5**.
* 16 integration panels are assumed to be sufficient.

* Real variable used:
* **area** - cross-sectional area of elliptical tank
* **olddepth** - depth of previous calibration mark

* Ensure valid range of arguments to tank function.

if y > 200 **then**
$\quad \left[\; y \leftarrow 200 \right.$
area ← simp(−200+olddepth, y, 16, tank)
tankvol ← (7*area/5000) − 5
end module

This module tankvol assumes that the function tank has been defined. The same function module from the depth gauge problem may be used here.

h) Translation of the algorithm to FORTRAN/77   These refinements are collected and translated to FORTRAN/77 to give the program of Figure 10.18. The output follows in Figure 10.19.

```
C Figure 10.18 -- The Volume Gauge Problem
C                 A program to compute the location of calibration
C                 markings for a volume gauge, marked every
C                 5 cubic meters of oil in an elliptical tank.

C*********************************************************************

C VOLUME - current volume for calibration mark
C ODEPTH - previous calibration mark
C NDEPTH - new calibration mark
C YL, YR - left, right end points of next calibration mark interval
C NEWY   - computed y coordinate of the new mark
C ERROR  - error indicator from BISECT module

C*********************************************************************

      INTEGER N
      REAL VOLUME, ODEPTH, NDEPTH, YL, YR, NEWY, TANKVOL
      LOGICAL ERROR
      COMMON ODEPTH
      EXTERNAL TANKVOL

C Prepare column headings for volume gauge.
      PRINT *, '   VOLUME           DEPTH'
```

```
C Figure 10.18 (continued)

C Calibrate depth levels corresponding to volumes of oil from
C 5 cubic meters to 175 cubic meters in steps of 5 cubic meters.
        ODEPTH = 0.0
        ERROR = .FALSE.
        VOLUME = 5.0
  100 IF (VOLUME .LE. 175.0 .AND. .NOT.ERROR) THEN

C          Calculate the level for the current oil volume.

        YL = -200.0 + ODEPTH + 7.0
        YR = -200.0 + ODEPTH + 30.0

        CALL BISECT(YL,YR,0.05,TANKVOL,ERROR,NEWY)

        IF (ERROR) THEN
            PRINT *, 'ERROR IN BISECT. TERMINATE THE ALGORITHM.'
        ELSE

C          Record the current level and prepare for the next one.

            NDEPTH = 200.0 + NEWY
            PRINT *, VOLUME, NDEPTH, ' CM.'
            ODEPTH = NDEPTH
            VOLUME = VOLUME + 5.0
        ENDIF
        GOTO 100
      ENDIF
      STOP
      END
C***********************************************************************
C Function TANKVOL -- Volume increment function.
C***********************************************************************
      REAL FUNCTION TANKVOL(Y)
      REAL ODEPTH, TANK, SIMP
      COMMON ODEPTH
      EXTERNAL TANK

C Ensure valid range of arguments to tank function.
      IF (Y .GT. 200.0) THEN
          Y = 200.0
      ENDIF
      TANKVOL = (7.0*SIMP(-200.0+ODEPTH, Y, 16, TANK)/5000.0) - 5.0
      RETURN
      END
C***********************************************************************
C Function TANK -- Given a value for X, evaluate elliptical
C                  tank function.
C***********************************************************************
      REAL FUNCTION TANK(X)
      REAL X, SQRT
      TANK = SQRT(160000.0*(1.0 - X*X/40000.0))
      RETURN
      END
```

Program Notes

- Variable ODEPTH is declared to be COMMON to the main program and to the function TANKVOL. This permits the use of the variable in both places, without appearing as a parameter of TANKVOL. Since TANKVOL is used as an argument to BISECT, to be compatible it can have only one parameter. For a complete discussion of COMMON, see Appendix D.

Figure 10.19 Output from the calibration of a volume gauge of Figure 10.18.

VOLUME	DEPTH	
5.000000	26.54102	CM.
10.00000	42.48047	CM.
15.00000	56.08398	CM.
20.00000	68.42969	CM.
25.00000	79.87695	CM.
30.00000	90.78516	CM.
35.00000	101.2441	CM.
40.00000	111.3438	CM.
45.00000	121.1738	CM.
50.00000	130.8242	CM.
55.00000	140.2949	CM.
60.00000	149.5859	CM.
65.00000	158.7871	CM.
70.00000	167.8984	CM.
75.00000	176.9199	CM.
80.00000	185.8516	CM.
85.00000	194.7832	CM.
90.00000	203.7148	CM.
95.00000	212.6465	CM.
100.0000	221.5781	CM.
105.0000	230.5996	CM.
110.0000	239.7109	CM.
115.0000	248.9121	CM.
120.0000	258.2031	CM.
125.0000	267.5840	CM.
130.0000	277.1445	CM.
135.0000	286.9746	CM.
140.0000	297.0742	CM.
145.0000	307.4434	CM.
150.0000	318.2617	CM.
155.0000	329.6191	CM.
160.0000	341.7852	CM.
165.0000	355.1191	CM.
170.0000	370.5195	CM.
175.0000	391.9650	CM.

10.5 Summary

The theme of this chapter has been the use of modules bisect and simp in several applications which require the use of zero-finding or area-finding algorithms.

One of the important lessons of these examples was the approach to problem-solving used in algorithm development. It is often very useful to mold one's thinking about a solution to permit the use of well-tested procedures for standard tasks. Large numbers of such procedures are usually readily available in program libraries.

By thinking in terms of modules for program development, the resulting algorithms may often be quite short and consist primarily of several module invocations. Such a short and elegant description of the tasks to be done by the algorithm promote easy understanding of the algorithm. However, even with an extensive program library, the solution of large problems is still a formidable task. The reason for this is that the large problems are not always stated in terms that allow immediate application of known techniques. Thus, the problems have to be carefully examined, decomposed, and refined until they can be solved with existing tools.

10.6   References

Forsythe, G.E.; Malcolm, M.A.; and Moler, C.B. *Computer Methods for Mathematical Computations.* Englewood Cliffs, N.J.: Prentice-Hall, 1977.

Freeman, P. "Software Reliability and Design: A Survey." *13th Design Automation Conference*, New York: IEEE Computer Society and Association for Computing Machinery, 1976.

I.M.S.L., "Library Reference Manual," Houston: I.M.S.L. Inc., 1980.

Leavenworth, K. "Modular Design of Computer Programs." *Data Management*, July 1974, pp. 14-19.

Maynard, J. *Modular Programming.* Philadelphia: Auerbach Publishers, 1972.

Meyers, G.J. "Characteristics of Composite Design." *Datamation*, September, 1973, pp. 100-102.

10.7   Exercises

In most of the following exercises a program is requested to solve a specific problem. For each problem it is recommended that step-wise refinement be used in developing a pseudocode algorithm to solve the problem.   This algorithm should then be translated into FORTRAN/77 and run on the computer.   Where appropriate, the program should be tested with a variety of data sufficient to ensure that the program does what it is supposed to do.

10.1   The following curves cross the x axis in two places.   Develop a program which will compute the area between the curve and the x axis.   Your program should be general enough to compute the area under any of the curves by merely changing the function definition and the initial parameters.

a) $f(x) = -x^2 + 10.9x - 20.4$
b) $f(x) = x^2 - x - 15.75$
c) $f(x) = -x^2 + 14.31x - 33.4$

10.2   The following function pairs completely enclose an area or areas by their curves. Develop a program which will compute the enclosed area or areas.   Your program should be general enough that it may be used for any function pair by changing only the function definitions and the initial parameters.

a) $f(x) = \sqrt{6.25 - (x + 1.5)^2}$, $g(x) = \sqrt{9 - (x - 1)^2}$
b) $f(x) = x^4 - 5$, $g(x) = -2x + 6$
c) $f(x) = \sin x$, $g(x) = 0.1 + 0.2x$
    (Find the enclosed area within the range 0 to π)

   d) $f(x) = \cos x$, $g(x) = -.5$
      (Find the enclosed area within the range 0 to π)
   e) $f(x) = 1 + x^2$, $g(x) = \sqrt{4 - x^2}$

10.3   The following function pairs completely enclose two separate areas. Develop a program which will determine the total enclosed area.

   a) $f(x) = x^3 - 2x^2 - 5x + 6$, $g(x) = -x$
   b) $f(x) = 2.0\sin(x - \pi)$, $g(x) = 0.2 - 0.2x$

10.4   The following sets of three curves enclose at least one area. Develop a program which will compute the enclosed area.

   a) $f(x) = x^2 - 10x + 9$, $g(x) = .5x + 4$, $h(x) = -.25x - 7$
   b) $f(x) = -0.2 - 0.2x$, $g(x) = 2 - x^2$, $h(x) = 2\sin(x - \pi)$
      (Compute the enclosed area within the range -0.5 to -4)

10.5   The following two curves intersect in two places.

   a) $f(x) = 2x^2 - 20x + 55$
   b) $g(x) = -4x^2 + 20x - 5$

Develop a program which will use the printer-plot routines to plot the curves in the range $[-1.5, +1.5]$ and then fill in the enclosed area with the character A.

10.6   Increasing the number of intervals in the Trapezoidal and Simpson's Rule calculations will, within limits, increase the accuracy of the result.

   a) Develop a main program which will plot the error (difference between the exact and calculated value) versus the values of n := 2, 4, 8, 16, . . . , 1024. Test your program on the curve $f(x) = 7 - 7x^6$ whose exact area between 0 and 1 is 6. Because of the range of n and the error, a $\log_{10}$-$\log_{10}$ scale should be used for the plot. (Hint: use a built-in function to take the $\log_{10}$ of the argument to be plotted.)
   b) Explain the resulting curves in the graph of part a).

10.7   a) Using step-wise refinement, develop a pseudocode module to approximate the area enclosed between the zeros of any given polynomial function and the x axis over a given interval. The diagram in Figure 10.20 shows the shaded areas to be computed for a cubic polynomial which has three zeros between the interval $[a,b]$. Hints: 1) Refer to the algorithm which searched for sign changes in a function so that you may compute starting points for a zero-finding algorithm. 2) Design the module interface to pass back useful information to the caller, such as the number of zeros found, the approximated area (obviously), and an indication of any error situations encountered.
      b) Translate the algorithm from part a) into FORTRAN/77. Test the program by running some known integrations, for example, the test cases for the numerical integration programs from Chapter 8.
      c) Once you feel confident that the area-finding program of part b) is working, attempt the following test cases. For each test case, explain the result. You

Figure 10.20   An example of the shaded areas to be computed (Exercise 10.7).

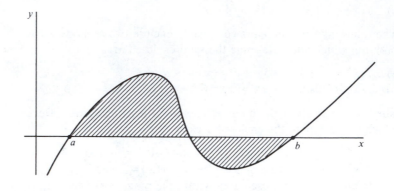

may find that providing a hand-drawn graph is useful in describing your program's actions.

i) $f(x) = x^2 + 1, [-1, +1]$
ii) $f(x) = x^3 - x^2 + x - 1, [0,2]$
iii) $f(x) = x^4 - 7.65x^3 + 21.075x^2 - 24.5x + 9.9, [0,4]$
iv) $f(x) = x^3 - 4.75x^2 + 7x - 3, [0,3]$
v) $f(x) = \sin 12x, [-.01, +1.01]$
vi) $f(x) = 1 + \sin 12x, [-.01, +1.01]$
vii) $f(x) = x^3 - 6x^2 + 11x - 6, [1,3]$

d)   The function $f(x) = 1/(x - 1)$ is undefined for $x = 1$. Explain what kind of problem this would create in an area-finding program, and where the problem should be handled.

10.8   A graph of the function $\log x$ appears as shown in Figure 10.21.

Figure 10.21   A graph of the function $f(x)$ (Exercise 10.8).

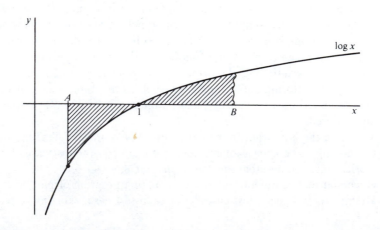

For every fixed value of A, $0 < A \leq 1$, there is a value of B so that the $\int_A^B \log x \, dx = 0$. Develop a program to find values of B for several values of A.

10.9   The cubic polynomial $f(x) = x^3 - 3x^2 + x - 2$ is depicted in Figure 10.22

Figure 10.22   A graph of the cubic polynomial $x^3 - 3x^2 + x - 2$ (Exercise 10.9).

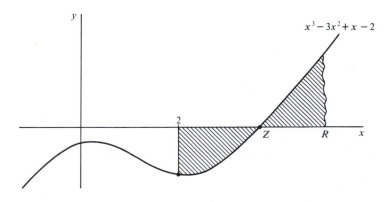

a)   Somewhere between $x = 2$ and $x = 4$ there is a zero of $f(x)$, called Z. Find this point Z using the Bisection method to an accuracy epsilon, (given as data).

b)   Having found Z, then determine the point R, to the right of Z, such that

$$\int_2^Z f(x) \, dx = -\int_Z^R f(x) \, dx$$

using Simpson's Rule to evaluate the areas. The point R is estimated initially to be 4. This guess is modified by successively adding $eps\,2$ to it until

$$\left| \left| \int_2^Z f(x) \, dx \right| - \left| \int_Z^R f(x) \, dx \right| \right| \leq eps\,3$$

where $eps\,2$ and $eps\,3$ are also read as data. You may assume that this condition is always attainable for the $eps\,2$ read as data. Develop a FORTRAN/77 program to accomplish a) and b).

10.10   The function $\dfrac{1}{x^2} \cos\left(\dfrac{x}{1 + 0.1e^{-x}}\right)$ has the form shown in Figure 10.23
Compute $I = \int_I^\infty f(x) \, dx$. Note that

$$I = A_1 - A_2 + A_3 - A_4 \quad \cdots \quad ,$$

where A_i are the areas labeled on the graph. It is known that the difference between successive values of x_i (the zeros of $f(x)$) is $\pi \leq |x_{i+1} - x_i| \leq \dfrac{3\pi}{2}$, and

Figure 10.23 A graph of $\dfrac{1}{x^2}\cos\left(\dfrac{x}{1+0.1e^{-x}}\right)$ (Exercise 10.10).

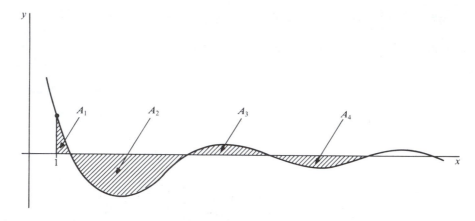

$0 \le x_i \le \pi$. Develop a FORTRAN/77 program to compute an approximate value for I by computing successively $A_1, A_2, A_3, \ldots$ and terminating when $|A_k| \le 10^{-2}$.

10.11 A car manufacturer is about to install a new type of gas tank having a slightly irregular cross-sectional shape, as illustrated in Figure 10.24. The tank will be 1.5 meters across and have the same odd shape from end to end. The company would like to calibrate the volume (in liters) of the tank at 1 centimeter depth intervals. Develop a program to determine these volumes and list them in table form.

Figure 10.24 Cross-section of an irregularly shaped gas tank .

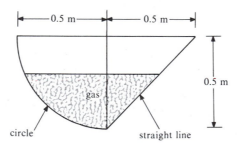

10.12 Assume that a water trough has the shape shown in Figure 10.25. Its cross-section is a segment of a parabola and its ends are perpendicular to the liquid surface. The general equation of the parabolic segment is given. For this problem, assume that $a = 40$ cm. and $b = 20$ cm., and that the trough is 2 m. long. It is desired to have a volume calibration in liters (1 liter = 1000 cubic centimeters) marked on one end of the tank in 2 cm. steps from bottom to top. Develop a FORTRAN/77 program to tabulate the appropriate volume markings, based on the Trapezoidal Rule.

Figure 10.25   A parabolically shaped water trough (Exercise 10.12).

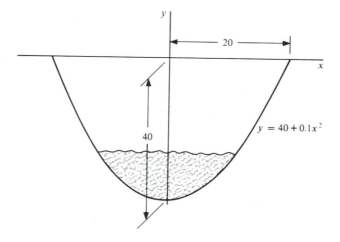

$$y = 40 + 0.1x^2$$

10.13   An architect has designed an asymmetric storage shed having the cross-sectional shape as shown in Figure 10.26.   The shed is to be 50 meters in length.   It is designed such that both roof/side structures, y_1 and y_2, are curves from parts of two circles.   The radii of the circles are 20 meters and 30 meters, respectively. The centers of the circles are 30 meters apart and are located at ground level. The architect needs to compute the volume of air contained by the storage building in order to determine the heating requirements.   Develop a program, using zero-finding and numerical integration techniques, to help the architect in this computation.   *Note:* The equation of a circle with center (h, k) and radius r is $(x - h)^2 + (y - k)^2 = r^2$.

Figure 10.26   Cross-section of a storage shed (Exercise 10.13).

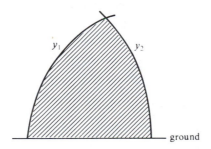

10.14 An architect has designed a building to be built on a slope with the cross-section shown in Figure 10.27. The ends are square and the length of the building (perpendicular to the cross-section) is 12 meters.

Figure 10.27 Cross-section of a building to be built on a slope (Exercise 10.14).

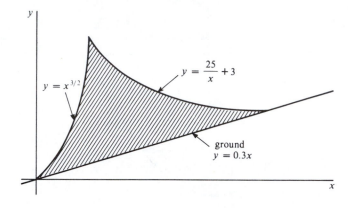

Develop a FORTRAN/77 program to find the volume contained in the structure which lies above the sloping ground.

10.15 A civil engineer wishes to plan the excavation of a roadway along the side of a hill, as shown in the diagram in Figure 10.28. The roadway must be banked at 4 degrees and the side must be sloped at 60 degrees to control erosion. With respect to an origin taken at the intersection of the slope and the road, the equation of the hill is

$$\frac{y^2}{5} + \left[\frac{x}{10} \right]^2 = 1 + \frac{\sqrt{x + 10}}{4}$$

Develop a FORTRAN/77 program which will determine the cross-sectional area of the portion of the hill to be removed.

Figure 10.28 Plan for a roadway excavation (Exercise 10.15).

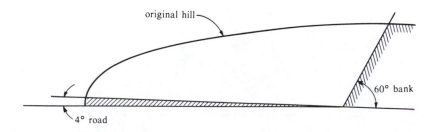

11
Efficiency of Algorithms

11.1 Introduction

As was intimated in the last chapter, the development of a correct algorithm does not automatically mean that the algorithm is efficient.   Despite the tremendous advances being made in the power and size of computers, the topic of algorithm efficiency is still important.   Awaiting any advances in computing speed are larger and larger problems to be solved.   In terms of efficiency, the difference between a bad algorithm and a good algorithm can make even the computer solution of a problem entirely intractable.

In the simplest of terms, achieving efficiency usually means performing a minimum number of operations to compute the required result.   Once an algorithmic technique is known to be efficient for certain tasks, that technique may be used with confidence in other similar situations.

It is the intent of this chapter to provide only a brief introduction to the topic of efficiency and how efficiency is measured.   An extensive discussion of *algorithm complexity*, as it is called, is certainly beyond the scope of an introductory text.   There are excellent texts which pursue this topic further, and the interested reader is directed to the references at the end of this chapter.

11.2 Measures of Efficiency

The efficiency of an algorithm is usually measured in terms of the rate of growth of its time and space requirements with an increase in the size of the problem.   That is, if an algorithm is to operate on a problem of twice a previous size, how many more operations (time) will the algorithm have to perform, and how much more data will have to be stored (space)?   The answers to these questions give a means of predicting and comparing algorithm efficiency.

The size of a problem is denoted by n.   In a general sense, n represents the amount of data to be processed.   For the prime number classification algorithm of Figure 4.5, n would be the number being classified, and the main concern would be how the number of operations increases as this number gets larger.   For the quadratic equation algorithm of Figure 9.10, the number of coefficient groups is the problem size n.   Finding all of the real zeros of a polynomial of degree n is another problem for which one might wish to know the time requirements as a function of n.

The usual measure for the efficiency of an algorithm is called the *order* of the algorithm.   If the size of a problem doubles and the time to solve this new problem also doubles, then the algorithm is said to be linear and of order n, written $O(n)$.   An algorithm of $O(n^2)$ is one for which every doubling of the problem size roughly quadruples the solution time.

The diagrams in Figure 11.1 illustrate possible time complexities for different algorithms, plotted against problem size n.   Figure 11.1 a) shows the time growth curves for two different algorithms.   The curves are straight lines with equations of the form:

$$time_1 = a_1 + b_1 \times n$$

for algorithm 1, and

$$time_2 = a_2 + b_2 \times n$$

for algorithm 2.   The slope of the line gives the linear factor.   If these algorithms performed the same computations, then algorithm 2 would be preferred over algorithm 1 on a time complexity basis, since its rate of growth is smaller $(b_2 < b_1)$.   Figure 11.1 b) shows a graph for an algorithm of complexity $O(n^2)$.   The equation of this curve is of the form:

$$time = a + bn + cn^2$$

Figure 11.1   Examples of time complexity graphs.

a) algorithms of $O(n)$

b) algorithms of $O(n^2)$

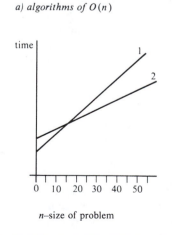

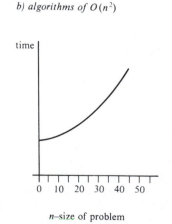

It is important to note that algorithms of low order of complexity may not always be the best choice over the entire range of problem sizes. This usually occurs with small problem sizes. For instance, Figure 11.2 illustrates possible time complexities for $O(n)$ and $O(n^2)$ algorithms which perform the same computation. According to these graphs, the algorithm A_1 of $O(n^2)$ is best for an initial range of problem sizes less than forty, the algorithm A_2 of $O(n)$ is best for a range of problem sizes between forty and one hundred, and algorithm A_3 of $O(n)$ is best for all larger problems.

Figure 11.2 Time complexity curves for two algorithms performing the same computation.

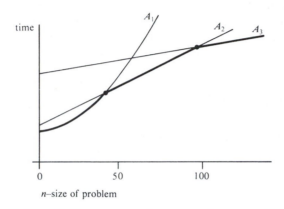

It should also be noted that, for a problem of a given size, the input data may be different, and this can have an effect on the number of computations performed. In these cases some assumptions must be made about the occurrences and distribution of the data to aid in the estimation of complexity. Through these assumptions, it is often possible to compute a best, an average, and a worst case complexity.

There are essentially two levels at which both time and space efficiency may be examined and discussed.

At the primary level, the concern is with the overall structure of the mathematical technique which the algorithm uses. This usually determines its order of complexity. Attention is given to the computational approach and the organization and access of data. There is often a tradeoff with respect to time and space, when time efficiency may be improved by using more space to store data.

As an example, if one wishes to test a number n for primeness, it is necessary to test as trial divisors only the prime numbers $\leq \sqrt{n}$, rather than all odd integers in this range. The disadvantage of such an algorithm is obviously the need to store a very large table of primes available for use in the tests. The *space* needed to store these primes may be a more valuable resource than the extra *time* required to do the divisions.

As a second level of improvement in efficiency, algorithm implementation is examined to eliminate unnecessary computations. Unfortunately, it is all too easy to implement an efficient algorithm in an inefficient manner. The space/time tradeoff is also present at this level, but usually to a lesser extent.

In general, the greatest gain in efficiency will be obtained by examining the overall structure and this is where the major effort in the design process should be expended. Since the step-wise refinement process does not guarantee an efficient algorithm, it is often necessary to modify the algorithm structure to improve efficiency. The initial effort spent in developing the algorithm is definitely not wasted, since the experience gained should facilitate these modifications. In most cases, improvements in the algorithm implementation may be performed independently of the overall algorithm structure.

When improving the efficiency of an algorithm, the level at which the optimization is being done is often not obvious. Since both levels have the same objective of producing a more efficient algorithm, a distinction is not usually necessary.

In most of the problems discussed in this and succeeding chapters, the major concern will be with time complexity. Thus, unless otherwise stated, all references to complexity will be taken to mean the time complexity.

11.3   Determining Efficiency

Evaluating the efficiency of an algorithm involves determining the number of operations performed for a problem of size n. The order of complexity of an algorithm can often be obtained without an extensive analysis. To illustrate how efficiency may be measured, a factoring algorithm, the prime number classification algorithm of Chapter 4, and a Pythagorean triples algorithm are examined. In each case, several versions of each algorithm are considered with the discussions about efficiency leading to improved versions of the algorithms.

11.3.1   Efficiency of a Factoring Algorithm

This first example deals with an algorithm to find all distinct, nontrivial factors of a given positive number. This is a relatively simple problem and an abbreviated algorithm for it is shown in Figure 11.3. The algorithm tests all positive numbers between 2 and $n - 1$ inclusive as trial divisors of the given number n by checking for a zero remainder. It is very similar to the prime number classification algorithm of Figure 4.5. To obtain a measure of its complexity, it is necessary to consider the number of operations performed for different values of n.

Analyzing the algorithm one can see that, for any n ($n \geq 2$) the body of the **while**–loop will be repeated $n - 2$ times. The **while** condition will be evaluated $n - 2 + 1$ or $n - 1$ times since it needs one final evaluation to terminate the loop. The number of operations performed each time through the body of the loop is essentially constant. The algorithm will perform an extra operation for each factor, namely the **put**, but the maximum number of times that this will occur is once per iteration. Thus, the number of operations performed by the loop is the maximum number of operations in the body of the loop and in evaluating the condition, call it p, times the $n - 2$ repetitions of the loop. Let q be the number of operations outside the loop, including the final evaluation of the **while** condition. This gives the expression $p(n - 2) + q = pn + (q - 2p)$. Since p and q do not depend on n, this expression varies linearly with n, and thus the algorithm is called a linear or $O(n)$ algorithm.

Figure 11.3   Factoring algorithm — no optimizations.

* Find all distinct, nontrivial factors of a positive number.

get n
put 'The number being factored is', n

*   Test possible divisors from 2 to n−1 for a zero remainder.

m ← 2
while m ≤ n−1 **do**
    ⎡ **if** rem(n, m) = 0 **then**
    | ⎡ **put** m, 'is a factor'
    | m ← m + 1
stop

To improve the efficiency of this algorithm it is necessary to reduce the n iterations required.   Observe that for any given factor m of n, there will be a corresponding cofactor c such that $m \times c = n$. Thus, the cofactor c can be found from m by $c = n/m$. Also, the properties of the factor and cofactor guarantee that if $m \leq \sqrt{n}$ then $c \geq \sqrt{n}$. Thus, the algorithm need only test divisors up to the $\sqrt{n}$.   Therefore, this algorithm may be improved by recording both the factor and its cofactor at the same time.   Such a change to the structure of the algorithm, shown in Figure 11.4, requires only $\sqrt{n}$ iterations and thus reduces the order to $O(\sqrt{n})$.

The **while** statement is executed $\lfloor \sqrt{n} \rfloor$ times, for test divisors 2, 3, . . . $\lfloor \sqrt{n} \rfloor$, plus a final evaluation of the condition on termination.   The notation $\lfloor \sqrt{n} \rfloor$ refers to the largest integer less than or equal to $\sqrt{n}$, and is called the floor function applied to the square root of n.   For each factor recorded an extra division and assignment operation are required, but again they are to be performed at most once for each iteration. The increase in space required by this change is negligible.

Figure 11.4   Factoring algorithm — optimized version 1.

* Find all distinct, nontrivial factors of a positive number.
* Test for divisibility by all divisors from 2 to √n and record the cofactor as well as factor.

get n
put 'The number being factored is', n
m ← 2
while m ≤ √n **do**
    ⎡ **if** rem(n,m) = 0 **then**
    | ⎡ c ← n/m
    | | **put** m, c, 'are factors'
    | m ← m + 1
stop

Further reduction in the number of operations may be accomplished by reducing the number of operations performed within each iteration. As was observed with the prime number classification algorithm in Chapter 4, the $\sqrt{n}$ term can be moved outside the **while** statement. Now the algorithm performs only one square root calculation instead of $\lfloor \sqrt{n} \rfloor$ of them. This is a change in the implementation of the algorithm and does not affect the order of the algorithm. Again, the space increase is negligible.

Figure 11.5 Factoring algorithm — optimized version 2.

* Find all distinct, nontrivial factors of a positive number.

* Test for divisibility by all divisors from 2 to $\sqrt{n}$ and record the cofactor as well as factor.
* Move the square root calculation out of the loop.

```
get n
put 'The number being factored is', n
m ← 2
k ← √n
while m ≤ k do
    ⎡ if rem(n, m) = 0 then
    ⎢     ⎡ c ← n/m
    ⎢     ⎣ put m, c, 'are factors'
    ⎣ m ← m + 1
stop
```

For the above algorithms, it was possible to establish their order without doing a detailed analysis. However, sometimes a detailed computation count is necessary to gain better insight into the effect of the optimizations. To facilitate this process, all arithmetic operations and the assignment operation may be normalized to the time of an addition operation. The table in Figure 11.6 gives reasonable normalization factors for present day computers. The expression rem(n, m) = 0 which appears in the table may be evaluated using integer arithmetic as $n - n/m \times m = 0$, which accounts for the equivalent six add operations. (In many cases, the rem operation may be performed internally in the computer by using only an integer division, and thus the rem operation could be as fast as two equivalent add operations.)

Figure 11.6 Normalization factors for algorithmic operations.

Operation	Time equivalent (number of adds)
←	1
−	1
*	2
/	2
$<, \leq, =, \neq, >, \geq$	1
¬, &, |	1
$\sqrt{n}$	10
rem(n, m) = 0	6

The **get** and **put** operations are more difficult to normalize so they will be counted separately.

The following tables give a detailed breakdown of the actual number of computations performed by the algorithms of Figures 11.3, 11.4, and 11.5. The column entitled *cost* contains either the normalized operation count or a code to indicate a **get** or a **put** operation. It has been assumed that the difference between recording one value and two values in a **put** operation is negligible. The repetition factor indicates the number of times the operations are repeated.

The first table in Figure 11.7 provides a count of each operation in the algorithm of Figure 11.3. To obtain this complete analysis, it was necessary to make an assumption about the number of factors that any number may have. As a first estimate, the number of distinct, nontrivial factors cannot exceed $n - 2$ since this is the length of the range between 1 and n. A little more thought though will reveal that in fact $2(\lfloor \sqrt{n} \rfloor - 1)$ is a tighter upper bound on the number of factors. All factors may be obtained by finding the factors $m \leq \sqrt{n}$ ($\lfloor \sqrt{n} \rfloor - 1$ possible factors) and for each of these a cofactor may be found (another $\lfloor \sqrt{n} \rfloor - 1$ possible factors). Thus, the total number of factors must be less than or equal to $2(\lfloor \sqrt{n} \rfloor - 1)$.

Figure 11.7   Operation count for the unoptimized factoring algorithm of Figure 11.3 for an arbitrary number being tested.

	Cost	Repetition factor	Total operations
get	g	1	g
put	p	1	p
m ← 2	1	1	1
m ≤ n−1	2	$n - 1$	$2n - 2$
rem(n, m) = 0	6	$n - 2$	$6n - 12$
put	p	$2(\lfloor \sqrt{n} \rfloor - 1)$	$2p(\lfloor \sqrt{n} \rfloor - 1)$
m ← m+1	2	$n - 2$	$2n - 4$
		worst case	$10n + g + 2p\lfloor \sqrt{n} \rfloor - p - 17$

The table of Figure 11.8 gives an analysis of the algorithm of Figure 11.4. For this algorithm, the number of iterations through the **while**–loop is $\lfloor \sqrt{n} \rfloor - 1$, as determined by the **while** condition. Since the maximum number of factors in this range is also $\lfloor \sqrt{n} \rfloor - 1$, the statements within the **if** action are performed a maximum of $\lfloor \sqrt{n} \rfloor - 1$ times.

Figure 11.9 gives the operation counts for the algorithm of Figure 11.5. Remember that the major difference between this algorithm and the previous one is that the square root calculation has been moved outside of the loop. As may be seen from the table, the effect of this change is to reduce the operation count by a total of $10\lfloor \sqrt{n} \rfloor - 11$ equivalent add operations.

Although the above tables give a worst case estimate of the time efficiency for each algorithm, the efficiencies implied by these formulas are still a bit intangible. Better insight may be achieved by tabulating these formulas for different problem sizes. The table in Figure 11.10 shows the operation counts in terms of the number of normalized

Figure 11.8 Operation count for the first optimized factoring algorithm of Figure 11.4 for an arbitrary number being tested.

	Cost	Repetition factor	Total operations
get	g	1	g
put	p	1	p
m ← 2	1	1	1
m ≤ √n	11	$\lfloor\sqrt{n}\rfloor$	$11\lfloor\sqrt{n}\rfloor$
rem(n, m) = 0	6	$\lfloor\sqrt{n}\rfloor - 1$	$6\lfloor\sqrt{n}\rfloor - 6$
c ← n/m	3	$\lfloor\sqrt{n}\rfloor - 1$	$3\lfloor\sqrt{n}\rfloor - 3$
put	p	$\lfloor\sqrt{n}\rfloor - 1$	$p(\lfloor\sqrt{n}\rfloor - 1)$
m ← m+1	2	$\lfloor\sqrt{n}\rfloor - 1$	$2\lfloor\sqrt{n}\rfloor - 2$

worst case $22\lfloor\sqrt{n}\rfloor + g + p\lfloor\sqrt{n}\rfloor - 10$

Figure 11.9 Operation count for the second optimized factoring algorithm of Figure 11.5 for an arbitrary number being tested.

	Cost	Repetition factor	Total operations
get	g	1	g
put	p	1	p
m ← 2	1	1	1
k ← √n	11	1	11
m ≤ k	1	$\lfloor\sqrt{n}\rfloor$	$\lfloor\sqrt{n}\rfloor$
rem(n, m) = 0	6	$\lfloor\sqrt{n}\rfloor - 1$	$6\lfloor\sqrt{n}\rfloor - 6$
c ← n/m	3	$\lfloor\sqrt{n}\rfloor - 1$	$3\lfloor\sqrt{n}\rfloor - 3$
put	p	$\lfloor\sqrt{n}\rfloor - 1$	$p(\lfloor\sqrt{n}\rfloor - 1)$
m ← m+1	2	$\lfloor\sqrt{n}\rfloor - 1$	$2\lfloor\sqrt{n}\rfloor - 2$

worst case $12\lfloor\sqrt{n}\rfloor + g + p\lfloor\sqrt{n}\rfloor + 1$

Figure 11.10 Operation counts for the three factoring algorithms for various numbers being tested.

	Figure 11.3 Unoptimized Version	Figure 11.4 Optimized Version 1	Figure 11.5 Optimized Version 2
n	$10n + g + 2p\lfloor\sqrt{n}\rfloor - p - 17$	$22\lfloor\sqrt{n}\rfloor + g + p\lfloor\sqrt{n}\rfloor - 10$	$12\lfloor\sqrt{n}\rfloor + g + p\lfloor\sqrt{n}\rfloor + 1$
4	$23 + g + 3p$	$34 + g + 2p$	$25 + g + 2p$
10	$83 + g + 5p$	$56 + g + 3p$	$37 + g + 3p$
100	$983 + g + 19p$	$210 + g + 10p$	$121 + g + 10p$
500	$4983 + g + 43p$	$474 + g + 22p$	$265 + g + 22p$
1000	$9983 + g + 61p$	$672 + g + 31p$	$373 + g + 31p$

add operations and the number of **get** and **put** actions for different values of n. As may be seen from this table, the optimizations result in a substantial reduction in the number of required operations.   For the factoring algorithm, the best case, worst case and average times are all the same, except for the number of **put**s needed, which depends on the input data.   The number of operations to find all the distinct, nontrivial factors of the number 1000 has been reduced by 9610 equivalent add operations, and the number of **put** operations has been reduced by half.   Notice that moving the square root from the **while** statement to a position before the loop reduced the number of operations from 672 to 373 equivalent add operations.   Thus, a relatively simple change turned out to have considerable impact upon the algorithm speed.   This illustrates the potential for improvement that exists when dealing with loops.

11.3.2   Efficiency of the Prime Number Classification Algorithms

The prime number classification algorithm of Figure 4.5 processed a single number to determine if it was prime or composite and that algorithm was optimized to give the algorithm of Figure 4.6. These optimizations were closely paralleled by those of the factoring algorithms. The major difference is that the **while**–loop in the prime number classification algorithm may stop looping early when a divisor is found.   If the number being tested is a prime then the **while**–loop will test all values of $m \leq \sqrt{n}$ before terminating.   Thus, the worst case efficiency occurs when n is a prime and has not been improved.   If the number is composite, fewer calculations will be performed in almost all circumstances.   Thus, it is the average and the best case efficiencies that are improved.

An analysis of the average complexity of the prime number classification algorithm is quite complicated.   It depends upon the numbers being tested, and would require some knowledge of the expected distribution of primes versus nonprimes in the numbers to be tested.   The tables in Figures 11.11 and 11.12 give a detailed analysis of the two prime number classification algorithms.   In Figure 11.11 the operation counts are given for the unoptimized algorithm of Figure 4.5.   The table gives an analysis for the case that the number n is prime.   (Since this unoptimized algorithm cannot terminate early, the analysis will be the same for both prime and composite numbers.   This means that the algorithm will perform $n - 2$ divisions, and that the statement prime ← **false** will not be performed.)

Figure 11.11   Operation count for the prime number classification algorithm of Figure 4.5 when the number being tested is a prime.

	Cost	Repetition factor	Total operations
get	g	1	g
prime ← **true**	1	1	1
m ← 2	1	1	1
m ≤ n−1	2	$n - 1$	$2n - 2$
rem(n, m) = 0	6	$n - 2$	$6n - 12$
prime ← **false**	1	0	0
m ← m+1	2	$n - 2$	$2n - 4$
prime	1	1	1
put	p	1	p
		worst case	$10n + g + p - 15$

The algorithm of Figure 4.6 contains three optimizations from the previous algorithm. First, for prime numbers the algorithm divides by numbers only up to the square root of n (calculated outside of the loop). Second, for composite numbers the algorithm terminates immediately after the first factor is found. Third, only odd divisors are allowed in the loop. The analysis for this algorithm, shown in Figure 11.12, assumes the worst case when n is prime. (The operations performed for a composite n will depend upon the value of n itself.) Again, the statement prime ← **false** will not be executed.

Figure 11.12   Operation count for the prime number classification algorithm of Figure 4.6 when the number being tested is a prime.

	Cost	*Repetition factor*	*Total operations*
get	g	1	g
prime ← **true**	1	1	1
rem(n, 2) = 0 **and** n ≠ 2	8	1	8
prime ← **false**	1	0	0
m ← 3	1	1	1
k ← $\sqrt{n}$	11	1	11
m ≤ k **and** prime ≠ 0	3	$(\lfloor\sqrt{n}\rfloor)/2$	$3(\lfloor\sqrt{n}\rfloor)/2$
rem(n, m) = 0	6	$(\lfloor\sqrt{n}\rfloor-1)/2$	$6(\lfloor\sqrt{n}\rfloor-1)/2$
prime ← **false**	1	0	0
m ← m+2	2	$(\lfloor\sqrt{n}\rfloor-1)/2$	$2(\lfloor\sqrt{n}\rfloor-1)/2$
prime	1	1	1
put	p	1	p
		worst case	$5.5\lfloor\sqrt{n}\rfloor+g+p+18$

The worst case expressions from the above tables have been evaluated for different values of n and are listed in Figure 11.13. Each value of n in this table is a prime number. The calculated values in the table give the exact number of operations required to verify that the values of n are prime.

Figure 11.13   Operation counts for the prime number classification algorithm in its original and optimized versions for various prime numbers being tested.

n	*Figure 4.5* *Unoptimized Version* $10n+g+p-15$	*Figure 4.6* *Optimized Version* $6\lfloor\sqrt{n}\rfloor+g+p+18$
5	$35+g+p$	$30+g+p$
11	$95+g+p$	$36+g+p$
101	$995+g+p$	$78+g+p$
503	$5015+g+p$	$150+g+p$
1013	$10115+g+p$	$204+g+p$

As may be seen from the table in Figure 11.13, the optimizations have reduced the number of required operations tremendously.   The number of equivalent add operations required to verify that the number 1013 is prime has been reduced to approximately 1/50 of the previous value for the unoptimized algorithm.   To further illustrate the improvement in efficiency of the algorithms, the table of Figure 11.14 shows the operation counts when testing various composite numbers. It can be seen that the optimized algorithm achieves the most dramatic improvement when the composite number being tested has a small factor. The least improvement occurs when the number is the square of a prime, such as demonstrated by 5041.

Figure 11.14   Operation counts for the prime number classification algorithm in its original and optimized versions for various composite numbers being tested.

n	First Factor	Figure 4.5 Unoptimized Version	Figure 4.6 Optimized Version
35	5	$335 + g + p$	$43 + g + p$
667	23	$6655 + g + p$	$142 + g + p$
1739	37	$17375 + g + p$	$219 + g + p$
5041	71	$50395 + g + p$	$406 + g + p$
5065	5	$50635 + g + p$	$43 + g + p$

11.3.3   Efficiency of Algorithms for the Pythagorean Triples Problem

As a further example of algorithmic efficiency, consider a problem which requires several nested loops. A Pythagorean triple consists of three integers of which the square of the largest equals the sum of the squares of the other two. Since these integers could be the sides of a right-angled or Pythagorean triangle, such a combination is referred to as a Pythagorean triple. The sum of the three integers corresponds to the perimeter of such a triangle.

Example 11.1   Pythagorean Triples Problem
    Find all Pythagorean triples such that their sum is less than a given value.

For instance, if the perimeter limit is chosen to be 50, then Figure 11.15 shows examples of some valid Pythagorean triples.

Figure 11.15   Examples of integer triples which form a Pythagorean triangle with perimeter less than 50.

Triple	Perimeter
3:4:5	12
6:8:10	24
5:12:13	30
9:12:15	36
8:15:17	40
12:16:20	48

This problem is one which is suitable for step-wise refinement. However, in the interests of brevity, the refinement details will be omitted and only an abbreviated final algorithm will be presented.

In a first attempt at developing an algorithm for this problem, one might test all possible combinations of three integers by varying each integer in the triple and testing for the Pythagorean property. Such a scheme would test triples 1:1:1, 1:1:2, 1:1:3 and so on. A simple limit for each side would be the value of the perimeter itself. An algorithm patterned on these lines is shown in Figure 11.16. This algorithm increments each side in turn and checks each resulting triple to see if it forms a Pythagorean triangle. The Pythagorean test in the **if** statement is accompanied by a test to ensure that the total of the sides is also less than the perimeter.

Figure 11.16   Pythagorean triples algorithm – unoptimized version.

* An algorithm to find all Pythagorean Triples with a perimeter less than a given value.

```
get perimeter
side1 ← 1
while side1 ≤ perimeter do
    ⌈  side2 ← 1
    │  while side2 ≤ perimeter do
    │      ⌈  hyp ← 1
    │      │  while hyp ≤ perimeter do
    │      │      ⌈  if side1² + side2² = hyp² and side1 + side2 + hyp ≤ perimeter then
    │      │      │      ⌈  put 'Triple is ', side1, side2, hyp
    │      │      └  hyp ← hyp + 1
    │      └  side2 ← side2 + 1
    └  side1 ← side1 + 1
stop
```

The efficiency of this algorithm is quite easy to determine. The looping structure of three nested **while**–loops each with the loop limit of **perimeter** causes the innermost statements to be executed **perimeter**^{3} times. Thus, the value of the perimeter, say p, controls the order of the algorithm which would be $O(p^3)$.

The simple analysis used to get the order of the algorithm is, in fact, sufficient for our purpose so far. The individual operations could have been counted but such numbers will just act as constant additive or multiplier terms and not change the p^3 property.

An algorithm which is of $O(p^3)$ may require excessive computer time for large p since the time requirements accelerate as the cube of the problem size. Although some problems are intrinsically demanding in their computational requirements, any improvements at all in the algorithms for such problems are welcome.

By examining the results or thinking about the operation of the algorithm of Figure 11.16, it is possible to suggest several improvements which will make it more efficient. For example, the limits for the **while**–loops are unnecessarily large. In any triangle, the largest side must be less than one-half of the perimeter. Thus the loop limit can be perimeter/2. Just this simple observation results in an algorithm which requires one-eighth the number of operations.

More detailed examination of the algorithm would show that repetitions occur. For example, the combinations 3:4:5, 4:3:5 and 5:4:3, etc. would all be generated. Only one of these six triples would suffice, since the other five represent equivalent triangles.

To avoid these equivalent triples, one should ensure that the sides are ordered side1 ≤ side2 ≤ hyp. To achieve this ordering the loop limits must be 1 ≤ side1 < perimeter/2, side1 ≤ side2 < perimeter/2, and side2 ≤ hyp < perimeter/2. Even with these loop limits it is still possible that the sum of the sides will exceed the given value. Thus, some method of eliminating those combinations is still needed. The unoptimized algorithm used a second condition in the **if** statement in the innermost **while**–loop to prevent this. However, a moment's reflection should convince the reader that as soon as the perimeter is exceeded by the sum of the sides then the innermost **while**–loop can be terminated. Incorporating these changes gives the algorithm shown in Figure 11.17. The efficiency of this algorithm has been improved somewhat.

Figure 11.17   Pythagorean triples algorithm – optimized version 1.

* An algorithm to find all Pythagorean Triples with a perimeter less than a given value.

get perimeter

* Test values of **side1** from 1 to **perimeter/2**.

side1 ← 1
while side1 ≤ perimeter/2 **do**

> * Test values of **side2** from **side** to **perimeter/2**.
>
> side2 ← side1
> **while** side2 ≤ perimeter/2 **do**
>
>> sumside ← side1 + side2
>>
>> * Test hypotenuse values from **side2** to **perimeter/2**.
>> * Terminate loop if **perimeter** is exceeded.
>>
>> hyp ← side2
>> **while** hyp ≤ perimeter/2 **and** sumside + hyp ≤ perimeter **do**
>>
>>> **if** side1^2 + side2^2 = hyp^2 **then**
>>>
>>>> **put** 'Triple is ', side1, side2, hyp
>>>
>>> hyp ← hyp + 1
>>
>> side2 ← side2 + 1
>
> side1 ← side1 + 1

stop

By a detailed counting argument, it may be shown that in terms of the perimeter p, the number of executions of the statements in the innermost loop is

$$\frac{p^3}{48} + \frac{p^2}{8} + \frac{p}{6} \; ,$$

if the possibility of early termination side1 + side2 + hyp $\geq$ perimeter is ignored.

Although the coefficient has been reduced to 1/48, the algorithm is still $O(p^3)$. It should be apparent to the reader that the algorithm will remain $O(p^3)$ if the structure of the algorithm involves three nested **while**–loops, each of which is executed for a range of parameter values which grows with p. Could one of these loops be eliminated?

Consider the inner loop. Is it really necessary? Since the hypotenuse of a right-angled triangle can be calculated from the other two sides, why bother trying to find it by searching. Rather, why not simply calculate the hypotenuse and determine if the sum of the squares of the two sides is a perfect square. An algorithm using this idea is shown in Figure 11.18.

Figure 11.18   Pythagorean triples algorithm – optimized version 2.

* An algorithm to find all Pythagorean Triples with a perimeter less than a given value.

get perimeter

* Test values of **side1** from 1 to **perimeter/2**.

side1 ← 1
while side1 ≤ perimeter/2 **do**

> * Test values of **side2** from **side1** to **perimeter/2**.
>
> side2 ← side1
> sidesq ← 2*side1^2
> **while** side2 ≤ perimeter/2 **and** sidesq ≤ perimeter^2/4 **do**
>
> > sidesq ← side1^2 + side2^2
> > hyp ← int($\sqrt{\text{sidesq}}$)
> > **if** hyp^2 = sidesq **then**
> >
> > > **put** 'Triple is ', side1, side2, hyp
> >
> > side2 ← side2 + 1
>
> side1 ← side1 + 1

stop

The efficiency of this algorithm is improved over the last one by eliminating the inner **while**–loop. The two remaining loops determine the order of the algorithm as $O(p^2)$. The number of executions of the statements which replaced the innermost loop is given by $\dfrac{p^2}{8} + \dfrac{p}{4}$.

The innermost **while**–loop structure for which the limits increased with perimeter p has been eliminated, but it has been replaced by a single calculation involving a square root. A detailed operation count could give precise data on this effect. The $O(p^3)$ will be more efficient for small values of p, when it costs less to check a few extra values than to compute a square root.

11.4   Optimizations in General

These examples have illustrated that the efficiency of some algorithms may be greatly improved by relatively simple optimizations.   The largest gains in efficiency are achieved by reducing the number of **while**–loop iterations.   The remaining gains are accomplished by minimizing the number of operations performed within the **while** loops. The design of an efficient algorithm is the first step towards achieving an efficient computer program.

When large computer programs are being designed, it is not clear how much time should be spent performing extensive algorithm optimizations.   The reason for this uncertainty is that in large systems it is not easy to predict which parts of the system will be used most.   In many systems, a common observation is that 10% of the code consumes 90% of the execution time.   Thus, an extensive optimization effort would be best performed on that 10% of code.   Any effort spent on optimizing the remaining 90% of the code will show only a small return on the effort.

One method of measuring the activity of a computer program is called *profiling*. In the simplest sense, an execution profile of a program gives the number of times each statement is executed.   Thus, by comparing these numbers the sections of a program which are executed most frequently may be found.   Special programs, called *profilers*, exist to perform these measurements.

The intended use of a program also affects the optimization effort.   If a program is only going to be used once, then extensive optimization may not be warranted.   On the other hand, a program which is liable to undergo very frequent use should be made as efficient as possible.

11.5   Summary

This chapter has given a brief introduction to the topic of algorithm and program efficiency.   This is an important topic as more people are using computer programs, and the problems to be solved are becoming larger.

For the size of problems and algorithms presented here, a simple way to determine and compare the efficiencies is to count the number of operations each algorithm performs.   The result of such analysis allows insight into the relative performance of algorithms and can determine which algorithm is best for the current problem.

Measurements of programs can be performed in a somewhat more automatic manner using computer profiling techniques.   These measurements allow one to obtain precise information about the execution behavior of the program to identify the heavily used parts.   However, the ability to profile programs does not remove the necessity for algorithm efficiency analysis.   An algorithm analysis can remove the need for programming and profiling the various alternatives.

11.6 References

Aho, A.V.; Hopcroft, J.E.; and Ullman, J.D. *The Design and Analysis of Computer Algorithms.* Reading, Mass.: Addison-Wesley Pub. Co., 1974.

Van Tassel, D. *Program Style, Design, Efficiency, Debugging, and Testing.* Englewood Cliffs, N.J.: Prentice-Hall, 1974.

Weide, B. "A Survey of Analysis Techniques for Discrete Algorithms." *Computing Surveys* 9(1977): 291-313.

11.7 Exercises

11.1 If two different algorithms for the same problem have the following equations for the number of equivalent add operations, which algorithm would you prefer? Discuss your answer.

a) algorithm 1: $x - 10y + 50$
b) algorithm 2: $x - 2y + 2$

11.2 The equivalent operation counts for three versions of the factoring algorithm are shown in Figure 11.10. Ignoring the **get** and **put** counts, plot the operation counts versus the problem size and compare the resulting curves.

11.3 Determine the expression for the equivalent number of add operations for the algorithms of Figures 11.3, 11.4, and 11.5 assuming that the remainder operation rem(n,m) is equivalent to only two add operations.

11.4 Determine the number of equivalent add operations (worst case) which the quadratic equation algorithm of Figure 9.10 will require for:

a) one set of a, b, c values,
b) two sets of a, b, c values,
c) three sets of a, b, c values.

Plot a graph of the above counts versus the problem size (1, 2, and 3) ignoring the **get** and **put** counts.

11.5   The following algorithm determines the sum of a set of numbers in a data list. A data count indicates the number of values to be summed.

> * Algorithm to sum the numbers in a data list.
>
> **get** n
> sum ← 0
> i ← 0
> **while** i < n **do**
> >   **get** value
> >   sum ← sum + value
> >   i ← i + 1
>
> **put** 'The sum of the', n, 'values is', sum
> **stop**

Determine the number of equivalent add operations required by this algorithm to sum 10, 15, 20, and 25 numbers.   Plot the operation count versus the size of the problem.

11.6   The following algorithm calculates the factorial of a given number.   Determine an expression which gives the number of equivalent add operations which the algorithm performs for a number n.

> * An algorithm to calculate the factorial of n.
>
> **get** n
> prod ← 1
> i ← 1
> **while** i ≤ n **do**
> >   prod ← prod*i
> >   i ← i + 1
>
> **put** 'The factorial of', n, 'is', prod
> **stop**

Plot the number of operations required versus the problem size when $n = 5, 10, 15, 20$ (ignore the **get** and **put** times).   Is this algorithm linear with respect to its time?

11.7   Develop an algorithm, using step-wise refinement, which will test all the integer numbers from 2 to n to determine if they are prime or composite.   For the algorithm as a whole, determine the equivalent number of add operations the algorithm would require.

a)   if the prime number classification algorithm of Figure 4.5 is used,
b)   if the prime number classification algorithm of Figure 4.6 is used.

Is the difference significant in this case? Discuss your answer.

11.8   The following algorithm calculates n terms of the following series.

$$x + x^2 + x^3 + x^4 + \cdots + x^n$$

in a somewhat inefficient manner.

* Algorithm to evaluate n terms of a series whose general term is x^n.

get n, x
put 'The values for n and x are', n, x
sum ← 0
i ← 1
while i ≤ n **do**

    prod ← 1
    j ← 1
    while j ≤ n **do**

        prod ← prod*x
        j ← j + 1

    sum ← sum + prod
    i ← i + 1

put 'The sum of the series is', sum
stop

a) Determine the expression for the equivalent number of add operations for the algorithm.

b) Rewrite the algorithm to make it more efficient and determine its equivalent add expression. Compare your answer to that of part a).

11.9 Perform a detailed operation count (ignoring **get**s and **put**s) for the optimized Pythagorean algorithms of Figures 11.17 and 11.18. Plot the curves for different values of the perimeter.

11.10 Translate the first optimized Pythagorean algorithm of Figure 11.17 into a FORTRAN/77 program. Insert counters within each loop to determine the exact number of loop iterations for different values of perimeter.

Part D
Handling Large Masses of Data

12 Handling Large Masses of Data *271*

13 Searching and Sorting Techniques *303*

14 Statistics *349*

15 Vectors, Matrices, and Linear Equations *391*

12
Handling Large Masses of Data

12.1   Introduction

In previous chapters the problems being solved did not require the retention of very much information to achieve the desired result.   However, many mathematical problems, such as analyzing experimental results, gathering statistical information, plotting graphs, and solving systems of equations, do involve the manipulation of large quantities of data.   Fortunately, computers are useful not only for their computational speed but also for their facility in handling data in such volumes.

A variety of techniques are available for handling masses of data.   In terms of storage the options include internal computer memory and external devices such as magnetic tapes and discs.   The differing speeds, capacities, and other attributes of these devices have considerable influence on the choice of a best method for dealing with the data for a particular problem.   In terms of manipulating data the choice of algorithm varies according to the storage medium used.

The entire topic of storage techniques is very important.   With most real-life applications the amount of data is quite large, and as a result the processing of such data on even the largest computers may take several hours.   Consequently, much research has been done on devising techniques for storing and manipulating this data to minimize this processing time.   One way of improving processing time is to arrange the data in storage to reflect any inherent structure in the data itself or to reflect any obvious order in the way the data will be accessed.   A more thorough discussion of this topic falls under the heading of *data structures* or *file structures*.

This chapter is concerned with only a small portion of this entire field, that is, the use of internal storage as applied to simple one- and two-dimensional arrays.   For other aspects of this topic, the reader is directed to the references at the end of this chapter.

12.2   One-Dimensional Arrays in Pseudocode

In many applications it is necessary to deal with each element of a set of numbers in a similar way or to deal with the entire set as a unit.   Such sets are often ordered as first element, second element, third element, and so on.   This ordering provides the means to uniquely identify which element of an *array* of numbers is to be dealt with.

In problems involving sets of numbers it is sometimes possible to process one element of the set completely before continuing with another.   Thus, as the algorithm obtains a new value, the old one can be forgotten, and a single variable will suffice. Frequently, however, the original value is required at a later stage; in such cases it is necessary to remember all the values in a convenient storage area, and to recall any value when needed.   Thus, techniques are necessary to retain and access elements of simple arrays of numbers.

12.2.1   Representation

The representation of a simple ordered array in pseudocode is similar to the commonly used mathematical notation.   A complete array is referenced by writing its name in upper case letters.   To refer to individual elements of an array, the array name is written in lower case letters while the position of the element in the array is indicated by a subscript.   Consider representing a collection of daily temperature readings for one week.

Sun.	Mon.	Tues.	Wed.	Thurs.	Fri.	Sat.
12	15	16	14	21	25	30

If the complete array is called T, the temperature on Sunday is t_1, on Monday t_2, ... , and on Saturday t_7.   In general, the i-th element of the array is referenced by t_i.   Notice that the natural order of days of the week is retained in this representation of the array as summarized below.

	t_1	t_2	t_3	t_4	t_5	t_6	t_7
T	12	15	16	14	21	25	30

12.2.2   Input and Output

The pseudocode to input the elements of an array X could be written quite simply as:

get X

Though this statement may be useful for early refinements of an algorithm, it is deceptive in that no information is given about the size of the array.   Assuming that the set X has 10 elements, reading the 10 values for X is expressed more clearly by a **while**–loop using a counter or index to specify the array element in which the data item is to be stored.

```
i ← 1
while i ≤ 10 do
   ┌ get xᵢ
   │ i ← i + 1
```

This loop can be abbreviated further using the **for**–loop:

```
for i from 1 to 10 do
   ┌ get xᵢ
```

The above methods of expressing input for an array may also be used for describing the **put** action. Again, it is preferable to use an explicit loop to refer to each element individually in the final refinement of an algorithm, so that it is clear how many elements are being processed.

Another concern with printing array elements is the ability to print many of them on the same output line. While each pseudocode **put** action normally produces a separate output line, the following *implied loop* demonstrates a convention by which all ten x_i output values could be printed on one line:

put (x_i, i **from** 1 **to** 10)

12.2.3 Processing

The manipulation of elements of an array may take on many forms. In early refinements of an algorithm it may again be useful to simply refer to the entire array by name. For example, finding the sum of the 25 entries in an array called LIST might be written as

$$\text{sum} \leftarrow \sum \text{LIST}$$

However, the actions inherent in the above statement are more clearly expressed by the following pseudocode expansion:

```
sum ← 0
for index from 1 to 25 do
   ┌ sum ← sum + listᵢₙdₑₓ
```

The summation must be initialized outside the loop and then each array element accumulated inside the loop.

12.2.4 Applications of Simple Arrays

Ordered arrays or lists are useful in solving a variety of mathematical problems. This section investigates one simple example, which is developed using step-wise refinement. Later chapters will study arrays used in statistics as well as in sorting and searching techniques.

Example 12.1   Average Temperature Problem
Given the temperature readings for seven days of a week, record the number of degrees which the daily temperature is above or below the average temperature for the week.

a) Problem Discussion   To find the difference between the temperature on each day and the average for the week, it is necessary to compute the average first and then subtract the temperature for each day from the average.   Thus, the daily temperature readings are required twice, and it is useful to store them in an array.

b) Selection of Initial Decomposition   Since the entries of the set must be available before processing can begin, the initial sequence-decomposition is a good way to start.   As stated previously, finding the number of degrees above or below the average requires finding the average first and then computing the difference for each day.   A first version is given as Figure 12.1.

Figure 12.1   First version of a pseudocode algorithm for the average temperature problem.

1.   Acquire the daily temperature readings.
2.   Compute and record the average temperature for the week.
3.   Compute the temperature difference for each day and record the results.
4.   **stop**

---

c) Refining Step **1.**   Let the name of the array for the seven daily temperatures be TEMP.   Then reading the entries from input values may be written as follows:

   * Acquire the daily temperature readings.

   for i **from** 1 **to** 7 **do**
   $\quad\Big[$ **get** $temp_i$

d) Refining Step **2.**   Computing the average temperature involves summing all the daily temperatures and dividing by the total number of days.

   * Compute and record the average temperature for the week.

   sum $\leftarrow$ 0
   for i **from** 1 **to** 7 **do**
   $\quad\Big[$ sum $\leftarrow$ sum + $temp_i$
   average $\leftarrow$ sum/7
   put 'The average temperature is', average

e) Refining Step **3.**   To compute the number of degrees above or below the average, it is necessary to create a loop to subtract the average from the temperature for each day. These differences could be written out directly.   Although this might be more efficient in this case, it is instructive to use a new array, HILO, which will store the differences above or below the average temperature. This serves to isolate the output of data as a logical unit of the algorithm and to illustrate the creation of an array as part of processing data.

3.1 Compute the temperature difference for each day.
3.2 Record the temperature and difference for each day.

The refinements of these two steps can be based on previous work and are completed below:

* Compute the temperature difference for each day.

for i **from** 1 **to** 7 **do**

$\lceil$ $hilo_i \leftarrow temp_i - average$

* Record the temperature and difference for each day.

put 'Temperature   Difference'
for i **from** 1 **to** 7 **do**

$\lceil$ **put** $temp_i$, $hilo_i$

f) Final Version of the Algorithm   The refinements for the various steps of the algorithm can now be collected and are presented in Figure 12.2.

12.3   One-Dimensional Arrays in FORTRAN/77

12.3.1   Representation

Just as the use of ordinary or scalar variables is more formal in FORTRAN/77, so is the definition and use of arrays. The type of data to be stored in the elements of an array must be declared. In fact, only values of this type may be stored in the array. In addition, it is necessary to specify the subscript range for the array. Thus, for example, if the array TEMP is to have 7 integral entries the declaration would be:

```
INTEGER TEMP(1:7)
```

This statement instructs the compiler to reserve 7 consecutive locations for the array called TEMP, to check that subscripts belong to the range from 1 to 7 inclusive, and that all values stored there will be integers. Note that if the lower subscript limit is omitted in the declaration, a value of 1 is assumed. Subscripts are also used to reference individual entries in the array. However, in FORTRAN/77, the subscript or array index is placed in parentheses immediately following the array name. The subscript must be either an integer or an integer-valued expression with a value between 1 and the size of the array, inclusive. The diagram which follows illustrates this naming convention for the array of 7 temperatures encountered in the previous section. As with the pseudocode, TEMP(I) is used to reference the temperature on the *i*-th day.

Figure 12.2 Final version of the pseudocode algorithm for the average temperature problem.

```
* Average Temperature Problem
* Given a set of temperature readings for each day of a week find
* the number of degrees above or below the average for each day.

* Variables used:
* TEMP - array of daily temperatures
* HILO - array of temperature differences
* sum - sum of readings for averaging
* average - average temperature for the week

* Acquire the daily temperature readings.
```

for i **from** 1 **to** 7 **do**

$\quad$ $\lbrack$ **get** temp$_i$

* Compute and record the average temperature for the week.

sum ← 0
for i **from** 1 **to** 7 **do**

$\quad$ $\lbrack$ sum ← sum + temp$_i$

average ← sum/7
put 'The average temperature is', average

* Compute the temperature difference for each day.

for i **from** 1 **to** 7 **do**

$\quad$ $\lbrack$ hilo$_i$ ← temp$_i$ − average

* Record the temperature and difference for each day.

put 'Temperature   Difference'
for i **from** 1 **to** 7 **do**

$\quad$ $\lbrack$ **put** temp$_i$, hilo$_i$

stop

12, 15, 16, 14, 21, 25, 30

TEMP

TEMP(1)	TEMP(2)	TEMP(3)	TEMP(4)	TEMP(5)	TEMP(6)	TEMP(7)
12	15	16	14	21	25	30

12.3.2 Input and Output

There are a variety of ways of expressing input and output of array elements in FORTRAN/77. To begin with, the READ and PRINT statements are two of the few instances in which it is legal to use the name of an array by itself. Consider the following brief example which reads and prints the first 10 known prime numbers.

```
      INTEGER PRIME(1:10)
      READ *, PRIME
      PRINT *, PRIME
      STOP
      END
```

The read statement causes ten values to be read into the array PRIME while the PRINT statement causes these same ten values to be printed. In each case the number of entries is specified by the declared size of the array.

Though the above convention is easy to use, it requires knowledge of the number of elements to process, a number which may be known explicitly as in the average temperature problem above. Frequently, however, the exact number of entries to be processed is supplied as data. In cases like this it is necessary to guess at an upper bound for the size of the array (using information supplied in the statement of the problem if possible) and to use a DO–loop to read in the values. For example, the following FORTRAN/77 fragment allows a variable number of known prime numbers to be input for processing, up to a maximum of 100 primes. The actual number of primes provided will be expected as a first item of input data. This actual number is assumed to be less than 100, although additional FORTRAN/77 statements to verify this assumption could easily be inserted. Most FORTRAN/77 compilers provide a check during execution-time which causes an error message if a reference is made to an array with an out-of-range subscript value.

```
      INTEGER PRIME(1:100), I, N
C Determine the actual number of primes to process.
      READ *, N
C Acquire the values of the N primes supplied.
      DO 100 I = 1, N
         READ *, PRIME(I)
  100 CONTINUE
```

In this example the READ statements are encountered 1+N times and therefore, there must be at least 1+N data lines: the number of primes, and the N prime numbers.

As with pseudocode, the DO–loop in this example can be written in an abbreviated form such as the following.

```
      READ *, (PRIME(I), I = 1, N)
```

In fact, it may be convenient to include the input of N in the same statement.

```
      READ *, N, (PRIME(I), I = 1, N)
```

Here a value of N is read before it is needed to control the reading of values for the array PRIME. This implied DO–loop has the advantage that, since the READ statement is encountered only once, several data values may be placed on one line.

When the values of an array are to be printed, using an explicit DO–loop will cause each value to be printed on a separate line. An implied DO–loop will print the values across the page, continuing on subsequent lines as necessary.

12.3.3   Applications of Simple Arrays

To illustrate the application of arrays, the algorithm of Figure 12.2 will be translated to FORTRAN/77. Translation of this algorithm requires a little care in choosing the data types. Though the daily temperature readings are probably integral, it is quite likely that the average and, therefore, the differences are not. Thus, the array TEMP could be of type INTEGER while the array HILO should be of type REAL. The complete program is listed in Figure 12.3, while the corresponding output is presented in Figure 12.4.

```
C Figure 12.3 -- Average Temperature Problem.
C                 Given a set of temperature readings
C                 for each day of a week, find the number of
C                 degrees above or below the average for each day.
C**********************************************************************
C TEMP    - array of daily temperatures
C HILO    - array of temperature differences
C SUM     - sum of temperature readings for averaging
C AVER    - average temperature for the week
C I       - loop counter for each day of the week
C**********************************************************************
        INTEGER TEMP(1:7), SUM, I
        REAL HILO(1:7), AVER
C Acquire the daily temperature readings.
        DO 100 I = 1, 7
            READ *, TEMP(I)
    100 CONTINUE
C Compute and record the average temperature for the week.
        SUM = 0
        DO 200 I = 1, 7
            SUM = SUM + TEMP(I)
    200 CONTINUE
        AVER = SUM/7.0
        PRINT *, 'THE AVERAGE TEMPERATURE IS', AVER
C Compute the temperature difference for each day.
        DO 300 I = 1, 7
            HILO(I) = TEMP(I) - AVER
    300 CONTINUE
C Record the temperature and difference for each day.
        PRINT *, ' '
        PRINT *, 'TEMPERATURE  DIFFERENCE'
        PRINT *, ' '
        DO 400 I = 1,7
            PRINT *, TEMP(I), HILO(I)
    400 CONTINUE
        STOP
        END
```

Program Notes

- Most of the programs presented thus far were designed to accept input in an interactive manner. Since arrays can be large in size, programs involving arrays will instead expect the input to be stored in a file. This is particularly useful during the debugging stages.

Figure 12.4   Input and output files for the temperature analysis program of Figure 12.3.

a) Input file:

```
12
15
16
14
21
25
30
```

b) Output file:

```
THE  AVERAGE  TEMPERATURE  IS      19.00000

TEMPERATURE   DIFFERENCE
        12   -7.000000
        15   -4.000000
        16   -3.000000
        14   -5.000000
        21    2.000000
        25    6.000000
        30   11.00000
```

This first example has illustrated but a few of the operations commonly applied to ordered sets or lists.   Further examples are suggested in the exercises.

12.4   Multidimensional Arrays

Simple ordered arrays are useful in solving many mathematical problems.   However, not all data is inherently one-dimensional in structure.   Consider the data presented in Figures 12.5 and 12.6.   The table in Figure 12.5 lists the precipitation readings taken over each of the 12 months of the year at 4 locations in the same region.   To retain the relationship between region and month it would be desirable to organize the array with two dimensions having 12 rows, one for each month, and 4 columns, one for each region. The second table of Figure 12.6 gives 4 nicotine measurements for each of 3 tests applied to each of 5 brands of cigarettes.   To represent this data adequately would require a three-dimensional array.

12.5   Multidimensional Arrays in Pseudocode

The basic techniques required to handle multidimensional arrays in pseudocode are illustrated in this section by using arrays with only two dimensions.   Extension of these ideas to arrays with three or more dimensions is straightforward and is not done explicitly in this chapter.

Figure 12.5 Precipitation for one year at 4 locations.

		Location		
Month	*North*	*East*	*South*	*West*
January	12.4	13.5	12.1	12.6
February	8.2	9.5	8.0	7.5
March	14.9	13.5	12.9	15.3
April	30.0	35.5	40.2	37.7
May	24.5	26.1	23.4	24.0
June	10.0	9.0	8.5	7.9
July	4.0	.5	2.3	3.2
August	3.4	0.0	4.5	6.1
September	7.8	7.9	7.6	7.8
October	10.1	10.6	10.9	12.0
November	12.3	12.5	12.1	12.6
December	14.1	15.2	12.8	9.5

Figure 12.6 Nicotine levels in 5 brands of cigarettes by 4 measurements in 3 tests.

	Test 1	Test 2	Test 3
A	2.1, 2.3, 1.9, 2.0	2.3, 2.4, 2.3, 2.5	2.0, 1.9, 2.0, 2.1
B	4.5, 4.6, 4.7, 4.8	4.0, 3.9, 4.1, 4.3	4.4, 4.4, 4.5, 4.4
C	0.5, 0.5, 0.5, 0.5	0.4, 0.6, 0.5, 0.5	0.6, 0.6, 0.4, 0.5
D	6.1, 6.5, 6.7, 6.3	6.5, 6.5, 6.7, 6.9	5.9, 6.0, 6.2, 6.0
E	3.7, 3.8, 3.7, 3.6	3.8, 3.6, 3.7, 3.7	3.6, 3.7, 3.5, 3.8

12.5.1 Representation

The representation of multidimensional arrays in pseudocode can be handled in a manner similar to ordinary arrays. A name written in upper case will refer to the entire array, whereas individual elements in the set will be referenced by using a lower case letter with a subscript for each dimension. For example, the data given in Figure 12.5 could be labeled PRECIP, and the elements can be referenced as illustrated by the following diagram.

$precip_{1,1}$	$precip_{1,2}$	$precip_{1,3}$	$precip_{1,4}$
$precip_{2,1}$	$precip_{2,2}$	$precip_{2,3}$	$precip_{2,4}$
.	.	.	.
.	.	.	.
.	.	.	.
$precip_{12,1}$	$precip_{12,2}$	$precip_{12,3}$	$precip_{12,4}$

12.5.2 Input and Output

There are several ways in which data can be acquired and recorded for arrays of multiple dimensions. Any order which exists in these data items must be modeled by the loop structures which **get** or **put** the array elements. In all likelihood the data is not organized at random but rather in either *row-major* or *column-major* order. If the data is in row-major order, all the column entries for row 1 are followed by the column entries for row 2, and so on. Row-major order would require an outer loop which varies the row index, and an inner loop which varies the column index.   On the other hand, if the data is in column-major order, the row entries for column 1 are followed by the row entries for column 2, and so on.   Column-major order would require the outer loop to vary the column index and the inner loop to vary the row index.   Most algorithmic segments can easily be changed from row to column order by rearranging the inner and outer loop structure.   For simplicity the illustrations for input will only use row-major order for the data.

Consider reading the 12×4 precipitation values from the table in Figure 12.5.

* PRECIP - precipitation array 12×4 elements
* r - the row index
* c - the column index

for r **from** 1 **to** 12 **do**

     get (precip$_{r,c}$, c **from** 1 **to** 4)

The recording of values stored in multidimensioned arrays may be coded in an analogous fashion by replacing the word **get** with the word **put**.

12.5.3   Processing

The computations performed on elements of a multidimensional array can vary considerably.   When all the elements are to be involved, it is necessary to use a double loop structure similar to that used for reading the entries of the array.   Several examples will be given in the following section on applications.

12.5.4   Applications

The following example will demonstrate a variety of loop structures for analyzing the weather data presented in Figure 12.5.

Example 12.2   Rainfall Analysis Problem

    For the table of precipitation levels observed at four locations over a 12-month period, find the average rainfall per month over the entire region as well as the wettest location over the year.

a) Problem Discussion   Since the problem requires that the weather data be examined several times, it is appropriate to retain the table in storage.   A natural arrangement is a two-dimensional array.

b) Selection of Initial Decomposition   While the data represent several observations, only one such set of data is to be analyzed, and an initial sequence decomposition can be used.   The algorithm will first input the entire set of data into the array and then analyze the data as required, as shown in Figure 12.7.

Figure 12.7   First version of a pseudocode algorithm for the rainfall analysis problem in Example 12.2.

1.   Acquire the precipitation measurements.
2.   Find the average rainfall for each month and the wettest location over the year.
3.   **stop**

---

c) Refining Step **1.**   Assume that the data are to be entered in row-major order, that is, on 12 lines with the 4 readings for each month on the same line.   Therefore, it is convenient to use an outer loop to process each line.   Within this loop, an inner loop is used to input the 4 readings for each month.   Finally, these input values should be recorded to verify the data, and it is easiest to echo the values as they are obtained.

> * Acquire and record the precipitation measurements.

> **put** 'Month North East South West'
> **for** r **from** 1 **to** 12 **do**
>> **get** ($precip_{r,c}$, c **from** 1 **to** 4)
>> **put** r, ($precip_{r,c}$, c **from** 1 **to** 4)

d) Refining Step **2.**   There are two distinct analyses required as part of Step **2.**   It is most convenient to record each as it is found.   This is reflected in the next decomposition:

> **2.1** Find and record the average rainfall for each month.

> **2.2** Find and record the wettest location over the year.

e) Refining Step **2.1**   To find the average rainfall for each month the averaging process must be repeated 12 times, once for each month.   This is done using a loop for row-major order as shown below:

> * Find and record the average rainfall for each month.

> **2.1.1 for** r **from** 1 **to** 12 **do**
>> **2.1.2** Find and record the average for the r-th month.

f) Refining Step **2.1.2**   The averaging process involves summing the elements along each row of the array.   This, in turn, requires a loop to advance along the 4 column entries for the row.   The average can be computed by dividing by the number of elements summed, and can be recorded along with the current month number r.

> sum ← 0
> **for** c **from** 1 **to** 4 **do**
>> sum ← sum + $precip_{r,c}$
> avg ← sum/4
> **put** 'The average rainfall for month', r, 'is', avg

g) Refining Step **2.2**   Finding the wettest location over the year first requires finding the total rainfall at each location then searching for the largest total and recording the result.

> **2.2.1** Find the total rainfall for each location.

> **2.2.2** Search for the largest total and record the wettest location.

h) Refining Step **2.2.1**   Finding the total rainfall for each location can be done very easily by observing that it involves a rearrangement of the summing used in the previous averaging process, that is, using column-major instead of row-major order.   It will be necessary to retain the values of these rainfall totals in order to find the wettest location later.   They are stored in a one-dimensional array called LOCTOT for location totals. These totals are recorded as a check that the largest total found later is indeed correct.

> * Find the total rainfall for each location.

for c **from** 1 **to** 4 **do**

    $loctot_c \leftarrow 0$
    for r **from** 1 **to** 12 **do**
        $loctot_c \leftarrow loctot_c + precip_{r,c}$
    put 'The total rainfall for location', c, 'is', $loctot_c$

i) Refining Step **2.2.2**   Several ways exist to determine the largest element in an array, but one which is quite straightforward will suffice here.   Since all the rainfalls must be nonnegative, initialize the maximum rainfall at a negative number, and then check each of the location totals for a better estimate.   However, it is necessary to remember where this largest rainfall occurred, so whenever a larger estimate is found, a second variable **where** will be assigned the current location index.

> * Search for the location with largest total rainfall.

$rain \leftarrow -1$
$where \leftarrow 0$
for c **from** 1 **to** 4 **do**

    if $loctot_c \geq rain$ **then**
        $rain \leftarrow loctot_c$
        $where \leftarrow c$

> * Record the wettest location.

put 'The wettest location is', where

Notice that this code will determine the last location with the largest total if several should have the same value.

j) Final Version of the Algorithm   The various sections of the algorithm are presented together in Figure 12.8.

12.6   Multidimensional Arrays in FORTRAN/77

12.6.1   Representation

Implementation of multidimensional arrays in FORTRAN/77 is similar to the way one-dimensional arrays were defined and used.   Elements of a multidimensional array are referred to by the array name, with the subscripts, one for each dimension and separated

Figure 12.8 Pseudocode algorithm for the rainfall analysis problem.

```
* Given a table of precipitation at four locations
* over a 12-month period, find the average rainfall
* per month, and the wettest location over the year.

* Variables used:
* PRECIP - monthly precipitation in four locations
* LOCTOT - total rainfall in a location for the year
* r, c - row (month) and column (location) indices
* sum - total rainfall for a location in a month
* avg - average rainfall for the month
* rain - current largest rainfall in a location
* where - location of largest rainfall

* Acquire and record the precipitation measurements.
put 'Month  North  East  South  West'
for r from 1 to 12 do
     ⌈  get (precip_{r,c}, c from 1 to 4)
     ⌊  put r, (precip_{r,c}, c from 1 to 4)
* Find and record the average rainfall for each month.
for r from 1 to 12 do
     ⌈  sum ← 0
     |  for c from 1 to 4 do
     |       ⌊  sum ← sum + precip_{r,c}
     |  avg ← sum/4
     ⌊  put 'The average rainfall for month', r, 'is', avg
* Find the total rainfall for each location.
for c from 1 to 4 do
     ⌈  loctot_c ← 0
     |  for r from 1 to 12 do
     |       ⌊  loctot_c ← loctot_c + precip_{r,c}
     ⌊  put 'The total rainfall for location', c, 'is', loctot_c
* Search for the location with largest total rainfall.
rain ← −1
where ← 0
for c from 1 to 4 do
     ⌈  if loctot_c ≥ rain then
     |       ⌈  rain ← loctot_c
     ⌊       ⌊  where ← c
* Record the wettest location.
put 'The wettest location is', where
stop
```

by commas, placed within brackets immediately after it. The first subscript refers to the row number, the second to the column number, and so on. The type of value to be stored in an array and the subscript range for each dimension must be included in the declaration. Thus, the storage for the precipitation table of Figure 12.5 could be declared as follows:

```
REAL PRECIP(12,4)
```

This causes the compiler to set aside 12×4 or 48 spaces for the real values of the array.

12.6.2   Input and Output

FORTRAN/77 has features for reading and writing set entries that correspond to those discussed for pseudocode. Again, this is one of the few places where an array name can be used by itself. Thus, the entire 48 entry array of precipitations can be read in by the following statement.

```
READ *, PRECIP
```

All 48 data values for PRECIP must be arranged in *column-major* order. This form always requires enough data values (that is, 48) to fill each element in the array.

To provide flexibility in the range of problem sizes handled by a program, an array is usually declared with a maximum size of rows and columns sufficiently large to handle all expected cases. When working with such a general program, whether reading or manipulating elements of the array, it is necessary to specify the limits on the rows and columns appropriate for the current problem. For example, the number of rows and columns actually desired might be input as two additional data items preceding the array entries themselves. In the following program segment the initial READ statement obtains the number of rows and columns, NR and NC, from the first two data items and proceeds to read NR*NC values for the array in row-major order.

```
        READ *, NR, NC
        DO 200 R = 1, NR
            DO 100 C = 1, NC
                READ *, PRECIP(R,C)
100         CONTINUE
200 CONTINUE
```

The data stored in multidimensioned arrays is often presented in tabular form. Since printed output is produced one line at a time, the loop structures used will always generate a line of output from the innermost loop. To accumulate printed values on the same output line, the FORTRAN/77 implied DO–loop may be used. The following segment of FORTRAN/77 creates a simple table of the precipitation data stored in the array PRECIP:

```
        DO 100 R = 1, 12
            PRINT *, (PRECIP(R,C), C = 1, 4)
100 CONTINUE
```

If the table were to contain the row number on each line, then this value would have to be printed within the row loop, but before the innermost column loop, as follows:

```
      DO 100 R = 1, 12
         PRINT *, R, (PRECIP(R,C), C = 1, 4)
  100 CONTINUE
```

Headings for each of the table columns would have to be produced outside this entire loop structure, as has been done in the FORTRAN/77 program shown later in Figure 12.9. These input and output structures model the natural tabular form of multidimensional data.

The most flexible of all input/output statements involves the use of nested implied DO–loops such as:

```
  READ *, (PRECIP(R,C), C = 1, 4), R = 1, 12)
  PRINT *, (PRECIP(R,C), C = 1, 4), R = 1, 12)
```

in which the inner loop varying C is repeated for each value of R.

12.6.3 Processing
When processing entries of multidimensional arrays it is always necessary to specify a subscript for each dimension. The control of these subscript values will be handled by various loop structures. Examples of several loop structures are given in the next section.

12.6.4 Applications
To illustrate the use of arrays in FORTRAN/77, the rainfall analysis algorithm for Example 12.2, presented in pseudocode in Figure 12.8 has been translated into FORTRAN/77 as shown in Figure 12.9. The output produced by the program using the data from Figure 12.5 is listed in Figure 12.10.

12.7 Arrays and Modules

The idea of organizing commonly used routines as modules was first presented in Chapter 5. It is often desirable to create modules which make use of arrays of data.

In pseudocode, modules may use arrays without any special attention. Array names may appear in argument or parameter lists just as any other type of variable.

However, using arrays in FORTRAN/77 subprograms may require extra care when these arrays form part of the argument/parameter list. Naturally, the type, such as REAL or INTEGER, of an array used in an argument list must be the same as the type declared in the parameter list in the subprogram. Furthermore, it is important that the declared size and number of dimensions of the array be the same in both the calling program and the subprogram[1].

---

[1] There are exceptions to this rule which will not be discussed in this introduction.

```
C Figure 12.9 -- Rainfall Analysis Problem.
C               Given a table of rainfall readings at four locations
C               over a 12-month period, find the average rainfall
C               over that 12-month period and the wettest location
C               over the year.

C***********************************************************************

C PRECIP - precipitation in four locations
C R      - row index (month)
C C      - column index (location)
C SUM    - total rainfall for a location in a month
C AVG    - rainfall for the month
C LOCTOT - total rainfall for a location in a month
C RAIN   - current largest rainfall in a location
C WHERE  - location of largest rainfall

C***********************************************************************

      INTEGER R, C, WHERE
      REAL PRECIP(12,4), SUM, AVG, LOCTOT(4), RAIN

C Acquire and record the precipitation measurements.

      PRINT *, '        MONTH      NORTH           EAST           SOUTH',
     +'        WEST'
      PRINT *, ' '
      DO 100 R = 1, 12
          READ *, (PRECIP(R,C), C=1,4)
          PRINT *, R, (PRECIP(R,C), C=1,4)
  100 CONTINUE

C Find and record the average rainfall for each month.

      PRINT *, ' '
      DO 300 R = 1, 12
          SUM = 0.0
          DO 200 C = 1, 4
              SUM = SUM + PRECIP(R,C)
  200     CONTINUE
          AVG = SUM/4.0
          PRINT *, 'THE AVERAGE FOR MONTH', R,' IS', AVG
  300 CONTINUE

C Find the total rainfall for each location.

      PRINT *, ' '
      DO 500 C = 1, 4
          LOCTOT(C) = 0.0
          DO 400 R = 1, 12
              LOCTOT(C) = LOCTOT(C) + PRECIP(R,C)
  400     CONTINUE
          PRINT *, 'THE TOTAL RAINFALL FOR LOCATION', C,' IS', LOCTOT(C)
  500 CONTINUE

C Search for the largest total.

      PRINT *, ' '
      RAIN = -1.0
      WHERE = 0
      DO 600 C = 1, 4
          IF (LOCTOT(C) .GE. RAIN) THEN
                RAIN = LOCTOT(C)
                WHERE = C
          ENDIF
  600 CONTINUE
```

```
C Figure 12.9 (continued)
C Record the wettest location.
      PRINT *, 'THE WETTEST LOCATION IS', WHERE
      STOP
      END
```

Figure 12.10 Input and output files for the rainfall analysis program of Figure 12.9. (Spacing edited)

a) Input file:

```
12.4 13.5 12.1 12.6
 8.2  9.5  8.0  7.5
14.9 13.5 12.9 15.3
30.0 35.5 40.2 37.7
24.5 26.1 23.4 24.0
10.0  9.0  8.5  7.9
 4.0   .5  2.3  3.2
 3.4  0.0  4.5  6.1
 7.8  7.9  7.6  7.8
10.1 10.6 10.9 12.0
12.3 12.5 12.1 12.6
14.1 15.2 12.8  9.5
```

b) Output file:

MONTH	NORTH	EAST	SOUTH	WEST
1	12.40000	13.50000	12.10000	12.60000
2	8.200000	9.500000	8.000000	7.500000
3	14.90000	13.50000	12.90000	15.30000
4	30.00000	35.50000	40.20000	37.70000
5	24.50000	26.10000	23.40000	24.00000
6	10.00000	9.000000	8.500000	7.900000
7	4.000000	0.5000000	2.300000	3.200000
8	3.400000	0.0000000E+00	4.500000	6.100000
9	7.800000	7.900000	7.600000	7.800000
10	10.10000	10.60000	10.90000	12.00000
11	12.30000	12.50000	12.10000	12.60000
12	14.10000	15.20000	12.80000	9.500000

```
THE AVERAGE FOR MONTH        1  IS   12.65000
THE AVERAGE FOR MONTH        2  IS   8.300000
THE AVERAGE FOR MONTH        3  IS   14.15000
THE AVERAGE FOR MONTH        4  IS   35.85000
THE AVERAGE FOR MONTH        5  IS   24.50000
THE AVERAGE FOR MONTH        6  IS   8.850000
THE AVERAGE FOR MONTH        7  IS   2.500000
THE AVERAGE FOR MONTH        8  IS   3.500000
THE AVERAGE FOR MONTH        9  IS   7.775001
THE AVERAGE FOR MONTH       10  IS   10.90000
THE AVERAGE FOR MONTH       11  IS   12.37500
THE AVERAGE FOR MONTH       12  IS   12.90000

THE TOTAL RAINFALL FOR LOCATION        1  IS   151.7000
THE TOTAL RAINFALL FOR LOCATION        2  IS   153.8000
THE TOTAL RAINFALL FOR LOCATION        3  IS   155.3000
THE TOTAL RAINFALL FOR LOCATION        4  IS   156.2000

THE WETTEST LOCATION IS            4
```

At compile time the translated version of the subprogram is designed to handle arrays of the declared size. However, no space is set aside to contain the array entries. Rather, at execution time, the subprogram uses the space for the array in the calling program. Note that this may be different from the way in which ordinary or scalar variables are handled. However, the effect is the same; any change made to a parameter in a subprogram affects the value of the corresponding argument in the calling program. All of this activity is hidden from the FORTRAN/77 user and is, therefore, of minimal concern provided the array is properly declared.

The following example will provide some insight into the design and development of modules which use arrays. Both pseudocode and FORTRAN/77 versions of the module will be discussed.

Example 12.3 Minimum/Maximum Problem

Develop a module to find the largest and smallest entries in a given set of numbers. Test this module on the following three sets of data:

1) 12, 15, 18
2) 25, 25, 25
3) 10, 20, 0, 50

a) Problem Discussion Since very few guidelines are specified, the problem solver is given a lot of flexibility in approaching the problem. In such circumstances, it is tempting to be guided by the sample data. Assuming that the routine might be useful elsewhere, a good approach is to provide a module with few limitations on the user. Thus the number of elements contained in the array should be supplied by the caller. However, the type of data handled will have to be decided, and in this example, integer data will suffice. The module does not need to handle several sets of numbers at once, since the caller can invoke this module once for each different set.

b) A Minimum/Maximum Module The minimum/maximum module interface design must be based on the data imported and exported. Obviously two exports can be the smallest and the largest integers found. This forces the module to be a subroutine module, since more than a single result is computed from the array of numbers. The set of numbers must be accepted as an import parameter. The number of elements actually contained in the array must also be expected from the caller as an import parameter. The following module interface will suffice for the minmax module:

smodule minmax (**imports**: SET, num; **exports**: small, large)

In order to find the minimum and maximum values it will be necessary to scan all the entries in the array. To begin such a scan, some initial value must be assumed. In the rainfall analysis problem earlier, an initial negative value was chosen because it was known that all the rainfall data was nonnegative. One similar possibility is to use an arbitrary large guess for the smallest and an equivalent small guess for the largest. Another alternative which avoids guessing at the range of values is to assume that the first number in the array is both the smallest and largest and then to search for smaller or larger values in the remainder of the array. This second alternative is preferable since it removes any uncertainty about the range of numbers, although it assumes that there will always be a first element in the array. The pseudocode module minmax in Figure 12.11 uses this technique.

Figure 12.11   A pseudocode module to find the minimum and maximum elements in an array.

smodule minmax (**imports**: LIST, num; **exports**: small, large)

* Module **minmax** to find the smallest and
* largest entries in a given array of data.

* Variables used:
* **LIST** - given array of numbers
* **num** - number of entries in the array
* **small** - smallest entry found in the array
* **large** - largest entry found in the array

* Initialize the smallest and largest as the first entry.

small ← list$_1$
large ← list$_1$

* Search the rest of the array for better values.

for i **from** 2 **to** num **do**

⎡   **if** list$_i$ < small **then**

⎢   ⎡   small ← list$_i$

⎢   **else**

⎢   ⎡   **if** list$_i$ > large **then**

⎣   ⎣   ⎡   large ← list$_i$

end module

---

c) Main Module to Test the Three Sets of Numbers   Since the main module must handle several sets of numbers, an initial iterative decomposition can be used. Since the number of values in each set is not constant, the actual number must precede each set of input values. To provide an arbitrary number of sets of data, an end-of-data sentinel such as a negative count of values will mark the end of the last set. A pseudocode algorithm to use the module minmax to find the smallest and largest values in sets of data input this way is presented in Figure 12.12.

Figure 12.12   A pseudocode algorithm to test module minmax of Figure 12.11 on several sets of data.

```
* Main module to find the largest and smallest
* number in several sets of data.

* Variables used:
* LIST - the current list of data being searched
* count - the number of entries in the current list
* small - the smallest entry in the current list
* large - the largest entry in the current list

* Continue processing sets as long as the count is positive.

get count
while count > 0 do
    get (listᵢ, i from 1 to count)
    put 'The list of', count, 'numbers is:'
    put (listᵢ, i from 1 to count)
    call minmax(LIST, count; small, large)
    put 'The smallest entry is', small
    put 'The largest entry is', large
    get count
stop
```

d) Translation of minmax *into a* FORTRAN/77 *Subroutine*   With the previous discussions about defining arrays used with modules, the translation of minmax into FORTRAN/77 can proceed smoothly.   A little forethought about the maximum size of the array is required.   Since no specifications are given a limit of 100 is arbitrarily chosen.   It will also be assumed that the entries are integral.   The FORTRAN/77 version of MINMAX is presented in Figure 12.13.

e) A Mainline Program to Use Subroutine MINMAX   Translation of the main pseudocode module to FORTRAN/77 again requires introducing the type declarations for each variable.   Since the subprogram is designed to handle sets of maximum size 100 the mainline should use the same size for the array.   Organizing the input data also requires some care.   The length of each array to follow should be typed on a separate line since it is read separately.   This program is shown as Figure 12.14.   As a check that the program functions properly the output for the sample data is given in Figure 12.15.

```
C Figure 12.13 -- A Minimum/Maximum Module for an Array
C                  Subroutine MINMAX to find the smallest and largest
C                  entries in a given array of data.
C LIST     - given array of numbers
C NUM      - number of entries in the array
C SMALL    - smallest entry in the array
C LARGE    - largest entry in the array
C**********************************************************************
        SUBROUTINE MINMAX(LIST,NUM,SMALL,LARGE)

        INTEGER LIST(100), NUM, SMALL, LARGE, I
C Initialize the smallest and largest as the first entry.
        SMALL = LIST(1)
        LARGE = LIST(1)

C Search the rest of the array for better values.
        DO 100 I = 2, NUM
           IF (LIST(I) .LT. SMALL) THEN
              SMALL = LIST(I)
           ELSE
              IF (LIST(I) .GT. LARGE) THEN
                 LARGE = LIST(I)
              ENDIF
           ENDIF
   100  CONTINUE
        RETURN
        END
```

```
C Figure 12.14 -- A Largest/Smallest Array Element Problem.
C                  Program to find the largest and smallest
C                  numbers in several data lists.
C LIST     - the current list
C N        - the number of entries in the current list
C SMALL    - the smallest entry in the current list
C LARGE    - the largest entry in the current list
C**********************************************************************
        INTEGER LIST(100), N, SMALL, LARGE, I
C Continue processing arrays as long as N is positive.
        READ *, N
   100  IF (N .GT. 0) THEN
           READ *, (LIST(I), I = 1, N)
           PRINT *, 'THE LIST OF', N, ' NUMBERS IS:'
           PRINT *, (LIST(I), I = 1, N)
           CALL MINMAX(LIST,N,SMALL,LARGE)
           PRINT *, 'THE SMALLEST ENTRY IS', SMALL
           PRINT *, 'THE LARGEST  ENTRY IS', LARGE
           PRINT *, ' '
           READ *, N
           GOTO 100
        ENDIF
        STOP
        END
C Subroutine MINMAX is placed here.
```

Figure 12.15 Input and output files for the minimum/maximum program of Figure 12.14.

a) Input file:

```
3
12  15  18
3
25  25  25
4
10  20  0  50
-1
```

b) Output file:

```
THE  LIST  OF                3   NUMBERS  IS:
         12            15                18
THE  SMALLEST  ENTRY  IS              12
THE  LARGEST   ENTRY  IS              18

THE  LIST  OF                3   NUMBERS  IS:
         25            25                25
THE  SMALLEST  ENTRY  IS              25
THE  LARGEST   ENTRY  IS              25

THE  LIST  OF                4   NUMBERS  IS:
         10            20               0          50
THE  SMALLEST  ENTRY  IS               0
THE  LARGEST   ENTRY  IS              50
```

12.8 Summary

This chapter has introduced the problem of handling large amounts of data which must be retained in storage for processing more than once. A natural organization, called an array, which models a mathematical vector or matrix, was introduced. The use of arrays in both pseudocode and FORTRAN/77 covered several examples of typical algorithms. Special considerations when arrays are used in modules provide the means to create flexible modules that process large amounts of data. Further chapters will extend the applications in which arrays will be useful.

12.9 References

Aho, A.V.; Hopcroft, J.E.; and Ullman, J.D., *Data Structures and Algorithms*, Reading, Ma.: Addison-Wesley Publishing Co., 1983.

Horowitz, E. and Sahni, S., *Fundamentals of Data Structures*, Woodland Hills, Ca.: Computer Science Press, 1976.

Tremblay, J.P. and Sorenson, P.G. *An Introduction to Data Structures with Applications.* New York: McGraw-Hill Book Co., 1976.

Wirth, N.   *Algorithms + Data Structures = Programs.* Englewood Cliffs, N.J.:
   Prentice-Hall, 1976.

12.10   Exercises

In most of the following exercises a program is requested to solve a specific problem.
For each problem it is recommended that step-wise refinement be used in developing a
pseudocode algorithm to solve the problem.   This algorithm should then be translated
into FORTRAN/77 and run on the computer.   Where appropriate, the program should be
tested with a variety of data sufficient to ensure that the program does what it is
supposed to do.   In some cases, this will involve writing a main program to test the
required module.

12.1   Give the output produced by the following pseudocode algorithm, and explain
the difference between the two lines of output.

```
get n, (listᵢ, i from 1 to n)
put LIST
limit ← int(n/2)
i ← 1
while i ≤ limit do
    ┌ temp ← listᵢ
    │ listᵢ ← listₙ₋ᵢ₊₁
    │ listₙ₋ᵢ₊₁ ← temp
    └ i ← i + 1
put LIST
stop
5, 10, 20, 30, 40, 50
```

12.2   Consider the following FORTRAN/77 program.

```
C Exercise 12.2
        INTEGER LIST(50), N, I, ENTRY
        LOGICAL FLAG
        N = 0
        READ *, ENTRY
 100 IF (ENTRY .NE. 0) THEN
            I = 1
            FLAG = .FALSE.
 200    IF (I .LE. N .AND. .NOT. FLAG) THEN
            IF (ENTRY .EQ. LIST(I)) THEN
                FLAG = .TRUE.
            ELSE
                I = I + 1
            ENDIF
            GOTO 200
        ENDIF
        IF (.NOT. FLAG) THEN
            N = N + 1
            LIST(N) = ENTRY
        ENDIF
        READ *, ENTRY
        GOTO 100
    ENDIF
    DO 300 I = 1, N
        PRINT *, LIST(I)
 300 CONTINUE
    STOP
    END
```

a)   What output would the program produce if the data was supplied in the following order?

            10 10 20 30 20 40 40 50 0

b)   In general, what is the purpose of the program? A one sentence answer should be sufficient.

12.3   For each of the following FORTRAN/77 programs, circle and briefly explain the error(s) (there may be more than one). Also specify whether each error would be detected at compile-time or execution-time.

```
        INTEGER I, SUM
        SUM = LIST(1)
        I = 2
 100 IF (I < 5) THEN
            SUM = SUM + LIST(I)
            I = I + 1
            GOTO 100
        ENDIF
        PRINT *, SUM
        STOP
        END
order of data values:
4 1 2 5 3
```

```
          INTEGER N, I
          N = 10
          INTEGER SET(N)
          I = 11
    100 IF (I .GT. 0) DO
             READ *,
             PRINT *, LIST(11-I)
             I = I - 1
             GOTO 100
          ENDIF
          STOP
          END
     order of data values:
     6, 12, 4, 13, 2, 5, 20, 18, 7, 4
```

12.4   The prime number classification algorithm presented in Chapter 4 involved test-ing odd divisors from 2 to the square root of the number. Ideally, it is only necessary to check for divisibility by the prime numbers less than the square root. This can only be accomplished if the necessary primes are stored in a list. Develop a program to generate a list of the first 100 prime numbers by taking advantage of numbers already in the list.

12.5   A popular exercise in generating primes was suggested by the Greek mathemati-cian, Eratosthenes, and is called the Sieve of Eratosthenes. As an illustration of how the method works, consider confining the search to the integers from 1 to 200. The algorithm begins with an ordered list of the integers. Starting with the first prime (2), all further multiples of this prime are eliminated from consideration (perhaps by setting these list entries to zero). The next prime will be the first integer following the current prime which has not been eliminated. Multiples of this prime are then eliminated, and again the remaining integers are searched for the next prime. The algorithm continues until the current prime is greater than $\sqrt{200}$. Develop a program to simulate this method of generating primes.

12.6   In the physical sciences the term *vector* is often used to denote a quantity such as force or velocity, which has both a magnitude and direction. Geometrically, vectors can be represented by directed line segments. With every such vector v can be associated a triplet of numbers, (v_x, v_y, v_z) called the components of the vector. The length of the vector, v, denoted by $|v|$, is defined as:

$$|\mathbf{v}| = \sqrt{v_x^2 + v_y^2 + v_z^2}$$

The inner product of two vectors, $\mathbf{u}$ and $\mathbf{v}$, denoted $\mathbf{u} \cdot \mathbf{v}$, is defined as:

$$\mathbf{u} \cdot \mathbf{v} = u_x \times v_x + u_y \times v_y + u_z \times v_z$$

The angle between any two vectors $\mathbf{u}$ and $\mathbf{v}$ is given by:

$$\cos^{-1} \left[\frac{\mathbf{u} \cdot \mathbf{v}}{|\mathbf{u}| \; |\mathbf{v}|} \right]$$

a)   Write a program to find the angle between two 3-dimensional vectors. The program should handle an arbitrary number of such pairs.

b)   Generalize the program of part a) to find the angle between two
n-dimensional vectors.

12.7   Given n points on the Euclidean plane with coordinates (x_i, y_i), $i = 1, 2, \ldots , n$,
then the perimeter of the enclosed area is given by the following formula.

$$\sum_{i=1}^{n-1} \sqrt{(x_{i+1} - x_i)^2 + (y_{i+1} - y_i)^2} + \sqrt{(x_1 - x_n)^2 + (y_1 - y_n)^2}$$

Develop a program to compute the perimeter of the area enclosed by a given set
of n coordinate pairs.

12.8   Given n points on the Euclidean plane with coordinates (x_i, y_i), $i = 1, 2, \ldots , n$,
then an approximation to the enclosed area is given by the following formula.

$$\frac{1}{2} \sum_{i=1}^{n-1} [(x_{i+1} - x_i) \times (y_{i+1} + y_i)] + \frac{1}{2} [(x_1 - x_n) \times (y_1 + y_n)]$$

Develop a program to compute this approximation to the area enclosed by a
given set of n coordinate pairs.

12.9   Give the output produced by the following pseudocode algorithm, and give the
meaning of the variable x.

```
get m, n
get ((ar,c, c from 1 to n), r from 1 to m)
x ← 0
row ← 0
col ← 0
for r from 1 to m do
        for c from 1 to n do
                if x < ar,c then
                        x ← ar,c
                        row ← r
                        col ← c
put x, row, col
stop
3, 2, 10, 16, 14, 16, 16, 12
```

12.10   Suppose that a checkerboard is represented by an 8 by 8 array called **BOARD**.
Thus, $board_{1,1}$ represents the upper left-hand corner, $board_{1,8}$ represents the upper
right-hand corner, $board_{8,1}$ represents the lower left-hand corner, and $board_{8,8}$
represents the lower right-hand corner.

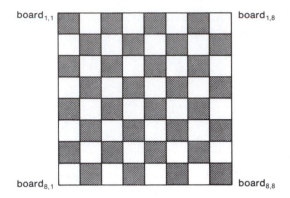

board$_{1,1}$ ... board$_{1,8}$

board$_{8,1}$ ... board$_{8,8}$

A 0 could be stored in board$_{i,j}$ if position (i,j) is empty; a 1 could be stored in board$_{i,j}$ if position (i,j) contains a red piece or red king, and a 2 could be stored in board$_{i,j}$ if position (i,j) contains a black piece or black king.

a) Write a FORTRAN/77 program that "sets" some checkers on **BOARD** (this could be accomplished by reading 64 digits into the array). Then the program should scan the matrix to count how many squares are empty, how many are occupied by red checkers, and how many are occupied by black checkers. Finally, the program should record the respective totals.

b) Modify your solution to part a) to verify that the checkers are correctly located and that no checkers are on the wrong colored square. Any erroneous locations should be recorded and added to a separate total.

12.11   A magic square is a square array such that each of the following quantities has the same value:

• the sum of the elements in each row
• the sum of the elements in each column
• the sum of the elements along each diagonal.

The following 3 × 3 array is an example since all of the above quantities have the sum 15.

$$\begin{bmatrix} 4 & 9 & 2 \\ 3 & 5 & 7 \\ 8 & 1 & 6 \end{bmatrix}$$

Develop a module to determine if a given array is a magic square.

12.12   a) Develop a module to produce a list of the divisors (including 1 and itself) for any given integer.

b) It has been conjectured that for any integer the sum of the cubes of its divisors is equal to the square of the sum of its divisors. Write a program to test this conjecture on the integers from 1 to 100.

12.13   a) Develop a module to remove all the negative entries from a given list. Do not make use of a second list in this process.

b) Develop a program to test the module of part a) on the following lists.

1)   12, 14.5, 5.4, 9.56
2)   − 3.4, 4.5, 5.6, − 4.2, − 7.8, 6.7, − 8.9
3)   − 1, − 2, − 3, − 4, − 5

12.14 a) Develop a module to take a given list and produce a second list with the entries of the first list in reverse order.

  b) Modify the module of part a) to return the reversed entries in the same list. Do not use a second list to reverse the entries. It should only be necessary to use one other variable for storage.

12.15 When considering investments it is useful to have access to tables listing the compounded amount over a number of years for a variety of interest rates. Develop a program to produce such a table for an initial investment of one dollar at rates of 5%, 6%, 7%, 8%, 9%, and 10% invested for 1, 2, 3, . . . , and 20 years.

12.16 One method of normalizing a set of data consists of reducing the range of data to between 0 and 1. Thus, the smallest value becomes 0, the largest becomes 1, and all other values are between the two. Develop a module to normalize a given set of data.

12.17 The greatest common divisor (GCD) of a group of numbers is the largest integer that will divide evenly into each number, for example,

  a) the GCD of 45, 295, 75, and 1900 is 5,
  b) the GCD of 42, 63, and 84 is 21, and
  c) the GCD of 7, 13, 17, and 25 is 1.

  Develop a module to find the GCD for an arbitrary group of numbers.

12.18 Develop a function module called REPEAT to perform a repeated operation on successive elements of a list and return the result as the value of the function. The function is given a, the list of entries, n, the number of entries in a, and oper, the name of a function module designed to take two arguments and perform the required operation on them. For example, if the elements of the list are:

$$a_1, a_2, a_3, . . . , a_n$$

then the function will calculate:

$$a_1 \square a_2 \square a_3 \square \cdots \square a_n$$

where $\square$ represents the operation to be performed. For instance, to calculate the product of the elements of a list it would be necessary to write a function module such as the one given below and then use it in the call to function REPEAT.

```
REAL FUNCTION MULT(X,Y)
REAL X, Y
MULT = X*Y
RETURN
END
```

12.19   In some mathematical problems it is desirable to perform arithmetic to higher accuracy than is possible using available computing machinery. In cases like this the individual digits of a number are stored in a list and arithmetic operations are performed using the list entries. Develop a series of modules to add, subtract, multiply, and divide n-digit integers. The modules should be able to handle at least 25-digit integers.

12.20   A real polynomial of degree n is an expression of the form:

$$p(x) = a_1 + a_2 x + a_3 x^2 + \cdots + a_i x^{i-1} + \cdots + a_{n+1} x^n,$$

where the a_i are real numbers called coefficients. The x's are merely symbols used as "place-holders" and in themselves have no meaning. For computer implementation, it is convenient to think of polynomials as just a finite sequence of real numbers

$$(a_1, a_2, a_3, \ldots, a_{n+1})$$

which can be stored as entries of an array A of length $n + 1$.

a)   In Chapter 6, Horner's rule was introduced as an efficient way to evaluate polynomials. Develop a module which uses Horner's rule to evaluate a given n-th degree polynomial for a specific given value of x.

b)   The derivative of an n-th degree polynomial is given by the following expression.

$$p'(x) = a_2 + 2a_3 x + 3a_4 x^2 + \cdots + (i-1)a_i x^{i-2} + \cdots + na_{n+1} x^{n-1}$$

Develop a module which uses Horner's rule to evaluate the derivative of a given n-th degree polynomial for a specific value of x.

c)   Chapter 7 includes a discussion of Newton's method for approximating the zero of a function. Develop a module to use Newton's method to approximate a zero of a given n-th degree polynomial function for a given starting value.

d)   Develop a program to use the modules of parts a), b), and c) to approximate as many zeros as possible for any n-th degree polynomial of size $n \leq 25$. Test the program on the following polynomials.

1) $p(x) = -25.25 - 17.75x + 17.25x^2 + 9.75x^3 + x^4$
2) $p(x) = -254 + 5078x - 40x^2 - 242x^3 + 2x^5$

e)   There is a rule in algebra called the "Descartes Rule of Signs" which states that:

1)   the maximum number of positive real zeros of a polynomial is given by the number of sign changes in the coefficents

2)   the maximum number of negative real zeros of a polynomial is given by the number of sign changes in the coefficents when x is replaced by $-x$.

Develop a program to use this rule to determine the maximum number of positive and negative real zeros for an n-th degree polynomial.

f)   Develop a module to find the sum polynomial, $C = A + B$, of two polynomials A (of degree m) and B (of degree n).

g)   Develop a module to find the product polynomial, $C = A \times B$, of two polynomials A (of degree m) and B (of degree n). The i-th term of the product polynomial will be the sum of all terms of the form $a_q b_r$ with $q + r = i + 1$, that is,

$$c_i = a_1 b_i + a_2 b_{i-1} + a_3 b_{i-2} + \cdots + a_i b_1$$

h)   If A is a polynomial of degree m, B is a polynomial of degree n, and C is a polynomial of degree p, then develop a program which uses the modules of parts f) and g) to compute the polynomial $A^2 + B \times C$.

12.21   In mathematics, the term matrix is often used to describe a rectangular array of numbers. An $m \times n$ matrix A is a rectangular array having m rows and n columns

$$A = \begin{bmatrix} a_{1,1} & a_{1,2} & \cdots & a_{1,n} \\ a_{2,1} & a_{2,2} & \cdots & a_{2,n} \\ \cdot & \cdot & & \cdot \\ \cdot & \cdot & & \cdot \\ \cdot & \cdot & & \cdot \\ a_{m,1} & a_{m,2} & \cdots & a_{m,n} \end{bmatrix}$$

Develop modules to perform each of the following tasks.

a)   Create an $n \times n$ identity matrix.

b)   Find the sum of two $m \times n$ matrices.

c)   Find the product of an $m \times n$ and an $n \times p$ matrix.

d)   Determine if a given $n \times n$ matrix is upper triangular.

e)   Find the transpose of a given $n \times n$ matrix.

f)   Determine if a given $n \times n$ matrix is symmetric.

g)   Interchange the two diagonals of a given $n \times n$ matrix.

h)   Exchange two rows of a given $m \times n$ matrix.

i)   Exchange two columns of a given $m \times n$ matrix.

12.22   A *Latin square* of order n consists of n distinct symbols, each occurring n times, arranged in the form of a square matrix in such a way that every row and every column is a permutation of the n symbols. Illustrated below are a 3 by 3 and a 5 by 5 Latin square.

```
A   B   C              0   1   2   3   4

C   A   B              1   2   3   4   0

B   C   A              2   3   4   0   1

                       3   4   0   1   2

                       4   0   1   2   3
```

Two Latin squares of order *n* are called *orthogonal* if, when the squares are superimposed, each element of the first square occurs exactly once with each element of the second square. Consider the following two 4 by 4 Latin squares.

```
a   b   c   d          a   b   c   d

b   a   d   c          c   d   a   b

c   d   a   b          d   c   b   a

d   c   b   a          b   a   d   c
```

When superimposed, the following pairs occur in each cell. Notice that each pair only occurs once.

```
a,a   b,b   c,c   d,d

b,c   a,d   d,a   c,b

c,d   d,c   a,b   b,a

d,b   c,a   b,d   a,c
```

Using top-down design and step-wise refinement, develop a pseudocode algorithm to obtain any two square arrays and to determine whether or not they represent orthogonal Latin squares. Your algorithm should be able to specify which combinations occurred more than once and which did not occur. For simplicity, you may assume that the symbols used for an order *n* Latin square are the digits from 1 to *n*. It is necessary to verify that each square is a Latin square, perhaps through the use of a module.

Translate your algorithm into FORTRAN/77 and test it using the two squares above (note that a 1 can be substituted for the a's, a 2 for the b's, etc.). Also test your program with your attempts to find an orthogonal Latin square for the following 5 by 5 Latin square. Include at least one listing that demonstrates the error diagnosing abilities of your algorithm.

```
3   4   5   1   2

1   2   3   4   5

4   5   1   2   3

2   3   4   5   1

5   1   2   3   4
```

13
Searching and Sorting Techniques

13.1 Introduction

The topic of organizing and manipulating collections of data was first introduced in Chapter 12. This chapter will discuss two types of operations frequently applied to a list of data, namely, searching and sorting.

Naturally, the idea of a search is to find something. Each day a person spends time looking for things, whether it be for a matching sock in a drawer, a particular car in a parking lot, or a word in a dictionary. With computer applications the item sought is usually a value such as a specific entry in a list of numbers, or the largest number in a list. Computers can be quite useful because they can deal with very large lists. For example, a request by the police to identify the owner of a particular vehicle with a given license number requires the search of potentially several million items on file.

Ordering information according to a predetermined criterion is also common in everyday life and provides the motivation for sorting. For example, playing cards are organized by rank within suit for convenience in playing such games as hearts or bridge. Names in a telephone directory must be listed in alphabetical order within towns or cities for easy reference. Of course, the telephone company also maintains lists ordered by telephone number as well as by street. The large size of these telephone lists necessitates the use of a computer in their production and maintenance.

The two topics of searching and sorting are usually discussed together since some searching techniques require a presorted list, and many sorting methods involve searching for values. Since searching and sorting are such common operations in computer processing, many different algorithms and approaches have been developed. One factor in the choice of algorithm is the storage medium for the data. Algorithms for *internally* stored data rely on the fast access times for data in random access computer memory. Algorithms for *externally* stored data must contend with the longer access times and the larger capacities of external storage media, such as magnetic tape and disk files.

Although searching and sorting techniques exist for both internally and externally stored data, the discussion here will be limited to internal sorting techniques. Algorithms for externally stored data are included in the texts referenced at the end of the chapter.

13.2   Searching Techniques

The problem of searching a list of data may take many forms. The purpose of the search may be to determine the absence or presence of an entry, to locate its position in the list, or to find the frequency of occurrence.

The choice of a searching technique depends on several factors such as the order and size of the list and whether or not the search must be repeated. If there is no order to the entries in a list, then the items must be examined one at a time until the desired item is found (a linear search). However, if the list is ordered (such as an alphabetical listing of words in a dictionary), it may be possible to use a more sophisticated approach such as a binary search. Intuitively, for short lists and infrequent searches, one would expect a simple method to be sufficient. However, for long lists and frequent references, a more elaborate method involving a prior ordering of the list may be appropriate.

This section examines two approaches to locating the position of a particular item in a list of numbers: the linear and binary search techniques. Each technique is discussed and implemented as a module to allow for inclusion in a library. The label of the item being sought is usually referred to as a *key*. Hence, these modules are all designed to locate a value called key in a list named LIST having n entries. The position of key will be returned in an export parameter called place.

13.2.1   Simple Linear Searches

The most straightforward method of finding the position of a specific value in a list of numbers is to compare the key value with each entry in the list, checking for equality. A first approach is illustrated by the following pseudocode. This segment compares key with each of the n elements in LIST. When a match is found, place is given the value of the location, loc.

for loc **from** 1 **to** n **do**
    if key = list$_{loc}$ **then**
        place ← loc

Several observations can be made about this approach. Firstly, should the key not appear at all, the variable place will remain undefined. Secondly, even if a match is found, the algorithm stubbornly continues to the end of the list, an obvious inefficiency.

The linear search module of Figure 13.1 illustrates a solution to both of these problems. This module, named linear, accepts as imports LIST, n, and key and returns, as exports, place and found. The variable found has been introduced to reflect whether or not the key has been located. The logical variable found is initialized to **false** prior to the search, then changed to **true** when the position of key is found. The **while**–loop uses **found** to terminate the search if a match is found before the list is exhausted.   It is important to realize that such a compound condition precludes the use of a **for**–loop. Furthermore, the counter loc is incremented within an **else** action which could not be done in a **for**–loop.

Figure 13.1   A pseudocode module for a linear search.

smodule linear (**imports**: LIST, n, key; **exports**: place, found)

```
* Module to use a linear search to find the place of a given key value
* in a given LIST of length n.
* The found export is true if key is found in the list, otherwise is false.

* Variables used:
* LIST - given list of numbers
* n - given number of entries in the list
* key - given value to be found in the list
* place - position of key in the list
* found - truth of 'key is found in list'
* loc - location of current entry in the list
```

found ← **false**
loc ← 1
while loc ≤ n **and not** found **do**
⎡ **if** key = list$_{loc}$ **then**
⎢ ⎡ place ← loc
⎢ ⎣ found ← **true**
⎢ **else**
⎣ ⎡ loc ← loc + 1

end module

This module will determine the correct position of a value regardless of the order of the entries in the list.   Thus, for an *unordered* list, the algorithm will require an average of n/2 iterations through the loop and, therefore, n/2 comparisons between the key and LIST entries.   If the value is not located, exactly n comparisons will be made.

If the list is *ordered*, then improvements to the module are possible.   The condition used to terminate the **while**–loop can be expanded to take advantage of the ordering for items not found in the list.   For instance, if the list is sorted in ascending order, the search can be terminated as soon as a LIST value is greater than key.   Likewise, if the list is in descending order, the search ends when a LIST value is less than key.   Thus, for an *ordered* list, the average number of comparisons is always n/2 regardless of whether the item is found or not.

13.2.2   A Binary Search

The linear search techniques presented in the previous section, while simple to understand and easy to write, are time consuming for long lists of numbers.   This is undesirable, particularly if the search operation is to be applied frequently.   In such situations it is usually expedient to maintain the list sorted in ascending or descending order and to use a more sophisticated but faster search technique. Such an improved search technique can be modeled on the way a person looks for a name in a telephone directory or the way in which the bisection algorithm approached the problem of zero-finding, as discussed in Chapter 7.

The technique is called a *binary search* and starts by comparing the key with the middle entry in the current sorted list. Note that there may be two middle entries for lists of even length but nothing is lost by choosing either arbitrarily. If a match is found, the search is over. Otherwise, if the key is less than the middle entry, the search can be confined to the first half of the list. Similarly, if the key is greater than the middle entry, the search is confined to the second half of the list. In either case, the same logic is then applied to the middle entry in the new list. This new list will be approximately half the size of the previous list. The process continues until either a match is found or until the list can no longer be subdivided. In the latter case the key is not in the original list.

Consider the list of 15 numbers

5, 6, 9, 12, 13, 20, 23, 29, 30, 41, 45, 49, 60, 65, 78

which have been sorted into ascending order. Suppose that it is necessary to determine the locations of several values in the list. The diagram in Figure 13.2 shows the actions involved in performing a binary search on the list for the key value **20**. The complete list is indexed as it would be for computer processing. The key is compared to the middle or eighth entry and is found to be less than the value **29**. Thus, the first half of the list becomes the subject of the next search. This time the middle entry is in position four, and since the key is greater than **12**, the second half of this list, that is, positions five through seven, form the subsequent list. After another comparison, the key is found to be equal to the value of the middle entry (position six).

Figure 13.2 A binary search for the value **20** in a sorted list. The shaded portion of the list represents the current sublist after successive comparisons.

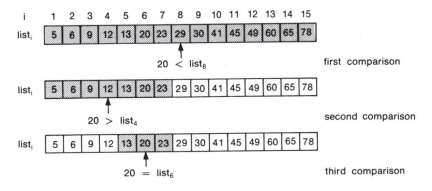

As a second example, Figure 13.3 demonstrates an attempt to find the key value **40** in the same list of 15 numbers.   In this case, however, the value does not appear in the list and the search terminates when the key value fails to match the only entry remaining in the sublist.

Figure 13.3   A binary search for the (absent) value **30** in a sorted list. The shaded portion of the list represents the current sublist after successive comparisons.

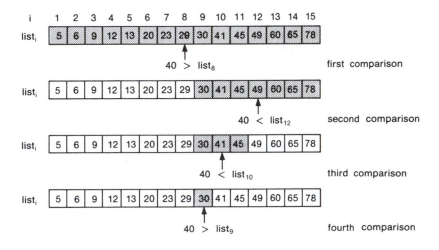

a) Developing the Algorithm   With the understanding gained from these numerical examples, an algorithm for the binary search can now be developed.   The binary search algorithm will also be developed as a module and will have the same parameters as module linear, namely LIST, n, and key as imports and place and found for exports.   The initial description of the binary search module is given in Figure 13.4.

Figure 13.4   First version of a pseudocode module for a binary search.

smodule binary (**imports**: LIST, n, key; **exports**: place, found)

1.   Find the place of key in LIST of n entries using a binary search technique.

end module

b) Refining Step **1.**   While considering the previous numerical examples it was clear that the portion of the list being considered at any stage of the search kept changing. It is therefore necessary to retain some means of referring to each end of the current list. These references are called *pointers* and are simply variables whose values indicate a position in a list.   In this case two pointers will be used, called low and high.   The search for the key will continue as long as a list exists, that is, as long as low ≤ high.

However, the search should stop if the key is found. As with the linear search, a logical variable called found will be used to terminate the search when the key has been found. It will be set to **false** prior to the search to indicate that the key has not been located yet and changed to **true** if the key value is found. The resulting refinement of Step **1**. follows.

> * Initialize the sublist to search, and the found flag.

low ← 1
high ← n
found ← **false**

> * Continue to search as long as key has not yet been
> * found, and the sublist has not been exhausted.

while not found **and** low ≤ high **do**

> **1.3** Perform a binary search for key on the sublist bounded by low and high setting found and place if key is found.

c) Refining Step **1.3** At each stage in a binary search it is necessary to determine the middle entry of the current list and compare the middle entry of LIST with key. Either key will be equal to the middle entry or it will be necessary to choose the left or right sublist for further consideration. The appropriate refinement follows.

> * Compute the position of the middle entry.

middle ← int [(low + high)/2]
if key = list$_{middle}$ **then**

> **1.3.2** Remember the position of the key and indicate that it has been found.

else

> **1.3.3** Refine the list for the subsequent search.

d) Refining Step **1.3.2** The position of key is given by the current value of middle. To indicate that key has been found, found is set to **true**.

> * key has been found: remember where and set flag.

place ← middle
found ← **true**

e) Refining Step **1.3.3** For the subsequent search, the list is confined to the first or second half of the current list. If the key is less than the current middle entry, move the high pointer to the left of the middle entry, that is to middle−1. Otherwise the key must be greater than the middle entry and the low pointer is moved to the right of the middle entry, that is to middle+1.

* Refine the sublist by eliminating top or bottom half.

if key < list$_{middle}$ **then**

$\left[\right.$ high $\leftarrow$ middle $-$ 1

else

$\left[\right.$ low $\leftarrow$ middle $+$ 1

f) The Final Algorithm   The algorithm is now complete and is presented in Figure 13.5.

Figure 13.5   Final version of the pseudocode module for a binary search.

smodule binary (**imports**: LIST, n, key; **exports**: place, found)

* Module to search a given list of length n for a
* given key, and to return a flag whether the key was
* found and the place it was found.}

* Variables used:
* **LIST** - given list of numbers
* **n** - length of given list
* **key** - given value to find in list
* **place** - list index of **key**, if found
* **found** - truth of 'key is in the list'
* **low** - index of first entry in the current sublist
* **high** - index of last entry in the current sublist
* **middle** - index of middle entry in the current sublist

* Initialize the sublist to seach, and the found flag.

low $\leftarrow$ 1
high $\leftarrow$ n
found $\leftarrow$ **false**

* Continue to search as long as **key** has not yet been
* found, and the sublist has not been exhausted.

while not found **and** low $\leq$ high **do**

$\left[\right.$ * Compute the position of the middle entry.

middle $\leftarrow$ int [(low + high)/2]
if key = list$_{middle}$ **then**

$\left[\right.$ * key has been found: remember where and set flag.

place $\leftarrow$ middle
found $\leftarrow$ **true**

else

$\left[\right.$ * Refine the sublist by eliminating top or bottom half.

if key < list$_{middle}$ **then**

$\left[\right.$ high $\leftarrow$ middle $-$ 1

else

$\left[\right.$ low $\leftarrow$ middle $+$ 1

end module

---

g) Program for the Final Version of the Algorithm   Whereas a linear search is relatively easy to write, a binary search is somewhat longer and would be a valuable addition to a personal library of programs if not available elsewhere.   A FORTRAN/77 implementation of module binary is presented in Figure 13.6.

```
C Figure 13.6 -- A Binary Search Module.
C                 A subprogram to search a given list of length N
C                 for a given KEY, and to return a flag to indicate
C                 whether or not the key was found and the place
C                 it was found.
C***********************************************************************
C LIST    - given list of numbers
C N       - length of given list
C NMAX    - given maximum value for N
C KEY     - given value to find in list
C PLACE   - list index of KEY if found
C FOUND   - truth of 'KEY is in the list'
C LOW     - index of first entry in the current sublist
C HIGH    - index of last entry in the current sublist
C MIDDLE  - index of the middle entry in the current sublist
C***********************************************************************
        SUBROUTINE BINARY(LIST, NMAX, N, KEY, PLACE, FOUND)
        INTEGER NMAX, LIST(NMAX), N, KEY, PLACE
        INTEGER LOW, HIGH, MIDDLE
        LOGICAL FOUND
C Initialize the sublist to search and the found flag.
        LOW = 1
        HIGH = N
        FOUND = .FALSE.
C Continue to search as long as KEY has not yet been found
C and the sublist has not been exhausted
   100 IF (.NOT.FOUND .AND. LOW .LE. HIGH) THEN
C        Compute the position of the middle entry.
        MIDDLE = (LOW + HIGH)/2
        IF (KEY .EQ. LIST(MIDDLE)) THEN
C          KEY has been found; remember where and set flag.
          PLACE = MIDDLE
          FOUND = .TRUE.
        ELSE
C          Refine the sublist by eliminating top or bottom half.
          IF (KEY .LT. LIST(MIDDLE)) THEN
             HIGH = MIDDLE - 1
          ELSE
             LOW = MIDDLE + 1
          ENDIF
        ENDIF
        GOTO 100
      ENDIF
      RETURN
      END
```

Program Notes

- An additional import parameter, NMAX, has been added to represent the maximum size of LIST as declared in the calling program.   This allows the subroutine to specify a variable size for LIST and yet agree with the calling program.   This feature of FORTRAN/77 is called *variable dimensioning*. A variable dimension can only be used in a subprogram.   The dimension must be an import parameter, and its value must be less than or equal to the declared size of the list in the calling program.

13.2.3   Efficiency of Linear Versus Binary Searches

The principle of the binary search is repeated division of the list into two sublists.   The maximum number of comparisons needed to find an entry or to determine that the key is not in the list is, therefore, the number of times the length of the list can be divided by two.   Mathematically this can be expressed as

$$\lfloor \log_2 n \rfloor + 1$$

This formula gives the maximum number of comparisons required.   While it is possible to derive an expression for the average number of comparisons necessary, that formula is complex and gives little added information.

The table below contrasts the *average* number of comparisons required by the linear search with the *maximum* number of comparisons needed for a binary search for several lists of length *n*.   In each case it is assumed that the list is presorted.

n	4	8	16	128	512	1024	1048576	
linear	2	4	8	64	256	512	524288	*average*
binary	3	4	5	8	10	11	21	*maximum*

Notice how much better the binary search is for larger values of *n*.   It should be remembered, however, that a binary search can only be used with an ordered list.

13.3   Sorting Techniques

Since sorting is such a common and necessary activity in computer applications there are literally dozens of sorting techniques described in the literature.   There are two overall classes of techniques, those involving only internal storage and those that also use external storage devices.   The discussion to follow will investigate examples of several classic algorithms which use only internal storage.   These are a selection method, an exchange method, and an insertion method.   A relatively modern method called Quicksort which is a combination of these techniques is also discussed.   In all cases, the sorting method will be developed to sort the numbers in ascending order.

13.3.1   A Simple Selection Sort

A simple selection sort most closely approximates how a list of numbers might be sorted by hand using pencil and paper.   The given list of numbers is scanned from beginning to end to find the smallest value.   This number is copied to a new list while its entry in the old list is destroyed to remove it from further consideration (by hand the entry might be crossed out; by computer the entry might be replaced by a very large number). Then the modified old list is searched again to find the next smallest number. When found, this number is placed at the end of the new list and its original in the old list is destroyed. The selection process continues until the old list is depleted.

This technique is illustrated for a sample list of numbers in Figure 13.7. During the first pass the smallest value of 3 is found in position four. Thus 3 becomes the first entry in the new list, and the fourth entry in the old list is removed from consideration. On the second pass the number 4 in position five is smallest. It is appended to the new list, and its entry in the old list is destroyed. In this way the algorithm continues selecting 7, 7, 8, and 9 to form the sorted new list.

Figure 13.7 Example of a simple selection sort. The shaded portion of the list represents the current sublist after successive comparisons.

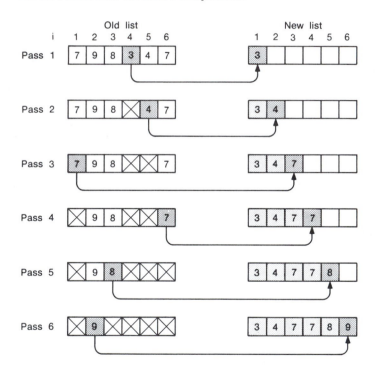

---

a) Developing the Algorithm   Since this algorithm may be of value in other algorithms, it will be developed as a module designed to accept an unsorted list, OLD, of n numbers and produce a second list, NEW, sorted in increasing order. A first version is given in Figure 13.8.

Figure 13.8   First version of a pseudocode module for a selection sort.

smodule select (**imports**: OLD, n; **exports**: NEW)
1.   Sort the entries of list OLD into list NEW using a simple selection sort.
end module

---

b) Refining Step **1.**   The selection process is repeated once for each number in the original list.   For each pass through the original list it is necessary to find the smallest number in the old list, copy it to the new list, and remove it from the old list.   In the refinement below, these three steps are imbedded in a loop controlled by a counter variable, **pass**, that will increment from 1 to n.

> * During each **pass**, find the smallest entry in OLD,
> * copy it to list NEW, and destroy it in list OLD.

1.1 for pass **from** 1 **to** n **do**

> **1.2** Find the smallest value in OLD.
>
> **1.3** Copy this smallest value to NEW.
>
> **1.4** Destroy the original in OLD.

c) Refining Step **1.2**   Finding the smallest value in a list was described as part of the module minmax in Chapter 12.   Unfortunately, this module does not return the position of the smallest element.   However, such a modification to do this is easy to incorporate.   As well, the code to find the largest entry can be deleted from the module.   A modified module called min is presented in Figure 13.9.

With this module available, Step **1.2** of the algorithm can be expressed by the following module reference:

>   min(OLD, n; small, place)

d) Refining Step **1.3**   During each pass, another number will be appended to list NEW. Its position is given quite simply by the value of **pass**.   Thus, the refinement of Step **1.3** becomes

> $new_{pass} \leftarrow small$

e) Refining Step **1.4**   Destroying the smallest value in the old list can be accomplished by changing it to a very large number, for example,

> $old_{place} \leftarrow \infty$

f) The Final Algorithm   Collecting the pieces of the algorithm together results in the description given in Figure 13.10.

Figure 13.9 Pseudocode module for locating the smallest value in a list.

smodule min (**imports**: LIST, n; **exports**: small, place)

* Module to find the smallest entry **small** and its position **place** in a given **LIST** of length n.

* Variables used:
* **LIST** - given list of numbers
* **n** - given number of entries in the list
* **small** - smallest entry in the list
* **place** - position of the smallest
* **i** - current location being examined

* Initialize the smallest as the first entry.

small ← $list_1$
place ← 1

* Search the rest of the list for a better value updating
* **small** and **place** each time a better estimate is found.

for i **from** 2 **to** n **do**

    if $list_i$ < small **then**

        small ← $list_i$
        place ← i

end module

Figure 13.10 Final version of the pseudocode module for a selection sort.

smodule select(**imports**: OLD, n; **exports**: NEW)

* Module to use a simple selection process to sort the n entries of list **OLD**
* into list **NEW** in increasing order.

* Variables used:
* **OLD** - original list of numbers
* **n** - number of entries in the list
* **NEW** - resulting sorted list
* **pass** - current pass number
* **small** - current smallest entry in OLD
* **place** - position of the smallest in OLD

* During each pass, find the smallest entry in **OLD**, copy it to list **NEW**,
* and destroy it in list **OLD**.

for pass **from** 1 **to** n **do**

    min(OLD, n; small, place)
    new_{pass} ← small
    old_{place} ← ∞

end module

---

g) Final Discussion   The selection sort will always require *n* passes over the list being sorted. During each pass the first entry in the old list is assumed to be the smallest and is then compared to each of the remaining entries in the old list. The number of comparisons is therefore $n - 1$ for each of the *n* passes for a total of $n(n - 1)$. These comparisons will be necessary regardless of how the entries are initially ordered. Some improvement in the number of comparisons needed can be realized by using a single list and storing the partially sorted entries at the beginning of the same list (see Exercise 13.5 c). With such a strategy, the number of entries to scan for the smallest decreases by one after each pass resulting in an algorithm which requires approximately half the number of comparisons.

13.3.2   An Exchange Sort

Techniques involving exchanges form the second group of internal sorting methods. In an exchange sort, pairs of entries in the list are compared, and if the entries are out of order, they are interchanged. The comparison process is repeated systematically until no more exchanges are necessary. The order in which pairs are examined varies from algorithm to algorithm, but all methods make several passes over all or part of the list in some systematic fashion.

The most common exchange method is known as the bubble sort. It employs the obvious pairing of consecutive entries in the list. During the first pass through the list, the comparison begins with the items in locations one and two. If out of order, these two items are interchanged. This process is then repeated for the items in locations two and three, three and four, . . . , up to $n - 1$ and *n*. After this pass, the largest entry will have "bubbled" to position *n*, even if it started at position one. Thus, pass two need only examine the first $n - 1$ entries in the list as the same sequence of comparisons is carried out. The algorithm continues passing through the list, reducing the size of the list each time, until all of the entries are in order.

Figure 13.11 illustrates the bubble sort technique as it is applied to the list of numbers 7, 9, 8, 3, 4, 7. At each stage of the algorithm the pair of numbers being examined or exchanged is highlighted. From this diagram, note that five comparisons and four exchanges are made during the first pass as the algorithm examines all six numbers. Pass two requires only four comparisons, and three exchanges are made in moving the number 8 into position. Three comparisons are made in pass three and two interchanges occur. Finally, pass four makes two comparisons but no exchanges and thus the numbers have been sorted.

a) Developing the Algorithm   The bubble sort algorithm will also be designed as a module. Module bubble will accept as import parameters an unsorted list called LIST and the number of entries in the list, n. The sole export parameter will be LIST sorted in ascending order. A first version is given as Figure 13.12.

b) Refining Step **1.**   The bubble sort algorithm makes a series of passes over the list and bubbles the largest element to the top of the list during each pass. Thus, a loop is required to repeat the comparison/exchange sequence for each element to be bubbled into place. During the first pass, n−1 pairs must be examined. Since each pass succeeds in moving the next largest entry into position near the end of the list, the

Figure 13.11   Example of a bubble sort. The heavy shading highlights the current pair of numbers being compared. The arrows underneath specify the exchanges that take place as a result. The lighter shading indicates the current extent of the sorted list.

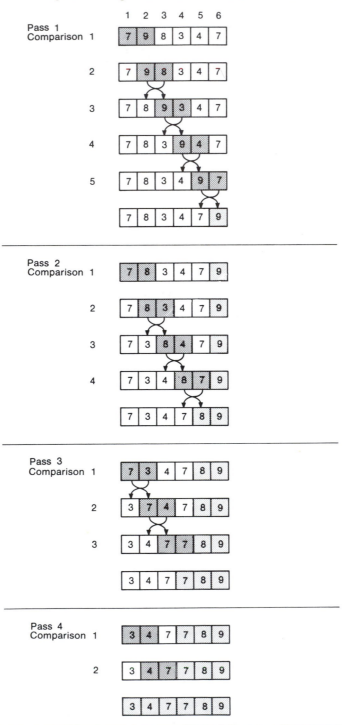

Figure 13.12 First version of a pseudocode module for a bubble sort.

smodule bubble (**imports**: LIST, n; **exports**: LIST)

1. Sort the entries of LIST into ascending order using the bubble sort technique.

end module

---

maximum number of pairs for each subsequent pass can be reduced by one using an in-crement of −1. The loop continues as long as there are pairs to examine. Thus, the refinement of Step **1.** follows.

> **1.1 for** maxpairs **from** n−1 **to** 1 **by** −1 **do**
>
> $\lceil$ **1.2** Compare entries in pairs exchanging the pair if the values are out of order.

c) Refining Step **1.2**   There are maxpairs pairs of numbers to be compared, thus a loop is necessary to begin at the first pair and perform the compare/exchange on each pair up to maxpairs.

> * For each pass, compare the LIST entries in pairs.
> * Exchange entries that are out of order.
>
> **1.2.1 for** pair **from** 1 **to** maxpairs **do**
>
> $\lceil$ **1.2.2** Compare entries pair and pair+1 and if out of order, exchange them.

d) Refining Step **1.2.2**   The exchange of two numbers was discussed in Chapter 5 in the sort2 module. Such a module could be used, although to refresh the idea of performing an exchange, the code will be copied here.

> **if** $\text{list}_{pair} > \text{list}_{pair+1}$ **then**
>
> $\lceil$ $\text{temp} \leftarrow \text{list}_{pair}$
> $\text{list}_{pair} \leftarrow \text{list}_{pair+1}$
> $\text{list}_{pair+1} \leftarrow \text{temp}$

e) Improving the Efficiency of the Bubble Sort   The outer loop controls the number of passes over the list. Frequently, the list becomes sorted before all passes have been made. Such was the case in the previous numerical example. This condition can be detected by remembering whether or not any exchanges take place during the current pass. This can be accomplished by using a logical exchange flag (called xflag) which is initialized before each pass to the value **false** and is changed to **true** whenever an exchange takes place. The outer loop must be redesigned to continue as long as the previous pass required at least one exchange. Therefore a **while**–loop which tests xflag must replace the **for**–loop. These improvements are incorporated in the final algorithm.

f) The Final Algorithm   The complete module to accomplish the bubble sort is present-ed in Figure 13.13.

Figure 13.13   Final version of the pseudocode module for a bubble sort.

smodule bubble (**imports**: LIST, n; **exports**: LIST)

* Module to sort the entries of **LIST** into ascending order using the bubble sort technique.

* Variables used:
* **LIST** - list of numbers before and after sorting
* **n** - number of entries in the list
* **maxpairs** - maximum number of pairs for current pass
* **pair** - comparison pair counter
* **xflag** - exchange flag, truth of 'exchange took place'

* Initialize the number of comparisons and exchange flag.

maxpairs ← n − 1
xflag ← **true**

* Continue passing over the list until there are no exchanges.

while xflag **do**

> * For each pass, compare the LIST entries in pairs.
> * Exchange entries that are out of order and set **xflag**.
>
> xflag ← **false**
> **for** pair **from 1 to** maxpairs **do**
>
> > **if** list$_{pair}$ > list$_{pair+1}$ **then**
> >
> > > temp ← list$_{pair}$
> > > list$_{pair}$ ← list$_{pair+1}$
> > > list$_{pair+1}$ ← temp
> > > xflag ← **true**
>
> * After each pass, reduce the comparisons by 1.
>
> maxpairs ← maxpairs − 1

end module

---

g) Final Discussion   The bubble sort algorithm requires one less comparison for each subsequent pass through the list.   Thus, for a list of *n* numbers, the maximum number of comparisons is

$$(n-1) + (n-2) + \cdots + 2 + 1 = \frac{n(n-1)}{2} \ .$$

Though this maximum number would only be required if the smallest number appeared last in the original list, it can be shown that even for random lists of numbers, the average does not deviate much from this formula.   The one distinct advantage, however, is that if the list is already in increasing order, only one pass entailing *n* − 1 comparisons is necessary.

13.3.3 An Insertion Sort

The third family of sorting techniques involves taking elements sequentially from a given list and inserting them in their correct relative positions in a new list.

The diagram in Figure 13.14 illustrates the building of a sorted list from the list of numbers 7, 9, 8, 3, 4, 7. The new list is initially given its first entry, 7, from the old list. To insert the second entry, 9, no shifting is necessary since 9 is greater than the last entry of the new list. Thus, 9 is simply added to the end. For the third entry, the 9 in the new list is shifted to make room for the 8 from the old list. The insertion continues for the entries 3, 4, and 7. Figure 13.15 gives a more detailed look at the movement of data to make room for the insertion of the last entry, 7.

Figure 13.14   An example of an insertion sort. The current entry being inserted is shaded more heavily.

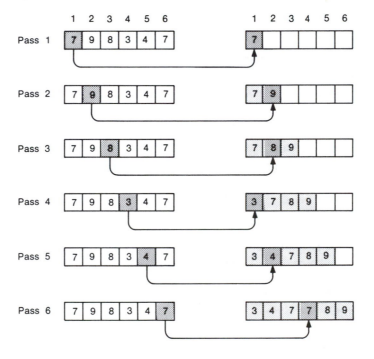

a) Developing the Algorithm   The algorithm for linear insertion will be written as a module called insert and will have import parameters OLD, the unsorted list, and n, the number of entries in this list. The export parameter will be the list NEW containing the values sorted in ascending order. A first version of the algorithm is shown as Figure 13.16.

Figure 13.15   Inserting the second 7 in the last step of the previous example.

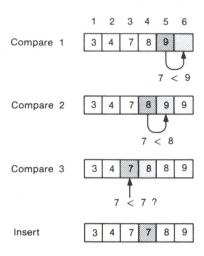

Figure 13.16   First version of a pseudocode module for a linear insertion sort.

smodule insert (**imports**: OLD, n; **exports**: NEW)

1.   Sort the entries of list OLD into ascending order in list NEW using a linear insertion sort.

end module

b) Refining Step **1.**   The insertion process is repeated once for each of the n entries in the list OLD.   This is controlled by an outer loop using the index i.   Each time through the loop, the i-th entry in the list will be correctly positioned in the current list NEW.

* Repeat the insertion for each entry in OLD.

1.1 for i **from** 1 **to** n **do**

1.2 Insert the i-th entry of the old list into the correct position of the new list using a linear search from the end of the list.

c) Refining Step **1.2**   To find the correct position for the current entry, it is necessary to adapt the linear search written earlier in this chapter, to proceed backwards through list NEW.   The current length of the new list is given by the number of entries already inserted, one less than the position of the current key (i−1).   Using variable j as the index in the new list, the search will start at position i−1 and continue backwards until either the correct position is found (set found to **true**) or until the list is exhausted (j=0). The correct position for the current key is preceding all entries that are larger.   Thus, each larger entry is advanced one location to eventually make room for the key.   When a smaller entry is found or if all entries are larger, the key can be placed in location j+1, already vacated by previous shifting.   These refinements are given in the correct sequence below.

* Search **NEW** backwards for position of **OLD** entry
* until the position is found or the list exhausted.

found ← **false**
j ← i − 1
while j > 0 **and not** found **do**

> **if** new$_j$ > old$_i$ **then**
>
> > * **OLD** entry must appear before **NEW** entry.
> > * Advance the **NEW** entry and move on to the next.
> >
> > new$_{j+1}$ ← new$_j$
> > j ← j − 1
>
> **else**
>
> > * Correct position found.
> >
> > found ← **true**

* Place the entry in the last vacated slot.

new$_{j+1}$ ← old$_i$

d) The Final Algorithm   Now that all the refinements are complete, the final algorithm can be presented in Figure 13.17.

e) Final Discussion   The number of comparisons needed to locate the position for each entry changes as the length of the new list changes.   Each time one would expect, on the average, to search halfway through the new list.   Thus, to insert the *i*-th entry, $(i − 1)/2$ comparisons would be expected.   For a list of *n* entries the average number of comparisons would be

$$\frac{1}{2}(0 + 1 + 2 + \cdots + n − 1) = \frac{1}{2}\left[\frac{n(n − 1)}{2}\right] = \frac{n(n − 1)}{4} \ .$$

The maximum number of comparisons would be required if the list were in exactly reverse order.   In this case twice the above number would be required since each old entry would always be inserted at the first of the new list.   Conversely, if the list were already sorted, each old entry would be added to the end of the new list and only $n − 1$ comparisons would be needed.   In general, some improvement in efficiency can be made by using a binary search rather than a linear search.   This suggestion is left as an exercise (see Exercise 13.7d).

13.3.4   Quicksort

Quicksort is a relatively modern and fast sorting algorithm devised by C.A.R. Hoare. It is essentially an insertion/exchange scheme which at each stage succeeds in correctly positioning at least one number in the list.   The knowledge that this element is so positioned is used to reduce the number of comparisons needed to position subsequent entries.

Figure 13.17 Final version of the pseudocode module for a linear insertion sort.

smodule insert (**imports**: OLD, n; **exports**: NEW)

* Module to sort the entries of list **OLD** into ascending order in list **NEW**
* using a linear insertion sort.

* Variables used:
* **OLD** - original list of numbers
* **n** - number of entries in the list
* **NEW** - resulting sorted list
* **i** - position of OLD entry being inserted
* **j** - current entry being compared in NEW
* **found** - truth of 'entry found by backward search'

* Repeat the insertion for each entry in **OLD**.

for i **from 1 to** n **do**

> * Search NEW backwards for position of OLD entry until the position is found
> * or the list exhausted.
>
> found ← **false**
> j ← i − 1
> **while** j > 0 **and not** found **do**
>
> > **if** new_j > old_i **then**
> >
> > > * OLD entry must appear before NEW entry.
> > > * Advance the NEW entry and move on to the next.
> > >
> > > new_{j+1} ← new_j
> > > j ← j − 1
> >
> > **else**
> >
> > > * Correct position found.
> > >
> > > found ← **true**
>
> * Place the entry in the last vacated slot.
> new_{j+1} ← old_i

end module

The object of Quicksort is to rearrange or *partition* the list of numbers relative to a specific entry called the *pivot* so that in the resulting partitioned list, all entries preceding the pivot are less than or equal to the pivot and all entries following the pivot are greater than or equal to the pivot.

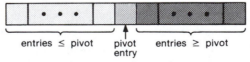

As a result of the partitioning, the pivot entry has its correct final position. The same partitioning process is then applied to the two sublists on either side of the pivot entry. In this way the original list is systematically reduced to a number of sublists each of length one which are, of course, sorted and, more importantly, correctly positioned relative to each other.

Consider the same list of numbers used earlier and, for convenience, choose the first entry as the pivot.

One possible partitioning relative to this entry is:

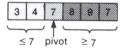

The two elements preceding 7 are less in magnitude while the three elements following 7 are greater or equal.   Furthermore, when this list is finally sorted, 7 should be in this position.   The partitioning process would now be applied to the two sublists, 3, 4 and 8, 9, 7.

The most important feature of the algorithm is the partitioning.   The entry selected as the pivot entry is usually the first entry, but other selections are also possible (see Exercise 13.8).   Having chosen the pivot entry, the algorithm scans the list from each end, looking for the first element on each side which does not belong on that side of the pivot.   These two elements are then exchanged and the scans resume with the adjacent elements.

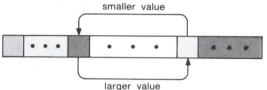

When the two scans meet, the pivot entry is positioned between the two sublists to maintain the relative ordering.

To illustrate the partitioning process the following larger list of numbers will be used.

54, 13, 56, 95, 21, 94, 31, 69, 46, 19, 55, 65, 72, 81, 74

Figure 13.18 illustrates the partitioning relative to the first entry, 54.   The list is scanned from each end, from the right to find an entry less than or equal to the pivot, and from the left to find an entry greater than or equal to the pivot.   The left scan starts in position two and stops at position three locating the value 56.   The right scan starts in position fifteen and stops at position ten locating the value 19 as shown in stage i) of the diagram.   Notice that the entries in the positions before three are all ≤54 and that those in positions after ten are all ≥54.   To extend the patterns, the 19 and 56 exchange positions.   Then the two scanning procedures move on.   Advancing from the left locates 95 ≥ 54 in position four and from the right finds 46 in position nine (see stage ii).   These two entries are also exchanged.   The next scans stop at 94 in position six and 31 in position seven (see stage iii).   Following their exchange, 31 will be in position six and 94 in position seven.   If the scanning is allowed to continue, the left scan

Figure 13.18 Partitioning a set relative to the pivot element in the first entry. Shading identifies elements partitioned so far: darkest for elements greater than the pivot, medium for the pivot, lightest for elements less than the pivot.

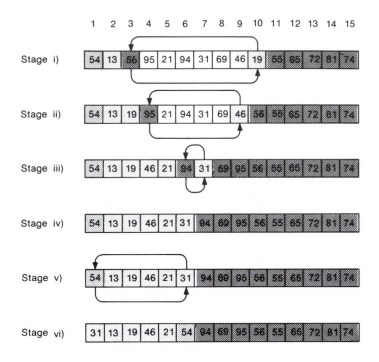

for larger values stops at position seven, the rightmost entry greater than or equal to the pivot, while the right scan stops at position six, the leftmost entry less than or equal to the pivot (see stage iv). At this point the two scans have overlapped.

It is now time to correctly position the pivot between the sublists. One alternative is to shuffle all the entries in the left sublist down one position to make room for the pivot. However, since the partitioned sublist is in no particular order as yet, the pivot can be exchanged with the rightmost entry in the left sublist containing the smaller elements. Since the pivot is in position one, among the entries less or equal, it is exchanged with the entry in position six, where the right scan ended (see stage v). This places the pivot in its correct ultimate position thus providing the required partitioning (see stage vi). The resulting two sublists, [31, 13, 19, 46, 21] and [94, 69, 95, 56, 65, 72, 81, 74] can now be partitioned in the same way. The partitioning at any stage terminates when a sublist is of length one or less.

a) Developing the Quicksort Algorithm The Quicksort algorithm will be designed as a module called quicksort. Recall that the algorithm begins by partitioning the complete list to form two sublists. These two sublists could now be sorted by reapplying the quicksort module to each in turn. It is, therefore, desirable to design the module to be flexible enough to handle a portion of a list as well as the entire list. Thus, the import parameter list for module quicksort includes the LIST entries as well as the pointers left and right, the left and right limits of the current portion of LIST to be considered. Since the partitioning leaves the pivot in its correct sorted position, the sort will export the sorted LIST. A first version of the module appears in Figure 13.19.

Figure 13.19 First version of a pseudocode module for Quicksort.

smodule quicksort (**imports**: LIST, left, right; **exports**: LIST)

1. Sort the entries of LIST into ascending order using the Quicksort technique.

end module

---

b) Refining Module quicksort *Step* **1.** The essential step in the Quicksort algorithm is the partitioning of the list so that:

$$list_{left} \ldots list_{p-1} \leq list_p \leq list_{p+1} \ldots list_{right}$$

After this partitioning is complete, the same process must then be applied to the sublist entries left, left+1, . . . , p−1 and p+1, p+2, . . . , right. Of course, this process should only be performed if there is a list to partition, that is, if left < right. These steps can be described by the following pseudocode:

```
* If the list contains more than a single element, then
* sort it, otherwise, there is nothing to do.
```

1.1 if left < right **then**

> **1.2** Partition $list_{left}$ . . . $list_{right}$ into two smaller sublists:
> $list_{llleft}$ . . . $list_{rlleft} \leq list_p \leq list_{llright}$ . . . $list_{lllleft}$
>
> * Sort each of these smaller sublists.
>
> **1.3** quicksort(LIST, llleft, rlleft; LIST)
> **1.4** quicksort(LIST, llright, rlright; LIST)

This algorithm decomposition suggests something new, the use of a module reference to itself. Such a module is called self-referencing or *recursive.* A recursive module must be able to remember the current status of the module, including which statement is being executed within the module and the current values of all variables, so that the module can be invoked with a different set of argument values. While recursive module references are supported by some programming languages, such is not the case with FORTRAN/77. It is, therefore, necessary to program such references explicitly.

Module quicksort begins by partitioning the original list. Then this same partitioning must be applied to the two partitions. This process must be repeated until all partitions are of length one or less and thus are sorted. To remember which sublists require further partitioning, it is expedient to introduce an algorithmic tool called a *stack.* A stack is essentially a list in which the last or top entry is always the current entry. All additions to or deletions from the stack are made only at the top.

In module quicksort, therefore, it is necessary to maintain two stacks, one for each endpoint of the sublist, as well as a variable pointing to the current top of the stacks. The current list being partitioned will appear at the top of the stacks. At the end of each partitioning process, the current list is deleted from the stacks and the two sublists are added. The partitioning will continue as long as there are lists on the stacks. Lists of length one or less are completely partitioned and so are immediately removed from the stacks.

Module quicksort can now be restated as described in Figure 13.20. Notice that import parameters left and right are no longer appropriate and that n, the length of the original list, has taken their place.

Figure 13.20 Version 2 of a pseudocode module for a non-recursive Quicksort.

smodule quicksort (**imports**: LIST, n; **exports**: LIST)

1.1 Stack the original LIST.

1.2 while there are more lists on the stacks **do**

      1.3 if length of current stacked list is 0 or 1 **then**

           The current list is partitioned; remove it from the stacks.

      else

           1.4 Partition the list currently on top of the stacks.

           1.5 Delete the current list from the stacks and add the left and right sublists to the stacks.

end module

---

c) Refining Module quicksort *Step* **1.1** The essential things to remember about each list or sublist are the two endpoints. Consequently two stacks called lstack and rstack will be maintained for the left and right endpoints respectively. Variable nstack will be the number of lists currently on the stacks and, therefore, represents a pointer to the top of the stacks. Thus, stacking the original list in step **1.1** requires that:

    * Stack the original list.

    $nstack \leftarrow 1$
    $lstack_{nstack} \leftarrow 1$
    $rstack_{nstack} \leftarrow n$

d) Refining Module quicksort *Step* **1.2** Deciding whether or not there are more lists on the stacks simply involves checking the value of nstack. Consequently step **1.2** can be written as:

    * Keep partitioning as long as stacked lists remain.

    while $nstack > 0$ **do**

e) Refining Module quicksort *Step* **1.3**   The length of the current list can be calculated from the two endpoints.   To remove the list from the top of the stacks, decrement the stack pointer.   In pseudocode these steps can be described by:

* If the length of the current list is **0** or **1**, remove it from the stacks; it is partitioned.

if $lstack_{nstack} \geq rstack_{nstack}$ **then**

$\left[\; nstack \leftarrow nstack - 1 \right.$

f) Refining Module quicksort *Step* **1.4**   Step **1.4** is the all important partitioning process. Since it has a logically distinct role in the algorithm, it is appropriate to define a module called **partition** which will take the portion of a list from a left limit, **left**, to a right limit, **right**, and partition it as required.   The necessary import parameters are therefore LIST, **left**, and **right**.   The exports from the module **partition** are the positions of the two sublists created by the partitioning process.   This information will be conveyed by specifying the endpoints of the sublists, **llleft** and **rlleft** for the left sublist and **llright** and **rlright** for the right sublist.

The definition of module **partition** is given in Figure 13.21.

Figure 13.21   First version of a pseudocode module for partitioning a list.

smodule partition (**imports**: LIST, left, right; **exports**: LIST, llleft, rlleft, llright, rlright)

1.   Partition the portion of LIST from left to right so that:
$list_{llleft} \cdots list_{rlleft} \leq list_p \leq list_{llright} \cdots list_{rlleft}$

end module

With the aid of module **partition**, Step **1.4** in module **quicksort** is easy to refine.   The left endpoint of the current list is given by the top of **lstack** and the right endpoint is on top of **rstack**.   The appropriate reference to module **partition** is:

    call partition(LIST, left, right; LIST, llleft, rlleft, llright, rlright)

g) Refining Module quicksort *Step* **1.5**   Now that the current list has been partitioned it can be removed from the stacks and the two sublists added.   To remove the current list from the stacks, the pointer to the top of the stacks is decremented by one.   Finally, the two sublists created by the partitioning must be added to the stacks.   The operation of adding to a stack is called *pushing* the stack.   In contrast, the operation of deleting the top entry of a stack is called *popping* the stack.   To minimize the number of lists that are stacked waiting to be partitioned, the shortest list will always be stacked last so that it is attacked first.   Thus, the stacking process is refined as follows.

* Remove the current list from the stack.

nstack ← nstack − 1

* Add the left and right sublists to the stack adding the shortest list last.

llength ← rlleft − llleft + 1
rlength ← rlright − llright + 1
if llength ≤ rlength **then**

> nstack ← nstack + 1
> lstack$_{nstack}$ ← llright
> rstack$_{nstack}$ ← rlright
> nstack ← nstack + 1
> lstack$_{nstack}$ ← llleft
> rstack$_{nstack}$ ← rlleft

else

> nstack ← nstack + 1
> lstack$_{nstack}$ ← llleft
> rstack$_{nstack}$ ← rlleft
> nstack ← nstack + 1
> lstack$_{nstack}$ ← llright
> rstack$_{nstack}$ ← rlright

h) The Final quicksort *Module*   The complete algorithm to implement Quicksort is presented as the quicksort module in Figure 13.22, and as the FORTRAN/77 subroutine QUICK in Figure 13.23.

Figure 13.22   The final version of the pseudocode module for Quicksort.

smodule quicksort (**imports**: LIST, n; **exports**: LIST)

* Module to sort the entries of LIST into ascending order using the Quicksort algorithm.

* Variables used:
* **LIST** - given list of numbers to sort
* **n** - given number of entries in the list
* **lstack/rstack** - stack of pointers to the left/right end of a list
* **nstack** - number of entries on each stack; pointer to current top of each stack
* **llleft/rlleft** - left/right limit of the left sublist
* **llright/rlright** - left/right limit of the right sublist
* **llength/rlength** - length of left/right sublist

* Stack the original list.

nstack ← 1
lstack$_{nstack}$ ← 1
rstack$_{nstack}$ ← n

* Keep partitioning as long as stacked lists remain.

while nstack > 0 **do**

> * If the length of the current list is 0 or 1,
> * remove it from the stacks; it is partitioned.
>
> **if** lstack$_{nstack}$ ≥ rstack$_{nstack}$ **then**
>
>> nstack ← nstack − 1
>
> **else**
>
>> * Otherwise, employ the partitioning process.
>>
>> **call** partition (LIST, lstack$_{nstack}$, rstack$_{nstack}$; LIST, llleft, rlleft, llright, rlright)
>>
>> * Remove the current list from the stacks.
>>
>> nstack ← nstack − 1
>>
>> * Add the left and right sublists to the stacks, adding the shortest list last.
>>
>> llength ← rlleft − llleft + 1
>> rlength ← rlright − llright + 1
>> **if** llength ≤ rlength **then**
>>
>>> nstack ← nstack + 1
>>> lstack$_{nstack}$ ← llright
>>> rstack$_{nstack}$ ← rlright
>>> nstack ← nstack + 1
>>> lstack$_{nstack}$ ← llleft
>>> rstack$_{nstack}$ ← rlleft
>>
>> **else**
>>
>>> nstack ← nstack + 1
>>> lstack$_{nstack}$ ← llleft
>>> rstack$_{nstack}$ ← rlleft
>>> nstack ← nstack + 1
>>> lstack$_{nstack}$ ← llright
>>> rstack$_{nstack}$ ← rlright

end module

```
C Figure 13.23 -- A Quicksort Module.
C                 Subroutine QUICK to sort the N entries of LIST into
C                 ascending order using Quicksort.

C************************************************************************
C LIST            - given list of numbers to sort
C N               - given number of entries in the list
C NMAX            - given maximum value for N
C LSTACK/RSTACK   - stack of pointers to left/right end of list
C NSTACK          - number of entries on each stack
C                 - pointer to the current top of each stack
C LLLEFT/RLLEFT   - left/right limit of the left sublist
C LLRITE/RLRITE   - left/right limit of the right sublist
C LLEN/RLEN       - length of the left/right sublist
C************************************************************************
        SUBROUTINE QUICK(LIST,N,NMAX)

        INTEGER NMAX, LIST(NMAX), N, LSTACK(20), RSTACK(20), NSTACK
        INTEGER LLLEFT, RLLEFT, LLRITE, RLRITE, LLEN, RLEN
C Stack the original list.
        NSTACK = 1
        LSTACK(NSTACK) = 1
        RSTACK(NSTACK) = N
C Keep partitioning as long as stacked lists remain.
  100 IF (NSTACK.GT.0) THEN

C         If the length of the current list is 0 or 1,
C         remove it from the stack - it is partitioned.

        IF (LSTACK(NSTACK).GE.RSTACK(NSTACK)) THEN
            NSTACK = NSTACK - 1
        ELSE
C         Otherwise, employ the partitioning process.

        CALL PARTIT(LIST,NMAX,LSTACK(NSTACK),RSTACK(NSTACK),
     +              LLLEFT,RLLEFT,LLRITE,RLRITE)
C         Remove the current list from the stack.

        NSTACK = NSTACK - 1
C         Add the left and right sublists to the stack,
C         adding the shortest list last.

        LLEN = RLLEFT - LLLEFT + 1
        RLEN = RLRITE - LLRITE + 1
        IF (LLEN.LE.RLEN) THEN
            NSTACK = NSTACK + 1
            LSTACK(NSTACK) = LLRITE
            RSTACK(NSTACK) = RLRITE
            NSTACK = NSTACK + 1
            LSTACK(NSTACK) = LLLEFT
            RSTACK(NSTACK) = RLLEFT
        ELSE
            NSTACK = NSTACK + 1
            LSTACK(NSTACK) = LLLEFT
            RSTACK(NSTACK) = RLLEFT
            NSTACK = NSTACK + 1
            LSTACK(NSTACK) = LLRITE
            RSTACK(NSTACK) = RLRITE
        ENDIF
```

C Figure 13.23 (continued)
```
        ENDIF
           GOTO 100
     ENDIF
     RETURN
     END
```

Program Notes

- Variable dimensions have been used for the list in the subroutine.   Recall that the value of NMAX must agree with the declared size of the list in the calling program.
- The maximum size for the stacks has been chosen as 20.   This size is large enough to handle lists of size one million or less.   For proof of this fact, see Exercise 13.8 g).

i) Refining Module partition *Step* **1.**   The partitioning process revolves around the pivot element, arbitrarily chosen as the first in the list.   The remainder of the list is scanned relative to this value.   The scanning proceeds from each end exchanging entries as required until the scans overlap.   At this point it is possible to correctly position the pivot element.   These essential steps can be phrased in the following way.

1.1 Choose the pivot element.

1.2 While the scans don't overlap

⌈ Scan the list from both ends exchanging values as needed to partition the list.

1.3 Position the pivot element.

1.4 Compute the sublist endpoints.

j) Refining Module partition *Step* **1.1**   For this partitioning module the first or leftmost entry of the current list is selected as the pivot element.

* Choose the pivot element.

pivot ← list$_{left}$

k) Refining Module partition *Step* **1.2**   To scan the list from each end, two indices or pointers, appropriately called lindex and rindex, are used to maintain the current scanning position in each case.   The two scans do not overlap as long as lindex is less than rindex. The first question to ask is where should these two scanning processes start.   In order to make this decision, consider the following schematic diagram depicting the list at some arbitrary stage in the process.

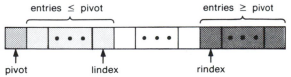

The entries in positions lindex and rindex have just been exchanged, and the scanning is about to continue.   Since the entries at lindex and at rindex are correctly positioned, the left scan should continue at position lindex+1 and the right scan should continue with the entry in position rindex−1. In order for the first left scan to start at position left+1, lindex must be initialized at left. Similarly, for the first right scan to begin at position right, rindex must be initialized at right+1.

The next question becomes, when should the two scanning processes terminate? The left scan stops when an entry greater than or equal to the pivot entry is found. What if all entries are less than pivot? In this isolated case, the left scan must be stopped when it reaches position right, before it tries to access entries beyond the end of the list. However, if the left scan is performed first, it could conceivably still reach right+1 (the initial value of rindex) and try to examine this nonexistent entry. A simple solution to avoid this potential problem is to perform the right scan prior to the left scan.

The right scan is halted when an entry less than or equal to pivot is located. Since pivot is chosen as the leftmost entry in the list, even if all other entries are greater than pivot, the right scan will terminate before it goes beyond the left end of the list.

The final question concerns the exchange of entries. As long as the scan pointers have not overlapped, the entries they point to should be exchanged. Though either or both entries may be equal to pivot and would not have to be moved, little is gained by avoiding such instances. However, once the scans overlap, no interchange should take place. The mechanism to exchange entries was already discussed as part of the bubble sort technique. The refinement for step **1.1** can now be written in detail.

* Initialize the scan pointers.

lindex ← left
rindex ← right + 1

* Proceed as long as the endpoints do not overlap.

while lindex < rindex **do**

$\quad$ * Scan from the right looking for entries ≤ pivot element.

$\quad$ rindex ← rindex − 1
$\quad$ **while** list$_{rindex}$ > pivot **do**

$\quad\quad$ rindex ← rindex − 1

$\quad$ * Scan from the left looking for entries ≥ pivot element.

$\quad$ lindex ← lindex + 1
$\quad$ **while** list$_{lindex}$ < pivot **and** lindex < rindex **do**

$\quad\quad$ lindex ← lindex + 1

$\quad$ * Exchange current left entry with current right entry
$\quad$ * provided the scans have not overlapped.

$\quad$ **if** lindex < rindex **then**

$\quad\quad$ temp ← list$_{lindex}$
$\quad\quad$ list$_{lindex}$ ← list$_{rindex}$
$\quad\quad$ list$_{rindex}$ ← temp

l) Refining Module partition *Step* **1.3**   This final step concerns the positioning of the element pivot. Following the scanning process, the list is described by the following diagram.

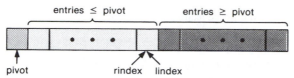

Thus, the entry pivot and the entry in position rindex must be exchanged to produce the final partitioning.   The final position of the pivot element, p, is given by the value of rindex.   The pseudocode description is therefore:

> * Exchange the pivot element with the one at the end of the left sublist.

> $list_{left} \leftarrow list_{rindex}$
> $list_{rindex} \leftarrow pivot$
> $p \leftarrow rindex$

Notice that pivot serves as the temporary location for the entry in position left during the exchange.

m) Refining Module partition *Step* **1.4**   Computing the sublist endpoints is straightforward and is given by the following refinement.

> * Compute the sublist endpoints.

> $llleft \leftarrow left$
> $rlleft \leftarrow p - 1$
> $llright \leftarrow p + 1$
> $rlright \leftarrow right$

n) The Final partition *Module*   The complete module for partitioning the list is presented in Figure 13.24, and the FORTRAN/77 version in Figure 13.25.

o) Efficiency Discussion   A thorough and detailed discussion of the efficiency of Quicksort is relatively complicated.   It can be shown that the average number of comparisons required is approximately

> $2n \log_e n$ or about $1.4n \log_2 n$.

Thus, Quicksort is theoretically much faster than any of the methods discussed previously.   The maximum number of comparisons required is $n(n - 1)/2$.   Unfortunately, this occurs for lists that are already sorted.   Finally, it can also be shown that the minimum number of comparisons is about

> $0.5n \log_2 n$.

Figure 13.24 Final version of the pseudocode module for partitioning a list.

smodule partition (**imports**: LIST, left, right; **exports**: LIST, llleft, rlleft, llright, rlright)

```
* Partition the portion of LIST from left to right so that
* elements listleft . . . listp-1 ≤ listp ≤ listp+1 . . . listright
* Variables used:
* LIST - given list of numbers
* left,right - left,right limits of sublist to be partitioned
* lindex,rindex - left,right indices for scanning process
* pivot - first element in the list to be partitioned
* p - final pivot position in partitioned list
* llleft,rlleft - left,right limits of the left sublist
* llright,rlright - left,right limits of the right sublist
```

```
* Choose the pivot element and initialize the scan pointers.
pivot ← listleft
lindex ← left
rindex ← right + 1
```

```
* Proceed as long as the endpoints do not overlap.
while lindex < rindex do
        * Scan from the right looking for entries ≤ pivot element.

        rindex ← rindex − 1
        while listrindex > pivot do
                [ rindex ← rindex − 1

        * Scan from the left looking for entries ≥ pivot element.

        lindex ← lindex + 1
        while listlindex < pivot and lindex < rindex do
                [ lindex ← lindex + 1

        * Exchange the current left entry with the right entry provided the scans have not
        overlapped.

        if lindex < rindex then
                [ temp ← listlindex
                  listlindex ← listrindex
                  listrindex ← temp
```

```
* Exchange the pivot element with the one at the end of the left sublist,
* which rindex points to due to overlap of the scans.

listleft ← listrindex
listrindex ← pivot
p ← rindex
```

```
* Compute the sublist endpoints.

llleft ← left
rlleft ← p − 1
llright ← p + 1
rlright ← right
end module
```

```
C Figure 13.25 -- A Partitioning Module.
C                       Subroutine PARTIT to partition a list of numbers so
C                       that elements LIST(LEFT), ..., LIST(P-1) <= LIST(P),
C                       and LIST(P) <= LIST(P+1), ..., LIST(RIGHT).
C*************************************************************************
C LIST            - given list of numbers to partition
C N               - given number of entries in the list
C NMAX            - maximum value for N
C LEFT/RIGHT      - left/right limit of sublist to be partitioned
C LINDEX/RINDEX   - left/right indices for scanning process
C PIVOT           - first element in the list to be partitioned
C P               - final pivot position in partitioned list
C LLLEFT/RLLEFT   - left/right limits of the left sublist
C LLRITE/RLRITE   - left/right limits of the right sublist
C*************************************************************************
        SUBROUTINE PARTIT(LIST,NMAX,LEFT,RIGHT,LLLEFT,RLLEFT,
       +                                        LLRITE,RLRITE)
        INTEGER NMAX, LIST(NMAX), LEFT, RIGHT, LLLEFT, RLLEFT
        INTEGER LLRITE, RLRITE, LINDEX, RINDEX, PIVOT, P, TEMP
C Choose the pivot element and initialize the scan pointers.
        PIVOT = LIST(LEFT)
        LINDEX = LEFT
        RINDEX = RIGHT + 1
C Proceed as long as the endpoints do not overlap
   100  IF (LINDEX .LT. RINDEX) THEN
C            Scan from the right looking for entries less than or
C            equal to the pivot element.
             RINDEX = RINDEX - 1
   200       IF (LIST(RINDEX) .GT. PIVOT) THEN
                 RINDEX = RINDEX - 1
                 GOTO 200
             ENDIF
C            Scan from the LINDEX looking for entries greater than or
C            equal to the pivot element.
             LINDEX = LINDEX + 1
   300       IF (LIST(LINDEX) .LT. PIVOT .AND. LINDEX .LT. RINDEX) THEN
                 LINDEX = LINDEX + 1
                 GOTO 300
             ENDIF
C            Exchange the current left entry with the right entry
C            provided that the scans have not overlapped.
             IF (LINDEX .LT. RINDEX) THEN
                 TEMP = LIST(LINDEX)
                 LIST(LINDEX) = LIST(RINDEX)
                 LIST(RINDEX) = TEMP
             ENDIF
             GOTO 100
        ENDIF
```

```
C Figure 13.25 (continued)
C Exchange the pivot element with the one at the end of the left
C sublist which RINDEX points to due to overlap of the scans.
      LIST(LEFT) = LIST(RINDEX)
      LIST(RINDEX) = PIVOT
      P = RINDEX
C Compute the sublist endpoints.
      LLLEFT = LEFT
      RLLEFT = P - 1
      LLRITE = P + 1
      RLRITE = RIGHT
      RETURN
      END
```

13.3.5   Comparison of Sorting Methods

The discussion of each sorting method included calculation of the number of comparisons required to sort a list of length n.   Counting the number of comparisons required is one of the standard methods for comparing the efficiency of various sorting techniques (other criteria include a measure of the data movement involved).   The table in Figure 13.26 presents the average, maximum, and minimum number of comparisons required by each of the four methods discussed in this chapter.   Since such formulas are sometimes difficult to grasp, the average number of comparisons is tabulated for several values of n in Figure 13.27.   For relatively short lists ($n < 30$) the insertion sort exhibits the best characteristics.   Thereafter, Quicksort is clearly the fastest method to use.

Figure 13.26   Comparison of the efficiency of sorting techniques.

Method	Average	Number of Comparisons Maximum	Minimum
Selection	$n(n-1)$	$n(n-1)$	$n(n-1)$
Exchange	$< \dfrac{n(n-1)}{2}$	$\dfrac{n(n-1)}{2}$	$n-1$
Insertion	$\dfrac{n(n-1)}{4}$	$\dfrac{n(n-1)}{2}$	$n-1$
Quicksort	$1.4n\log_2 n$	$\dfrac{n(n-1)}{2}$	$.5n\log_2 n$

13.4   Using Sorts in Applications

The previous sorting section presented an idealized approach to the task of sorting.   In each case the algorithm was applied to a single list of integers.   Since the algorithms are fundamentally sound they can be applied to floating point numbers or alphabetic

Figure 13.27 Tabulation of the average number of comparisions for several sorting techniques.

Method	16	32	64	Length of the List 128	256	512	1024
Selection	240	992	4032	16256	65280	261632	1047552
Exchange	120	486	2016	8128	37640	130816	523776
Insertion	60	243	1008	4064	18820	65408	261888
Quicksort	90	224	538	1255	2868	6452	14336

information equally well with only minor changes to the FORTRAN/77 declarations. Similarly, to change the sort sequence from ascending to descending order would require the appropriate modifications to the comparisons made in each algorithm.   However, when performing sorts of real-life data, or when sorting the data several different ways, more substantial changes may be needed.

Consider the tables of data listed in Appendix L.   When such collections are presented as data for a program, they are usually referred to as files.   Each line in a table is called a *record* in the file.   Furthermore, each piece of information in a record is called a *field* of that record.   Finally, the field or piece of information that forms the basis for sorting the file is called the *key* or *sort key*. For instance, the table of hockey statistics recorded in Appendix L could be labeled the NHL file since it represents the performance of hockey players in the National Hockey League.   Each line in the table is appropriately a record in the file and coincidentally represents the record of a player during the 1980/1981 hockey season.   The fields for each record or player include the player's name, team, position, games played, goals, assists, total points, and penalty minutes.

The problems encountered in working with such a file are twofold.   A sort usually requires that additional information be presented to identify the field chosen as the sort key.   For example, a list sorted by total points is more meaningful if it includes the players' names.   The second problem is that the sort often involves more than one field in each record thus requiring a *compound sort key*. It is not unreasonable, for example, to desire a list of players sorted by total points with players having an equal number of points being ranked by goals scored.   The following discussion will present solutions to both of these problems.

13.4.1 Sorting With Added Information

There are several ways to manage the additional information during a sort.   One possibility is to manipulate the entire record in the sorting process.   However, this suggestion can be discarded quickly since it involves a great deal of data movement each time it is necessary to rearrange entries in the sorting process.   An alternative means of ordering the records without actually moving them is required.   A frequent technique used in such situations is to prepare a table of indices or pointers and access the records *indirectly* through these pointers.   Then, during the sorting process these pointers rather than the actual data are exchanged.   For instance, Figure 13.28 shows a series of records to be sorted.   Each record has a key and additional information.   Shown to the left of the records is the pointer list before sorting.   On the right is the pointer list after sorting is completed.   The pointer list after sorting indicates where the records may be found in the original file for the file to be ordered.   Thus, the first item can be found in position four (the key 3 and its fields), the second in position five (the key 4 and its fields), and so on.   The file itself does not change; only the pointers are manipulated.

Figure 13.28   An example of a pointer sort.

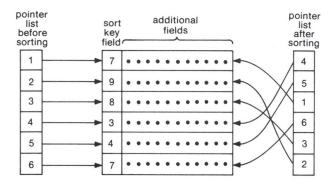

All of the sorting modules developed earlier in this chapter can be changed to manipulate pointers rather than the actual data.   As an example, consider making such modifications to module bubble.   The module still accepts LIST and n as import parameters but now returns PTR, the resulting list of pointers, as the export parameter.

smodule bubble (**imports**: LIST, n; **exports**: PTR)

Before the sorting process starts, the module bubble must create the initial PTR list from the integers 1 through n as follows.

for p **from** 1 **to** n

$\left[\quad ptr_p \leftarrow p \right.$

As the list is sorted, all references to LIST are done through the PTR list, for example,

if $list_{ptr_{pair}} > list_{ptr_{pair+1}}$ **then**

Whenever successive entries are out of order, their pointers are exchanged,

temp $\leftarrow ptr_{pair}$
$ptr_{pair} \leftarrow ptr_{pair+1}$
$ptr_{pair+1} \leftarrow$ temp

rather than the entries themselves.   These modifications will be presented later in this section when discussing an example.

13.4.2   Sorting With a Compound Sort Key

The second problem of a compound key is relatively easy to solve.   The comparisons must now be expanded to handle the tie breaking fields.   This involves modifying the sort algorithm to accept more than one import list.   Whenever a decision must be made and the first pair of keys is equal, the comparison process continues with successive pairs of keys, until the tie is broken or the compound keys are found to be identical.

Consider making further modifications to module bubble to accomodate a record consisting of two fields contained in the lists FA and FB.   The corresponding elements of FA and FB form the compound sort key.   Naturally, LIST is replaced in the parameter list by the lists FA and FB.   The decision about when to exchange pointers is expanded to include instances when the FA entries are equal.   The revised test can be written as:

if $\text{fa}_{\text{ptr}_{\text{pair}}} > \text{fa}_{\text{ptr}_{\text{pair}+1}}$ **or**
$(\text{fa}_{\text{ptr}_{\text{pair}}} = \text{fa}_{\text{ptr}_{\text{pair}+1}}$ **and** $\text{fb}_{\text{ptr}_{\text{pair}}} > \text{fb}_{\text{ptr}_{\text{pair}+1}})$ **then**

The next example will require the use of such modifications.

13.4.3   Application to a Specific Example

Sorting many of the files in Appendix L would require the use of the modifications suggested in this section.   Consider the following example.

Example 13.1   NHL Player Standings Problem
   Given the file of information for players in the NHL as contained in Appendix L,
   produce a listing of players ranked by total points.   Players with the same number
   of total points should be ranked by goals scored.

a) Problem Discussion   In order to solve this problem it will be advantageous to use a pointer sort that can handle a compound sort key.   In addition, it will be necessary to process alphabetic information.   FORTRAN/77 allows for the definition of a CHARACTER data type to make such processing easier.   The succeeding discussion will first develop modifications to module bubble, now called PTRBUB, and then outline the mainline program to use PTRBUB to produce the desired sorted list.

b) A Modified Bubble Sort   This example obviously requires a sort that can handle additional information as well as a compound sort key.   In addition, the ranking requested is in decreasing order.   Listed in Figure 13.29 is a subroutine PTRBUB which combines all of these requirements.   The fields FA and FB have replaced LIST in the import parameter list.   A pointer list, PTR, is used to refer to the data fields, and these pointers are manipulated rather than the actual data.   Successive pointers are exchanged if the FA entries are out of order or if the FA entries are equal but the FB entries are out of order.   The result is a list of pointers to the data indicating the required order.

c) A Mainline to Produce the Listing   A mainline program to input the file, sort it according to the specified criteria, and output the resulting sorted list is presented in Figure 13.30.   In order to handle the character information in the file, the CHARACTER

```
C Figure 13.29 -- A Pointer Bubble Sort Module.
C               Subroutine PTRBUB to use a combination pointer and
C               bubble sort to sort a file with a compound
C               sort key having two fields, FA and FB.

C***********************************************************************
C FA      - first part of the compound sort key
C FB      - second part of the compound sort key
C N       - number of records in the file
C NMAX    - maximum value of N
C PTR     - resulting list of pointers to sort the file
C MAXPAR  - maximum number of pairs for current pass
C PAIR    - comparison pair counter
C XFLAG   - exchange flag, truth of 'exchange took place'
C TEMP    - temporary used to exchange out-of-order pointers

C***********************************************************************
      SUBROUTINE PTRBUB(FA,FB,N,NMAX,PTR)

      INTEGER N, NMAX, P, MAXPAR, PAIR, TEMP
      INTEGER FA(NMAX), FB(NMAX), PTR(NMAX)
      LOGICAL XFLAG

C Set up the pointer list to point to the initial positions
C of the records in the file, that is, 1, 2, 3, ..., N.

      DO 100 P = 1, N
         PTR(P) = P
  100 CONTINUE

C Initialize the number of comparisons and exchange flag.

      MAXPAR = N - 1
      XFLAG = .TRUE.

C Continue passing over the list until there are no exchanges.

  200 IF (XFLAG) THEN

C         For each pass, compare the records in pairs.
C         If the records are out of order, exchange the pointers
C         to the records and set the exchange flag.
C         After each pass, reduce the comparisons by 1.

         XFLAG = .FALSE.
         DO 300 PAIR = 1, MAXPAR
            IF(FA(PTR(PAIR)) .LT. FA(PTR(PAIR+1)) .OR.
     +        (FA(PTR(PAIR)) .EQ. FA(PTR(PAIR+1)) .AND.
     +         FB(PTR(PAIR)) .LT. FB(PTR(PAIR+1)))) THEN
               TEMP = PTR(PAIR)
               PTR(PAIR) = PTR(PAIR+1)
               PTR(PAIR+1) = TEMP
               XFLAG = .TRUE.
            ENDIF
  300    CONTINUE
         MAXPAR = MAXPAR - 1
         GOTO 200
      ENDIF
      RETURN
      END
```

data type has been introduced.   The variable lists to represent a player's name, team, and position of play are declared to be of type CHARACTER.   Each entry in these lists is given a specific length to correspond to the maximum length for that field.   In order to prepare the file for input to the program, quotes are used to delimit the character fields. For more details on the character data type, read Appendix G.

```
C Figure 13.30 -- NHL Player Standings Problem.
C                  Program to produce a listing of the NHL file
C                  sorted by goals within total points.
C                  Use a bubble sort which returns a list of
C                  pointers to the records in the correct order.

C*********************************************************************

C PLAYER - the player's name (CHARACTER*19)
C TEAM    - the player's team (CHARACTER*12)
C POSITN  - the player's playing position (CHARACTER*1)
C GAMES   - the number of games played
C GOALS   - the number of goals scored
C ASSIST  - the number of assists scored
C POINTS  - the total number of points scored
C PENALT     - the number of penalties in minutes
C PTR     - the pointer list to position the records in order
C N       - the number of players in the file
C NMAX    - the maximum number of players planned for
C I, P    - miscellaneous indices and pointers

C*********************************************************************

        CHARACTER PLAYER(600)*19, TEAM(600)*12, POSITN(600)*1
        INTEGER GAMES(600), GOALS(600), ASSIST(600), POINTS(600)
        INTEGER PENALT(600), PTR(600), N, NMAX, I, P
C Allow for a maximum of 600 players on file.
C Input the actual number of players and their records.
        NMAX = 600
        READ *, N
        DO 100 I = 1, N
           READ *, PLAYER(I), TEAM(I), POSITN(I), GAMES(I),
     +           GOALS(I), ASSIST(I), POINTS(I), PENALT(I)
   100 CONTINUE
C Invoke the sorting routine to sort the file.
        CALL PTRBUB(POINTS,GOALS,N,NMAX,PTR)
C Output the file in order using the pointer list
C to access the records in the correct order.
        PRINT *, 'NAME                   ','TEAM        ','POS',
     +        '              GP',',             G',',             A',
     +        '            PTS',',             PM'
        PRINT *, ' '
        DO 200 I = 1, N
           P = PTR(I)
           PRINT *, PLAYER(P), TEAM(P), POSITN(P), GAMES(P),
     +           GOALS(P), ASSIST(P), POINTS(P), PENALT(P)
   200 CONTINUE
        STOP
        END
C Subroutine PTRBUB is placed here.
```

A portion of the output generated by this sort program is presented in Figure 13.31. The horizontal spacing has been altered slightly to fit the information on the page of text.

Figure 13.31 Partial output from the program of Figure 13.30. (Spacing edited)

NAME	TEAM	POS	GP	G	A	PTS	PM
Gretzky, Wayne	Edmonton	C	80	55	109	164	28
Dionne, Marcel	Los Angeles	C	80	58	77	135	70
Nilsson, Kent	Calgary	C	80	49	82	131	26
Bossy, Mike	Islanders	W	79	68	51	119	32
Taylor, Dave	Los Angeles	W	72	47	65	112	130
Stastny, Peter	Quebec	C	77	39	70	109	37
Simmer, Charlie	Los Angeles	W	65	56	49	105	62
Rogers, Mike	Hartford	C	80	40	65	105	32
Federko, Bernie	St. Louis	C	78	31	73	104	47
Richard, Jacques	Quebec	W	78	52	51	103	39
Middleton, Rick	Boston	W	80	44	59	103	16
.							
.							
Logan, Dave	Vancouver	D	7	0	0	0	13
Oddleifson, C.	Vancouver	C	8	0	0	0	6
Johnston, John	Washington	D	2	0	0	0	9
Chartier, Dave	Winnipeg	C	1	0	0	0	0
Whelton, Bill	Winnipeg	D	2	0	0	0	0

13.5 Summary

This chapter has investigated several methods of searching and sorting.   In each case both elementary and sophisticated methods have been presented.   The binary search technique is one of the best available and should be used whenever a list is presorted or the searches are sufficiently frequent to warrant sorting the file.

Several approaches to sorting were presented to provide an insight into the many methods available.   There is no best method of sorting - it usually depends on the characteristics of the data presented.   Often existing methods can be modified to work well for the specific data at hand.   Except for isolated cases, the Quicksort algorithm provides excellent characteristics as a general purpose sorting technique.

13.6 References

The amount of literature on sorting and searching techniques is too voluminous to list exhaustively.   The references listed below are some of the better sources of additional information.   Each reference in turn includes listings of appropriate articles in the journals.

Aho, A.V.; Hopcroft, J.E.; and Ullman, J.D.   *The Design and Analysis of Computer Algorithms.* Reading Mass: Addison-Wesley Publishing Co., 1974, pp. 76-105.

Kernighan, B.W. and Plauger, P.J.   *Software Tools*. Reading Mass: Addison-Wesley Publishing Co., 1976, pp. 105-116.

Knuth, D.E.   *The Art of Computer Programming - Volume 3 - Sorting and Searching*. Reading Mass: Addison-Wesley Publishing Co., 1973.

Page, E.S. and Wilson, L.B.   *Information Representation and Manipulation in a Computer*. Cambridge: Cambridge University Press, 1973, pp. 152-216.

13.7   Exercises

In most of the following exercises a program is requested to solve a specific problem. For each problem it is recommended that step-wise refinement be used in developing a pseudocode algorithm to solve the problem.   This algorithm should then be translated into FORTRAN/77 and run on the computer.   Where appropriate, the program should be tested with a variety of data sufficient to ensure that the program does what it is supposed to do.

13.1   a)   Translate module linear into a FORTRAN/77 subroutine.

b)   Write a FORTRAN/77 main program to test subroutine LINEAR by trying to find the positions of

       1, 2, 7, 8, 23, 29

in the following list of numbers.

       2, 3, 5, 7, 11, 13, 17, 19, 21, 23

c)   Modify subroutine LINEAR of part a) to take advantage of the ordering in the given list of numbers and then rerun the program of part b).

d)   Another approach to searching involves a linear search from both ends of a list.   Such a search would alternately compare the key to entries at the beginning and the end of the list until either the position of the key is found or the two searches intersect.   Again modify subroutine LINEAR of part a) and rerun the program of part b).

e)   Module linear (see Figure 13.1) is designed to return the place of a given key value in a given list of length n.   If the key value appears more than once in LIST, only the first occurrence would be found.   Consider *modifying* module linear to return the positions of *all* occurrences of the key value in LIST.

    i)   What changes would be required to the module interface?
    ii)   What changes would be required to the body of the module?

13.2   a)   If subroutine BINARY is not available in machine readable form, then prepare it in machine readable form suitable for FORTRAN/77.

b)   Create a list of the first 100 prime numbers and write a FORTRAN/77 main program to find various entries in this list using subroutine BINARY of part a).

c)   Modify subroutine LINEAR of Exercise 13.1 c) and subroutine BINARY of part a) to include an export parameter for the number of comparisons needed to either find an entry or determine that it does not appear in the list. Modify the program of part b) to compare the performance of these two modules.

13.3   Assume that you have two lists of data which are already sorted, one in ascending order and the other in descending order. Each list of data is preceded by a data count.

Develop a pseudocode algorithm which will check the two lists to determine if one is a reversed copy of the other. Your algorithm should be reasonably efficient and should stop as soon as possible. Your algorithm should output appropriate messages on termination.

13.4   The ternary search is similar to the binary search with one variation. Given a list sorted in ascending order of magnitude, the ternary search divides the list into *three* parts. For lists of length not evenly divisible by 3, the 3 sublists will be of unequal length which is acceptable. For instance, a list of length 17 yields sublists of length 5, 6 and 6 since $17/3 = 5$ and $2/3 \times 17 = 11$.

The ternary search uses the one-third entry and two-thirds entry for comparison with the key in order to find a match or to determine the portion of the current list which should be used for the continuation of the search.

Develop a FORTRAN/77 subroutine called TERNRY which implements the ternary search procedure described above. TERNRY should import the list itself, the size of the list and the key, and export the position of the key in the list and a flag which indicates the presence or absence of the key in the list.

13.5   a)   Translate modules min and select into FORTRAN/77 subprograms.
       b)   Write a FORTRAN/77 main program to test these modules on several lists of randomly chosen numbers.
       c)   Module select was designed to sort the entries of a list OLD into a second list NEW. By exchanging the smallest entry with the first entry, the second smallest with the second entry, . . . , the list can be sorted in place without the need for a second list. Furthermore, less effort is required to find the current smallest since the initial portion of the list will already be sorted.

            Make the necessary changes to modules min and select and test them with the program of part b).
       d)   An alternate selection sort is based on choosing the largest entry at each stage rather than the smallest. These larger entries are placed towards the end of the list in such a fashion that it is constructed backwards.

            Write a max module to find the largest, then modify select, and test it with the program of part b).

13.6   a)   Translate module bubble into a FORTRAN/77 subroutine.
       b)   Write a FORTRAN/77 main program to test subroutine BUBBLE on several lists of randomly chosen numbers.
       c)   Module bubble is designed to make one less comparison with each subsequent pass, on the premise that at least the current largest entry has

moved into the correct position.   Depending on the specific entries in the list, more than one entry may have "bubbled" into position.   In fact, all entries from the point of the last interchange to the end of the list will be in the proper order.

Modify subroutine BUBBLE to remember the position of the last interchange and to use this information to reduce the number of comparisons.   Rerun the program of part b) with this subroutine as a test of your revisions.

d)   Module bubble is designed to start at the beginning of a list and "bubble" the larger entries to the end of the list.   It is also feasible to take the reverse approach and start the comparisons at the end of the list and therefore "bubble" the smaller entries to the beginning of the list.   Redevelop module bubble to take this bottom-up approach.   Translate the revised subroutine into FORTRAN/77 and test it with an appropriate main program.

e)   Redesign module bubble to perform odd numbered passes top-down and even numbered passes bottom-up.   Translate the revised subroutine into FORTRAN/77 and test it with an appropriate main program.

f)   Assess the relative merits of each version of subroutine BUBBLE.   Modify each version to compute the number of comparisons involved.   Then write a single main program to test each version on

1)   a list already sorted in ascending order.
2)   a list sorted in descending order.
3)   several partially order lists.
4)   several randomly ordered lists.

State your conclusions.

13.7   a)   Translate module insert into FORTRAN/77.

b)   Write a FORTRAN/77 main program to test subroutine INSERT on several appropriate lists of numbers.

c)   Module insert was designed to sort the entries of a list OLD into a second list NEW.   By removing the current entry to be inserted, it is possible to retain the sorted portion of the list in the initial section of the list without using a second list.   Make the necessary changes to module insert so that it sorts the entries using only the given list.   Translate the revised subroutine to FORTRAN/77 and test the resulting subroutine with the program of part b).

d)   Redesign module insert to use a binary rather than a linear search to find the correct position for each entry.   Note that this will require some slight modifications to module binary.   Translate the revised module into FORTRAN/77 and again test the subroutine with the program of part b).

13.8   a)   If subroutines QUICK and PARTIT are not available in machine readable form, then prepare them in a form suitable for FORTRAN/77.

b)   Write a FORTRAN/77 program to test subroutines QUICK and PARTIT on several appropriate lists of numbers.

c)   An alternate pivoting strategy for the partitioning in Quicksort involves choosing the last entry rather than the first.   Rewrite subroutine PARTIT to pivot about the last entry. Rerun the program of part b) to test the revisions.

d) Still another pivoting strategy for the partitioning in Quicksort chooses the median of three of the entries in the list, for example, the first, the middle, and the last. Again rewrite subroutine PARTIT and rerun the program of part b).

e) Though Quicksort is very fast for longer lists of numbers, it does not perform as well for short lists. Redesign the module quicksort to use an insertion sort whenever the length of the current sublist is less than or equal to 30. Test the revisions by rerunning the program of part b).

f) As presented, module quicksort does not take advantage of the fact that at any stage of the partitioning process, there may be several list elements equal to the pivot. Ideally these elements should be grouped together so that:

$$list_{ll} \leq \ldots \leq list_{m-1} < list_m$$
$$list_m = \ldots = list_p = \ldots = list_q$$
$$list_q < list_{q+1} \leq \ldots \leq list_{rl}$$

Successive partitioning is then carried out on entries ll through m−1 and q+1 through rl. Make the necessary changes to the quicksort algorithm, then translate the resulting module to FORTRAN/77, and compare its performance with the original version.

g) Prove that the maximum number of recursive calls in the Quicksort technique is given by

$$\lfloor \log_2 n \rfloor + 1$$

13.9 Consider an array which contains only numbers ≥ 0. It is necessary to move all nonzero entries to the start of the array. Develop an appropriate pseudocode algorithm and translate the algorithm to a FORTRAN/77 program. Demonstrate the program for several examples including the following.

0, 2, 0, 3, 6, 9, 3, 9, 3, 9, 0, 15, 0, 0, 1

Output the number of nonzero entries as well as the resulting list.

Hint: Although this problem can be handled by using sorting techniques, it is a special case which can be handled in order n.

13.10 Suppose A and B are two lists of integral entries. It is necessary to know which entries are in:

1) both A and B.
2) A but not B.
3) B but not A.

Develop a pseudocode algorithm to get the two lists, A and B, and produce three lists of entries satisfying each of the three criteria. Translate the algorithm into FORTRAN/77 and test the program on the following two lists of entries.

$$A = (2, -5, 8, 4, -7, 1, -6, 10)$$
$$B = (9, 8, 4, -10, 3, -5, 12, 11, -3)$$

13.11   Given two lists of numbers,

$$X = (x_1, x_2, \ldots, x_n)$$

and

$$Y = (y_1, y_2, \ldots, y_m)$$

develop a pseudocode algorithm to create a single list

$$Z = (z_1, z_2, \ldots, z_k)$$

which contains each distinct element of X and Y, with no repetitions, and arranged in ascending order, that is,

$$z_1 < z_2 < \cdots < z_k$$

For example, if $X = (5, 2, 6, 2, 6)$ and $Y = (1, 5, 2, 5, 3, 5)$, then the resulting list should be $Z = (1, 2, 3, 5, 6)$.

13.12   Given a sorted list with possible duplicates, develop a pseudocode algorithm to produce a list of the entries with duplicates removed.

13.13   Modify each sorting module to produce an additional export parameter representing the number of comparisons needed to sort the given list.   Next, write a single main program to use these methods for

- a list of about 100 entries already sorted in ascending order.
- a list of about 100 entries sorted in descending order.
- several lists of random entries, choosing lengths from 10 to 100.

13.14   Create a program to rank teams in the National Hockey League by most "goals for" and least "goals against."   This ranking can be accomplished by sorting the number of goals in each column and later searching for each team's number of goals.   The resulting table would be printed in the input order (you do not need to implement a pointer sort therefore).   An example of the first few lines of the table would be:

Team Name	GF	Rank	GA	Rank
Boston	316	9	272	6
Buffalo	327	7	250	3
⋮	⋮	⋮	⋮	⋮

Your program should take advantage of existing modules for sorting and searching.

13.15   Given the file of NHL team statistics for the 1980–1981 season, produce a listing of the teams ranked

a)   in decreasing order by goals for.
b)   in ascending order by goals against.

13.16 Given the file of NHL player statistics for the 1980–1981 season, produce a listing of

    a)   the top 10 players by points scored.

    b)   the 5 worst "bad guys" (those with highest penalty minutes).

    c)   all the defencemen ranked by points scored.

    d)   the best player at each position in the league.

    e)   the best player at each position for each team.

13.17 Given the file of NHL goalie statistics for the 1980–1981 season, produce a listing of:

    a)   the goalies ranked by average.

    b)   the summary performance of all goalies for each team.

14
Statistics

14.1   Introduction

The collection and analysis of information is a pervasive activity in today's society and is performed by a variety of individuals, agencies, and institutions.   Scientists collect data from their experiments, financial firms collect data about credit ratings and profit margin, and governments collect data about food prices and unemployment.   However, for these data to be easily understood, they must be analyzed, condensed, and summarized.   The results of such analyses are often used to develop and support hypotheses, to make policy decisions, and to predict trends.   Such analyses and predictions are called *descriptive* and *inductive* statistics respectively.

When information is collected, the set of possible measurements is called the *population.* Since in many cases the entire population may not be tested, a representative subset or *sample* of the population must be used.   Assuring that the sample is indeed representative is a challenging and important task since far-reaching decisions may be based on the results.   For instance, the results of samplings performed for political polls and television ratings can affect government actions and program scheduling respectively.

Almost everyone is familiar with statistical measures in one form or another. Statistics are kept in sports such as hockey, baseball, and football to describe team or individual performances.   Statistical measures are used in the actuarial mathematics of insurance companies to determine life insurance premiums.   Pharmaceutical houses use statistical techniques to compute the effectiveness of new drugs.   Closer to home, everybody has received, perhaps too frequently, a statistical measure of scholastic performance; that is, he or she has had an average grade computed for his or her courses.   That the study of statistics is broadly based is evidenced by the diversity of disciplines which include an introductory statistics course as part of their basic curriculum.

Statistics is a very important topic. Unfortunately, it is very easy to misinterpret or misuse statistical results. Many television advertisements quote statistics to imply that their product is superior. The fact that some of the given statistics are incomplete and have other interpretations is often missed by an uninformed viewer. Campbell (1974) gives an interesting discussion of this topic.

The limited space available in this chapter allows only an introduction to some of the standard statistical techniques and terminology such as collection of data, computation of descriptive measures, and the use of tools for analysis. In many cases computer programs will be developed to facilitate these calculations.

14.2   Tables and Graphs

The data which are collected, called the *raw data*, are often presented in the form of a table. For instance, consider the typical table of data given in Figure 14.1. Such data are very difficult to analyze visually since humans usually have a limited ability to remember numbers. (Without looking at the table again, how many of the numbers in Figure 14.1 can you remember? For that matter, how many of them would you really want to remember?) When the data are arranged in a table, the first piece of information one usually knows about is the total number of data values (33 in this case).

Figure 14.1   Typical table of raw data.

4.90	1.75	5.01	6.30	3.01	8.50
6.19	5.02	2.37	7.90	5.64	9.77
9.63	7.41	5.32	3.35	6.10	10.28
10.11	6.91	8.61	9.14	10.42	6.05
2.10	6.89	9.45	9.63	12.51	11.34
12.17	15.99	11.89			

The next thing which can be determined about the data is the maximum and minimum values. In this case, they are 15.99 and 1.75 respectively. (The module **minmax** of Chapter 12 could be used to determine these attributes.) From the values of the maximum and minimum, one may obtain the *range* of the data which is simply the difference between the maximum and minimum values, $15.99 - 1.75 = 14.24$.

To obtain more insight into the data requires a little more effort. A common technique is to count the number of data values which fall into several predetermined, consecutive intervals or *classes* which cover the range of the numbers. The number of values in each class is called the *class frequency*. The collection of class frequencies is called a *frequency distribution*. Data summarized in such a manner are called *grouped data*. Conversely, raw data are often referred to as *ungrouped data*. Grouped data may be presented in several ways, and these are discussed in the following sections.

14.2.1   Frequency Tables

When a frequency distribution is presented in tabular form it is called a *frequency table*. A frequency table for the data of Figure 14.1 is shown in Figure 14.2. In this case, the *class width* is 2.0 for each of the 8 classes.

Figure 14.2   A frequency table for the data of Figure 14.1.

class boundaries	class frequency
0.0–2.0	1
2.0–4.0	4
4.0–6.0	5
6.0–8.0	8
8.0–10.0	7
10.0–12.0	5
12.0–14.0	2
14.0–16.0	1

The number of classes used is somewhat arbitrary and may require several attempts to achieve reasonable values. The number of classes is commonly between 8 and 25. Some people make use of Sturge's formula

$$k = 1 + 3.3\log_{10}n \tag{14.1}$$

where k is the number of classes and n is the total number of data values. The class widths are usually, but not necessarily, uniform and are determined by the number of classes and the range. It is important to assign data values to classes in a unique way. This requires a decision as to whether a data value which occurs on a boundary will be assigned consistently to the next higher or next lower class.

Consider the design of a module to classify raw data and to produce a frequency table.

Example 14.1   Frequency Table Module

Develop a general classification module to generate a frequency table for a given table of raw data.

a) Problem Discussion   Before discussing the details of an interface for a classify module, consider the mechanics of producing the frequency table. To establish the necessary class boundaries, the range of values in the table is needed, namely the minimum and maximum values.

Presumably this range and Sturge's formula can be used to establish class widths and class boundaries. Frequently, however, real data would give unnatural break points for these classes. For the raw data in Figure 14.1, the range is from 1.75 to 15.99, which is 14.24, and could be divided into $1 + 3.3\log_{10}33$ or about 11 classes, each of width 1.29. Often these computed values make it difficult for the reader to appreciate the class boundaries. To improve these choices of class boundaries, a better design involves allowing the user to specify the number of classes as well as the low and high limit for the range of values.

Given these user specified parameters, it will be the task of the module classify to map or convert each given observation (raw data value) into a class number. Some thought should be given to the handling of invalid class numbers resulting from out-of-range observations. The ostrich approach is to simply ignore them, but this leaves the user in the dark and vulnerable to execution errors. Another option is to collect out-of-range values in the two extreme classes at the endpoints of the supplied range, but this may result in distorted frequencies at either or both ends. Regardless of which of these two options is implemented, some indication of out-of-range values should be reported to the user. Since module classify should not produce printed messages, it will notify the user of out-of-range values via a logical error flag and leave such values unclassified.

b) Module interface To begin the formal development of module classify, consider the form of the module interface. Since there are several export parameters, classify must clearly be a subroutine module. The import parameters are the array of raw data values, RAW, the number of observations, nobs, and the class specifications, namely, the number of classes, nclass, and the low and high limits for the range, clow and chigh. As exports, the module classify will produce an array of frequency counts of the observations, COUNTS, which fall into each class as well as a logical flag, error, which reports whether or not any observations fell out of the given range. The resulting interface is given below:

> **smodule** classify(**imports**: nobs, RAW, nclass, clow, chigh;
>   **exports**: COUNTS, error)

c) Module Decomposition The frequency count classification algorithm has three basic steps:

1. Initialize the error flag and frequency counts.
2. Compute the class width.
3. Classify the observations.

The first two steps may be easily refined into pseudocode by initializing the export parameters and using the import class specifications as follows:

* Initialize the error flag and frequency counts.

error ← **false**
for class **from** 1 **to** nclass **do**
    $\lceil$ $\text{count}_{\text{class}}$ ← 0
* Compute the class width.

width ← (chigh - clow)/nclass

The third step, classifying the observations, is the major step in the algorithm. It is repeated for each of the nobs observations. For each observation, a check must be made for out-of-range values. Thus, the decomposition of Step **3.** is as follows:

* Classify the observations.

3.1 for i **from** 1 **to** nobs **do**

> **3.2** If the observation is out of range, then set the error flag.
> **3.3** Otherwise, determine the class for this observation and increment the class frequency count.

Determining the class for an observation requires computing the number of class widths between the observation and the low endpoint of the range. This computation is shown below along with the final refinement of Step **3**.

* Classify the observations.

for i **from** 1 **to** nobs **do**

> * Check for data out of range and set the error flag.
>
> **if** (raw_i < clow) **or** (raw_i > chigh) **then**
>
> > error ← **true**
>
> **else**
>
> > * Determine the class for this observation,
> > * and increment its frequency count.
> >
> > class ← int(raw_i - clow)/width + 1
> > $counts_{class}$ ← $counts_{class}$ + 1

d) Conversion to FORTRAN/77   The pseudocode fragments are collected together and translated into the FORTRAN/77 subroutine CLSIFY, shown in Figure 14.3. Its use will be demonstrated in the next section.

14.2.2 Histograms

Another method of presenting data which has been grouped into classes is to use a *histogram*. A histogram presents the same information as a frequency table but uses a more graphic representation. A histogram is essentially a graph which uses rectangles to present the class and frequency information. The width of the rectangle is equal to the class width and the height of the rectangle corresponds to the class frequency. Figure 14.4 shows a histogram corresponding to the frequency table of Figure 14.2. As may be seen from the diagram, a histogram provides a summary of the data allowing relative class frequencies to be better appreciated.

Alternate ways of scaling the height of the histogram rectangles are to divide the class frequency by *n* or to divide the class frequency by the class width. The latter is the only correct way when the classes have unequal widths.

With respect to the choice of the classes themselves, there is some flexibility. For the sample data, a different number of classes could be chosen, different class widths are possible, and different class boundaries may be used. It is conceivable that a change in the choice of these parameters will produce a histogram which conveys an entirely different impression of the data. For instance, Figure 14.5 shows a histogram for the same data with only the class boundaries changed. Although this histogram does not present as pleasing a diagram as the previous one, it is nevertheless an equally valid summary of the data.

```
C FIGURE 14.3 -- Frequency Table Module
C                 Subroutine CLSIFY to classify data according to a given
C                 number of classes within a given range, and to
C                 produce an array of frequency counts for each class.

C***********************************************************************

C NOBS    - number of observations
C RAW     - array of observed data
C NCLASS  - number of classes
C CLOW    - lower limit of class range
C CHIGH   - upper limit of class range
C COUNTS  - array of class counts
C ERROR   - .TRUE. if raw data out of range
C WIDTH   - class width
C COUNTS  - current class number
C I       - loop counter

C***********************************************************************

      SUBROUTINE CLSIFY(NOBS, RAW, NCLASS, CLOW, CHIGH, COUNTS, ERROR)

      INTEGER NOBS, NCLASS, COUNTS(NOBS), CLASS, I
      REAL RAW(NOBS), CLOW, CHIGH, WIDTH
      LOGICAL ERROR

C Initialize the error flag and frequency counts.

      ERROR = .FALSE.
      DO 100 CLASS = 1, NCLASS
         COUNTS(CLASS) = O
  100 CONTINUE

C Compute the class width.

      WIDTH = (CHIGH - CLOW)/NCLASS

C Classify the observations.

      DO 200 I = 1, NOBS

C         Check for data out of range and set the error flag.

         IF (RAW(I) .LT. CLOW .OR. RAW(I) .GT. CHIGH) THEN
            ERROR = .TRUE.
         ELSE

C            Determine the class for this observation, ensure
C            that it is within limits, due to round-off error,
C            and increment its frequency count.

            CLASS = IFIX((RAW(I) - CLOW)/WIDTH) + 1
            IF (CLASS .GT. NCLASS) THEN
               CLASS = NCLASS
            ENDIF
            COUNTS(CLASS) = COUNTS(CLASS) + 1
         ENDIF
  200 CONTINUE
      RETURN
      END
```

Figure 14.4   A histogram for the data of Figure 14.1.

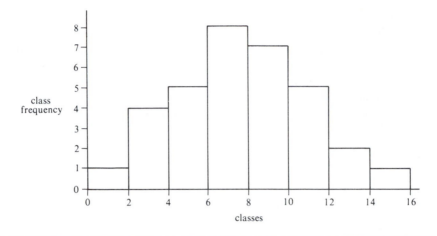

Figure 14.5   An alternate histogram for the data of Figure 14.1.

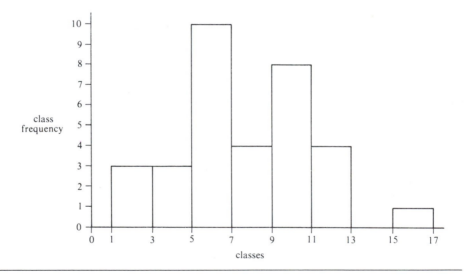

An algorithm to construct a histogram is a natural sequel to the module which classifies data and produces a frequency table.   Such a histogram algorithm, which uses a frequency table as input, is developed in the following discussion.

Example 14.2   Histogram Module
Develop a module which will construct a histogram from a given set of frequency counts.

a) Problem Discussion   There are many approaches to constructing a histogram. One simple approach would be to use the plotting routines from Chapter 6. While it would be possible to draw multiple parallel lines to represent the histogram bars, labelling the bars cannot be done by the printer-plot routines.

A more direct approach is to print the histogram bars for each class frequency. A graphic way to represent these frequency counts is to use a box of asterisks, several print lines wide and several print columns high for each unit of the frequency count, such as:

```
****
****
****
****
```

Positioning such bars vertically across the page is somewhat difficult with a line printer, but consider rotating the histogram 90° and printing the histogram bars across the page. This significantly eases the problem of determining what to print on each line.

Another concern is handling histograms of various sizes. It will be necessary to consider how to adjust the actual size of a histogram so that it fits nicely on an output page. This can be done by scaling or selecting the number of asterisks in each unit of the bar corresponding to a frequency count or counts.

b) Defining the Module Interface   Since a histogram is a visual representation of a frequency table, it is evident that such a table is a necessary import parameter. From the interface design of module classify, the frequency table consisted of the number of classes, nclass, the table of frequency counts, COUNTS, and the low and high limits for the class range, clow and chigh. A histogram module does not need any explicit export parameters, since the module prints its only results, the histogram. Thus, the module interface would be:

smodule histogram(**imports**: nclass, COUNTS, clow, chigh)

c) Developing the Module Algorithm   The histogram module has two basic steps:

1.   Compute scale factors and class boundaries.
2.   Print the histogram bars for each class.

To refine these steps, it is necessary to visualize the form of the final histogram. In particular, the histogram bar must indicate the frequency count for that class, but also the class boundaries. A rather complete form of the histogram bar might look like the following:

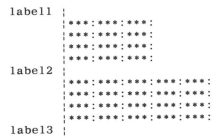

```
label1  |
        |***:***:***:
        |***:***:***:
        |***:***:***:
        |***:***:***:
label2  |
        |***:***:***:***:***:
        |***:***:***:***:***:
        |***:***:***:***:***:
        |***:***:***:***:***:
label3  |
```

where `label1`, `label2`, and `label3` will be the printed numerical values of the class boundaries for the histogram bar, and the histogram bar will be represented by four lines of asterisks. Each unit of the frequency count will contain several asterisks, in this case three, and a colon to indicate the end of each unit.

To scale the histogram, it is necessary to know the maximum line length on the line printer. This length must be reduced by the number of print positions reserved for the labels and axis characters, '|'. The available maximum length will be assumed to be the variable linesize.

If the largest frequency count, maxcnt, exceeds linesize, then it is reasonable to have the counts scaled down such that each character printed represents 2, 3 or more counts. An appropriate divisor for the frequency counts is obtained by the calculation:

$$\text{divisor} \leftarrow \text{int}(\text{maxcnt}/(\text{linesize}+1)) + 1$$

For example, with linesize equal to 40 and maxcnt equal to 40, no scaling occurs as divisor will be 1. But if maxcnt is between 41 and 81, counts are divided by 2.

Another possibility occurs when the maximum frequency count is quite small, when one would wish to spread the histogram over the full line length. In this case, each count corresponds to several asterisk characters followed by the colon. The number of characters per unit will be called nstar which can be determined from the calculation:

$$\text{nstar} \leftarrow \text{int}(\text{linesize}/\text{maxcnt})$$

d) Refining Step **1.** From the previous discussion, computing the scale factors and class boundaries can be refined as follows:

* Compute the scale factors and class boundaries.

1.1 Find the maximum frequency count.
1.2 Compute the scale factors.
1.3 Compute the class width for class boundaries.

The refinement into pseudocode can follow immediately:

* Compute the scale factors and class boundaries.

* Find the maximum frequency count.

maxcnt ← count$_1$
for i **from** 2 **to** nobs **do**
⎡ **if** maxcnt < count$_i$ **then**
⎢   ⎡ maxcnt ← count$_i$
⎣

* Compute the scale factors.

divisor ← int(maxcnt/(linesize+1)) + 1
nstar ← int(linesize/maxcnt)

* Compute the class width for class boundaries.

width ← (chigh - clow)/nclass

e) Refining Step **2.**   This step involves printing out a histogram bar for each class. Recall that the form of a histogram bar includes labelling the class boundary both before and after the histogram bar.   The following decomposition uses a loop to print a bar for each class:

* Print a histogram bar for each class.

2.1 Print the initial class boundary.
2.2 for i **from** 1 **to** nclass **do**
⎡ **2.3** Print a histogram bar for this frequency count.
⎢ **2.4** Print the next class boundary.
⎣

Refining Steps **2.1** and **2.4** requires a variable, say class, which corresponds to the current class boundary value.   This variable would be initialized to the low end of the class range, clow, and be incremented by the class width, width.   Thus, Step **2.1** becomes:

* Print the initial class boundary.

class ← clow
put class, '¦'

and Step **2.4** becomes:

* Print the next class boundary.

class ← class + width
put class, '¦'

Refining Step **2.3** to print each histogram bar involves an inner loop to print the four identical lines of the bar.   The scaling factors are applied to the number of asterisks printed in each unit, and to the number of units printed for each bar.

* Print a histogram bar for this frequency count.

for b **from** 1 **to** 4 **do**

$\left[\begin{array}{l}\textbf{put } `\qquad`,\ `¦`,\ ((`*`,\ \text{s } \textbf{from } 1 \textbf{ to } \text{nstar-1}),\ `:`), \\ \qquad \text{u } \textbf{from } 1 \textbf{ to } \text{count}_i/\text{divisor})\end{array}\right.$

Note that in the **put** statement, implied loops are used to ensure that all the printed information appears on the same line.   The first field of blanks should match the size of the printed label, class.

f) Translation into FORTRAN/77   These pseudocode fragments have been collected together to form the FORTRAN/77 module shown in Figure 14.6.   The maximum available line length, LSIZE, was defined to be the constant 40 which is suitable for the width of the pages in this book.

A FORTRAN/77 main program to use these two subroutines, CLSIFY and HISTGM, is shown in Figure 14.7.   Note that the design of the subroutine HISTGM requires the classification of the raw data as generated by subroutine CLSIFY.   One might have incorporated both the classification and printing of the histogram in a single, somewhat larger and more complex, module.   However, this separation of function into two modules provides extra flexibility when a frequency table alone is desired, or when histograms of frequency tables produced by other means are desired.   Figure 14.8 contains the printed output produced by this main program when executed with the raw data from Figure 14.1.

14.2.3   Frequency Polygons and Curves

A third way of presenting the frequency information is through the use of line graphs. In the simplest case, a *frequency polygon* is obtained by joining the center points on the top of each histogram rectangle.   Such a graph is shown in Figure 14.9 for the histogram of Figure 14.4.

In the case of a very large mass of data, it is possible to make the class widths very small and still have a representable frequency in each class.   This reduction in class width will have the effect of smoothing out the frequency polygon into a *frequency curve.* Figure 14.10 shows three such frequency curves exhibiting properties often found in data.   Frequency curves such as these are quite important and much analysis has been done to determine their properties.

```
C Figure 14.6 -- Histogram Module.
C                Subroutine HISTGM to construct a histogram, given
C                a set of class frequency counts
C***********************************************************************
C NCLASS   - number of classes
C COUNTS   - frequency for each class
C CLOW     - lower limit of class range
C CHIGH    - upper limit of class range
C LSIZE    - number of characters in a histogram bar
C CLASS    - label for class boundary
C WIDTH    - class width
C NSTAR    - number of astericks per unit height
C I,B,U,S  - loop indices - I, BAR, UNIT, STAR
C MAXCNT   - maximum frequency count
C DIVISR   - scale factor for histogram units
C***********************************************************************
      SUBROUTINE HISTGM(NCLASS, COUNTS, CLOW, CHIGH)

      INTEGER NCLASS, COUNTS(NCLASS), NSTAR, I, B, U, S, MAXCNT, DIVISR
      INTEGER LSIZE
      REAL CLOW, CHIGH, CLASS, WIDTH
C Initialize the line size.
      LSIZE = 40
C Find the maximum frequency count.
      MAXCNT = COUNTS(1)
      DO 100 I = 2, NCLASS
         IF (MAXCNT .LT. COUNTS(I)) THEN
            MAXCNT = COUNTS(I)
         ENDIF
  100 CONTINUE
C Compute the scale factors.
      DIVISR = MAXCNT/(LSIZE+1) + 1
      NSTAR = LSIZE/MAXCNT
C Compute the class width and first class boundary.
      WIDTH = (CHIGH - CLOW)/NCLASS
      CLASS = CLOW
      PRINT *, ' '
      PRINT *, CLASS, ' ¦'
C Print a histogram bar for each class.
      DO 500 I = 1, NCLASS
C        Print out the required number of bars.
         DO 400 B = 1, 4
            PRINT 9000, '¦', (('*', S = 1, NSTAR), ':',
     +                                U = 1, COUNTS(I)/DIVISR)
  400    CONTINUE
C Print the next class boundary.
         CLASS = CLASS + WIDTH
         PRINT *, CLASS, ' ¦'
  500 CONTINUE
      RETURN
 9000 FORMAT(17X,116A1)
      END
```

Program Notes

- In order to display the components of the histogram bar in adjacent output columns in FORTRAN/77, it was necessary to introduce a simple example of a FORMAT statement. The statement FORMAT(17X,116A1) when referenced by a PRINT statement allows for initial spacing and all of the characters in a histogram bar to be displayed in consecutive columns. Appendix F is devoted to the study of formatting.

```
C Figure 14.7 -- A Frequency Classification/Histogram Problem.
C               Program to use subroutines CLSIFY and HISTGM to
C               produce a frequency table and a histogram for a
C               given set of raw data.
C*********************************************************************
C X      - array of observations
C COUNTS - set of class counts
C NOBS   - number of observations
C NCLASS - number of classes
C CLOW   - lower limit of class range
C CHIGH  - upper limit of class range
C ERROR  - .TRUE. if data out of class range
C I, J   - loop counters

C*********************************************************************
        INTEGER COUNTS(20), NOBS, NCLASS, I, J
        REAL X(100), CLOW, CHIGH
        LOGICAL ERROR

C Acquire observations, preceded by a data count.

        READ *, NOBS
        PRINT *, 'THE NUMBER OF OBSERVATIONS IS', NOBS
        READ *, (X(I), I = 1, NOBS)

C Acquire classification parameters.

        READ *, CLOW, CHIGH, NCLASS
        PRINT *, 'THE CLASS RANGE IS', CLOW, ' TO ', CHIGH
        PRINT *, 'THE NUMBER OF CLASSES IS', NCLASS
        PRINT *, ' '

C Classify the raw data.

        CALL CLSIFY(NOBS,X,NCLASS,CLOW,CHIGH,COUNTS,ERROR)

C Provided no error occurred during classification, record
C the frequency table and produce a histogram.

        IF (ERROR) THEN
            PRINT *, 'RANGE ERROR IN CLASSIFICATION'
        ELSE
            PRINT *, '     CLASS          COUNT'
            DO 100 I = 1, NCLASS
                PRINT *, I, COUNTS(I)
100         CONTINUE

            CALL HISTGM(NCLASS,COUNTS,CLOW,CHIGH)

        ENDIF
        STOP
        END

C Subroutines CLSIFY and HISTGM would be placed here.
```

Figure 14.8 Printed output produced by the main program of Figure 14.7 when executed on the
data from Figure 14.1.

```
THE NUMBER OF OBSERVATIONS IS              33
THE CLASS RANGE IS   0.0000000E+00   TO      16.00000
THE NUMBER OF CLASSES IS              8
         CLASS          COUNT
           1              1
           2              4
           3              5
           4              8
           5              7
           6              5
           7              2
           8              1

0.0000000E+00    ┊
                 ┊*****:
                 ┊*****:
                 ┊*****:
                 ┊*****:
   2.000000      ┊
                 ┊*****:*****:*****:*****:
                 ┊*****:*****:*****:*****:
                 ┊*****:*****:*****:*****:
                 ┊*****:*****:*****:*****:
   4.000000      ┊
                 ┊*****:*****:*****:*****:*****:
                 ┊*****:*****:*****:*****:*****:
                 ┊*****:*****:*****:*****:*****:
                 ┊*****:*****:*****:*****:*****:
   6.000000      ┊
                 ┊*****:*****:*****:*****:*****:*****:*****:*****:
                 ┊*****:*****:*****:*****:*****:*****:*****:*****:
                 ┊*****:*****:*****:*****:*****:*****:*****:*****:
                 ┊*****:*****:*****:*****:*****:*****:*****:*****:
   8.000000      ┊
                 ┊*****:*****:*****:*****:*****:*****:*****:
                 ┊*****:*****:*****:*****:*****:*****:*****:
                 ┊*****:*****:*****:*****:*****:*****:*****:
                 ┊*****:*****:*****:*****:*****:*****:*****:
  10.00000       ┊
                 ┊*****:*****:*****:*****:*****:
                 ┊*****:*****:*****:*****:*****:
                 ┊*****:*****:*****:*****:*****:
                 ┊*****:*****:*****:*****:*****:
  12.00000       ┊
                 ┊*****:*****:
                 ┊*****:*****:
                 ┊*****:*****:
                 ┊*****:*****:
  14.00000       ┊
                 ┊*****:
                 ┊*****:
                 ┊*****:
                 ┊*****:
  16.00000       ┊
```

Figure 14.9   A frequency polygon for the data of Figure 14.1.

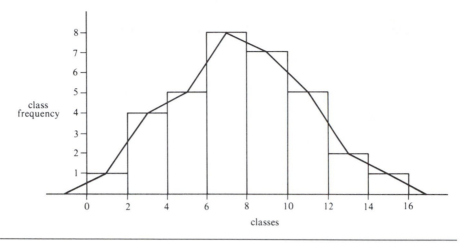

Figure 14.10   Examples of frequency curves.

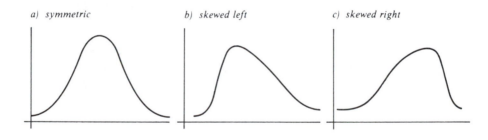

14.3   Measures of Central Tendency

Statistical measures which tend to predict where the central region of the data lies are called *measures of central tendency*. The mean, median, and the mode all fall into this category.

14.3.1   The Mean

There are several different types of means, the most common of which is the *arithmetic mean* or simply the *mean*. The mean or *average* is computed by summing all data values and dividing the total sum by the number of data values in the sum.   Thus, for a set of data values X, the arithmetic mean $\bar{x}$ (called *xbar*) is computed by

$$\bar{x} = \frac{x_1 + x_2 + x_3 + \cdots + x_n}{n} = \frac{1}{n} \sum_{i=1}^{n} x_i \tag{14.2}$$

As an example, for the data 1, 7, 4, 6, 9, 5, 4, the arithmetic mean is

$$\bar{x} = \frac{(1 + 7 + 4 + 6 + 9 + 5 + 4)}{7} = 5.14 \ .$$

Two less commonly used means are called the *geometric mean, GM*

$$GM = (x_1 x_2 x_3 x_4 \cdots x_n)^{1/n} \tag{14.3}$$

and the *harmonic mean, HM*

$$HM = \frac{1}{\frac{1}{n} \left[\frac{1}{x_1} + \frac{1}{x_2} + \frac{1}{x_3} + \cdots + \frac{1}{x_n} \right]}$$

$$= \frac{1}{\frac{1}{n} \sum_{i=1}^{n} \frac{1}{x_i}} \ . \tag{14.4}$$

These latter means are used in special circumstances and are presented here only to inform the reader as to their existence and how they are calculated.

14.3.2 The Median

The *median* of a set of data values is the data value which occupies the middle position when the data have been sorted into either ascending or descending order. In the case when there are two middle values (*n* even), the median is the average of these two middle values.

$$\text{Median} = \begin{cases} x_{(n+1)/2} & n \text{ is odd} \\ \\ \dfrac{x_{n/2} + x_{(n+2)/2}}{2} & n \text{ is even} \end{cases} \tag{14.5}$$

The seven data values 1, 7, 4, 6, 9, 5, 4 would have to be sorted into the order 1, 4, 4, 5, 6, 7, 9 (or 9, 7, 6, 5, 4, 4, 1) from which the median is in the $(7 + 1)/2$-th $= 4$-th position. Thus, the median is the value 5.

14.3.3 The Mode

The *mode* of a set of data values is the data value(s) which occur(s) the most number of times. The mode is not necessarily a unique value and, in fact, may not even exist. The numbers 1, 7, 4, 6, 9, 5, 4 have a mode of 4 since that value occurs most often. The numbers 1, 7, 4, 6, 9, 5 do not have a mode. For a frequency curve, the mode is the value of *x* corresponding to the maximum point on the curve. Curves with two maxima are called *bimodal* and those with more than two maxima are called *multimodal*.

14.4   Measures of Dispersion

The measures of the above section described where the central region of the data was but they did not tell anything else about the distribution. For example, the curves of Figure 14.11 have the same arithmetic mean, median, and mode (all falling at the same place in this case) but still have vastly different distributions. Looking at the curves one could say that one curve is more spread out or *dispersed* than the other. Thus, some measures to describe this dispersion are also desired. Note that the range is in fact one measure of dispersion but even it is the same for the given curves. However, what does distinguish the above curves from each other is the frequency of data values at different distances or *deviations* from the mean. Many measures of dispersion compute some average of these deviations.

Figure 14.11   Two distributions with the same mean, median, and mode.

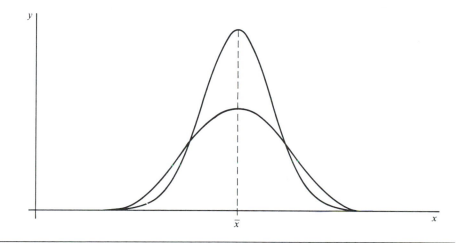

14.4.1   Mean Deviation

The first dispersion measure is the *mean deviation* which simply computes the average of the magnitude of the deviation. This calculation is indicated by the equation below.

$$MD = \frac{|x_1 - \overline{x}| + |x_2 - \overline{x}| + |x_3 - \overline{x}| + \cdots + |x_n - \overline{x}|}{n}$$

$$= \frac{1}{n} \sum_{i=1}^{n} |x_i - \overline{x}| \tag{14.6}$$

Notice that this equation takes the absolute value (magnitude) of the deviation in order that all summed terms are positive. If this were not done both positive and negative values would be summed, and the mean deviation would be zero, which is useless.

14.4.2   The Standard Deviation

The standard deviation also computes the deviation from the mean, but in this case the square root of the average of the squares of the deviations is used as given by the following formula.

$$S = \left(\frac{(x_1 - \bar{x})^2 + (x_2 - \bar{x})^2 + (x_3 - \bar{x})^2 + \cdots + (x_n - \bar{x})^2}{n - 1} \right)^{1/2}$$

$$= \left(\frac{1}{n - 1} \sum_{i=1}^{n} (x_i - \bar{x})^2 \right)^{1/2} \tag{14.7}$$

The motivation for this measure is similar to the previous mean deviation in that the summed terms should all be positive. The squaring operation accomplishes this, and although it is not obvious from the formulas, the standard deviation is much easier to work with in mathematical analysis. The use of $n - 1$ instead of n as the divisor is also motivated by advanced mathematical considerations, and there is little numerical difference in the final result when n is large (say, $n > 10$).

There is another version of the standard deviation formula which may also be used. It is derived from the above equation as shown below.

$$S = \left(\frac{1}{n - 1} \sum_{i=1}^{n} (x_i - \bar{x})^2 \right)^{1/2}$$

$$= \left(\frac{1}{n - 1} \sum (x_i^2 - 2x_i\bar{x} + \bar{x}^2) \right)^{1/2}$$

$$= \left(\frac{1}{n - 1} \left[\sum x_i^2 - \sum 2x_i\bar{x} + \sum \bar{x}^2 \right] \right)^{1/2}$$

$$= \left(\frac{1}{n - 1} \left[\sum x_i^2 - 2n\bar{x} \left(\frac{\sum x_i}{n} \right) + n\bar{x}^2 \right] \right)^{1/2}$$

$$= \left(\frac{1}{n - 1} \left[\sum x_i^2 - 2n\bar{x}\,\bar{x} + n\bar{x}^2 \right] \right)^{1/2}$$

$$= \left(\frac{1}{n - 1} \left[\sum x_i^2 - n\bar{x}^2 \right] \right)^{1/2} \tag{14.8}$$

$$= \left(\frac{1}{n - 1} \left[\sum x_i^2 - \frac{1}{n} \left(\sum x_i \right)^2 \right] \right)^{1/2} \tag{14.9}$$

Although formulas (14.7) and (14.9) are algebraically equivalent there is, as often happens, quite a difference when they are used in computations. For instance, formula

(14.7) requires processing the data values twice, once to compute $\bar{x}$ and once more to compute the n values of $(x_i - \bar{x})^2$. Formula (14.9) requires only one processing of the data since $\sum x_i^2$ and $(\sum x_i)^2$ may be calculated at the same time. Thus, formula (14.9) would require approximately half the data handling of formula (14.7).

On the other hand, notice that formula (14.7) has potential for better accuracy. If the standard deviation is small relative to the data values, both sums in equation (14.9) may be so large that any difference between them is lost due to the limited number of digits in computer and calculator arithmetic. Equation (14.7) does not suffer from this difficulty as long as the x_i's may be distinguished from $\bar{x}$. For example, consider computing the standard deviation of the following numbers on an IBM 4341 computer (7 digits and truncated arithmetic).

$$1000.00, \ 1000.01, \ 1000.02, \ 1000.03, \ \ldots, \ 1000.50$$

There are 51 data values in total, and their mean is 1000.25. The first formula computes the standard deviation as follows.

$$s_1 = \left(\frac{1}{50} [(-.25)^2 + (-.24)^2 + (-.23)^2 + \cdots + (.25)^2] \right)^{1/2}$$

$$= \sqrt{.02211243}$$

$$= .1487024$$

The second formula computes

$$s_2 = \left(\frac{1}{50} \left[(1000.00)^2 + (1000.01)^2 + \cdots + (1000.50)^2 - \frac{1}{51}(51012.75)^2 \right] \right)^{1/2}$$

$$= \sqrt{-2.240000}$$

Thus, the second formula gives a completely erroneous result in a case such as this when the standard deviation is small with respect to the mean.

In all fairness to the second formula, however, this difficulty may be negated if one can reduce the value of each data value by a constant amount Δx before the calculations. This magnitude reduction does not affect the dispersion of the curve; rather it just shifts the curve towards the y axis such that the new mean is much smaller. Both the standard deviation and the mean will now be small, and there should be no difficulty with the calculation. This situation is shown in Figure 14.12. The formula for this calculation is as follows.

$$s = \left(\frac{1}{n-1} \left[\sum_{i=1}^{n} (x_i - \Delta x)^2 - \frac{1}{n} \left(\sum_{i=1}^{n} (x_i - \Delta x) \right)^2 \right] \right)^{1/2} \tag{14.10}$$

The ideal amount to shift the curve would, of course, be $\Delta x = \bar{x}$, but $\bar{x}$ is unknown before the one pass computation. In fact, if it was known, the first standard deviation formula would be used instead. An informed guess about a good value for Δx could be made from previous knowledge about the data values or by analyzing the first few data

Figure 14.12 Shifting a curve by a constant value.

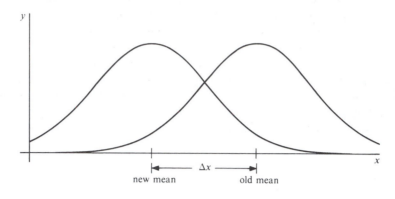

values and assuming that they are representative of the remaining values. The fact that the introduction of the Δx term does not change the value of the standard deviation may be proven algebraically.

14.4.3 The Variance
The variance of a set of data values is defined as the square of the standard deviation.

$$variance = s^2 \qquad\qquad (14.11)$$

Notice that both formulas for the standard deviation compute the variance first and then take its square root to get the standard deviation.

14.5 Computing the Statistical Measures

The computation of the most common statistical measures of mean, variance, and standard deviation on computers is a relatively simple task. As a result, a step-wise refinement and presentation of an algorithm have not been included. Figures 14.13 and 14.14 present two subroutines, called STATS1 and STATS2 respectively, which compute these statistics. STATS1 uses the standard deviation formula of equation (14.7) and STATS2 uses equation (14.9).

```
C Figure 14.13 -- A Statistical Measures Module.
C                 Subroutine STATS1 calculates the mean, variance, and
C                 standard deviation of the values in an array.

C**********************************************************************
C X      - one-dimensional array containing raw data
C N      - number of data values in the array X
C XBAR   - mean
C VAR    - variance
C STDEV  - standard deviation
C SUMX   - sum of the X values
C SUMDIF - sum of the squares of the differences

C**********************************************************************
       SUBROUTINE STATS1(X, N, XBAR, VAR, STDEV)

       INTEGER I, N
       REAL X(N), XBAR, VAR, STDEV, SUMX, SUMDIF, SQRT
C Calculate the sum of the X values and the mean.

       SUMX = 0.0
       DO 100 I = 1,N
          SUMX = SUMX + X(I)
  100 CONTINUE
       XBAR = SUMX/N

C Calculate the sum of the differences squared, the variance,
C and the standard deviation.

       SUMDIF = 0.0
       DO 200 I = 1,N
          SUMDIF = SUMDIF + (X(I) - XBAR)**2
  200 CONTINUE

       VAR = SUMDIF/(N-1)
       STDEV = SQRT(VAR)
       RETURN
       END
```

```
C Figure 14.14 -- A Second Statistical Measures Module.
C                  Subroutine STATS2 calculates the mean, variance, and
C                  standard deviation of the values in an array.

C*********************************************************************

C X      - one-dimensional array containing raw data
C N      - number of data values in the array X
C XBAR   - mean
C VAR    - variance
C STDEV  - standard deviation
C SUMX   - sum of the X values
C SUMXSQ - sum of the squares of the X values

C*********************************************************************

      SUBROUTINE STATS2(X, N, XBAR, VAR, STDEV)

      INTEGER I, N
      REAL X(N), XBAR, VAR, STDEV, SUMX, SUMXSQ, SQRT
C Calculate the sum and sum of squares of the X values.
      SUMX = 0.0
      SUMXSQ = 0.0
      DO 100 I = 1,N
         SUMX = SUMX + X(I)
         SUMXSQ = SUMXSQ + X(I)*X(I)
  100 CONTINUE
C Compute the mean, variance, and standard deviation.
      XBAR = SUMX/N
      VAR = (SUMXSQ - SUMX*SUMX/N)/(N-1)
      STDEV = SQRT(VAR)
      RETURN
      END
```

14.5.1 Analyzing Some Real-Life Data

To illustrate the use of the above modules to calculate summary statistics of an array of data, the National Hockey League data from Appendix L will be used. A program to compute the average number of points scored by an NHL player during the 1980–1981 season is presented in Figure 14.15. Each player record from the data file is read, and the points scored value saved for each player. A counter of the current number of players ensures that the array entries are filled successively, and that a total number of entries is available for the statistics modules. The results of processing the player data from Appendix L are shown in Figure 14.16. The computed average is 33.5 points for 504 NHL players, with a standard deviation of 27.5 points. Such a high value for the standard deviation indicates that there is considerable variation in the scoring abilities of NHL players. It might be more interesting to repeat these calculations for only those players who played at least 10 or 20 games, or for those players at each position.

```
C Figure 14.15 -- NHL Player Scoring Statistics Problem.
C                      Determine the average and standard deviation for
C                      the number of points scored by all players.
C***********************************************************************
C NAME    - player's name
C POSITN  - position normally played: 'C'=center, 'W'=winger, 'D'=defense
C TEAM    - team of hockey player
C GAMES   - games played by hockey player
C GOALS   - goals scored by hockey player
C ASSIST  - assists obtained by hockey player
C POINTS  - total points earned by hockey player
C PENALT  - penalty minutes incurred by hockey player
C POWPLY  - power play goals scored
C SHORT   - short-handed goals scored
C GAMWIN  - game winning goals scored
C PLAYER  - number of players
C AVG     - average points scored
C VAR     - variance in points scored
C STDEV   - standard deviation in points scored
C***********************************************************************
      CHARACTER NAME*19, TEAM*12, POSITN

      INTEGER GAMES, GOALS, ASSIST, POINTS, PENALT
      INTEGER POWPLY, SHORT, GAMWIN, PLAYER, I
      REAL TPOINT(600), AVG, VAR, STDEV
C Print out the headings.
      PRINT *, '    NAME            TEAM        POS        GP',
     +'          G          A        PTS        PM',
     +'          PP        SH        GW'
      PRINT *, ' '
C Initialize the count of players.
      PLAYER = 0
C While an end-of-file has not been encountered, read a player record.
  100 READ(*, *, END=150)  NAME, TEAM, POSITN, GAMES, GOALS, ASSIST,
     +           POINTS, PENALT, POWPLY, SHORT, GAMWIN
      PLAYER = PLAYER + 1
      PRINT *, NAME, TEAM, POSITN, GAMES, GOALS, ASSIST,
     +                POINTS, PENALT, POWPLY, SHORT, GAMWIN
      TPOINT(PLAYER) = POINTS
      GOTO 100
  150 CONTINUE
C Compute the summary scoring statistics for all players.
      CALL STATS1(TPOINT,PLAYER,AVG,VAR,STDEV)
      PRINT *, ' '
      PRINT *, 'THE', PLAYER, ' PLAYERS AVERAGED', AVG,
     +         'POINTS WITH STANDARD DEVIATION', STDEV
      STOP
      END
C Subroutine STATS1 is placed here.
```

Program Notes

- A more general form of the READ statement has been introduced to take advantage of the END= option. Both counting the number of players in the file and adding an end-of-data sentinel are impractical here. The END= option allows for the input loop to terminate gracefully.   For more details see Appendices D and F.

Figure 14.16   Scoring statistics for players in the National Hockey League showing the average and standard deviation for all players, input and output for the program of Figure 14.15

a) Input file:

```
'Middleton, Rick    ' 'Boston    ' 'W' 80 44  59 103  16  16  4  7
'McNab, Peter       ' 'Boston    ' 'C' 80 37  46  83  24  16  0  4
'Park, Brad         ' 'Boston    ' 'D' 78 14  52  66 111  10  0  2
.
.
.
'Cory, Ross         ' 'Winnipeg  ' 'D'  5  0   1   1   9   0  0  0
'Chartier, Dave     ' 'Winnipeg  ' 'C'  1  0   0   0   0   0  0  0
'Whelton, Bill      ' 'Winnipeg  ' 'D'  2  0   0   0   0   0  0  0
```

b) Output file (spacing editted):

NAME	TEAM	POS	GP	G	A	PTS	PM	PP	SH	GW
Middleton, Rick	Boston	W	80	44	59	103	16	16	4	7
McNab, Peter	Boston	C	80	37	46	83	24	16	0	4
Park, Brad	Boston	D	78	14	52	66	111	10	0	2
.										
.										
Cory, Ross	Winnipeg	D	5	0	1	1	9	0	0	0
Chartier, Dave	Winnipeg	C	1	0	0	0	0	0	0	0
Whelton, Bill	Winnipeg	D	2	0	0	0	0	0	0	0

THE   504 PLAYERS AVERAGED   33.5281 POINTS WITH STANDARD DEVIA-
TION   27.53555

14.6   The Normal Distribution

There are several frequency distributions which are used in statistical computations. These distributions have been developed because they bear a close resemblance to distributions which occur naturally.   The most important of these is a bell-shaped distribution called the *normal* or *Gaussian distribution*. The normal distribution has the general shape shown in Figure 14.17.

The equation for the general normal curve is

$$y = \frac{e^{-\frac{(x-m)^2}{2s^2}}}{s\sqrt{2\pi}} \tag{14.12}$$

Figure 14.17 The general shape of the normal distribution.

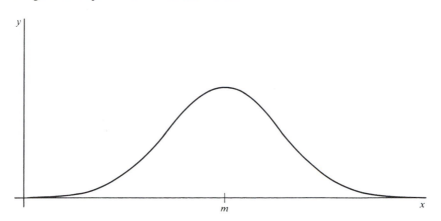

where e $\simeq$ 2.718283, π $\simeq$ 3.141593, m = mean, s = standard deviation, and $-\infty < x < +\infty$.   From this formula it should be obvious that there is not just one normal curve.   If the mean is varied, the curve is just displaced along the x axis (an effect which was mentioned earlier).   If the standard deviation is increased, the curve will flatten out but still retain its bell shape and contain the same area.   Figure 14.18 indicates the effect of changing these parameters of the equation.   However, regardless of the changes, the area under the curve remains at 1.   All normal distributions have the property that 68.26% of the area lies within one standard deviation of the mean; 95.44% of the area lies within two standard deviations of the mean; and 99.74% of the area lies within three standard deviations of the mean.   This property is illustrated in Figure 14.19 and can easily be verified through numerical integration (see Exercise 14.6).

The above properties of the normal distribution may be quite useful.   If a frequency distribution of raw data is known to be normally shaped then one may use these percentages to make statements about the data.   For instance, assume that a class of 150 students writes an exam, which when graded results in marks which are assumed to be normally distributed.   If the mean mark is 65 and the standard deviation is 15, then one would expect that 102 students (68% of 150) have marks between 50 (65 $-$ 15) and 80 (65 + 15) and that approximately 143 students (95% of 150) have marks between 35 (65 $-$ 2 $\times$ 15) and 95 (65 + 2 $\times$ 15).

By looking at the above areas from a different perspective one can determine the relative position of a data value in its set.   For instance, one could say that a student who obtained a mark of 80 performed better than approximately 84% of the class (the area under the curve less than the mean plus 1 standard deviation).   This calculation is straightforward since the mark of 80 occurs at the 1 standard deviation position.   However, if one chooses a mark which is not quite so conveniently placed, a bit more work is required.   Since a computer is not always available (or appropriate) statisticians have traditionally used tables to obtain the percentage area information.   However, since one can not describe tables for all possible distributions, statisticians provide a table for just

Figure 14.18 Changes in the normal distribution formula.

a) Effect of increasing the mean from m_1 to m_2

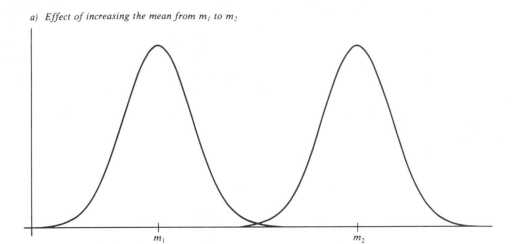

b) Effect of increasing the standard deviation

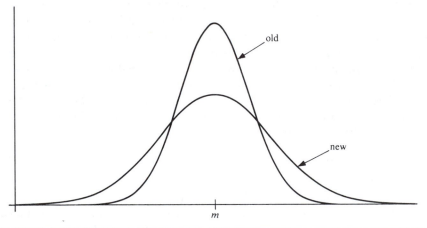

one normal distribution and describe how to convert other normal distributions to it. Currently, good numerical approximations for the normal distributions are available on most computers and even on some hand-held calculators.

14.6.1 Standard Form of the Normal Distribution

The normal distribution used by statisticians has a mean of zero and a standard deviation of one. The formula of this *standardized normal distribution* or *z-distribution* is given by

$$y = \frac{e^{-\frac{z^2}{2}}}{\sqrt{2\pi}} \tag{14.13}$$

Figure 14.19 Areas under a normal distribution curve.

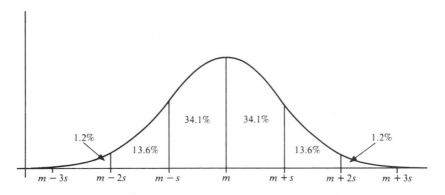

Other normal distributions may be converted to this standard form by the formula

$$z = \frac{(x - m)}{s} \tag{14.14}$$

which gives what is called a *z-score*.   (This conversion is used when *m* and *s* have been computed for a fairly large sample, that is, 20 or 30 measurements.) The standard normal curve is shown in Figure 14.20.   z-scores of ± 1, ± 2, and ± 3 correspond to positions which are ± 1, ± 2, and ± 3 standard deviations away from the mean.

Figure 14.20 The standardized normal curve.

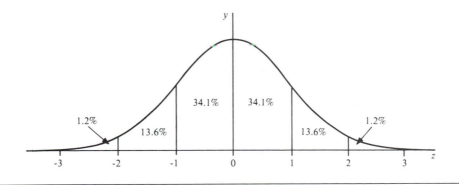

With respect to ordinary normal distributions one can see from equation (14.14) that a value of $x = m$ will map onto $z = 0$, $x = m + s$ will map onto $z = 1$, and so on. The majority of the area under a normal curve (99.74%) lies between $-3 \leq z \leq +3$, and thus, z-scores outside this range are not often encountered.

The z-score is thus a nondimensional description of where a data value lies with respect to the mean of its set.   Since all normally distributed measurements may be converted into a z-score, only the standard distribution needs to be tabulated. Appendix M contains such a table.

14.7 Relationships Between Sets of Measurements

From a given sample of a population, it is possible to measure several different attributes. For instance, one could measure the height and weight of university students, the weight and gas mileage of cars, or the size and cost of textbooks in the bookstore. When one measure accompanies another measure as in the above examples, one may wish to determine whether there is any relationship between the two. The degree to which measurements are linearly related is called their *correlation*. If two measurements are correlated then it may be possible to determine an equation to describe this relationship and thereby use one measure to predict the other. This process is called *simple linear regression*.

Correlation and regression calculations are relatively easy to perform with the use of a computer. Unfortunately, this is exactly what causes some problems. The fact that one can perform these calculations for almost any set of data does not guarantee that the results are meaningful.

One of the simpler ways to gain insight into this problem is to generate an $x - y$ graph, called a *scatter plot*, of the data points. Such a plot may reveal characteristics of the data which will suggest whether a correlation or regression calculation would be appropriate.

14.7.1 Scatter Plots and Correlation

The simplest way to determine if two measurements are related is to plot the measurements on an $x - y$ graph. One measurement is taken as the x value (abscissa) and the other measurement is taken as the y value (ordinate). The graph so obtained is the scatter plot. If the points on a scatter plot seem to form a straight line then they are *correlated*. Figure 14.21 shows three scatter plots in which graph a) shows a negative correlation (as x gets larger y gets smaller), graph b) shows no correlation, and graph c) shows a positive correlation (as x gets larger y gets larger). If all points should happen to lie exactly on a straight line then measurements are said to be *perfectly correlated*.

Figure 14.21 Scatter plots showing different correlation possibilities.

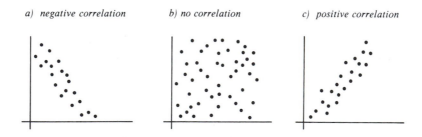

a) *negative correlation*   b) *no correlation*   c) *positive correlation*

The measure of correlation is called the *correlation coefficient* which takes on values of -1.0 (perfect negative correlation) to $+1.0$ (perfect positive correlation). Values of the correlation coefficient near 0.0 imply no correlation at all. The correlation coefficient for Figure 14.21 a) would be near -1, for b) it would be near 0, and for c) it would be near $+1$. It should be pointed out that a correlation between two measurements does not imply a causative effect. That is, one does not necessarily cause the other to happen.

To be able to compute the correlation coefficient between two sets of measurements, it is necessary to determine if there is a consistent relationship between corresponding individual measurements. The way this can be done is to compare each measurement with respect to its mean. The three scatter plots of Figure 14.22 show data points which have a perfect negative correlation, no correlation, and a perfect positive correlation respectively. On each plot the deviation from the mean and the sign of the deviation are indicated for each point. For graph a), when the x deviation is small, the y deviation is also. When the x deviation is large, the y deviation is large. In both cases, the x and y deviations have opposite signs. A similar situation exists in graph c) except that the signs are the same. In graph b) there is no such consistent relationship between the signs of deviations.

Figure 14.22   Relationships between data points and their mean for correlation.

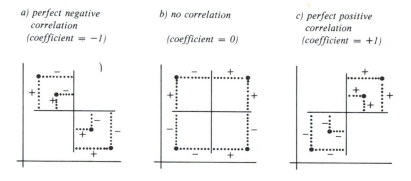

Thus, when a correlation does exist there is a consistent relationship between the x and y deviations and their means. A method is now needed to quantify this relationship and to take into account that correlations may have to be performed on measurements which vary greatly in scale relative to each other. It turns out that the z-score serves this purpose exactly since it is a nondimensional indication of where a data value lies with respect to its mean.

The correlation coefficient r is computed by determining the average of the products of the z-scores according to the following formula.

$$r = \frac{\sum\limits_{i=1}^{n} \left(z_{x_i} z_{y_i} \right)}{n - 1} \tag{14.15}$$

where the z_x are z-scores for abscissa measurements, and the z_y are z-scores for ordinate measurements.

As an example, consider the values in Figure 14.23 which give two measurements, the number of pages and the price for some softcover textbooks.

Figure 14.23 Number of pages and prices for some softcover textbooks.

Book	Pages	Price	Book	Pages	Price
1	166	6.75	6	335	15.50
2	195	10.25	7	370	11.75
3	200	9.00	8	450	14.75
4	260	9.00	9	517	19.00
5	265	11.25	10	552	16.50

A scatter plot of these measurements shown in Figure 14.24 implies that there is some positive correlation between the price and number of pages for the books. Therefore, it seems reasonable to compute the correlation coefficient.

Figure 14.24 Scatter plot of prices and pages for some softcover textbooks.

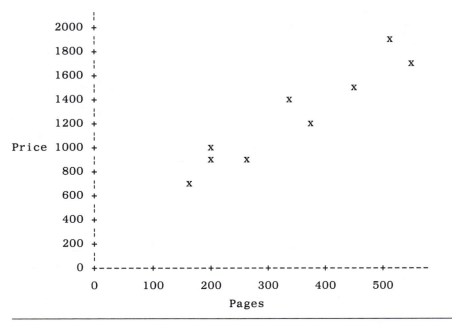

To determine the correlation coefficient between the prices and pages, it is necessary to determine the z-scores and then use equation (14.15). (For illustrative purposes, the z-score calculations are being allowed here with only 10 measurements instead of demanding the 20 or more which are usually required.) The z-scores for these measurements are calculated in Figure 14.25 along with the product of the z-scores.

Figure 14.25 z-scores for pages and prices for some softcover textbooks.

Measure-ment	Pages(x)	z_x	Price(y)	z_y	$z_x z_y$
1	166.	−1.20	6.75	−1.44	1.72
2	195.	−0.99	10.25	−0.51	0.50
3	200.	−0.95	9.00	−0.84	0.80
4	260.	−0.51	9.00	−0.84	0.43
5	265.	−0.48	11.25	−0.25	0.12
6	335.	0.03	15.50	0.35	0.01
7	370.	0.28	11.75	−0.11	−0.03
8	450.	0.86	14.75	0.68	0.59
9	517.	1.35	19.00	1.81	2.44
10	552.	1.60	16.50	1.15	1.84

					8.41

$\bar{x} = 331.0$, $\bar{y} = 12.0$, $s_x = 138.01$, $s_y = 3.77$

The correlation coefficient may now be calculated as follows.

$$r = \frac{\sum_{i=1}^{n} z_{x_i} z_{y_i}}{n-1} = \frac{8.41}{9} = .93$$

Thus, there is a large positive correlation of .93 between the price and number of pages in the softcover books which were sampled. However, to emphasize again, this high correlation value does not necessarily mean that the number of pages is the only factor in the price of the books. There are other factors which can contribute greatly to the price such as the number of copies printed per run, the market demand, and competition.

The more common forms of the equation for the correlation coefficient may be obtained by first substituting equation (14.14) into equation (14.15).

$$r = \frac{1}{n-1} \sum_{i=1}^{n} \left[\frac{(x_i - \bar{x})}{s_x} \times \frac{(y_i - \bar{y})}{s_y} \right]$$

$$= \frac{\sum(x_i - \bar{x})(y_i - \bar{y})}{(n-1)s_x s_y}$$

Then, by substituting equation (14.7) for s_x and s_y gives

$$r = \frac{\sum(x_i - \bar{x})(y_i - \bar{y})}{\left(\sum(x_i - \bar{x})^2 \sum(y_i - \bar{y})^2 \right)^{1/2}} \tag{14.16}$$

while substituting equation (14.8) gives

$$r = \frac{\sum x_i y_i - \frac{1}{n} \sum x_i \sum y_i}{\left(\left[\sum x_i^2 - \frac{1}{n} (\sum x_i)^2 \right] \left[\sum y_i^2 - \frac{1}{n} (\sum y_i)^2 \right] \right)^{1/2}} \qquad (14.17)$$

This latter equation, of course, is prone to round-off error as is equation (14.8).

14.7.2 Regression

In many circumstances it is not enough to know that two measurements are correlated. What is needed is a description of the actual functional relationship between the variables. A technique for obtaining such a function is called regression.

Simple linear regression is used when the underlying relationship between the variables seems to be truly linear and when the data is of roughly constant variance. This may be interpreted visually to mean that the data points should lie in a band of approximately constant width as is the case in Figures 14.21 a) and 14.21 c). In Figure 14.21 b) a regression is useless since r is 0 (that is, one can not use x to predict y). The graphs of Figure 14.26 show two scatter plots of data for which computation of a regression line would be meaningless. In Figure 14.26 a), the two data points which are remote from the others can have a large effect on the line. When data like this occur, the first inclination is to go back and check these points to see if they are correct. Another alternative is to collect more data because there may indeed be a relationship between the points, but it may be a nonlinear one. In the case of Figure 14.26 b), if there really are no data values between the two groups, the data are not correlated even though a computed correlation coefficient would be near -1. There are merely two distinct pairs of observations with some clustering around them.

Figure 14.26 Scatter plots for which linear correlation is questionable.

a) *two data points remote
   from the rest of the data*   b) *two distinct clusters of data*

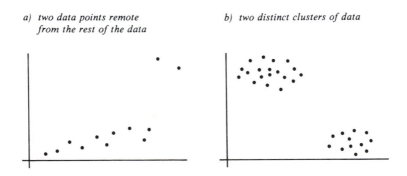

The curve which is fitted to a set of data values may be a straight line, a quadratic, or some higher order curve. The scatter plot can give some indication as to which type of curve (if any) should be fitted. Regardless of which curve is being used, the objective is to determine the best one. The curve which best fits the data values is usually taken to be the one which minimizes the sum of squared vertical distances between the data points and the curve itself.   The individual vertical deviations are referred to as the *residuals*. The diagram of Figure 14.27 illustrates the residual values for an arbitrary curve.   Minimization of the sum of squares of the residuals is called the *least squares method*.

Figure 14.27   Residuals of a curve fitted to a set of data points.

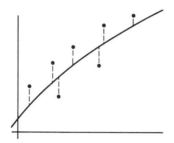

---

a) Least Squares Lines   If a straight line is being fitted to the data points, the equation of the line will be of the following form.

$$y = a + bx$$

The *y residual* for the *i*-th data point is then given by the following.

$$y \ residual \ = \ y_i - (a + bx_i)$$

According to the least squares criterion, the values of *a* and *b* are those for which the sum of squared residuals is minimized.   That is, minimize

$$ls_1 = (y_1 - (a + bx_1))^2 + (y_2 - (a + bx_2))^2 + \cdots + (y_n - (a + bx_n))^2 \qquad (14.18)$$

$$= \sum_{i=1}^{n} (y_i - (a + bx_i))^2$$

It can be shown using calculus that a minimum value of ls_1 results when the following equations are solved for *a* and *b*. (Note that *a* and *b* are the unknowns in these equations.)

$$na + b\sum x_i = \sum y_i \qquad (14.19)$$

$$a\sum x_i + b\sum x_i^2 = \sum x_i y_i$$

These equations may be solved through elimination techniques (see Chapter 15) and transformed to give the following expressions for *a* and *b*.

$$b = \frac{\sum (x_i - \overline{x})(y_i - \overline{y})}{\sum (x_i - \overline{x})^2} \qquad (14.20)$$

$$a = \overline{y} - b\overline{x}$$

The equations of (14.20) can easily be evaluated by a computer program. Figure 14.28 gives a program which does exactly this. In addition, the program generates a scatter plot and also plots the regression line so that one can see if it is a good fit. The program assumes that the data pairs are preceded by a data count.

```
C Figure 14.28 - Scatter Plot Problem.
C                 Program to generate a scatter plot of the input data
C                 pairs and to calculate a least squares regression line
C                 for the data, and to plot this line on the graph.

C**********************************************************************
C X,Y         - storage for the input data point pairs
C N           - number of data points to process
C SUMX, SUMY  - summation of X and Y values
C SUMXY       - summation of X*Y terms
C SUMXDS      - summation of (X-XBAR)*(Y-YBAR) terms
C XMIN, XMAX  - minimum and maximum values of X for plotting
C A, B        - coefficients of the regression line
C XINCR       - size of increment for plot of regression line
C XP, YP      - X and Y points for plotting the regression line
C XBAR, YBAR  - means for X and Y values

C**********************************************************************
      INTEGER I, N
      REAL X(1000), Y(1000)
      REAL XBAR, YBAR, SUMX, SUMY, XDIFF, SUMXY, SUMXDS
      REAL A, B, XMIN, XMAX, XINCR, XP, YP, AMIN1, AMAX1
C Initialize the plotting routines and read in the data.
      CALL SETPLT(51,21)
      READ *, N
      DO 100 I = 1, N
         READ *, X(I), Y(I)
         CALL STOPNT(X(I),Y(I),'X')
  100 CONTINUE
C Calculate the terms of the least-squares line and the
C maximum and minimum X values.
      SUMX = 0.0
      SUMY = 0.0
      XMIN = X(1)
      XMAX = X(1)
      DO 200 I = 1, N
         SUMX = SUMX + X(I)
         SUMY = SUMY + Y(I)
         XMIN = AMIN1(XMIN,X(I))
         XMAX = AMAX1(XMAX,X(I))
  200 CONTINUE
      XBAR = SUMX/N
      YBAR = SUMY/N
```

```
C Figure 14.28 (continued)
C Calculate the sum of products of the X and Y differences
C and the sum of the X differences squared.
      SUMXY = 0.0
      SUMXDS = 0.0
      DO 300 I = 1, N
         XDIFF = X(I) - XBAR
         SUMXY = SUMXY + XDIFF*(Y(I) - YBAR)
         SUMXDS = SUMXDS + XDIFF**2
  300 CONTINUE
C Compute the actual linear regression coefficients.
      B = SUMXY/SUMXDS
      A = YBAR - B*XBAR
      PRINT *, 'THE LEAST SQUARES LINE IS:'
      PRINT *, ' '
      PRINT *, 'Y =', A, '+', B, 'X'
C Add the least squares line to the plot.
      XINCR = (XMAX - XMIN)/16
      DO 400 XP = XMIN, XMAX, XINCR
         YP = A + B*XP
         CALL STOPNT(XP, YP, '0')
  400 CONTINUE
C Generate the scatter plot.
      CALL PLOT(1)
      STOP
      END
```

The output from the program for the textbook data of Figure 14.23 is shown in Figure 14.29. The equation of the line is also given there preceding the actual plot. From the plot it appears that the least squares line is a reasonable fit for the given data.

b) Least Squares Quadratic Curves   To compute a least squares quadratic curve for a set of data points, similar reasoning may be used. In this case, one wishes to use a quadratic equation of the form

$$y = a + bx + cx^2 \tag{14.21}$$

and to minimize

$$ls_2 = \sum_{i=1}^{n} (y_i - (a + bx_i + cx_i^2)) \tag{14.22}$$

which requires solving the equations

$$\begin{aligned}
na &+ b\sum x_i &+ c\sum x_i^2 &= \sum y_i \\
a\sum x_i &+ b\sum x_i^2 &+ c\sum x_i^3 &= \sum x_i y_i \\
a\sum x_i^2 &+ b\sum x_i^3 &+ c\sum x_i^4 &= \sum x_i^2 y_i
\end{aligned} \tag{14.23}$$

The solution of these equations in a general form is certainly not recommended.   Even

---

Figure 14.29 Computer-generated scatter plot and regression line, input and output for the program of Figure 14.28.

a) Input file:

```
10
166   6.75
195  10.25
200   9.00
260   9.00
265  11.25
335  15.50
370  11.75
450  14.75
517  19.00
552  16.50
```

b) Output file:

```
THE LEAST SQUARES LINE IS:
Y =    3.902266      +   2.5597384E-02 X
  NUMBER OF POINTS : SUBMITTED          27  PLOTTED            27


 1.90000+                                              X
        !
        !                                                  0
        !                                             0
        !                                          0     X
 1.59375+
        !                         X                     0
        !                                      0   X
        !                                  0  X
        !                               0
 1.28750+
        !                           0
        !                      0
        !                  0        X
        !              X  0
 0.98125+        X           0
        !        X  0     X
        !     0
 0.67500*---------+---------+---------+---------+---------+
             1.6600     2.4320     3.2040     3.9760     4.7480     5.5200

     THE Y - AXIS SCALE FACTOR IS 10**           1
            THE X - AXIS SCALE FACTOR IS 10**                  2
```

---

if the coefficients are computed and the equations then solved, it is still a tedious task. Chapter 15 presents a subroutine which when given the coefficients of such equations will perform the solution for the unknowns.

c) General Least Squares Curves This technique of formulating linear equations for the coefficients does extend to making higher degree polynomials fit the data. However, special numerical techniques are needed to solve these problems accurately. If desired, one may also fit more complicated functions than polynomials.   Programs for these techniques exist in many program libraries.

14.8   Special Languages for Statistical Analysis

Since the people who use statistical analysis in their work are not necessarily computer programmers, special languages have been developed to allow them to still use the computer but with a minimum of effort.   Perhaps the best known of these is the SPSS (Statistical Package for the Social Sciences) language, Klecka et al. (1975) and Nie (1970), developed during the late 1960's.

This language allows users to specify, in more-or-less statistical terms and English phrases, the actions and analyses which are to be performed on their data.   SPSS language statements consist of single word commands which are accompanied by some parameters.   These commands are simple but quite powerful.   For instance, only one command is needed to specify each of the following actions.

- Production of frequency tables.
- Generation of scatter plots.
- Calculation of the standard statistical measures of mean, median, mode, standard deviation, variance, range, maximum, and minimum.

In addition, many other options exist including basic data and file manipulation commands.   Figure 14.30 shows a simple SPSS program which processes the book data of Figure 14.23.   These statements are all that are necessary to generate a scatter plot, calculate the statistical measures listed above, and perform a regression calculation.

```
COMMENT            Figure 14.30 SPSS program to process the book data.
RUN NAME           BOOKDATA
COMMENT            Provide the data for the program.
DATA LIST          FIXED/ 1 PAGES 1-3, PRICE 5-9
INPUT MEDIUM       CARD
N OF CASES         10
READ INPUT DATA
166   6.75
195  10.25
200   9.00
260   9.00
265  11.25
335  13.50
370  11.75
450  14.75
517  19.00
552  16.50
COMMENT            Perform the plots and statistical computations.
SCATTERGRAM        PRICE WITH PAGES
STATISTICS         ALL
REGRESSION         VARIABLES = PRICE,PAGES/
                   REGRESSION=PRICE WITH PAGES(2) RESID=0 /
STATISTICS         6
FINISH
```

Thus, this language has some very attractive features and is heavily used. However, the same caution must again be issued with the interpretation and use of the statistical results. In fact, the cautions may be even more important here since so much information may be generated so easily. The ability to perform a variety of statistical analyses does not guarantee that the results generated are meaningful.

14.9   Summary

Statistical analysis is very important and widely used. It allows one to summarize data to gain insight into its characteristics. As well, it is used to detect relationships between measurements and to predict other results on the basis of these relationships.

It is relatively easy to perform statistical calculations. One may either write one's own programs, use a special language such as SPSS, or use library modules. However, interpretation of statistical results and the making of inferences from them can be difficult. Consultation with a statistician is often advisable before setting out to acquire the data. Such expert advice can ensure that the proper quantity and quality of data is collected to provide the information sought. Statisticians will also be aware of the most accurate and efficient computational procedures to use in the analysis of the data.

14.10   References

Anscombe, F.J. "Graphs in Statistical Analysis." *The American Statistician* 29, no.1 (1973).

Campbell, S.K.   *Flaws and Fallacies in Statistical Thinking.* Englewood Cliffs, N.J.: Prentice-Hall, 1974.

Ehrenberg, A.S.C.   *Data Reduction – Analyzing and Interpreting Statistical Data.* New York: John Wiley and Sons, 1971.

Kalbfleisch, J.G.   *Probability and Statistical Inference.* Volumes 1 and 2. New York: Springer-Verlag New York Inc., 1979.

Klecka, W.R.; Nie, N.H.; and Hull, C.H.   *SPSS Primer.* New York: McGraw-Hill Book Co., 1975.

Nie, N.H.   *SPSS - Statistical Package for the Social Sciences.* New York: McGraw-Hill Book Co., 1970.

Spiegal, M.R.   *Theory and Problems of Statistics.* New York: Schaum Publishing Co., 1961.

14.11   Exercises

In most of the following exercises a program is requested to solve a specific problem. For each problem it is recommended that step-wise refinement be used in developing a pseudocode algorithm to solve the problem. This algorithm should then be translated into FORTRAN/77 and run on the computer. Where appropriate, the program should be tested with a variety of data sufficient to ensure that the program does what it is supposed to do.

14.1 The following data represent the heights (in centimeters) of a number of university professors.

157	158	160	161	161	161	165	166	166
116	167	168	169	171	171	171	171	171
171	171	172	172	172	172	172	172	172
172	173	173	173	174	174	174	174	174
175	175	175	177	177	177	177	178	178
179	179	180	183	184	187	189	190	190
191	191	193						

Use the modules CLSIFY and HISTGM to produce a frequency table and histogram for this data. Experiment with different class ranges and note the various shapes of histogram that occur.

14.2 The following data values represent the term-work averages (out of 50) of a class of 18 students.

29.7	29.9	26.9	29.2	33.0	31.1	27.1	24.0
28.9	29.0	27.2	28.0	32.5	33.0	24.5	29.7
27.0	26.7						

Develop a program which will perform the following tasks.

a) Compute the mean and standard deviation of the class averages using the subroutine STATS1 of Figure 14.13.
b) Determine the median mark of the class.

14.3 Prove algebraically that the standard deviation of equation (14.10) is equivalent to the standard deviation formula of equation (14.9).

14.4 Develop a program which will compute the standard deviation using the formula of equation (14.10). The program should assume that the first data value is representative of the remaining data. Test your program on suitable data to be sure that it works. Compare the results of this program with the results from the other standard deviation formulas on the same data.

14.5 Some statisticians believe that the extreme values in a sample of data should not be used in the calculation of the sample mean and variance. Assuming that an array X contains data values in ascending order, then the data values from x_1 to x_{k-1} and from x_{l+1} to x_n ($1 \le k < l \le n$) are the extreme values and hence are ignored. Thus, for an array X, which contains n data values, they would use the following equations

$$\bar{x}_t = \frac{\sum\limits_{i=k}^{l} x_i}{l - k + 1} \quad \text{and} \quad s_t^2 = \frac{\sum\limits_{i=k}^{l} (x_i - \bar{x}_t)^2}{l - k}$$

to compute the mean $\bar{x}_t$ and variance s_t^2 from x_k to x_l.

a) Develop a FORTRAN/77 subroutine with module interface

SUBROUTINE SAMPT(X, K, L, N, XBART, SSQT)

which when given the vector X (the data values have already been sorted in ascending order) and the index values K and L will compute XBART $= \bar{x}_t$ and SSQT $= s_t^2$ as defined above.

b) Develop a main program which will use the above subroutine to compute the sample mean and standard deviation of the data of Exercise 14.2.

14.6 Develop a program which will perform numerical integration on the normal curve, equation (14.12), to determine the area within 1, 2, and 3 standard deviations of the mean.   Assume different values for the mean and standard deviation including a mean of 0 and standard deviation of 1.

14.7 Develop a program which will plot the following normal distributions.   There should be one graph for part a) and a different one for part b).

a) $m = 10.0$, $s = 0.5$; $m = 10.0$, $s = 2.5$; $m = 10.0$, $s = 5.0$
b) $m = 10.0$, $s = 1.0$; $m = 8.0$, $s = 1.0$; $m = 6.0$, $s = 1.0$

Plot the curves in the range of ± 3 standard deviations.

14.8 The following list contains 15 student identification numbers together with 4 course grades for each.

83000001	82	63	92	43
83000002	83	73	77	58
83000003	72	51	64	24
83000004	45	80	67	29
83000005	59	35	74	54
83000006	97	84	94	89
83000007	85	41	86	63
83000008	74	74	72	59
83000009	83	94	97	92
83000010	93	78	88	60
83000011	76	84	63	89
83000012	100	78	100	82
83000013	80	92	91	81
83000014	74	84	91	68
83000015	71	58	63	68

Develop a program which will process this data to produce the following two tables.

I.D number	Average Mark	Standard Deviation
83000001	-----	-----
83000002	-----	-----
83000003	-----	-----
.	.	.
.	.	.
.	.	.
83000015	-----	-----

Course Number	Average Mark	Standard Deviation
1	-----	-----
2	-----	-----
3	-----	-----
4	-----	-----

14.9   Develop a program which will process the student data file of Appendix L and determine the average and standard deviation marks for each student and for each assignment.

14.10   a)   Show algebraically that the use of the z-scores in the correlation calculation of equation (14.15) will give it a value of ± 1 for points which lie on a nonhorizontal straight line.   What happens if the line is horizontal?

b)   Compute by hand the correlation coefficient for the data points $(1,1)$, $(3,2)$, and $(5,3)$.

14.11   Develop a program which will process the Indianapolis 500 race data of Appendix L and plot the least squares linear regression line for the data.   The largest departures of the data from the regression line tend to occur after the resumption of the races in 1945.   Can you suggest a change in application of the linear regression technique to fit the data more closely?

14.12   Develop a program which will calculate the least squares quadratic polynomial for the following data values.   Plot both the data values and the quadratic polynomial to compare the fit.

a) $(x_i, y_i) = (0,6)$, $(1,9)$, $(2,12)$, $(3,13)$, $(4,10)$, $(5,6)$, $(6,5)$, $(7,0)$

b) $(x_i, y_i) = (-6,6)$, $(-5,4)$, $(-4,2)$, $(-3,-1)$, $(-2,-3)$, $(-1,-3)$, $(0,-2)$, $(1,-1)$, $(2,1)$, $(3,2)$, $(4,3)$, $(5,5)$, $(6,5)$

14.13   Use the program developed in Exercise 6.7 to create a frequency polygon corresponding to the histogram in Figure 14.8.

15
Vectors, Matrices, and Linear Equations

15.1 Introduction

In this chapter, some problems will be considered which can be handled by the use of matrix and vector notation. A simple marketing example will be developed, and aspects of problems arising from this example will be used as a theme for the entire chapter. The main mathematical ideas involve matrix-vector multiplication, matrix multiplication, and the solution of linear systems of equations. Simple modules will be constructed which will enable the reader to perform the computations associated with the problems simply and elegantly. One would find these modules useful in a wide variety of physical problems. Structural analysis of buildings, bridges or vehicles, electrical networks, analysis of studies of the allocation and distribution of resources and economic models are just a few examples of problems which rely on such tools.

15.2 A Marketing Example

As an introduction to the use of vectors and matrices, consider the following competitive marketing problem.

Example 15.1   Two Bakery Problem
    Assume that two bakeries A and B compete for the bread market in a particular
    city. A certain exchange of customers occurs between the two firms: each month
    98% of bakery A's customers stay and 2% switch to B; at the same time, 96% of B's
    customers stay and 4% switch to A.

If the objective of the study is a determination of the way in which the market shares evolve with time, then the first step should be the construction of a model. Bakery A's fraction of the market will be represented by x and B's share by y, so that $x + y = 1$, assuming that A and B share the entire market between them.

Letting x' and y' be the shares after one month, it is seen that

$$x' = 0.98x + 0.04y \tag{15.1}$$

$$y' = 0.02x + 0.96y \ .$$

In matrix notation, this could be written as

$$Z' = T \times Z, \tag{15.2}$$

where

$$T = \begin{bmatrix} 0.98 & 0.04 \\ 0.02 & 0.96 \end{bmatrix} \ , \ Z' = \begin{bmatrix} x' \\ y' \end{bmatrix} \ , \ Z = \begin{bmatrix} x \\ y \end{bmatrix} .$$

Matrix T is the representation of the *transformation* which changes Z to Z'. The *vector* of market shares Z with elements x and y is changed to Z' by multiplying Z by the *matrix* T.

The rule for this multiplication is that the elements in the first row of matrix T are multiplied, element by element, with the corresponding elements of vector Z. The first element of Z' is the sum of these products. Similarly, the second element of Z' is the sum of products of elements of the second row of T with the corresponding elements of vector Z.

For example, if the initial shares are $x = 0.40$ and $y = 0.60$ then the shares after one month will be

$$Z' = \begin{bmatrix} 0.98 & 0.04 \\ 0.02 & 0.96 \end{bmatrix} \times \begin{bmatrix} 0.40 \\ 0.60 \end{bmatrix} = \begin{bmatrix} 0.98 \times 0.40 + 0.04 \times 0.60 \\ 0.02 \times 0.40 + 0.96 \times 0.60 \end{bmatrix} = \begin{bmatrix} 0.416 \\ 0.584 \end{bmatrix} .$$

That is, $x' = 0.416$ and $y' = 0.584$.

15.3   Matrix-Vector Multiplication

The rule for performing the multiplication in the previous section may be generalized for matrices and vectors of any size. Suppose that the multiplication is to be done for a matrix of size $n \times n$ and a vector of size n, represented by

$$T = \begin{bmatrix} t_{11} & t_{12} & t_{13} & \cdots & t_{1n} \\ t_{21} & t_{22} & t_{23} & \cdots & t_{2n} \\ t_{31} & t_{32} & t_{33} & \cdots & t_{3n} \\ \cdot & \cdot & \cdot & & \cdot \\ \cdot & \cdot & \cdot & & \cdot \\ \cdot & \cdot & \cdot & & \cdot \\ t_{n1} & t_{n2} & t_{n3} & \cdots & t_{nn} \end{bmatrix} \quad \text{and} \quad Z' = \begin{bmatrix} z_1 \\ z_2 \\ z_3 \\ \cdot \\ \cdot \\ \cdot \\ z_n \end{bmatrix} \qquad (15.3)$$

The rule for multiplication of $T \times Z$ to give Z' is that the corresponding elements in row r of matrix T and in vector Z are multiplied in pairs and these n products are summed to give element r of Z'. This is done for $r = 1, 2, \ldots, n$. A formula for the operation is

$$z'_r = t_{r1} \times z_1 + t_{r2} \times z_2 + t_{r3} \times z_3 + \cdots + t_{rn} \times z_n, \quad r = 1, 2, \ldots, n.$$

It is convenient to represent such sums by a summation symbol and an equivalent form is then

$$z'_r = \sum_{i=1}^{n} t_{ri} \times z_i, \quad r = 1, 2, \ldots, n. \qquad (15.4)$$

15.3.1 A Module for Matrix-Vector Multiplication

This matrix-vector multiplication is a good candidate for the construction of a module, since the operation is an important tool in solving many problems. The interface of the module will be

smodule matvec(**imports**: n, T, Z; **exports**: V)

This module accepts as import an integer n, a matrix T of dimension n×n, and a vector Z of dimension n. Its export is a vector V of dimension n, the matrix-vector product of T with Z. A first version of this module follows as Figure 15.1.

Figure 15.1   First version of a pseudocode module for matrix-vector multiplication.

smodule matvec(**imports**: n, T, Z; **exports**: V)

1.   For each v_r compute the sum of products of elements of row r of T with elements of Z.

end module

---

a) *Refining Step* **1.**   To account for all elements of vector V, a **for**–loop is used to vary the row r from 1 to n and to compute the elements of V as follows:

* For each row r, compute the sum of products of elements of row r of T with vector Z.

1.1 for r from 1 to n do

$$\left[\quad \textbf{1.2} \quad v_r \leftarrow \sum_{i=1}^{n} t_{ri} * z_i \right.$$

b) Refining Step **1.2**   To compute the elements of V, another **for**–loop is used to accumulate the sums of the products of corresponding elements in row r of matrix T and vector Z.

sum ← 0
for i **from** 1 **to** n **do**
$$\left[\quad \text{sum} \leftarrow \text{sum} + t_{ri} * z_i \right.$$
$v_r \leftarrow$ sum

c) Final Version of the Algorithm   The complete algorithm may now be assembled, and is shown as Figure 15.2.

Figure 15.2   Final version of the pseudocode module for matrix-vector multiplication.

smodule matvec(**imports:** n, T, Z; **exports:** V)

* Module to multiply matrix T by vector Z to produce result vector V.

* Variables used:
* n - import dimension of arrays
* T - import matrix (n×n)
* Z - import vector (n×1)
* V - export vector (n×1)

* For each row r, form the sum of products of the elements of row r of T with vector Z.

for r from 1 to n do
$$\left[\begin{array}{l} \text{sum} \leftarrow 0 \\ \textbf{for i from 1 to n do} \\ \quad \left[\quad \text{sum} \leftarrow \text{sum} + t_{ri} * z_i \right. \\ v_r \leftarrow \text{sum} \end{array} \right.$$
end module

---

d) Conversion to FORTRAN/77   A FORTRAN/77 version of the module is given as a subroutine in Figure 15.3.

e) Testing the Subroutine   The use of this module is illustrated by using the numerical data of the example at the end of Section 15.2 in the program of Figure 15.4.   The appropriate input file and resulting output file appear in Figure 15.5.

```
C Figure 15.3 -- Matrix-Vector Multiplication Module.
C                  Subroutine MATVEC to multiply matrix T by vector Z to
C                  produce result vector V.

C***************************************************************************
C N       - dimension of all arrays
C T       - import matrix (NxN)
C Z       - import vector (Nx1)
C V       - export vector (Nx1)

C***************************************************************************
        SUBROUTINE MATVEC(N,T,Z,V)
        INTEGER N, R, I
        REAL T(N,N), Z(N), V(N), SUM
C For each row R, form the sum of the products of the elements of
C row R of T with the elements of vector Z.
        DO 100 R = 1, N
           SUM = 0.
           DO 200 I = 1, N
              SUM = SUM + T(R,I)*Z(I)
200        CONTINUE
           V(R) = SUM
100     CONTINUE
        RETURN
        END
```

15.3.2 Applications of Matrix-Vector Multiplication

The matrix-vector multiplication module may be used to answer a number of questions about the behavior of the bread marketing model. For example, it may be used to determine the market shares after two years, given the transition rules for each month. Alternately, the effects of an advertising campaign designed to alter the brand-switching behavior could be studied as could the effects of a third competitor in the market.

Determination of the market shares after two years may be addressed by a simple modification to the program of Figure 15.4. Solution of this problem requires that the monthly transformation be applied 24 times to the initial vector. To do this requires that the line CALL MATVEC(N,T,Z,ZP) of Figure 15.4 be replaced by the following loop:

```
        DO 300 I = 1, 24
           CALL MATVEC(N,T,Z,ZP)
           DO 200 J = 1, N
              Z(J) = ZP(J)
200        CONTINUE
300     CONTINUE
```

Notice that the outer loop invokes the matrix-vector multiplication 24 times. The inner loop copies the results of one transformation into Z where it may be used as input for the next transformation.

Figure 15.6 contains the results from the modified program and demonstrates the distribution of market shares after an extended period of time. The advertising campaign problem could be dealt with using this model by altering the definition of the transformation matrix. The alterations in the model would reflect an increase or

```
C Figure 15.4 -- The Two Bakery Problem.
C                 Program to compute the market shares of two bakeries
C                 after one month.
C*************************************************************************
C T       - transformation matrix
C Z       - vector to be transformed
C ZP      - transformed vector
C BAKERS  - number of bakeries
C I,J     - loop counters
C*************************************************************************
      INTEGER I, J, BAKERS
      REAL T(2,2), Z(2), ZP(2)
C Input and echo matrix T and vector Z.
      BAKERS = 2
      READ *, ((T(I,J), J = 1, BAKERS), I = 1, BAKERS)
      READ *, (Z(I), I = 1, BAKERS)
      PRINT *, '          MATRIX T              VECTOR Z'
      DO 100 I = 1, BAKERS
         PRINT *, (T(I,J), J = 1, BAKERS), Z(I)
  100 CONTINUE
C Form the matrix-vector product ZP = T*Z.
      CALL MATVEC(BAKERS,T,Z,ZP)
C Print out the transformed vector.
      PRINT *, ' '
      PRINT *, 'THE MARKET SHARES AFTER ONE MONTH ARE',
     +                              (ZP(I), I = 1, BAKERS)
      STOP
      END
C Subroutine MATVEC is placed here.
```

Figure 15.5 Input and output for the first month of the two bakery program of Figure 15.4.

a) Input file:

```
0.98, 0.04
0.02, 0.96
0.40, 0.60
```

b) Output file:

```
          MATRIX T              VECTOR Z
  0.9800000       3.9999999E-02 0.4000000
  2.0000000E-02   0.9600000     0.6000000

THE MARKET SHARES AFTER ONE MONTH ARE   0.4160000        0.5840001
```

decrease of market share as a result of advertising, and would only be put into effect for the duration of the campaign.

Figure 15.6 Output for 24 months of the modified two bakery program of Figure 15.4

```
           MATRIX T                  VECTOR Z
  0.9800000        3.9999999E-02  0.4000000
  2.0000000E-02    0.9600000      0.6000000
```

THE MARKET SHARES AFTER 24 MONTHS ARE   0.6062668   0.3937332

The effect of a third competitor is a bit more complicated and will now be examined in detail.

Example 15.2   Three Bakery Problem

Suppose that bakeries A and B compete with each other and that brand-switching occurs each month according to the transformation T of the two bakery problem. Suppose further that a new bakery C starts operations after a market survey which indicates that it could attract the business of half of all switching customers, and 2% of all other customers of A and B.   The survey also suggests that bakery C could retain 92% of its customers each month and lose 4% to each of A and B. Assuming that A and B each have the market share corresponding to the end of the 24 month period when C starts operations, what will be the distribution of market shares after the next 1, 2, 3, and 4 years?

a) Problem Analysis   If the market shares of A, B, and C are represented by x, y, z and x', y', z' at the beginning and end of a month respectively, then the information given produces the following equation for the new value of x:

$$x' = 0.9604x + 0.02y + 0.04z .$$

The terms in this equation are found by observing that A previously retained 98% of its market but now 2% of the 98% or 1.96% switches to C, leaving A with 96.04%.   This gives the term $0.9604x$.   A previously gained 4% of B's customers each month but now half go to C, producing the term $0.02y$.   C loses 4% of its market to A, producing the term $0.04z$.

Similar arguments are applied to deduce the system of equations:

$$x' = 0.9604x + 0.02y + 0.04z \qquad (15.5)$$

$$y' = 0.01x + 0.9408y + 0.04z$$

$$z' = 0.0296x + 0.0392y + 0.92z .$$

As before, this may be represented as a matrix-vector multiplication $Z' = T \times Z$, where

$$T = \begin{bmatrix} 0.9604 & 0.02 & 0.04 \\ 0.01 & 0.9408 & 0.04 \\ 0.0296 & 0.0392 & 0.92 \end{bmatrix}, \quad Z' = \begin{bmatrix} x' \\ y' \\ z' \end{bmatrix}, \quad \text{and} \quad Z = \begin{bmatrix} x \\ y \\ z \end{bmatrix} . \qquad (15.6)$$

b) Developing the Algorithm   The general structure of an algorithm for the solution of the problem should now be clear.   A first version is shown as Figure 15.7.

Figure 15.7   First version of a pseudocode algorithm for the three bakery problem.

* Algorithm to compute the market shares of the three bakery problem.

* Variables used:
* T - transformation matrix of size number of bakers × number of bakers
* Z - vector of market shares at the start of a month
* ZP - transformed vector of shares at the end of a month

* Input and echo-print the elements of the transformation matrix
* and the vector of initial shares.

get T, Z
put 'The transformation matrix T is', T
put 'The initial vector of market shares Z is', Z

* Compute the market shares for 1, 2, 3, and 4 years.

for years **from** 1 **to** 4 **do**

  1. For each of the 12 months, transform the old vector of market shares Z to the new vector ZP using matvec, then copy ZP to Z.

  2. Record the year-end market position.

end

---

c) Refining Step **1.**   This step corresponds closely to the FORTRAN/77 code added to solve the first problem.   In pseudocode:

  * For each of the 12 months, transform Z to ZP and copy ZP to Z.

  for months **from** 1 **to** 12 **do**

    matvec(n, T, Z; ZP)
    Z ← ZP

d) Refining Step **2.**   This refinement is straightforward.

  * Record the year-end market position.

  put 'After year', years
  put 'Market shares are'
  put (z_i, i **from** 1 **to** 4)

e) Final Program   The complete algorithm may now be assembled and converted to FORTRAN/77 as shown in Figure 15.8.   The input for and the output from the FORTRAN/77 program follow as Figure 15.9.

```
C Figure 15.8 -- The Three Bakery Problem.
C                Program to compute the market shares of three
C                bakeries for each of four years.

C**********************************************************************
C T      - transformation matrix
C Z      - market shares at the start of a month
C ZP     - market shares at the end of a month
C BAKERS - number of bakeries
C MONTH  - loop counter for months
C YEAR   - loop counter for years

C**********************************************************************
      INTEGER I, J, MONTH, YEAR, BAKERS
      REAL T(3,3), Z(3), ZP(3)
C Input and echo-print the elements of the transformation
C matrix and vector of initial shares.
      READ *, BAKERS
      READ *, ((T(I,J), J = 1, BAKERS), I = 1, BAKERS)
      READ *, (Z(I), I = 1, BAKERS)
      PRINT *, '               MATRIX T               VECTOR Z'
      DO 100 I = 1, BAKERS
         PRINT *, (T(I,J), J = 1, BAKERS), Z(I)
  100 CONTINUE
C Compute the market shares for 1, 2, 3, and 4 years.
      PRINT *, ' '
      DO 400 YEAR = 1, 4
C        Transform the monthly market shares 12 times.
         DO 300 MONTH = 1, 12
            CALL MATVEC(BAKERS,T,Z,ZP)
C           Copy ZP to Z.
            DO 200 I = 1, BAKERS
               Z(I) = ZP(I)
  200       CONTINUE
  300    CONTINUE
C        Print the year-end market position.
         PRINT *, 'AFTER YEAR', YEAR, 'THE MARKET SHARES ARE',
     +                        (ZP(I), I = 1, BAKERS)
  400 CONTINUE
      STOP
      END
C Subroutine MATVEC is placed here.
```

Figure 15.9 Input and output files for the three bakery problem program of Figure 15.8.

a) Input file:

```
3
0.9604, 0.0200, 0.0400
0.0100, 0.9408, 0.0400
0.0296, 0.0392, 0.9200
0.6060, 0.3940, 0.0000
```

b) Output file:

```
                 MATRIX T                        VECTOR Z
   0.9604000      2.0000000E-02   3.9999999E-02   0.6060000
   9.9999998E-03  0.9408000       3.9999999E-02   0.3940000
   2.9600000E-02  3.9200000E-02   0.9200000       0.0000000E+00

AFTER YEAR   1 THE MARKET SHARES ARE   0.4898522   0.2861892   0.2239586
AFTER YEAR   2 THE MARKET SHARES ARE   0.4544229   0.2689440   0.2766331
AFTER YEAR   3 THE MARKET SHARES ARE   0.4422551   0.2683843   0.2893607
AFTER YEAR   4 THE MARKET SHARES ARE   0.4376096   0.2698039   0.2925867
```

---

f) Discussion of Results   After four years, bakery C has steadily increased its share of the market to about 29%, although there was less change from the third to fourth years. At the same time, bakeries A and B have had their shares of the market reduced to about 44% and 27% respectively.   These shares should be compared with the initial market shares shown by the vector Z.

15.4   Multiplication of Matrices

In the previous section, the transformation of a vector Z to another vector Z′ was represented by Z′ = T × Z.   T was called the transformation matrix and the formation of T × Z was called a matrix-vector multiplication.   In many circumstances, there will be more than one transformation involved, say Z″ = U × Z′, where U is another matrix. This could be written in two ways:

$$Z'' = U \times (T \times Z), \quad \text{or} \quad Z'' = (U \times T) \times Z.$$

Although very similar in appearance, the brackets radically alter the interpretation of the equations.   In the first equation the *matrix* U multiplies the *vector* T × Z, that is, the transformations U and T are applied in turn to the vector Z.   In the second equation the *matrix* U × T multiplies the *vector* Z, that is, a single transformation U × T is formed and is applied to the vector Z.   The notation suggests that U × T be called the *product* of U and T, but the rules for its computation may be deduced by asking that the results be the same.

Example 15.3   Matrix Multiplication Problem
Find a single transformation matrix which is equivalent to the successive application of two monthly transformations from the two bakery problem of Example 15.1.

From the equation (15.2), one monthly transformation is $Z' = T \times Z$, and a second application gives $Z'' = T \times Z'$.   Using the rules for matrix-vector multiplication gives

$$Z'' = T \times Z'$$

$$= \begin{bmatrix} 0.98 & 0.04 \\ 0.02 & 0.96 \end{bmatrix} \times \begin{bmatrix} 0.98x + 0.04y \\ 0.02x + 0.96y \end{bmatrix}$$

$$= \begin{bmatrix} 0.98(0.98x + 0.04y) + 0.04(0.02x + 0.96y) \\ 0.02(0.98x + 0.04y) + 0.96(0.02x + 0.96y) \end{bmatrix}$$

The x and y terms in this vector may be factored and the result expressed as the matrix vector product $Z'' = R \times Z$.

$$Z'' = \begin{bmatrix} 0.98 \times 0.98 + 0.04 \times 0.02 & 0.98 \times 0.04 + 0.04 \times 0.96 \\ 0.02 \times 0.98 + 0.96 \times 0.02 & 0.02 \times 0.04 + 0.96 \times 0.96 \end{bmatrix} \times \begin{bmatrix} x \\ y \end{bmatrix}$$

Closer inspection reveals that the *first column* of R is simply the matrix-vector product of matrix T with the vector consisting of the *first column* of T.   Similarly, the *second column* of R is the matrix-vector product of T with the *second column* of T.   R would be referred to as T^2.

Matrix multiplication makes sense in some applications even when the matrices have different dimensions; it is necessary that the number of *columns of the matrix on the left* should match the number of *rows of the matrix on the right*.   The general formula for the product of a matrix A having m rows and n columns with a matrix B having n rows and k columns is

$$c_{rs} = \sum_{i=1}^{n} a_{ri} \times b_{is} \; ; \quad r = 1, 2, \ldots, m; s = 1, 2, \ldots, k. \tag{15.7}$$

Note that the product $C = A \times B$ has m rows and k columns.

15.4.1   A Matrix Multiplication Module
Conversion of the formula for matrix multiplication to a module is desirable, since such a module may be useful in many applications.   The module will have the form

smodule matmpy(**imports**: m, n, k, A, B; **exports**: C)

The module accepts as imports the integers m, n, and k, a matrix A (dimension m×n), and a matrix B (dimension n×k), and produces for export the matrix C (dimension m×k). A first version is shown as Figure 15.10.

Figure 15.10   First version of a pseudocode module for matrix multiplication.

smodule matmpy(**imports**: m, n, k, A, B; **exports**: C)

1.   For each element c_{rs} of matrix C, compute $c_{rs} \leftarrow$ sum of products of elements of row r of A with column s of B.

end module

---

a) Refining Step **1.**   Matrix C will have m rows and k columns.   An outer loop is needed to produce each of the m rows.   Within this outer loop, an inner loop is used to compute each of the k column entries for the current row.

```
* For each row r of A and column s of B, sum the products
* of the row vector times the column vector.
```

for r **from** 1 **to** m **do**

$$\text{for s from 1 to k do}$$
$$c_{rs} \leftarrow \sum_{i=1}^{n} a_{ri} * b_{is}$$

Formation of this sum is quite straightforward.

```
sum ← 0
for i from 1 to n do
    sum ← sum + ari * bis
crs ← sum
```

b) Final Version of the Matrix Multiplication Algorithm   This algorithm is assembled in Figure 15.11.

c) A FORTRAN/**77** *Matrix Multiplication Module*   A FORTRAN/**77** version follows as Figure 15.12.

15.4.2   Applications of Matrix Multiplication

Matrix multiplication provides the tool needed to construct a single transformation which corresponds to a sequence of other transformations.

Example 15.4   *Three Bakery Problem Using A One-Year Transformation*
      Solve the three bakery problem by developing a single transformation representing a one-year evolution of the market.

a) Background   From the previous discussion, the desired one-year transformation will correspond to 12 applications of the original one-month transformation T.   Thus, the one-year transformation will correspond to T^{12}.   The three bakery problem may be solved for the three years by three applications of T^{12}.

Figure 15.11   Final version of the pseudocode module for matrix multiplication.

smodule matmpy(**imports:** m, n, k, A, B; **exports:** C)

* Module for matrix multiplication.

* Variables used:
* A - import matrix m×n
* B - import matrix n×k
* C - export matrix m×k
* sum - temporary storage for sum of products

* For each row r of A and column s of B, sum the products
* of the row vector times the column vector.

for r **from** 1 **to** m **do**

    for s **from** 1 **to** k **do**

        sum ← 0
        for i **from** 1 **to** n **do**

            sum ← sum + a_{ri} * b_{is}

        c_{rs} ← sum

end module

```
C Figure 15.12 -- A Matrix Multiplication Module.
C                 Subroutine MATMPY to form the matrix product C = A*B.
C**********************************************************************
C A   - import matrix (MxN)
C B   - import matrix (NxK)
C C   - export matrix (MxK)
C SUM - temporary storage for sum of products
C**********************************************************************
        SUBROUTINE MATMPY(M,N,K,A,B,C)

        INTEGER M, N, K, R, S, I
        REAL A(M,N), B(N,K), C(M,K), SUM
C For each row R of A and column S of B, form the product
C of the row vector and the column vector.
        DO 100 R = 1, M
           DO 200 S = 1, K
              SUM = 0.0
              DO 300 I = 1, N
                 SUM = SUM + A(R,I)*B(I,S)
  300         CONTINUE
              C(R,S) = SUM
  200      CONTINUE
  100   CONTINUE
        RETURN
        END
```

A slight modification of the algorithm in Figure 15.7 for solving the three bakery problem is given below:

1. Compute the one-year transformation T^{12}.
2. Compute and record the market shares after 1, 2, 3, and 4 years.

b) Refining Step **1.**   In order to retain the transformation T, it is necessary to use another matrix to hold the successive powers of T. This matrix, T12, can be initialized to T×T by one invocation of matmpy. Successive powers of T can be formed by using matmpy to form T×T12 in TEMP.

    * Compute the one-year transformation in T12.
    * Form T^2 in T12 initially.

matmpy(n, n, n, T, T; T12)

    * Form the twelfth power of T in T12.

for power **from** 3 **to** 12 **do**
   ⎡ matmpy(n, n, n, T, T12; TEMP)
   ⎣ T12 ← TEMP

c) Refining Step **2.**   This step involves repeated application of the one-year transformation, T12, to the market shares vector Z.

for year **from** 1 **to** 4 **do**
   ⎡ matvec(n, T12, Z; ZP)
   | Z ← ZP
   ⎣ **put** 'Market share after ', year, ' years is ', Z

d) A FORTRAN/77 *Final Version*   This algorithm is given as a FORTRAN/77 program in Figure 15.13. The output follows as Figure 15.14. Comparing these results to those contained in Figure 15.9 confirms that the one-year transformation, T^{12}, produces the same results as T applied twelve times.

```
C Figure 15.13 -- Three Bakery Problem Using a One-year Transformation.
C                 Program to compute market shares of three bakeries
C                 using the one-year transformation T**12 and
C                 applying this in four successive years.
C*******************************************************************************
C T       - transformation matrix
C T12     - matrix in which powers of T are developed
C TEMP    - temporary matrix storage
C Z       - market shares vector for each year
C ZP      - new market shares vector at end of year
C BAKERS  - number of bakers
C I,J,YEAR,POWER - loop indices
C*******************************************************************************
```

```
C Figure 15.13 (continued)
      INTEGER BAKERS, I, J, YEAR, POWER
      REAL T(3,3), T12(3,3), TEMP(3,3), Z(3), ZP(3)
C Input and echo the data.
      READ *, BAKERS
      READ *, ((T(I,J), J = 1, BAKERS), I = 1, BAKERS)
      PRINT *, 'MATRIX T'
      DO 100 I = 1, BAKERS
         PRINT *, (T(I,J), J = 1, BAKERS)
  100 CONTINUE
C Compute the one-year transformation in T12.
C Form T**2 in T12 INITIALLY.
      CALL MATMPY(BAKERS,BAKERS,BAKERS,T,T,T12)
C Form the twelfth power of T in T12.
      DO 400 POWER = 3, 12

         CALL MATMPY(BAKERS,BAKERS,BAKERS,T,T12,TEMP)

C        Copy TEMP to T12 for the next step.

         DO 300 I = 1, BAKERS
            DO 200 J = 1, BAKERS
               T12(I,J) = TEMP(I,J)
  200       CONTINUE
  300    CONTINUE
  400 CONTINUE
      PRINT *, ' '
      PRINT *, 'ONE YEAR TRANSFORMATION'
      DO 500 I = 1, BAKERS
         PRINT *, (T12(I,J), J = 1, BAKERS)
  500 CONTINUE
C Input the initial market share data.
      READ *, (Z(I), I = 1, BAKERS)
      PRINT *, ' '
      PRINT *, 'INITIAL VECTOR OF MARKET SHARES'
      PRINT *, (Z(I), I = 1, BAKERS)
C Compute the market shares for 1, 2, 3, and 4 years.
      PRINT *, ' '
      DO 700 YEAR = 1, 4
         CALL MATVEC(BAKERS,T12,Z,ZP)
         PRINT *, 'MARKET SHARES AFTER YEAR', YEAR, 'ARE ',
     +                                (ZP(J), J = 1, BAKERS)
         DO 600 J = 1, BAKERS
            Z(J) = ZP(J)
  600    CONTINUE
  700 CONTINUE
      STOP
      END
C Subroutines MATMPY and MATVEC are placed here.
```

Figure 15.14 Output from the program of Figure 15.13 for the three bakery problem using a one-year transformation.

```
MATRIX  T
  0.9604000         2.0000000E-02   3.9999999E-02
  9.9999998E-03     0.9408000       3.9999999E-02
  2.9600000E-02     3.9200000E-02   0.9200000

ONE  YEAR  TRANSFORMATION
  0.6761243         0.2033525       0.2903421
  0.1163685         0.5473855       0.2468531
  0.2075070         0.2492622       0.4628049

INITIAL  VECTOR  OF  MARKET  SHARES
  0.6060000         0.3940000          0.0000000E+00

MARKET  SHARES  AFTER  YEAR    1  ARE    0.4898522   0.2861892   0.2239586
MARKET  SHARES  AFTER  YEAR    2  ARE    0.4544229   0.2689441   0.2766331
MARKET  SHARES  AFTER  YEAR    3  ARE    0.4422551   0.2683843   0.2893607
MARKET  SHARES  AFTER  YEAR    4  ARE    0.4376096   0.2698038   0.2925866
```

15.5   Undoing a Transformation or Solving Equations

The previous problems have been concerned with predicting the future evolution of a market.   Sometimes it is also necessary to use similar information about the present state of a system to deduce its previous state.

Suppose, for instance, that you are a tax investigator with the assignment of deducing the market shares of the three bakeries one month ago, given the present distribution of the market and the matrix T governing the monthly change in market shares.   Such information might be necessary to determine if reported incomes are unreasonable.

In this problem, the notation of the previous sections will be used.   Z will represent the vector of market shares one month ago, and Z' will represent the present vector of shares.   As before, $T \times Z = Z'$, but now it is Z' which is known, and Z which is to be found.   Looking first at the two bakery model of Section 15.2, it is seen that $(x',y') = (0.416, 0.584)$ with (x,y) to be determined from

$$\begin{bmatrix} 0.98 & 0.04 \\ 0.02 & 0.96 \end{bmatrix} \times \begin{bmatrix} x \\ y \end{bmatrix} = \begin{bmatrix} 0.416 \\ 0.584 \end{bmatrix}. \tag{15.8}$$

Doing the matrix-vector multiplication gives

$$0.98x + 0.04y = 0.416 \tag{15.9}$$

$$0.02x + 0.96y = 0.584.$$

Written in this way, the two equations in two unknowns present a problem familiar to all readers from high school mathematics courses.   The solution, also familiar, involves the elimination of one unknown from one equation.   For example, *both sides* of the second equation of (15.9) might be multiplied by 49, that is, 0.98/0.02, to give

$$0.98x + 47.04y = 28.616 .$$

Subtracting the first equation (left side from left side and right side from right side) gives

$$(0.98 - 0.98)x + (47.04 - 0.04)y = 28.616 - 0.416, \quad \text{or} \quad 47.0y = 28.2.$$

Now it is clear that $y = 0.6$, and substituting this into the first equation of (15.9) gives

$$0.98x + 0.04 \times 0.6 = 0.416 \quad \text{or} \quad x = (0.416 - 0.024)/0.98 = 0.4.$$

15.5.1   Solving Triangular Systems of Equations

Reflecting upon what was done to solve the system of equations, it is seen that the system was transformed to the *triangular form* shown below.

$$0.98x + 0.04y = 0.416 \tag{15.10}$$

$$47.0y = 28.2$$

The solution was then easy to deduce from this form of the equations.

The general form of n equations in n unknowns is

$$
\begin{bmatrix}
a_{11} & a_{12} & a_{13} & \cdots & a_{1n} \\
a_{21} & a_{22} & a_{23} & \cdots & a_{2n} \\
a_{31} & a_{32} & a_{33} & \cdots & a_{3n} \\
\cdot & \cdot & \cdot & & \cdot \\
\cdot & \cdot & \cdot & & \cdot \\
\cdot & \cdot & \cdot & & \cdot \\
a_{n1} & a_{n2} & a_{n3} & \cdots & a_{nn}
\end{bmatrix}
\times
\begin{bmatrix}
z_1 \\ z_2 \\ z_3 \\ \cdot \\ \cdot \\ \cdot \\ z_n
\end{bmatrix}
=
\begin{bmatrix}
c_1 \\ c_2 \\ c_3 \\ \cdot \\ \cdot \\ \cdot \\ c_n
\end{bmatrix}
. \tag{15.11}
$$

Observe that the solution to the system will be easy if it has the triangular form

$$
\begin{bmatrix}
t_{11} & t_{12} & t_{13} & \cdots & t_{1n} \\
0 & t_{22} & t_{23} & \cdots & t_{2n} \\
0 & 0 & t_{33} & \cdots & t_{3n} \\
\cdot & \cdot & \cdot & & \cdot \\
\cdot & \cdot & \cdot & & \cdot \\
\cdot & \cdot & \cdot & & \cdot \\
0 & 0 & 0 & \cdots & t_{nn}
\end{bmatrix}
\times
\begin{bmatrix}
z_1 \\ z_2 \\ z_3 \\ \cdot \\ \cdot \\ \cdot \\ z_n
\end{bmatrix}
=
\begin{bmatrix}
c_1 \\ c_2 \\ c_3 \\ \cdot \\ \cdot \\ \cdot \\ c_n
\end{bmatrix}
. \tag{15.12}
$$

The solution proceeds by observing that

$$z_n = \frac{c_n}{t_{nn}}.$$

Knowing this value permits solution for

$$z_{n-1} = \frac{(c_{n-1} - t_{n-1,n} \times z_n)}{t_{n-1,n-1}}.$$

Knowing z_n and z_{n-1} then permits solution for $z_{n-2}, z_{n-3}, \ldots, z_1$. This process of *back-substitution* continues until all unknowns have been determined. Note, however, that the process fails if any one of the diagonal elements of T is zero, since a division by each diagonal element occurs once.

15.5.2   A Module for Solving Triangular Systems of Equations

Using the notation of the previous section, a module will be developed to solve the linear system of equations

$$T \times Z = C,$$

where T is a triangular transformation matrix. A first version of the module is presented in Figure 15.15.

Figure 15.15   First version of a pseudocode module to solve triangular linear equation systems.

smodule backsolve (**imports:** n, T, C; **exports:** Z)

1.   For each element of Z, starting at z_n, compute $z_i \leftarrow (c_i - \sum_{j=i+1}^{n} t_{ij} * z_j) / t_{ii}$

end module

---

a) Refining Step **1.**   It is necessary to solve for the elements of Z in reverse order, starting with n and going to 1. Therefore, a **for**–loop is constructed which reduces index i from n to 1. The solution for each of the Z entries is left as a summation formula for expansion at the next step.

> * Starting with $z_n = c_n/t_{nn}$, solve for $z_{n-1}, z_{n-2}, \ldots, z_1$.
>
> **for** i **from** n **to** 1 **by** −1 **do**
> $$z_i \leftarrow (c_i - \sum_{j=i+1}^{n} t_{ij} * z_j)/t_{ii}$$

The operations involved in this summation may now be expanded. The portion of the formula in parentheses is called sum, which is initialized to the i-th component of vector C. Then, an inner **for**–loop controls the substitution of "known" Z entries from i+1 to n in calculating sum.

> sum ← c_i
> **for** j **from** i+1 **to** n **do**
> $$sum \leftarrow sum - t_{ij} * z_j$$
> $z_i \leftarrow sum/t_{ii}$

b) Final Version of the Algorithm   The complete algorithm may now be assembled and is shown as Figure 15.16.   A FORTRAN/77 version follows as Figure 15.17.   Output from tests of this module will be presented in a later section.

Figure 15.16   Final version of the pseudocode module to solve triangular linear systems.

smodule backsolve (**imports**: n, T, C; **exports**: Z)

```
* Module to solve a triangular system
* of n linear equations in n unknowns using a
* given coefficient matrix T and right-hand side C,
* to produce the solution vector Z.
```

```
* Variables used:
* n - import dimension of all arrays
* T - upper triangular coefficient matrix
* C - right-hand side of the system
* Z - solution vector to the system
* sum - temporary storage for sum of products
```

* Starting with $z_n = c_n/t_{nn}$, solve for $z_{n-1}, z_{n-2}, \ldots, z_1$.

for i **from** n **to** 1 **by** −1 **do**
$$\begin{array}{|l} \text{sum} \leftarrow c_i \\ \textbf{for } j \textbf{ from } i{+}1 \textbf{ to } n \textbf{ do} \\ \quad \begin{array}{|l} \text{sum} \leftarrow \text{sum} - t_{ij} * z_j \end{array} \\ z_i \leftarrow \text{sum}/t_{ii} \end{array}$$

end module

15.5.3   Solving General Systems of Linear Equations.

In the previous section it was shown that the solution of triangular systems of linear equations was quite easy using the back-substitution algorithm.   Therefore, the first step in solving a general linear system is to transform the system to an equivalent triangular system having the same solution.

To do this, it is necessary to examine some possible changes which could be made to a system of equations without changing its solution.   Each equation in the system represents a valid statement about a relationship among the unknowns.   If enough equations are given, then a solution may be found.   In general, if there are *n* unknowns, *n* equations are needed.   However, none of the equations is permitted to contradict the others, nor should any equation be a consequence of the others, if a unique solution is expected.

There are really only two valid operations which may be applied to a single equation.   Both sides may be *multiplied* by the same nonzero constant or the same quantity may be *added* to both sides.

If there are *two* equations, one of them may be replaced by a new equation formed by adding a constant multiple of one equation to another.   This was the process which lead to the conclusion earlier that

```
C Figure 15.17 -- Module to Solve Triangular Linear Systems.
C                  Subroutine BSOLVE to solve a triangular system
C                  of N linear equations in N unknowns using a given
C                  coefficient matrix T and right-hand side C, to
C                  produce the solution vector Z. T is assumed to be
C                  non-singular.

C*************************************************************************

C N    - the actual size of all arrays
C NDIM - the variable dimension of all arrays
C T    - upper triangular coefficient matrix of size NxN
C        (assumed to be non-singular)
C C    - right-hand side of the system
C Z    - solution of the system of equations
C SUM  - temporary storage for sum of products

C*************************************************************************

      SUBROUTINE BSOLVE(NDIM,N,T,Z,C)

      INTEGER NDIM, N, I, J
      REAL T(NDIM,NDIM), Z(NDIM), C(NDIM), SUM
C Starting with Z(N) = C(N)/T(N,N),
C solve for Z(N-1), Z(N-2), ... , Z(1).

      DO 200 I = N, 1, -1
         SUM = C(I)
         DO 100 J = I+1, N
            SUM = SUM - T(I,J)*Z(J)
100      CONTINUE
         Z(I) = SUM/T(I,I)
200   CONTINUE
      RETURN
      END
```

$$0.98x + 0.04y = 0.416$$

$$0.02x + 0.96y = 0.584$$

had the same solution as

$$0.98x + 0.04y = 0.416$$

$$47.0y = 28.2 \ .$$

For the general linear system

$$
\begin{bmatrix}
a_{11} & a_{12} & a_{13} & \cdots & a_{1n} \\
a_{21} & a_{22} & a_{23} & \cdots & a_{2n} \\
a_{31} & a_{32} & a_{33} & \cdots & a_{3n} \\
\cdot & \cdot & \cdot & & \cdot \\
\cdot & \cdot & \cdot & & \cdot \\
\cdot & \cdot & \cdot & & \cdot \\
a_{n1} & a_{n2} & a_{n3} & \cdots & a_{nn}
\end{bmatrix}
\times
\begin{bmatrix}
z_1 \\ z_2 \\ z_3 \\ \cdot \\ \cdot \\ \cdot \\ z_n
\end{bmatrix}
=
\begin{bmatrix}
c_1 \\ c_2 \\ c_3 \\ \cdot \\ \cdot \\ \cdot \\ c_n
\end{bmatrix}
\qquad (15.13)
$$

the reduction to triangular form may be carried out systematically.   Any equation may
be altered by adding to it a multiple of any other equation.   Notice that this
corresponds to adding a multiple of one row of the coefficient matrix, A, to another row,
with the same operations done on the right hand side, C.

Provided that the first element of the first row is not zero, multiples of this row may
be added to subsequent rows to produce zeros in the first position of the subsequent
rows.   The elements of these rows are changed and this is denoted by the use of primes.

$$
\begin{bmatrix}
a_{11} & a_{12} & a_{13} & \cdots & a_{1n} \\
0 & a'_{22} & a'_{23} & \cdots & a'_{2n} \\
0 & a'_{32} & a'_{33} & \cdots & a'_{3n} \\
\cdot & \cdot & \cdot & & \cdot \\
\cdot & \cdot & \cdot & & \cdot \\
0 & \cdot & \cdot & & \cdot \\
0 & a'_{n2} & a'_{n3} & \cdots & a'_{nn}
\end{bmatrix}
\times
\begin{bmatrix}
z_1 \\ z_2 \\ z_3 \\ \cdot \\ \cdot \\ \cdot \\ z_n
\end{bmatrix}
=
\begin{bmatrix}
c_1 \\ c'_2 \\ c'_3 \\ \cdot \\ \cdot \\ \cdot \\ c'_n
\end{bmatrix}.
\tag{15.14}
$$

Similarly, if the second element of row two is not zero, multiples of row two may be added to subsequent rows to produce

$$
\begin{bmatrix}
a_{11} & a_{12} & a_{13} & \cdots & a_{1n} \\
0 & a'_{22} & a'_{23} & \cdots & a'_{2n} \\
0 & 0 & a''_{33} & \cdots & a''_{3n} \\
\cdot & \cdot & \cdot & & \cdot \\
\cdot & \cdot & \cdot & & \cdot \\
0 & 0 & \cdot & & \cdot \\
0 & 0 & a''_{n3} & \cdots & a''_{nn}
\end{bmatrix}
\times
\begin{bmatrix}
z_1 \\ z_2 \\ z_3 \\ \cdot \\ \cdot \\ \cdot \\ z_n
\end{bmatrix}
=
\begin{bmatrix}
c_1 \\ c'_2 \\ c''_3 \\ \cdot \\ \cdot \\ \cdot \\ c''_n
\end{bmatrix}.
\tag{15.15}
$$

This process may be continued to give a triangular system, provided that the diagonal
elements remain nonzero at each step.

If a diagonal element should happen to be zero, it is a simple matter to exchange
that row with a subsequent row whose first entry is not zero.   If no subsequent row has
a nonzero initial entry, then the equations do not have a unique solution. It is acceptable
to interchange rows of the coefficient matrix since this corresponds to writing down the
original equations in a different order, which should not affect the solution.

The process of creating a triangular coefficient matrix is called *Gaussian Elimination*. It will now be developed more formally as a pseudocode algorithm.

a) Developing a Gaussian Elimination Algorithm   The previous discussion permits the
first version of the algorithm to be outlined directly as a module, as shown in
Figure 15.18.

Figure 15.18 First version of a pseudocode module for Gaussian Elimination.

smodule gauss (**imports**: n, T, C; **exports**: T, C, error)

* Module to convert the linear system T*Z = C to triangular form.

* Variables used:
* n - import dimension of all arrays
* T - import (general) and export (triangular) matrix
* C - import and export vector
* error - returns **true** if no unique solution possible

1. For each diagonal element t_{ii}, transform the elements $t_{i+1,i}$, $t_{i+2,i}$, . . . , $t_{n,i}$ to zero by row operations.
end module

---

b) Refining Step **1.** This first refinement will incorporate the double loop structure required to step along the diagonal and to create zeros in subdiagonal positions.

> * Create zeros below t_{ii}, for i ← 1, 2, . . . , n−1.

1.1 for i **from** 1 **to** n **do**
> **1.2 for** j **from** i + 1 **to** n **do**
>> **1.3** Create a zero in position (j,i) by a row operation.

c) Refining Step **1.3** A zero may be created in position i of row j if row j is replaced by (row j) − (row i) * t_{ji}/t_{ii}

This requires another loop to step along all elements of row j.

> * Do the row operation (first attempt).

for k **from** i+1 **to** n **do**
> $t_{jk} \leftarrow t_{jk} - t_{ik}*(t_{ji}/t_{ii})$

$t_{ji} \leftarrow 0$
$c_j \leftarrow c_j - c_i*(t_{ji}/t_{ii})$

Since the ratio in parentheses is independent of k, it should be computed only once for each entry to this loop. This is an implementation optimization, as described in Chapter 11. The more efficient refinement follows:

* Do the row operation (second attempt).

ratio ← t_{ji}/t_{ii}
for k **from** i+1 **to** n **do**
$$\left[\; t_{jk} \leftarrow t_{jk} - t_{ik}\text{*ratio}\right.$$
$t_{ji} \leftarrow 0$
$c_j \leftarrow c_j - c_i\text{*ratio}$

d) Further Refinements   The algorithm as refined to this point will fail if the diagonal or *pivot* element is zero.   For reasons beyond the scope of this text, the algorithm may also produce inaccurate results if the pivot element is small.

For these reasons, a good Gaussian Elimination algorithm incorporates row interchanges so that the row with the largest possible element in position *i* (at the *i*-th stage) is moved to row *i*.   This may be accomplished by adding an additional step, say **1.1.1**, in the refinement of Step **1.**, as follows

for i **from** 1 **to** n **do**
> **1.1.1** Search for the row with maximum i-th element and exchange with row i.
>
> **for** j **from** i + 1 **to** n **do**
>> * Do the row operation.
>>
>> ratio ← t_{ji}/t_{ii}
>> **for** k **from** i + 1 **to** n **do**
>>> $t_{jk} \leftarrow t_{jk} - t_{ik}\text{*ratio}$
>>
>> $t_{ji} \leftarrow 0$
>> $c_j \leftarrow c_j - c_i\text{*ratio}$

e) Refining Step **1.1.1**   This pseudocode segment will be presented directly in Figure 15.19, since such search algorithms were fully described in Chapter 13.   Note that an error flag was introduced to protect against the possibility that a pivot element may be zero.   If this went undetected, then computing ratio would result in a divide-by-zero error.   Such matrices which result in a zero pivot element are called *singular* matrices.

f) Final Version of the Gaussian Elimination Algorithm   The preceding refinements may now be assembled and the complete module is presented in Figure 15.20.

g) A FORTRAN/77 *Gaussian Elimination Module*   The final version of the module is presented as a FORTRAN/77 subroutine in Figure 15.21.

Both the pseudocode and FORTRAN/77 versions use the arrays T and C for both import and export parameters.   This means that the original information in the arrays is destroyed by the module, so if the original values will be needed by the calling module, it will be the responsibility of the caller to make copies of these arrays.

Figure 15.19 Search and row interchange pseudocode for the Gaussian Elimination module.

* Find the maximum $t_{index,i}$ of t_{ii}, $t_{i+1,i}$, . . . , t_{ni} to be pivot element.

index ← i
pivot ← abs(t_{ii})
for j **from** i + 1 **to** n **do**

> **if** abs(t_{ji}) > pivot **then**
>> pivot ← abs(t_{ji})
>> index ← j

* If index > i, exchange rows i and index.

if index > i **then**

> **for** k **from** i **to** n **do**
>> temp ← t_{ik}
>> t_{ik} ← $t_{index,k}$
>> $t_{index,k}$ ← temp
>
> temp ← c_i
> c_i ← c_{index}
> c_{index} ← temp

* If the pivot is zero, then no unique solution is possible.

if pivot = 0 **then**

> error ← **true**

Figure 15.20   Final version of the pseudocode module for Gaussian Elimination.

smodule gauss (**imports**: n, T, C; **exports**: T, C, error)

* Module to convert the linear system $T*Z = C$ to triangular form.
* Variables used:
* n - size of linear system
* T - coefficient matrix (import) to be reduced to triangular form (export)
* C - right-hand side vector which will also be reduced
* error - returns **true** if matrix is singular
* pivot - largest (in magnitude) subdiagonal element
* index - row index of pivot element
* ratio - ratio of subdiagonal to diagonal element

error ← **false**
for i **from** 1 **to** n **do**

$\quad$ * Find the maximum $t_{index,i}$ of $t_{ii}, t_{i+1,i}, \ldots, t_{ni}$ to be pivot element.

$\quad$ index ← i
$\quad$ pivot ← abs(t_{ii})
$\quad$ **for** j **from** i + 1 **to** n **do**

$\quad\quad$ **if** abs(t_{ji}) > pivot **then**

$\quad\quad\quad$ pivot ← abs(t_{ji})
$\quad\quad\quad$ index ← j

$\quad$ * If index > i, exchange rows i and index.

$\quad$ **if** index > i **then**

$\quad\quad$ **for** k **from** i **to** n **do**

$\quad\quad\quad$ temp ← t_{ik}
$\quad\quad\quad$ t_{ik} ← $t_{index,k}$
$\quad\quad\quad$ $t_{index,k}$ ← temp

$\quad\quad$ temp ← c_i
$\quad\quad$ c_i ← c_{index}
$\quad\quad$ c_{index} ← temp

$\quad$ * If the pivot is zero, then no unique solution is possible.

$\quad$ **if** pivot = 0 **then**

$\quad\quad$ error ← **true**

$\quad$ **else**

$\quad\quad$ **for** j **from** i + 1 **to** n **do**

$\quad\quad\quad$ * Create a zero in position (j,i) by a row operation.

$\quad\quad\quad$ ratio ← t_{ji}/t_{ii}
$\quad\quad\quad$ **for** k **from** i + 1 **to** n **do**

$\quad\quad\quad\quad$ t_{jk} ← $t_{jk} - t_{ik} *$ ratio

$\quad\quad\quad$ t_{ji} ← 0
$\quad\quad\quad$ c_j ← $c_j - c_i*$ratio

end module

```
C Figure 15.21 -- A Gaussian Elimination Module.
C                Subroutine GAUSS to convert the linear system
C                T*X = C to triangular form.
C***********************************************************************
C NDIM  - variable dimension of all arrays
C N     - actual size of all arrays
C T     - import matrix(general) and export matrix(triangular)
C C     - import and export form of right-hand-side vector
C ERROR - .TRUE. if matrix is singular
C PIVOT - largest (in magnitude) subdiagonal element
C INDEX - row containing the largest subdiagonal element
C RATIO - ratio of subdiagonal to diagonal element
C***********************************************************************
        SUBROUTINE GAUSS(NDIM,N,T,C,ERROR)

        INTEGER NDIM, N, I, J, K, INDEX
        REAL T(NDIM,NDIM), C(NDIM), PIVOT, TEMP, RATIO, ABS
        LOGICAL ERROR
C Create zeros in subdiagonal positions of columns 1 to N.
C Check for zero diagonal elements in the reduction.
        ERROR = .FALSE.
        DO 100 I = 1, N

C        Find the maximum T(INDEX,I) of T(I,I), T(I+1,I), ..., T(N,I)
C        to be the pivot element.

         INDEX = I
         PIVOT = ABS(T(I,I))
         DO 200 J = I+1, N
            IF (ABS(T(J,I)) .GT. PIVOT) THEN
                PIVOT = ABS(T(J,I))
                INDEX = J
            ENDIF
  200    CONTINUE

C        If INDEX exceeds I, exchange rows I and INDEX.

         IF (INDEX .GT. I) THEN
            DO 400 K = I, N
               TEMP = T(I,K)
               T(I,K) = T(INDEX,K)
               T(INDEX,K) = TEMP
  400       CONTINUE
            TEMP = C(I)
            C(I) = C(INDEX)
            C(INDEX) = TEMP
         ENDIF
```

```
C Figure 15.21 (continued)
C         If the pivot is zero, then no unique solution is possible.
          IF (PIVOT .EQ. 0.0) THEN
              ERROR = .TRUE.
          ELSE
C             Create a zero in position (J,I) by a row operation.
              DO 300 J = I+1, N
                  RATIO = T(J,I)/T(I,I)
                  DO 500 K = I+1, N
                      T(J,K) = T(J,K) - T(I,K)*RATIO
      500         CONTINUE
                  C(J) = C(J) - C(I)*RATIO
      300     CONTINUE
          ENDIF
  100 CONTINUE
      RETURN
      END
```

15.5.4 Using the Linear Equation Modules

To test these linear equation modules, it is necessary to form a matrix equation and to compute its solution. The market shares data for the three bakery problem using a one-year transformation shown in Figure 15.14 provides a good example.

Example 15.5   Initial Market Shares Problem

For the three bakery problem described earlier, and given a one-year transformation matrix T and the resulting market shares vector C, determine what the market shares were at the beginning of the year.

This problem can be formulated as the matrix equation

$$T \times Z = C$$

where T and C are known and Z is unknown. The program will input the coefficient matrix and the right-hand side vector and then use the BSOLVE and GAUSS modules to compute a solution. After GAUSS is invoked, the error flag must be checked in case the coefficient matrix was singular. Such a program is presented in Figure 15.22 with the input data and computed results shown in Figure 15.23. The test data was designed to produce a known result which was the initial market shares of (0.606, 0.394, 0.0) from the three bakery problem. The computed results using the linear equation modules are as expected with the limited accuracy of computer arithmetic.

```
C Figure 15.22 -- The Initial Market Shares Problem.
C                 Program to use the linear equation modules GAUSS
C                 and BSOLVE to determine the initial market shares
C                 in the three bakeries problem.

C**********************************************************************
C T      - coefficient matrix
C Z      - solution vector
C C      - right-hand-side vector
C BAKERS - number of bakeries
C ERROR  - error flag for singular matrix in GAUSS

C**********************************************************************
      INTEGER BAKERS, I, J
      REAL T(5,5), C(5), Z(5)
      LOGICAL ERROR
C Input and echo the data.
      READ *, BAKERS
      READ *, ((T(I,J), J = 1, BAKERS), I = 1,BAKERS)
      READ *, (C(I), I = 1, BAKERS)
      PRINT *, 'MATRIX T'
      DO 100 I = 1, BAKERS
          PRINT *, (T(I,J), J = 1, BAKERS)
  100 CONTINUE
      PRINT *, ' '
      PRINT *, 'MARKET SHARE AFTER ONE YEAR :', (C(I), I = 1, BAKERS)
C Reduce the system to triangular form.
      CALL GAUSS(5,3,T,C,ERROR)
C If no solution, print an error message.
      IF (ERROR) THEN
          PRINT *, ' '
          PRINT *, 'NO SOLUTION, SINCE THE MATRIX IS SINGULAR'
      ELSE
C         Find the solution by back-substitution.
          CALL BSOLVE(5,3,T,Z,C)

          PRINT *, ' '
          PRINT *, 'INITIAL MARKET SHARES WERE', (Z(I), I = 1, BAKERS)
      ENDIF
      STOP
      END
C Subroutines GAUSS and BSOLVE are placed here.
```

Figure 15.23   Input and output for the initial market shares program of Figure 15.22.

a) Input file:

```
3
0.6761243 0.2033525 0.2903421
0.1163685 0.5473855 0.2468531
0.2075070 0.2492622 0.4628049
0.4898522 0.2861892 0.2239586
```

b) Output file:

```
 MATRIX T
   0.6761243        0.2033525        0.2903421
   0.1163685        0.5473855        0.2468531
   0.2075070        0.2492622        0.4628049

 MARKET SHARE AFTER ONE YEAR :  0.4898522  0.2861892  0.2239586

 INITIAL MARKET SHARES WERE  0.6059999  0.3940000  1.7275276E-07
```

15.6   Summary

This chapter has given a brief introduction to the use of a few modules which facilitate matrix computations.   The program libraries of typical computing centers contain dozens of modules, which enable the programmer to produce efficient solutions to a wide variety of problems which arise in practical applications.

It is hoped that the reader of this chapter will be starting to feel comfortable with the idea of manipulating matrices and vectors as freely as simple variables in pseudocode algorithm development.   Translation of the algorithm to FORTRAN/77 may then proceed, making full use of any available library modules.

It should be noted that matrix notation is merely a powerful shorthand for mathematical ideas which can be discussed without it.   However, many such ideas would be completely lost in a morass of technical details without this tool.   In a sense, the use of matrices shares many ideas with structured program design and fits in nicely with pseudocode algorithm development.   In mathematical analysis, matrices shield the user from the need to cope with large numbers of mathematical relationships.   In developing pseudocode algorithms, one is shielded from immediate worries about detailed conventions required in the final programming language.

15.7   References

There is a vast amount of literature on matrix computations and the solution of linear systems of equations.   A small selection is listed here, with much more extensive lists appearing in the bibliographies of some of these references.

Barrodale, I.; Roberts, F.D.K.; and Ehle, B.L.   *Elementary Computer Applications.* New York: John Wiley and Sons, 1971.

Dahlquist, G.; Bjorck, A. *Numerical Methods.* Translated by N. Anderson. Englewood Cliffs, N.J.: Prentice-Hall, 1974.

Forsythe, G.E.; Malcolm, M.A.; and Moler, C.B. *Computer Methods for Mathematical Computations.* Englewood Cliffs, N.J.: Prentice-Hall, 1977.

Forsythe, G.E.; Moler, C.B. *Computer Solution of Linear Algebraic Systems.* Englewood Cliffs, N.J.: Prentice-Hall, 1967.

Noble, B. *Applied Linear Algebra.* Englewood Cliffs, N.J.: Prentice-Hall, 1969.

15.8   Exercises

In most of the following exercises a program is needed to solve a specific problem.   For each problem it is recommended that step-wise refinement be used in developing a pseudocode algorithm to solve the problem.   This algorithm should then be translated into FORTRAN/77 and run on the computer.   Where appropriate, the program should be tested with a variety of data sufficient to ensure that the program does what it is supposed to do.

It is suggested that the reader become familiar with the matrix manipulation programs available at the local computing center.   It may be useful to compare them to the programs presented in this chapter.   These programs are often in the form of modules which may be used to make the program development task much easier.

15.1   a)   Develop FORTRAN/77 modules to do the following matrix operations:

1)   Read in the elements of an n*n matrix by rows;
2)   Print out the elements of the matrix in 1).

b)   Rewrite the program in Figure 15.13 using these modules.

15.2   Compute and plot the monthly market shares for each bakery over a four-year period for the matrix T and initial vector of Figure 15.9.

15.3   Construct a transformation matrix which corresponds to the three bakery problem of Section 15.3.2 with the additional assumption that the total market starts to grow by 3% per month when C starts operations, with 2% of the new customers going to C and 1% to A.   Follow the market for 3 years, tabulating the output for each month.

15.4   Assume that 5 countries, A, B, C, D, and E, share the world newsprint market with present shares 0.15, 0.18, 0.35, 0.25, and 0.07 respectively.   Assume that each one retains 96% of its market each year and loses 1% to each of its competitors.

a)   Formulate a model and use it to compute and plot the market shares over a 25-year period.

b)   Repeat the calculation starting with an initial state in which A has 10% of the market, C has 87%, and the others have 1% each.   What do you conclude about the relative importance of the initial state and the transformation in the ultimate behavior of the market?

15.5   Find the transformation which corresponds to a five-year period in the newsprint marketing example of the previous problem. Test the supposition that five applications of this transformation give the same results as 25 applications of the one-year transformation.

15.6   Consider the following pseudocode algorithm. Note that A and B are n×n matrices.

```
get n, A, B
i ← 1
while i+1 < n-1 do
    ┌ j ← 1
    │ while j-1 ≤ i do
    │     ┌ if bᵢᵢ ≥ 0 then
    │     │     [ bᵢⱼ ← bᵢⱼ + aᵢⱼ * bᵢᵢ²
    │     │ else
    │     │     [ bᵢⱼ ← bᵢⱼ - aᵢⱼ * bᵢᵢ²
    │     └ j ← j+1
    └ i ← i+1
put B
```

a)   Rewrite this algorithm to improve its efficiency by reducing the number of arithmetic operations and comparisons as much as possible.

b)   Write a FORTRAN/77 subroutine for the improved algorithm.

15.7   Use the programs developed in the text to solve the following linear systems:

a)
$$
\begin{aligned}
4x_1 & - x_2 & & - x_4 & = 0 \\
-x_1 & + 4x_2 & - x_3 & & = 5 \\
& - x_2 & + 4x_3 & - x_4 & = 5 \\
-x_1 & & - x_3 & + 4x_4 & = 0
\end{aligned}
$$

b)
$$
\begin{aligned}
2.713x + 8.356y + 3.259z &= 5.222 \\
1.997x + 4.347y + 7.558z &= 4.386 \\
9.854x + 3.656y + 4.775z &= 7.547
\end{aligned}
$$

c)
$$
\begin{aligned}
1.000x_1 + 0.500x_2 + 0.333x_3 + 0.250x_4 &= 2.083 \\
0.500x_1 + 0.333x_2 + 0.250x_3 + 0.200x_4 &= 1.283 \\
0.333x_1 + 0.250x_2 + 0.200x_3 + 0.167x_4 &= 0.950 \\
0.250x_1 + 0.200x_2 + 0.167x_3 + 0.143x_4 &= 0.760
\end{aligned}
$$

15.8   a) Solve the following system of linear equations for $t = 0, 0.5, 1.0, 1.5, 2.0$.

$$
\begin{aligned}
25.5x_1 &- 1.50x_2 &+ 2.00x_3 & &= 30(1 + t) \\
1.50x_1 &+ 30.5x_2 & &+ 2.00x_4 &= 35(1 + t) \\
-10.0x_1 &+ 2.00x_2 &+ 20.5x_3 &+ 3.50x_4 &= 15(1 + t) \\
1.00x_1 &- 3.50x_2 &- 3.00x_3 &+ 40.0x_4 &= 30(1 + t)
\end{aligned}
$$

b) How would you modify the elimination program so that all five problems are solved at once? (Hint: Think about how you might replace vector C by five vectors in the elimination phase of the solution.)

15.9   A patient recovering from a long illness requires that his food each day contain 11 units of vitamin A, 9 units of vitamin B, and 20 units of vitamin C. Food 1 has 1 unit of vitamin A, 3 units of vitamin B, and 4 units of vitamin C (per gram).   Food 2 has 2 units of vitamin A, 3 units of vitamin B, and 5 units of vitamin C (per gram).   Food 3 has 3 units of vitamin A, 3 units of vitamin B, and 3 units of vitamin C (per gram).

Let x_1 be the amount (in grams) of food 1 eaten by the patient on one day. Let x_2 be the amount (in grams) of food 2 eaten by the patient that day. Let x_3 be the amount (in grams) of food 3 eaten by the patient that day.

a) Give a linear equation involving x_1, x_2, and x_3 which represents the amounts of foods 1, 2, and 3 that the patient must eat one day so as to consume precisely the required amount of vitamin A. Give a similar equation for vitamin B. Give a similar equation for vitamin C.

b) Write a main program in FORTRAN/77 to determine the amounts of each food which will satisfy these three equations. Use subroutines GAUSS and BSOLVE.   Show the data which would be required for the problem given above.

15.10   Solve the system of linear equations:

$$
\begin{aligned}
-2x_1 &+ x_2 & & & &= 0.01 \\
x_1 &- 2x_2 &+ x_3 & & &= 0 \\
&x_2 &- 2x_3 &+ x_4 & &= 0 \\
& & &\cdot & &\cdot \\
& & &\cdot & &\cdot \\
& & &\cdot & &\cdot \\
x_{98} &- 2x_{99} &+ x_{100} & & &= 0 \\
&x_{99} &- 2x_{100} & & &= 0.05
\end{aligned}
$$

You will probably find that your computer system will not permit you to store the 10,000 coefficients of a system of 100 linear equations. Observing that only 298 of the coefficients are nonzero, devise a suitable storage scheme for this system and modify the elimination and back-substitution algorithms appropriately. (Pivoting is not necessary.) How large a system of the above structure could be solved using the computing facilities available to you?

15.11 Suppose that you wish to find the polynomial

$$a_0 + a_1 x + a_2 x^2 + \cdots + a_k x^k$$

which is the best least squares approximation to data given in the form of coordinate pairs

$$(x_j, y_j), \ j = 1, 2, 3, \ldots, m$$

It can be shown that the vector A of values of the polynomial coefficients satisfies the equation

$$T \times T' \times A = T \times Y, \quad \text{where}$$

$$T = \begin{bmatrix} 1 & 1 & 1 & \cdots & 1 \\ x_1 & x_2 & x_3 & \cdots & x_m \\ x_1^2 & x_2^2 & x_3^2 & \cdots & x_m^2 \\ \cdot & \cdot & \cdot & & \cdot \\ \cdot & \cdot & \cdot & & \cdot \\ \cdot & \cdot & \cdot & & \cdot \\ x_1^k & x_2^k & x_3^k & \cdots & x_m^k \end{bmatrix}, \quad A = \begin{bmatrix} a_0 \\ a_1 \\ a_2 \\ \cdot \\ \cdot \\ \cdot \\ a_k \end{bmatrix} \quad \text{and} \ Y = \begin{bmatrix} y_1 \\ y_2 \\ y_3 \\ \cdot \\ \cdot \\ y_k \\ \cdot \\ \cdot \\ y_m \end{bmatrix}$$

T' is the transpose of T; that is, the matrix whose first row is the first column of T, second row is the second column of T, etc.

Write a program which uses the modules MATMPY, MATVEC, GAUSS, and BSOLVE of this chapter (or alternatives) to find the best least squares approximation of degree 2 ($k = 2$) to the data:

$$(x_j, y_j) = (0, 1.00), (30, 0.75), (45, 0.50), (60, 0.27), (90, 0.00)$$

15.12 The temperature distribution over a rectangular plate, with given temperature prescribed at its edges is known to satisfy Laplace's equation.

If a uniform grid is drawn over the plate, giving nodes at a number of interior points, an approximation to the solution may be found by determining the temperature only at the node points. The solution is determined from the rule that the temperature at any interior point must be the average of the temperatures at the four adjacent points — up, down, left, and right. (This is a discrete version of Laplace's equation.)

a) Formulate the equations to be solved for the temperatures at the 12 interior points of the following diagram.

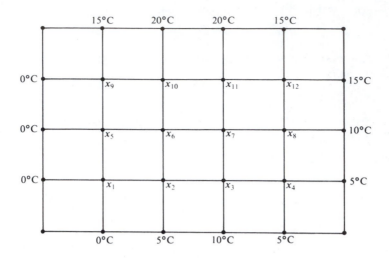

b) Calculate the approximate temperature distribution over the plate by solving the 12 equations.

Part E
Simulation Techniques

16 Deterministic Simulation *427*

17 Probabilistic Simulation *463*

16
Deterministic Simulation

16.1 Introduction

Simulation is the process of making a model of a real system and then performing experiments on the model. The purpose of simulation is to understand the behavior of the system; one may wish simply to predict its future behavior or to evaluate alternate means of operating or controlling the system.

An important example of the first objective is the prediction of weather. Today, there exist mathematical models of the atmosphere which may be solved on large-scale computers to give weather forecasts valid for a few days. An example of the second kind would be a model of an economy which is sensitive to many different factors. A government may gain some insight into appropriate policy actions by observing the effects of such actions on a simulation model. Experimenting with the real system in this case can be (and sometimes is!) catastrophically expensive.

In these two examples, the corresponding models may be very sophisticated and very expensive to develop and run. Even so, the importance of the insight gained through the simulation may make such an investment worthwhile. In the next two chapters, elementary models of simpler systems will be developed which should give the reader some feeling for the way in which simulation models are designed and used.

16.2 Simulation Models

A simulation involves a description of the way in which a system changes over some period of time. A quantitative *representation* of the system at some instant of time is called the *state* of the system. Thus, the heart of any simulation model is a description of the way in which values of state variables of the system change with time.

Continuous models examine the rate of change of state variables with time. *Discrete* models give rules for the way in which the state variables change over a specified time increment. One usually needs to examine the state of the system only at a sequence of discrete time intervals, so that continuous models are usually approximated by discrete models. For this reason, such discrete time models will be the only kind dealt with here.

The rules governing the change of state may be either *deterministic* or *probabilistic*. In a deterministic model, the new state may be completely deduced from the old state by applying well-defined rules. In a probabilistic model, a variety of new states are all possible, but the one which actually occurs is subject to some predefined laws of chance. Deterministic models are discussed in the remainder of this chapter and probabilistic models in Chapter 17.

16.3   Structure of Simulation Model Programs

All programs which are examined in this chapter and the next have a general structure similar to that shown in Figure 16.1.

Figure 16.1   General structure of a simulation algorithm.

1. Obtain simulation parameters and initial states.

2. While termination criterion is not met

   $\begin{bmatrix} \text{time} \leftarrow \text{time} + \text{time step} \\ \text{Change the state variables and record the state of the system.} \end{bmatrix}$

3. Summarize the system behavior.

4. **stop**

In the case of the weather example alluded to in the introduction, the initial conditions would be the observed state of the weather at the time when the forecast is made. The innocent looking line Change the state variables and record the state of the system would correspond to the use of a massive program module which involves the solution of literally thousands of equations. The same structure applies to simple programs. For example, a program is developed in Section 16.6 which plots the path of a bouncing ball. In this case, the initial state is the initial location and velocity of the ball. The line Change the state variables and record the state of the system represents an application of simple physical laws to deduce the changes in the location and velocity of the ball after a short time step. The summary involves recording the computed points and subsequently plotting the trajectory.

16.4   An Investment Example

To illustrate the steps involved in the construction of a simulation model and program, a simple investment plan is examined.

Example 16.1   Investment Simulation Problem
A person who has a present annual salary of $15,000 wishes to plan an investment program. If the salary increases by 8% at the end of each year, and 10% of the old salary is invested then at an interest rate of 12% compounded annually, what is the status of the investment at the end of 5, 10, 15, . . . , 30 years?

a) Problem Discussion   In this example, the output desired is a simple table showing the amount of money saved at the end of each five-year period. The state variables are the current salary and the amount of savings. The simulation parameters are the salary increase, the fraction of salary invested, and the interest rate. Although fixed values of these quantities are given in the statement of the problem, it is useful to regard them as parameters which may be varied, so that the effect of changes to them may be studied.

For the specific 8% increase in the example, the new salary at the end of each year is easily computed as

$$salary\,(t+1) = salary\,(t) + 0.08 \times salary\,(t).$$

The new savings may be found by adding together the old savings, interest on the old savings, and the current amount of salary saved.

$$savings\,(t+1) = savings\,(t) + 0.12 \times savings\,(t) + 0.10 \times salary\,(t).$$

b) Initial Decomposition   The general algorithm structure of Figure 16.1 is appropriate for this problem. This gives the initial version of the algorithm shown as Figure 16.2, with the steps labeled for subsequent refinement.

Figure 16.2   First version of a pseudocode algorithm for the investment problem.

1.   Obtain investment parameters and initial states.

2.   While termination criterion is not met

⌈   time ← time + timestep
⌊   Change the investment variables and record the state of the system.

3.   Summarize the investment behavior.

4.   **stop**

---

c) Refining Step **1.**   The simulation parameters are the salary increase, perinc, the fraction of salary invested, persav, and the interest rate, perint, all expressed as percentages. The refinement is as follows:

get perinc, persav, perint

Initial values must be given for the state variables, salary and savings. This is expressed as:

> **get** salary, savings

Recall that good programming practice dictates that there be prompting messages preceding a request for input for programs processed interactively or echo-checking of input values for programs using input from a file. In the simulation chapters this latter approach will be demonstrated in the pseudocode development. The FORTRAN/77 programs will be converted for use interactively. A final refinement of Step **1.** is given below. Note that the state variable year has also been added to identify the salary and savings information.

> * Obtain and record the simulation parameters.
>
> **get** perinc, persav, perint
> **put** 'Percent salary increase is', perinc
> **put** 'Percent of salary saved is', persav
> **put** 'Percent interest on savings', perint
>
> * Obtain and record the initial state values.
>
> **get** salary, savings
> year ← 0
> **put** 'Year', 'Salary', 'Savings'
> **put** year, salary, savings

d) Refining Step **2.** For this example, the simulation ends when the elapsed time is 30 years. Thus, a **while**–loop will be used with control variable year, which was initialized to 0 in Step **1.**

> * Simulate the system for 30 years, tabulating the state at 5 year intervals.
>
> **2.1 while** year < 30 **do**
>
> > **2.2** year ← year + 1
> > **2.3** Compute new salary and savings.
> > **2.4** Record the salary and savings if the year is a multiple of 5.

e) Refining Step **2.3** Using the formulas given in a), but generalized to use the simulation parameters, the refinement of **2.3** is:

> * Compute new salary and savings.
>
> savings ← savings + (perint*savings + persav*salary)/100
> salary ← salary + perinc*salary/100

Note that the new values of salary and savings replace the old values. Observe that it would be wrong to reverse the order of these two statements. Why?

f) Refining Step **2.4**   An appropriate way to express Step **2.4** is:

> * Record the salary and savings if the year is a multiple of 5.
>
> **if** year(mod 5) = 0 **then**
>
>   ⌈ **put** year, salary, savings

g) Refining Step **3.**   No summary is needed in this example since the generated table will contain all the necessary information.

h) The Final Algorithm   The various refinements may now be combined to give the final version of the algorithm.   The translation of this algorithm into FORTRAN/77 is straightforward and is presented in Figure 16.3.

```
C Figure 16.3 - Investment Simulation Problem.
C                Program to simulate a simple investment problem
C                involving the saving of a fixed percentage of
C                salary at a fixed interest rate while the
C                salary increases by a fixed percent each year.

C**********************************************************************

C SALARY - the current salary
C SAVING - the current savings
C YEAR   - the current year of the simulation
C PERINC - the percentage increase in salary
C PERSAV - the percent of salary put into savings
C PERINT - the percentage interest earned on savings

C**********************************************************************

      REAL SALARY, SAVING, PERINC, PERSAV, PERINT
      INTEGER YEAR, MOD
C Obtain the simulation parameters.
      PRINT *, 'ENTER THE % SALARY INCREASE:'
      READ *, PERINC
      PRINT *, 'ENTER THE % OF SALARY SAVED:'
      READ *, PERSAV
      PRINT *, 'ENTER THE % INTEREST ON SAVINGS:'
      READ *, PERINT
C Obtain the initial conditions.
      PRINT *, 'ENTER THE INITIAL SALARY AND SAVINGS:'
      READ *, SALARY, SAVING
      PRINT *, ' '
      PRINT *, '      YEAR      SALARY           SAVINGS'
      PRINT *, ' '
      PRINT *, YEAR, SALARY, SAVING
C Simulate the system for 30 years, tabulating
C the state at 5 year intervals.
      DO 100 YEAR = 1, 30
         SAVING = SAVING + (PERINT*SAVING + PERSAV*SALARY)/100.0
         SALARY = SALARY + PERINC*SALARY/100.0
         IF (MOD(YEAR,5) .EQ. 0) THEN
              PRINT *, YEAR, SALARY, SAVING
         ENDIF
  100 CONTINUE
      STOP
      END
```

The output for the program is listed in Figure 16.4.   Though the accumulated investment is more than $746,000, the salary has also increased to more than $150,000. Thus, the savings amount to a considerable sum of money, roughly equivalent to five years salary.   It is easy to modify the simulation parameters and run the simulation again to study variations in the savings plans.   The next chapter will also investigate this problem to study variable increases in salary.

Figure 16.4   Output from the investment simulation program of Figure 16.3.

```
ENTER THE % SALARY INCREASE:
8.0
ENTER THE % OF SALARY SAVED:
10.0
ENTER THE % INTEREST ON SAVINGS:
12.0
ENTER THE INITIAL SALARY AND SAVINGS:
15000.0 0.0
```

YEAR	SALARY	SAVINGS
0	15000.00	0.0000000E+00
5	22039.92	10988.01
10	32383.88	35509.63
15	47582.54	86302.39
20	69914.38	186950.1
25	102727.2	380684.7
30	150939.9	746147.7

16.5   Pursuit Problems

In a pursuit problem one body is chasing or pursuing another.   The objective of simulation in such a problem is the computation of the paths followed, with a view to determining the outcome.   One may also wish to study the effects of various strategies of pursuit or evasion.

The example developed in detail is that of a bull chasing a hiker, but with different parameter values and variable names it could equally well be a missile pursuing an aircraft or the coast guard trying to intercept a drug smuggler. The main tool needed to develop the algorithms is elementary geometry.

16.5.1   The Bull-Hiker Pursuit Problem

Example 16.2   Bull-Hiker Pursuit Problem
While a hiker is walking in an open area towards some trees 400 meters distant, an angry bull starts to pursue him.   The bull is initially at a point 100 meters directly opposite a point on the path 50 meters ahead of the hiker.   The bull's pursuit strategy is rather simple-minded.   It moves directly towards the hiker, rather than

trying to intercept him. The bad news is that the bull has a speed advantage. The bull can run at 8.5 meters/second, whereas the hiker can only manage 8.0 meters/second over this distance. Does the story have a happy ending?

a) Problem Discussion   A simple mathematical model of the pursuit process can be developed to study this situation. The objective will be to compute and plot the paths of both the bull and the hiker and to check if they remain safely separated until the hiker gets to the trees.

The first stage in such a process is to make a diagram, including some reference coordinate system. The system is chosen to be as simple as possible. For instance, the hiker's path will be taken as the *x* axis, with his initial location as the origin. This is shown in Figure 16.5.

Figure 16.5   Diagram for the bull-hiker pursuit problem.

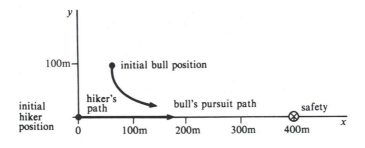

The second step is to make a detailed description of the way in which the bull and hiker positions change with time. These positions will be denoted $(x_b(t), y_b(t))$ and $(x_h(t), y_h(t))$ respectively, with initial values (in meters):

$$x_b(0) = 50, \quad y_b(0) = 100, \quad x_h(0) = 0, \quad y_h(0) = 0.$$

Note that subscripts *b* and *h* refer to the bull and hiker respectively. The argument *t* specifies the time. These coordinates are *state variables* and represent the *state* of the *system* at any time *t*. The hiker's change of position over a short time step δt may be described quite simply as

     new position   ←   *old position* + *distance traveled*.

Symbolically, the *x* and *y* components are isolated and written in the following way:

$$x_h(t + \delta t) \leftarrow x_h(t) + velocity \, \times \, time \; step$$

$$\leftarrow x_h(t) + v_h \times \delta t$$

$$y_h(t + \delta t) \leftarrow y_h(t) \leftarrow 0.$$

The bull's motion is dependent upon the hiker's position, since the bull always moves directly towards the hiker. It will be assumed that the bull's change in position over a *short* time step δt will be adequately described by motion in a straight line. The direction of this line is determined at the start of the time interval δt. At this point, reference to the diagram of Figure 16.6 may help to clarify the relative positions of the bull and hiker at an arbitrary time t. This diagram illustrates the situation at the beginning of the chase when the bull is located to the *right* of the hiker (larger x coordinate). The reader should confirm that the same equations may be derived from a diagram showing the bull to the *left* of the hiker (smaller x coordinate) (see Exercise 16.6).

Figure 16.6   Diagram of the relative bull and hiker positions.

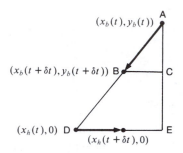

The distance AB from $(x_b(t), y_b(t))$ to $(x_b(t + \delta t), y_b(t + \delta t))$ is the distance traveled by the bull in the time step δt and is known to be $8.5 \times \delta t$. The distance between the bull and hiker at time t may be computed from the Pythagorean relation (triangle ADE) as:

$$s(t) = \sqrt{(x_b(t) - x_h(t))^2 + (y_b(t) - y_h(t))^2}$$

In the diagram, it will be observed that triangle ABC is similar to triangle ADE. This fact may be used to compute CB and AC, the changes in the x and y coordinates of the bull. Since

$$\frac{CB}{AB} = \frac{ED}{AD} \quad \text{and} \quad \frac{AC}{AB} = \frac{AE}{AD}$$

it follows that

$$\frac{x_b(t + \delta t) - x_b(t)}{x_h(t) - x_b(t)} = \frac{v_b \times \delta t}{s(t)} \quad \text{and}$$

$$\frac{y_b(t + \delta t) - y_b(t)}{y_h(t) - y_b(t)} = \frac{v_b \times \delta t}{s(t)}.$$

Rearranging these equations for the motion of the bull gives

$$x_b(t + \delta t) = x_b(t) + \frac{x_h(t) - x_b(t)}{s(t)} \times v_b \times \delta t \quad \text{and}$$

$$y_b(t + \delta t) = y_b(t) + \frac{y_h(t) - y_b(t)}{s(t)} \times v_b \times \delta t .$$

Recall that the equations for the motion of the hiker are

$$x_h(t + \delta t) = x_h(t) + v_h \times \delta t \quad \text{and} \quad y_h(t + \delta t) = 0.$$

Together, these equations for the bull and hiker give a complete description of the change of state which occurs from time t to time $t + \delta t$, and form the basis for the simulation model. It is conventional to eliminate the arguments t and $t + \delta t$ in developing algorithms using these formulas; it is then understood that new coordinate values replace old values as they are computed.

b) Initial Decomposition   For this simulation problem the general algorithm structure of Figure 16.1 may be used. It gives the initial version of the algorithm shown in Figure 16.7, with the steps labeled for subsequent refinement.

Figure 16.7   First version of a pseudocode algorithm for the bull-hiker pursuit problem.

1.   Obtain the pursuit parameters and initial states.

2.   While termination criterion is not met

> time ← time + timestep
>
> Change the pursuit variables and record the state of the system.

3.   Summarize the results of the pursuit.

4.   **stop**

---

c) Refining Step **1.**   The simulation parameters in this case are: the time step, the speeds of the bull and the hiker, and the distance to safety in the trees. The initial states are the initial coordinates of the bull and hiker. Thus, the refinement is as follows.

> * Obtain and record the simulation parameters and initial states.
>
> **get** tstep, xb, yb, xh, yh, vb, vh, xmax
> **put** 'The bull coordinates are', xb, yb
> **put** 'The hiker coordinates are', xh, yh
> **put** 'The velocity of the bull is', vb
> **put** 'The velocity of the hiker is', vh
> **put** 'The time increment is', tstep
> **put** 'The distance to safety is', xmax
> t ← 0

Notice that the subscripts used in the problem discussion have been changed to constitute part of the variable name.

In addition to defining these variables, it is also necessary to initialize the plotting process and to record the initial positions for plotting. These steps are written as:

```
call setplt(41, 11)
call stopnt(xb, yb, 'B')
call stopnt(xh, yh, 'H')
```

d) Refining Step **2.** ⟍ The simulation comes to an end if either the hiker reaches safety or the bull overtakes him. An appropriate elaboration of this **while**–loop and its termination criterion is:

* Simulate the motion of the bull and hiker until the hiker is overtaken
* or reaches safety.

2.1 $s \leftarrow \text{sqrt}((xh-xb)^2 + (yh-yb)^2)$

2.2 while $xh <$ xmax **and** $s > 1$ **do**

> **2.3** $t \leftarrow t + tstep$
>
> **2.4** Change the positions of the bull and hiker (state variables).
>
> **2.5** Record the positions of the bull and hiker (state of the system).

This means that the bull is assumed to have overtaken the hiker if the distance between them, s, becomes one meter or less. Note that both xh and s change with time t, and that both must be initialized before the **while** statement.

e) Refining Step **2.4** The change in the state variables is accomplished by using the formulas developed earlier.

* Change the positions of the bull and hiker.

```
xb ← xb + (xh−xb)*vb*tstep/s
yb ← yb + (yh−yb)*vb*tstep/s
xh ← xh + vh*tstep
s ← sqrt((xh−xb)² + (yh−yb)²)
```

Notice that these statements simply replace the old coordinates by their new values.

f) Refining Step **2.5** For this problem, the state of the system at the end of each time step may be recorded using the plotting routines.

* Record the positions of the bull and hiker.

```
call stopnt(xb, yb, 'B')
call stopnt(xh, yh, 'H')
```

g) Refining Step **3.** The final summary for this problem can be restricted to a message as to whether the hiker made it to the trees or not, and the generation of a plot.

* Record the final outcome and plot the paths.

put 'At time', t
if xh ≥ xmax **then**

> **put** 'The hiker reached safety'
> **put** 'The distance between the bull and hiker is', s

else

> **put** 'The hiker was overtaken at x =', xh

call plot(1)

h) Final Version of the Algorithm   A FORTRAN/77 version of the algorithm is assembled from the pseudocode fragments and appears in Figure 16.8.   The output from the program is shown in Figure 16.9.   For the given parameters, the hiker did manage to beat the bull to the safety of the trees.   Notice that the paths of the bull and the hiker overlap for a portion of the chase, as indicated by the asterisks along a portion of the hiker's path.   This does not mean that the bull actually caught the hiker, but that the bull followed the same path at a later time.

Exercises 16.8 and 16.9 suggest some variations on this example which may be of interest.

```
C Figure 16.8 -- Bull-Hiker Pursuit Problem.
C                  Program to simulate a bull chasing a hiker across
C                  a field.
C*******************************************************************************
C T       - the time
C XB,YB   - the coordinates of the bull's position
C XH,YH   - the coordinates of the hiker's position
C VB      - the velocity of the bull
C VH      - the velocity of the hiker
C S       - the distance of the bull from the hiker
C TSTEP   - the time increment
C XMAX    - the x coordinate of safety
C*******************************************************************************
        REAL T, TSTEP, XB, YB, XH, YH, VB, VH, XMAX, S, SQRT
C Obtain and record the simulation parameters and initial states.
        PRINT *, 'ENTER THE INITIAL COORDINATES OF THE BULL:'
        READ *, XB, YB
        PRINT *, 'ENTER THE INITIAL COORDINATES OF THE HIKER:'
        READ *, XH, YH
        PRINT *, 'ENTER THE VELOCITY OF THE BULL:'
        READ *, VB
        PRINT *, 'ENTER THE VELOCITY OF THE HIKER:'
        READ *, VH
        PRINT *, 'ENTER THE TIME INCREMENT:'
        READ *, TSTEP
        PRINT *, 'ENTER THE DISTANCE TO SAFETY:'
        READ *, XMAX
C Initialize plotting and store the initial coordinates.
        CALL SETPLT(41,11)
        CALL STOPNT(XB,YB,'B')
        CALL STOPNT(XH,YH,'H')
C Simulate the motion of the bull and hiker until
C the hiker is overtaken or reaches safety.
        S = SQRT((XH-XB)**2 + (YH-YB)**2)
        T = 0.0
  100 IF (XH.LT.XMAX .AND. S.GT.1.0) THEN
C          Change the positions of the bull and hiker.
           T = T + TSTEP
           XB = XB + (XH-XB)*VB*TSTEP/S
           YB = YB + (YH-YB)*VB*TSTEP/S
           XH = XH + VH*TSTEP
           S = SQRT((XH-XB)**2 + (YH-YB)**2)
C          Record the current positions of the bull and hiker.
           CALL STOPNT(XB,YB,'B')
           CALL STOPNT(XH,YH,'H')
           GOTO 100
        ENDIF
```

```
C Figure 16.8 (continued)
C Record the final outcome and plot the paths.
      PRINT *, ' '
      PRINT *, 'AT TIME =',T
      IF (XH .GE. XMAX) THEN
          PRINT *, 'THE HIKER REACHED SAFETY'
          PRINT *, 'THE DISTANCE BETWEEN THE BULL AND HIKER IS', S
      ELSE
          PRINT *, 'THE HIKER WAS OVERTAKEN AT X =', XH
      ENDIF
      CALL PLOT(1)

      STOP
      END
```

Figure 16.9   Output from the bull-hiker pursuit program of Figure 16.8.

```
ENTER THE INITIAL COORDINATES OF THE BULL:
50.0 100.0
ENTER THE INITIAL COORDINATES OF THE HIKER:
0.0 0.0
ENTER THE VELOCITY OF THE BULL:
8.5
ENTER THE VELOCITY OF THE HIKER:
8.0
ENTER THE TIME INCREMENT:
0.125
ENTER THE DISTANCE TO SAFETY:
400.0

AT TIME =    50.00000
THE HIKER REACHED SAFETY
THE DISTANCE BETWEEN THE BULL AND HIKER IS    8.727783

 NUMBER OF POINTS : SUBMITTED          802  PLOTTED          802


 1.00000+     B
        ¦     BB
        ¦     B
        ¦     B
        ¦     B
 0.50000+     B
        ¦     B
        ¦      B
        ¦      BB
        ¦        BBBB
 0.00000*HHHHHHHH*****************************H
       0.0000    1.0000    2.0000    3.0000    4.0000

   THE Y - AXIS SCALE FACTOR IS 10**          2
         THE X - AXIS SCALE FACTOR IS 10**          2
```

16.6   Problems in Dynamics

Simulation problems in dynamics are concerned with the motion of physical objects under the action of external forces.   There is a standard approach to all such problems. A coordinate system is chosen, and a diagram, called the *free body diagram*, is drawn which shows the object and all forces acting upon it.   The forces are decomposed into components in the coordinate directions, and converted to accelerations.   Finally, the knowledge of accelerations is used to calculate changes in velocity components over a short time step, and these in turn are used to calculate changes in coordinates.   The basic rules, which are applied in each coordinate direction, are:

1)   *force* = *mass* × *acceleration* or *acceleration* = *force* / *mass*;
2)   *change in velocity* = *average acceleration* × *time step*;
3)   *change in coordinate* = *average velocity* × *time step*.

16.6.1   The Bouncing Ball Problem
As an example of a dynamics simulation, consider the following problem involving a bouncing ball.

Example 16.3   Bouncing Ball Problem
    Calculate and plot the path of a ball for several bounces along a level floor, given its initial location and velocity.   Assume that the only external force is gravity and that the acceleration due to gravity is 9.8 meters/second^2.   The bouncing characteristics of the ball may be assumed to follow the rule that 10% of the vertical velocity is lost when the ball bounces, but no loss in horizontal velocity occurs.

a) Problem Discussion   A natural choice of coordinate system in this case is the direction along the floor as the *x* coordinate and the vertical height as the *y* coordinate.   The *free body diagram* is very simple in this case, and is shown in Figure 16.10.

Figure 16.10   Free-body diagram for the bouncing ball problem.

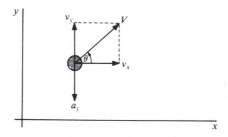

The state variables in this example will be the *x* and *y* coordinates of the ball and its velocity components in the *x* and *y* directions.   The initial state of the simulation will be the initial coordinates and velocity components.

The change of state of the system is described by using the simple physical laws governing motion under acceleration. Since no forces act to alter the motion in the x direction, the velocity will remain constant at its initial value. If the ball is projected at v meters/second at an angle θ to the horizontal, this initial velocity in the x direction is $v_x = v \cos \theta$. Similarly, the motion in the y direction is initially $v_y = v \sin \theta$, but this velocity changes as the ball is accelerated under the force of gravity.

Since acceleration is the rate of change of velocity, the new velocity component will be

$$v_y(t + \delta t) = v_y(t) + a_y \times \delta t \ .$$

In this case, the acceleration a_y is due to gravity in the negative y direction, so $a_y = -9.8$ meters/second^2.

This velocity may be used to calculate the new y coordinate. For motion under constant acceleration, an elementary physics text will provide the formula

$$y(t + \delta t) = y(t) + \frac{1}{2}\left[v_y(t + \delta t) + v_y(t) \right] \times \delta t \ .$$

The new x coordinate follows simply from

$$x(t + \delta t) = x(t) + v_x \times \delta t \ .$$

There remains the problem of what to do when the ball hits the floor. The assumption that 10% of the velocity is lost when the bounce occurs is implemented as:

if y (t+dt) $<$ 0 **then**
$$\left[\ v_y(t+dt) \leftarrow |0.9 \ * \ v_y(t+dt)| \right.$$

This assumption is obviously not quite correct, since it allows the ball to move slightly below floor level before its direction is changed. The error caused by this assumption will be negligible if δt is small enough. Alternatively, one could use a zero-finding program such as the bisection routine of Chapter 7 to find that fraction of δt which will produce a zero value of y.

b) Development of the Algorithm   Working from an initial decomposition such as Figure 16.1, the various steps of the algorithm may be refined to give the FORTRAN/77 program of Figure 16.11 for the bouncing ball problem. For brevity the intermediate steps are omitted. Notice that the subscripts used to indicate direction have been incorporated into the variable names and that the times have been dropped except for the velocities in the y direction. In this case, VYOLD and VYNEW have been used. Notice that the angle must be changed from degrees to radians in order to use the built-in SIN and COS functions. The graphical output of the program follows as Figure 16.12.

```
C Figure 16.11 - Bouncing Ball Simulation Problem.
C                    Program to simulate the motion of a bouncing ball
C                    for a given number of bounces.  Assume that gravity
C                    is the only external force.

C***********************************************************************
C T       - the time
C TSTEP   - the time increment
C NBOUNC  - the number of bounces to be simulated
C BOUNCE  - the current number of bounces
C X,Y     - the x and y coordinates of the ball
C V       - the initial velocity of the ball
C VX      - the x component of the velocity
C VYOLD   - the y component of the velocity at the start of TSTEP
C VYNEW   - the y component of the velocity at the end of TSTEP
C AY      - the y component of the acceleration
C ANGLE   - the angle at which the ball is thrown (in degrees)
C THETA   - the angle at which the ball is thrown (in radians)

C***********************************************************************
        REAL T, TSTEP, X, Y, V, VX, VYOLD, VYNEW, AY
        REAL ANGLE, PI, THETA, SIN, COS, ABS
        INTEGER BOUNCE, NBOUNC
C Initialize and calculate the simulation parameters and states.
        PRINT *, 'ENTER THE INITIAL VELOCITY OF THE BALL:'
        READ *, V
        PRINT *, 'ENTER THE ANGLE AT WHICH THE BALL IS THROWN:'
        READ *, ANGLE
        PRINT *, 'ENTER THE NUMBER OF BOUNCES:'
        READ *, NBOUNC
        PRINT *, 'ENTER THE TIME INCREMENT:'
        READ *, TSTEP

        PI = 3.1415926
        AY = -9.8
        THETA = ANGLE*PI/180.0
        VX = V*COS(THETA)
        VYOLD = V*SIN(THETA)
C Initialize the state variables and plot package.
        X = 0.0
        Y = 0.0
        T = 0.0
        CALL SETPLT(51,31)
        CALL STOPNT(X,Y,'B')
C Perform the simulation for NBOUNC bounces of the ball. A bounce
C occurs only when the ball hits the floor, at which time it changes
C direction and loses 10% of its velocity.
        BOUNCE = 0
    100 IF (BOUNCE .LT. NBOUNC) THEN
            T = T + TSTEP
            X = X + VX*TSTEP
            VYNEW = VYOLD + AY*TSTEP
            Y = Y + (VYOLD+VYNEW)*TSTEP/2.0
            VYOLD = VYNEW
            CALL STOPNT(X,Y,'B')
            IF (Y .LE. 0.0) THEN
                VYOLD = ABS(0.9*VYOLD)
                Y = 0.0
                BOUNCE = BOUNCE + 1
            ENDIF
            GOTO 100
        ENDIF
```

```
C Figure 16.11 (continued)
C The simulation is complete.  Plot the path.
      CALL PLOT(1)
      STOP
      END
```

Figure 16.12 Output from the bouncing ball program of Figure 16.11.

```
ENTER THE INITIAL VELOCITY OF THE BALL:
10.0
ENTER THE ANGLE AT WHICH THE BALL IS THROWN:
45.0
ENTER THE NUMBER OF BOUNCES:
5
ENTER THE TIME INCREMENT:
0.01

  NUMBER OF POINTS : SUBMITTED          606  PLOTTED          606


           ¦      BBB
           ¦      B B
           ¦     BB BB
           ¦      B   B
 2.17309+     B     B
           ¦    BB    BB          BB
           ¦    B      B         BBBB
           ¦    B      B         B  B
           ¦    B      B        BB  B
 1.73848+    B      B      B     B        BB
           ¦ BB       BB      B    B      B B
           ¦ B         B      B    B      BB BB
           ¦ B         B     BB    B      B  B
           ¦ B         B      B   BB    B    B        BBB
 1.30386+ B         B      B      B    BB    B      B BB
           ¦ B         B      B      B    B    BB    B  B
           ¦ B         B      B      B    B      B  B    B      BBB
           ¦B          B      B      B    B      B  B   BB    BB B
           ¦B          B  B      B    B      B    B      B    B  BB
 0.86924+B          B  B     BB  B      B    BB    B      B    B
           ¦B          B  B        B  B      B    B      B    BB    B
           ¦B          B  B        B  B      B  B      B    B      BB
           ¦B          B  B        B  B      B  B      B  B    B
           ¦B          B  B        B  B      B  B      B  B    B
 0.43462+B          B  B        B  B      B  B      B  B    B
          B          BB          BB          BB          BBB      B
          B          B           BB          BB          BB      BB
          B          B           B           BB          BB      B
          B          B           B           B           B       B
 0.00000*---------+-B-------+--B------+--B------+--B-------+--B-------B
           ¦          B           B           B           B       B
            0.0000    0.8556    1.7112    2.5668    3.4224    4.2780

      THE Y - AXIS SCALE FACTOR IS 10**          0
            THE X - AXIS SCALE FACTOR IS 10**              1
```

16.7 Population Dynamics

An interesting class of simulation problems arises when the variations in the numbers of members of interdependent populations are studied as they vary with time. In this section, some simple population models will be developed and programmed. Although very simple, the models demonstrate some of the essential features of the complex models of world economies, which have received so much publicity in recent years.

16.7.1 A Model for Single Species Populations

In this section, a model will be developed which may be used to predict the future numbers of members of a single species population. Naturally, such predictions depend upon the assumptions made, such as the rate at which members of the population reproduce or die and whether or not these rates depend on the presence of other members of the population.

The purpose of this and the next section is to show how verbal statements of these assumptions may be converted to simple mathematical models, suitable for use in simulation programs.

Example 16.4   Population Growth Problem
Develop a model for a single species population, in which the relative growth rate is constant.

a) Development of the Mathematical Model   The number of members of a single population at time t will be represented by $P(t)$. A simple birth (or death) process means that a certain fraction of the population reproduces (or dies) in a particular time interval, say δt. Such a process may be modeled by an equation of the form

$$P(t + \delta t) = P(t) + c \times P(t)\delta t$$

In this case, c is called the relative growth rate. The words relative and rate imply that c must be multiplied by the actual population $P(t)$ and by the time increment δt to produce the actual growth during δt of $P(t + \delta t) - P(t)$. If c is negative, the population is, of course, decreasing.

One may rearrange this equation to produce

$$P(t + \delta t) = (1 + c \times \delta t) \times P(t)$$

and, by induction, obtain the solution

$$P(t) = P(0) \times (1 + c \times \delta t)^n, \text{ where } t = n \times \delta t.$$

Solutions to this equation are shown in Figure 16.13.

16.7.2 A Model for Single Species Populations with Competition

This equation would be a poor description of a large population which is competing for a limited food supply.

Figure 16.13   Solutions to the simple population growth equation.

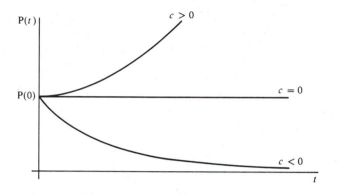

Example 16.5   Population Growth with Competition Problem
Develop a model for a single species population with a limited food supply which is sufficient to support a population P_{max}, but not adequate to allow reproduction at this level.

a) Modifications to the Mathematical Model   The solution is to arrange that the relative growth rate c' should decrease to 0 as $P(t)$ increases to P_{max}.   A simple formula which achieves this is

$$c' = c \times \left[\frac{P_{max} - P(t)}{P_{max}} \right]$$

which has the value c for the limiting case $P(t) \rightarrow 0$ and vanishes for $P(t) = P_{max}$. Thus, the single species model with competition is

$$P(t + \delta t) = P(t) + c \times \left[\frac{P_{max} - P(t)}{P_{max}} \right] \times P(t) \times \delta t .$$

A simplification of this equation results if both sides of the equation are divided by P_{max} and if the ratio $P(t)/P_{max}$ is denoted by $p(t)$.   This process of *normalization* is a useful tool in making mathematical models; here it results in the elimination of one parameter, P_{max}, from the model, thereby simplifying any simulation study.   The normalized equation is

$$p(t + \delta t) = p(t) + c \times [1 - p(t)] \times p(t) \times \delta t$$

When rewritten in the form of a differential equation, this equation is sometimes called the fundamental equation of ecology.

b) Development of the Algorithm   An algorithm will now be developed to test the model.   The general structure of the simulation algorithm will follow the outline of Figure 16.1.   The state variables are the time and the normalized population p.   The time is initialized to zero, and an initial population pinit can be acquired from input data. The simulation parameters are the relative growth rate, c, the time increment, dt, and the time limit on the simulation, tlimit, all of which may have initial values acquired from input.   Changing the state variables requires implementing the fundamental equation of ecology.   The recording of the state of the system at each time interval is accomplished by appropriate calls to the plotting package.   Since this problem very closely follows the general simulation algorithm, it may be implemented in FORTRAN/77 directly, shown in Figure 16.14.   The graphical output from this program follows as Figure 16.15.

It is clear that the model has the behavior which was expected.   The population rises quickly but stabilizes as $p(t)$ approaches 1.   Recall that this corresponds to P(t) approaching P_{max}.   Additional experiments with the model would reveal that this same limiting behavior is observed for all starting values, including those for which the initial population values are slightly larger than P_{max}.   The reader is invited to try a number of such starting values and various growth rates to see the effect on the solutions (see Exercise 16.22).

16.7.3   A Prey-Predator System

A more complex simulation problem is the study of the interactions between two (or more) species, one of which (the predator) depends upon another (the prey) as a primary food source.   Such a system is called a prey-predator ecological system and the one which will be examined here is a hypothetical rabbit/fox system.

Example 16.6   Rabbit/Fox Problem

Consider a population of foxes and rabbits.   The rabbits' food supply is vegetation and the environment will support R_{max} rabbits. The foxes in turn feed on the rabbits.   Develop a model under suitable assumptions to simulate the interaction of the two populations.

a) Development of the Mathematical Model   It is assumed that the rabbits exist in an environment in which vegetable food sources suffice to support a maximum population of R_{max} rabbits.   The model developed in the last section may be applied to this problem to give a *rabbit* equation:

$$R(t + \delta t) = R(t) + c \times \delta t \times \left[\frac{R_{max} - R(t)}{R_{max}} \right] \times R(t)$$

The fractional growth rate c for the rabbit population would have to be found by experimental observation in an actual environment.   For the hypothetical situation discussed here, it will be assumed that the increase, with no competition, is four rabbits per month for each rabbit pair, corresponding to $c = 2$ when δt is measured in months.

It is also assumed that, in the presence of R_{max} rabbits and few foxes, the foxes will reproduce at the rate of four fox cubs per year per pair of foxes, corresponding to $c = 0.167$ when δt is in months.   However, if the foxes increase or the rabbits decline in

```
C Figure 16.14 - Population Growth with Competition Problem.
C                 Program to simulate the growth of a single
C                 species population.
C*********************************************************************
C P      - the normalized population ratio P/Pmax
C T      - the time
C DT     - the time increment
C C      - the relative growth rate
C PINIT  - the initial population (normalized)
C TLIMIT - the time limit for the simulation
C*********************************************************************
      REAL P, T, DT, C, PINIT, TLIMIT
C Obtain the simulation parameters and initial states.
      PRINT *, 'ENTER THE RELATIVE GROWTH RATE:'
      READ *, C
      PRINT *, 'ENTER THE TIME INCREMENT:'
      READ *, DT
      PRINT *, 'ENTER THE INITIAL POPULATION RATIO:'
      READ *, PINIT
      PRINT *, 'ENTER THE TIME LIMIT:'
      READ *, TLIMIT
C Initialize the system.
      T = 0.0
      P = PINIT
      CALL SETPLT(41,21)
      CALL STOPNT(T,P,'*')
      CALL STOPNT(0.0,0.0,'-')
      CALL STOPNT(0.0,1.0,'-')
C Compute and plot population values at time-steps DT.
  100 IF (T.LE.TLIMIT) THEN
          T = T + DT
          P = P + C*(1.0 - P)*P*DT
          CALL STOPNT(T,P,'*')
          GOTO 100
      ENDIF

      CALL PLOT(1)
      STOP
      END
```

Program Notes

- Two additional calls to STOPNT are included to place a dash at the 0 and 1 ratio levels.   This ensures that the scale runs from 0 to 1 in the *y* direction.

---

numbers, the model must allow for the reproduction rate of the foxes to slow down.   At the level of 15 rabbits per fox, it is assumed that the foxes will no longer reproduce at all.   If the rabbit supply is even lower, then the foxes will die off.   If the rabbit supply is higher, then foxes will reproduce at the rate $[R(t) - 15 \times F(t)]/R_{max}$.   Notice that when there are fewer than 15 rabbits per fox, this term will be negative reflecting a decreasing population.   A possible equation which incorporates these assumptions to model the number of foxes, $F(t)$, at time t is:

Figure 16.15 Simulation of population growth with competition, output from the program of Figure 16.14.

```
ENTER THE RELATIVE GROWTH RATE:
1.0
ENTER THE TIME INCREMENT:
0.25
ENTER THE INITIAL POPULATION RATIO:
0.05
ENTER THE TIME LIMIT:
9.99
 NUMBER OF POINTS : SUBMITTED           43   PLOTTED            43

   1.00000-                       *************
          !                    ****
          !                 ***
          !                *
          !               *
   0.75000+              *
          !             *
          !            *
          !           *
          !          *
   0.50000+         *
          !        *
          !       *
          !      *
          !     *
   0.25000+    *
          !   *
          !  **
          ! ***
          !**
   0.00000+---------+---------+---------+---------+
         0.0000     0.2500    0.5000    0.7500    1.0000

     THE Y - AXIS SCALE FACTOR IS 10**           0
           THE X - AXIS SCALE FACTOR IS 10**            1
```

$$F(t + \delta t) = F(t) + 0.167 \times \delta t \times \left[\frac{R(t) - 15 \times F(t)}{R_{max}} \right] \times F(t)$$

All rates have to be related to the same time scale, of course, which is months for this model.

The model still needs to allow for the decrease in rabbits due to consumption by the foxes. The first model will assume that the foxes will consume 15 rabbits per month when there are R_{max} rabbits, but that the foxes will ration themselves to a consumption proportional to the number of rabbits when there are fewer rabbits. The modification to the rabbit equation which accomplishes this is

$$R(t + \delta t) = R(t) + 2 \times \delta t \times R(t) \times \left[\frac{R_{max} - R(t)}{R_{max}} \right] - 15 \times \delta t \times \left[\frac{R(t)}{R_{max}} \right] \times F(t)$$

Rather than deal with absolute numbers of rabbits and foxes it is convenient to deal with them as fractions of R_{max}.   Letting $r(t) = R(t)/R_{max}$ and $f(t) = F(t)/R_{max}$ leads to the equations

$$r(t + \delta t) = r(t) + 2 \times \delta t \times r(t) \times (1 - r(t)) - 15 \times \delta t \times r(t) \times f(t)$$

$$f(t + \delta t) = f(t) + 0.167 \times \delta t \times f(t) \times (r(t) - 15 \times f(t))$$

A simulation program may now be produced for the rabbit/fox system using these latter two equations to change the state of the system, namely the values of $r(t)$ and $f(t)$, over the time-step δt.   In this case, the initial states are $r(0)$ and $f(0)$ and the simulation parameters are δt and the time limit *tmax*.   One could also regard the growth rates and consumption rates as parameters, rather than fixing their values and imbedding them in the equations.

b) Development of the Program   The structure of this program is so similar to that of the program for single species simulation that a step-wise refinement and pseudocode algorithm will not be repeated.   It will be assumed that a study is to be carried out over a five-year period, and that the state of the system is to be recorded each month for plotting.   A time step of one month does not prove to be satisfactory, however, due to the large changes which could occur in the rabbit population in one month (see Exercise 16.23).   Ten time steps are used between calls on the plotting procedure, with each step of size 1/10 month or 3 days (approximately).   A FORTRAN/77 program follows as Figure 16.16.

The reader is invited to try the program with a variety of plausible initial data. Two examples are given in the output listed in Figure 16.17.   It is apparent that both of these populations stabilize after a few years at $r = 0.67$ and $f = 0.045$ approximately. The actual values are $r = 2/3$ and $f = 2/45$, since substitution of these values in the equations produces no change in the state of the system.

This model is said to be stable, in the sense that the same final population values are reached regardless of the starting values.   A mathematician could predict this property of the model using advanced techniques, but simulation allows the same result to be seen in an elementary way.

16.7.4   An Alternate Prey-Predator Model

Another version of the rabbit/fox model will now be developed to demonstrate that the behavior of such models may be a bit more subtle than the previous output would suggest.   This version will be called the greedy fox model since it incorporates the assumption that a fox continues to consume rabbits at the rate of fifteen per month, as long as any rabbits remain.   Another assumption is that if all the rabbits disappear, the foxes may survive in small numbers by consuming chipmunks, if all the rabbits disappear.

Example 16.7   Greedy Fox Problem

Develop a prey-predator model for a rabbit/fox population in which the foxes do not ration their consumption of rabbits, and can subsist on chipmunks if all the rabbits disappear.

```
C Figure 16.16 - Rabbit/Fox Simulation Problem.
C                   Program to simulate a two species population problem.
C*********************************************************************
C R       - the normalized rabbit population ratio R(t)/Rmax
C RNEW    - temporary value of R
C F       - the normalized fox population ratio F(t)/Rmax
C T       - the time
C DT      - the time increment
C TMAX    - the number of months to run the simulation
C NSTEPS  - the number of time steps per month
C MONTHS  - index for number of months
C ISTEP   - index for number of steps
C*********************************************************************
      REAL R, F, T, DT, RNEW
      INTEGER TMAX, MONTHS, NSTEPS, ISTEP
C Obtain the simulation parameters and initial states.
      TMAX = 60
      NSTEPS = 10
      T = 0.0
      DT = 1.0/NSTEPS
      PRINT *, 'ENTER THE INITIAL RABBIT RATIO:'
      READ *, R
      PRINT *, 'ENTER THE INITIAL FOX RATIO:'
      READ *, F
C Initialize plotting.
      CALL SETPLT(51,21)
      CALL STOPNT(T,R,'R')
      CALL STOPNT(T,10.0*F,'F')
      CALL STOPNT(0.0,0.0,'-')
      CALL STOPNT(0.0,1.0,'-')
C Compute the populations at tenth of a month intervals.
C Plot the population at the end of each month.
      DO 200 MONTHS = 1, TMAX
          DO 100 ISTEP = 1, NSTEPS
              T = T + DT
              RNEW = R + 2.0*DT*R*(1.0 - R) - 15.0*DT*R*F
              F = F + 0.167*DT*F*(R - 15.0*F)
              R = RNEW
              IF (R.LE.0.0) THEN
                  R = 0.0
              ENDIF
  100     CONTINUE
          CALL STOPNT(T,R,'R')
          CALL STOPNT(T,10.0*F,'F')
  200 CONTINUE
      CALL PLOT(1)
      STOP
      END
```

Program Notes

• Since the fox population is small compared to the rabbit population, the graph for the foxes will be lost if not rescaled. Multiplication of the fox numbers by 10 in the calls to STOPNT solves this problem.

Figure 16.17   Two examples of the rabbit/fox simulation, output from the program of
Figure 16.16.

a) Graph for an initial rabbit ratio of 0.1 and a fox ratio of 0.002:

```
1.00000-   R
          :   RRRRRRRR
          :            RRRR
          : R              RRR
          :                   RRR
0.75000+                        RRRR
          :                         RRRRRRRRRR
          :                                   RRRRRRRRRRRRRRRRR
          :
          :
0.50000+
          :                                  FFFFFFFFFFFFFFFFFFFFF
          : R                         FFFFFFF
          :                        FFF
          :                     FFF
          :                  FFF
0.25000+               FF
          :             FFF
          :           FF
          : R       FFF
          :   FFFFFF
0.00000*FF-------+---------+---------+---------+---------+
        0.0000     1.2000     2.4000     3.6000     4.8000     6.0000

      THE Y - AXIS SCALE FACTOR IS 10**               0
            THE X - AXIS SCALE FACTOR IS 10**               1
```

b) Graph for an initial rabbit ratio of 0.1 and a fox ratio of 0.1:

```
1.00000*
          :
          :
          :
          : F
0.75000+
          : F
          :              RRRRRRRRRRRRRRRRRRRRRRRRRRRRRRRRRRRRRRRRRRRRRR
          :   F RRR
          :   F*
0.50000+   R FFFF
          :             FFFFFFFFFFFFFFFFFFFFFFFFFFFFFFFFFFFFFFFFFFFFFFFF
          :
          :   R
          :
0.25000+ R
          :
          : R
        R
          :
0.00000+---------+---------+---------+---------+---------+
        0.0000     1.2000     2.4000     3.6000     4.8000     6.0000

      THE Y - AXIS SCALE FACTOR IS 10**               0
            THE X - AXIS SCALE FACTOR IS 10**               1
```

The first assumption is incorporated by altering the term $-15 \times r(t) \times f(t) \times \delta t$ to $-15 \times f(t) \times \delta t$ in the first equation. The second assumption is modeled by changing $0.167 \times f \times (r - 15 \times f) \times \delta t$ to $0.167 \times f \times (c + r - 15 \times f) \times \delta t$ where c is a small constant. For example, $c = 0.01$ and $r = 0$ implies that the fox population would eventually become $R_{max}/1500$, if all rabbits should disappear. These changes are made in the FORTRAN/77 program which follows as Figure 16.18.

The output for three different sets of data is presented in Figures 16.19 and 16.20. In the top example of Figure 16.19, for the initial values $r = 0.1$, $f = 0.002$, and $c = 0$, the study indicates that the rabbits and foxes may coexist indefinitely in this greedy fox model. Note, however, that the limiting values of the rabbit and fox populations are $R_{max}/2$ and $R_{max}/30$, somewhat lower than for the previous model.

In the lower example of Figure 16.19, the results are given for the same initial values of r and f but with a small c value of 0.01. It may surprise the reader to observe that this apparently minor change results in the collapse of the system. The rabbit population rises to roughly R_{max} as before, but as the foxes become established, the rabbit population is completely destroyed. Then, the fox population dwindles away to the small residual value $R_{max}/1500$. This effect is perhaps more dramatic in Figure 16.20. Here the initial values $r = 0.49$, $f = 0.033$, with $c = 0.03$ represent values at which the system should be nearly in equilibrium, with very little change of state in any one time-step.

Note how the rabbit population oscillates with the small initial fluctuation increasing until the rabbit population shows a precipitate disappearance at about four years. The fox population then dwindles to about $R_{max}/500$.

There are many ways in which these models may be varied or improved. One possibility would be the incorporation of the assumption that the populations may reproduce only after a certain age has been reached. This will not be pursued here, but the reader is invited to think about ways in which this might be done.

16.8   Summary

This chapter presented a few simple simulation problems and developed models and programs to investigate them. The principles used are valid, however, for the much more complex problems encountered in the real world.

An important aspect which was only addressed briefly was that of testing the models and programs for a range of parameters and initial conditions to gain insight into some real system. The variety and unpredictability of the results from the prey-predator model should make the reader cautious about accepting the results of any simulation study without extensive investigation.

```
C Figure 16.18 -- Greedy Fox Simulation Problem.
C                  Program to simulate a three species population in
C                  which the foxes do not ration their consumption of
C                  rabbits and can subsist on chipmunks if the rabbits
C                  disappear.
C*************************************************************************
C R      - the normalized rabbit population ratio R(t)/Rmax
C RNEW   - temporary value of R
C F      - the normalized fox population ratio F(t)/Rmax
C T      - the time
C C      - the chipmunk parameter
C DT     - the time increment
C MONTHS - the index for number of months
C I      - the index for number of steps
C TMAX   - the number of months to run the simulation
C NSTEPS - the number of time steps per month

C*************************************************************************
      REAL R, F, T, DT, RNEW
      INTEGER TMAX, MONTHS, NSTEPS, ISTEP
C Obtain and record the simulation parameters and initial states.
      TMAX = 60
      NSTEPS = 10
      T = 0.0
      DT = 1.0/NSTEPS
      PRINT *, 'ENTER THE INITIAL RABBIT RATIO:'
      READ *, R
      PRINT *, 'ENTER THE INITIAL FOX RATIO:'
      READ *, F
      PRINT *, 'ENTER THE CHIPMUNK PARAMETER:'
      READ *, C
C Initialize plotting.
      CALL SETPLT(51,21)
      CALL STOPNT(T,R,'R')
      CALL STOPNT(T,10.0*F,'F')
      CALL STOPNT(0.0,0.0,'-')
      CALL STOPNT(0.0,1.0,'-')
C Compute the populations at tenth of a month intervals.
C Plot the population at the end of each month.
      DO 200 MONTHS = 1, TMAX
         DO 100 I = 1, NSTEPS
            T = T + DT
            RNEW = R + 2.0*DT*R*(1.0 - R) - 15.0*DT*F
            F = F + 0.167*DT*F*(C + R - 15.0*F)
            R = RNEW
            IF (R.LE.0.0) THEN
                 R = 0.0
            ENDIF
  100    CONTINUE
         CALL STOPNT(T,R,'R')
         CALL STOPNT(T,10.0*F,'F')
  200 CONTINUE

      CALL PLOT(1)
      STOP
      END
```

Figure 16.19   First two examples of a greedy fox simulation, output from the program of
Figure 16.18.

a) Graph for an initial rabbit ratio of 0.1, an initial fox ratio of 0.002 and a chipmunk parameter of 0.0:

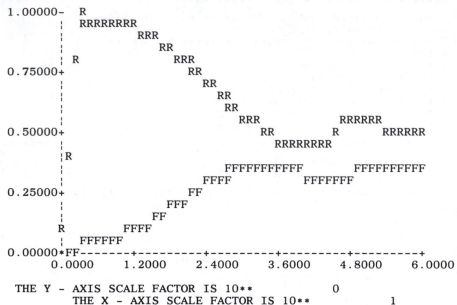

b) Graph for an initial rabbit ratio of 0.1, an initial fox ratio of 0.002 and a chipmunk parameter of 0.01:

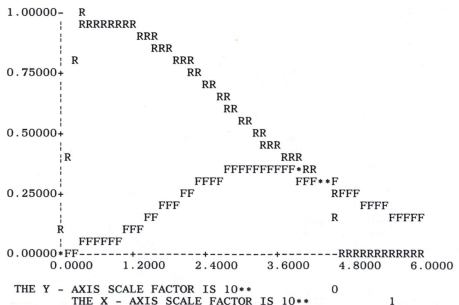

Figure 16.20   Third example of a greedy fox simulation, output from the program in Figure 16.18.

Graph for an initial rabbit ratio of 0.49, an initial fox ratio of 0.033 and a chipmunk parameter of 0.03:

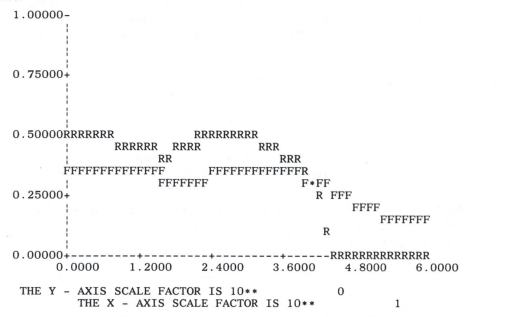

```
1.00000-
        ÷
        ÷
        ÷
0.75000+
        ÷
        ÷
        ÷
        ÷
0.50000RRRRRRR             RRRRRRRRR
        ÷        RRRRR   RRRR          RRR
        ÷           RR                 RRR
        · FFFFFFFFFFFFF       FFFFFFFFFFFFFFR
        ÷           FFFFFFF        F*FF
0.25000+                           R  FFF
        ÷                              FFFF
        ÷                                 FFFFFFF
        ÷                           R
        ÷
0.00000+---------+---------+---------+------RRRRRRRRRRRRRR
        0.0000    1.2000    2.4000    3.6000   4.8000    6.0000

     THE Y - AXIS SCALE FACTOR IS 10**          0
          THE X - AXIS SCALE FACTOR IS 10**          1
```

16.9   References

The following references provide greater elaboration of the ideas presented in this chapter.   Barrodale et al.   (1971) provides additional elementary material and Braun (1975, 1978) is a good source for a variety of interesting problems.   Forrester (1971) and Meadows (1972) extend the ideas of simulation to predictions about the evolution of the world.

Barrodale, I.; Roberts, F.D.K.; and Ehle, B.L.   *Elementary Computer Applications.* New York: John Wiley and Sons, 1971.

Braun, M.   *Differential Equations and Their Applications.* New York: Springer-Verlag, 1975 and 1978.

Forrester, J.W.   *World Dynamics.* Cambridge, Mass.: Wright-Allen Press, 1971.

Gordon, G.   *System Simulation.* Englewood Cliffs, N.J.: Prentice-Hall, Second Edition 1978.

Meadows, D., et al.   *The Limits to Growth.* New York: Universe Books, 1972.

16.10 Exercises

In most of the following exercises a program is requested to solve a specific problem. For each problem it is recommended that step-wise refinement be used in developing a pseudocode algorithm to solve the problem.   This algorithm should then be translated into FORTRAN/77 and run on the computer.   Where appropriate, the program should be tested with a variety of data sufficient to ensure that the program does what it is supposed to do.

16.1   a)   Generalize the investment example of Section 16.4 to allow for interest on the investment to be compounded semiannually.

   b)   Generalize the investment example of Section 16.4 to allow for interest on the investment to be compounded quarterly.

16.2   Modify the investment example of Section 16.4 to determine, to the nearest tenth of a percent, the minimum interest rate required to have an accumulated investment of at least three times the final salary.

16.3   Modify the investment example of Section 16.4 to determine, to the nearest tenth of a percent, the minimum percentage of the income that must be saved in order that the final investment be $1,000,000.

16.4   Investment problems have been discussed several times in this text. Now consider simulating a retirement plan. Suppose a person has accumulated $150,000 by his retirement. The money is invested at 12% per annum, compounded annually. He plans to withdraw $2000 each month the first year, but plans to increase his withdrawals by 10% each year to handle inflation.

   a)   What are the state variables in this problem?
   b)   What are the values of the initial parameters?
   c)   What are the equations that describe the transition from one state to the next?
   d)   Provide successive step-wise refinements to develop a simulation algorithm starting with the initial decomposition of the form shown in Figure 16.1.

16.5   Banks and trust companies have introduced daily interest savings accounts (DISA) to complement their conventional savings accounts (CSA). With a CSA, the interest is calculated on a *monthly* basis. The amount of interest paid is based on the minimum (daily) balance during the specific month (called the *minimum monthly balance*. (The *daily* implies that if a withdrawal is followed by a deposit later the same day, the final balance for the day is the relevant amount, not the presumably lower balance between the withdrawal and the deposit.) These interest payments are accumulated (without further interest) and are actually deposited to the account semiannually (say June 30 and December 31).

   With a DISA, the interest is calculated on a *daily* basis. The amount of interest to be paid is based on the minimum daily balance. These interest payments are accumulated (without further interest) and are deposited to the account monthly (say the first day of the next month).

a) Since DISA's have an obvious advantage to the customer over CSA's, banks
    compensate by offering higher interest rates for CSA's (for example, the
    rate for a DISA might be 10% per annum whereas the rate for a CSA
    might be 11% per annum). Therefore, the choice between the two types of
    accounts is no longer as clear. To some extent, it depends on the banking
    habits of the individual customer.

    Suppose a person's banking is characterized by the following figures:

- The net monthly income (paid on the last day of each month) is $2000.
- There are *monthly* bills of $1100, on the average (mortgage, utilities,
  credit card payments, etc., paid on the twenty-fifth day of each month).
- There are *weekly* bills of $150, on the average (groceries, clothes, enter-
  tainment, gas, etc.).

Assume a balance of $2000 from the previous year.

    Using step-wise refinement develop a FORTRAN/77 program to simulate
    this person's banking record for one year to determine which of the two
    account types is best. Your program should be as general as possible
    (though you may ignore leap years) and should produce meaningful output.

b) The banking model presented in part a) is rather simplified since there are a
    variety of expenses that occur at only specific times of the year. The list
    below gives some typical items.

Date	Item	Amount
Mar. 1	House Taxes	$300
Aug. 1	House Taxes	$250
Nov. 1	House Taxes	$250
June 15	House Insurance	$200
Sept. 1	Car Insurance	$350
Apr. 15	Spouse's Birthday	$100
July 7	Friend's Birthday	$200
Dec. 1	Christmas Gifts	$500
June 15	Wedding Anniversary	$100

    Incorporate this type of expense into the banking model and modify the
    program from part a).

16.6 Derive the equations for the motion of the bull and hiker in the example of
      Section 16.5 with the bull located to the left of the hiker.

16.7 For the bull-hiker problem of Section 16.5, what is the minimum speed for the
      hiker so that he may reach the trees safely, if the bull can run at 9
      meters/second?

16.8 Derive the equations for the motion of the bull and hiker under the assumption
      that the hiker initially runs at right angles to the line joining the bull and hiker.
      When the hiker's direction is straight towards the trees, he continues in this
      direction. Does this strategy improve the hiker's chances?

16.9   Recall the program for the bull-hiker pursuit problem in Figure 16.8. Assume that the bull tires easily and that his speed may be represented by

$$V_B(t) = 10e^{-.01t} .$$

The hiker, on the other hand, warms up slowly but eventually tires. His speed is described by

$$V_h(t) = 8 + 2\sin\left(\frac{\pi}{40}t\right) .$$

Modify the given algorithm to incorporate these changes.

16.10   A hawk perches at the peak of a 30 meter tree, watching for field mice in a nearby pasture to move far enough from their burrows to be caught. The mice can run at two meters/second and the hawk flies at a constant 20 meters/second directly towards any mouse which is a potential meal.

   a)   If a mouse is initially at a point 35 meters from the base of the tree and his burrow is 5 meters further away in a direct line, does the mouse reach safety?
   b)   If the mouse is not caught, how much closer to the tree could he forage and remain safe?
   c)   What if the burrow is 5 meters away but perpendicular to the line between the mouse and tree? (This is harder, since you must work in three dimensions.)

16.11   A short sighted owl makes its home at the peak of a 35 meter tree. When it dimly perceives any flying object passing within 30 meters, the owl pursues it at a speed of 20 meters/second. The pursuit is stopped and the owl returns home if the object passes out of range. Some children enjoy teasing the owl by throwing a ball from the base of the tree at various angles to the horizontal at a speed of 25 meters/second.

       Develop a program to determine and plot the path of the ball and of the owl (if he pursues the ball). The owl takes the ball home if he catches it and abandons the pursuit if he has not caught it before it returns to ground after bouncing once (losing 20% of its vertical velocity). Do the simulation for angles of 30, 45, 60, and 75 degrees.

16.12   Four cockroaches are initially placed at the corners of a square room with sides of length 3 meters. At a given time, each roach starts to pursue the one adjacent to it in a counter-clockwise direction, at a speed of 0.3 meters/second. Plot the four trajectories, terminating when the separation between the roaches is less than 0.05 meters.

16.13   Generalize the previous problem to n (≤ 10) roaches placed uniformly about the periphery of a circle of radius 2 meters.

16.14   A stock car demolition derby is to be organized according to the following weird rules.

a)   Seven cars are to be placed at 45 degree intervals (clockwise) around the perimeter of a circular field of radius 150 meters, in order of increasing maximum speed. The speeds are 10, 11, 13, 14, 14, 15, and 17 meters/second.

b)   Each car attempts to overtake the car adjacent to it in a clockwise direction (that is, the next faster car except for #7 which attacks #1).

c)   Upon impact (separation < 2 meters), the overtaken car is knocked out. The overtaking car is somewhat damaged, however, and is assumed to suffer a 2.5 meters/second reduction in maximum speed.   It continues and attacks the next car in a clockwise direction.

d)   When there are only two cars left, the faster one is declared to be the winner.

Develop a program to simulate the demolition derby. Modify the program to allow a rerun of the derby with car #4 scratched at the start and the remaining cars fixed.

16.15   In 1943 London was attacked by V-1 "buzz-bombs" which flew over the English Channel at a constant altitude of 2,500 meters at a speed of 195 meters/second. In defense, the R.A.F. patrolled at this altitude in their fastest aircraft, the Tempest, which could do 175 meters/second indefinitely, and 200 meters/second for a period of 20 seconds without overheating. Assuming that the Tempests patrol at right angles to the missiles' anticipated paths, can sight an incoming missile at a range of 1,500 meters, and can turn at a maximum rate of 15°/second, how closely must the Tempests be spaced so as to be able to intercept any V-1? (A Tempest pilot is deadly at 150 meters.)

16.16   A ship moves towards a cliff to deposit soldiers on a beach at the base of the cliff. The ship's velocity is a constant 6 meters/second in a direction directly towards the cliff. A gun which can fire shells with a muzzle velocity of 500 meters/second is situated 30 meters up the cliff. The angle of projection of the shell is measured in degrees to the horizontal.

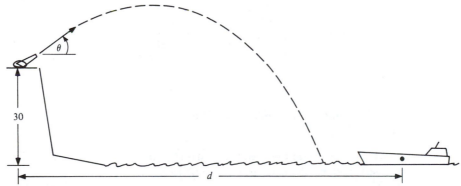

For any shot the angle θ is chosen as the angle of the previous shot plus or minus a small angle $\delta\theta$, the sign being chosen according to whether the previous shot was too long or too short respectively. Exceptions to this rule are that the angle of projection can never be less than the initial angle of projection which is always

45°, (if the shot is too short with this angle of projection the gun keeps firing at maximum range) and the angle θ is never allowed to exceed 90°.

A new shot is not fired until the previous shell reaches the ship or water, and a new angle of projection can be determined. A 'hit' occurs when the shell lands within 10 meters of the ship.

The initial position of the ship is 3000 meters directly out to sea from a point vertically below the gun. The ship can be considered safe when it is within 100 meters of the cliff.

The model assumes no air resistance to the shell; the only acceleration acting is gravity at 9.8 meters/second² in a vertical direction (downwards).

a) Construct the mathematical model for this problem.
b) Write a FORTRAN/77 program to simulate the motion, plotting the position of the ship and shells. The program should allow the incremental angle $\delta\theta$ and the discrete time step of the simulation to be read as data.

16.17 Water flows into a regular shaped tank as depicted below. The inflow of water is a constant 10 liters/minute. The *maximum* outflow of water through the outflow pipe is 3.5 liters/minute. If the height of the water above the bottom of the outflow pipe is h meters, then the volume of water flowing out of the outflow pipe is given as

$$3.5 * \frac{2}{\pi} \arccos(1 - 2h) \text{ liters/minute.}$$

Thus, if the depth of the water in the tank is less than or equal to 0 meters, the outflow is zero, and if the depth of the water is greater than or equal to .5 meters, the outflow is a maximum 3.5 liters/minute.

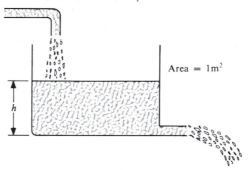

Simulate the filling of the tank, initially empty, to determine at what time the tank overflows.

a) Write a pseudocode algorithm to perform this task.
b) Convert your pseudocode to FORTRAN/77.

16.18 Simulate the motion of a ball bouncing down a 25 meter corridor with a three meter ceiling. Assume that the ball is thrown at a speed of 15 meters/second at an angle of − 45 degrees (downwards). Follow the motion for a distance of 10 meters beyond the end of the corridor, where the floor but not the ceiling is assumed to continue. Assume that the acceleration due to gravity is -9.8 meters/second^2 and that the ball retains 85 percent of its vertical velocity when it bounces from the floor or ceiling.

16.19   A boy stands 4 meters from a high wall bouncing a 0.1 kilogram ball once before it hits the wall at a point half way to the wall. As the ball hits the wall it rebounds back towards the boy. If the boy who is 1.5 meters tall can reach up .5 meters, how fast must he throw the ball so it rebounds low enough for him to catch it. The ball loses 5% of its velocity both when it bounces on the ground and on the building.

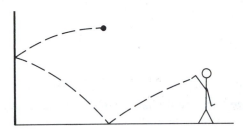

16.20   A ball of mass 0.1 kilogram is tethered to the ground by a light elastic cord of length one meter when unstretched. The force required to stretch the elastic is proportional to the distance stretched and is given by the formula

$$f = 0.75 \times \text{elongation(kilogram-meter/sec/sec)}.$$

Develop a program to simulate the motion of the ball if the ball is initially at rest at a point three meters above a point on the ground which is one meter away from the tether point. Assume that the acceleration due to gravity is -9.8 meters/second^2, and that the ball loses five percent of its vertical velocity when it bounces. Follow the motion for six bounces.

16.21   A baseball team is considering a move from Oakland to Denver. The commissioner agrees, subject among other things, to the fences being located far enough away that home run hitters do not gain any advantage due to Denver's thin air. Assuming that the Oakland fence is 135 meters from home plate, how far away should the Denver fence be? It is known that the force due to air resistance (drag) is proportional to the cross-sectional area and to the square of the velocity. That is,

$$f = k \times a \times v^2$$

At sea level, $k = 0.080$ and in Denver, $k = 0.065$ (approximately), when a is in meters^2 and v is in meters/second. Assume that the mass of the ball is 0.1 kilogram and that its diameter is 0.07 meters.

a)   First, find the initial velocity required for a ball to travel 135 meters, when hit at an angle of 45 degrees at sea level.

b)   Then, find the distance the same initial conditions will produce in Denver.

16.22 a) Modify the single species population program of Figure 16.14 to simulate several populations with different initial populations but with the same growth rate. The program should produce a single graph.
   b) Modify the single species population program of Figure 16.14 to simulate several populations with different growth rates but with the same initial populations. The program should only produce a single graph.

16.23 It was suggested in Section 16.7.3 that a time step of one month would not be appropriate. Try running the program in Figure 16.16 with NSTEPS = 1 and observe what happens.

16.24 A river system contains two distinct fish populations - a species of large fish and another of small fish. The current population of small fish, which eat other small marine life, is $0.2p$, where the environment could support p small fish. The small fish would double in numbers each month with unlimited food resources.

The large fish currently number $0.01p$ and consume 3 small fish per day each. The large fish would double each year with abundant small fish, but their reproduction falls to 0 if the ratio of small fish to large fish falls to 100 or less.

   a) Construct a model of this system.
   b) Construct a program to simulate the system for ten years with a variety of initial conditions.

16.25 An isolated lake could support a maximum population of 500,000 whitefish, which feed on various vegetable and marine life. With no competition, the whitefish would triple each year.

A government agency decides to promote a sport fishing industry by introducing a species of salmon to the lake. The salmon prey on whitefish and would increase at the rate of 50% per year in the presence of abundant whitefish. The salmon growth rate shrinks to 0 as their numbers grow to exceed 10% of the whitefish population. Salmon consume 10 whitefish per month.

   a) Develop a program to simulate the growth of the whitefish from an initial level of 5,000, with no salmon predation.
   b) Three years after the start of the simulation of a), introduce 2,000 salmon to the lake and follow the system for 20 years.

16.26 In the previous whitefish-salmon system, assume that each of the populations is reduced at a relative rate of 0.2% per day for a six-month fishing season each year. That is, 2 fish per 1000 of each species are caught each day. Start the fishing season 2 years after the introduction of the salmon and follow the system behavior for 18 years. How do the numbers compare to the previous problem? If the numbers surprise you, investigate the question in, for example, Braun (1975, 1978).

17
Probabilistic Simulation

17.1 Introduction

Probabilistic or *stochastic* models are used in the simulation of systems whose change in state is affected by chance. Although analytical techniques do exist for analyzing idealized versions of such systems, stochastic processes are often quite complex and thus simulation is an attractive tool.

The simulation of stochastic processes had its origin in the 1940s when it was used to solve nuclear reaction and shielding problems. The term *Monte Carlo* was coined at that time to describe some of the analysis techniques by analogy to games of chance. Since then, the use of simulation techniques has spread to almost all fields of science. Currently, probabilistic simulation techniques are used in the analysis and solution of problems in communications, transportation, industrial production, business, economics, marketing strategy, physical and chemical processes, performance of computer systems, and many other fields. These simulation techniques may also be used in the playing of games which range from simple coin and dice tossing to extremely complex military games played by governments.

Although most of the above systems are too complex to be considered here, this chapter introduces some of the basic terminology and concepts of probabilistic simulation. For further information, the reader may consult the references at the end of the chapter.

17.2   Simulating Stochastic Processes — Random Numbers

A stochastic process is characterized by the fact that the state of the system changes in response to random stimuli.   This element of randomness is introduced in a simulation through the use of a random number generator and some distribution function.   The random numbers, usually generated over a fixed range, provide the randomness; the distribution functions describe the relative frequencies of possible outcomes, that is, how the random numbers should be interpreted for each specific problem.

Consider the simulation of a simple coin toss.   If the coin does not land on its edge, there are only two possible outcomes of a toss, either heads or tails.   Over many tosses, the order of occurrence of heads and tails would be random but, if the coin is fair, one would expect approximately the same total number of heads and tails to be produced. In this case the distribution of heads and tails is said to be uniform.

In the simulation of a gas station, discussed later in this chapter, the arrival times of cars will be random according to some distribution which describes the overall arrival process.   The service times also show some pattern with a few cars requiring either very long or very short periods of service.   The mathematical descriptions of these variations in service times and arrivals are called distributions.

There are many ways in which random numbers may be generated.   Manual techniques such as spinning a roulette wheel or drawing numbers from a hat are possible generation techniques, but they are not suitable for use in a computer simulation. Another possibility is to have library tables of random numbers such as those produced by the RAND Corporation.   However, the use of such tables is limited by storage requirements and access times.   Furthermore, there is always the chance of requiring more numbers than are contained in the tables.   Thus, for simulation purposes the random numbers are usually generated internally in the computer as they are required.

When generating random numbers for simulation there is a requirement that the numbers be *reproducible* (for comparison and testing purposes) but not *predictable*, and that the sequence of random numbers so produced should be as long as possible before it repeats itself (all such random number generators eventually repeat the sequence). Further requirements are that the random numbers be statistically independent of each other and that they be produced quickly with minimal storage requirements.

To achieve reproducibility, the random numbers must be generated by some deterministic method and as a result are called *pseudo-random* numbers.   The "goodness" of such pseudo-random numbers is determined by whether or not they pass a series of statistical tests of randomness (see Exercise 17.3).   In all subsequent discussions it will be assumed that a reference to random numbers refers to such pseudo-random numbers.

Random numbers may be produced in many different distributions for a variety of possible applications.   The following sections describe several different types of random numbers, their generation, and their use.

17.3   Uniformly Distributed Random Numbers

The simplest and most basic random number distribution is the uniform distribution. These random numbers may be used in the generation of all other distributions using suitable transformations. The key property of uniformly distributed random numbers is that all numbers within a given range are equally likely to occur. A FORTRAN/77 subroutine called RANDOM, developed later and shown in Figure 17.2, will generate such random numbers. The reader who is interested in finding out more about how they are generated should continue with the remaining parts of this section. *Other readers should go to Section 17.4 directly.*

17.3.1   Generation of Uniformly Distributed Random Numbers

The most common ways of generating random numbers are the *congruential* methods. The three basic methods of this type are the *additive, multiplicative,* and *mixed congruential* techniques. The first two use only addition or multiplication respectively in the calculation of the random numbers while the mixed method uses a combination of both. Each of these methods generates a sequence $\{n_i\}$ of nonnegative integers each less than some positive value m. In the mixed congruential method each random number n_{i+1} is derived (deterministically) from the previous random number by the relationship

$$n_{i+1} \leftarrow [a \times n_i + c](\bmod m)$$

where a and c are nonnegative integers and m is a large positive integer closely related to the word size of the machine. Thus, to generate a sequence of random numbers, one needs a starting value or *seed* n_0 and values for the constants a, c, and m. The values chosen for these quantities are quite important since they affect the *period* or length of the sequence before it repeats and other statistical properties of the random number sequence. For a given m, the values of a and c should be selected such that n_0 may be chosen arbitrarily.

As an example to illustrate what is happening, consider the generation of single digit numbers using decimal arithmetic ($m = 10$). It should be obvious that $a = 0$ and $c = 0$ are not good choices and that $a = 1$ would probably not introduce the desired randomness. It also turns out that $a = 5$ is a disastrous choice. Ignoring these possibilities for the constants, sequences of period 1, 2, 4, and 5 may be generated. The table of Figure 17.1 illustrates the sequences for several a, c, and n_0 choices. As may be seen from the table, some values of a and c are better than others. The best sequences are those generated when $a = 6$ as they have the longest period. As an added bonus, which is not obvious from the few examples in the table, the choice of $a = 6$ and $c \neq 1$ or 6 allows *any* value to be chosen for the seed, and the sequence of random numbers will still have a period of 5. This characteristic does not hold for any other a and c combination as in those cases the choice of n_0 does affect the period.

As a result of their importance, the a and c values are usually predetermined for a particular random number generator. Even from this very simple example it may be seen that the choice of multiplier and addend must be made carefully.

Figure 17.1   One-digit random number sequences for different choices of a, c and n_0.

a	c	n_0	*next 6 digits of sequence*	*period*
2	3	3	9, 1, 5, 3, 9, 1	4
2	3	5	3, 9, 1, 5, 3, 9	4
2	3	7	7, 7, 7, 7, 7, 7	1
3	7	1	0, 7, 8, 1, 0, 7	4
3	7	2	3, 6, 5, 2, 3, 6	4
3	7	4	9, 4, 9, 4, 9, 4	2
6	3	2	5, 3, 1, 9, 7, 5	5
6	3	3	1, 9, 7, 5, 3, 1	5
6	3	4	7, 5, 3, 1, 9, 7	5
6	6	3	4, 0, 6, 2, 8, 4	5
7	9	3	0, 9, 2, 3, 0, 9	4

For binary computers, m is usually chosen to give the maximum possible range, that is, from 0 to the largest positive number that can be represented. This usually means that $m = 2^{b-1}$ where b is the number of binary digits (bits) in the computer word. The maximum possible period, given suitable values for a and c, is 2^{b-3} or $m/4$. To obtain the maximum period and the minimum amount of correlation between the numbers, a and c should be chosen such that:

1) $a = 8t \pm 5$ (t a positive integer);
2) $m/100 < a < m - \sqrt{m}$;
3)   the binary digits of a have no obvious pattern;
4) c should be an odd integer with $c/m \simeq 0.21132$.

The seed n_0 may be chosen arbitrarily. For more discussion, see Forsythe et al. (1977), page 242.

17.3.2   Uniformly Distributed Random Numbers in the Range [0,1)

The integer valued random numbers generated by the mixed congruential technique described above will have a range determined by the word size of the computer. In order to provide a measure of standardization over different computers, these random numbers are usually mapped into the range [0,1).[1] This mapping is performed by dividing each integer random number by m. The pseudocode statements below indicate the calculations necessary to generate the next random number r in a sequence in the range [0,1).

    n ← [n * a + c] (mod m)
    r ← n / m

When implementing this algorithm on a computer one can take advantage of the fact that (mod 2^b) calculations are performed automatically in integer arithmetic. Because of the internal representation of integer numbers (an intrinsic property of computers) the

---

[1] The notation [0,1) means that 0 is included in the range and 1 is not.

(mod 2^b) calculation may generate either a positive or negative number.   If the number is positive then it is, in fact, a (mod 2^{b-1}) value which is desired.   If the number is negative it may be converted to a (mod 2^{b-1}) positive value by simply adding to it the *magnitude* of the largest negative number (2^{b-1}).

A FORTRAN/77 subroutine to generate uniformly distributed random numbers is given in Figure 17.2.   The constants in the procedure are for the VAX or IBM computers, which have a 32-bit word length.   Thus, the values are derived from

$m = 2^{b-1} = 2^{31} = 2147483648$

$1/m = .4656612E - 9$ (value truncated)

range of integers $= -2147483648$ to $+2147483647$

and appropriate choices for the multiplier and addend are

$a = 843314861$ and

$c = 453816693$.

The maximum possible period is $2^{29} = 536,870,912$ random numbers, many more than could be stored in a table of random numbers.   The equivalent constants for Honeywell 36-bit computers are $m = 2^{35} = 34359738368$, $1/m = 0.29103830E - 10$, $a = 13493037709$, and $c = 7261067085$.

```
C Figure 17.2 -- A Random Number Module.
C               Subroutine RANDOM to generate uniformly distributed
C               random numbers over the range 0.0 to 1.0 on a
C               32-bit word computer.  It will generate 2**29
C               random numbers before repeating. Constants chosen
C               from Forsythe, Malcolm, and Moler.
C*********************************************************************
C N     - previous integer valued random number (initially the seed)
C U     - real valued random number where U is in [0,1)
C*********************************************************************
        SUBROUTINE RANDOM(N,U)
        REAL U
        INTEGER N

        N = N * 843314861 + 453816693
        IF (N .LT. 0) THEN
             N = N + 2147483647 + 1
        ENDIF
        U = N * .4656612E-9
        RETURN
        END
```

Program Notes

- The addition of the magnitude of the largest negative number must be done by adding the value of the largest positive number and then adding one.
- This program is *not* portable to any computer. The values of the constants must be chosen with care to match the arithmetic properties of the machine used. A FORTRAN program which chooses the constants automatically is given in Forsythe, Malcolm, and Moler.

The random numbers produced by the mixed congruential method are statistically reasonable, reproducible, and generated quickly. Also, the method requires little storage. Thus, the technique is quite suitable for the majority of applications.

17.4   Using Uniformly Distributed Random Numbers

In most simulation problems it is not sufficient to just generate uniformly distributed random numbers (variates) in the standardized range [0,1). The specific requirements of each problem must be taken into consideration. Usually this means that the generated variates will be transformed through either a continuous or discrete mapping function onto a range of possible outcomes. The specification of the possible outcomes is given by a distribution curve such as described in Chapter 14. Stating this in another way, one is given a distribution function and one wants to generate random variates with that distribution. The following sections describe two mapping operations for the uniform distribution.

17.4.1   Continuous Mappings of Standard Uniform Variates

Consider the situation in which a simulation problem requires random variates to be distributed uniformly in the range [a,b). The distribution function for these numbers is given in Figure 17.3.

Figure 17.3   Uniform distribution function.

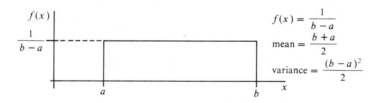

$$f(x) = \frac{1}{b-a}$$

$$\text{mean} = \frac{b+a}{2}$$

$$\text{variance} = \frac{(b-a)^2}{2}$$

The required mapping operation is performed by the following expression.

$$x = u \times (b-a) + a$$

Thus, the mapping function needs only a standard uniform variate u and the limits of the required range [a,b). For instance, if random numbers which are uniformly distributed over the range [5,8) are desired, then the equation would be

$$x = u \times 3 + 5 \ .$$

The table of Figure 17.4 shows the mapping performed by this equation for selected values of u.

Figure 17.4   Examples of a continuous mapping of uniform variates from [0,1) to [5,8).

u	x
0.0	5.0
0.25	5.75
0.5	6.5
0.75	7.25
0.999999	7.99999

17.4.2   Discrete Mappings of Standard Uniform Variates

Suppose that a simulation process is controlled by an event which has only 4 possible outcomes and that they occur randomly with the following probabilities.

$$\left.\begin{array}{l} \text{probability of outcome } 1 = p_1 \\ \text{probability of outcome } 2 = p_2 \\ \text{probability of outcome } 3 = p_3 \\ \text{probability of outcome } 4 = p_4 \end{array}\right\} \text{ where } p_1 + p_2 + p_3 + p_4 = 1.0$$

What these probabilities mean is that outcome 1 should occur $p_1 \times 100\%$ of the time; outcome 2 should occur $p_2 \times 100\%$ of the time; outcome 3 should occur $p_3 \times 100\%$ of the time; and outcome 4 should occur $p_4 \times 100\%$ of the time.

The diagrams in Figure 17.5 show possible histograms for two different probability weightings for the four outcomes.   The weightings are indicated below each diagram.

Figure 17.5   Frequency histograms for two hypothetical processes.

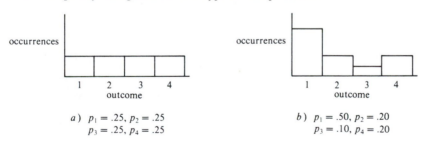

$$a)\ \ p_1 = .25, p_2 = .25$$
$$p_3 = .25, p_4 = .25$$

$$b)\ \ p_1 = .50, p_2 = .20$$
$$p_3 = .10, p_4 = .20$$

To obtain a mapping of standard uniform variates such that the above distributions occur is relatively simple.   All that is necessary is to divide up the range of the uniform variate into classes, one for each outcome.   The width of each class corresponds to the probability that a particular outcome will occur.   The rationale behind this scheme is that since the random variates are uniformly distributed over the entire range, then the number of times a random variate falls in a given class is determined by the width of the class.

The diagrams in Figure 17.6 illustrate classifications for the probabilities given above, and an interpretation is provided below each diagram.   These classifications will result in each outcome occurring the required percentage of the time.

Figure 17.6   Subdivision of the range [0,1) for the processes of Figure 17.5.

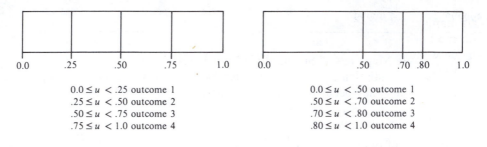

$0.0 \le u < .25$ outcome 1
$.25 \le u < .50$ outcome 2
$.50 \le u < .75$ outcome 3
$.75 \le u < 1.0$ outcome 4

$0.0 \le u < .50$ outcome 1
$.50 \le u < .70$ outcome 2
$.70 \le u < .80$ outcome 3
$.80 \le u < 1.0$ outcome 4

To perform these mappings it is only necessary to check the value of the random variate.   The following pseudocode segment shows how to do this mapping for distribution b) in Figure 17.6.

if u < 0.50 **then**
⌈ Specify outcome 1 for random numbers between 0 and 0.50.
else
⌈ **if** u < 0.70 **then**
⌈ Specify outcome 2 for random numbers between 0.50 and 0.70.
else
⌈ **if** u < 0.80 **then**
⌈ Specify outcome 3 for random numbers between 0.70 and 0.80.
else
⌈ Specify outcome 4 for random numbers between 0.80 and 1.00.

If the mapping was to be done for distribution a) in Figure 17.6, the pseudocode would have an identical structure with only the probabilities changed.   Of course, if the number of outcomes was changed the pseudocode could be modified to accommodate it.

Up to now, there has been no qualification on exactly what an outcome is.   In fact, an outcome may just determine a specific value for a variable, or an outcome may be that an entire set of actions is performed.   The technique described above is suitable for all such possibilities.   However, a more specific mapping is possible for a restricted class of outcomes.   For instance, when the set of outcomes is a set of consecutive integer values, (a, a+1, a+2, . . . , b), then the mapping of the standard uniform variate onto this range may be performed by the following equation.

x = int (u * (b−a+1)) + a

For example, if the set of possible outcomes is the integers (5, 6, 7, 8), then the following equation will perform the mapping.

x = int (u * 4) + 5

This mapping will give the same result as when the previous technique is used with each outcome having a probability of 0.25.   The table of Figure 17.7 demonstrates this mapping on what would be the class limits in the previous method.   Remember that the random variate 1.0 is never generated.

Figure 17.7   Examples of mapping uniform variates onto integer sequences.

class #	u	u*4	int(u*4)	int(u*4)+5
1	0.00	0.0	0	5
	0.2499999	0.9999996	0	5
2	0.25	1.0	1	6
	0.4999999	1.9999996	1	6
3	0.50	2.0	2	7
	0.7499999	2.9999996	2	7
4	0.75	3.0	3	8
	0.9999999	3.9999996	3	8

17.5   The Investment Problem Revisited

The investment problem of Chapter 16 was made quite simple by assuming that the simulation parameters were constant.   Perhaps the most unrealistic assumption was that the increase in salary would be a constant percentage.   It would be more likely that this figure would vary with the performance of the individual and with inflation.   One could accept a constant value for the percentage of the salary put into savings since this is more-or-less under the direct control of the individual.   A constant value for the percentage interest earned on savings could be rationalized on the grounds that it represents an average investment objective.

This section examines the investment problem when the percentage salary increase is not a constant, but is subject to random perturbations.

Example 17.1   Probabilistic Investment Problem

Develop a program to simulate the investment problem of Example 16.1 when the yearly percentage salary increase varies uniformly over the range 6.5 to 12%.

a) Problem Discussion   Since the percentage salary increase varies uniformly over the continuous range of 6.5% to 12%, a probabilistic simulation and the mapping technique of Section 17.4.1 can be used.

b) Development of a Program   Since this problem is very similar to Example 17.1, the program of Figure 17.3 may be used in this example with small modifications.

Since the percentage salary increase is no longer constant, it is not possible to obtain a value for PERINC from the data list.   Instead, it must be computed for each year from the upper and lower bounds for the percentage increase.   Letting the variables PERHIG and PERLOW represent these values respectively, the program statements to obtain the simulation parameters become as shown below.

```
PRINT *, 'ENTER THE % SALARY INCREASE RANGE:'
READ *, PERLOW, PERHIG
PRINT *, 'ENTER THE % OF SALARY SAVED:'
READ *, PERSAV
PRINT *, 'ENTER THE % INTEREST ON SAVINGS:'
READ *, PERINT
PRINT *, 'ENTER THE RANDOM NUMBER SEED:'
READ *, SEED
```

With respect to the percentage salary increase, perinc, the following statements will perform the required calculation.

```
CALL RANDOM(SEED,U)
PERINC = U*(PERHIG - PERLOW) + PERLOW
```

These changes are incorporated into the program of Figure 17.8.   The output of this program using two different random number seeds is shown in Figure 17.9.   While the absolute results differ, both sets of results show the same trend.   The time limit of 30 years smooths the effects of the random number generator somewhat.   Notice that for the data given, the salary increase varies from 6.5% to 12%, as requested.   However, despite this difference from the example in Chapter 16, the final amount saved, though larger, is a smaller multiple of the final salary.

17.6   Rolling a Die

As another simple example of probabilistic simulation consider the roll of a die.

Example 17.2   Single Die Problem
Develop a program to simulate rolls of a die.   Count the number of occurrences of each side.

a) Problem Discussion   For this problem the system being simulated is a six-sided die, and the state of the system is determined by which side of the die is facing upwards. The system has six possible states, one state for each side of the die, and a change in state depends upon the event of rolling the die.   Of course, this event also has six possible outcomes.   In particular, the outcomes are that the die may show the numbers 1, 2, 3, 4, 5, or 6 on any roll.   Assuming that the die is fair, each of these six outcomes has a probability 1/6 of occurring.   Note the similarity to the example of Section 17.4.2.   In order to keep track of the occurrences of each side, six counters must exist, the correct one being incremented after each roll.

```
C Figure 17.8 - Probabilistic Investment Problem.
C               Program to simulate the investment problem
C               involving the saving of a fixed percentage of
C               salary at a fixed interest rate while the salary
C               increases vary uniformly over a given range.
C**************************************************************************
C SALARY - the current salary
C SAVING - the current savings
C YEAR   - the current year of the simulation
C PERLOW - the lower bound for the percentage salary increase
C PERHIG - the upper bound for the percentage salary increase
C PERINC - the percentage increase in salary
C PERSAV - the percent of salary put into savings
C PERINT - the percentage interest earned on savings
C SEED   - the seed for the random number generator
C U      - uniformly distributed random number
C**************************************************************************
      REAL SALARY, SAVING, PERLOW, PERHIG, PERINC, PERSAV, PERINT
      REAL U
      INTEGER YEAR, MOD, SEED
C Obtain the simulation parameters.
      PRINT *, 'ENTER THE % SALARY INCREASE RANGE:'
      READ *, PERLOW, PERHIG
      PRINT *, 'ENTER THE % OF SALARY SAVED:'
      READ *, PERSAV
      PRINT *, 'ENTER THE % INTEREST ON SAVINGS:'
      READ *, PERINT
      PRINT *, 'ENTER THE RANDOM NUMBER SEED:'
      READ *, SEED
C Obtain the initial conditions.
      PRINT *, 'ENTER THE INITIAL SALARY AND SAVINGS:'
      READ *, SALARY, SAVING
      YEAR = 0
      PERINC = 0.0
      PRINT *, ' '
      PRINT *, '        YEAR    INCREASE        SALARY        SAVINGS'
      PRINT *, ' '
      PRINT *, YEAR, PERINC, SALARY, SAVING
C Simulate the system for 30 years, tabulating
C the state at 5 year intervals.
      DO 100 YEAR = 1, 30
C         Calculate the increase in savings.
          SAVING = SAVING + (PERINT*SAVING + PERSAV*SALARY)/100
C         Calculate the percentage increase in salary.
          CALL RANDOM(SEED,U)
          PERINC = U*(PERHIG - PERLOW) + PERLOW
          SALARY = SALARY + PERINC*SALARY/100.0
          IF (MOD(YEAR,5) .EQ. 0) THEN
              PRINT *, YEAR, PERINC, SALARY, SAVING
          ENDIF
  100 CONTINUE
      STOP
      END
```

Figure 17.9 Output from the investment program of Figure 17.8 using two different random
number seeds.

a) First choice of seed:

```
ENTER THE % SALARY INCREASE RANGE:
6.5 12.0
ENTER THE % OF SALARY SAVED:
10.0
ENTER THE % INTEREST ON SAVINGS:
12.0
ENTER THE RANDOM NUMBER SEED:
9418537
ENTER THE INITIAL SALARY AND SAVINGS:
15000.0 0.0
```

YEAR	INCREASE	SALARY	SAVINGS
0	0.0000000E+00	15000.00	0.0000000E+00
5	8.419737	21862.18	10851.96
10	8.615856	34896.36	35686.60
15	10.14109	55812.82	89395.25
20	7.006038	85027.38	198885.1
25	10.97596	134545.0	413517.5
30	7.706339	196016.6	826066.4

b) Second choice of seed:

```
ENTER THE % SALARY INCREASE RANGE:
6.5 12.0
ENTER THE % OF SALARY SAVED:
10.0
ENTER THE % INTEREST ON SAVINGS:
12.0
ENTER THE RANDOM NUMBER SEED:
512527
ENTER THE INITIAL SALARY AND SAVINGS:
15000.0 0.0
```

YEAR	INCREASE	SALARY	SAVINGS
0	0.0000000E+00	15000.00	0.0000000E+00
5	6.683468	22696.77	11230.94
10	11.74834	36805.32	36938.53
15	9.946734	55297.77	92163.11
20	11.67349	91667.78	204736.3
25	8.415586	148682.0	431166.4
30	8.771918	227882.6	871482.6

b) Initial Decomposition   For this simulation, the general simulation model of
Figure 16.1 can be used as a starting point.   For this particular problem, however, it is
somewhat artificial to associate a time step with the intervals between rolls of the die.
Thus, the statement which increments the time will be omitted from the general form.
The result is shown in Figure 17.10.

Figure 17.10 Initial version of a pseudocode algorithm for the single die problem.

1. Obtain simulation parameters and initial states for rolling the die.

2. While termination criterion is not met

⎡ Change the state variables by rolling the die and record the state of the system.

3. Summarize the system behaviour.

4. stop

---

c) Refining Step **1.** For maximum generality, the number of rolls of the die and the seed are made simulation parameters and are obtained from a data list.

> * Obtain the number of rolls and the random number seed.
>
> **get** nrolls, seed
> **put** 'Number of rolls to be simulated is', nrolls
> **put** 'Random number seed is', seed

d) Refining Step **2.** The criterion for termination is that all the rolls of the die must have been completed. Rolling the die involves determining the side which is facing up and keeping track of the number of occurrences of each side. Counting the occurrences of each side may be done using a six-element array with the side numbers as the index of the array. This counter array must be initialized before the simulation starts.

> * Initialize the counters.
>
> **2.1.1 for i from 1 to 6 do**
>
> ⎡ **2.1.2** $count_i \leftarrow 0$
>
> * Roll the die and collect statistics.
>
> **2.2.1 for i from 1 to nrolls do**
>
> ⎡ **2.2.2** Roll the die and count the result.

e) Refining Step **2.2.2** The rolling of the die is simulated using the techniques of Section 17.4. A standard uniform variate is mapped onto the set of face numbers (1, 2, 3, 4, 5, 6) to determine which side is showing. This face number is then used as the index into the array COUNT.

> **call** random(seed; u)
> side $\leftarrow$ int(u * 6) + 1
> $count_{side} \leftarrow count_{side} + 1$

f) Refining Step **3.** The array COUNT contains the total occurrences for each face so it must be recorded. In order to make these statistics more readable, they are recorded on separate lines using a loop.

* Record the number of times each side occurred.

put 'The statistics on rolling the die are:'
for i **from** 1 **to** 6 **do**

> [**put** 'Side', i, 'occurred', count$_i$, 'times'

g) Program for the Final Version of the Algorithm Collecting all the refinements together and translating them to FORTRAN/77 gives the program shown in Figure 17.11. The output from the program is shown in Figure 17.12. As expected, the number of occurrences of each side is approximately the same. One should never expect these occurrences to be exactly the same. In fact, one would be suspicious if they were.

```
C Figure 17.11 - Single Die Problem.
C                 Program to count the number of occurrences of each
C                 side of a die when rolled a given number of times.
C********************************************************************
C NROLLS - number of rolls of the die to be simulated
C SEED   - seed for the random number generator
C COUNT  - table of 6 elements to count the number of times each
C          side occurs
C SIDE   - randomly chosen side of the die
C U      - uniformly distributed random number
C********************************************************************
      INTEGER NROLLS, SEED, I, COUNT(6), SIDE, IFIX
      REAL U
C Obtain the number of rolls and the random number seed.
      PRINT *, 'ENTER THE NUMBER OF ROLLS TO BE SIMULATED:'
      READ *, NROLLS
      PRINT *, 'ENTER THE RANDOM NUMBER SEED:'
      READ *, SEED
      PRINT *, ' '
C Initialize the side counters.
      DO 100 I = 1, 6
         COUNT(I) = 0
  100 CONTINUE
C Roll the die and count occurrences of each side.
      DO 200 I = 1, NROLLS
         CALL RANDOM(SEED,U)
         SIDE = IFIX(U * 6) + 1
         COUNT(SIDE) = COUNT(SIDE) + 1
  200 CONTINUE
C Record the number of times each side occurred.
      PRINT *, 'THE STATISTICS ON ROLLING THE DIE ARE:'
      PRINT *, ' '
      DO 300 I = 1, 6
         PRINT *, 'SIDE', I, 'OCCURRED', COUNT(I), 'TIMES'
  300 CONTINUE
      STOP
      END
```

Figure 17.12   Results of rolling a die, output from the program of Figure 17.11.

```
ENTER THE NUMBER OF ROLLS TO BE SIMULATED:
3000
ENTER THE RANDOM NUMBER SEED:
7498631

THE STATISTICS ON ROLLING THE DIE ARE:
SIDE            1 OCCURRED           501 TIMES
SIDE            2 OCCURRED           488 TIMES
SIDE            3 OCCURRED           501 TIMES
SIDE            4 OCCURRED           489 TIMES
SIDE            5 OCCURRED           514 TIMES
SIDE            6 OCCURRED           507 TIMES
```

17.7   Other Distributions

In the investigation of real-life phenomena it has been observed that not all systems may be modeled using the uniform variates. There are several other distributions which have been found necessary. The following sections describe some of these.

17.7.1   Generating Normally Distributed Variates

The normal or Gaussian distribution is one of the more commonly used distributions in stochastic modeling. The normal distribution has the shape illustrated in Figure 17.13.

Figure 17.13   The shape of the normal distribution.

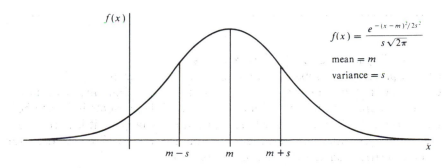

$$f(x) = \frac{e^{-(x-m)^2/2s^2}}{s\sqrt{2\pi}}$$

mean $= m$

variance $= s$

The generation of normally distributed random variates is given by the following equation. Note that it is necessary to generate several standard uniform variates, in this case 12, to obtain one normally distributed variate.

$$x = \left[\sum_{i=1}^{12} u_i - 6 \right] \times s + m$$

Thus, it is necessary to supply a mean and standard deviation for use in the generation of the normal variates. A FORTRAN/77 subroutine to generate normally distributed variates using the above technique is shown in Figure 17.14.

```
C Figure 17.14 -- A Normally Distributed Random Number Module.
C                 Subroutine NORMAL to generate normally distributed
C                 random numbers with a desired mean and standard
C                 deviation.

C***********************************************************************
C SEED    - seed for random procedure
C MEAN    - desired mean
C STDEV   - desired standard deviation
C XN      - generated normally distributed random number
C U       - uniformly distributed random number
C SUM     - sum of the random numbers

C***********************************************************************
        SUBROUTINE NORMAL(SEED,MEAN,STDEV,XN)

        REAL MEAN, STDEV, XN, U, SUM
        INTEGER SEED, I

        SUM = 0.0
        DO 100 I = 1, 12
           CALL RANDOM(SEED,U)
           SUM = SUM + U
  100   CONTINUE

        XN = MEAN + (SUM - 6)*STDEV
        RETURN
        END
```

17.7.2 Generating Exponentially Distributed Variates

If, in a stochastic process, the probability that an event will occur in a small time interval is quite small and if the occurrence of an event is statistically independent of other events, then the time interval between occurrences of these events is said to be exponentially distributed. Thus, in order to simulate these processes, it is necessary to generate random variates with an exponential distribution. Figure 17.15 shows a graph of the exponential distribution and the position of its mean.

The mapping of the standard uniform variates into the exponential distribution is given by

$$x = -m \times \log_e(u_i)$$

Thus, it is necessary to supply a mean and only one uniform random number for generating exponentially distributed random numbers. The FORTRAN/77 subroutine of Figure 17.16 performs the above computation.

Figure 17.15   The shape of the exponential distribution.

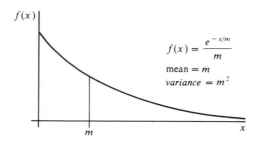

$$f(x) = \frac{e^{-x/m}}{m}$$

$$\text{mean} = m$$

$$variance = m^2$$

```
C Figure 17.16 -- An Exponentially Distributed Random Number Module.
C                   Subroutine EXPON to generate exponentially
C                   distributed random numbers with a desired mean.

C*******************************************************************************
C N       - seed for the uniformly distributed random number generator
C U       - uniformly distributed random number
C MEAN    - desired mean for the exponentially distributed random numbers
C E       - the exponentially distributed random number

C*******************************************************************************
      SUBROUTINE EXPON(N,MEAN,E)

      REAL MEAN, E, ALOG, U
      INTEGER N

      CALL RANDOM(N,U)
      E = -MEAN * ALOG(U)
      RETURN
      END
```

17.7.3   Generating Poisson Distributed Variates

The Poisson distribution is a discrete distribution related to the exponential distribution and is concerned with predicting the total number of events which will occur in a given time interval, if the time between events is exponentially distributed. The Poisson distribution function is shown in Figure 17.17. Note that the ordinate $f(n)$ gives the probability that a particular integer variate n occurs. The generation of a Poisson variate n is done by forming the products of successive standard uniform variates until the following relationship holds.

$$\prod_{i=0}^{n} u_i > e^{-m} > \prod_{i=0}^{n+1} u_i$$

In this case, just the mean must be provided for the calculation. The FORTRAN/77 subroutine of Figure 17.18 calculates Poisson variates.

Figure 17.17 Two Poisson distributions with different mean values.

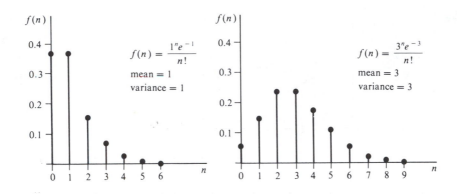

```
C Figure 17.18 -- A Poisson Distributed Random Number Module.
C                  Subroutine POISSN to generate random numbers which
C                  have a Poisson Distribution with a desired mean.

C***********************************************************************
C N      - seed for the uniformly distributed random number
C          generator
C MEAN   - desired mean for the Poisson variates
C P      - Poisson distributed random number
C PROD   - product of uniformly distributed random numbers
C U      - uniformly distributed random number

C***********************************************************************
        SUBROUTINE POISSN(N,MEAN,P)

        REAL MEAN, PROD, U, B, EXP
        INTEGER N, P

        P = 0.0
        B = EXP(-MEAN)
        PROD = 1.0
        CALL RANDOM(N,U)
        PROD = PROD * U
  100 IF (PROD .GE. B) THEN
            CALL RANDOM(N,U)
            PROD = PROD * U
            P = P + 1.0
            GOTO 100
        ENDIF
        RETURN
        END
```

17.8   Queuing Systems

Waiting in a line or queue has become almost a daily experience for everybody.   One waits in line for the teller's window in a bank, for the gas pumps in a gas station, for the cashiers in a grocery store, for food and the cashiers in a cafeteria, and especially at student registration time.   In industry, one may have queues of items awaiting assembly, or a queue may exist for the services of a forklift truck or an overhead crane.   Queues also exist in computer systems where many programs are waiting to be read in, waiting for execution, or waiting to be printed.   These are but a few examples.

The motivation for waiting in a queue is that a common service or action is required by many persons or things.   Thus, the basic elements of queuing systems are *servers* and *queues*. The server performs some service and the queue provides an ordering for those things awaiting service.   A queuing system will usually have *arrivals* and *departures*. Arrivals enter the queuing system for service and departures leave the queuing system hopefully, but not necessarily, having been serviced.

There are many possible organizations for queuing systems.   It is possible for queuing systems to have one or more servers and one or more queues.   The diagram of Figure 17.19 illustrates several simple possibilities.   In examples a) and b) the arrivals to the system enter into the single queue.   Queuing systems often consist of many single-server single-queue systems in which case an arrival must make a decision as to which queue is to be entered.   The organization and rules governing the operation of such queuing systems is called the *queuing strategy*.

Figure 17.19   Simple examples of possible queuing organizations.

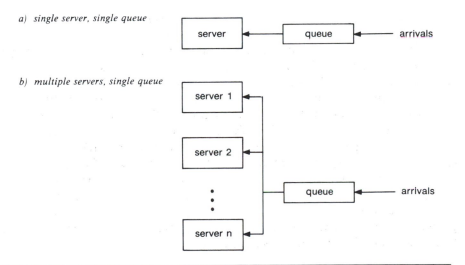

In most queuing systems there is a desire to obtain a cost effective means of providing service.   The objectives in providing the actual service are somewhat contradictory. It is desired that:

1)   the server(s) be as highly utilized as possible and the number of servers be kept to a minimum,

2)   the average waiting time be kept within a reasonable limit.

The utilization of the servers has a direct influence on the cost of providing the service. An acceptable average waiting time is sometimes determined by potential customer irritation (indeed a difficult thing to predict) and in other systems, such as in industry, may be determined by the fact that some processes need service within a specified time to prevent production losses.

To simulate such systems one needs to determine which of the numerous possible parameters have an influence on the operation of the system, specifically at the level on which it is to be simulated.   The minimum information needed is the number of servers and queues, the number of events and how they affect the system, and the distributions of arrival times and expected service times.   The following section gives an example of a simple queuing system.

17.8.1   Simulation of a Single-Pump Gas Station
As a first example of a queuing system consider the gas station problem stated below.

Example 17.3   Single-Pump Gas Station Problem
>   Simulate a gas station which has one gas pump and one queue. Assume that from observations made during an overload period, the arrivals to the system are uniformly distributed with an average of 15 cars arriving per hour and that the service time is constant at 5 minutes.   Statistics are to be gathered about the maximum and average queue lengths.

a) Problem Discussion   Although this problem as stated represents a simplification of a real gas station both in terms of the queuing strategies and the statistics requested, it can illustrate some important concepts.   The arrival and service times clearly indicate that the gas station will be overloaded as there will be 15 cars arriving but only 12 cars being serviced during the one-hour period.   The purpose of the simulation might be to study the behavior of the waiting queue during such an overload period.

Since the arrivals to the system are uniformly distributed at a rate of 15 cars per hour, this means that one car will arrive approximately every 4 minutes.   Thus, in a one-minute time period, there is a 0.25 probability of a car arriving, and the techniques of the section on mapping of uniform variates may be used.   The generation of service times in this problem is easy since it is a fixed value, namely 5 minutes.

The state of the gas pump will be described by the amount of time remaining to serve the current car.   The statistics concerning the average queue length must be gathered by summing the queue lengths at every time step.   The maximum queue length must also be checked at every time step.

b) Selection of an Initial Decomposition   Since in this problem there is just one simulation to be performed on the gas station, the general simulation model of Figure 16.1 may be used, as shown in Figure 17.20.

Figure 17.20   Initial version of a pseudocode algorithm for the single-pump gas station problem.

1.   Obtain simulation parameters and initial states for the gas station.

2.   While termination criterion is not met

> time ← time + tstep
>
> Change the state variables of the gas station.

3.   Summarize the queue behavior at the gas station.

4.   stop

---

c) Refining Step **1.**   The simulation parameters necessary for this problem include the simulation time step, the time limit, the service time, the arrival probability, and the seed for the random number generator.   These values may be obtained as input data.

> * Obtain the simulation parameters for the gas station.
>
> **get** tstep, tlimit, prarr, stime, seed
> **put** 'The time step is', tstep
> **put** 'The time limit is', tlimit
> **put** 'The probability of arrival is', prarr
> **put** 'The service time is', stime
> **put** 'The random number seed is', seed
> **1.2** Initialize the simulation state variables.

The initial states for the gas station will be determined as the state variables are more clearly defined.   At this stage of development, the only known state variable is time which is initialized to zero.   Step **1.2** will be supplied later when all state variables are known.

d) Refining Step **2.**   During each time interval it is necessary to modify the system state variables.   This requires a check for possible arrivals to the system, a check for the status of the pump, and the collection of queue length statistics during each time interval.   The system should terminate when the time limit is exceeded.   The following pseudocode refinement does this.

> * Change the state variables of the gas station.
>
> **2.1 while** time < tlimit **do**
>
> > **2.2** time ← time + tstep
> > **2.3** Check for arrivals to the system.
> > **2.4** Check the status of the pump.
> > **2.5** Collect the queue length statistics.

e) Refining Step **2.3**   If one knows that the probability of a car arriving in one minute is some value prarr, then as long as the simulation time step is fixed at one minute, this probability may be checked against a standard uniform variate.   However, if the simulation time step were to be reduced to a fraction of a minute, then the probability must be similarly adjusted.   This may be done by generating a standard uniform variate and considering an arrival to occur if the random number is less than prarr*tstep. The queue length may be maintained as a counter called queue. The initial value of queue will be zero, and this assignment should be provided in Step **1.2**.

> * Check for arrivals to the system and add them to queue.
>
> random(seed; u)
> **if** u < prarr*tstep **then**
> $\Big\lceil$ queue ← queue + 1

f) Refining Step **2.4**   On each time step the pump must be checked to see whether it is busy or free. If it is busy, then the service time remaining can be decremented by one time step and a check performed as to whether the car has finished service. Since the pump may become free during a time step, a separate check must be made again as to whether it is free or not. If the pump is free and the queue is not empty, a car is taken from the queue and placed at the pump.

> **2.4.1** If the pump is busy then
> $\Big\lceil$ Decrement the service time remaining and check if the car is finished.
> **2.4.2** If the pump is free and the queue is not empty then
> $\Big\lceil$ Take a car out of the queue, assign it a service time, and place it at the pump.

g) Refining Step **2.4.1**   The pump status and the service time remaining can be deduced from the same variable, tpump. If the pump is free, then the service time must be zero. If the pump is busy, then tpump is the service time remaining. When the pump is busy, the service time remaining must be decremented each time step by an amount of time equal to the time step. Subtracting the time step may result in a negative value for tpump which indicates that the service has been completed and the pump is now free. This state variable tpump must be initialized to zero in Step **1.2**.

> * If the pump is busy, decrement the service time remaining
> * and check if the car is finished.
>
> **if** tpump > 0 **then**
> $\Bigg\lceil$ tpump ← tpump − tstep
>   **if** tpump < 0 **then**
> $\Big\lceil$ tpump ← 0

h) Refining Step **2.4.2**   When the pump is free and there are cars in the queue, it is necessary to take a car from the queue (just decrement the counter queue), assign it the service time, and place the car at the pump. This may be done as follows.

* If the pump is free and the queue is not empty, take a car out
* of the queue, and assign it a service time.

if tpump = 0 **and** queue ≠ 0 **then**

> queue ← queue − 1
> tpump ← stime

i) Refining Step **2.5**   In order to determine the average queue length, it is necessary to sum the queue lengths at the end of each time interval.   The sum is accumulated in a variable totque, which must be initialized to zero in Step **1.2**.   The maximum queue length will be remembered in the variable maxque which may be initialized to zero.

* Collect the queue statistics.

totque ← totque + queue
if maxque < queue **then**

> maxque ← queue

j) Refining Step **3.**   The calculation of the average queue length is accomplished by dividing the sum of the queue lengths in each time interval by the total number of time intervals

* Summarize the queue behavior at the gas station.

avgque ← totque / (tlimit/tstep)
put 'The average queue length was', avgque
put 'The maximum queue length was', maxque

k) Backtracking to Refine Step **1.2**   The initialization of the state variables must still be refined.   The variables, queue, totque, maxque, tpump, and of course, time represent the state of the gas station at each time step.   These are initialized as follows:

* Initialize the simulation state variables.

queue ← 0
totque ← 0
maxque ← 0
tpump ← 0
time ← 0

l) Program for the Final Version of the Algorithm   Putting all the refinements together gives the FORTRAN/77 program in Figure 17.21.   A statement which prints out the state of the system at each time step has been inserted into the program.   A variable ARRIVE was introduced to remember how many arrivals occurred during each time step.   This printed information allows some insight into the operation of the gas station.

The output of the program given in Figure 17.22 shows a simulation of the gas station over a 60-minute time period with a one-minute time step.   The arrival rate of 15 cars per hour was used, giving the probability of arrival as 0.25.   The record of arrivals and service time demonstrate the random behavior of the simulation with idle periods and bunches of arrivals both occurring.   As may be seen from the queue length, the gas station was barely able to keep up with the number of cars arriving.   The average queue length was about 1.9 with the number of cars waiting fluctuating from 1 to a maximum of 4. At least in the first hour the expected buildup in the queue did not materialize. However, when the length of the simulation is extended to two hours and the seed is changed to 7421263 the queue grows in length to an average of 2.8 and a maximum of 7.

In a real-life situation the length of the queue would probably deter many customers from arriving. Thus, the effective arrival rate of cars to the system would drop, and the queue would probably stabilize at some reasonable length. This sort of situation could also be simulated by making the model more sophisticated.

```
C Figure 17.21 - Single-Pump Gas Station Problem.
C                 Simulate a single-queue, single-pump gas station
C                 and determine the maximum and average queue length
C                 during an overload period.
C*************************************************************************
C TIME      - the time expressed in minutes
C TSTEP     - the time increment expressed in minutes
C TLIMIT    - the time limit expressed in minutes
C TPUMP     - the service time in minutes that a car has left
C QUEUE     - the number of cars in the queue
C TOTQUE    - the totals of the queue lengths
C AVEQUE    - the average queue length
C MAXQUE    - the maximum queue length
C U         - uniformly distributed random number
C PRARR     - the probability of a car arriving in any minute
C ARRIVE    - number of cars arrived in a minute
C STIME     - the service time
C SEED      - starting value for the random number generator
C*************************************************************************
      INTEGER QUEUE, MAXQUE, TOTQUE, ARRIVE, SEED
      REAL TIME, TSTEP, TLIMIT, TPUMP, AVEQUE, PRARR, STIME, U
C Obtain the simulation parameters for the filling station.
      PRINT *, 'ENTER THE TIME STEP:'
      READ *, TSTEP
      PRINT *, 'ENTER THE TIME LIMIT:'
      READ *, TLIMIT
      PRINT *, 'ENTER THE PROBABILITY OF ARRIVAL:'
      READ *, PRARR
      PRINT *, 'ENTER THE SERVICE TIME:'
      READ *, STIME
      PRINT *, 'ENTER THE RANDOM NUMBER SEED:'
      READ *, SEED
      PRINT *, ' '
      PRINT *, '      TIME         ARRIVALS      QUEUE   TIME LEFT'
      PRINT *, ' '
C Initialize the simulation state variables.
      QUEUE = 0
      TOTQUE = 0
      MAXQUE = 0
      TPUMP = 0.0
      TIME = 0.0
```

```
C Figure 17.21 (continued)
C Continue the simulation for TLIMIT minutes.
   100 IF (TIME .LT. TLIMIT) THEN
           TIME = TIME + TSTEP
C          Check for arrivals to the system and add them to the queue.
           ARRIVE = 0
           CALL RANDOM(SEED,U)
           IF (U .LT. PRARR*TSTEP) THEN
              ARRIVE = 1
           ENDIF
           QUEUE = QUEUE + ARRIVE
C          If the pump is busy, decrement the service time remaining
C          and check if the car is finished.
           IF (TPUMP .GT. 0.0) THEN
               TPUMP = TPUMP - TSTEP
               IF (TPUMP .LT. 0.0) THEN
               TPUMP = 0.0
               ENDIF
           ENDIF
C          If a pump is free and the queue is not empty, then take a car
C          out of the queue and assign it a service time.
           IF (TPUMP .EQ. 0.0 .AND. QUEUE .NE. 0) THEN
               QUEUE = QUEUE - 1
               TPUMP = STIME
           ENDIF
C          Collect the queue statistics.
           TOTQUE = TOTQUE + QUEUE
           IF (MAXQUE .LE. QUEUE) THEN
              MAXQUE = QUEUE
           ENDIF
           PRINT *, TIME, ARRIVE, QUEUE, TPUMP
           GOTO 100
       ENDIF
C Calculate the average queue length and record queue statistics.
       AVEQUE = TOTQUE / (TLIMIT/TSTEP)
       PRINT *, ' '
       PRINT *, 'THE AVERAGE QUEUE LENGTH WAS ', AVEQUE
       PRINT *, 'THE MAXIMUM QUEUE LENGTH WAS ', MAXQUE
       STOP
       END
```

Figure 17.22   Output from the single-pump gas station program of Figure 17.21.

```
ENTER THE TIME STEP:
1.0
ENTER THE TIME LIMIT:
60.0
ENTER THE PROBABILITY OF ARRIVAL:
0.25
ENTER THE SERVICE TIME:
5.0
ENTER THE RANDOM NUMBER SEED:
7948317
```

TIME	ARRIVALS	QUEUE	TIME LEFT
1.000000	1	0	5.000000
2.000000	1	1	4.000000
3.000000	0	1	3.000000
4.000000	0	1	2.000000
5.000000	1	2	1.000000
6.000000	0	1	5.000000
7.000000	0	1	4.000000
8.000000	0	1	3.000000
9.000000	1	2	2.000000
10.00000	0	2	1.000000
11.00000	0	1	5.000000
12.00000	0	1	4.000000
13.00000	0	1	3.000000
14.00000	1	2	2.000000
15.00000	1	3	1.000000
16.00000	1	3	5.000000
17.00000	0	3	4.000000
18.00000	0	3	3.000000
19.00000	1	4	2.000000
20.00000	0	4	1.000000
21.00000	0	3	5.000000
22.00000	0	3	4.000000
23.00000	0	3	3.000000
24.00000	0	3	2.000000
25.00000	0	3	1.000000
.	.	.	.
.	.	.	.
.	.	.	.
46.00000	0	1	5.000000
47.00000	0	1	4.000000
48.00000	1	2	3.000000
49.00000	1	3	2.000000
50.00000	0	3	1.000000
51.00000	0	2	5.000000
52.00000	0	2	4.000000
53.00000	0	2	3.000000
54.00000	0	2	2.000000
55.00000	0	2	1.000000
56.00000	0	1	5.000000
57.00000	0	1	4.000000
58.00000	1	2	3.000000
59.00000	0	2	2.000000
60.00000	0	2	1.000000

```
THE AVERAGE QUEUE LENGTH WAS     1.883333
THE MAXIMUM QUEUE LENGTH WAS            4
```

17.9   Simulation of a Multiple-Pump Gas Station

The previous gas station model contained many simplifications concerning the number of pumps (one), the distribution of arrivals (uniform), and the service time (constant). In spite of these, the model does illustrate the concepts and general structure of a queuing problem. Extensions to that model may be incorporated relatively easily in the simulation program. Consider the following extension to that problem.

Example 17.4   Multiple-Pump Gas Station Problem
Develop a program to simulate a multiple-pump, single-queue gas station in which the arrivals have a Poisson distribution and the service time depends upon the number of liters of gas required by a car. The number of liters required is normally distributed.

a) Problem Discussion   If the multiple pumps are to be incorporated, the actions on each pump will be identical to that of the single pump example. The program would probably best simulate multiple pumps with an array for the service time remaining on each pump. The changes required for the new arrivals and service time distributions will just replace the previous calculations.

b) Changes to the Single-Pump Gas Station Program   In order to generate Poisson arrivals, it is necessary to have a seed and a mean. Note that the mean is the expected number of arrivals in the chosen time interval. The number of liters calculation requires another seed and the mean and standard deviation of that distribution. Variables for these quantities must be declared and values obtained for them.

To gain some confidence and insight into the use of distributions for these quantities, statistics on the number of arrivals and the average service times have been included in the program design.

To handle multiple pumps, it is necessary to be able to store the service time left for the car at each pump. For this problem it has been assumed that the number of pumps is a simulation parameter and may have a maximum value of 10. The following FORTRAN/77 program segment shows the changes to the program of Figure 17.21 necessary to declare and obtain the simulation parameters.

```
      INTEGER NPUMPS, QUEUE, MAXQUE, ARRIVE, TOTQUE
      INTEGER PSEED, NSEED, I
      REAL TIME, TSTEP, TLIMIT, AVGLIT, STDLIT, LITERS, TPUMP(10)
      REAL TOTSERV, AVGSERV, AVGQUE, ARRPR

C Obtain the simulation parameters for the filling station.

      PRINT *, 'ENTER THE TIME STEP:'
      READ *, TSTEP
      PRINT *, 'ENTER THE TIME LIMIT:'
      READ *, TLIMIT
      PRINT *, 'ENTER THE NUMBER OF PUMPS TO BE SIMULATED:'
      READ *, NPUMPS
      PRINT *, 'ENTER THE EXPECTED ARRIVAL RATE:'
      READ *, ARRPR
      PRINT *, 'ENTER THE POISSON GENERATOR SEED:'
      READ *, PSEED
      PRINT *, 'ENTER THE AVERAGE LITERS PUMPED:'
      READ *, AVGLIT
      PRINT *, 'ENTER THE STANDARD DEVIATION:'
      READ *, STDLIT
      PRINT *, 'ENTER THE NORMAL GENERATOR SEED:'
      READ *, NSEED
```

The initialization of the service time array now requires a loop to zero the service time of each pump as follows:

```
      DO 100 I = 1, NPUMPS
         TPUMP(I) = 0.0
  100 CONTINUE
```

The arrivals to the system are generated using the Poisson random number generator poisson described earlier. It is only necessary to supply the expected value to the procedure and add the generated number of arrivals to the queue.

```
      CALL POISSN(PSEED,ARRPR*TSTEP,ARRIVE)
      QUEUE = QUEUE + ARRIVE
```

The number of liters required by each car is generated by supplying the normal random number generator normal with the mean and standard deviation for the desired service distribution. It is assumed that the service time is composed of a constant term of 1 minute and a term of 1/10 minute per liter pumped.

```
      CALL NORMAL(NSEED,AVGLIT,STDLIT,LITERS)
      TPUMP(I) = 1.0 + 0.1*LITERS
```

In order to check the status of each pump, the statements which perform this checking must be placed in a loop. This change and all the changes above are shown, together with the additional statistics collection for the number of arrivals and average service times, in the complete program of Figure 17.23.

```
C Figure 17.23 - Multiple-Pump Gas Station Problem.
C                 Simulate a multiple-pump gas station with a given
C                 number of pumps and a single queue. Arrivals are
C                 Poisson and service times are normally distributed.

C**********************************************************************

C TIME      - current time expressed in minutes
C TSTEP     - time increment expressed in minutes
C TLIMIT    - simulation time limit expressed in minutes
C AVGLIT    - mean number of liters of gas requested
C STDLIT    - standard deviation in number of liters
C LITERS    - number of liters of gas to be pumped
C TPUMP(I)  - service time left for car at each pump
C NPUMPS    - number of pumps given for this model
C TOTSER    - total service time for all cars
C AVGSER    - average service time
C QUEUE     - number of cars waiting in the queue
C TOTQUE    - total number of cars in queue
C MAXQUE    - maximum number of cars in queue
C AVEQUE    - average number of cars in queue
C ARRPR     - Poisson mean number of arrivals/minute
C ARRIVE    - number of cars arrived in a minute
C TOTARR    - total number of cars arrived
C NSEED     - seed for the normal random number generator
C PSEED     - seed for the Poisson random number generator
C I         - loop counter

C**********************************************************************

      INTEGER NPUMPS, QUEUE, MAXQUE, ARRIVE, TOTQUE
      INTEGER PSEED, NSEED, I
      REAL TIME, TSTEP, TLIMIT, AVGLIT, STDLIT, LITERS, TPUMP(10)
      REAL TOTSER, AVGSER, AVGQUE, ARRPR
C Obtain the simulation parameters for the filling station.
      PRINT *, 'ENTER THE TIME STEP:'
      READ *, TSTEP
      PRINT *, 'ENTER THE TIME LIMIT:'
      READ *, TLIMIT
      PRINT *, 'ENTER THE NUMBER OF PUMPS TO BE SIMULATED:'
      READ *, NPUMPS
      PRINT *, 'ENTER THE EXPECTED ARRIVAL RATE:'
      READ *, ARRPR
      PRINT *, 'ENTER THE POISSON GENERATOR SEED:'
      READ *, PSEED
      PRINT *, 'ENTER THE AVERAGE LITERS PUMPED:'
      READ *, AVGLIT
      PRINT *, 'ENTER THE STANDARD DEVIATION:'
      READ *, STDLIT
      PRINT *, 'ENTER THE NORMAL GENERATOR SEED:'
      READ *, NSEED
      PRINT *, ' '
      PRINT *, '      TIME          ARRIVE      QUEUE   SERVICE TIME',
     +         'AT EACH PUMP'
      PRINT *, ' '

      QUEUE = 0
      TOTQUE = 0
      MAXQUE = 0
      TOTSER = 0
      TOTARR = 0
      TIME = 0
```

```
C Figure 17.23 (continued)
C Initialize the pump time parameters.
      DO 100 I = 1, NPUMPS
         TPUMP(I) = 0.0
  100 CONTINUE
C Continue the simulation for TLIMIT minutes.
  200 IF (TIME .LT. TLIMIT) THEN
         TIME = TIME + TSTEP
C        Randomly select how many cars arrive during this time
C        step and add them to the queue.
         CALL POISSN(PSEED,ARRPR*TSTEP,ARRIVE)
         QUEUE = QUEUE + ARRIVE
         TOTARR = TOTARR + ARRIVE
C        Check each pump to see if it is still busy this time step.
         DO 300 I = 1, NPUMPS
C           If the pump is busy, decrement the service time left,
C           and if finished, set time to zero.
            IF (TPUMP(I) .GT. 0.0) THEN
               TPUMP(I) = TPUMP(I) - TSTEP
               IF (TPUMP(I) .LT. 0.0) THEN
                  TPUMP(I) = 0.0
               ENDIF
            ENDIF
C           If this pump is free and the queue is non-empty, take a
C           car from the queue and compute the service time based on
C           the number of liters to be pumped.
            IF (TPUMP(I) .EQ. 0.0 .AND. QUEUE .NE. 0) THEN
               QUEUE = QUEUE - 1
               CALL NORMAL(NSEED,AVGLIT,STDLIT,LITERS)
               TPUMP(I) = 1.0 + 0.1*LITERS
               TOTSER = TOTSER + TPUMP(I)
            ENDIF
  300    CONTINUE
C        Collect the queue statistics.
         TOTQUE = TOTQUE + QUEUE
         IF (MAXQUE .LT. QUEUE) THEN
            MAXQUE = QUEUE
         ENDIF
         PRINT *, TIME, ARRIVE, QUEUE, (TPUMP(I), I = 1, NPUMPS)
         GOTO 200
      ENDIF
C Summarize the queue behaviour at the station.
      AVEQUE = TOTQUE / (TLIMIT/TSTEP)
      PRINT *, ' '
      PRINT *, 'THE AVERAGE QUEUE LENGTH WAS ', AVEQUE
      PRINT *, 'THE MAXIMUM QUEUE LENGTH WAS ', MAXQUE
      AVGSER = TOTSER / (TOTARR - QUEUE)
      PRINT *, 'THE AVERAGE SERVICE TIME WAS ', AVGSER
      PRINT *, 'THE NUMBER OF ARRIVALS WAS   ', TOTARR
      STOP
      END
```

The output from this program is given in Figure 17.24 for a gas station with 3 gas pumps. Again the simulation was over a 60-minute period, but with a higher probability of arrival corresponding to 30 cars per hour. The normally distributed gas requirements have a mean of 40 liters and a standard deviation of 10 liters. Thus, the service time would have a mean of 5 minutes as before.

As may be seen from the record of the simulation activity and the summary statistics at the end of the output, the three gas pumps were sufficient to handle this demand. While the simulation took several time steps to get its first arrival, several multiple arrivals of two cars in the same time step occurred, with even three cars arriving at once. The average service time was very close to the expected mean of 5 and the number of arrivals was quite close to the expected number of 30. Different results with different random number seeds should be anticipated but all within reasonable bounds of the expected means.

17.10   Summary

A simulation of a probabilistic system has many similarities with a deterministic simulation, the major difference being that a probabilistic system selects which of its next possible states to enter in a random manner. This randomness is controlled according to the characteristics of the individual systems.

17.11   References

Forsythe, G.E.; Malcolm, M.A.; and Moler, C.B.   *Computer Methods for Mathematical Computations.* Englewood Cliffs, N.J.: Prentice-Hall, 1977.

Knuth, D.E.   *The Art of Computer Programming,* Vol.2: *Semi-Numerical Algorithms.* Reading, Mass.: Addison-Wesley Publishing Co., 1969.

Naylor, T.H.; Balintfy, J.L.; Burdick, D.S; and Chu, K., *Computer Simulation Techniques.* New York: John Wiley and Sons, 1966.

RAND Corporation.   *A Million Random Digits with 100,000 Normal Deviates.* Glencoe, Ill.: The Free Press, 1955.

Shannon, R.E.   *Systems Simulation.* Englewood Cliffs, N.J.: Prentice-Hall, 1975.

Figure 17.24 Output from the multiple-pump gas station program of Figure 17.23.

```
ENTER THE TIME STEP:
1.0
ENTER THE TIME LIMIT:
60.0
ENTER THE NUMBER OF PUMPS TO BE SIMULATED:
3
ENTER THE EXPECTED ARRIVAL RATE:
0.6
ENTER THE POISSON GENERATOR SEED:
5347211
ENTER THE AVERAGE LITERS PUMPED:
40.0
ENTER THE STANDARD DEVIATION:
10.0
ENTER THE NORMAL GENERATOR SEED:
7421263
```

TIME	ARRIVE	QUEUE	SERVICE TIME AT EACH PUMP		
1.000000	0	0	0.0000000E+00	0.0000000E+00	0.0000000E+00
2.000000	0	0	0.0000000E+00	0.0000000E+00	0.0000000E+00
3.000000	0	0	0.0000000E+00	0.0000000E+00	0.0000000E+00
4.000000	1	0	4.979331	0.0000000E+00	0.0000000E+00
5.000000	0	0	3.979331	0.0000000E+00	0.0000000E+00
6.000000	0	0	2.979331	0.0000000E+00	0.0000000E+00
7.000000	0	0	1.979331	0.0000000E+00	0.0000000E+00
8.000000	1	0	0.9793305	4.301390	0.0000000E+00
9.000000	0	0	0.0000000E+00	3.301390	0.0000000E+00
10.00000	0	0	0.0000000E+00	2.301390	0.0000000E+00
11.00000	2	0	5.129200	1.301390	5.167133
12.00000	0	0	4.129200	0.3013897	4.167133
.	.	.	.	.	.
27.00000	2	1	1.261404	1.382586	2.618265
28.00000	2	3	0.2614036	0.3825860	1.618265
29.00000	1	2	3.108816	4.038772	0.6182652
30.00000	0	1	2.108816	3.038772	4.076767
31.00000	0	1	1.108816	2.038772	3.076767
32.00000	3	4	0.1088157	1.038772	2.076767
33.00000	0	3	4.307665	3.8771629E-02	1.076767
.	.	.	.	.	.
53.00000	0	4	1.666352	2.020765	3.116265
54.00000	0	4	0.6663518	1.020765	2.116265
55.00000	1	4	5.019773	2.0764828E-02	1.116265

```
THE AVERAGE QUEUE LENGTH WAS        1.600000
THE MAXIMUM QUEUE LENGTH WAS               6
THE AVERAGE SERVICE TIME WAS       4.707222
THE NUMBER OF ARRIVALS WAS         36.00000
```

17.12   Exercises

In most of the following exercises a program is requested to solve a specific problem. For each problem it is recommended that step-wise refinement be used in developing a pseudocode algorithm to solve the problem. This algorithm should then be translated into FORTRAN/77 and run on the computer. Where appropriate, the program should be tested with a variety of data sufficient to ensure that the program does what it is supposed to do.

17.1   a)   Locate information about random number generators available on your computing system. If none is available, construct a FORTRAN/77 procedure similar to that of Figure 17.2 to generate random numbers which are uniformly distributed in the range 0.0 to 1.0. The expected mean of these numbers is 0.5 with a standard deviation of 0.289.

   b)   Develop a FORTRAN/77 program which will plot the mean versus N, the number of random numbers being tested, for N = 1, 11, 21, . . . , 1001.

   c)   Develop a FORTRAN/77 program that, for a given seed, will calculate the mean and standard deviation for 5 consecutive groups of random numbers, each group containing 200 random numbers.

17.2   Develop a FORTRAN/77 program to compute the mean and standard deviation for random numbers generated according to the normal, exponential, and Poisson distributions. Compute the percentage difference between the calculated values and the expected values.

17.3   There are many ways available to test the "goodness" of a uniformly distributed, random number generator. Two of the simplest tests are described below.

   a)   Divide the range [0,1] into l equal classes. Generate n random numbers and count how many fall into each class. The class frequencies should be approximately the same and equal to n/l.

   b)   Count the number of upward runs (that is, sequential runs of random numbers in ascending order) of length k and count the number of downward runs (that is, sequential runs of random numbers in descending order) of length k. For each value of k the counts should be approximately the same.

   Develop and test FORTRAN/77 subroutines, one for each of a) and b), that will test the random numbers produced by the random number generator RANDOM.

17.4   The probability density function illustrates the shape of the curve for each random number distribution. Develop a program that will draw a curve corresponding to the histogram of the values generated by the uniform, normal, exponential, and Poisson distributed random numbers.

17.5   The game of ODDS and EVENS involves tossing 2 coins. The result of each toss may be either ODDS (that is, one HEAD and one TAIL) or EVENS (that is, two HEADS or two TAILS). Develop a program to simulate this game for 1000 tosses and determine the number of ODDS and EVENS that occur.

17.6   The following game is played by two people using coins. In each play of the game, each person *shows* one side of a coin (that is, either HEADS or TAILS). The payoff on each play is determined by the following rules.

Person 1	Person 2	result
HEADS	HEADS	person 2 pays person 1 $20
HEADS	TAILS	person 1 pays person 2 $30
TAILS	HEADS	person 1 pays person 2 $10
TAILS	TAILS	person 2 pays person 1 $20

a)   Assuming that there is an equal chance of each person choosing HEADS or TAILS the amount of money lost by either player should be approximately zero. Develop a program to simulate this game over 1000 plays.

b)   Assume that person 1 is a crafty individual who recognizes that if he can show TAILS more often than HEADS (without alerting person 2), he can minimize the amount of money he gives away (that is, he will give away $10 more often than $30 when he loses). Person 1 decides to show TAILS 5/8 of the time and HEADS 3/8 of the time. Develop a program to simulate 1000 plays of this game and determine the wins and losses. Compare these results to those of part a).

17.7   Assume that you are a passenger in a car driving down a highway. The driver of the car suggests a friendly wager which involves keeping track of the last two digits of the license plates of passing cars. He will bet you $10 that within the next twenty cars that pass, the same two digit number (00-99) will occur more than once. Develop a program that will simulate this game to determine whether or not you should have taken the bet. Perform the simulation 100 times and determine the amount of money you would have won or lost.

17.8   Jack Spratt's wife has introduced the following domestic procedure to reduce the amount of money they spend on meat. If Jack is served meat today, his wife randomly selects one ball from a box containing three black balls and one white ball. If the selected ball is white, he is served meat tomorrow; if the ball is black, he goes vegetarian. On the other hand, if Jack is a vegetarian today, she randomly chooses one ball from another box containing three black and two white balls. Again, a white ball signifies meat tomorrow and a black ball signifies no meat tomorrow. The rules are suspended on Fridays, when fish is served (and counted as meat).

Develop a program to simulate Jack's diet for one year, recording the number of vegetable and meat days. Start your simulation on a Friday.

17.9   The weather in a region is somewhat peculiar. According to the local weather office, the winter weather has the property that if it snows on one day, then the probability is 0.7 that it will snow the next day. If it does not snow on a certain day, then the probability is 0.2 that it will snow the next day.

Develop a program that will simulate the weather in this region over 150 days of winter and count the number of snowy days. Assume that the probability is 0.5 that it will snow on the first day of the simulation.

17.10   One of the authors has been coerced into reducing his smoking habits according to the following scheme.   Sixteen times a day, his wife will break one of his 100 millimeter filterless cigarettes into three distinct pieces.   If the author can form a triangle from the three pieces, he then smokes the pieces; otherwise he throws them away.

The author believes that his wife is deliberately attempting to break each cigarette in such a way as to prevent him from smoking the pieces.   Develop a program to check the validity of his suspicion.   The program should determine the number of cigarettes the author would be able to smoke if the cigarettes were broken in a random manner with the breaks distributed uniformly over the length of the cigarette.   Perform the simulation for a 100-day period.   *Ed. note: The scheme was marvellously successful.   He has quit smoking since the previous version of the book was published!*

17.11   Assume that the following diagram represents the street layout of a section of a city.

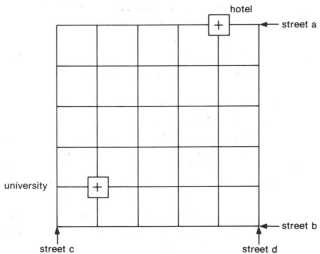

One evening two groups of students were out drinking at the hotel.   At closing time, both groups left the hotel to walk back to the university and realized that they had forgotten the way.   Thus, each group decided that in order to get back, they would adopt the following strategy.   To start they would choose a street at random and walk to the next intersection.   There they would again decide at random which street to choose next and walk one more block, and so on.   Fortunately, both groups were able to remember the main streets indicated and thus did not go beyond them.

Each group started off by itself, and immediately a difference in their strategy became apparent.   When group 1 reached an intersection, they could not remember which street they used to get there and thus had to choose their next direction from all streets leading into the intersection.   Group 2, however, was in a little better shape and could remember the street they just took and thus always took a different street from the intersection.

Develop a program that will simulate the above problem and determine which group gets to the university first. Perform several simulations varying the random number seed.

17.12   Consider a gas station which has only one pump. Cars arrive at an average rate of 20 per hour. The service time for a car is either one minute or ten minutes, with probabilities of 4/5 and 1/5 respectively. In order to optimize the service, the gas station owner has two queues for the single pump. A car requiring one minute of service enters the first queue, and other cars enter the second queue. The first queue is a priority queue, and whenever the pump becomes free a car from this queue has priority.

Develop a program which will simulate the operation of this gas station over a period of three hours. Determine the average number of cars in the queues.

17.13   A university has a computer on which student jobs are run. Students arrive at an average rate of 200 per hour and queue if necessary. When they reach the front of the queue, they hand their program to the operator. Student jobs are of two types. Type 1 jobs fail to run and these take 10 seconds. Type 2 jobs are jobs which run successfully and these take 20 seconds. On average, half the student jobs fail and half run successfully.

Develop a program to simulate this process for one hour using a five-second time step. Your program should print out the status of the system at the end of each time step and determine the time at which the computer is next free.

Determine the average queue length over the complete simulation.

17.14   A local supermarket is considering setting up a single cash register express checkout for all customers with eight items or less. By observation it has been determined that in any one-minute time period the probability is 0.3 that such a customer will arrive at the checkout. The service time for a customer is observed to be one minute half the time, two minutes a quarter of the time, and three minutes one quarter of the time.

Develop ε program which will simulate the operation of this express checkout lane for an 8-hour period with a one-minute time increment. Determine the maximum number of people in the queue.

17.15   A regular tetrahedron is a four-sided solid, with each side an equilateral triangle. A game is based on casting tetrahedra with sides numbered 1–4, four at a time and recording the spots facing down. Develop a FORTRAN/77 program to simulate the throwing of the set of tetrahedra 5000 times. Your program should list the relative frequencies of "four of a kind" (all spots the same) and "straight" (spots 1, 2, 3, 4 indicated).

17.16   The game of Yahtzee is a game involving five dice. On any round, a player is allowed to roll the dice a maximum of three times. Of course, all five dice are thrown the first time. On rolls two and three, the player may decide which and how many dice to roll again.

In a normal game, a player must try for each of about 12 different combinations of dice on successive rounds (for example, at least three ones, . . . , at least three sixes, four of a kind, five of a kind, full house, short straight, and long straight, etc.).

Develop a FORTRAN/77 program to simulate 100 rounds of Yahtzee (involving three rolls maximum per round) and to estimate the chances of obtaining

a)   all five dice the same
b)   four of any kind
c)   five of any kind
d)   a full house (2 of one number, 3 of another)
e)   a short straight (1, 2, 3, 4 or 2, 3, 4, 5 or 3, 4, 5, 6)
f)   a long straight (1, 2, 3, 4, 5 or 2, 3, 4, 5, 6)
g)   a complete set of:
   - five ones at least once
   - five twos at least once
   - five threes at least once
   - five fours at least once
   - five fives at least once
   - five sixes at least once.

17.17   A company wants to market one of its products by including a prize in each box. The prizes are to be uniformly distributed over all boxes to be packaged during the duration of the promotion scheme.

   The company wants to know how many unique prizes there should be to give a customer a reasonable chance to collect a complete set of prizes.

   Develop a FORTRAN/77 program to simulate collecting random prizes from a box and to determine the average number of boxes required in say 100 trials to collect a complete set of n prizes for $n = 2, 3, 4$ and 5.

17.18   In the game of Nim, any number of objects, for example, six matches, are arranged in three piles. Two players, Starch and Husky, draw in turn, each taking *any* number of matches from any *one* pile. Whoever takes the last match is the winner. For example, if six matches are placed in three piles containing one, two and three matches, and Starch draws first, the game could proceed as follows:

	1	2	3
Initial pile sizes:	1	2	3
After Starch's 1st turn	1	1	3
After Husky's 1st turn	1	1	0
After Starch's 2nd turn	1	0	0
After Husky's 2nd turn	0	0	0

Husky wins.
   Write a FORTRAN/77 program to play the game of Nim.

a)   Design two modules which will have their interfaces as follows:

```
SUBROUTINE STARCH(NPILE,IWIN)
SUBROUTINE HUSKY(NPILE,IWIN)
```

where NPILE is a one-dimensional array of length three which contains the current number of matches in each pile, and IWIN is a logical variable set by the module to .TRUE. if no matches remain (that is, that person wins the game), or .FALSE. if any matches remain. These modules will, when invoked, perform *one* turn for Starch and Husky respectively according to different strategies.

i)   Starch's playing strategy will be such that on each of her turns she removes only *one* match from the largest pile.

ii) Husky's playing strategy is to be determined by yourself. (Be sure to document, using comments, the strategy you are using.)

b) The program will use these modules to play the game of Nim for three piles. Your main program must:

1.   read in the initial pile sizes into a one-dimensional array of size three,

2.   play the game until someone wins, and

3.   print out the name of the winner and the number of the turn on which he or she won.

Run your program for several different pile sizes and check if the results vary depending upon who goes first. (If you think that the playing strategy you develop is good, test it against your friends.)

17.19   In ancient Rome, many gladiator contests were held in the Colosseum. One such contest could have been like the following. There is a line-up of gladiators waiting to fight tigers. There are seven doors. Four of them have hungry tigers behind them, and the other three have doves. The first gladiator in line chooses a door. If there is a tiger behind it, he is eaten alive and dies. The tiger is put back in his cage. But if he chooses a door with a dove, the man is set free, the dove is put back in his cage, and a tiger is killed. So now there is one less door to choose from; 3 have doves and 3 have tigers.

Men will keep on choosing doors until all the tigers are killed. After that, the men are kept as slaves.

Simulate this gladiator contest several times. How many men died and how many were set free in each contest?

Appendices

A   A Summary of Pseudocode Algorithms   *503*

B   Algorithms Expressed in Flowcharts   *511*

C   Translation of Pseudocode to FORTRAN/77   *519*

D   Summary of FORTRAN/77 Statements and Rules   *529*

E   Internal Representation of Data in FORTRAN/77   *587*

F   Formatted Input and Output   *595*

G   Character Manipulation   *619*

H   Manipulation of Logical Values   *631*

I   Manipulation of Extended-Precision Values   *639*

J   Manipulation of Complex Values   *649*

K   The Plotting Package   *657*

L   Data Files   *665*

M   Areas Under the Standard Normal Curve   *681*

N   Built-in FORTRAN/77 Functions   *683*

A
A Summary of Pseudocode Algorithms

An algorithm describes a sequence of operations which may be followed to solve a particular problem. Pseudocode is a language used to describe the individual steps of the algorithms in this text. This appendix briefly summarizes the pseudocode statements and their rules.

A.1 Constants

A constant is just a decimal number. For instance, the numbers 10, -5, 0, 846.94, -7.12, $.56 \times 10^{-3}$ are all constants.

A.2 Variables

A variable is simply a name which is used to represent or remember an integer or real value. The value represented by a variable may change, but a variable may have only one value at any given time. Variable names are written in lower-case characters. A variable is considered to be undefined until it has been given a value. A variable may not be used in a calculation until it has been assigned some value, that is, until it has been defined. As examples, the names sum, i, j, count, and price are all valid pseudocode variable names.

A.3 Arrays

An array is an indexed collection of numeric values. The name of the entire array is referenced by an upper-case name. Individual values or elements of the array are referenced by using the array name in lower-case followed by a subscript to indicate the position of the particular element in the array. Multidimensional arrays are defined in a similar fashion to follow standard mathematical notation. Examples are given in Figure A.1.

Figure A.1   Examples of references to an array and array elements.

X	- refers to an entire array of values which has the name X
x_1	- refers to the 1st element of the array X
x_2	- refers to the 2nd element of the array X
x_j	- refers to the jth element of the array X
$y_{k,l}$	- refers to the element in the k-th row and l-th column of array Y

A.4 Expressions

There are two types of expressions: arithmetic and logical.

a) Arithmetic Expressions   An *arithmetic* expression describes required arithmetic calculations. The result of such an expression is a single numeric value. The arithmetic operations have a priority to describe the order in which these operations are performed. If adjacent operations have the same priority, they are performed from left to right. A summary and some examples appear in Figure A.2.

Figure A.2   Arithmetic operators and arithmetic expressions.

arithmetic operators:	*	multiplication	higher priority
	/	division	.
			.
	+	addition	.
			.
	−	subtraction	lower priority
example:	$a^2 + b/c - d_i{*}2$		

---

b) Logical Expressions   A *logical* expression or *condition* is used for testing purposes and contains relational and logical operators. The result of a logical expression is either **true** or **false**. A relational operator tests the relationship between two arithmetic expressions. If the relation holds, then that relation has the logical value **true**; otherwise it has the logical value **false**. A logical operator performs Boolean logic on logical values.

The relational and logical operators, Boolean logic, and operator priority are all listed in Figure A.3 along with several examples.

Figure A.3   Operators and Boolean logic for logical expressions.

relational operators:		
	$=$	equal
	$\neq$	not equal
	$<$	less than
	$\leq$	less than or equal
	$>$	greater than
	$\geq$	greater than or equal

logical operators:			
	not	not	highest priority
	and	and	
	or	or	lowest priority

Boolean logic:

not false $\rightarrow$ **true**
not true $\rightarrow$ **false**

false and false $\rightarrow$ **false**
false and true $\rightarrow$ **false**
true and false $\rightarrow$ **false**
true and true $\rightarrow$ **true**

false or false $\rightarrow$ **false**
false or true $\rightarrow$ **true**
true or false $\rightarrow$ **true**
true or true $\rightarrow$ **true**

Priority between types of operations:
1. arithmetic operations (highest priority)
2. relational operations
3. logical operations (lowest priority)

examples:

$x \neq y$
$r < s$ **or** $r > t$
$(a+b \leq c^2-7)$ **and not** $(d \geq 5)$

The **and** and **or** logical operators are binary in that they require two operands, one on either side.   The **not** logical operator is unary because it needs only one operand placed to the right of it.

A.5   Assignment Statements

Assignment statements are used to assign the value of an expression to a variable or an array element.   The general form and an example are given in Figure A.4.   The expression to the right of the assignment operator ($\leftarrow$) is evaluated completely before the resultant value is assigned to the variable on the left-hand side (LHS).

Figure A.4   Assignment statements.

general form: variable $\leftarrow$ arithmetic expression

example: $r \leftarrow a^2 + b/c - d_i * 2$

A.6   The stop Statement

The **stop** statement is used to specify that execution of the algorithm is to terminate. Examples of this statement are shown in the following sections.

A.7   Comment Statements

Comment statements are used to provide an English description of a pseudocode algorithm.   Each such line starts with an * to distinguish it from the regular pseudocode statements (see Figure A.5).   A good algorithm includes comment lines to describe:

1)   A brief English description of what the algorithm does.
2)   A list of variables and their purpose in the algorithm.
3)   A running commentary about important aspects in the algorithm itself.

Figure A.5   Comment statements.

general form: * Comment information.

example: * Algorithm to calculate a simple expression.

$x \leftarrow 5$
$y \leftarrow x^3 + 5x^2 - 3.7x + 11$
put x, y
stop

A.8   The get Statement

These statements are used to obtain data values from a data list and to assign these values to the variables in the input list of the **get** statement.   The data list is usually shown following the last statement of the algorithm.   When executed, the **get** statement implies that the next data values in the data list are assigned to the values in the input list.   Values on the data list are not reused.   In the Figure A.6, x and y obtain the values 1 and 5.7 respectively.   Variable z receives the value 4, while d_1 and d_2 receive the values 3 and 6.

Figure A.6   The **get** statement.

general form: **get** input list

example: * Algorithm to illustrate the **get** statement.

get x, y
get z
get $(d_i, i \leftarrow 1$ to 2)
stop
1, 5.7, 4, 3, 6

A.9 The put Statement

A **put** statement is used to indicate when messages and values are to be recorded by the algorithm (see Figure A.7). When executed, the **put** statement implies that the values of the variables and the messages in the output list are to be recorded.

Figure A.7 The **put** statement.

general form: **put** output list

example: **put** 'The values are:', x, y

A.10 The while–do Statement

These statements are used to indicate that a group of statements is to be executed repeatedly while some condition is **true**. All statements enclosed by the large left bracket are repeated while the condition (logical expression) in the **while–do** statement has a value of **true**. When the condition is **false** the statement following the body of the **while**–loop is executed. The general form and an example appear in Figure A.8.

Figure A.8 The **while–do** statement.

general form:

    while condition **do**

$$\left[\text{ S - a sequence of statements to be repeated} \right.$$

example:

```
* This algorithm calculates the squares
* of the numbers from 1 to 10.
i ← 1
while i ≤ 10 do
    ⎡ j ← i * i
    ⎢ put i, j
    ⎣ i ← i + 1
stop
```

A.11 The for Statement

Many loop structures in algorithms require that the loop be repeated under control of a simple counter. Although this may be accomplished in a straightforward way using the **while–do** construction, it is considered to be worthwhile to have a special simple structure for this purpose, called the **for** statement. This statement is particularly useful when dealing with arrays. The general form and an example appear in Figure A.9. Note that when the step is 1, the clause **by 1** is often omitted.

Figure A.9   The **for** statement.

general form:
        for index **from** start **to** finish **by** step **do**

$$\left[\; \text{S - a sequence of statements to be repeated}\right.$$

example:
        * This algorithm assigns the squares
        * of the integers 1 to 10
        * to the elements of an array.
        for i **from** 1 **to** 10 **by** 1 **do**

$$\left[\; a_i \leftarrow i * i \right.$$

        stop

A.12   The if–then–else Statement

These statements are used to select alternate statements for execution depending on whether a condition is **true** or **false** (see Figure A.10).   Only one of the sequences S_1 or S_2 is executed.   After one of them is executed, the statement following the **if–then–else** is executed.   The **if–then–else** does not imply repetition.

Figure A.10   The **if–then–else** statement.

general form:
        if condition **then**

$$\left[\; S_1 \text{ - statements executed if ''condition'' is } \textbf{true}\right.$$

        else

$$\left[\; S_2 \text{ - statements executed if ''condition'' is } \textbf{false}\right.$$

example:
        if x $\leq$ 0.0 **then**

$$\left[\; z \leftarrow x + y \right.$$

        else

$$\left[\; z \leftarrow x - y \right.$$

Note: If S_2 is null, the **else** clause is left off, resulting in an **if–then** statement.

A.13   Modules

A module is used to contain a segment of pseudocode which is logically distinct in the task that it performs.   This allows for clean design of algorithms and allows a module to be executed from many different places.   There are two types of modules, a subroutine module and a function module.

a) Subroutine Modules   Subroutine modules are the more common type of module. The general form of definition and usage is shown in Figure A.11. An example involving the definition and use of a subroutine module is presented in Figure A.12.

Figure A.11   General form of a subroutine module.

definition:

           smodule name (**imports**: import parameters;
                      exports: export parameters)

           : S - statements executed when this module is referenced
           .

           end module

use:

           call name (import arguments; export arguments)

Figure A.12   Example of a subroutine module.

```
* Subroutine module to calculate m ← k*k.
smodule square (imports: k; exports: m)
m ← k * k
end module
* Use a subroutine module to square the numbers from 1 to 10.
i ← 1
while i ≤ 10 do
   ⌈  call square (i; j)
   |  put i, j
   ⌊  i ← i + 1
stop
```

---

b) Function Modules   Function modules are used when the single export from the module is to be part of an arithmetic expression. The general form of definition and usage is shown in Figure A.13. An example involving the definition and use of a function module is presented in Figure A.14.

Figure A.13   General form of a function module.

definition:

           fmodule name (**imports**: import parameters)

           : S - statements executed when this module is referenced
           .

           name ← expression
           end module

use:

           name (import arguments)

Figure A.14   Example of a function module.

* Function module to calculate k*k.

fmodule square (**imports:** k)
square ← k * k
end module

* Use a function module to square the numbers from 1 to 10.

i ← 1
while i ≤ 10 **do**
  ⎡ j ← square (i)
  ⎢ **put** i, j
  ⎣ i ← i + 1
stop

B
Algorithms Expressed in Flowcharts

B.1 Introduction

A flowchart, sometimes called a block diagram or flow diagram, is simply a pictorial representation of an algorithm. Boxes of different shapes are used to depict the various actions. Lines with arrows are used to connect the boxes and to indicate the sequence of operations.

Flowcharts were one of the first ways of describing algorithms and still have many supporters. Although international standards have been established, numerous flowcharting symbols and conventions are used in practice. In addition, new flowcharting techniques are continually being developed in an attempt to keep them current with structured programming practices. The discussion of flowcharts in this appendix is neither extensive nor rigorous, presenting only one set of basic concepts and symbols.

B.2 Basic Flowchart Symbols

In flowcharting, the shape of each box is used to indicate a particular type of operation. The basic shapes used in this discussion are summarized in Figure B.1. Typically, each box will have lines leading to it (called *entries*) and lines leading from it (called *exits*) to indicate the sequence of operations or *flow of control*.

Figure B.1   The basic flowchart symbols.

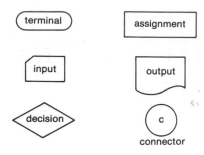

B.3   Terminal Elements

In a pseudocode algorithm, the problem solver always begins with the topmost action and proceeds sequentially, unless otherwise instructed, until the **stop** action is encountered.   Though a flowchart algorithm normally flows from top to bottom, this is not a strict requirement.   Thus a flowchart normally includes both a start and stop symbol.   Both are depicted in an oval box as shown in Figure B.2.

Figure B.2   The start and stop elements.

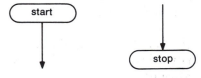

Naturally, each flowchart must have only one start symbol, located at the top of the diagram, but may include several stop symbols.   Again, good practice should limit the algorithm to one **stop** symbol, preferably located at the bottom of the diagram.

B.4   Assignment Operations

Expressing calculations and assignment of values in a flowchart is very similar to pseudocode.   The same notation is used inside a rectangle, as illustrated in Figure B.3. It is conventional to express several related calculations and corresponding assignments within the same rectangle where appropriate.

Figure B.3   The assignment element.

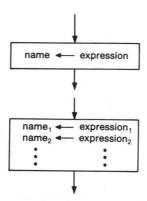

B.5   The get Element

To express the **get** action in a flowchart, the list of names requiring values is written inside a rectangle with the top left corner cut off — presumably to approximate the appearance of a punched card on which data historically has been recorded.   Thus, the shape of the input box replaces the word **get** in pseudocode.   The **get** element is illustrated in Figure B.4.

Figure B.4   The get element.

B.6   The put Element

Since the most common output medium is the printer, the flowchart output symbol is designed to resemble the end of a long piece of paper.   The names of the quantities to be recorded are listed inside the box.   The word **put** used in pseudocode is implied by the shape of the output box, illustrated in Figure B.5.

Figure B.5   The **put** element.

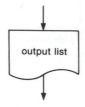

B.7   The **while–do** Element

Unlike the basic elements expressed so far, the **while–do** action requires several flowchart symbols, as described in Figure B.6.

Figure B.6   The **while–do** element.

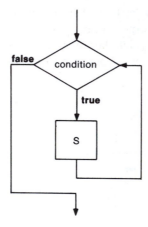

The condition, placed in a diamond-shaped box, is evaluated when the symbol is encountered.   If the condition is **true**, the path labeled **true** is followed and the sequence of symbols S is performed.   Then the flow returns to test the condition.   When the condition becomes **false**, the flow jumps around the action sequence S along the line labeled **false**, to continue with the actions following the **while–do**.   Notice that the S placed in the square box indicates any sequence of flowchart elements.

As with the pseudocode version of the **while–do**, the same three conditions must be satisfied for the flowchart version of the **while–do** to function properly.   Specifically, it is necessary to initialize the **while–do** control variables before entering the **while–do**, the condition must be properly phrased, and the action sequence S must at some point change the parameters.

B.8   The if–then–else Element

The **if–then–else** action is also expressed using several flowchart symbols as illustrated in Figure B.7.   Again the diamond box contains the condition to be evaluated.   If the condition is **true**, the path labeled **true** is followed, and action sequence S_1 is performed. Otherwise, the condition must be **false** and the path labeled **false** is followed to action sequence S_2.   In both cases, the procedure continues with the operations which follow the **if–then–else**.

Figure B.7   The **if–then–else** element.

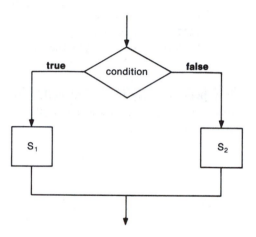

B.8.1   The if–then Element
In cases when the **else** action of an **if–then–else** is null, the flowchart description would be drawn as demonstrated in Figure B.8.

Figure B.8   The **if–then** element.

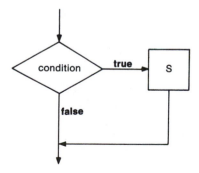

Notice that, for each diamond box, there are two "exit" arrows, one labeled **true** indicating the flow if the condition is **true**, the other labeled **false** specifying the flow for a **false** condition.

B.9   Drawing a Complete Flowchart

In the preceding sections, the flowchart elements for each of the six basic actions have been presented.   It is now appropriate to combine these elements into a complete diagram.   Consider the composite Example 2.5 discussed in Chapter 2.

Example B.1   Indianapolis 500 Winning Speeds
Draw a flowchart for an algorithm which will list the winning speeds at the Indianapolis 500 race and will indicate the amount that each speed is up or down from the previous race.

Since this example has already been presented in pseudocode form, the correspondence between the pseudocode constructs and the flowchart elements is easy to see.   The complete flowchart is presented in Figure B.9.

Figure B.9   Flowchart for Example 2.5 — the Indianapolis 500 problem.

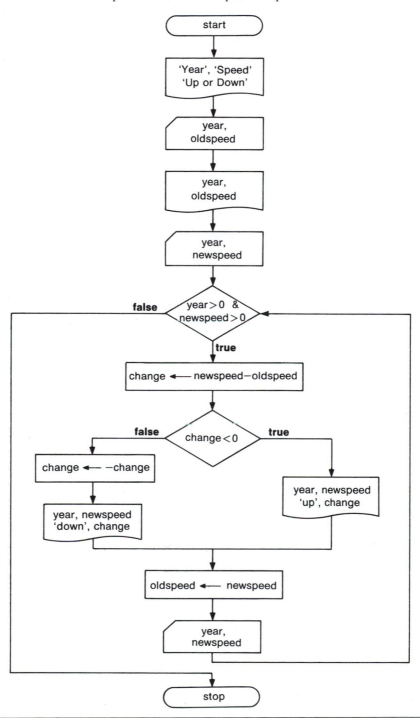

C
Translation of Pseudocode to FORTRAN/77

The development of algorithms in this text is done independently of a programming language.   In the place of a real programming language, a simple hypothetical language, called pseudocode, is used to describe algorithms.   When it comes time to run the algorithms on the computer, the pseudocode may be translated very simply into a FORTRAN/77 program.

Because a programming language runs on a computer, there are always more details to be considered.   For instance, a computer imposes restrictions on the size of values that may be used.   It often needs additional information, such as specification statements and control cards, and has rules regarding where statements may be placed.   The diagram in Figure C.1 illustrates some of the general considerations in the translation.

Figure C.1   General form of pseudocode to FORTRAN/77 translation.

```
                                    :    specification statements
                                    .

    statements of a                      FORTRAN/77 statements which
  . pseudocode                      :       correspond to statements
  . algorithm                       .       of the algorithm

  stop                              STOP
                                    END

  : data
  .
```

To run a FORTRAN/77 program on the computer, the program must be prepared in a machine readable form, traditionally punched cards, but now more probably on some type of terminal with the aid of a text-editing system. In most cases lines of FORTRAN/77 code are 80 characters long, though only columns 1–72 are used since file sequence numbers usually occupy columns 73–80. The actual FORTRAN/77 statements begin in column 7. Columns 1–5 are reserved for statement label numbers and column 6 is used to continue previous lines when necessary. Comment lines begin with a letter C in column 1. Many compilers require the use of upper case letters. This rule and those for statement placement are sometimes relaxed by some compilers.

This appendix describes the conversion process for each type of pseudocode statement. Since Appendix A gives a summary of the pseudocode, the same order of discussion has been followed here. This appendix does not give an exhaustive set of rules for FORTRAN/77 since these are given in Appendix D. For more details on the FORTRAN/77 features, please refer to the appropriate sections of that appendix.

C.1   Constants

The numeric constants in FORTRAN/77 are similar to those in pseudocode except that FORTRAN/77 makes a distinction between integer- and real-valued constants.

a) Integer Constants   An integer-valued constant is a constant which does not contain a decimal point. The numbers 10, –5, 0, and 76319 are all integer constants. Integer constants are also called *fixed-point* numbers since the decimal point is assumed to be fixed immediately to the right of the number.

b) Real Constants   A real constant is a number which does contain a decimal point and thus may have fractional decimal values. The numbers 846.94, 0.0, –7.12, and .56E–3 are all real constants. Real constants are also called *floating-point* constants since the decimal point may appear anywhere in the number.

The distinction between integer and real numbers originated because it is easier for a computer to perform integer arithmetic than arithmetic on real values. In fact, in the early days of computing, integer arithmetic was performed by special electronic circuits (hardware), and real arithmetic was performed by programs (software). This situation still exists today but only in small computers.

In FORTRAN/77 there is a physical limit (determined by the computer) to the size of both types of constants, and there are some alternate ways of specifying real constants.

C.2   Variables

FORTRAN/77 also has variables, but it distinguishes between those variables that may store integer values and those that may store real values. There are rules to determine which type of value a variable may store as well as rules on what constitutes a valid variable name. A valid variable name is composed of up to six characters. The first character must be an alphabetic character (A-Z), while the remaining characters may be alphanumeric (A-Z, 0, 1, 2, 3, 4, 5, 6, 7, 8, 9).   The type of variable is specified in a special declaration statement.   For example, the following statements declare that the variables COUNT and INDEX are to store integer values and that the variables ITEM and COST are to store real values:

```
INTEGER COUNT, INDEX
REAL ITEM, COST
```

C.3   Arrays

In FORTRAN/77, arrays are just variables which have been declared to contain a certain number of elements.   The maximum size of arrays must be predefined in FORTRAN/77 using a specification statement.   The entire array may be referred to by just using the name of the array by itself (allowed only in a limited number of places) and elements of the array are referenced by indicating the position with a subscript enclosed in parentheses.

Figure C.2   Referencing elements of an array in pseudocode and FORTRAN/77.

Pseudocode	FORTRAN/77
x_1	X(1)
x_2	X(2)
x_j	X(J)
$y_{1,5}$	Y(1,5)
$y_{i,j}$	Y(I,J)

C.4   Expressions

As with pseudocode, FORTRAN/77 contains arithmetic and logical expressions.   The differences are very few and are detailed below.

a) Arithmetic Expressions   An arithmetic expression in FORTRAN/77 has all the arithmetic operators of pseudocode and one additional operator to explicitly define the exponentiation operation.   The priorities of these operators are identical to those of pseudo code, with exponentiation being the highest of all.   Like pseudocode, adjacent operators of equal priority are normally executed from left to right.   Exponentiation is an exception since adjacent exponentiation operators are executed right to left.   These operators are shown in Figure C.3.

Figure C.3   Translation of arithmetic expressions from pseudocode to FORTRAN/77.

a) Operators

x^2	exponentiation	X**2
*	multiplication	*
/	division	/
+	addition	+
−	subtraction	−

b) Example

$a^2 + b/c + 7{\cdot}c^2 - d_i^2$ A**2 + B/C + 7.0*C**2 - D(I)**2

---

b) Logical Expressions   A logical expression in FORTRAN/77 differs from that in pseudocode only in that the symbols for the operators are different.   FORTRAN/77 requires the symbols shown in Figure C.4.

Figure C.4   Translation of logical expressions from pseudocode to FORTRAN/77.

a) Relational Operators

$\le$	equal	.EQ.
$\ne$	not equal	.NE.
$<$	less than	.LT.
$\le$	less than or equal	.LE.
$>$	greater than	.GT.
$\ge$	greater than or equal	.GE.

b) Logical Operators

not	not	.NOT.
and	and	.AND.
or	or	.OR.

c) Examples

$x \ne y$	X .NE. Y
$r < s$ **or** $r > t$	R .LT. S .OR. R .GT. T
$a+b \le c^2 - 7$ **and** $d \ge 5$	A+B .LE. C**2-7 .AND. D .GE. 5

C.5   Assignment Statements

The most visible difference between the assignment statements of pseudocode and FORTRAN/77 is that in FORTRAN/77 the assignment operator is the = symbol.   A less obvious, but very important, difference results from the distinction FORTRAN/77 makes between integer and real values.   This results when the LHS and RHS of an assignment statement are of different types, that is, REAL = INTEGER or INTEGER = REAL.   In these cases, after the RHS has been completely evaluated, the result is converted into the type of the variable on the LHS, truncating the fractional part of a REAL value if necessary.

Figure C.5   Translation of assignment statements from pseudocode to FORTRAN/77.

$r \leftarrow a^2 + b/c - d_i^2$ R = A**2 + B/C - D(I)**2

C.6   The **stop** and STOP Statements

The **stop** statement converts directly into the STOP statement of FORTRAN/77.   Both statements have the same role of halting the algorithm or program.

Figure C.6   Translation of the **stop** statement from pseudocode to FORTRAN/77.

stop   STOP

C.7   Comment Statements

In FORTRAN/77, a comment statement is any statement which begins with a C in column 1.   Such statements are ignored by FORTRAN/77 and are simply printed with the program listing.

Figure C.7   Translation of comment statements from pseudocode to FORTRAN/77.

* These are pseudocode   C THESE ARE FORTRAN/77
* comments.   C COMMENTS.

C.8   The **get** and READ Statements

The input statement in FORTRAN/77 is the READ statement.   There are many forms of the READ statement, but the simplest version is very similar in form to the pseudocode **get** statement and is called the *free-format* READ statement.   The actions of the **get** and READ statements, however, are slightly different.   In pseudocode, the data is considered to be in one big list, and when a new **get** statement is encountered, the data for it is taken from the next values on the list.   In FORTRAN/77 the data may be presented in several ways, on a series of punched cards, in separate lines of a computer file, or on separate lines at a computer teminal.   However, care must be used in determining how many values may be placed on each line.   Each time a new READ statement is encountered, a new data line is read.   When the computer reads a new data line, it starts scanning the line in column 1 looking for the data.   The individual items of data are separated from each other by one or more blanks, a comma, or both.   The computer assigns the first data value to the first variable in the input list, the second data value to the second variable in the input list, and so on.   If there are not enough data values on the first data line, the computer automatically reads the next one and continues by scanning it.   If the number of data values on a data line exceeds the number of variables in the input list, then the extra data values are ignored and lost.

Figure C.8   Translation of the **get** statement from pseudocode to FORTRAN/77.

a) General Form

get input list

```
READ *, input list
```

b) Example

get x, y, z, (d$_i$, i **from 1 to 2**)

```
READ *, X, Y, Z, (D(I), I = 1, 2)
```

C.9   The put and PRINT Statement

The PRINT statement in FORTRAN/77 corresponds to the **put** statement.   The form of the PRINT statement illustrated in Figure C.9 is called the *free-format* PRINT statement. Each time a PRINT statement is encountered, the computer starts printing on a new line. If the output list contains too many values to be printed on that line, the computer automatically advances to the next line and continues printing there.

Figure C.9   Translation of the **put** statement from pseudocode to FORTRAN/77.

a) General Form

put output list

```
PRINT *, output list
```

b) Example

put 'The values are', x, y

```
PRINT *, 'THE VALUES ARE', X, Y
```

C.10   The if-then-else and IF-THEN-ELSE Statements

The **if-then-else** statement of pseudocode may be translated directly into the IF-THEN-ELSE statement of FORTRAN/77.   The only difference is that an ENDIF statement must be used to indicate the end of the IF statement.   As with pseudocode, the ELSE clause of FORTRAN/77 may be omitted.   In this case, the ENDIF statement is used to terminate the THEN clause.

Figure C.10 Translation of the **if-then-else** statement from pseudocode to FORTRAN/77.

a) General Form

```
if condition then                    IF(condition) THEN
    ⌈ S₁                                  :    FORTRAN/77 statements for S₁
                                          :
    else                             ELSE
    ⌈ S₂                                  :    FORTRAN/77 statements for S₂
                                          :
                                     ENDIF
```

b) Example

```
if a ≤ b then                        IF(A .LE. B) THEN
    ⌈ r ← a + s                          R = A + S
    else                             ELSE
    ⌈ r ← a + t                          R = A + T
                                     ENDIF
```

C.11   The **while-do** and FORTRAN/77 **Equivalents**

The **while-do** construct is not explicitly supported in FORTRAN/77. Instead the **while-do** must be simulated using a block IF-THEN with a GOTO statement or using the FORTRAN/77 DO statement, equivalent to the pseudocode **for** statement (see the next section).

The general form of the simulated **while-do** is given in Figure C.11 with a corresponding example to illustrate its use. The label, formally called a *statement number*, is a unique 1–5 digit number (between 1 and 99999) placed at the beginning of a line for identification purposes. The GOTO statement, called an *unconditional branch* or *transfer*, is used to alter the sequential ordering of statement execution. The use of the GOTO branch to the labelled beginning of the loop is an explicit representation of the implied return to the **while** condition at the completion of the sequence of statements S in pseudocode.

C.12   The **for** and DO **Statements**

A **for** loop is a succinct and elegant method of describing loops which are controlled by a single control variable (cv) which changes from an initial value (iv) to a test value (tv) by a constant increment or stepping value (sv) for each repetition. The corresponding feature in FORTRAN/77 is the DO loop. The general form of each is shown in Figure C.12 with an example following. Notice the use of a statement label on the CONTINUE statement as well as in the DO statement itself to explicitly indicate the end of the range of the DO loop. The DO parameters, cv, iv, tv, and sv, have the same function as in the pseudocode **for**. cv must be an INTEGER or REAL variable. However, iv, tv, and sv may be any valid INTEGER or REAL constants, variables, or expressions.

Figure C.11   Simulating the **while-do** statement from pseudocode in FORTRAN/77 using an IF-THEN block and GOTO.

a) General Form

```
while condition do          label  IF (condition) THEN
  ⌈ S                                :  FORTRAN/77 statements for S
                                     .
                                   GOTO label

                                   ENDIF
```

b) Example

```
* This algorithm calculates    C This program calculates
* the squares of the           C the squares of the
* numbers from 1 to 10.         C numbers from 1 to 10.
                                       INTEGER I, J
i ← 1                                  I = 1
while i ≤ 10 do                 100    IF (I .LE. 10) THEN
  ⌈  j ← i * i                             J = I * I
  |  put i, j                              PRINT *, I, J
  |  i ← i + 1                             I = I + 1
                                           GOTO 100

                                       ENDIF
stop                                   STOP
                                       END
```

Figure C.12   Translation of the pseudocode **for** statement to the FORTRAN/77 DO statement.

a) General Form

```
for cv from iv to tv by sv do        DO label cv = iv, tv, sv
  ⌈ S                                      :  FORTRAN/77 statements for S
                                           .
                                     label CONTINUE
```

b) Example

```
* This algorithm calculates          C This program calculates
* the squares of the even            C the squares of the even
* numbers from 2 to 10.              C numbers from 2 to 10.
                                           INTEGER I
for i from 2 to 10 by 2 do                 DO 100 I = 2, 10, 2
  ⌈ put i, i*i                                 PRINT *, I, I*I
                                     100    CONTINUE
stop                                       STOP
                                           END
```

C.13   Modules and Subprograms

In pseudocode there are two ways to define a module and two ways in which modules can be used. The two module types are subroutine modules and function modules. In FORTRAN/77, these modules are called subprograms, and there are the same two ways of defining and referencing a subprogram. Thus, there is a subroutine subprogram and a function subprogram.

    The FORTRAN/77 action of transferring the data values between the arguments and parameters is similar to that in pseudocode. However, FORTRAN/77 does not make any distinction between **import** and **export** arguments or parameters. The values of all FORTRAN/77 arguments are copied into the corresponding subprogram parameters when the subprogram is invoked. On return from a subprogram, the values of all parameters are copied back into the corresponding argument. The exception to this rule is that arrays are not copied down and back. Because of their potential size, the invoking program and invoked subprogram share the same memory locations for arrays.

Figure C.13   Translation of pseudocode subroutine modules into FORTRAN/77.

a) General Form

smodule name (**imports**: import list; **exports**: export list)	SUBROUTINE name(parameter list)
⋮ S	⋮ FORTRAN/77 statements for S
end module	RETURN
	END

b) Example

```
* Use a subroutine module           C Use a subroutine subprogram
* to square the numbers             C to square the numbers
* from 1 to 10.                     C from 1 to 10.
                                           INTEGER I, J
for i from 1 to 10 do                      DO 100 I = 1, 10
   ┌  call square (i;j)                         CALL SQUARE(I,J)
   └  put i, j                                  PRINT *, I, J
                                       100 CONTINUE
stop                                       STOP
                                           END

* Subroutine module to             C Subroutine subprogram to
* calculate the square of k.       C calculate the square of K.
smodule square (imports: k; exports: m)    SUBROUTINE SQUARE(K,M)

                                           INTEGER M, K
m ← k * k                                  M = K*K
                                           RETURN
end module                                 END
```

Figure C.14 Translation of pseudocode function modules into FORTRAN/77.

a) General Form

fmodule name (**imports**: import list)	FUNCTION name(parameter list)
: S	: FORTRAN/77 statements for S
name ← ''results''	NAME = "results"
	RETURN
end module	END

b) Example

* Use a function module	C Use a function subprogram
* to square the numbers	C to square the numbers
* from 1 to 10.	C from 1 to 10.
	INTEGER I, J, SQUARE
for i **from** 1 **to** 10 **do**	DO 100 I = 1, 10
j ← square (i)	J = SQUARE(I)
put i, j	PRINT *, I, J
	100 CONTINUE
stop	STOP
	END
*Function module to	C Function subprogram to
*calculate the square of k.	C calculate the square of K.
fmodule square (**imports**: k)	INTEGER FUNCTION SQUARE(K)
	INTEGER K
square ← k * k	SQUARE = K*K
	RETURN
end module	END

D
Summary of
FORTRAN/77
Statements and Rules

This appendix provides a summary of FORTRAN/77. The acronym FORTRAN comes from FORmula TRANslation, the first description of the FORTRAN language appearing in 1954. Since then many versions of the FORTRAN language have been developed with FORTRAN/77 being the latest of these. The FORTRAN/77 specifications are described in the American National Standards Institute's document ANSI X3.9-1978. Compared to the previous standard ANSI 3.9-1966, FORTRAN/77 has many additional features. As well, there are some changes that create conflicts with the previous standard but this was done "only when such changes were necessary to correct an error in a significant manner." The ANSI X3.9-1978 standard details the conflicts.

For the most part, if a FORTRAN program written for compilers of the 1966 standard is straight forward then it should compile and execute under a compiler for the 1978 standard. If an old FORTRAN program does contain some conflicting statements then in most instances the compiler will detect these and inform the user. However, some of the changes have to do with execution methods and are not detectable by a compiler. Thus it is a good idea to test the program on known data on the new compiler and compare the results with those from the old compiler.

The following pages describe most features of FORTRAN/77. Many of these statements have not been mentioned elsewhere in the text because they are not necessary at the introductory level. However, for each statement a description is now given, usually along with an example of its use. The descriptions here are based upon the FORTRAN/77 standard itself. Since many manufacturers modify or enhance their FORTRAN/77 compilers some differences may be noted. If there are different implementation schemes possible for some of the FORTRAN/77 features, the simplest scheme is presented for the reader. For instance, the transfer of arguments to subprograms may be done either through call-by-value result or call-by-reference, while the standard just says that the arguments become associated. Here it was decided to describe the call-by-value result scheme for single variables and call-by-reference for arrays.

Many of the more important features of the FORTRAN/77 language are given a more detailed discussion in a later appendix.

D.1   Arithmetic Expressions

1) They are composed of operands separated by arithmetic operators.   The general form of an arithmetic expression is

    A op B op C . . .

    where op refers to an arithmetic operator and A, B, and C are called *operands* and may be constants, symbolic names of constants, variables, array elements and/or function references.

2) Valid operators are **, *, /, +, and –.   These operators are called *binary* because they require two operands, one on each side.   The + and – may also be used as *unary* operators, in which case only one operand is used and is placed to the right of the operator.

3) Expressions may also contain parentheses to remove ambiguity or improve readability.

4) Expressions are evaluated according to a priority scheme.   The priority means that, whenever an operand has an arithmetic operator on both sides, the operator with the highest priority is done first.

    a) Expressions in parentheses are evaluated first.   If parentheses are nested, evaluation of the innermost level precedes the others.

    b) Exponentiation has the highest priority of the operators.   Consecutive exponentiation operators are performed starting from the right.

    c) Multiplication and division are the next highest and are of equal priority. They are performed in the order they are encountered going from left to right in the expression.

    d) Addition and subtraction are the lowest priority and are of equal priority. They are performed in the order in which they are encountered going from left to right in the expression.

5) The result of an integer division (integer by integer) is always an integer.   Any fractional part is truncated (that is, ignored).

6) Division by zero is an error.

7) If an expression contains both integer and real values, it is called a mixed-mode expression.

    a) In all mixed-mode calculations other than exponentiation, the integer value is converted to real immediately before each individual calculation takes place.

    b) In exponentiation, a value which is raised to an integer exponent is calculated by performing repetitive multiplication.   If a value is raised to a real exponent, logarithms are used to compute the result.   Note that the FORTRAN/77 standard does not allow an integer value to be raised to a real exponent.

8)   In comparison with the other operators the priority of the arithmetic ones is highest as shown below.

Operator Type	*Priority*
arithmetic	highest
character	:
relational	:
logical	lowest

Examples

1) `5 + 3*4` → `5 + 12` → `17`
2) `5 + 2**3*7` → `5 + 8*7` → `5 + 56` → `61`
3) `-4**2` → `-16`   (unary operator -)
4) `(- 4)**2` → `+16`   (unary operator -)
5) `5/2` → `2`
6) `5/-2` → error   (two operators together)
7) `2**3**2` → `2**9` → `512`
8) `3*5/4*2` → `15/4*2` → `3*2` → `6`
9) `2.0**3` → `2.0*2.0*2.0` → `8.0`
10) `2.0**3.0` → antilog(3.0*log(2.0)) → `8.0`
11) `(-2.0)**3` → `(-2.0)*(-2.0)*(-2.0)` → `-8.0`
12) `(-2.0)**3.0` → antilog(3.0*log(-2.0)) → error (log(-2.0))
13) `2 + 3.0` → `2.0 + 3.0` → `5.0`
14) `7/3*4.0` → `2*4.0` → `2.0*4.0` → `8.0`
15) `4.0*7/3` → `4.0*7.0/3` → `28.0/3` → `28.0/3.0` → `9.333333`

D.2   Arithmetic IF

Purpose

This statement branches to one of three executable statements, depending on the value of an arithmetic expression.   (See also block IF and logical IF.)

General Form

```
IF(arithmetic expression) stno1, stno2, stno3
```

The next statement executed will be one of the statements labeled `stno1`, `stno2`, or `stno3` depending on the value of the arithmetic expression.   If the arithmetic expression has the value:

< 0	transfer to	stno1
= 0	transfer to	stno2
> 0	transfer to	stno3.

Rules
1) stno1, stno2, and stno3 are statement numbers on executable statements in the same program unit.
2) Any or all of the statement numbers may be similar. If they are all the same, the statement is an unconditional transfer statement, that is, it always branches to the same place regardless of the value of the arithmetic expression.

Examples
1) IF(I) 21,51,42
    The next statement executed will be the statement labeled 21 if the value of I is less than 0, the statement labeled 51 if the value of I is equal to 0, or the statement labeled 42 if the value of I is greater than 0.
2) IF(A+5.0) 100,100,200
    The next statement executed will be the statement labeled 100 if the value of A+5.0 is less than or equal 0.0 or the statement labeled 200 if the value of A+5.0 is greater than 0.0.

D.3 Arrays

Purpose
To enable a large number of data elements to be stored and processed in an efficient manner.

General Form of Definition

    specification statement arrayname $(d_1,d_2,d_3,\ldots,d_7)$

where the arrayname is the name of the entire array. The d_1, d_2, ..., d_7 are the dimensions of the array.

General Form of Usage

    arrayname $(s_1,s_2,s_3,\ldots,s_7)$

where $(s_1$, s_2, s_3,..., $s_7)$ are subscripts to identify which data element is being referenced. In special circumstances the arrayname may be used by itself.

Rules
1) An array is defined in a DIMENSION, INTEGER, REAL, CHARACTER, LOGICAL, DOUBLE, COMPLEX, or COMMON statement and all data elements in any one array are of the same type. An array must be defined in each program unit in which it is used. Transfer of array data between program units is done through arguments and parameters or through COMMON blocks.
2) The rules for array names follow the rules for variable names, including the default typing rules.

3) In the simplest cases, an array dimension is of the form $d_1 : d_u$ where d_1 is the optional lower bound of the array and d_u is the upper bound of the array.   Both d_1 and d_u may be expressions in which the constants and symbolic names of constants are of type INTEGER.

4) A dimension bound may have a value which is negative, zero, or positive but d_u must be greater than or equal to d_1.   If d_1 is omitted it has an assumed value of 1.

5) An array may be specified with anywhere from 1 to 7 dimensions.   The size of a dimension is the value $d_u - d_1 + 1$.

6) A subscript is an integer expression which in relation to the corresponding dimension must have a value $d_1 \leq s \leq d_u$.   An array element reference must have exactly the same number of subscripts as was defined in the array declaration.

7) Arrays from 1 to 3 dimensions are easily represented graphically as indicated in the following examples.

Specification Description	*Graphic Representation*

DIMENSION LIST(10)
or
DIMENSION LIST(1:10)

LIST is an integer array with 10 data elements numbered 1 to 10.

LIST(1)
LIST(2)
.
.
.
LIST(10)

DIMENSION LIST(-5:7)

LIST is an integer array with 13 data elements numbered -5 to +7.

LIST(-5)
LIST(-4)
.
.
LIST(0)
.
.
.
LIST(7)

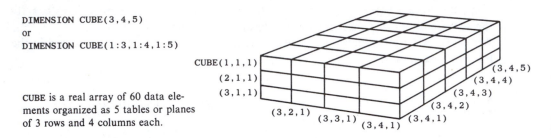

```
DIMENSION TABLE(4,5)
or
DIMENSION TABLE(1:4,1:5)
```

TABLE is a real array with 20 data elements organized as 4 rows and 5 columns.

```
DIMENSION CUBE(3,4,5)
or
DIMENSION CUBE(1:3,1:4,1:5)
```

CUBE is a real array of 60 data elements organized as 5 tables or planes of 3 rows and 4 columns each.

8) Since computer memories are essentially 1-dimensional, it is necessary to store the multi-dimensional arrays in a form other than how they are visualized, as shown in Figure D.1.   There are two options: row-major (row-by-row) or column-major (column-by-column) order with the latter method being used in FORTRAN/77.

9) Arrays must be declared in each program where they are to be used. Array data can be transmitted between program units either through COMMON or as actual arguments in an argument list and as a dummy argument (formal parameter) in a parameter list.

10) By varying the actual argument and the dummy argument definition in the called subprogram either

   a) the entire array may be passed
   b) a contiguous portion (in the internal storage sense) of the array may be passed.

11) In an argument list of the calling program unit, an array name may be used as follows:

   a) the array name by itself: used to pass all or a contiguous portion of the array starting at the first data element
   b) the array name followed by a subscript: used to pass a contiguous portion of the array starting at the data element indicated by the subscript.

12) In the parameter list of the called subprogram, only the array name itself is ever used with a declaration of that array's size following in a specification statement.

13) For subprograms, FORTRAN/77 allows adjustable or variable dimensions in which the dimension expression may contain integer variables provided these variables are either in the parameter list or in COMMON.

14) The upper bound of the last dimension may be an asterisk which means that the computer will calculate the upper bound to reference as much of the actual argument as is possible.

Figure D.1   Storage visualization of multi-dimensional arrays in FORTRAN/77.

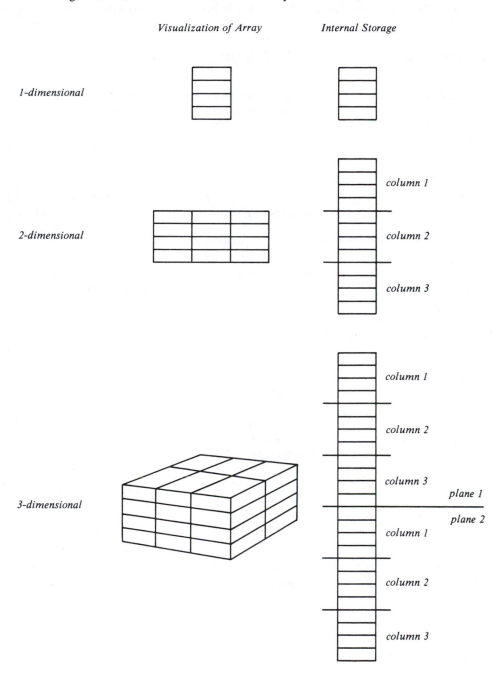

15)   In the following examples, type specification statements could be used in place of the DIMENSION statements and the rules indicated apply to FUNCTION subprograms also.

Calling Program Unit	*Called Program Unit*	*Action*
a) DIMENSION X(10) . . . CALL SUB1(X) CALL SUB1(X(1)) . . .	SUBROUTINE SUB1(A) DIMENSION A(10) . . .	in both calls of SUB1, array A will reference all data elements of X. A(1) ≡ X(1) etc.
CALL SUB2(X) . . .	SUBROUTINE SUB2(B) DIMENSION B(7) . . .	array B will reference the first 7 data elements of array X. B(1) ≡ X(1) etc.
CALL SUB3(X(3)) . . .	SUBROUTINE SUB3(C) DIMENSION C(4) . . .	array C will reference 4 data elements of array X starting at X(3). C(1) ≡ X(3) etc.
b) DIMENSION R(2,3) . . .		
CALL SUB4(R) . . .	SUBROUTINE SUB4(T) DIMENSION T(2,3) . . .	array T will reference all 6 data elements of R in the expected manner.
CALL SUB5(R) . . .	SUBROUTINE SUB5(U) DIMENSION U(3,2) . . .	array U will reference all 6 data elements of R. U(1,1) ≡ R(1,1) U(2,1) ≡ R(2,1) U(3,1) ≡ R(1,2) U(1,2) ≡ R(2,2) U(2,2) ≡ R(1,3) U(3,2) ≡ R(2,3)
CALL SUB6(R(1,2)) . . .	SUBROUTINE SUB6(V) DIMENSION V(2) . . .	array V will reference the 2nd column of array R. V(1) ≡ R(1,2) V(2) ≡ R(2,2)

c) DIMENSION X(5,10)   SUBROUTINE SUB7(D,L,M)
   DIMENSION Y(20,100)   DIMENSION D(L,M)
   CALL SUB7(X,5,10)   array D will be of size 5×10
                                                        to match array X.
   CALL SUB7(Y,20,100)   array D will be of size
                                                        20×100 to match array Y.
   CALL SUB7(Y,20,5)   array D will be of size 20×5
                                                        to match the 1st 5 columns
                                                        of array V.
   CALL SUB7(Y(1,8),20,5)   array D will be of size 20×5
                                                        and refer to columns 8 to 12
                                                        of array Y.
   CALL SUB7(Y,4,7)   array D will be of size 4×7
                                                        and overlap column 1 and 8
                                                        data elements of column 2.

d) DIMENSION C(2:11)   SUBROUTINE SUB8(P)   array P will overlap array C
   DIMENSION D(5,10)   DIMENSION P(-4:5)   exactly. P(-4) ≡ C(2),
   CALL SUB8(C)   .   ... P(5) ≡ C(11)
                              .
                              .
   CALL SUB9(D(2,2))   SUBROUTINE SUB9(Q)   array D has 44 data ele-
                            DIMENSION Q(3:*)   ments (D(2,2) to D(5,10))
                                                        available and thus the array
                                                        Q becomes Q(3:46).

16) The name of the array may be used without a subscript:

   a) in an argument or parameter list
   b) in COMMON or type statement
   c) in an EQUIVALENCE statement
   d) in a DATA statement
   e) in the list of an input or output statement
   f) as the unit identifier for an internal file in an input or output statement
   g) as a format identifier in an input or output list.

D.4   ASSIGN **Statement**

Purpose

This statement assigns a statement number to an integer variable for use with the assigned GOTO statement.

General Form

    ASSIGN stno TO name

This statement is used only in conjunction with the assigned GOTO statement.   The rules and example of its use are given with that statement.

D.5   Assigned GOTO Statement

Purpose
This statement branches to one of several statements depending on the statement number that was assigned to a variable in an ASSIGN statement.

General Form

```
ASSIGN stno TO name
  .
  .
  .
GOTO name,(stnol,stno2, . . . ,stnok)
```

The name in the ASSIGN and the assigned GOTO statement is an INTEGER variable.

Rules
1)   The statement number used in the ASSIGN statement must be defined in that program unit.
2)   The statement number must be the label of an executable statement or a FORMAT statement.
3)   The integer variable name may contain either a statement number or an integer value. When used in an assigned GOTO or as a FORMAT identifier the variable must be defined with a statement number and must not be referenced in any other way.
4)   If the statement number list is present then the statement label value of name must be in the list. The name may be a variable, an array element or character substring.

Example

```
C This program sums the first 10 integers.
      INTEGER BACK, I, N, SUM
      N = 10
      SUM = 0.0
      I = 1
      ASSIGN 100 TO BACK
  100    SUM = SUM + I
         I = I + 1
         IF(I .GT. N)ASSIGN 300 TO BACK
         GOTO BACK,(100,300)
  300 PRINT *, 'THE SUM OF THE FIRST', N, 'INTEGERS IS', SUM
      STOP
      END
```

D.6 Assignment Statements

Purpose

Assignment statements are used to assign the value of an arithmetic expression to a variable.

General Form

```
name = expression
```

The expression on the right-hand side (RHS) is completely evaluated and then the result is assigned to the variable on the left-hand side (LHS).   The = symbol is referred to as the assignment operator.

Rules

1) The assignment statement may be

   a) an arithmetic assignment statement: LHS and RHS must both be arithmetic (integer, real, double precision, complex).
   b) a logical assignment statement: LHS and RHS must both be of type logical. (See also Appendix H.)
   c) a character assignment statement: LHS and RHS must both be of type character. (See also Appendix I.)

2) If in an arithmetic assignment statement the types of the LHS and the RHS do not agree, then the value of the RHS is converted automatically to that of the LHS before assignment is done.   This is called mixed-mode assignment.   For example, if B is REAL and K is INTEGER,

   ```
   B = 9        → B is assigned the value 9.0, and
   K = 4.9      → K is assigned the value 4
   ```

3) Special conventions are needed if either side of the assignment operator involves a complex quantity. See Appendix J.
4) Blanks may be used to improve readability.   The authors have a convention of placing blanks around the assignment operator and around the lower priority operators.

Examples

```
1)  R = S*T + 5.0*Y
2)  A = 0.0
3)  I = J + 17
4)  LOGICAL R, S, T, U
    R = .TRUE.
    S = .FALSE.
    T = X .GE. Y  .AND.  X .LE. Z
```

5) CHARACTER A*10, B*20
    A = 'ABCDEF'
    B(4:15) = A // 'RSTUV'

D.7 BACKSPACE **Statement**

Purpose
This statement is used to position the file to the record before the one where it is currently positioned.

General Form

```
BACKSPACE u
BACKSPACE (cilist)
```

The u is an external unit specifier; the cilist contains specifiers from the following list:

```
[UNIT =] u
IOSTAT = ios
ERR = s
```

These specifiers are discussed in more detail in Section D.39, Input/Output Statement Specifiers.

Rule
1) The external unit must be connected for sequential access.

D.8 BLOCK DATA **Subprogram**

Purpose
This feature provides a means of initializing named and unnamed COMMON blocks.

General Form

```
BLOCK DATA
COMMON/common name/ common list

:    initialization and specification statements only
.

END
```

Rules
1) BLOCK DATA subprograms may not contain any executable statements. They may only contain IMPLICIT, COMMON, DATA, DIMENSION, PARAMETER, END, EQUIVALENCE, the type declaration statements (INTEGER, REAL, etc.), and comment statements.
2) All initialization must be performed following the COMMON declaration.

Example

```
C This program segment has a named COMMON which
C is initialized by a BLOCK DATA subprogram.
      INTEGER I, J, K
      REAL X, Y
      COMMON/CHARLY/ I, J, X(10), K(7), Y

      .
      .
      .

      STOP
      END

      BLOCK DATA
      COMMON/CHARLY/ I, J, X(10), K(7), Y
      INTEGER I/0/, J/1/
      REAL X/10*0.0/
      DATA K/7*0/, Y/2.0/
      END
```

D.9   Block IF Statement

Purpose

This statement allows the selection of alternate statements for execution.   (See also arithmetic IF and logical IF.)

General Form

```
      IF(logical expression) THEN
      .
          statements S1
      .
      ELSE
      .
          statements S2
      .
      ENDIF
```

The logical expression is evaluated and if it has the value .TRUE., then the statements S1 are executed.   If the logical expression has a value .FALSE., the statements S2 are executed.   Following execution of either S1 or S2, execution continues with the statement following the ENDIF.   (See also ELSEIF.)

Rules
1)   Only one of the statement groups, S1 or S2 is executed.
2)   The THEN word must be on the same line (or a continuation thereof) as the IF(logical expression).
3)   The ENDIF must always be included.
4)   The ELSE and its statements S2 may be omitted to give the IF-THEN statement. The ENDIF is still necessary.
5)   Transfer of control into the range of a block IF is not allowed.

Example

```
C This program reads in 10 records.  Each record contains 1
C integer and 2 real values. It performs arithmetic on the
C real numbers as determined by the integer value.
C If the integer is: 1 - add A+B
C                     2 - subtract A-B
C         anything else - print a warning message
      INTEGER I, NUM
      REAL A, B
      DO 500 I = 1,10
         READ *, NUM, A, B
         IF (NUM .EQ. 1) THEN
             PRINT *, 'THE SUM OF', A, B, 'IS', A+B
         ELSE
             IF (NUM .EQ. 2) THEN
                 PRINT *, 'THE DIFFERENCE OF', A, B, 'IS', A-B
             ELSE
                 PRINT *, 'BAD CODE', NUM
             ENDIF
         ENDIF
  500 CONTINUE
      STOP
      END
```

D.10 CALL **Statement**

Purpose

The CALL statement allows a user to invoke a subroutine subprogram from another program.

General Form

```
CALL name (argument list)
```

A detailed description and examples of this statement accompany the discussion of the SUBROUTINE statement.

D.11 CHARACTER **Expressions**

Purpose

To allow character strings to be manipulated.

Rules

1) A character expression may be a character constant, the symbolic name of a character constant, a character variable, a character substring, or a character function.
2) The only valid character operator is the concatenation operator //.
3) The priority of the // operator is indicated below:

Operator Type	Priority
arithmetic	highest
character	:
relational	:
logical	lowest

with evaluation of this concatenation operator proceeding from left to right.

4)   See Appendix G for further rules and information on the CHARACTER data type.

D.12   CHARACTER **Statement**

Purpose

This statement allows a user to define specific variable or array names to be of type CHARACTER.

General Form

```
CHARACTER*n list
```

The list contains variable or array names separated by commas.   The *n ($1 \leq n \leq 255$) indicates the number of characters each item in the list may store.   If omitted the default number of characters is 1.   Alternately the length specification may follow the variable name or array specification.   For example:

```
CHARACTER*10 A, B(20)
CHARACTER A*10, B(20)*10
```

are equivalent declarations.   This statement and the entire topic of character data types are discussed in Appendix G.

D.13   CLOSE **Statement**

Purpose

This statement is used to terminate the connection of a unit to a particular file.

General Form

```
CLOSE (cilist)
```

The cilist contains specifiers to control the termination of the unit to the file.   The specifiers may be:

```
[UNIT =] u
IOSTAT = ios
ERR = s
STATUS = sta
```

of which there must be exactly one external unit specifier and may contain at most one of each of the other specifiers.   These specifiers are discussed in more detail in Section D.39, Input/Output Statement Specifiers. The valid values for `sta` are:

KEEP   keep file on closing
DELETE   delete file on closing

Refer to the processor's FORTRAN/77 manual for further information.

D.14   COMMENT Line

Purpose
A comment line allows a user to insert textual information into a program for the purpose of documenting the program and clarifying the program structure.

General Form

```
C text information
or
* text information
or
ƀƀƀƀƀƀƀ . . . ƀƀƀƀƀƀƀ
▲                   ▲
col 1           col 72
```

The text information extends from column 2 through 72 and may contain any character capable of representation in the FORTRAN processor.

Rules
1) A comment line may appear anywhere in a program unit and may precede the initial statement of a program unit.
2) Comment lines may appear between continuation statements.
3) Comments do not affect the execution of a program in any way.

D.15   COMMON Statement

Purpose
This statement provides an alternate communication method between main programs and subprograms, other than through the argument/parameter lists.

General Form

```
COMMON/common name/ common list
```

The common list is composed of variable and array names.   A COMMON statement reserves a block of memory large enough to contain all the common list variables in order of appearance in the list. When a COMMON statement of the same name appears in another program unit, the exact same area of memory is used for both. Thus the subprograms have access to a 'common' area of memory.

Rules
1) The common name may be up to six symbols in length and must begin with an alphabetic character.
2) A common name and a variable name may not be the same.
3) If a common block contains a character variable or a character array then all other entities in that common block must be of type CHARACTER.
4) If many COMMON statements with the same common name appear in the same program segment, then the common lists are appended. Of the following statements, those on the left are equivalent to the one on the right, for example:

        COMMON/SAM/ A,B,C   COMMON/SAM/ A,B,C,D,E
        COMMON/SAM/ D,E

5) If the /common name/ is omitted, then the resulting area is called an unnamed or blank common. (Consider it to be a named common with an internal name defined by the compiler.) For example:

        COMMON R,S,T   or   COMMON // R, S, T

6) COMMON is a compile-time feature. It is completely established before execution begins.
7) Variables may not be initialized in the COMMON statement nor may a variable that has been previously initialized through compile-time initialization be placed in a common list.
8) Variable and array names may appear in type specification statements as well as COMMON. Also, the size of an array may be declared in a COMMON statement, but an array must not be given a size twice. For example:

        INTEGER A, B(10)
        REAL X
        COMMON/ARNOLD/ A(15),B,X

   is legal but

        INTEGER X(10)
        COMMON/SALLY/ X(10)

   is not legal.
9) An array name in the common list may not have variable dimensions.
10) Neither a function name nor subprogram parameters may appear in a COMMON statement.
11) The common list acts as a template which tells how the associated common area is to be accessed. Thus a particular common area may be accessed in different ways by different program segments. For example, if the following COMMON statements appear in different program segments,

```
COMMON/HARRY/ I(10),J(3),K
COMMON/HARRY/ L(6),M(8)
```

then they both refer to the same 14 words of memory. Array L and I(1) ... I(6) use the same 6 locations, while array M uses the same locations as I(7) ... I(10), J(1), ... ,J(3), and K.

12) The size of a common block is determined by the sum of the sizes of the entities in its common list(s) including any extension from EQUIVALENCE. The size of a named common block must be the same in all program units that define it. Blank common blocks need not be the same size.

13) Entities in a named common block may be initially defined, valuewise, in a BLOCK DATA subprogram.

D.16   Compile-time Initialization of Variables

Purpose
This feature allows the user to assign values to variables at compile time.

General Form
Compile-time initialization of variables is performed in the type specification statements. The following shows its use in the INTEGER and REAL specification statements. (See also the DATA statement, and for other data types, see Appendices G, H, I, and J.)

```
REAL rname/real constant/
INTEGER iname/integer constant/
```

The first statement implies that the real variable rname is to be assigned the value of the real constant. In the second statement, the integer variable iname is to be assigned the value of the integer constant.

Rules
1) The type of the variable and the value must usually be the same. One exception to this rule is that a constant may be a character string (see Appendix G).

2) Many variable initializations may be performed at the same time.

```
REAL X/5.0/, Y/10.0/, Z/123.54/
```

3) Arrays may be declared and initialized at the same time.

```
REAL A(3)/0.0,0.0,0.0/, B(2)/5.0,27.0/
```

4) A shorthand notation of n* may be used to indicate that a constant is to be repeated n times. The repetition factor n must be a nonnegative, nonzero integer constant.

```
INTEGER I(1000)/1000*0/, J(128)/100*1,28*2/
```

5) Initialization of multidimensional arrays is performed in column order. For instance, the following statement will initialize all elements in the first column of A to 1.0, the second column of A to 2.0, and the third column to 3.0.

    REAL A(10,3)/10*1.0,10*2.0,10*3.0/

6) This initialization takes place once only at compile time.

D.17 COMPLEX Statement

Purpose
This statement allows the user to declare a specific variable, array, or function name to be of type COMPLEX.

General Forms

    COMPLEX list
    COMPLEX*8 list
    COMPLEX*16 list

The latter two lines represent extensions to the standard in several implementations including the IBM and VAX systems. The lists contain variable, array, or function names separated by commas. The first two statements perform the same operation of declaring the items in the list to be single-precision complex (that is, two single-precision values). The last statement declares the items in its list to be extended-precision complex (that is, two extended-precision values). This statement and the entire topic of complex data types are discussed in Appendix J.

D.18 Computed GOTO

Purpose
The computed GOTO statement is used to branch to one of several statements depending on the value of an INTEGER variable.

General Form

    GOTO(stno1,stno2, . . . ,stnok),i

The stno1, stno2,..., stnok are statement numbers on executable statements in the same program unit, and i is an INTEGER variable. When executed the statement has the following action:

a) If: i has the value 1, branch to stno1
         i has the value 2, branch to stno2

> .
> .
> .

i has the value k, branch to stnok

b) If: i is outside the range i<1 or i>k, then control is passed to the statement following the computed GOTO.

Example

```
C This program reads in 10 records.  Each record contains 1
C integer and 2 real values. It performs arithmetic on the
C real numbers as determined by the integer value.
C If the integer is: 1 - add A+B
C                    2 - subtract A-B
C                    3 - multiply A*B
C                    4 - divide A/B
C         anything else - print a warning message
      INTEGER I, NUM
      REAL A, B

      DO 500 I = 1, 10
          READ *, NUM, A, B
          GOTO(100,200,300,400),NUM
          PRINT *, 'BAD CODE', NUM
             GOTO 500
100       PRINT *, 'THE SUM OF', A, B, 'IS', A+B
             GOTO 500
200       PRINT *, 'THE DIFFERENCE OF', A, B, 'IS', A-B
             GOTO 500
300       PRINT *, 'THE PRODUCT OF', A, B, 'IS', A*B
             GOTO 500
400       PRINT *, 'THE QUOTIENT OF', A, B, 'IS', A/B
500 CONTINUE
      STOP
      END
```

D.19   Constants

Integer Constants

1)   Integer constants are numbers written without a decimal point.

2)   They may take on only integer values.   For example:

   17, -5, 0, +25, 94786

3)   They are stored internally in the computer as 32-bit binary numbers and thus are limited in range from -2147483648 to +2147483647.   (See Appendix E for more information.)

Real Constants

1)   Real constants are numbers written with a decimal point and may have many forms. All of the following numbers have the same value:

by hand: 12.74, .0001274 × 10^5, 12740 × 10^{-3}
FORTRAN/77: 12.74, .0001274E5, 12740E-3

2)   They are stored internally as 32-bit binary numbers in an exponent form and contain up to 7 decimal digits.   See Appendix E for more information.

D.20   CONTINUE **Statement**

Purpose
This is a do-nothing statement which is often used as the object of a DO loop and in conversion from pseudocode into standard FORTRAN.

General Form

```
nnnnn CONTINUE
```

The nnnnn is a statement number and is optional, but the statement has no use without one.

Rules
1)   This statement by itself causes no action.
2)   In all cases other than when a CONTINUE is the object of a DO loop, a branch to a CONTINUE statement causes the computer to proceed immediately to the statement following it.

Examples
1)   See the section on the DO statement in this appendix for more information concerning the CONTINUE as the object of a DO loop.
2)   See Appendix C for use of the CONTINUE in translation of pseudocode into FORTRAN/77.

D.21   DATA **Statement**

Purpose
This statement allows variables, arrays, and array elements to be initialized at compile time.   (See also the section in this appendix on the compile-time initialization of variables.)

General Form

```
DATA vlist1/clist1/, vlist2/clist2/, . . .
```

The vlist1 and vlist2 are lists of variables and clist1 and clist2 are lists of constants.   The variable lists contain one or more variables, array names, or array elements which are to be initialized. The constant list contains the initialization values. The type of the variable and its corresponding constant must be the same.

Rules
1) The DATA statement may appear anywhere in a program unit following the specification statements. It is nonexecutable, and the initializations are performed only once before any execution begins. The names of dummy arguments, functions, and entities in blank COMMON may not appear in a DATA statement. The entities in a named COMMON may appear in a DATA statement only in a BLOCK DATA subprogram.
2) The type of the vlist entity and the constant must agree for character and logical types. For integer, real, double precision and complex, the constant will be converted into the correct type if necessary.
3) The operation of the DATA statement is similar to that of initialization in the INTEGER and REAL statements. For example:

```
REAL X, A
INTEGER I, J
DATA X/5.0/, A/3.0/, I,J/7,10/
```

is equivalent to

```
REAL X/5.0/, A/3.0/
INTEGER I/7/, J/10/
```

4) The variable list may contain more than one name for initialization. The constant list must contain the correct number of constants to initialize all of the variables in the variable list. For arrays the values are assigned in storage order. (See also section D.3 on arrays.)

```
LOGICAL R
REAL X, A
INTEGER I, J
DATA X, A, I, J/5.0,3.0,7,10/, R/.TRUE./
```

5) If in the initialization of a character entity, the length of that entity and the constant do not match, then the constant is either truncated on the right or padded on the right with blanks. Thus from the following

```
CHARACTER*5 R, S*7
DATA R, S/2*'ABCDEF'/
```

R is assigned ABCDE and S is assigned 'ABCDEFb'.
6) When arrays are initialized, the size of the array must have been declared previously. The following DATA statement initializes the three elements of A to 0.0 and only the third element of B to 7.9.

```
DIMENSION A(3), B(5)
DATA A/0.0,0.0,0.0/, B(3)/7.9/
```

7) To help in the initialization, a replication factor of the form n* may be used as well as an implied DO structure. The following statements initialize all elements of X to 0.0, the odd elements of Y to 0.0, and the even elements of Y to 1.0. The variables R, S, and T are all initialized to 5.0.

```
REAL X(1000), Y(2000), R, S, T
DATA X/1000*0.0/, (Y(I), I=1,1999,2)/1000*0.0/
DATA (Y(I), I=2,2000,2)/1000*1.0/, R,S,T/3*5.0/
```

The implied DO loops may be nested.

8) A variable, array element or substring must not be defined more than once.

D.22 DIMENSION **Statement**

Purpose

This statement provides an alternate way to define the size of arrays. (For most uses this statement may be replaced by REAL and/or INTEGER statements.)

General Form

```
DIMENSION array list
```

The array list contains the names of arrays and their sizes.

Rules

1) An array may only have its size defined once.
2) If the size of an array is declared in a DIMENSION statement, it may also have its type defined in a specification statement. The following statements are equivalent:

```
REAL IRVING                  REAL IRVING(10)
DIMENSION IRVING(10)
```

3) Refer to Section D.3 for more information on arrays and more examples.

D.23 DO **Statement and** DO **Loop**

Purpose

This feature is used to provide a convenient way to perform looping with automatic incrementing of the index.

General Form

```
DO nnnnn i = e₁, e₂, e₃

   :  statements
   .

nnnnn CONTINUE
```

In the DO statement, i is an integer, real, or double precision variable and is called the DO-variable or index of the loop. As well, e_1, e_2, and e_3 are called the parameters of the DO loop and may be integer, real, or double precision expressions.

e_1 - is the initial expression
e_2 - is the test value expression
e_3 - is the increment expression
nnnnn CONTINUE - is the terminal statement or object of the DO loop

The statements which follow the DO statement up to and including the object of the DO loop are said to be within the *range* of the DO loop. The DO loop operates in the following way:

1) The initial value expression, test value expression, and the increment expression are evaluated and converted to the type of the DO-variable if necessary giving initial parameter M_1, terminal parameter M_2, and incrementation parameter M_3 respectively.
2) The DO-variable is assigned the value M_1.
3) The iteration count (IC) is calculated from the following expression

$$IC = MAX(INT((M_2-M_1+M_3)/M_3),0)$$

which means that the iteration count is zero when

$M_1>M_2$ and $M_3>0$ or
$M_1<M_2$ and $M_3<0$.

4) The iteration count is calculated and if it is zero the DO-loop becomes inactive with control passing to the statement following the terminal statement. If the iteration count is not zero then the statements in the range of the DO-loop are processed until the terminal statement is reached.
5) When the terminal statement has been processed the following steps take place:

a) the DO-variable is incremented by M_3,
b) the iteration count is decremented by 1,
c) the iteration count testing of step 4 is repeated.

Rules
1) The increment is optional and if it is omitted, it is assumed to have the value 1.
2) The DO-variable may not be redefined by the program inside the DO-loop.
3) A DO loop may only be entered by way of the DO statement. A branch into the range of a DO loop may not be made from outside the range of that loop.
4) A branch may be made from inside the range of a DO loop to outside the range of that DO, and the value of the index is the last value defined.

5) If an exit is made from a DO loop by way of the object of the DO, (that is, all repetitions are done) the value of the index is the last value defined.

6) The terminal statement of the DO-loop must be an executable statement but may not be a GOTO, assigned GOTO, arithmetic IF, block IF, ELSEIF, ENDIF, RETURN, STOP, END, or DO statement.

7) DO-loops may be nested. An inner DO-loop must be entirely within the range of the outer DO-loop.

8) Nested DO-loops may have the same terminal statements.

Points

1) It is good programming practice to always use a CONTINUE statement as the object of the DO loop.

2) Indentation of the statements inside a DO loop makes the program easier to read.

Examples

1)
```
C This program sums the first 10 integers.
      INTEGER I, N, SUM

      N = 10
      SUM = 0
      DO 100 I=1, N, 1
         SUM = SUM + I
  100 CONTINUE
      PRINT *, 'THE SUM OF THE FIRST', N, 'INTEGERS IS', SUM
      STOP
      END
```

2)
```
C This program sums the numbers from 10.50 to
C 25.75 in steps of .25.
      REAL X, SUM
      SUM = 0.0
      DO 1500 X = 10.50, 25.75, .25
         SUM = SUM + X
 1500 CONTINUE
      PRINT *, 'THE SUM OF THE NUMBERS IS', SUM
      STOP
      END
```

3)
```
C This program reads in 50 data values which are
C arranged one per record or line in a file and stores
C them in a two-dimensional array.  It then prints out
C the array in reverse order.
      REAL X(10, 5)
      DO 200 I = 1, 10
         DO 100 J = 1, 5
            READ *, X(I,J)
  100    CONTINUE
  200 CONTINUE
      DO 300 I = 10, 1, -1
         PRINT *, (X(I,J),J=5, 1, -1)
  300 CONTINUE
      STOP
      END
```

D.24   DOUBLE PRECISION **Statement**

Purpose
This statement allows a user to declare specific variable, array, or function names to be of type double precision.

General Form

```
DOUBLE PRECISION list
```

The list contains variable, array, or function names separated by commas.   This statement and the entire topic of double precision arithmetic (also called extended precision) are discussed in Appendix I.

D.25   ELSEIF **Statement**

Purpose
To allow simplification of nested block IF structures.

General Form

```
IF (logical expression) THEN
   : statements S1
   .
ELSEIF (logical expression) THEN
        : statements S2
        .
    ELSE
        : statements S3
        .
ENDIF
```

The ELSEIF statement functions similar to a block IF statement. It does not however have an ENDIF statement associated with it.

Example
Compare this example to the block IF example.

```
C This program reads in 10 records.  Each record contains 1
C integer and 2 real values.  It performs arithmetic on the
C real numbers as determined by the integer value.
C If the integer is: 1 - add A+B
C                     2 - subtract A-B
C         anything else - print a warning message
      INTEGER I, NUM
      REAL A, B
      DO 500 I = 1,10
         READ *, NUM, A, B
         IF (NUM .EQ. 1) THEN
             PRINT *, 'THE SUM OF', A, B, 'IS', A+B
         ELSEIF (NUM .EQ. 2) THEN
                 PRINT *, 'THE DIFFERENCE OF', A, B, 'IS', A-B
             ELSE
                 PRINT *, 'BAD CODE', NUM
         ENDIF
  500 CONTINUE
      STOP
      END
```

D.26   END **Statement**

Purpose

The END statement indicates the end of a main program or the end of a subprogram to the compiler.

General Form

```
END
```

When this statement is encountered by the compiler, the compiler ends compilation of the current program segment.

Rule

1) In FORTRAN/77 the END statement is also executable. That is, if it is executed in the main program, the program terminates as if a STOP statement had been executed. If it is executed in a subprogram, then it has the effect of a RETURN statement.

D.27   ENDFILE **Statement**

Purpose

This statement is used to write an end-of-file record to the file.

General Form

```
ENDFILE i
ENDFILE(cilist)
```

The u is an external unit specifier; the `cilist` contains specifiers from the following list:

```
[UNIT=] u
IOSTAT = ios
ERR = s
```

These specifiers are discussed in more detail in Section D.39, Input/Output Statement Specifiers.

Rule
1) The external unit must be connected for sequential access.

D.28 ENTRY **Statement**

Purpose
This statement allows a user to define additional entry points to a subroutine or function subprogram.

General Form

```
ENTRY name(parameter list)
```

The name, is any valid FORTRAN/77 name, and the parameter list consists of variable, array, or function names.

Rules
1) The ENTRY statement defines an alternate entry point to a subprogram and an alternate parameter list.   The type of entry point, that is, a SUBROUTINE or FUNCTION which determines how it is referenced, is decided by the subprogram type.
2) The ENTRY statement is placed within the body of the subprogram but is not an executable statement in the normal sense.   An ENTRY statement is ignored if it occurs in a sequence of statements being executed.
3) The ENTRY statement may not be placed in the range of a DO or WHILE loop.
4) Any variable in the subprogram not in the ENTRY parameter list has the last value it was assigned.

Example

```
C This program reads N integer values into the array
C VALUES.  It uses the subroutine SETUP to setup the
C argument and parameter correspondences for the array
C and its size.  Then it uses the subroutine entry SUM
C to sum the numbers in the array.
      INTEGER I, N, VALUES(1000), ANSWER

      READ *, N, (VALUES(I), I=1,N)
      CALL SETUP(VALUES, N)

      CALL SUM(ANSWER)
      PRINT *, 'THE SUM OF THE', N, 'NUMBERS IS =', ANSWER
      STOP
      END

      SUBROUTINE SETUP(ARRAY, N)
      INTEGER N, ARRAY(N), I, RESULT
      RETURN

      ENTRY SUM(RESULT)
      RESULT = 0
      DO 100 I = 1, N
         RESULT = RESULT + ARRAY(I)
100   CONTINUE
      RETURN
      END
```

D.29   EQUIVALENCE **Statement**

Purpose

This statement allows a user to declare that variables and arrays in the same program unit may be forced to occupy the same storage locations.

General Form

```
EQUIVALENCE (equivalence group1), (equivalence group2), . . .
```

The equivalence groups contain variable names, array element names, array names, and character substring names separated by commas.   The effect of the statement is that all those items within a group will be forced to overlap their storage locations.

Rules

1) The EQUIVALENCE statement is not executable.   It should be placed before all executable statements.
2) Since the items in an equivalence group share the same locations, they share the same values.   For example, in the following program:

```
EQUIVALENCE (A,B)
A = 1.0
PRINT *, B
STOP
END
```

when A is assigned the value 1.0, B also takes on this value and the value printed
will be 1.0.

3) Variables of different types may be equivalenced together.   However, no data type
conversion is done and thus, since internal representations for different types are not
the same, the results are somewhat unpredictable.   For instance, when the following
program was run on the IBM computer the value printed for I was 1091567616.
The internal representations for this number and 1.0 are the same.

```
EQUIVALENCE (I,X)
X = 1.0
PRINT *, I
STOP
END
```

4) Arrays may be equivalenced to simple variables and other arrays.   When an array
name is used it is the first element of the array that is used as the equivalence
point.   For the program segment

```
REAL A(5),B(4),C(3,2)
EQUIVALENCE (A,B),(A,R),(R,C)
```

the following storage sharing results

	A(1)	B(1)	R	C(1,1)
	A(2)	B(2)		C(2,1)
	A(3)	B(3)		C(3,1)
	A(4)	B(4)		C(1,2)
	A(5)			C(2,2)
				C(3,2)

5) Array elements may be used to specify equivalence points within the array.   For
example, consider the following program segment

```
REAL A(5),B(4),C(3,2)
EQUIVALENCE (B(4),A(1)),(A(3),C(2,1)),(B(3),R)
```

the storage would be shared as follows.

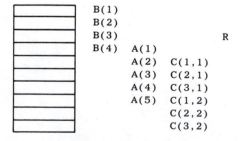

	B(1)			
	B(2)			
	B(3)		R	
	B(4)	A(1)		
		A(2)	C(1,1)	
		A(3)	C(2,1)	
		A(4)	C(3,1)	
		A(5)	C(1,2)	
			C(2,2)	
			C(3,2)	

6) The subscript of an array element in an equivalence statement may be an expression
but the expression may contain only integer constants.

7) Character entities may be equivalenced only to other character entities.

8) If compile-time initialization is to be performed on items to be equivalenced, it must be done after equivalence.

9) An EQUIVALENCE statement must not cause any item to be in two different positions. The following equivalence is illegal.

```
REAL  R(10)
EQUIVALENCE  (S,R(5)),  (S,R(4))
```

10) Items in COMMON may be equivalenced provided that the result does not try to extend past the beginning of the COMMON storage area. It is, however, legal to extend the length of the COMMON storage in the other direction. These situations are illustrated below.

   a) The following equivalencing is legal:

```
REAL  C(5),  D(6)
COMMON/JOE/  C
EQUIVALENCE  (C(3),D(1))
```

   b) The following equivalencing is illegal because it tries to extend back past the start of the COMMON area.

```
REAL  C(5),  D(6)
COMMON/JOE/  C
EQUIVALENCE  (C(1),D(3))
```

11) Neither function names nor subprogram parameters may appear in an EQUIVALENCE statement.

D.30   Executable and Non-Executable Statements

All statements in FORTRAN may be classified as being executable or non-executable. Executable statements cause some action to be performed by the computer. Non-executable statements are used to specify or define characteristics, data arrangement and organization of the program to the compiler. The following table classifies the FORTRAN statements.

Executable Statement

assignment statements
ASSIGN statement
GOTO statements
IF statements
CONTINUE statement
STOP, PAUSE statements
DO statements
READ, WRITE, PRINT statements
REWIND, BACKSPACE, ENDFILE, OPEN statements
CLOSE, INQUIRE statements
CALL, RETURN statements

Non-executable Statements

PROGRAM, FUNCTION, SUBROUTINE, ENTRY, and BLOCK DATA statements
DIMENSION, COMMON, EQUIVALENCE, IMPLICIT statements
PARAMETER, EXTERNAL, INTRINSIC statements
INTEGER, REAL, DOUBLE PRECISION, COMPLEX, LOGICAL, and CHARACTER statements
DATA statement
FORMAT statement
statement-function statement

D.31   Execution-Time Dimensioning of Arrays

Purpose
This feature allows a calling program to specify the size of an argument array to a subprogram.

Rules
1)   Execution-time dimensioning may be used only in a subprogram.
2)   Execution-time dimensioning is indicated by placing integer variables in place of constants for the array size in the array declaration in a subprogram.
3)   The array must be in the subprogram parameter list.   The variable dimensions must also be in the parameter list.
4)   A parameter array may have more than one variable dimension or may have constant and variable dimensions.

```
SUBROUTINE DOUG(X,L,M,Y,N)
INTEGER X(L,M), Y(2,N)
```

5)   The size of the argument array in the calling program is the maximum size allowed for the corresponding parameter arrays in the subprogram.

Example

```
C This program uses a subroutine to sum the elements of two
C arrays of different sizes. The name of the array to be summed
C and its size are included as arguments to the subroutine.
C The subroutine uses these to assign the corresponding
C parameter array the correct size.
      REAL X(10), Y(5), XSUM, YSUM

      READ *, X, Y
      CALL SUM(X,10,XSUM)
      CALL SUM(Y,5,YSUM)
      PRINT *, 'X AND Y SUMS ARE', XSUM, YSUM
      STOP
      END

      SUBROUTINE SUM(A,N,RESULT)
      INTEGER I, N
      REAL A(N), RESULT

      RESULT = 0.0
      DO 100 I = I, N
          RESULT = RESULT + A(I)
  100 CONTINUE
      RETURN
      END
```

D.32   EXTERNAL Statement

Purpose

The EXTERNAL statement indicates to the compiler that specific names are those of functions which are external to the current program such that the names may be used as an actual argument.

General Form

```
EXTERNAL external list
```

The external list contains function or subroutine names separated by commas. These names need only be in the external list when the function or subroutine name is being passed as an argument.

Rules

1) Statement function names may not be passed as an argument and, thus, may not appear in an external list.
2) A function or subroutine name may appear in an EXTERNAL statement only once per program unit.
3) If an intrinsic function name appears in an EXTERNAL statement then that name becomes the name of an external procedure and the intrinsic function of the same name is not available for use in that program unit.

Example

```
C Use the bisection program to determine a zero
C of the functions x**2+5x-204 and x**2-4x-77.
C The bisection program is assumed to be in the library
C as defined in the main body of the text.
      EXTERNAL SAM,GEORGE
      LOGICAL FLAG1, FLAG2
      REAL A, B, C, D, EPS, SAM, GEORGE, ROOT1, ROOT2

      READ, A, B, C, D, EPS
      CALL BISECT(A,B,EPS,SAM,FLAG1,ROOT1)
      CALL BISECT(C,D,EPS,GEORGE,FLAG2,ROOT2)
      PRINT *, 'THE ROOTS ARE', ROOT1, ROOT2
      STOP
      END

      REAL FUNCTION SAM(X)
      SAM = X**2 + 5.0*X - 204.0
      RETURN
      END

      REAL FUNCTION GEORGE(X)
      GEORGE = X**2 - 4.0*X - 77.0
      RETURN
      END
```

D.33 Files

A file is a sequence of records. A file may be either external or internal with the former being of primary concern. An external file resides on either a magnetic disk or magnetic tape. Files may be created and deleted. All input/output statements may refer to files that exist. The INQUIRE, OPEN, CLOSE, WRITE, PRINT, and ENDFILE statements may also refer to files that do not exist. A file may be named and the records in a file may be formatted or unformatted. There are two types of access methods, sequential and direct. At any point in time a file will have a current position which depends upon the previous input/output statements. In sequential access, the position determines which record will be accessed next. Refer to Section D.38, Input/Output Statements, of this appendix for more detail on the individual statements. Refer to the processor's FORTRAN/77 manual for more details on files and their properties.

D.34 FORMAT Statement

Purpose
This statement provides the user with complete control over how data is input to and output from a program.

General Form

```
nnnnn FORMAT(format codes)
```

The nnnnn is the statement number of the FORMAT statement. The FORMAT statement is not an executable statement as such but is used in conjunction with the READ, PRINT, and WRITE statements. Refer to Appendix F for a discussion of the FORMAT statement and its use.

D.35   FUNCTION **Subprograms**

Purpose
These subprograms allow the user to define multi-line functions.

General Form of Definition

```
FUNCTION name(parameter list)

:    statements
.

RETURN
END
```

The function name obeys the rules for FORTRAN/77 names. The parameter list contains variable, array, or function names separated by commas.

General Form of Usage

```
name(argument list)
```

This reference may appear anywhere an arithmetic expression is allowed. The argument list contains one or more arguments separated by commas. An argument may be a constant, an arithmetic expression, variable, array, function, or subroutine name. The number of arguments must be the same as the number of parameters, and each argument must be of the same type as its corresponding parameter.

When the reference is executed, the following happens:

1) The computer transfers to the first statement of the subprogram.
2) The values of the arguments are *copied* into the corresponding parameters. For arrays, only their location is passed, and the subroutine uses the same data area.
3) Execution of the subprogram begins at the first executable statement.
4) When a RETURN statement is executed

    a) the values of the parameters are *copied* back into the corresponding argument.

    b) the computer returns to the calling program and resumes execution in the same statement from which it came. The function reference is given the value that was last assigned to the function name in the subprogram.

Rules
1) The function name may be used as a variable in the subprogram and must be assigned a value before returning.
2) Function parameters may not be initialized at compile time.
3) Function references may not form a loop.
4) If an argument is a DO-loop index or a DO-loop parameter, the value of the corresponding parameter may not be changed in the function.
5) Variables and statement numbers are local to a subprogram. If the same names and numbers are used in another program segment, they are not considered the same by the compiler.
6) A function subprogram has a data type. A function subprogram may be of type INTEGER, REAL, DOUBLE PRECISION, COMPLEX, LOGICAL, or CHARACTER.
7) The type of a function is determined implicitly by the first letter rule of variables or by explicit declaration in the function statement.

```
REAL FUNCTION name (parameter list)
INTEGER FUNCTION name (parameter list)
```

(See Appendices G, H, I, and J for information on the function subprograms associated with the other data types.)
8) The type of a function in the calling program must be the same as in the definition.

Example

```
C Calculate L!/(M!*K!) using function subprograms.
      INTEGER L, M, K, FACT, ANSWER

      READ *, L, M, K
      ANSWER = FACT(L)/(FACT(M)*FACT(K))
      PRINT *, 'THE ANSWER IS', ANSWER
      STOP
      END

      INTEGER FUNCTION FACT(N)
      INTEGER I, N

      FACT = 1.0
      DO 100 I = N, 2, -1
         FACT = FACT*I
  100 CONTINUE
      RETURN
      END
```

D.36 GOTO **Statement**

Purpose
The GOTO statement is used to branch unconditionally to an executable statement. (See also COMPUTED GOTO).

General Form

```
    GOTO nnnnn
```

The nnnnn is the statement number on an executable statement in the same program unit.

Rule

1) It may be used by itself or may appear after a logical IF statement.

Example

```
C This program sums the first 10 integers.
        INTEGER I, N, SUM

        N = 10
        SUM = 0
        I = 1
    50 IF (I .GT. N) GOTO 1000
            SUM = SUM + I
            I = I + 1
            GOTO 50
  1000 PRINT *, 'THE SUM OF THE FIRST', N, 'INTEGERS IS', SUM
        STOP
        END
```

D.37   IMPLICIT Statement

Purpose

This statement allows a user to change the settings which are used to determine the default type of variable names.   (See the variables section of this appendix for information on the default settings.)

General Form

```
    IMPLICIT type1(letter list 1), type2(letter list 2), . . .
```

The type1, type2 each may be one of INTEGER, REAL, DOUBLE PRECISION, COMPLEX, LOGICAL, CHARACTER or CHARACTER*n.   The letter lists contain alphabetic letters separated by commas.   Each letter list gives the letters that will make all variables, arrays, symbolic names of constants, external functions, and statement functions that begin with those characters, to be of the specified type.

Rules

1) The IMPLICIT statements must precede all other statements in a program unit except PARAMETER statements.
2) The same letter must not be defined in IMPLICIT statements more than once in a program unit.

3) Those letters which are not changed in an IMPLICIT statement retain their previous settings. For example, the statement

        IMPLICIT INTEGER(O,P,Q,R,S,T)

   would result in the letters from I through T as defining integer variables by the first letter rule.

4) A letter list may specify a range of letters instead of the letters individually. For example, the actions of the statements in a) and b) directly below are equivalent. They make all variables beginning with I, J, K, L, M, and N of type REAL and those beginning with A through H and O through Z of type INTEGER.

   a) IMPLICIT INTEGER(A-H,O-Z), REAL(I-N)
   b) IMPLICIT REAL(I,J,K-M,N)
      IMPLICIT INTEGER(A-H,O-P,Q-Z)
   c) IMPLICIT LOGICAL(L)
      IMPLICIT CHARACTER(C),CHARACTER*20(D)

5) An IMPLICIT statement does not change the type of an intrinsic function.

D.38   Input/Output Statements

Purpose
The following statements are used to transfer data to and from external devices such as card readers, printers, terminals, and disk or magnetic tape files. These statements are described in greater detail under their own heading.

    READ   ⎫
    WRITE   ⎬ data transfer statements
    PRINT   ⎭

    OPEN   ⎫
    CLOSE   ⎬ file connection and inquiry statements
    INQUIRE ⎭

    BACKSPACE ⎫
    ENDFILE   ⎬ file positioning statements
    REWIND   ⎭

D.39   Input/Output Statement Specifiers

The input/output statements in FORTRAN/77 allow inclusion of specifiers to send parameters to the input/output process or receive status information about the input/output process or about a file. The common specifiers are described below. Specifiers which are unique to an input/output statement or that are uniquely used by an input/output statement are described with it.

1. [UNIT=] u   specifies the unit number which the current input/output statement is accessing.

    a)   u is the unit identifier which may be:

        i   - integer expression with zero or positive value
        *   - predetermined default unit number
        c   - character variable, character array, character array element, character substring.

    b)   UNIT= is optional but if omitted the unit specifier must be the first item in the list.

2. [FMT=] f   specifies where the formatting control is to be found.

    a)   f is the format identifier which may be:

        - statement label of a FORMAT statement
        - an integer variable name that has been ASSIGNED the statement label of a FORMAT statement
        - a character array name
        *   list directed formatting.

    b)   FMT= is optional but if omitted the format identifier must be the second item in the list and the first item must be the unit identifier without the UNIT=.

3. REC = rn   specifies the number of the record that is to be accessed for a direct access file.

4. IOSTAT = ios   retrieves the status of the input/output operation.

    a)   ios is the input/output status identifier and is an integer variable or integer array element.

    b)   The values of ios will be

        0 - input/output statement was successful
      +n - a processor-determined, positive integer value if the input/output statement encountered an error
      -n - a processor-determined, negative integer value if the input/output statement encountered an end-of-file condition and no error.

5. ERR = s   specifies the executable statement that is branched to when an error condition is encountered.

    a)   s is the statement label of the executable statement
    b)   If ERR = s does not appear in the input/output statement and an error is encountered, the program terminates.
    c)   If the input/output statement conains an input/output status indicator, the ios variable or array element will contain a positive valued processor code.

6. END = s   specifies the executable statement that is branched to when an end-of-file condition is encountered.

     a)   s is the statement label of the executable statement.
     b)   If END = s does not appear in the input/output statement and an end-of-file condition is encountered, the program terminates.
     c)   If the input/output statement contains an input/output status indicator, the ios variable or array element will contain a negative valued processor code.

7. FILE = fin   specifies the name of the file on the external storage device.

     a)   fin is a character expression whose value is the name of the file. Trailing blanks are removed and the resulting name must be a legal name for the processor.
     b)   If this specifier is omitted, the processor assigns an internal name for the file.

8. STATUS = sta   specifies the expected status of a file on an external storage device.

     a)   sta is a character expression the values of which are limited to predefined values.
     b)   The valid values for sta vary with the individual statements and thus are discussed with those statements.

9. ACCESS = acc   specifies the access method to be used on the file being connected.

     a)   acc is a character expression which must have a value of SEQUENTIAL or DIRECT.
     b)   The default value is SEQUENTIAL.
     c)   If the file exists, the access method must agree with the allowed access methods for the file.
     d)   Refer to the specifications or processor FORTRAN/77 manual for more information.

10. FORM = fm   specifies type of formatting that is to be used on the file being converted.

     a)   fm is a character expression which must have a value of FORMATTED or UNFORMATTED.
     b)   The default value is UNFORMATTED.
     c)   Refer to the specifications or processor FORTRAN/77 manual for more information.

11. BLANK = blnk   specifies how blanks are to be handled in numeric input fields.

     a)   blnk is a character expression which must have a value of NULL or ZERO.
     b)   The default value is NULL.
     c)   If the value is NULL, all blank characters in numeric formatted input fields are ignored.

      d)   If the value is ZERO, all non-leading blank characters in numeric formatted input fields are treated as zero.

12. RECL = rl   specifies the length of each record in a file being connected for direct access.

      a)   rl is the length of each record.

      b)   This specifier must be included for direct access and omitted for sequential access.

D.40   INQUIRE **Statement**

Purpose

This statement is used to inquire about the properties of a particular external file or the properties of the connection to a particular file.

General Form

```
INQUIRE (FILE = fin,flist) inquire by file
INQUIRE (UNIT = u,flist)    inquire by unit
```

The flist may contain at most one of each of the following inquiry specifiers.

IOSTAT = ios   ios is an integer variable or integer array element. It is assigned 0 if no error condition exists, otherwise it is assigned a processor determined positive number.

ERR = s   s is an error specifier. See section D.39.

EXIST = ex   ex is a logical variable or logical array element. File inquiry: .TRUE. if file exists, .FALSE. otherwise. Unit inquiry: .TRUE. if unit exists, .FALSE. otherwise.

OPENED = od   od is a logical variable or logical array element. File inquiry: .TRUE. if file connected to a unit, .FALSE. otherwise. Unit inquiry: .TRUE. if file connected to a file, .FALSE. otherwise.

NUMBER = num   num is an integer variable or integer array element. It is assigned the number of the unit that is connected to the file under inquiry. It is undefined if no unit is connected.

NAMED = nmd   nmd is a logical variable or array element. It is assigned .TRUE. if file has a name, .FALSE. otherwise.

NAME = fn   fn is a character variable or character array element that is assigned the name of the file.

ACCESS = acc   acc is a character variable or character array element. It is assigned the value SEQUENTIAL or DIRECT depending upon the connection method. It is undefined if there is no connection.

SEQUENTIAL = seq   seq is a character variable or character array element. It is assigned YES if file may be accessed sequentially, NO if the file may not be accessed sequentially, or UNKNOWN if the processor can not determine which.

DIRECT = dir	dir is a character variable or character array element. It is assigned YES if file may be accessed directly, NO if the file may not be accessed directly, or UNKNOWN if the processor can not determine which.
FORM = fm	fm is a character variable or character array element. It is assigned the value FORMATTED if file is connected for formatted input/output or UNFORMATTED if file is connected for unformatted input/output. It is undefined if there is no connection.
FORMATTED = fmt	fmt is a character variable or character array element. It is assigned YES if file allows formatted access, NO if file does not allow formatted access, or UNKNOWN if processor is unable to determine which.
UNFORMATTED = unf	unf is a character variable or character array element. It is assigned YES if file allows unformatted access, NO if file does not allow unformatted access, or UNKNOWN if processor is unable to determine which.
RECL = rcl	rcl is an integer variable or integer array element. It is assigned the record length of the file connected for direct access. It is undefined if there is no connection.
NEXTREC	nr is an integer variable or integer array element. It is assigned the number of the next record to be read or written on a file connected for direct access. It is undefined if there is no connection or if an error condition occurred.
BLANK = blank	blank is a character variable or a character array element. It is assigned NULL if null blank control is in effect or ZERO if zero blank control is in effect. It is undefined if there is no connection.

D.41   INTEGER **Statement**

Purpose
This statement is used to declare specific variable, array, or function names to be of type INTEGER.

General Forms

```
INTEGER list
INTEGER*4 list
INTEGER*2 list
```

The latter two lines represent extensions to the standard in several implementations including the IBM and VAX systems. The lists may contain variable names, function names, and array names. The first two statements are equivalent and declare the items in their lists to be full-word INTEGERs. The *4 notation refers to the fact that such integer values occupy 4 bytes of memory (a full word). The INTEGER*2 statement declares the items in its list to be half-word INTEGERs.   The *2 notation refers to the fact that such integer values occupy 2 bytes of memory (a half word).   (See also the section in this appendix on the compile-time initialization of variables.)

Rules
1) This statement should be placed before all executable statements.
2) This statement may be used to declare individual names to be of type INTEGER.

        INTEGER A, B, ISUM, COUNT

3) The size of arrays may be declared in this statement:

        INTEGER I(10), C(10,2)

4) Variables declared to be of type INTEGER*2 have a much reduced range of numbers that they may store (-32168 to +32167) and, thus, must be used carefully.   In addition, there are some restrictions on their use.

D.42   Intrinsic (Built-in) Functions

Purpose
Intrinsic functions provide a simple way for the user to perform common calculations.

General Form of Usage

        name(argument list)

This reference may appear anywhere an arithmetic expression is allowed.   The argument list consists of one or more arguments separated by commas.   An argument may be a constant, an arithmetic expression or a variable.   All intrinsic functions are predefined and a table of those available is given in Appendix N.   An intrinsic function may be a specific intrinsic function or a generic intrinsic function.

Examples
1)   A = SQRT(FLOAT(I))
2)   R = AMINO(A+5,S,X)
3)   C = SIN(ANGLE)
4)   PRINT *, ABS(T)+5.462

D.43 INTRINSIC **Statement**

Purpose

The INTRINSIC statement indicates to the compiler that the specified names are those of INTRINSIC functions such that the names may be used as an actual argument.

General Form

```
INTRINSIC intrinsic function name list
```

The intrinsic function name list contains names of intrinsic functions separated by commas. These names need only be in this name list when the intrinsic function name is being passed as an actual argument.

Rules
1) An intrinsic function name may appear in an INTRINSIC statement only once per program unit.
2) A name may not appear in both an INTRINSIC statement and an EXTERNAL statement.
3) A generic function does not loose its generic property if it appears in an INTRINSIC statement.
4) The names of the intrinsic functions for type conversion (INT, IFIX, IDINT, FLOAT, SNGL, REAL, DBLE, CMPLX, ICHAR, CHAR), lexical relationships (LGE, LGT, LLE, LLT), and for choosing the maximum or minimum value (MAX, MAX0, AMAX1, DMAX1, AMAX0, MAX1, MIN, MIN0, AMIN1, DMIN1, AMIN0, MIN1) must not be used as actual arguments.

D.44 **Logical Expressions**

Purpose

Logical expressions permit the expression of complicated logical relationships.

Rules
1) Logical expressions are composed of logical operators and logical operands. The logical operators in order of their priority are: .NOT., .AND., .OR., and .EQV., .NEQV.. The latter have an equal priority with each other.
2) The logical operands may be a logical constant, symbolic name of a logical constant, logical variable or array element, logical function reference, or relational expression.
3) The priority of the logical operators as a group is less than that of the relational expressions and thus, is also less than arithmetic expressions.
4) In a logical expression with operators of equal priority, the evaluation is performed left to right.

Examples

In the following, Example 1) is equivalent to Example 2), and Example 3) is equivalent to Example 4).   Note that the parentheses in Example 5) are necessary to preserve the intended meaning.   See also Appendix J.

1)   `A.LT.0.0 .AND. A.GT.10.0`
2)   `(A.LT.0.0) .AND. (A.GT.10.0)`
3)   `A**2+5.0+B+C.LT.25.0 .OR. D.GE.17.0`
4)   `(A**2+5.0+B+C.LT.25.0) .OR. (D.GE.17.0)`
5)   `.NOT.(X.GE.4 .AND. Y.LE.6)`
6)   `X.LT.5 .EQV. Y.GT.10`
7)   `LOGICAL A, B`
  `:`
  `:`
  `IF (A.NEQV.B) THEN`

D.45   Logical IF

Purpose

This statement allows some action to be taken as a result of some test or comparison. (See also arithmetic IF and block IF.)

General Form

```
IF (logical expression) executable statement
```

If the logical expression has the value `.TRUE.` then the statement following the IF is executed.   Otherwise the statement on the next line is executed.

Rule

1)   The executable statement may not be a DO statement, a block IF statement, ELSEIF, ELSE, ENDIF, END, or another logical IF.

Examples

1)   `IF(I .LT. 10) PRINT *, A, B`
2)   `IF(A+B .GT. C+D) GOTO 25`

D.46   LOGICAL **Statement**

Purpose

This statement is used to declare specific variable, array, or function names to be of type LOGICAL.

General Forms

```
LOGICAL list
LOGICAL*4 list
LOGICAL*1 list
```

The latter two lines represent extensions to the standard in several implementations including the IBM and VAX systems.   The lists may contain variable, array, or function names separated by commas.   The first two statements are equivalent and declare items in their list to be of type LOGICAL which occupies 4 bytes (*4) of memory.   The last statement declares items which occupy 1 byte (*1) of memory.   Refer to Appendix H for a discussion of these statements and the logical data types.

D.47   OPEN **Statement**

Purpose

This statement is used to create a file or to connect the program to an existing file for the purpose of READing or WRITEing data from/to the file.

General Form

```
OPEN (olist)
```

The olist contains specifiers to control the connection to the file.   The specifiers may be:

```
[UNIT=] u
IOSTAT = ios
ERR = s
FILE = fin
STATUS = sta
ACCESS = acc
FORM = fm
RECL = rl
BLANK = blnk
```

of which there must be one external unit specifiers and may contain at most one of each of the other specifiers.   These specifiers are discussed in more detail in Section D.39, Input/Output Statement Specifiers.   The valid values for sta are:

OLD   must have FILE= specifier, file must exist.
NEW   must have FILE= specifier, file must not exist.
SCRATCH   must not have FILE= specifier, temporary file used and deleted on CLOSE.

UNKNOWN   the default value.

Refer to the processor's FORTRAN/77 manual for further information.

D.48   PARAMETER **Statement**

Purpose
This statement allows a user to give a symbolic name to a constant which may then be used in place of a constant in that program.

General Form

```
PARAMETER (p1=e1, p2=e2, ...)
```

The p1 and p2 are symbolic names that are to represent the value of e1 and e2 respectively. e1 and e2 are constant expressions.

Rules
1) The constant expression may be arithmetic, character or logical.
2) The symbolic name and constant expression must be of the same type.
3) A constant expression may contain constants or previously defined symbolic names of constants.
4) A symbolic name of a constant may be defined only once.
5) Symbolic names of a constant are local to the program unit in which they are defined.
6) Symbolic names of a constant may not be used in a FORMAT statement, as part of another number, or as part of a complex constant.
7) If the symbolic name of a constant is not of the desired default type or is not of the correct length then the symbolic name must be specified prior to the PARAMETER statement and must not be changed by subsequent statements.

Example

```
C This program reads in and prints out 91 integer values.
      INTEGER START, END, IUNIT, OUNIT
      PARAMETER (START=10,END=100,IUNIT=5,OUNIT=6)
      INTEGER TABLE(START:END)

      READ(IUNIT,*) (TABLE(I),I=START,END)
      WRITE(OUNIT,*) (TABLE(I),I=START,END)
      STOP
      END
```

D.49   PAUSE **Statement**

Purpose
This statement is used to allow a temporary halt in the execution of a program to allow the computer operator to perform some task.

General Forms

```
PAUSE
PAUSE nnnnn
PAUSE 'message'
```

The 5-digit number or the character constant are printed on the terminal when the PAUSE statement is executed.   In computer installations which operate in a batch mode, the PAUSE statement is usually ignored.

D.50   PRINT **Statement**

Purpose
This statement allows a program to print messages and the values of variables, constants, and expressions.

General Form

```
PRINT *, iolist
```

This is the simplest form of the PRINT statement.   When executed, this statement will cause the computer to advance to a new line and print the messages and values in the iolist.   Other forms of this statement exist and are discussed in Appendix F.

Rules
1) Each PRINT statement starts printing on a new line.
2) The output list may contain variables, messages inside quotes, constants, and expressions.
3) If the output list contains too many values for all of them to be printed on one line, the computer automatically advances to the next line.   A print line usually contains from 120 to 133 characters, depending on the type of line printer installed.
4) If an array name is contained in the output list, then all elements of that array will be printed out in column order.
5) Implied DO loops are allowed to provide a shorthand notation for the output list. The following examples illustrate their use:

```
PRINT *, A(1),A(2),A(3),A(4)          PRINT *, (A(I), I=1,4)
PRINT *, B(1,1),B(1,2),B(2,1),B(2,2)  PRINT *, ((B(I,J), J=1,2), I=1,2)
PRINT *, 1, 3, 5, 7                   PRINT *, (I, I=1,7,2)
```

D.51 PROGRAM **Statement**

Purpose
To supply a user determined name to a main program.

General Form

```
PROGRAM program name
```

The program name is the symbolic name of the main program in which the PROGRAM statement appears.

Rules
1) The PROGRAM statement may appear only as the first statement of a main program.
2) The PROGRAM statement may be omitted.
3) The program name is global to the entire program and thus must be a unique program unit name and also may not be the same as the name of a COMMON block.
4) The program name may not be the same as any other name in the main program.

D.52 **Program Unit**

A program unit is a term which refers to a main program, a function subprogram, or a subroutine subprogram.

D.53 READ **Statement**

Purpose
This statement allows a program to obtain data either interactively or from a data file.

General Form

```
READ *, iolist
```

This is the simplest form of the READ statement.   When executed, this statement will cause the computer to read the next data record and assign the numbers or values on it to the variables in the iolist.   Other forms of this statement exist and are discussed in Appendix F.

Rules
1) The data values are supplied to the program either interactively or from a file.
2) Data values on the same line must be separated by a comma and/or one or more blanks.
3) In this program segment, A is assigned the value 3.0, I is assigned the value 4, and X is assigned the value 5.6.

```
READ *, A,I,X
      .
      .
supplied data
3 4.05 5.6
```

4) The iolist may contain only variable names. It may not contain constants or expressions.

5) The values on the data record should agree in type (REAL or INTEGER) with the corresponding variables in the iolist. If the variable type and the data type do not agree then the assignment of the data value to the variable follows the type conversion rules of mixed mode assignment statements. Data values may not be expressions.

6) Each READ statement encountered causes a new data record to be read. Thus, if there are more values per record than variables in the iolist, the remaining values are ignored.

7) If there are insufficient data values on a record, another record is read automatically. If there are not enough data records, an error message is issued.

8) If an array name is contained in the iolist, the computer will try to read in enough data for every element of the array and will assign them in column order.

9) Implied DO loops are allowed to provide a shorthand notation for the input list. The following examples illustrate their use:

```
READ *, A(1),A(2),A(3),A(4)            READ *, (A(I), I=1,4)
READ *, B(1,1),B(1,2),B(2,1),B(2,2)    READ *, ((B(I,J), J=1,2), I=1,2)
```

Examples

1) In the following program segment, two data records are read, and I is given the value 100, X is given the value 2.0, and Y is given the value 5.0.

```
READ *, I, X, Y
       .
       .
       .
supplied data
   100
2.0 5.0
```

2) In this program segment, an error will be issued since there are not enough data values. However, before the error is issued, X is assigned the value 2.0, A receives 3.0, and I is assigned 25. The value 4.0 is not used.

```
        READ *, X, A
        READ *, I, Z
        .
        :
        .
    supplied data
      2.0 3.0 4.0
      25
```

D.54   REAL **Statement**

Purpose
This statement is used to declare specific variable, array, or function names to be of type
REAL.

General Forms

```
    REAL list
    REAL*4 list
    REAL*8 list
```

The latter two lines represent extensions to the standards in several implementations
including the IBM and VAX systems.   The lists contain variable, array, or function
names separated by commas.   The first two statements are equivalent and declare all
items in their lists to be of type single-precision REAL.   The *4 notation refers to the
fact that a single-precision real number occupies 4 bytes of memory.   The last statement
declares the items in its list to be of type extended-precision REAL.   Refer to Appendix I
for more information on this data type.   (See also the section in this appendix on the
compile-time initialization of variables.)

Rules
1)   This statement should be placed before all executable statements.
2)   This statement may be used to declare individual names to be of type REAL.

```
    REAL ISUM, J, COUNT, JOE
```

3)   The size of an array may be declared in this statement.

```
    REAL R(10), JOE(20,5)
```

D.55   **Relational Expressions**

Purpose
Relational expressions are used to compare the values of arithmetic expressions.

General Form

```
expression REOP expression
```

where REOP stands for one of the six relational operators, .EQ., .NE., .LT., .LE., .GT., and .GE., and expression may be an arithmetic or character expression.

Rules
1) The priority of the relational operators is less than that of the arithmetic operators.
2) The result of a relational expression is either .TRUE. or .FALSE..

Examples
1) X .LT. 5.0
2) Y .GE. X**2 + 3*X + 1.5

D.56 RETURN **Statement**

Purpose
This statement is used to return from a subprogram to the program that called it.

General Form

```
RETURN
```

The operation of the RETURN varies slightly depending on whether the return is being made from a subroutine subprogram or a function subprogram.   See the discussion of the SUBROUTINE and FUNCTION statements for details.

Rules
1) A subprogram may have several RETURN statements.
2) A RETURN statement is an unconditional transfer statement.

Example
See the examples in this appendix for the SUBROUTINE and FUNCTION statements.

D.57 REWIND **Statement**

Purpose
This statement is used to reposition the file at its initial point for subsequent input/output.

General Form

```
REWIND u
REWIND (alist)
```

The u is an external unit specifier; the `alist` contains specifiers from the following list:

```
[UNIT=] u
IOSTAT = ios
ERR = s
```

These specifiers are discussed more detail in Section D.39, Input/Output Statement Specifiers.

Rule

1) The external unit must be connected for sequential access.

D.58   Statement Format

1) Columns 1-5 are reserved for statement numbers.   A statement number is a number from 1 to 99999 used to identify and refer to statements.   Only those statements which need to be referenced require a statement number.   The statement numbers need not be in ascending order, but it aids the readability of the program if they are.   A statement number may go anywhere within these five columns.

2) Column 6 is reserved for a continuation indicator.   Any nonzero or nonblank character in column 6 indicates that this statement is a continuation of the previous statement.   For instance, the following two statements are identical in operation.

```
col. 6                              col. 6
   ¦                                   ¦
   'X = A+B+C                          'X = A+B+C+D
 *+D
```

Multiple continuation statements are allowed. Often a FORTRAN processor will have some upper limit on the number allowed. The standard sets a maximum of 19. Columns 1 through 5 of a continuation line should be blank.

3) Program statements are punched in columns 7 to 72.

4) Columns 73 to 80 are reserved for sequence numbers.   These columns are not usually checked by FORTRAN processors.

D.59 **Statement** FUNCTIONS

Purpose
These subprograms allow users to write their own one-line functions.

General Form of Definition

```
name(parameter list) = expression
```

The `parameter list` contains one or more variable names, called parameters, separated by commas and `expression` must include at least these parameters in the calculations.

General Form of Usage

```
name(argument list)
```

This reference may appear anywhere an expression is allowed. The `argument list` contains one or more arguments separated by commas.   An argument may be a constant, an expression, or a variable.   The number of arguments must be the same as the number of parameters, and each argument value must be of the same type as its corresponding parameter.

When a statement function reference is executed the following actions occur:

1)   The values of the arguments are transferred into their corresponding parameters.
2)   The arithmetic expression of the statement function is evaluated, and the resultant value is assigned to the function name on the LHS of the statement function.
3)   The statement function reference is given the value of the statement function, and execution continues in the statement which contained the reference.

Rules
1)   Statement functions may appear in main programs and subprograms.   However, a statement function may only be used from within the program segment in which it is defined.
2)   Statement function names follow the same rules as variable names.
3)   Statement functions should be placed before all executable statements but after the declaration statements.
4)   Statement functions may be evaluated only by referencing their name in some other statement.   Thus, statement functions are not executable statements in the usual sense of the word.

Example

```
C This program uses a statement function to generate a table
C of Fahrenheit degrees versus Celsius degrees over the range
C of 0.0 to 212.0 degrees Fahrenheit.
      REAL FDEG, CEL, FAHREN
C Define the statement function CEL.
      CEL(FAHREN) = (FAHREN - 32.0)*5.0/9.0
      PRINT *, 'TABLE OF FAHRENHEIT VERSUS CELSIUS DEGREES'
      DO 100 FDEG = 0.0, 212.0, 1.0
         PRINT *, FDEG, CEL(FDEG)
  100 CONTINUE
      STOP
      END
```

D.60   Statement Ordering

1) A PROGRAM statement may appear only as the first statement of a main program.
2) FUNCTION, SUBROUTINE and BLOCK DATA statements may appear only as the first statement of a subprogram.
3) All specification statements must precede all DATA statements, statement function statements and executable statements. IMPLICIT specification statements must precede all other specification statements except PARAMETER.
4) DATA statements may appear anywhere after the specification statements.
5) Statement function statements must precede all executable statements.
6) ENTRY statements may appear anywhere in a subprogram except in the range of a block IF or a DO-loop.
7) An END statement is the last statement in a program unit.
8) FORMAT statements may appear anywhere.

D.61   STOP Statement

Purpose
The STOP statement is used to terminate execution of the program.

General Form

```
STOP
STOP nnnnn
STOP 'message'
```

When this statement is executed by the computer, it causes the computer to terminate the current program. When termination occurs, the 5-digit integer number or the character constant is usually printed to identify which STOP statement halted the program.

Rules
1) The nnnnn is optional and may be omitted.
2) Some installations may disable the nnnnn message.

Example
See any FORTRAN/77 program in this text.

D.62 SUBROUTINE **Subprograms**

Purpose
These subprograms allow a user to define a group of statements to be a separate program segment which may be invoked from within other program segments using the CALL statement.

General Form of Definition

```
SUBROUTINE name(parameter list)

:    statements

RETURN
END
```

The subroutine name obeys the rules for FORTRAN/77 names. The parameter list contains variable, array, or function names separated by commas.

General Form of Usage

```
CALL name(argument list)
```

The argument list contains one or more arguments separated by commas. An argument may be a constant, arithmetic expression, variable, array, or function name. The number of arguments must be the same as the number of parameters, and each argument must be of the same type as its corresponding parameter.

When, the CALL statement is executed, the following actions occur:

1) The computer transfers to the first statement of the SUBROUTINE.
2) The values of the arguments are *copied* into the corresponding parameters. For arrays, only their location is passed, and the subroutine uses the same data area.
3) Execution of the subroutine begins at the first executable statement.
4) When a RETURN statement is executed

   a) the values of the parameters are *copied* back into the corresponding arguments.
   b) the computer returns to the calling program and resumes execution at the statement following the CALL statement.

Rules
1) A Subroutine name may not be used as a variable in the subprogram.
2) Subroutine parameters may not be initialized at compile time.
3) Subroutine calls may not form a loop.
4) If an argument is a DO loop index or a DO loop parameter, the value of the corresponding parameter may not be changed in the subroutine.
5) Variables and statement numbers are local to a subroutine.   If the same names and numbers are used in another program segment, they are not considered the same by the compiler.

Example

```
C Calculate L!/(M!*K!) using subroutine subprograms
      INTEGER L, M, K, LFACT, MFACT, KFACT, ANSWER
      READ *, L, M, K
      CALL FACT(L,LFACT)
      CALL FACT(M,MFACT)
      CALL FACT(K,KFACT)
      ANSWER = LFACT/(MFACT*KFACT)
      PRINT *, 'THE ANSWER IS', ANSWER
      RETURN
      END
      SUBROUTINE FACT(N,IFACT)
      INTEGER I, N, IFACT
      IFACT = 1.0
      DO 100 I = N, 2, -1
         IFACT = IFACT*I
  100 CONTINUE
      RETURN
      END
```

D.63   Variables

1) A variable name may have up to 6 symbols.   The first symbol must be alphabetic A-Z, for example:

   A, X, COUNT, GEORGE, A1234

2) Operators and delimiters may not appear in a variable name.   Thus the following characters are illegal:

   * / + -) (. ' , & =

3) Blanks may appear in a variable name but are ignored by the compiler and not counted as one of the six symbols.

   WO MAN   is equivalent to   WOMAN

4) Both integer and real variables exist for storing integer and real values. There are two ways of determining the type of a given variable name.

   a) *Implicit Typing (first letter rule):* Variable names beginning with the symbols A-H, O-Z are REAL while those beginning with I, J, K, L, M, and N are INTEGER. If only these default rules are used, then the variable names JIM, MOE, and LESTER are of type INTEGER, and SAM, GEORGE, FRED, and X are of type REAL.

   b) *Explicit Typing:* This feature is used to override the default rules for individual variable names. The REAL and INTEGER specification statements are used.

```
REAL X, Y, FRED, JIM, JOE
INTEGER ABLE, GEORGE, JOKER
```

D.64 WRITE Statement

Purpose

This statement allows a user more control over the output of data.

General Form

```
WRITE(u,f)
```

This is the simplest form of the WRITE statement. The u is used to select the output device of the WRITE statement. It allows selection of a line printer, card punch, disks, and even magnetic tape units. The exact u used depends on the individual computer installation. The f refers to the statement number of the FORMAT statement which is to control the output. Refer to Appendix F for more information on the use of this statement.

E
Internal Representation of Data in FORTRAN/77

E.1 Number Systems

The decimal number system (base 10) used by humans has 10 different states (the decimal digits 0 to 9) and is not very convenient for computers. The technological properties of electronic components are much better suited to representing the two electrical states of 'on' and 'off'. As a result, most computers make use of a two-state number system called a base 2 or *binary* representation which has only the binary digits of 0 and 1. A binary digit is also called a *bit* and binary numbers consist of one or more bits. All data to be stored on a computer is converted into or represented by such numbers. The following are base 2 numbers of 8 bits each with their corresponding base 10 values. To prevent confusion, subscripts are given to indicate the base of the numbers.

$$00000000_2 = 0_{10}$$
$$01101111_2 = 111_{10}$$
$$11011110_2 = 222_{10}$$
$$11111111_2 = 255_{10}$$

The conversion between base 2 numbers and base 10 numbers may be accomplished in a straightforward manner. Conversion of a decimal number into binary may be done by repeatedly dividing the decimal number by 2, taking the remainder (0 or 1) at each stage to form the binary number. This is illustrated below for the decimal number 119.

	quotient	remainder
119/2 =	59	1
59/2 =	29	1
29/2 =	14	1
14/2 =	7	0
7/2 =	3	1
3/2 =	1	1
1/2 =	0	1

result $\longrightarrow 1\ 1\ 1\ 0\ 1\ 1\ 1_2$

To convert a binary number into a decimal number, it is first necessary to realize that the following equation holds for decimal numbers:

$$d_4 d_3 d_2 d_1 d_0 = d_4 \times 10_{10}^4 + d_3 \times 10_{10}^3 + d_2 \times 10_{10}^2 + d_1 \times 10_{10}^1 + d_0 \times 10_{10}^0,$$

where d_i represents a decimal digit. A simple example follows:

$$58764_{10} = 5 \times 10_{10}^4 + 8 \times 10_{10}^3 + 7 \times 10_{10}^2 + 6 \times 10_{10}^1 + 4 \times 10_{10}^0.$$

A similar equation holds for binary numbers,

$$b_4 b_3 b_2 b_1 b_0 = b_4 \times 2_2^4 + b_3 \times 2_2^3 + b_2 \times 2_2^2 + b_1 \times 2_2^1 + b_0 \times 2_2^0,$$

where b_i represents a binary digit. Of course, in base 2 arithmetic, multiplication by 2 means shifting the digit one place to the left, that is, $b_4 \times 2^4 = b_4 0000$. For example:

$$10101_2 = 1 \times 2_2^4 + 0 \times 2_2^3 + 1 \times 2_2^2 + 0 \times 2_2^1 + 1 \times 2_2^0$$

$$= 1000 + 0000 + 100 + 00 + 1.$$

Having established the above, it is only necessary to perform the evaluation of the binary digits using base 10 arithmetic.

$$10101_2 = 1 \times 2_2^4 + 0 \times 2_2^3 + 1 \times 2_2^2 + 0 \times 2_2^1 + 1 \times 2_2^0$$

$$= 1 \times 16_{10} + 0 \times 8_{10} + 1 \times 4_{10} + 0 \times 2_{10} + 1 \times 1_{10}$$

$$= 16_{10} + 4_{10} + 1_{10}$$

$$= 21_{10}$$

Since binary numbers are very difficult to remember, the individual binary digits are usually grouped together. The bit combinations in each group are represented by a different character. It is possible to take the bits in groups of 2,3,4, and so on. A group of 3 bits has $2^3 = 8$ different digits and is called the base 8 or *octal* representation. A group of 4 bits has $2^4 = 16$ different digits and is called the base 16 or *hexadecimal* representation. The octal representation is used on numerous computers including the Honeywell computers. The hexadecimal representation is used on all large IBM computers. The octal and hexadecimal forms are the two most common representation systems. It should be emphasized that grouping the bits together does not change how the computer stores the information but just allows a human to remember the numbers more easily.

The relationships between binary, octal, hexadecimal and decimal are shown in Figure E.1.

Figure E.1   Relationship between binary, octal, hexadecimal, and decimal values.

binary number	octal number	hexadecimal number	decimal value
00000	0	0	0
00001	1	1	1
00010	2	2	2
00011	3	3	3
00100	4	4	4
00101	5	5	5
00110	6	6	6
00111	7	7	7
01000	10	8	8
01001	11	9	9
01010	12	A	10
01011	13	B	11
01100	14	C	12
01101	15	D	13
01110	16	E	14
01111	17	F	15
10000	20	10	16
10001	21	11	17

Thus, by using the table, the following binary numbers may be written as indicated below.

$$10010111_2 = 227_8 = 97_{16}$$
$$10100101_2 = 245_8 = A5_{16}$$
$$000100111111_2 = 0477_8 = 13F_{16}$$

In large IBM computers, the basic unit of memory is the byte, which contains 8 bits and thus can store 2 hexadecimal digits. Since different data types have different memory requirements, several consecutive bytes are necessary to store some values. When 2 bytes are used, they form a unit of memory called a half word, when 4 bytes are used they are called a full word, and 8 bytes form a double word. The following table illustrates the relationship between these units of memory.

1 bit	= 0 or 1	
1 byte	= 8 bits	
1 half word	= 2 bytes	= 16 bits
1 word	= 4 bytes	= 32 bits
1 double word	= 8 bytes	= 64 bits

Typically, the storage of integer numbers, real numbers, and a character of information use multiples of bytes. For example

	Typical Large *IBM/DEC VAX*	*Typical* *Micros*
integer	4 bytes	2 bytes
real	4 bytes	4 bytes
character	1 byte	1 byte

E.2   Integer Numbers

An integer number may be either negative, zero, or positive.   Representing zero and positive numbers is not difficult.   It is the representation of negative numbers that is somewhat unusual.   Of the many ways of storing negative numbers, the most common method is the 2's complement notation.   In this notation, a positive number is converted into a negative number of the same magnitude by complementing all of the bits (change 0 to 1 and 1 to 0) and adding 1.   The hexadecimal representation (32 bits) for the decimal number 119 is given as follows.

$+119_{10}$	0	0	0	0	0	0	7	7_{16}	hex number
	0000	0000	0000	0000	0000	0000	0111	0111	binary form
	1111	1111	1111	1111	1111	1111	1000	1000	complement it
								+1	add 1
	1111	1111	1111	1111	1111	1111	1000	1001	negative binary form
-119_{10}	F	F	F	F	F	F	8	9_{16}	negative of hex number

The octal representation (36 bits) for the decimal number 119 is given as follows.

$+119_{10}$	0	0	0	0	0	0	0	0	0	1	6	7_8	octal number
	000	000	000	000	000	000	000	000	000	001	110	111	binary form
	111	111	111	111	111	111	111	111	111	110	001	000	complement it
												+1	add 1
	111	111	111	111	111	111	111	111	111	110	001	001	negative binary form
-119_{10}	7	7	7	7	7	7	7	7	7	6	1	1	negative of octal number

As it turns out, the left most bit of an integer number gives the sign (0 means positive, 1 means negative) of the integer value.

E.3   Real Numbers

The real number system requires not only negative, zero, and positive numbers but must also allow for a floating decimal point.   Thus computers must have a way of storing these numbers internally. If the general form of a decimal floating-point number can be said to be $0.d_{-1}d_{-2}d_{-3}d_{-4} \cdots \times 10^{dexp}$ then a hexadecimal representation of a number could have a general form of $0.h_{-1}h_{-2}h_{-3}h_{-4} \cdots \times 16^{hexp}$.   An octal representation of a real number can be represented by $0.o_{-1}o_{-2}o_{-3} \cdots \times 8^{oexp}$.   Conversion between the decimal and the other representations is not straightforward and, thus, will not be discussed here.   The storage of such real numbers involves reserving a portion of a computer word to store a sign, the exponent and the fractional or mantissa part.   A typical layout is shown by the following.

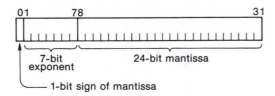

E.4   Character Information

In order that character information can be stored on a computer, each character must be converted into a number code which is used to represent it.   There are two common encoding schemes called EBCDIC — Extended Binary Coded Decimal Interchange Code, and ASCII — American Standard Code for Information Interchange.   These codes are arranged such that the numbers form a collating sequence for the characters, for example, A < B < C < . . . < Z, etc.

E.4.1   EBCDIC

Upper-case Letters			*Lower-case letters*			*Digits*		
Char	*Hex*	*Dec*	*Char*	*Hex*	*Dec*	*Char*	*Hex*	*Dec*
A	C1	193	a	81	129	0	F0	240
B	C2	194	b	82	130	1	F1	241
C	C3	195	c	83	131	2	F2	242
D	C4	196	d	84	132	3	F3	243
E	C5	197	e	85	133	4	F4	244
F	C6	198	f	86	134	5	F5	245
G	C7	199	g	87	135	6	F6	246
H	C8	200	h	88	136	7	F7	247
I	C9	201	i	89	137	8	F8	248
J	D1	209	j	91	145	9	F9	249
K	D2	210	k	92	146			
L	D3	211	l	93	147			
M	D4	212	m	94	148			
N	D5	213	n	95	149			
O	D6	214	o	96	150			
P	D7	215	p	97	151			
Q	D8	216	q	98	152			
R	D9	217	r	99	153			
S	E2	226	s	A2	162			
T	E3	227	t	A3	163			
U	E4	228	u	A4	164			

Upper-case Letters				*Lower-case letters*		
Char	*Hex*	*Dec*		*Char*	*Hex*	*Dec*
V	E5	229		v	A5	165
W	E6	230		w	A6	166
X	E7	231		x	A7	167
Y	E8	232		y	A8	168
Z	E9	233		z	A9	169

Special Symbols				*Special Symbols*		
Char	*Hex*	*Dec*		*Char*	*Hex*	*Dec*
¢	40	64		,	6B	107
.	4B	75		%	6C	108
<	4C	76		_	6D	109
(	4D	77		>	6E	110
+	4E	78		?	6F	111
¦	4F	79		:	7A	122
&	50	80		#	7B	123
!	5A	90		@	7C	124
$	5B	91		'	7D	125
*	5C	92		=	7E	126
)	5D	93		"	7F	127
;	5E	94		{	8B	139
~	5F	95		}	9B	155
–	60	96		[	AD	173
/	61	97		]	BD	189

E.4.2 ASCII

Upper-case Letters				*Lower-case Letters*				*Digits*		
Char	*Octal*	*Dec*		*Char*	*Octal*	*Dec*		*Char*	*Octal*	*Dec*
A	101	65		a	141	97		0	60	48
B	102	66		b	142	98		1	61	49
C	103	67		c	143	99		2	62	50
D	104	68		d	144	100		3	63	51
E	105	69		e	145	101		4	64	52
F	106	70		f	146	102		5	65	53
G	107	71		g	147	103		6	66	54
H	110	72		h	150	104		7	67	55
I	111	73		i	151	105		8	70	56
J	112	74		j	152	106		9	71	57
K	113	75		k	153	107				
L	114	76		l	154	108				
M	115	77		m	155	109				
N	116	78		n	156	110				
O	117	79		o	157	111				
P	120	80		p	150	112				
Q	121	81		q	161	113				

Upper-case Letters		
Char	Octal	Dec
R	122	82
S	123	83
T	124	84
U	125	85
V	126	86
W	127	87
X	130	88
Y	131	89
Z	132	90

Lower-case letters		
Char	Octal	Dec
r	162	114
s	163	115
t	164	116
u	165	117
v	166	118
w	167	119
x	170	120
y	171	121
z	172	122

Special Symbols		
Char	Octal	Dec
ƀ	40	32
!	41	33
"	42	34
#	43	35
$	44	36
%	45	37
&	46	38
'	47	39
(	50	40
)	51	41
*	52	42
+	53	43
,	54	44
-	55	45
.	56	46
/	57	47
:	72	58

Special Symbols		
Char	Octal	Dec
;	73	59
<	74	60
=	75	61
>	76	62
?	77	63
@	100	64
[	133	91
\	134	92
]	135	93
^	136	94
_	137	95
`	140	96
{	173	123
¦	174	124
}	175	125
~	176	126

F
Formatted Input and Output

F.1   Introduction

Most of the programs in the main body of this text used simple READ * and PRINT *
statements to handle the input and output of information in a program. The READ and
PRINT statements as they were used refer to a default external unit. The * character
specifies that the default formatting rules should be used to determine how the data is to
be read and displayed. Through the use of commands external to the FORTRAN/77
programming language, the default unit numbers can be converted to the terminal or to
an external disk file. However, in many cases the user wishes to control both the unit
selection and the formatting in the program itself.

A detailed discussion of unit number control and external devices is beyond the
scope of this text. Refer to Appendix D and the section titled Input/Output Statements
for a list of all the statements involved with advanced input/output techniques. With
respect to formatting of output, it is often desirable to present the output from a
program in a more readable form or to squeeze more information on each line or to
decide exactly what information should appear on each page.

In order to specify the layout of input data or the appearance of output lines, it is
necessary to introduce the FORMAT statement. By associating an input or output statement with a FORMAT statement, it is possible to control the operation of these statements
and the associated spacing of information. This appendix describes the basic details of
formatted input and output. Variations in exact implementation may be expected
depending on the compiler in use. The examples given demonstrate the results to be
expected from the majority of compilers.

F.2   Alternate Input and Output Statements

The card reader and printer are but two of many possible input/output devices.   To
allow for the flexibility of using other media, there are standard general input/output
statements, namely:

```
READ (cilist) [iolist]
READ f [,iolist]
WRITE (cilist) [iolist]
PRINT f [,iolist]
```

cilist   is a control information list which may be from the following list

```
[UNIT=] u
[FMT =] f
REC = rn
IOSTAT = ios
ERR = s
END = s
```

These specifiers are discussed in more detail in Appendix D under the title
Input/Output Statement Specifiers.   There must be exactly one unit specifier
u and at most one of each of the other specifiers.   If f is specified, the
input/output is formatted, otherwise it is unformatted.   If rn is specified, the
input/output is direct access, otherwise it is not.   If f is an * then the
input/output is called *list directed*.

f   is a format identifier.

iolist   is the list of variables to be supplied values on input or supplying values for
output.

F.3   The FORMAT Statement

FORMAT statements provide instructions on how information is to be read or printed.
The general form of the FORMAT statement is:

```
nnnnn FORMAT(codes)
```

The nnnnn is a 1–5 digit statement number in columns 1–5 of the line.   The codes
represent instructions about how the information in an input or output statment is to be
transmitted.   This includes information on horizontal as well as vertical spacing and
information about the column layout of constant values.   Normally, several codes
appear together and are separated by commas.

The following sections describe the individual FORMAT codes in detail.   Examples of
how to use these codes are given in Section F.22.

F.4   FORMAT Codes and FORMAT Masks

A wide variety of FORMAT codes or *masks* are provided for use in FORTRAN/77.   There
are summarized in Figure F.1 and described on succeeding pages.   The term mask is
used to describe the codes designed to handle numeric, character, and logical values.   It

describes the appearance of such values.   The protion of the input or output record containing the value is called the *field*, and the number of columns is called the *field width*.

Figure F.1   The FORTRAN/77 FORMAT codes.

Code	General Form	Purpose	Meaning	
A	Aw	Character strings	w =	total field width
B	BN	Blank handling		
	BZ			
D	Dw.d	Double- or extended-precision	w =	total field width
		floating-point values	d =	number of significant digits
E	Ew.d	Single-precision	w =	total field width
		floating-point values	d =	number of significant digits
F	Fw.d	Single- or extended-precision	w =	total field width
		floating-point values	d =	number of digits to the right of the decimal
G	Gw.d	General purpose	w =	total field width
		for D, E, F, I, or L	d =	see D, E, F-codes
H	nHs	Literal strings	n =	number of characters after H included in s
			s =	string following H to be included
I	Iw	Integer or fixed-point values	w =	total field width
	Iw.m		w =	total field width
			m =	minimum number of digits printed
L	Lw	Logical values	w =	total field width
P	kP	Scaling factor	k =	power of 10
S	S	Use default plus sign print setting		
	SP	Print optional plus sign		
	SS	Do not print plus sign		
T	Tc	Tabbing to specific columns	c =	absolute tab column position
	TLc	Tab to the left	c =	relative tab column position
	TRc	Tab to the right	c =	relative tab column position
X	nX	Horizontal spacing	n =	number of columns to skip
Z	Zw	Hexadecimal strings	w =	total field width (number of hex digits)
/	/	Vertical skipping		
'	's'	Enclosed literal string	s =	literal string
:	:	Terminate format control		

F.5   The A-Mask

Purpose

The A-mask is used to control the input and output of character information.   The information may be stored in variables of any data type including the FORTRAN/77 CHARACTER type.

General Form

Aw   w is an unsigned integer constant specifying the total field width or number of characters to be transmitted.

Input Rules

1) If the field width is shorter than the number of characters that can be stored in the receiving variable, blank characters are added on the right to fill the variable.
2) If the field width is longer than the number of characters that can be stored in the receiving variable, characters are truncated on the left.

Input Examples

Assume that the maximum number of characters to be stored in the variable is 4.

Characters in Input Field	Mask	Resulting Value Assigned
ABCD	A4	'ABCD'
ABC	A3	'ABCb'
ABCDE	A5	'BCDE'

Output Rules

1) If the field width is shorter than the number of characters stored in the variable, characters are truncated on the right.
2) If the field width is longer than the number of characters stored in the variable, the field is padded on the left with blank characters.

Output Examples

Assume that the maximum number of characters stored in the variable is 8.

Value to be Output	Mask	Characters in Output Field
'ZYXWVUTS'	A8	ZYXWVUTS
'ZYXWVUTS'	A6	ZYXWVU
'ZYXWVUTS'	A10	bbZYXWVUTS

Further examples may be found in the sample programs in Appendix G.

F.6   The BN and BZ Codes

Purpose

These codes are used to control the interpretation of blank characters encountered in numeric input fields.

General Form

BN

BZ

Rules

1) If a BN code is encountered in a FORMAT statement then all subsequent numeric input fields in that input statement will have blanks ignored.
2) If a BZ codes is encountered in a FORMAT statement then all numeric fields encounted in that input statement will have blanks interpreted as zeros.

F.7   The D-Mask

Purpose

The D-mask is used to control the input and output of extended-precision (double-precision) values in exponent notation.

General Form

Dw.d   w is an unsigned integer constant specifying the total field width.

d is an unsigned integer constant specifying the number of significant digits.

Rule

The D-mask functions in the same fashion as the E-mask except that up to 16 significant digits can be handled, and the letter D rather than E is used for the exponent.

Examples

The programs in Appendix I include examples of the D-mask.

F.8   The E-Mask

Purpose

The E-mask is used to control the input and output of single precision (REAL) floating-point values in exponent notation.

General Form

Ew.d   w is an unsigned integer constant specifying the total field width.

d is an unsigned integer constant specifying the number of significant digits and/or the number of digits appearing between the decimal point and the exponent.

Input Rules

Considerable freedom is allowed in specifying the value in the field.

1)   Any blank columns are treated as zeros unless explicitly set otherwise.
2)   If no exponent is specified, an exponent of zero is assumed.
3)   The exponent may be expressed in several ways so that 10^5 may be written as E+05, E05, E5, E+5, +05, or +5, and 10^{-4} may be written as E-04, E-4, -04, or -4.
4)   If the exponent is out of range, an error message is issued and execution halted.
5)   If a decimal point is specified, the value of d is ignored.
6)   If no decimal point is given, a decimal point is inserted d positions to the left of the exponent.

Input Examples

Characters in Input Field	Mask	Resulting Value Assigned
ҍҍҍ0.98765	E10.5	.98765
.98765E+05	E10.5	98765.
.98765Eҍҍҍ	E10.5	.98765
98.765E2	E8.2	9876.5
-98765+03	E9.4	-9876.5
-ҍ987ҍ5	E7.2	-987.05

Output Rules

1) The value is placed right justified in the w columns as illustrated below.

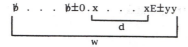

2) The rightmost 4 columns are normally used for the exponent, including the letter E, a sign column, and two columns for the numeric exponent.
3) The two-digit exponent includes a leading zero if necessary.
4) If the exponent is positive, the column reserved for the sign of the exponent is left blank. Similarly, if the value is positive, no sign is specified.
5) The d columns immediately to the left of the exponent are used to represent the fractional portion of the number.
6) A zero and decimal point always precede the fractional portion on the left.
7) Any additional columns to the left are set to blanks.
8) The number is represented as a normalized fraction with the exponent adjusted accordingly.
9) The value of w must be at least d+6 for positive values and at least d+7 for negative values to provide for the leading sign (if any), leading zero, decimal point and exponent.
10) If the value of w is too small to allow for all of the components of the number, the field is filled with asterisks.
11) If the value of d is less than 7, the fraction will be rounded.

Output Examples

Value to be Output	Mask	Characters in Output Field
123456.	E12.6	0.123456Eҍ06
-123.456	E12.5	-0.12346Eҍ03
-123.456	E12.6	************
-123.000	E12.4	ҍ-0.1230Eҍ00
-.000123	E12.4	ҍ-0.1230E-03

F.9   The F-Mask

Purpose
The F-mask is used to control the input and output of single- (REAL) or extended-precision (DOUBLE PRECISION) floating-point values without the exponent notation.

General Form
Fw.d   w is an unsigned integer constant specifying the total field width.

d is an unsigned integer constant specifying the number of digits to the right of the decimal point.

Input Rules
1) Only the digits 0 to 9, a sign, + or –, a decimal point . , or a blank may appear in the w columns.
2) Blank columns are treated as zeros, unless explicitly set otherwise.
3) If a decimal point appears anywhere in the w columns, the value of d is ignored.
4) If no decimal point appears, the value of d is used to insert a decimal point d+1 columns from the right end of the field.

Input Examples

Characters in Input Field	Mask	Resulting Value Assigned
ƀƀ1234	F6.2	12.34
ƀ12.34	F6.2	12.34
12.34ƀ	F6.2	12.34
ƀ12.34	F6.0	12.34
1ƀ2.34	F6.2	102.34
1234.5	F6.3	1234.5

Output Rules
1) The value is printed right justified in the w columns with the decimal point d+1 columns from the right.
2) If w is larger than necessary, blanks are placed to the left to fill the w columns.
3) Positive values are printed unsigned. Negative values have the minus sign placed immediately to the left of the most significant digit.
4) At least one digit appears to the left of the decimal, including a leading zero if the magnitude of the value is less than 1.
5) If necessary, zeros are supplied to fill the d columns to the right of the decimal.
6) The value is rounded to fit the columns specified.
7) If w is not sufficiently large, the w columns are filled with asterisks.

Output Examples

Value to be Output	Mask	Characters in Output Field
12.34	F5.2	12.34
-12.34	F6.2	-12.34
12.34	F8.4	ƀ12.3400
-12.34	F8.3	ƀ-12.340
12.34	F4.0	ƀ12.
12345.6	F7.0	ƀ12346.
12.34	F4.2	****
-12.34	F5.2	*****

F.10   The G-Mask

Purpose

The G-mask is used to control the input and output of a variety of data types including COMPLEX, DOUBLE PRECISION, INTEGER, LOGICAL, and REAL. This generalized mask is designing to save time in designing FORMAT masks, especially for beginning programmers.

General Form

Gw.d   w is an unsigned integer constant specifying the total field width.
   d is an unsigned integer constant specifying the number of digits to the right of the decimal point (if appropriate for the data type).

Input Rules

1) The rules that apply are determined by the variable type and the form of the input data.
2) For integer and logical values, the G-mask functions like the I- and L-masks, respectively. The d is ignored and may be omitted.
3) For real or complex values, the G-mask functions like the F- or E-mask, depending on whether or not an exponent is included in the input field.
4) For extended-precision values, the G-mask functions like the F- or D-mask, depending on whether or not an exponent is included in the input field.

Input Examples

Characters in Input Field	Mask	Variable Type	Resulting Value Assigned
ƀƀƀ12345	G8.3	I	12345
1ƀ2ƀ3ƀ4ƀ	G8	I	10203040
0.1234E4	G8.4	R	1234.
12345678	G8.0	R	12345670.
12345678	G8.0	D	12345678.

Output Rules

1) For integer and logical values, the G-mask performs like the I- or L-mask, respectively. The d may be omitted since it is ignored.

2) For floating-point values (real, complex, or extended-precision), the G-mask operates as a D-, E-, or F-mask depending on the value to be printed. For values outside the range $.1 \leq x < 10^d$ the value is printed in exponent notation with d significant digits. For values within the specified range, the value is printed with d digits to the right of the decimal. The rightmost 4 columns used for the exponent are left blank.

Output Examples

Value to be Output	Variable Type	Mask	Characters in Output Field
98765	I	G6	ƀ98765
.TRUE.	L	G6	ƀƀƀƀƀT
.098765	R	G10.4	0.9877E-01
.98765	R	G10.4	0.9876ƀƀƀƀ
98765.	R	G10.4	0.9877Eƀ05
9876.5	R	G10.4	ƀ9877.ƀƀƀƀ
.098765	D	G10.4	0.9876D-01
.98765	D	G10.4	0.9876ƀƀƀƀ
98765.	D	G10.4	0.9877Dƀ05

F.11   The H-Code

Purpose

The H-code is used to provide an alternate way of handling literal information on output (characteristic of early versions of FORTRAN). See also the ′-code.

General Form

nHs   n is an unsigned integer constant specifying the number of characters after H that form the literal string.

s is the literal character string of length n.

Output Rules

1) The value of n must be an exact count of the number of characters in the literal string.

2) Any character may appear in the literal string including single quotes.

Output Examples

Code	Characters in Output Field
4HXƀ=ƀ	Xƀ=ƀ
7HIT′Sƀok	IT′Sƀok

F.12   The I-Mask

Purpose

The I-mask is used to control the input and output of fixed-point (INTEGER) values.

General Form

Iw   w is an unsigned integer constant specifying the total field width.

Iw.m   m is an unsigned integer constant specifying the minimum number of digits to be printed on output.

Input Rules

1)   Only the numeric digits 0-9, a sign, + or -, or blanks are permitted in the w columns.   If, an invalid symbol appears, an error message is printed and execution halted.

2)   Blank columns are treated as zeros, unless explicitly set otherwise.

3)   The sign may appear anywhere to the left of the value.   A plus sign is optional and may be omitted.

4)   If the value is outside the range for an integer, an error message is printed and execution halted.

5)   The .m code does not have any effect on input.

Input Examples

Characters in Input Field	Mask	Resulting Value Assigned
123456	I6	123456
ƀƀ1ƀ2ƀ	I6	1020
ƀ-ƀ123	I6	-123
123.45	I6	123

Output Rules

1)   The value is printed right justified in the w columns.

2)   If .m is not specified, any extra columns to the left of the value are set to blanks. If .m is specified, the number of characters printed will be a minimum of m characters with leading zeros added if necessary.

3)   If the value is positive, the sign is omitted (see S codes).

4)   If the value is negative, the sign is placed immediately to the left of the most significant digit.

5)   If the value is too large to fit into the w columns, the w columns are filled with asterisks.   No error message is printed, and execution continues.

Output Examples

Value to be Output	Mask	Characters in Output Field
123456	I9	ƀƀƀ123456
−123456	I9	ƀƀ−123456
123456	I3	***
123	I7.5	ƀƀ00123

F.13   The L-Mask

Purpose
The L-mask is used to control the input and output of logical values.

General Form
Lw   w is an unsigned integer constant specifying the total field width.

Input Rules
1) The w columns are scanned from left to right looking for the first occurrence of a T or F.
2) If the letter T is encountered first, the value .TRUE. is assigned.   If the letter F is found first, a value of .FALSE. is assigned.
3) If the w columns are entirely blank, a value of .FALSE. is assumed.   Otherwise, if neither a T nor an F is found, an error message is issued, and execution is terminated.

Input Examples

Characters in Input Field	Mask	Resulting Value Assigned
T	L1	.TRUE.
ƀƀFƀ	L4	.FALSE.
WHATƀLUCK	L9	.TRUE.
BLANK	L5	error message
ƀ	L1	.FALSE.

Output Rule
1) A single letter T or F corresponding to the values .TRUE. and .FALSE., is placed in the rightmost column, and the remaining columns are filled with blanks.

Output Examples

Value to be Output	Mask	Characters in Output Field
.TRUE.	L1	T
.FALSE.	L3	ƀƀF

F.14 The P-Mask

Purpose

The P-mask is used to provide a scaling factor by powers of 10 for very large or very small values or to overcome accuracy problems caused by difficulties in expressing fractional values exactly. The authors have found little use for this mask.

General Form

kP k is an optionally signed integer constant specifying a scaling factor (power of 10).

Input Rules

1) When encountered in a FORMAT list, it applies to all subsequently interpreted D-, E-, F-, and G-masks until changed by another P-code.
2) The external value received is divided by 10 to the power k (equivalently, multiplied by 10 to the power -k) before it is assigned internally to the receiving variable.

$$External = 10^k * Internal$$

Input Examples

Characters in Input Field	Mask	Resulting Value Assigned
98765	F5.3	98.765
98765	0PF5.3	98.765
98765	1PF5.3	9.8765
98765	-2PF5.3	9876.5
98765432	-2P2F4.1	98760. & 54320.
98765432	-2PF4.1,F4.1	98760. & 54320.
98765432	-2PF4.1,0PF4.1	98760. & 543.2

Output Rules

The effect of a P-code depends on whether the mask is an E- or F-mask. In general:

1) When encountered in a FORMAT list, it applies to all subsequently interpreted D, E, F, and G edit descriptors until changed by another P code.

For an E-mask the following rules apply:

2) The P-code is used to change the appearance of the value on output, namely to shift the position of the decimal point relative to the most significant digit by k positions.
3) The d specifies the number of digits to appear between the decimal point, and the exponent (rather than the number of significant digits).
4) If k is negative, k zeros are inserted to the right of the decimal point, and the exponent is modified accordingly.
5) If k is zero, it is ignored.
6) If k is positive, k significant digits appear to the left of the decimal point, and the exponent is adjusted accordingly.

The next rule applies only to an F-mask.

7) The internal value is multiplied by 10^k before it is transmitted for external presentation.

The rules which apply for a G-mask depend on whether the value would include an exponent. See the description of the G-mask for details.

Output Examples

Value to be Output	*Mask*	*Characters in Output Field*
12.34	E13.5	ƀƀ0.12340Eƀ02
12.34	0PE13.5	ƀƀ0.12340Eƀ02
12.34	2PE13.5	ƀ12.34000Eƀ00
12.34	-2PE13.5	ƀƀ0.00123Eƀ04
12.34	F13.5	ƀƀƀƀƀ12.34000
12.34	3PF13.5	ƀƀ12340.00000
12.34	-2PF13.5	ƀƀƀƀƀƀ0.12340

F.15   The S-Code

Purpose
The S-code is used to control the printing of the optional plus sign for numeric fields.

General Forms
S
SP
SS

Rules
1) If the SP code is encountered in a FORMAT list then the optional plus sign will be printed in all subsequent numeric fields in that FORMAT statement.
2) If the SS code is encountered in a FORMAT list then the optional plus sign will *not* be printed in any subsequent numeric fields in that FORMAT statement.
3) If the S code is encountered in a FORMAT list then the optional plus sign is printed using the processor's default setting.
4) The S, SP, and SS codes have no effect on input.

F.16   The T-Code

Purpose
The T-code is used to position the next field in a specific column in a fashion similar to tabs on a typewriter.

General Forms

Tc   c is an unsigned integer constant representing the tab column position.

TLc

TRc

Rules

1)   The T code specifies absolute tab positioning.   TL and TR are tab positions relative to the current character position.

2)   Tc specifies that the next input or output will begin at character position c in the input or output buffer.

3)   TLc specifies that the next input or output will begin at character position c characters to the left of the current character position.

4)   TRc specifies that the next input or output will begin at character position c characters to the right of the current character position.

5)   For a line printer, the first character of the output buffer is used to control the line spacing and is not printed.   Thus the output is shifted to the left by one on the printed paper.

F.17   The X-Code

Purpose

The X-code is used to insert blanks between masked fields and, thus, provide horizontal spacing.

General Form

nX   n is an unsigned integer constant specifying the number of columns to skip.

Rule

This code is very easy to use, and no specific rules are required.   Note that the n precedes the letter X contrary to positioning for the FORMAT masks.

Examples

Examples of the X-code appear in Section F.21.

F.18   The /-Code

Purpose

The /-code is used to cause a skip to a new card, line, or record within a single string of FORMAT codes.

General Form

/   This indicates that the end of the relevant information on a card, printer line, or record has been reached and that processing should continue with the next.

Rules
1) No special caution is necessary except for the line printer.   In this case, it must be remembered that the first character of each line to be printed is used as the line spacing character and is not printed.
2) Slashes may be placed side by side to skip several records.   If the consecutive slashes appear in the middle of a string of FORMAT codes, n slashes will cause n−1 records to be skipped.   At the end of a FORMAT string, n records will be skipped.

F.19   The '-Code

Purpose
The '-code is used to output literal information, such as messages and identifying information.   Though this code can technically be used for input as well, this usage is rather obscure and will not be described.

General Form
's'   s the literal string to be transmitted.

Output Rule
To include a single quote within the string, two single quotes in adjacent columns are used.

Output Examples

Code	*Characters in Output Field*
'Xᴃ=ᴃ'	Xᴃ=ᴃ
'IT''SᴃOK'	IT'SᴃOK

F.20   The :-Code

Purpose
The :-code is used to terminate the output of character information when the FORMAT statement exhausts its list of output items.

General Form
:   Terminate format control.

Examples

The following statements

```
        I = 1
        J = 2
        K = 3
        WRITE (*,9000) I
        WRITE (*,9000) I, J
        WRITE (*,9000) I, J, K
   9000 FORMAT(1X,'I =',I5,:,' J =',I5,:,' K =',I5)
```

will produce the output below:

```
Ib=bbbb1
Ib=bbbb1bJb=bbbb2
Ib=bbbb1bJb=bbbb2bKb=bbbb3
```

F.21   Using FORMAT **Codes and Masks**

The previous sections presented the various FORMAT masks and codes in isolation.   A single FORMAT statement usually includes a combination of codes and masks to produce the desired effect.   Such a list is applied sequentially to the variables or values in the input or output list.   The FORMAT codes and masks are usually separated by commas to remove ambiguity and may also be separated by blanks to improve readability.   In the examples which follow, those variables beginning with the letter I are assumed to be INTEGER, those beginning with R are REAL, those with L are LOGICAL, those with DP are DOUBLE PRECISION, and those with CX are COMPLEX.

F.21.1   **Considerations for Printer Output**

Information on a line printer may be displayed in many different ways, depending on the physical characteristics of the printer.   The details of what is available should be checked with the individual computer center.   The most common width of a printer page is 132 characters.   (The output buffer is of size 133 to allow 1 character for carriage control.)

When a PRINT statement is being processed, a string of characters equal in length to the printer page is set up by the compiler.   This string of characters, called a *buffer,* is initialized to blanks, and a pointer is set to the first position.   As each FORMAT code and mask is processed, the pointer is advanced along the character string, and the characters produced by the FORMAT masks are placed in the buffer.   When all values have been converted and placed in the buffer, if a slash code is encountered, or if there are more values but not FORMAT masks, as discussed in Section F.21.5, the buffer is transmitted to the printer.   Of course, an attempt to place more than 133 characters in the buffer will result in an error message and termination of the program.

When applying FORMAT control for printed output, horizontal spacing is determined by the successive masks and codes used.   In addition, it is necessary to specify vertical spacing information.   By convention, the first character of each line is *not* printed but is used to determine how to vertically space the current line.   This first character is called the *carriage control character* (CCC).   Alternate names include printer or vertical control character.   The effect of specific characters is shown in table form below.   If none of these characters appear as the first to be printed, single spacing is assumed.

CCC	Effect	
+	no spacing	print the current line without advancing, that is, over the previous line of output
ƀ	single spacing	advance to the next line before printing the current line
0	double spacing	advance two lines before printing, thus leaving one blank line between
–	triple spacing	advance three lines before printing, thus leaving two blank lines between
1	new page	advance to the top of a new page before printing the current line

It should be emphasized that the first character on a line is used for this purpose, regardless of how it is produced.   Thus, it is feasible to generate the character as the first character of a masked field.   This is a dangerous practice, however, since the value placed in the masked field may produce unexpected results.   It is best to explicitly specify the carriage control character by one of the following methods (illustrated for single spacing):

        1X   1Hƀ   'ƀ'

Examples
1)   The following statements:

                I = 12345
                PRINT 9000, I
        9000 FORMAT(1X,I8)

will produce the following output:[1]

        ƀƀƀ12345ƀ . . .

2)   The following statements:
                R = 1234.5
                PRINT 9010, R
        9010 FORMAT('ƀ',F10.5)

will produce the following output:

        1234.50000ƀ . . .

---

[1] The use of an ellipsis indicates that the preceeding character, normally a blank (ƀ) is repeated for the remainder of the line.

3) The following statements:

```
      WRITE (*, 9020)
 9020 FORMAT(18H-ENDƀOFƀPROCESSING)
```

will produce the following output:

```
ƀ . . .           ←    two blank
ƀ . . .           ←        lines
ENDƀOFƀPROCESSINGƀ . . .
```

The first character in the literal string, –, is used to achieve triple spacing and, thus, does not appear as part of the message.

4) The following statements:

```
      PRINT 9030, 1, 2, 3
 9030 FORMAT('1','LINE',I2,/'0LINE',I2/1X,'LINE',I2)
```

will produce the following output:

```
LINEƀ1ƀ . . .     ←    first line on a new page
ƀ . . .           ←    blank line
LINEƀ2ƀ . . .
LINEƀ3ƀ . . .
```

5) The following statements:

```
      CX = (1., 2.)
      WRITE (*, 9040) 1234.5, 987, CX, 12345678.9
 9040 FORMAT(F6.1, 5X, I3 / '0', F5.1, F5.1 / '0', D20.12)
```

will produce the following output:

```
234.5ƀƀƀƀƀ987ƀ . . .    ←    first line on a new page
ƀ . . .                 ←    blank line
ƀƀ1.0ƀƀ2.0ƀ . . .
ƀ . . .                 ←    blank line
ƀƀ0.123456789000Dƀ08ƀ . . .
```

Since no control character was specified for the first line, the first character produced under the F-mask, the 1, was used as the carriage control character. Note that 5X,I3 is equivalent to I8 in this example.

F.21.2 Considerations for Input

The use of FORMAT control for input means that data values are no longer separated by commas or blanks. Since the standard input record contains 80 columns, an attempt to read information beyond column 80 results in an error message and program termination. Each execution of a READ statement from the input file automatically accesses the information on the next record.

Examples

1) Consider the effect of the following program segment:

                READ 8000, R
        8000 FORMAT(F8.1)

when given the following input record:

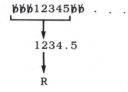

2) Consider the effect of the following program segment:

            READ (*, 8010), I, RONE, RTWO, L, CX
        8010 FORMAT(I5, E10.4, F5.2, L5, F4.0, F4.0)

when given the following input record:

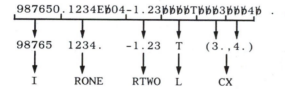

F.21.3   Field Counts

Frequently, the same FORMAT mask is to be used for a number of consecutive values. Rather than repeating the same mask several times, it is possible to precede the mask by an unsigned integer constant called a *field count* or *repeat factor*.

Examples

1) Consider the following program segment:

            READ (*, 8000) (R(I), I = 1, 6)
        8000 FORMAT(3F6.2, 3F6.3)

when given the following input record:

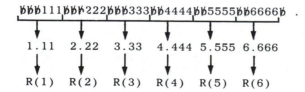

2)   The following statements:

```
        WRITE (*, 9000) (I, I = 1, 5)
   9000 FORMAT('ɓ', 5I4)
```

will produce the following output:

```
   ɓɓɓ1ɓɓɓ2ɓɓɓ3ɓɓɓ4ɓɓɓ5ɓ . . .
```

F.21.4   Group Counts

As well as repeating individual masks, it is often desirable to repeat groups of masks and/or codes.   This can be accomplished by surrounding the group with parentheses and placing an unsigned integer constant called a *group count* or *group factor* before the left parenthesis.   If the constant is missing, a group factor of one is assumed.

Examples

1)   Consider the effect of the following program segment:

```
        READ (*,8000) (R(I), I = 1, 6)
   8000 FORMAT(3(2F6.2,F6.3))
```

when given the following input record:

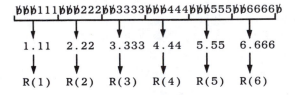

2)   The following statements assume the values from the previous example:

```
        WRITE (*, 9000) (R(I), I = 1, 6)
   9000 FORMAT('ɓ', 3('R(', I1, ')ɓ=', F6.3, 2X),
   +         /'ɓ', 3('R(', I1, ')ɓ=', F6.3, 2X) )
```

will produce the following output:

```
   R(1)ɓ=ɓ1.110ɓɓR(2)ɓ=ɓ2.220ɓɓR(3)ɓ=3.333ɓ . . .
   R(4)ɓ=ɓ4.440ɓɓR(5)ɓ=ɓ5.550ɓɓR(6)ɓ=6.666ɓ . . .
```

A continuation card is used to specify the FORMAT for the second line of output.

F.21.5   When the Number of Values and Masks Do Not Match

In a general program, it is not always feasible to design FORMAT statements that suit all possible situations.   Consequently, the number of FORMAT masks does not always match the number of items in the input or output list.   As a result, the following two problems arise:

a)   more masks than items
b)   more items than masks.

a) More Masks than Items   In order to handle this situation, it is helpful to know how a list of FORMAT codes and masks is processed.   Processing proceeds from left to right in the FORMAT list.   Codes are processed as they are encountered.   Each time a mask is found, the next entry in the input/output list is considered.   If the mask is not appropriate for the item, an error message is issued, and the program is terminated. Assuming the type is legal, the value is transmitted under control of the mask.   In this way, the processing continues until no variable is found for the current mask.   All codes and masks up to, but not including, this mask are processed.   This is summarized in a general form below, while the appropriate results are illustrated for several examples thereafter.

variable list var_1 var_2 . . . var_n

format list $(code_1, mask_1, code_2, mask_2, \ldots code_n, mask_n, code_{n+1}, mask_{n+1}, \ldots)$

processed

where var_i is a variable name, $code_i$ is zero, one, or more FORMAT codes, and $mask_i$ is one of the FORMAT masks.

Examples

1)   Consider the effect of the following program segment:

```
        READ 8000, I, R
   8000 FORMAT(I5,F5.0,I10,F10.5)
```

when given the following input record:

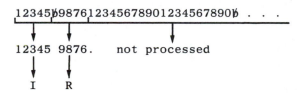

2)   The following statements assume the values from the previous example:

```
        PRINT 9000, I, R
   9000 FORMAT('b', 'Ib=', I5, 2X, 'Rb=', F6.0,2X,'GARBAGE', I3)
```

These statements produce the following output:

```
Ib=b12345bbRb=b9876.bbGARBAGEb  . . .
```

b) More Items than Masks The answer to this problem depends on whether the FORMAT list contains any group counts.

Consider first the absence of group counts. Recall that in processing a FORMAT list, each mask is associated with the next item in the input/output list. When the last right parenthesis is encountered, a check is made for additional items in the list. Should there be additional items, the process will advance to a new card or line and continue processing with the left end of the FORMAT list, thus recycling the codes and masks.

If the FORMAT list contains group counts, the answer is not quite as straightforward. In such cases, processing also advances to the next card or line. However, it continues with the group count corresponding to the group whose rightmost parenthesis is nearest to the closing parenthesis of the FORMAT statement. Several possible situations are illustrated below.

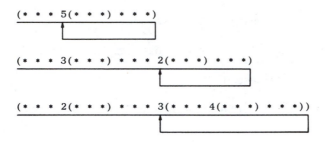

Examples

1) The following statements:

```
         R(1) = 1.
         R(2) = 2.
         R(3) = 3.
         PRINT 9000, (I, R(I), I = 1, 3)
    9000 FORMAT('0', 'R(', I1, ')ᵇ=', F3.0)
```

will produce the output below:

```
ᵇ . . .         ←   blank line
R(1)ᵇ=ᵇ1.ᵇ . . .
ᵇ . . .         ←   blank line
R(2)ᵇ=ᵇ2.ᵇ . . .
ᵇ . . .         ←   blank line
R(3)ᵇ=ᵇ3.ᵇ . . .
```

2) The following statements:

```
         R(1) = 1.
         R(2) = 2.
         R(3) = 3.
         PRINT 9010, (I, R(I), I = 1, 3)
    9010 FORMAT('0', 'OUTPUT', 2(2x,'R(', I1, ')ᵇ=', F3.0))
```

F.22.6 General Considerations

1) Since FORMAT statements are non-executable statements, only input and output statements may refer to them.

2) More than one input and/or output statement may refer to a single FORMAT statement.

3) FORMAT statements may be placed anywhere in the program or subprogram that uses them. Some programmers group them together at the beginning or at the end of the program segment. Others prefer to place each FORMAT statement with the input or output statement that uses it. The authors' preference is to place all FORMAT statements for a program between the declarations and the body of a program.

4) Good programming practice dictates that easily identifiable statement numbers be used for FORMAT statements. The authors' choice is to number FORMAT statements used for input as 8000, 8010, . . . and those for output as 9000, 9010, ...

G
Character Manipulation

G.1   Introduction

Though scientific and engineering problems primarily involve numerical computations, it is often desirable to include character information to supplement the numeric quantities. This has been evident in the programs throughout the text where titles and messages are used to identify the numeric output.   It is also useful to maintain portions of scientific data in character form when sorting files or presenting statistical data.   In fact, character quantities were necessary to plot the graphs in Chapter 6 and to draw the histograms in Chapter 13.

Computers were originally designed and built to perform numerical computations. Gradually, the storage and manipulation of character quantities were included in their repertoire, and, today, probably more computer processing involves character information than numerical quantities.   However, since FORTRAN was devised during the infancy of this transition, and since FORTRAN was originally designed to solve primarily numerical problems, the storage and handling of characters in standard FORTRAN are somewhat cumbersome.   More modern hybrids of FORTRAN, such as FORTRAN/77, enhance these facilities by providing for a CHARACTER data type.

This appendix introduces the basic notions of storing and manipulating character information in FORTRAN/77 as well as pointing out the equivalent methods for standard FORTRAN.   Unless otherwise stated in this appendix, rules given for FORTRAN/77 apply only for FORTRAN/77. On the other hand rules that are specified for FORTRAN apply to both FORTRAN and FORTRAN/77.

G.2   Character Constants

A character constant, often called a character *string*, is simply an ordered set of alphanumeric characters. The basic units of such a constant are the individual characters or symbols. The allowable symbols may vary depending on the computer, the programming language, the input medium, or the output medium. The basic FORTRAN character set usually includes the symbols:

```
A B C D E F G H I J K L M N O P Q R S T U V W X Y Z
0 1 2 3 4 5 6 7 8 9
0 - * / = ( ) . , \  % ' " @ blank
```

though lower-case letters and additional special symbols are often added. Refer to Appendix E which discusses the internal representation of information for more details on how computers store character information.

Since character constants may contain blank characters as well as various special symbols, a character string is usually delimited by single quote marks. Listed below are several examples of character constants. Notice that two single quotes, side by side, are used to represent a single apostrophe or quote within a character constant.

```
'ABC'
'1 PLUS 2 = 3'
'HE SAID, '' #% (EXPLETIVE DELETED)'''
'CARTER''S PEANUTS'
'REAGAN''S JELLYBEANS'
'ARNIE''S SUNFLOWER SEEDS'
```

G.3   Character Manipulation in FORTRAN/77

G.3.1   Character Variables and Arrays

Unlike standard FORTRAN, FORTRAN/77 allows for both character variables and character arrays. Since character data can be of various lengths, the declaration of variables and arrays specifies not only the type as character but also the maximum number of characters that can be represented.

The length for each variable and array in the declaration list can be specified all at once by the length specification after the keyword CHARACTER or the lengths may be specified individually for an item in the list by placing the length specification after that item. The length specification is of the form *len where len may be

a)   an unsigned, non-zero, integer constant
b)   an integer constant expression enclosed by parentheses and with a positive value
c)   an asterisk in parentheses

Listed below are several examples of character declarations.

```
CHARACTER A, ALPHA(26), CHKBRD(8,8)
CHARACTER*1 A, ALPHA(26), CHKBRD(8,8)
CHARACTER A*1, ALPHA(26)*1, CHKBRD(8,8)*1
CHARACTER SINGLE, NAME*20, BRAND(100)*30
```

Though different in form, the first three statements all produce the same result. A is defined as a simple character variable of length 1, ALPHA is a one-dimensional array having 26 entries each of length 1, and CHKBRD is a two-dimensional array having 8 rows and 8 columns for character length 1 entries. The last declaration defines SINGLE as a character variable of length 1, NAME as a character variable of length 20, and BRAND as an array of length 100, where each entry can contain a maximum of 30 characters.

G.3.2 Compile Time Initialization of Character Variables

Character variables may be initialized with character values at compile time in one of two ways. If the variables have already been declared as type CHARACTER, it is possible to use the DATA statement to assign values to the variables. General forms of the DATA statement are:

```
DATA name1 / value1 /, name2 / value2 /, . . .
DATA name1, name2, . . . / value1, value2, . . . /
```

An example of a character declaration and an appropriate DATA compile-time initialization is given below:

```
CHARACTER ONE, STARS*6
DATA ONE / '1' /, STARS / '******' /
```

It is also legal to declare and initialize variables in the same statement as follows:

```
CHARACTER ONE / '1' /, STARS*6 / '******' /
```

Note that, strings that are too long are truncated on the right, and strings that are too short are padded on the right with blanks.

G.3.3 Character Substrings

The manipulation of character values often requires the ability to manipulate portions or substrings of larger character strings. A character substring is a contiguous portion of a character variable and may be used in the same way as character variables themselves. A substring is specified as:

```
vname([e₁]:[e₂])            or
aname(s1,s2,...)([e₁]:[e₂])
```

where vname is the name of a character variable and aname is the name of a character array. e_1 and e_2 are integer expressions giving the starting character position and ending character position of the substring in the string. s1,s2,... are the array subscripts. Also, $1 \le e_1 \le e_2 \le$ len where len is the length of the string. Either, or both of e_1 and e_2 may be omitted. If e_1 is omitted, its default value is 1. If e_2 is omitted, its default value is len. For example, given the specifications

```
CHARACTER STRING*13/'ABCDEFGHIJKLM'/
CHARACTER TABLE(2)*5/'OPQRS', 'VWXYZ'/
```

the following illustrate the substring operation.

Reference	Value
STRING	'ABCDEFGHIJKLM'
STRING(:)	'ABCDEFGHIJKLM'
STRING(1:13)	'ABCDEFGHIJKLM'
STRING(:13)	'ABCDEFGHIJKLM'
STRING(1:)	'ABCDEFGHIJKLM'
STRING(5:7)	'EFG'
TABLE(1)	'OPQRS'
TABLE(1)(2:4)	'PQR'
TABLE(2)	'VWXYZ'
TABLE(2)(3:3)	'X'

G.3.4 Character Expressions, Operators and Assignment Statements

Character expressions may involve only character constants, symbolic names of character constants, character variables or character functions. The only character operator that exists is the concatenation operator '//' which allows concatenation of strings and substrings to form new character strings. This operator's priority is indicated below:

Operator Type	Priority
arithmetic	highest
character	:
relational	:
logical	lowest

with the evaluation of it being from left to right. As an example of concatenation, consider the following:

Expression	Result String
'A'//'B'	'AB'
'A'//'B'//'C'	'ABC'
('AB'//'C')//'D'	'ABCD'
'A//('B'//'C')//'D'	'ABCD'

And, given the following declarations

```
CHARACTER LINE*6/'ABCDEF'/
CHARACTER TABLE(3)*2/'AB','CD','EF'/
```

the following may also be done

Expression	*Result String*
LINE//'XYZ'	'ABCDEFXYZ'
LINE(2:3)//'.'//TABLE(2)(2:2)	'BC.D'

The concatenation operation proceeds from left to right taking into account the use of parentheses.

In the assignment of character data, the left-hand side may be a character variable, array element or substring and the right-hand side is a character expression. If the lengths are not the same, the expression is either truncated on the right or extended on the right with blanks. Note that none of the character positions referenced on the LHS may be referenced on the RHS.

As examples of character assignment, if the following definitions exist:

CHARACTER A*5/'ABCDE'/, B*2/'RS'/, D*3/'XYZ'/, E/'2'/, F*10

then

Assignment	*Result*
F = A//D//D	F contains 'ABCDEXYZXY'
A(3:4) = D	A contains 'ABXYE'
D(2:2) = B(1:1)	D contains 'XRZ'

Character data may be compared using relational expressions. When the lengths of the character strings being compared are not the same, the shorter string is considered to be padded on the right with blanks. The comparison operation is done character by character with the less than and greater than decision being made upon the first characters that are found that are not the same. For example, 'XYABDF' is less than 'XYACDF' since 'B'<'C' in the fourth character position.

G.3.5   Input and Output of Character Values

FORTRAN/77 allows for the input and output of character values with or without FORMAT control. The relevant rules are summarized below. Various examples are used in the problems discussed in the next section.

a) Free-format Input   Character values may be read without a FORMAT. Such data values must be specified with surrounding apostrophes. Successive values are separated by a comma and/or one or more blanks. Character strings that are too long are truncated with the leftmost characters being used, while strings that are too short are padded with blanks on the right. Apostrophes within character data must be represented by two apostrophes.

b) Formatted Input   A special FORMAT code called the A-mask is provided for character values. The general form is Aw where w specifies the width of the field. If the specified width is too short for the character value, the string is truncated on the left. However, if the value is shorter than the specified width, blanks are added on the right to fill the space.

c) Free-format Output   Character values can be printed without specifying a FORMAT. FORTRAN/77 assigns its own A-mask equal to the length of the value.   It does not delimit the value with either blanks or apostrophes.   Internal apostrophes are printed as a single character.   Thus, one blank will always precede the character value.

d) Formatted Output   The A-mask is also used to control the output of character values. If the value is too long for the mask, characters are truncated from the right.   If the value is too short for the mask, blank characters are added on the left to fill the mask.

G.3.6   Built-in Functions
There are several built-in functions for use with character strings.   They are listed in Appendix N with the other built-in functions.   Briefly, they are:

ICHAR(a)	returns the position of the character a in the collating sequence or in some processors the internal representation of the character.
CHAR(i)	returns the character which corresponds to the collating sequence position i or in some processors the internal representation i.
LEN(a)	returns the length of the character expression
INDEX(a_1,a_2)	returns the starting position of the first occurence of the character string a_2 in the string a_1. A value of zero is returned if the string is not found or if LEN(a_1) < LEN(a_2).

LGE(a_1,a_2)
LGT(a_1,a_2)   returns a TRUE or FALSE value depending upon the relative positions of
LLE(a_1,a_2)   the character strings as determined by the collating sequence.
LLT(a_1,a_2)

G.3.7   Function Subprograms
FORTRAN/77 allows the user to define character function subprograms.   These function subprograms behave in a manner similar to other function subprograms.   Examples of character function subprogram declarations are

```
CHARACTER FUNCTION RESULT (parameter list)
CHARACTER*10 FUNCTION SYMBOL (parameter list)
```

The above declare a character function called RESULT which will return a 1 character string and a character function SYMBOL which will return a 10 character string.
   The main program or other subprograms which reference a character function subprogram must declare the function name to be of the same size in a CHARACTER declaration statement.

G.3.8   Using Character Quantities
Character strings are a useful addition to many applications programs.   An important initial decision concerns the length of variable to use.   Since the length of each variable must be specified at compile time, it is not possible to react dynamically to the specific data encountered at execution time.   Typically, there are two choices.   A character string may be stored just in a character variable or it may be stored in a character array

with one character per array element. The individual problem determines which method is better. Two examples follow.

Example G.1   Data Validation

Given a file of 500 data lines supposedly containing only numeric information in columns 1–30, check the data for accuracy, and flag any invalid characters.

a) Problem Discussion   Very few guidelines are given for solving this problem.   It is obvious, though, that each character must be analyzed individually.   To do this, lets use a character array to store each character.   To check each character for numeric validity, all that is necessary is to check for a code between '0' and '9' inclusive.   To highlight invalid characters, an asterisk will be printed under the offending character. The structure of the algorithm involves an outer loop to control the input and processing of each of the 500 lines.   Within this outer loop is an inner loop to check each character for validity.   An array of characters is established to correspond to each character in the data line.   If the character is valid, a blank is assigned; if the character is invalid, an asterisk is assigned.   Since the data is keyed in successive columns, it is necessary to specify FORMAT masks for the input.

b) The FORTRAN/77 *Program*   The complete program is listed in Figure G.1, while some sample output appears in Figure G.2.

Example G.2   Character Encoding

Encode a given character string using a user defined recognition and code character sequence.

a) Problem Discussion   For this problem the user is to specify the characters that will be recognized by the encoding program and the corresponding characters that each recognized character will be encoded as.   Thus these two strings will have to be read in. We can assume that the recognition/code strings may vary in length for different encodings but that the maximum length is 80 characters.   The message to be encoded will also vary in length but again have a maximum length of 80 characters.

b) The FORTRAN/77 *Program*   The program to do the encoding is shown in Figure G.3 with sample output in Figure G.4.   The program reads in the RECOGN and CODE strings into character arrays storing 1 character per element.   It reads an 80–character message string into a character variable MESAGE and uses the character substring feature to determine the real length of the message.   It then picks up each character of MESAGE, searches the RECOGN list for that character, and if it finds it there, it substitutes the corresponding code character into MESAGE.   If the character is not found it inserts an *. When all characters have been encoded it puts out the new message.

In the data used as a test, the character encoding was obtained by just shifting the original character string by 8 characters to the right.   However, the encoding could be random.

```
C Figure G.1 -- Process a file of 500 data lines containing
C               numeric information in columns 1 to 30.
C               Check the lines for obvious typing errors
C               (non-numeric characters).
C**********************************************************************
C INPUT   - current set of input characters
C ERROR   - set of asterisks flagging errors in INPUT
C LINE    - position of current input line in the file
C CC      - current line column
C**********************************************************************
      CHARACTER INPUT(30), ERROR(30)
      INTEGER CC, LINE
 8000 FORMAT(30A1)
 9000 FORMAT('1',1X,A 8,1X,30A1)
 9010 FORMAT('0',I5,5X,30A1)
 9020 FORMAT(' ',10X,30A1)
C Record titles for the output.
      PRINT 9000, 'POSITION', ('=', CC = 1, 30)
C Process the 500 lines one at a time.
      DO 100 LINE = 1, 500
C         Input and echo output the current line.
          READ 8000, (INPUT(CC), CC = 1, 30)
          PRINT 9010, LINE, (INPUT(CC), CC = 1, 30)
C         Examine each character, flagging invalid characters.
          DO 200 CC = 1, 30
             IF (INPUT(CC).LT.'0' .OR. INPUT(CC).GT.'9') THEN
                ERROR(CC) = '*'
             ELSE
                ERROR(CC) = ' '
             ENDIF
  200     CONTINUE
C         Output the error symbols and proceed to the next line.
          PRINT 9020, (ERROR(CC), CC = 1, 30)
  100 CONTINUE
      STOP
      END
```

Figure G.2 Checking cards for obvious typing errors, output from the program of Figure G.1.

```
POSITION ==============================
    1      012345678901234567890123456789

    2      O1234567890I234567890O123456789
           *              *           **

    3      QWERTYUIOPASDFGHJKLZXCVBNM<>?
           *****************************
```

```
C Figure G.3 -- Program to encode a character string using a user
C                defined set of character codes.
C*********************************************************************
C N      - number of characters in the recognition array
C RECOGN - array of characters that are to be recognized
C CODE   - array of code characters corresponding to RECOGN array
C LENGTH - number of characters in the message
C MESAGE - message to be encoded
C CHAR   - temporary character storage
C NEWCHR - replacement character
C FOUND  - logical control variable
C*********************************************************************
      CHARACTER*80 MESAGE
      CHARACTER*1 CHAR, NEWCHR, RECOGN(80), CODE(80)
      LOGICAL FOUND
 8000 FORMAT(80A1)
 8001 FORMAT(A80)
C Input the number of characters to be recognized, the characters
C themselves, and the code characters.
      READ *, N
      READ (*,8000) (RECOGN(I), I = 1, N)
      READ (*,8000) (CODE(I), I = 1, N)
C Input the line to be converted.
      READ (*,8001) MESAGE
      PRINT *, 'THE ORIGINAL MESSAGE IS:'
      PRINT *, MESAGE
C Determine the length of the message by checking backwards from the end
C for the first non-blank character.
      LENGTH = 80
      CHAR = MESAGE(LENGTH:LENGTH)
  100 IF (LENGTH .GE. 1 .AND. CHAR .EQ. ' ') THEN
          LENGTH = LENGTH - 1
          CHAR = MESAGE(LENGTH:LENGTH)
          GOTO 100
      ENDIF
C Encode the message by looking up each character in turn and replacing
C it with its corresponding code.  If a character is not found in the
C recognition list then, code it with a '*'.
      DO 300 I = 1, LENGTH
          CHAR = MESAGE(I:I)
          FOUND = .FALSE.
          NEWCHR = '*'
          J    1
  200     IF (J .LE. N .AND. .NOT.FOUND) THEN
              IF (CHAR .EQ. RECOGN(J)) THEN
                  NEWCHR = CODE(J)
                  FOUND = .TRUE.
              ELSE
                  J = J + 1
              ENDIF
              GOTO 200
          ENDIF
          MESAGE(I:I) = NEWCHR
  300 CONTINUE
```

```
C Figure G.3 (continued)
C Print out the encoded message.
      PRINT *, ' '
      PRINT *, 'THE ENCODED MESSAGE IS:'
      PRINT *, MESAGE
      STOP
      END
```

Figure G.4   Input and output files for the character encoding program of Figure G.3

a) Input:

```
54
ABCDEFGHIJKLMNOPQRSTUVWXYZ0123456789 !@#$%^&()-+=:;<>?
-+=:;<>?ABCDEFGHIJKLMNOPQRSTUVWXYZ0123456789 !@#$%^&()
THE POSITION OF THE ENEMY SUBMARINES IS AS SUSPECTED; THERE ARE FOUR OF
THEM
```

b) Output:

```
THE ORIGINAL MESSAGE IS:
THE POSITION OF THE ENEMY SUBMARINES IS AS SUSPECTED; THERE ARE FOUR OF
THEM

THE ENCODED MESSAGE IS:
L?;2HGKALAGF2G<2L?;2;F;EQ2KM+E-JAF;K2AK2-K2KMKH;=L;:^2L?;J;2-
J;2<GMJ2G<2L?;E
```

G.4   Character Manipulation with Non-character Variables

G.4.1   Character Storage

Character data may also be manipulated in the non-character data types. In fact, since the early FORTRAN language did not have character variables, it was necessary to store character information in variables of one of the other data types, INTEGER, REAL, DOUBLE PRECISION, COMPLEX, or LOGICAL. The number of characters that a variable of each type can store depends on the word size of the computer being used. On the IBM 370 and VAX systems, a word of memory consists of 4 bytes and is, therefore, capable of storing 4 characters. The table in Figure G.5 lists the various data types and the number of characters that can be stored in a variable of each type.

Figure G.5   Number of characters for each data type.

Data Type	Characters
INTEGER	4
REAL	4
DOUBLE PRECISION	8
COMPLEX	8
LOGICAL	4

Though COMPLEX and DOUBLE PRECISION variables are sometimes useful for handling long character strings, the most common data type used is INTEGER. Because of the word length restrictions, it is necessary to divide longer character strings into variable-sized units. For INTEGER variables, this means substrings of length 4 or less must be used.

G.4.2   Assignment of Character Values

a) Execution-Time Assignment   Character constants cannot be assigned to non-character data types. However, variables being used to store character information can appear wherever such variables are normally valid, even though many of these uses, such as DO statement parameters, do not make sense. It is, therefore, permissible to use arithmetic means to create or manipulate character information. However, this can be tricky and should be avoided whenever possible.

b) Compile-Time Assignment   A convenient and often necessary way to initialize variables having character values is at compile time. The values may be assigned using a DATA statement or may be assigned in the appropriate declaration statement. Character constants may be specified by the H (Hollerith) code or by using apostrophes. For instance, the H code has the form nH where n specifies the number of characters immediately following the H that are part of the constant. Thus the statements:

```
INTEGER SENT(5)
DATA SENT / 4HTHIS, 4HbISb, 4HAbSE, 4HNTEN, 2HCE /
```

are equivalent to

```
INTEGER SENT(5) / 4HTHIS, 4HbISb, 4HAbSE, 4HNTEN, 2HCE /
```

which is equivalent to

```
INTEGER SENT(5) / 'THIS', 'bISb', 'AbSE', 'NTEN', 'CE' /
```

Note that it is necessary to subdivide the character string to fit the size of the variable in use.

G.4.3   Input and Output of Character Values

Since standard FORTRAN requires that formats be specified for all input and output, the A-mask must be used. The rules are the same as those described in the previous section. However, care must be exercised to divide the character string into word-size lengths.

G.4.4   Using Character Quantities

Manipulating character quantities in FORTRAN is somewhat cumbersome because of the restrictions imposed by the fixed number of characters that can be stored in each variable. When handling longer strings, it is necessary to store word-size pieces in separate variables or in entries of an array. As with FORTRAN/77 CHARACTER variables, if the application requires any character-by-character analysis, it is expedient to place each character in a separate entry of an array.

H
Manipulation of Logical Values

H.1   Introduction

Logical-valued expressions are an essential feature in all programming languages.   Their use in expressing conditions in the **if-then-else** and **while-do** constructs is essential to making decisions about the flow of operations in an algorithm.   A discussion of such expressions was given in Chapters 2 and 4.   As well, logical variables have also been introduced for the purpose of error flags for subprograms.   Such variables are also useful for solving problems in set theory and electrical circuit design.   The following sections will investigate the details of this data type.

H.2   Logical Constants

There are only two logical constants:

.TRUE. and .FALSE.

The periods on either side are necessary to distinguish these constants from potential variables with similar names.

H.3   Logical Variables

Like all special data types, any variable that will have logical values must be declared in a LOGICAL declaration statement such as:

```
LOGICAL FLAG, SCORE(100), TEST(20,25)
```

Notice that sets or arrays of logical variables can also be established. The amount of storage taken by a logical variable so declared depends upon the processor. Usually it would take 1 word or 4 bytes on IBM and VAX computers. Although not in the standards, some compilers also allow the definition of 1 byte, 2 bytes, or 4 bytes of storage to be specified.

```
LOGICAL*1 FLAG, SCORE(100), TEST(20,25)
LOGICAL*2 FLAG, SCORE(100), TEST(20,25)
LOGICAL*4 FLAG, SCORE(100), TEST(20,25)
```

The first statement declares that each logical variable or array element defined will have just 1 byte reserved for it. The second statement reserves 2 bytes each and the third statement reserves 4 bytes each.

H.4 Logical Operators

Logical values, by their nature, are different from arithmetic values and, thus, require a unique selection of operators. FORTRAN/77 provides five logical operators:

.NOT.   .AND.   .OR.   .EQV.   .NEQV.

for the manipulation of logical entities.

The .NOT. operator negates the value of its single operand. The .AND. operator produces a .TRUE. value if and only if both operands are .TRUE. while the .OR. operator gives a .TRUE. result if either or both of its two operands is true. The .EQV. operator produces a .TRUE. value if both of its operands have the same logical value. The .NEQV. operator produces a .TRUE. value only if both of its operands have different logical values.

The priority of these operators follows.

Operator	*Priority*
.NOT.	highest
.AND.	:
.OR.	:
.EQV. or .NEQV.	lowest

These operators are applied to logical variables P and Q in the table presented in Figure H.1.

Figure H.1   Logical operators and their operation.

P	.FALSE.	.FALSE.	.TRUE.	.TRUE.
Q	.FALSE.	.TRUE.	.FALSE.	.TRUE.
.NOT. P	.TRUE.	.TRUE.	.FALSE.	.FALSE.
.NOT. Q	.TRUE.	.FALSE.	.TRUE.	.FALSE.
P .AND. Q	.FALSE.	.FALSE.	.FALSE.	.TRUE.
P .OR. Q	.FALSE.	.TRUE.	.TRUE.	.TRUE.
P .EQV. Q	.TRUE.	.FALSE.	.FALSE.	.TRUE.
P .NEQV. Q	.FALSE.	.TRUE.	.TRUE.	.FALSE.

H.5   Relational Operators

Logical operators are not the only ones that produce logical-valued results.   The six relational operators, introduced in Chapter 4 and summarized in Figure H.2, are used to test the relationship between arithmetic quantities.   The result of a relational operation is either .TRUE. or .FALSE.

Figure H.2   The relational operators.

Symbol	*Operator*
=	.EQ.
≠	.NE.
>	.GT.
≥	.GE.
<	.LT.
≤	.LE.

H.6   Logical Expressions and Assignment Statements

Any expression involving logical variables, logical constants, logical operators, or relational operators is called a *logical expression*.   While such expressions are used primarily as conditions in IF-THEN-ELSE and WHILE-DO statements, their values may also be assigned to logical variables.

In evaluating expressions, recall that FORTRAN/77 employs a priority scheme to remove ambiguity between successive operators.   The scheme is extended in Figure H.3 to include logical and relational operators.   Of course, parentheses can be used to alter the order of operations.   Should two adjacent operators have the same priority, they are performed from left to right.   The sole exception to this rule is successive exponentiation, which is performed from right to left.   As examples consider the following program segment:

Figure H.3 FORTRAN/77 operator priority scheme.

highest	`**`
	`*,/`
	`+,-`
⋮	`.EQ., .NE., .GT., .GE., .LT., .LE.`
	`.NOT.`
	`.AND.`
	`.OR.`
lowest	`.EQV., .NEQV.`

```
INTEGER R, S, T, U, X, Y
LOGICAL A, B, C
  .
  .
A = .TRUE.
B = X .EQ. Y .OR. R .GT. S
C = T .LT. U
IF (B .EQV. C) THEN
  .
  .
```

H.7 Input and Output of Logical Values

Logical values may be read or printed with or without FORMAT control in FORTRAN/77.

a) Input Without FORMAT   Data values can be expressed in full as .TRUE. or .FALSE. or may be abbreviated to the single letters T or F respectively.   Naturally, pairs of values must be separated by a single comma, one or more blanks, or a combination of both.

b) Input With FORMAT   A specific L format code is provided for logical values.   The code is of the form Lw where w specifies the number of columns in the input field.   The input field may contain .TRUE., .FALSE., T or F anywhere in the w columns.

c) Output Without FORMAT   In FORTRAN/77 logical values may be printed without formal control.   The single letters T or F are printed for the values.

d) Output with FORMAT   A single letter T or F is printed in the rightmost of the w columns specified.

H.8 Built-in Functions

FORTRAN/77 does not provide any built-in functions for use with logical arguments.

H.9   Function Subprograms and Statement Functions

Function subprograms that produce a logical-valued result may be defined using any of the following declarations.

```
LOGICAL FUNCTION name   (parameter list)
LOGICAL FUNCTION name*4 (parameter list)
LOGICAL FUNCTION name*1 (parameter list)
```

The name of the function must be declared as a logical value of the same size in the calling program.   It is also possible to define logical-valued statement functions as illustrated in the example in the next section.

H.10   An Example Using Logical Variables

The following example involves making decisions about points on the cartesian coordinate plane:

Example H.1   Points on the Cartesian Plane
 Consider a circle centered at the origin with a given radius, and a rectangle, also centered at the origin with given width and height.   List all points in the first quadrant having integral coordinates that lie either strictly within the circle or strictly within the rectangle but not both.

a) Problem Discussion   A variety of possible situations is illustrated in Figure H.4. The required points are indicated for each of the four cases shown.   A number of approaches may be taken to find the necessary points.   One of the easiest involves checking all x coordinates from zero to the maximum of the radius and half the rectangle width.   For each x coordinate, all y coordinates from zero to the maximum of the radius and half the rectangle height must be checked.   The program will need to use a nested loop structure to test all integral points given by these computed limits.

c) Testing for Within the Circle and/or Rectangle   To illustrate several features of logical variables, the decision as to whether a point is within the circle can be made by a logical-valued statement function, such as the following:

```
CIRCLE(X,Y,R) = X**2 + Y**2 .LT. R**2
```

The decision relative to the rectangle is written as a logical function subprogram, although it also could be a statement function,

```
LOGICAL FUNCTION RECTGL(X,Y,WIDTH,HEIGHT)
```

which must check that the x coordinate is less than half the width and that the y coordinate is less than half the height.   The results of these functions are then used to determine whether the point is within one or the other but not both the circle and the

Figure H.4   Integral points within a circle or rectangle.

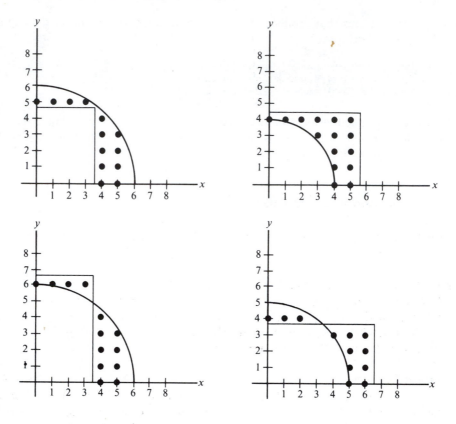

rectangle.   This relationship between two logical quantities is called the *exclusive-or* function.

c) The Program   The complete program to accomplish the requested task is presented in Figure H.5.   Take particular notice of the detailed notes at the end of the program.

Figure H.6 illustrates the output that is generated for a circle of radius 5 and a rectangle 6 units wide and 12 units high.

```
C Figure H.5 -- Program to list the integral points within
C                 a circle or a rectangle but not both.
C******************************************************************
C RADIUS - radius of the circle centered at the origin
C WIDTH  - width of the rectangle centered at the origin
C HEIGHT - height of the rectangle (y-direction)
C X,Y    - coordinate pairs tested
C XL     - maximum value of X to be tested
C YL     - maximum value of Y to be tested
C CIRCLE - logical function for inclusion in the circle
C RECTGL - logical function for inclusion in the rectangle
C INC    - logical flag for inside the circle
C INR    - logical flag for inside the rectangle
C EXORCR - logical exclusive or flag for inside one or other
C******************************************************************
      INTEGER X, XL, Y, YL, WIDTH, HEIGHT, RADIUS, MAX0, R
      LOGICAL CIRCLE, RECTGL, INC, INR, EXORCR
C The statement function for points within the circle.
      CIRCLE(X,Y,R) = X**2 + Y**2 .LT. R**2
C Input the circle radius and rectangle size.
      PRINT *, 'ENTER THE RADIUS OF THE CIRCLE:'
      READ *, RADIUS
      PRINT *, 'ENTER THE RECTANGLE SIZE:'
      READ *, WIDTH, HEIGHT
      PRINT *, ' '
C Print the output titles.
      PRINT *, '            X             Y'
      PRINT *, ' '
C Assuming that both the circle and the rectangle are centered
C at the origin, determine the range of (X,Y) pairs to check.
      XL = MAX0(RADIUS, WIDTH/2)
      YL = MAX0(RADIUS, HEIGHT/2)
C Generate and test points in the first quadrant.
      DO 100 X = 0,XL
         DO 200 Y = 0,YL
            INC = CIRCLE(X,Y,RADIUS)
            INR = RECTGL(X,Y,WIDTH,HEIGHT)
            EXORCR = INC .AND. .NOT.INR .OR. .NOT.INC .AND. INR
            IF (EXORCR) THEN
               PRINT *, X, Y
            ENDIF
200      CONTINUE
100   CONTINUE
      STOP
      END
```

```
C Figure H.5 (continued)
C Function RECTGL -- Logical function to determine if (X,Y)
C                    is within a rectangle WIDTH x HEIGHT
C                    centered at the origin.
C********************************************************************
      LOGICAL FUNCTION RECTGL(X,Y,WIDTH,HEIGHT)

      INTEGER X, Y, WIDTH, HEIGHT
      REAL XL, YL, FLOAT

      XL = FLOAT(WIDTH)/2.0
      YL = FLOAT(HEIGHT)/2.0
      RECTGL = FLOAT(X) .LT. XL .AND. FLOAT(Y) .LT. YL
      RETURN
      END
```

Program Notes

- Both CIRCLE and RECTGL must be declared as logical values in the main program.   Notice that even the dummy argument, R, used in the definition of CIRCLE must be declared as INTEGER.
- The expression for evaluating EXORCR could be written with parentheses to read more clearly.   However, the order of operations is correct without these parentheses.
- Since only integral coordinates are requested, INTEGER values are used for most of the numerical quantities.   Even though the width and height of the rectangle may not be evenly divisible by 2, the main program need only consider the next lowest integer.   However, function RECTGL must include the fractional portion for testing whether a point is within or on the rectangle.   The FLOAT function is used to emphasize this conversion.

Figure H.6 List of the integral points within a circle or a rectangle but not both, input for and output from the program of Figure H.5.

a) Input supplied:

5, 6, 12

b) Output produced:

X	Y
0	5
1	5
2	5
3	0
3	1
3	2
3	3
4	0
4	1
4	2

I
Manipulation of Extended-Precision Values

I.1 Introduction

The examples in several chapters, notably 7 and 8, have exposed the limitations of computer arithmetic. Though it is theoretically possible to obtain 7-significant-digit accuracy with 32-bit REAL arithmetic, such is rarely the case. Because many common decimal fractions are represented by truncating a repeating binary fraction, and because at most 7 significant digits are retained as the result of arithmetic operations, inaccuracies accumulate so that even the fourth or fifth significant digit is often suspect. To improve the accuracy of computation, most machines and the accompanying scientific programming languages include extended-precision capabilities that allow for up to 17-significant-digit accuracy. The sections of this appendix describe the elements of FORTRAN/77 to use for gaining this additional precision.

I.2 Extended-Precision Constants

Extended-precision constants are distinguished from single-precision or REAL constants by either writing more than 7 significant digits or by writing the number with a D exponent. The following are examples of valid extended-precision constants:

```
    2.718281828459045    0.052D 3      0.0D0
   -31.0062767           0.3665D-2    25.D+1
```

The maximum precision and limits on the size of extended-precision values vary depending on the computer in use. For an IBM 370, the maximum precision is 17 significant digits, the smallest non-zero value is 0.5397605346934028D-78, and the largest value is

0.7237005577332261D 76. On most computers, the size of the exponent does not differ between single and extended precision.

I.3 Extended-Precision Variables

All variables and arrays to be used for extended-precision values must be declared in a declaration statement. The FORTRAN/77 standard uses only the DOUBLE PRECISION declaration statement while many compilers also allow the use of an equivalent REAL*8 declaration statement. The use of the *8 notation stems from the fact that 8 units of memory called *bytes* are used to represent an extended-precision value in a 32-bit (4-byte) wordsize computer. (In this sense, single-precision REAL declarations may alternately be replaced by REAL*4 since 4 bytes are used to represent such values.) Thus, storing an extended-precision value requires twice the amount of space as a single-precision value. Hence the label DOUBLE PRECISION is used. In fact, since the portion of the space used for the exponent usually remains the same, all of the additional space is used to represent the fractional portion of the number. Thus, the improvement in precision from single to extended values is slightly greater than double. Both of the following declarations specify that SUM is to be a simple extended-precision variable, that ROWS is to be an array of 10 extended-precision values and that MATRIX is to be a 3×4 array having 12 extended-precision values.

```
DOUBLE PRECISION SUM, ROWS(10), MATRIX(3,4)
REAL*8 SUM, ROWS(10), MATRIX(3,4)
```

Rather than explicitly declaring variables as extended precision, it is sometimes advantageous to implicitly define all variables as extended precision using the IMPLICIT statement discussed in more detail in Appendix D.

I.4 Arithmetic Expressions and Assignment Statements

To achieve greater accuracy in the evaluation of arithmetic expressions, it is only necessary to declare all names as extended precision and to express all constants in extended-precision form. The same arithmetic operators and rules of evaluation used for single-precision quantities apply.

Any operation involving an extended-precision value and a nonextended-precision value causes the nonextended-precision value to be converted to extended-precision form before the operation takes place. Thus, the resulting value is always extended precision. The sole exception is exponentiation to an integer power. As with single precision, exponentiation to an integer power employs successive multiplication by the base to achieve the desired result, and, thus, no conversion of the exponent is necessary. In general, it is best to avoid mixed mode expressions whenever possible. This is particularly true for fractional values that cannot be represented exactly in binary notation. For instance, the number 0.1 does not have an exact internal representation. As a result, the approximations in single and extended precision differ. If the value of each of the following expressions is assigned to an extended-precision variable, the results are significantly different.

Expression	*Result* *(IBM)*
0.1E0 + 0.1E0	0.2000000476837158
0.1D0 + 0.1E0	0.2000000238418579
0.1D0 + 0.1D0	0.2000000000000000

While the representation of 0.1D0 uses 8 full bytes to represent 0.1, 0.1E0 uses only 4 bytes. When 0.1E0 is converted to extended precision, the additional 4 bytes are set to 0 rather than a more accurate representation of one tenth. This also means that the value of the following condition:

    0.1E0 .EQ. 0.1D0

is .FALSE. Sufficient inaccuracy is introduced by mixing single-precision and extended-precision constants to destroy the benefits of using extended precision. Forgetting to declare even one variable or to express one constant as extended precision is sufficient to invalidate the results of a program.

I.5   Input and Output of Extended-Precision Values

Very little additional caution is needed to read or print the value of an extended-precision variable. On input, the value may or may not include more than 7 significant digits and may be written with or without the D exponent. On output, extended-precision values are printed to 17 significant digits using the D exponent.

In order to better control the spacing for extended-precision values, two format codes are available. In addition to using the F-mask introduced in Appendix F, a D-mask of the form Dw.d, similar to the E-mask for single precision, can be used. Recall that w is an integer specifying the total number of character spaces to use, that d is the number of significant digits to be included, and that $w \geq d+7$.

I.6   Built-in Functions

A large number of built-in functions is available for use with extended-precision quantities. In most cases, these functions are similar and equivalent to their single-precision counterparts. There are both generic function and specific function names. For example, both ABS and DABS compute the extended-precision absolute value of the extended-precision argument. Both DABS and the argument variable must be declared as extended precision. Consult Appendix N for a complete list of such functions. Most non generic extended-precision functions start with the letter D and produce an extended-precision result (labeled r8 in the appendix).

I.7 Function Subprograms

To obtain more accurate results from user-defined function subprograms, it is possible to define the subprogram as an extended-precision function so that the value returned is extended precision. Such a declaration can be accomplished in either of the following two ways:

```
DOUBLE PRECISION FUNCTION name (parameters)
REAL FUNCTION name*8  (parameters)
```

Notice the positioning of the *8 in the second alternative. Of course, in the program that references such a function, the name must also be declared as extended precision.

I.8 Using Extended Precision in a Program

The use of extended-precision variables is best illustrated by translating a known program from single to extended precision. Listed in Figures I.1, I.2, I.4, and I.5 are the translations of subprograms BISECT and SIMP from Chapters 7 and 8 and mainline programs to use them. The translated subroutines are relabeled as DISECT and DSIMP. All single-precision declarations and constants have been changed to extended precision. FORMAT statements are used in the mainline programs to demonstrate the use of F- and D-masks for extended-precision quantities. The output produced by each program is given in Figures I.3 and I.6. The zero-finding program was executed with a much smaller value of the tolerance resulting in a significantly better approximation of the zero. The value of the function at the zero estimate is now approximately .0000000000000138 as opposed to -.0000277 with single precision. The area-finding program used from 2 to 8192 intervals to approximate the area. As can be seen from the output the double precision is more accurate than the single precision results due to the increased accuracy in the calculations and storage of the calculated values. As well, it is possible to increase the number of panels used far beyond the single-precision stage before round-off error contaminates the result.

```
C Figure I.1 -- The Bisection Zero-Finding Technique.
C                A main program to demonstrate the use of
C                subroutine DISECT to estimate the zero
C                of a given function within a given range.

C*********************************************************************
C A,B    - endpoints of the initial interval
C EPS    - desired tolerance
C ZERO   - resulting approximation to the zero
C FLAG   - exception flag from subroutine DISECT

C*********************************************************************
      EXTERNAL FUNC
      DOUBLE PRECISION A, B, EPS, ZERO, FUNC
      LOGICAL FLAG
 9000 FORMAT('0NO ZERO IN THIS INTERVAL.')
 9010 FORMAT('0THE ZERO IN THIS INTERVAL =',F20.16)
 9020 FORMAT(' THE FUNCTION VALUE THERE =',D25.17)
C Obtain the initial interval and tolerance.
      PRINT *, 'ENTER THE INITIAL INTERVAL:'
      READ *, A, B
      PRINT *, 'ENTER THE DESIRED TOLERANCE:'
      READ *, EPS
C Find a zero if possible and output an appropriate message.
      CALL DISECT(A,B,EPS,FUNC,FLAG,ZERO)

      IF (FLAG) THEN
         PRINT 9000
      ELSE
         PRINT 9010, ZERO
         PRINT 9020, FUNC(ZERO)
      ENDIF

      STOP
      END
C*********************************************************************
C Function FUNC -- Given a value for X, evaluate the function
C                    x**3 - 4x**2 - 4x + 15
C*********************************************************************
      DOUBLE PRECISION FUNCTION FUNC(X)
      DOUBLE PRECISION X
      FUNC = ((X - 4.0D0)*X - 4.0D0)*X + 15.0D0
      RETURN
      END
C Subroutine DISECT would be placed here.
```

```
C Figure I.2 -- The Double-Precision Bisection Zero-Finding Subroutine.
C                A subprogram to implement the bisection technique
C                for estimating a zero of a given function.
C***********************************************************************
C PL,PR  - endpoints of the initial interval
C XL,XR  - endpoints of successive intervals
C FL,FR  - function values at the endpoints
C XMID   - midpoint of the interval XL, XR
C FMID   - function value at the midpoint
C EPS    - given tolerance in the zero estimate
C F      - function containing a zero
C ERROR  - error flag: true if no sign change
C***********************************************************************
        SUBROUTINE DISECT(PL,PR,EPS,F,ERROR,XMID)

        REAL*8 PL, PR, XL, XR, FL, FR, XMID, FMID, F, EPS, ABS
        LOGICAL ERROR
C Set up the initial interval.
C Compute F(X) at the initial endpoints.
        XL = PL
        XR = PR
        FL = F(XL)
        FR = F(XR)

C Provided a zero exists in the given interval, bisect
C the interval and choose the subinterval with a sign
C change, until the interval width is within tolerance.
        IF (FL*FR .GT. 0.0D0) THEN
            ERROR = .TRUE.
        ELSE
            ERROR = .FALSE.
            XMID = (XL + XR)/2.0D0
 100        IF (ABS(XL - XMID) .GT. EPS) THEN
                FMID = F(XMID)
                IF (FL*FMID .LE. 0.0D0) THEN
C                   Choose the left subinterval.
                    XR = XMID
                ELSE
C                   Choose the right subinterval.
                    XL = XMID
                    FL = FMID
                ENDIF
                XMID = (XL + XR)/2.0D0
                GO TO 100
            ENDIF
        ENDIF
        RETURN
        END
```

Figure I.3   Finding a zero of a cubic polynomial, output from the program of Figure I.1.

```
ENTER THE INITIAL INTERVAL:
-2.5D0 -1.5D0
ENTER THE DESIRED TOLERANCE:
0.1D-14

THE ZERO IN THIS INTERVAL = -1.9575869857265653
THE FUNCTION VALUE THERE =  0.13766765505351941D-13
```

```
C Figure I.4 -- The Double-Precision Simpson's Rule Technique.
C              Main program to use function SIMP to find the area
C              under 7 - 7X**6 between 0 and 1, for 2, 4, 8, ...,
C              subintervals.
C***********************************************************************
C A,B    - endpoints of the integration interval
C PANEL  - current number of integration panels
C MAXPAN - maximum number of panels to compute
C AREA   - computed approximation to the area
C***********************************************************************
      EXTERNAL FUNC
      DOUBLE PRECISION A, B, AREA, FUNC, DSIMP
      INTEGER PANELS, MAXPAN
 9000 FORMAT('0    PANELS    AREA ESTIMATE'/)
 9010 FORMAT(1X, I11, D25.17)
C Obtain the interval and maximum number of panels.
      PRINT *, 'ENTER THE INTEGRATION INTERVAL:'
      READ *, A, B
      PRINT *, 'ENTER THE MAXIMUM NUMBER OF PANELS:'
      READ *, MAXPAN
C Compute the area for each number of panels up to the maximum.
      PRINT 9000
      PANELS = 2
  100 IF (PANELS .LE. MAXPAN) THEN
         AREA = DSIMP(A,B,PANELS,FUNC)
         PRINT 9010, PANELS, AREA
         PANELS = PANELS * 2
         GO TO 100
      ENDIF

      STOP
      END
C***********************************************************************
C Function FUNC -- Given a value for X, evaluate the function
C                  7.0 - 7.0*X**6
C***********************************************************************
      REAL FUNCTION FUNC*8(X)
      REAL*8 X
      FUNC = 7.0D0 - 7.0D0*X**6
      RETURN
      END
C Subroutine DSIMP would be placed here.
```

```
C Figure I.5 -- The Double-Precision Simpson's Rule Function.
C               Function subprogram to find the AREA under
C               the curve F between the endpoints A and B
C               using PANEL integration panels.

C***********************************************************************

C A,B     - endpoints of integration interval
C PANEL   - number of integration panels
C F       - function to integrate
C H       - subinterval width
C SUMEVN  - sum of F(X) values at even subintervals
C SUMODD  - sum of F(X) values at odd subintervals

C***********************************************************************

      DOUBLE PRECISION FUNCTION DSIMP(A,B,PANEL,F)

      REAL*8 A, B, F, H, SUMEVN, SUMODD, X
      INTEGER PANEL, I
C Calculate the subinterval width and initialize summations.
      H = (B - A)/(2*PANEL)
      SUMEVN = 0.0D0
      SUMODD = F(A+H)
C Sum function values at each subinterval.
      DO 100 I = 1, PANEL-1, 1
         X = A + 2.0D0*I*H
         SUMEVN = SUMEVN + F(X)
         SUMODD = SUMODD + F(X+H)
  100 CONTINUE
C Assemble the Simpson's Rule integration formula.
      DSIMP = (H/3.0D0) * (F(A) + 4.0D0*SUMODD + 2.0D0*SUMEVN + F(B))

      RETURN
      END
```

Figure I.6 Finding the area under a curve, output from the program of Figure I.4.

```
ENTER THE INTEGRATION INTERVAL:
0.0 1.0
ENTER THE MAXIMUM NUMBER OF PANELS:
8192

      PANELS    AREA ESTIMATE

           2   0.59825846354166667D+01
           4   0.59988733927408855D+01
           8   0.59999289909998577D+01
          16   0.59999955526242654D+01
          32   0.59999997218934975D+01
          64   0.59999999826160699D+01
         128   0.59999999989134686D+01
         256   0.59999999999320911D+01
         512   0.59999999999957554D+01
        1024   0.59999999999997349D+01
        2048   0.59999999999999821D+01
        4096   0.60000000000000000D+01
        8192   0.60000000000000020D+01
```

J
Manipulation of
Complex Values

J.1 Introduction

The complex number system is of theoretical interest to mathematicians and of practical importance to scientists and engineers. For these reasons, the FORTRAN family of programming languages has been endowed with the facilities for handling complex arithmetic.

In mathematics, a complex number consists of a pair of numbers; a real part, called x; an imaginary part y; and is written as $x + yi$, where $i^2 = -1$. The FORTRAN/77 standards define only single-precision complex values and just the COMPLEX statement. However, many FORTRAN/77 compilers include double-precision complex values also. The following discussion includes double-precision and variations on the complex statements as found in the VAX and IBM FORTRAN/77 compilers.

J.2 COMPLEX Constants

A COMPLEX constant is written as two single-precision or two extended-precision constants in parentheses with the two parts separated by a comma. The following are examples of valid COMPLEX constants (notice that either single- or extended-precision constants are legitimate):

COMPLEX *Constant*	*Meaning*
(2.5,-3.7)	$2.5 - 3.7i$
(0.5E1,2.4E-1)	$5 + 0.24i$
(-1.25,-9.8E+1)	$-1.25 - 98i$
(123456789.,1.D0)	$123456789 + i$

J.3   COMPLEX **Variables**

A variable is of type COMPLEX if it has been declared in a COMPLEX declaration statement.   Single-precision complex variables are declared as follows

        COMPLEX Z, PTS(25), TBELL(5,5)

Since, on a 32–bit (4–byte) wordsize computer, a COMPLEX value consists of two REAL values, each COMPLEX value requires 8 bytes of memory for single precision and 16 bytes for extended precision.   Thus, the following declaration is equivalent to the one above.

        COMPLEX*8 Z, PTS(25), TBELL(5,5)

In order to extend the precision of the above variables, the same variables are declared extended-precision COMPLEX by the following statement:

        COMPLEX*16 Z, PTS(25), TBELL(5,5)

Notice that one and two dimensional arrays can also be declared as COMPLEX variables.

J.4   **Arithmetic Expressions and Assignment Statements**

Any arithmetic expression involving one or more COMPLEX constants or variables is called a *complex expression*.   The rules governing COMPLEX arithmetic are summarized below for two complex values, (a,b) and (c,d), an integer value i, a real value r, and a double-precision value p.

$$(a,b) + (c,d) = (a + c, b + d)$$

$$(a,b) - (c,d) = (a - c, b - d)$$

$$(a,b) \times (c,d) = (ac - bd, ad + bc)$$

$$\frac{(a,b)}{(c,d)} = \left[\frac{ac + bd}{c^2 + d^2}, \frac{bc - ad}{c^2 + d^2} \right]$$

$$(a,b)^i = (a,b) \times (a,b) \times \cdots \times (a,b) \quad [i \text{ times}]$$

$$(a,b)^r = (a,b)^{(r,0)}$$

$(a,b)^p = (a,b)^{(p,0)}$ (prohibited by standards)

$(a,b)^{(c,d)} = \text{EXP}((c,d)*\text{LOG}((a,b)))$

It is possible to perform other operations on COMPLEX values using non-COMPLEX data types. The table below summarizes the type of result when any of the operations +, −, *, or / are applied. The first letter of each data type (plus length attribute if necessary) has been used in the table.

	INTEGER	REAL*4	REAL*8	COMPLEX*8	COMPLEX*16
COMPLEX*8	COMPLEX*8	COMPLEX*8	COMPLEX*16	COMPLEX*8	COMPLEX*16
COMPLEX*16	COMPLEX*16	COMPLEX*16	COMPLEX*16	COMPLEX*16	COMPLEX*16

Addition and subtraction by an INTEGER, REAL, or extended-precision quantity only affects the real part of the COMPLEX value, whereas multiplication and division affect both the real and imaginary components.

When COMPLEX values are assigned across an equals sign, the value is converted (if necessary) to the data type of the variable on the left. If variables of type INTEGER, REAL*4, or REAL*8 are being assigned a COMPLEX value, they take on the real component of the COMPLEX value (converted in type if necessary). Conversely, if such values are assigned to a COMPLEX variable, the value is assigned to the real component of the COMPLEX variable, and the imaginary component is set to zero. Note that COMPLEX values may be compared for equality and non-equality using the relational operators .EQ. and .NE.. COMPLEX values may *not* be compared with .LT., .LE., .GT., or .GE..

J.5   Input and Output of COMPLEX Values

Whenever values for a COMPLEX variable are read, 2 REAL constants must be provided for the real and imaginary components respectively. When a free format read is used, the constant must include the surrounding parentheses and a comma to separate the components. With a formatted read, the brackets and comma are omitted, and appropriate F-, E-, or D-codes are supplied for each component. Thus, two FORMAT masks must be supplied for each COMPLEX value.

COMPLEX values can also be printed with or without a FORMAT specification. On free-format output, the brackets and comma are included. If a FORMAT is specified, then an F-, E-, or D-code must be supplied for each component. If the brackets and comma are desired, then explicit formatting is required.

J.6   Built-in Functions

A variety of built-in functions are supplied for COMPLEX arithmetic. These are listed in Appendix N. As indicated there, many of the generic functions accept complex arguments. Generally speaking, single-precision functions for COMPLEX arithmetic normally begin with the letter C. Extended-precision COMPLEX functions (if available) begin with the letters CD. These functions must be declared with the corresponding length in the program segment using them. In fact, failure to do so will cause an error message to be issued.

Of particular note in the list of functions is CMPLX. In order to combine the value of two REAL variables, X and Y, into the real and imaginary parts of a COMPLEX variable, Z, it is necessary to write

```
Z = CMPLX(X,Y)
```

Expressions such as (X,Y), (0.0,Y), or (X,0.0) are invalid.

Two additional functions listed in Appendix N are useful when processing COMPLEX values. In order to isolate either part of a COMPLEX variable, the functions REAL and AIMAG must be used. Both functions produce real-valued results and should be declared appropriately. For instance, to assign the real part of a complex number Z to a real variable A and the imaginary part to a real variable B, one would write:

```
COMPLEX Z
REAL A, B
  .
  .
  .
A = REAL(Z)
B = AIMAG(Z)
```

J.7   Function Subprograms and Statement Functions

It is sometimes desirable to define COMPLEX-valued functions. Such functions may be defined in a single statement or may be introduced by one of the following declaration statements:

```
COMPLEX FUNCTION name (parameter list)
COMPLEX FUNCTION name*8 (parameter list)
COMPLEX FUNCTION name*16 (parameter list)
```

The first two alternatives declare a single-precision function, while the third specifies an extended-precision function. Whether a COMPLEX-valued function is defined as a subprogram or in a single statement, the name of the function must be declared in the program segment that uses it.

J.8   An Example Using COMPLEX Variables

Consider the following example involving the tabulation of a complex-valued function.

Example J.1   Tabulating a Complex Function
Evaluate the complex function:

$$f(z) = \begin{cases} e^z \times z^3 & \text{if } x > 0,\ y > 0 \\ \dfrac{3z}{(2 + 3.5i)z - 4.2} & \text{otherwise} \end{cases}$$

for a given value of x and for $y = -5, -4, \cdots, +5$.

Since the subject of function tabulation was discussed in detail in Chapter 6, no development of a solution is necessary. The sample program is presented in Figure J.1, while the resulting output is given in Figure J.2. Take particular note of the use of the built-in functions and the declarations of variable types.

```
C Figure J.1 -- Program to tabulate a complex-valued function.

C**********************************************************************

C Z      - a complex number
C X      - the real component of Z
C Y      - the imaginary component of Z
C F      - the complex-valued function
C CMPLX  - built-in function to combine components

C**********************************************************************

      COMPLEX Z, F, CMPLX
      REAL X, Y

C Read a value for X and tabulate F for this X and Y from -5 to +5.

      PRINT *, 'ENTER X VALUE FOR TABULATION:'
      READ *, X
      PRINT *, ' '
      DO 100 Y = -5.0, 5.0, 1.0
         Z = CMPLX(X,Y)
         PRINT *, Z, F(Z)
  100 CONTINUE

      STOP
      END

C**********************************************************************

C Function F -- Complex function defined by:
C                      z    3
C                     e  * z    if x>0 and y>0
C
C                       3z
C                 ---------------   otherwise.
C                 (2 +3.5i)z - 4.2

C**********************************************************************

C Z - value for which to evaluate the function
C CEXP, REAL, AIMAG - built-in functions

C**********************************************************************

      COMPLEX FUNCTION F*8(Z)
      COMPLEX Z, CEXP
      REAL REAL, AIMAG

      IF (REAL(Z).GT.0.0 .AND. AIMAG(Z).GT.0.0) THEN
         F = CEXP(Z)*Z**3
      ELSE
         F = 3.0*Z / ((2.0,3.5)*Z - 4.2)
      ENDIF

      RETURN
      END
```

Figure J.2   Tabulation of a complex-valued function, output from the program in Figure J.1.

```
ENTER X VALUE FOR TABULATION:
2.0
(2.000000,-5.000000)  (0.4826624,-0.7833533)
(2.000000,-4.000000)  (0.4951943,-0.8336816)
(2.000000,-3.000000)  (0.4930432,-0.9216547)
(2.000000,-2.000000)  (0.4127444,-1.064446)
(2.000000,-1.000000)  (0.1337420,-1.111730)
(2.000000,0.0000000E+00)  (-2.4469797E-02,-0.8564437)
(2.000000,1.000000)  (-60.40979,56.35091)
(2.000000,2.000000)  (-58.30268,-156.7005)
(2.000000,3.000000)  (327.1104,-113.8022)
(2.000000,4.000000)  (335.5503,569.3779)
(2.000000,5.000000)  (-758.1918,869.9078)
```

K
The Plotting Package

This appendix describes the plotting subroutines used in the main body of the text. A FORTRAN/77 version of the routines is listed on succeeding pages. A machine-readable version of the programs is available.

These routines generate a line-printer plot of maximum size 81 by 51 characters. The routines perform an automatic scaling of the data points such that they always fill the entire plot area. As a result, the user need not worry about data points accidentally exceeding the graph limits. There are three subroutines in total. A brief description of their use follows, and numerous examples of their use are given in Chapter 6.

K.1   SETPLT

This subroutine initializes the other plotting subroutines. It must be the first of the subroutines called and should be executed only once for each complete graph. The statement to use this subroutine is

```
CALL SETPLT(NROW,NCOL)
```

The variables NROW and NCOL represent the desired plotting surface size. NROW gives the number of character rows (the y direction) and valid sizes for it are 11, 21, 31, 41, 51. NCOL gives the number of character columns (the x direction) and valid sizes are 11, 21, 31, ... ,71, 81. If invalid values for NROW or NCOL are given, the subroutine automatically forces the size to be the next higher valid value or the maximum value.

K.2   STOPNT

This subroutine stores the points to be plotted until it comes time to actually generate the plot.   It must be executed at least once for each point that is to appear on the plot. For example, if the statement

```
CALL STOPNT(X,Y,'A')
```

is executed, then the letter A (it must be a single character) will be plotted at the point X,Y on the graph.   X and Y are the REAL cartesian coordinates of the point and must be assigned values in the program.   This subroutine will store only the first 1000 points for plotting.   If more than 1000 calls are made to STOPNT, the subroutine will issue a warning message and then ignore all points in excess of that number.

K.3   PLOT

This subroutine causes the stored points to be printed.   It should be executed after all points have been given to the STOPNT routine.   The statement to use this subroutine is

```
CALL PLOT(I)
```

The variable I controls whether or not axes are printed with the graph.   If I has the value 0, no axes are printed.   If I has any other value, axes are superimposed on top of the graph.

Note that more than one curve may be plotted on the same graph by simply calling STOPNT with a different character as the third argument.   If two different curves are being plotted on the same graph with different symbols, and the symbols coincide, an * will be printed in that position.

```
C Subroutine SETPLT -- Initialize the plotting package, and
C                      establish the actual number of rows and columns
C                      in the printed plot.
C***************************************************************************
C XLIMIT - maximum number of columns
C YLIMIT - maximum number of rows
C I      - loop counter
C BLANK  - character ' '
C***************************************************************************
      SUBROUTINE SETPLT(NCHARX,NCHARY)

      CHARACTER GRAPH(51,81), ZARRAY(1000)
      COMMON/ZGRID2/ GRAPH, ZARRAY

      INTEGER NROW, NCOL, N
      REAL XARRAY(1000), YARRAY(1000)
      LOGICAL INIT
      COMMON/POINTZ/ NROW, NCOL, N, INIT, XARRAY, YARRAY

      INTEGER I, J, XLIMIT/81/, YLIMIT/51/
      CHARACTER BLANK/' '/
C Statement function ADJUST(M) adjusts M to 11, 21, 31, ...
      ADJUST(M) = ((M + 8) / 10)*10 + 1
C Check supplied number of rows and columns. Adjust and set
C to default values if out of range.
      NCOL = ADJUST(NCHARX)
      IF (NCOL.LE.1) THEN
         NCOL = 11
         PRINT *, 'PLOT-WIDTH TOO SMALL, 11 CHARACTERS USED'
      ENDIF
      IF (NCOL.GT.XLIMIT) THEN
         NCOL = XLIMIT
         PRINT *, 'PLOT-WIDTH TOO LARGE, ', XLIMIT, ' CHARACTERS USED'
      ENDIF
      NROW = ADJUST(NCHARY)
      IF (NROW.LE.1) THEN
         NROW = 11
         PRINT *, 'PLOT-HEIGHT TOO SMALL, 11 CHARACTERS USED'
      ENDIF
      IF (NROW.GT.YLIMIT) THEN
         NROW = YLIMIT
         PRINT *, 'PLOT-HEIGHT TOO LARGE, ', YLIMIT, ' CHARACTERS USED'
      ENDIF
C Initialize elements of the array GRAPH to blanks. Zero the
C points counter and set the initialization flag.
      DO 100 I = 1, YLIMIT
         DO 100 J = 1, XLIMIT
            GRAPH(I,J) = BLANK
  100 CONTINUE
      N = 0
      INIT = .TRUE.
      RETURN
      END
```

```
C Subroutine STOPNT -- Stores x, y coordinates for later plotting.
C*********************************************************************
C X, Y  - X and Y coordinates of stored points
C Z     - character to be used for plotting the point
C*********************************************************************
      SUBROUTINE STOPNT(X,Y,Z)

      CHARACTER GRAPH(51,81), ZARRAY(1000)
      COMMON/ZGRID2/ GRAPH, ZARRAY

      INTEGER NROW, NCOL, N
      REAL XARRAY(1000), YARRAY(1000)
      LOGICAL INIT
      COMMON/POINTZ/ NROW, NCOL, N, INIT, XARRAY, YARRAY

      REAL X, Y
      CHARACTER Z
C Check for initialization.
      IF (.NOT. INIT) THEN
         PRINT *, 'WARNING - PLOT NOT INITIALIZED'
         CALL SETPLT(81,51)
      ELSE
         N = N + 1
         IF (N.LT.1001) THEN
            XARRAY(N) = X
            YARRAY(N) = Y
            ZARRAY(N) = Z
         ELSE
            IF (N.EQ.1001) THEN
               PRINT *, 'TOO MANY POINTS - FIRST 1000 USED.'
            ENDIF
         ENDIF
      ENDIF
      RETURN
      END
```

```
C Subroutine PLOT -- Perform the actual plotting. Coordinates are
C                    scaled and plotted. Axes are generated if CODE = 1
C*********************************************************************
C CODE   - if CODE=1 plot axes, otherwise do not plot axes
C GRAPH  - stores the image of the graph to be plotted
C NROW   - number of row positions in graph
C NCOL   - number of column positions in graph
C XARRAY - storage for x position of point to be plotted
C YARRAY - storage for y position of point to be plotted
C ZARRAY - storage for character to be plotted
C N      - number of points submitted for plotting
C INIT   - switch to ensure proper initialization is done
C LIMIT  - contains the number of points actually plotted
C XLOW, XHIGH - min and max of all x data point coordinates
C YLOW, YHIGH - min and max of all y data point coordinates
C ORD    - y coordinates for printing
C ABSCIS - x coordinates for printing
C*********************************************************************
```

```
      SUBROUTINE PLOT(CODE)

      CHARACTER GRAPH(51,81), ZARRAY(1000)
      COMMON/ZGRID2/ GRAPH, ZARRAY

      INTEGER NROW, NCOL, N
      REAL XARRAY(1000), YARRAY(1000)
      LOGICAL INIT
      COMMON/POINTZ/ NROW, NCOL, N, INIT, XARRAY, YARRAY

      CHARACTER VBAR/'¦'/, SPACE/' '/, PLUS/'+'/, STAR/'*'/, BAR/'-'/
      INTEGER I, J, CODE, IXX, IYY, IX, IY, LIMIT, FACTOR, YFACTOR
      REAL XLOW, XHIGH, XUNIT, YUNIT, RANGE, SCALE, CORR,
     + YLOW, YHIGH, XPOINT, YPOINT,
     + XSIZE, YSIZE, YORD, ABSCIS(9)
      CHARACTER C
 9000 FORMAT(9X, 81A1)
 9001 FORMAT(1X, F8.5, 81A1)
 9002 FORMAT(<I+3>X, 12F10.4)
C Check that the plot routines have initialized.
      IF (.NOT. INIT) THEN
          PRINT *, 'ERROR - NO INITIALIZATION'
          GOTO 999
      ENDIF
C Check the number of points to be plotted. If n > 1000
C only 1000 points have been stored.
      IF (N.EQ.0) THEN
          PRINT *, 'ERROR - ATTEMPT TO PLOT 0 POINTS'
          GOTO 999
      ENDIF
      LIMIT = N
      IF (LIMIT.GT.1000) LIMIT = 1000
      PRINT *, ' '
      PRINT *, ' NUMBER OF POINTS : SUBMITTED ', N, ' PLOTTED ', LIMIT
C Determine the high and low values for both X and Y coordinates.
      XLOW = XARRAY(1)
      XHIGH = XLOW
      YLOW = YARRAY(1)
      YHIGH = YLOW
      DO 500 I = 1, LIMIT
          XPOINT = XARRAY(I)
          YPOINT = YARRAY(I)
          IF (XPOINT.LT.XLOW) XLOW = XPOINT
          IF (XPOINT.GT.XHIGH) XHIGH = XPOINT
          IF (YPOINT.LT.YLOW) YLOW = YPOINT
          IF (YPOINT.GT.YHIGH) YHIGH = YPOINT
  500 CONTINUE
C If upper and lower limits are the same for either x or y axis,
C alter the high and low values so (high-low) is not zero.
      IF (XHIGH.EQ.XLOW) THEN
          XHIGH = XHIGH + 1.0
          XLOW = XLOW - 1.0
          PRINT *, 'WARNING - ALL POINTS HAVE SAME X-VALUE'
      ELSE
          PRINT *, ' '
      ENDIF
      IF (YHIGH.EQ.YLOW) THEN
          YHIGH = YHIGH + 1.0
```

```
              YLOW = YLOW - 1.0
              PRINT *, 'WARNING - ALL POINTS HAVE SAME Y-VALUE'
          ELSE
              PRINT *, ' '
          ENDIF

C Prepare locations for axes: if the origin would lie totally outside
C the graph, determined by plus or minus 10%, then force the axes along
C the edge of the graph.

          IF (LIMIT.LT.1000) LIMIT = LIMIT + 1
          XARRAY(LIMIT) = XLOW
          YARRAY(LIMIT) = YLOW
          ZARRAY(LIMIT) = PLUS
          IF (XLOW*XHIGH.LE.0) THEN

C         Put y-axis inside.

              XARRAY(LIMIT) = 0.0

          ELSEIF (XLOW.GE.0.0) THEN
                  IF ((XLOW.LE.0.1*XHIGH)) THEN
                      XARRAY(LIMIT) = 0.0
                      XLOW = 0.0
                  ENDIF
              ELSE
                  XARRAY(LIMIT) = XHIGH
                  IF ((-XHIGH.LE.-0.1*XLOW)) THEN
                      XARRAY(LIMIT) = 0.0
                      XHIGH = 0.0
                  ENDIF
          ENDIF
          IF (YLOW*YHIGH.LE.0) THEN

C         Put x axis inside.

              YARRAY(LIMIT) = 0.0

          ELSEIF (YLOW.GE.0.0) THEN
                  IF (YLOW.LE.0.1*YHIGH) THEN
                      YARRAY(LIMIT) = 0.0
                      YLOW = 0.0
                  ENDIF
              ELSE
                  YARRAY(LIMIT) = YHIGH
                  IF (-YHIGH.LE.-0.1*YLOW) THEN
                      YARRAY(LIMIT) = 0.0
                      YHIGH = 0.0
                  ENDIF
          ENDIF

C Mark the origin with a '+' if axes were requested and if the origin
C is within the plot area.

          IF (XARRAY(LIMIT).EQ.0.0 .AND. YARRAY(LIMIT).EQ.0.0
     +                            .AND. CODE.EQ.1) ZARRAY(LIMIT) = PLUS

C Compute the range of X and Y values, and the unit range for
C each printer position.

          XSIZE = XHIGH-XLOW
          YSIZE = YHIGH-YLOW
          XUNIT = XSIZE/(NCOL-1)
          YUNIT = YSIZE/(NROW-1)
          IXX = IFIX((XARRAY(LIMIT) - XLOW)/XUNIT + 1.5)
          IYY = IFIX((YARRAY(LIMIT) - YLOW)/YUNIT + 1.5)
```

```
C If axes are requested, build up the characters in the array graph.
      IF (CODE.EQ.1) THEN
C         Draw x - axis.
          DO 700 I = 1, NCOL
             GRAPH(NROW + 1 - IYY, I) = BAR
             IF (MOD(I-IXX,10).EQ.0) GRAPH(NROW+1-IYY,I) = PLUS
  700     CONTINUE
C         Draw y - axis.
          DO 800 I = 1, NROW
             GRAPH(NROW + 1 - I, IXX) = VBAR
             IF (MOD(NROW+IYY-I,5).EQ.1) GRAPH(NROW+1-I,IXX) = PLUS
  800     CONTINUE
      ENDIF
C Now generate the plot in the buffer. If the character position
C contains a character other than a space, "-", "¦", "+", or the
C current character, two curves have intersected, place a "*".
      DO 950 I = 1, LIMIT
          IX = IFIX((XARRAY(I)-XLOW)/XUNIT+1.5)
          IY = IFIX((YARRAY(I)-YLOW)/YUNIT+1.5)
          IY = NROW+1-IY
          C = GRAPH(IY,IX)
          IF ((C.NE.SPACE).AND.(C.NE.BAR).AND.(C.NE.VBAR).AND.
      +      (C.NE.PLUS).AND.(C.NE.ZARRAY(I))) THEN
                 GRAPH(IY,IX) =  STAR
          ELSE
              GRAPH(IY,IX) = ZARRAY(I)
          ENDIF
  950 CONTINUE
C Compute y - axis scale factor.
      YFACTOR = 0
      SCALE = 1.0
      RANGE = ABS(YHIGH)
      IF (ABS(YLOW).GE.RANGE) RANGE = ABS(YLOW)
  975 IF ((RANGE.GE.10).OR.(RANGE.LT.1)) THEN
          IF (RANGE.LT.1) THEN
              RANGE = RANGE*10
              SCALE = SCALE*10.0
              YFACTOR = YFACTOR - 1
          ELSE
              RANGE = RANGE/10.0
              SCALE = SCALE/10.0
              YFACTOR = YFACTOR + 1
          ENDIF
          GOTO 975
      ENDIF
      PRINT *, ' '
C Compute axis alignment correction.
      CORR = 0.0
      IF(YLOW*YHIGH.LT.0.0) CORR = (YLOW + (IYY - 1)*YUNIT)*SCALE
      DO 980 I = 1, NROW
          IF (MOD(NROW+1-IYY-I,5).NE.0) THEN
              PRINT 9000, (GRAPH(I,J), J=1,NCOL)
          ELSE
              YORD = (YLOW+(NROW - I)*YUNIT)*SCALE - CORR
              PRINT 9001, YORD, (GRAPH(I,J),J=1,NCOL)
```

```
            ENDIF
      980 CONTINUE
C Generate the abscissa coordinates.
          FACTOR = 0
          SCALE = 1.0
          RANGE = ABS(XHIGH)
          IF (ABS(XLOW).GE.RANGE) RANGE = ABS(XLOW)
      990 IF ((RANGE.GE.10).OR.(RANGE.LT.1)) THEN
              IF (RANGE.LT.1) THEN
                  RANGE = RANGE*10
                  SCALE = SCALE*10.0
                  FACTOR = FACTOR - 1
              ELSE
                  RANGE = RANGE/10.0
                  SCALE = SCALE/10.0
                  FACTOR = FACTOR + 1
              ENDIF
              GOTO 990
          ENDIF
C Compute axis alignment correction.
          CORR = 0.0
          IF (XLOW*XHIGH.LT.0.0) CORR = (XLOW + (IXX - 1)*XUNIT)*SCALE
          I = MOD(IXX,10)
C Label the abscissa axes.
          K = 0
          DO 1200 J = I, NCOL, 10
              K = K + 1
              ABSCIS(K) = (XLOW+(J-1)*XUNIT)*SCALE - CORR
     1200 CONTINUE
          PRINT 9002, (ABSCIS(J),J=1,K)
C Output abscissa labels displaced so that decimal points and
C ticks line up.
          PRINT *, ' '
          PRINT *, ' '
          PRINT *, '   THE Y - AXIS SCALE FACTOR IS 10**', YFACTOR
          PRINT *, '           THE X - AXIS SCALE FACTOR IS 10**', FACTOR
      999 RETURN
          END
```

L
Data Files

This appendix contains five data files for use with questions in the main body of this book.   The five data files are as follows:

1)   Ages and marks for a group of first-year university students;
2)   Year of graduation for a group of physicians;
3)   Winning speeds, drivers, and make of car at the Indianapolis 500 race;
4)   Tar and nicotine deliveries of some cigarette brands;
5)   National Hockey League player performance and team data for the 1980/81 season.

The information in these files is real data since it is more interesting to work with this data than contrived data.   It is not intended that the data be used for purposes other than this.   The authors have attempted to reproduce the original source data as carefully as possible and apologize if any errors have crept into these files.   Machine readable copies of the data files are available.

L.1   Student Data File

This file contains the identification numbers, birthdates and marks for a group of first-year university students.   The C#n notation refers to a course number.

Student Identification Number	Birthdate	Marks					
		C#1	C#2	C#3	C#4	C#5	C#6
82046106	22 08 57	88	65	83	69	60	70
82909691	21 02 60	98	76	80	83	71	85
82908418	02 09 60	62	79	62	72	69	68
82908227	18 09 59	95	95	93	90	92	94

82997936	15	11	59	95	85	82	73	73	81
82980681	19	11	59	50	52	65	70	65	71
82980778	03	11	58	98	91	77	85	75	82
82985368	11	12	59	100	100	99	100	95	90
82981705	03	02	59	85	95	95	83	76	88
82940532	13	02	60	89	81	73	72	78	83
82949973	22	10	59	84	72	72	68	68	70
82949275	29	07	59	78	95	67	88	83	65
82945924	31	05	59	78	78	80	71	79	70
82938416	22	05	60	51	55	47	65	80	70
82935063	01	05	59	78	89	80	86	80	80
82932244	03	05	59	60	82	95	78	75	68
82931240	28	06	59	72	78	70	72	72	69
82963635	05	04	58	81	93	84	91	93	86
82965832	23	07	59	75	95	70	84	71	69
82961977	14	04	60	88	69	75	92	80	83
82957512	15	06	60	80	96	79	95	88	73
82974880	25	12	59	92	90	83	80	79	81
82972844	31	10	59	83	72	80	89	90	64
82910855	13	10	59	100	100	71	78	77	88
82919961	26	05	59	73	95	65	73	65	61
82904633	24	03	60	58	45	61	60	55	70
82902922	27	02	60	79	81	67	59	78	75
82999877	04	08	60	62	69	60	71	59	61
82988276	29	08	61	83	68	79	71	74	80
82949305	20	06	61	73	90	94	82	79	83
82943620	27	06	60	75	60	88	81	58	76
82946946	03	11	60	68	53	67	79	76	74
82942214	06	09	60	96	85	75	83	80	76
82941467	01	04	61	83	82	87	75	83	79
82137228	11	01	59	80	95	73	90	81	78
82998659	19	05	62	80	77	83	78	87	81
82994160	21	01	61	77	83	60	77	75	68
82993361	26	05	61	77	81	82	64	76	75
82996573	07	09	61	92	89	97	82	75	79
82992740	25	01	62	54	60	60	75	39	59
82980707	12	05	62	93	90	82	76	80	75
82989277	31	10	61	72	83	72	72	65	77
82983096	06	02	62	90	95	100	79	78	83
82986726	28	07	61	67	67	65	68	65	87
82981351	21	10	61	45	50	46	21	57	68
82981731	03	10	61	67	75	66	78	78	75
82981750	18	07	61	87	65	82	87	78	75
82940392	11	09	61	67	77	95	75	75	75
82948531	16	10	61	96	83	70	62	76	75
82944146	01	09	61	87	80	78	99	75	66
82947837	16	11	61	43	70	50	70	75	72
82942038	22	05	61	63	76	67	55	75	68
82941176	27	11	62	89	62	75	75	67	88
82936352	09	01	62	85	96	80	75	78	83
82937050	07	12	62	95	95	91	85	83	96
82937646	05	09	62	100	78	78	88	87	83
82823862	24	07	54	70	58	75	74	75	72
82821091	10	01	60	52	68	43	84	75	69
82997106	16	01	62	70	61	74	83	75	72
82986424	27	03	62	90	75	75	85	76	78
82944847	15	03	64	90	89	82	78	88	89
82968629	14	01	62	83	79	71	91	58	82
82963181	08	06	62	58	75	72	69	76	72
82965843	30	04	62	86	72	84	80	75	59
82961309	29	06	62	71	68	78	72	83	74
82953950	26	12	62	82	77	78	78	65	62
82956564	01	09	62	78	75	73	76	58	68
82957447	01	04	62	72	54	82	88	82	70
82974973	21	10	62	67	83	65	76	74	75
82919888	20	08	62	87	77	74	76	75	78

L.2   Physician Data File

This file contains information concerning the graduation date of a group of local physicians.   The data is given by graduation year and the number of graduates in that year.

Year	#	Year	#	Year	#	Year	#	Year	#
1901	1	1934	1	1944	4	1954	6	1964	1
1910	1	1935	2	1945	3	1955	6	1965	3
1921	1	1936	2	1946	3	1956	1	1967	7
1922	2	1937	2	1947	2	1957	5	1968	7
1923	1	1938	1	1948	3	1958	5	1969	3
1924	1	1939	1	1949	3	1959	3	1970	6
1926	1	1940	3	1950	3	1960	7	1971	4
1929	2	1941	3	1951	3	1961	3	1972	2
1930	1	1942	3	1952	7	1962	4	1973	3
1932	3	1943	2	1953	5	1963	4		

L.3   Indianapolis 500 Data

This file contains the results of the Indianopolis 500 auto race for the years 1911 through 1982.   The race was not run during the war years 1917–1918 and 1942–1945. Listed are the year, the driver and make of car, the elapsed time for the winner, and the average speed.

Year	Driver, Make of Car	Time	Speed
1911	Ray Harroun, Marmon	6:42:08	74.59
1912	Joe Dawson, National	6:21:06	78.72
1913	Jules Goux, Peugot	6:35:05	75.93
1914	Rene Thomas, Delage	6:03:45	82.47
1915	Ralph DePalma, Mercedes	5:33:55	89.94
1916	Dario Resta, Peugot	3:34:17	84.00
1919	Howdy Wilcox, Peugot	5:40:42	88.05
1920	Gaston Chevrolet, Monroe	5:38:32	88.62
1921	Tommy Milton, Frontenac	5:34:44	89.62
1922	Jimmy Murphy, Murphy	5:17:30	94.48
1923	Tommy Milton, H.C.S. Special	5:29:50	90.95
1924	L.L. Corum & Joe Boyer, Duesenberg	5:05:23	98.23
1925	Peter DePaolo, Duesenberg	4:56:39	101.13
1926	Frank Lockart, Miller	4:10:14	95.90
1927	George Souders, Duesenberg	5:07:33	97.545
1928	Louis Meyer, Miller	5:01:33	99.482
1929	Ray Keech, Simplex Piston Ring Spl.	5:07:25	97.585
1930	Billy Arnold, Miller-Hartz Spl.	4:58:39	100.448
1931	Louis Schneider, Bowes Seal Fast Spl.	5:10:27	96.629
1932	Fred Frame, Miller-Hartz Spl.	4:48:03	104.144
1933	Louis Meyer, Tydol Spl.	4:48:00	104.162
1934	Bill Cummings, Boyle Spl.	4:46:05	104.863
1935	Kelly Petillo, Dilmore Spdwy Spl.	4:42:22	106.240
1936	Louis Meyer, Ring Free Spl.	4:35:03	109.069
1937	Wilbur Shaw, Shaw Gilmore Spl.	4:24:07	113.580
1938	Floyd Roberts, Burd Piston Ring Spl.	4:15:58	117.200
1939	Wilbur Shaw, Boyle Spl.	4:20:47	115.035
1940	Wilbur Shaw, Boyle Spl.	4:22:31	114.227
1941	Floyd Davis & Mauri Rose, Noc-Out Spl.	4:20:36	115.117
1946	George Robson, Thorne Eng. Spl.	4:21:26	114.820
1947	Mauri Rose, Blue Crown Spl.	4:17:52	116.338
1948	Mauri Rose, Blue Crown Spl.	4:10:23	119.814
1949	Bill Holland, Blue Crown Spl.	4:07:15	121.327
1950	Johnnie Parsons, Wynn's Spl.	2:46:55	124.002
1951	Lee Wallard, Belanger Spl.	3:57:38	126.244
1952	Troy Ruttman, Agajanian Spl.	3:52:41	128.922

1953	Bill Vukovich, Fuel Injection Spl.	3:53:01	128.740
1954	Bill Vukovich, Fuel Injection Spl.	3:49:17	130.840
1955	Bob Stewart, John Zink Spl.	3:53:59	128.209
1956	Pat Flaherty, John Zink Spl.	3:53:28	128.493
1957	Sam Hanks, Belond Exhaust Spl.	3:41:14	135.601
1958	Jimmy Bryan, Belond AP Spl.	3:44:13	133.791
1959	Rodger Ward, Leader Card 500	3:40:49	135.857
1960	Jim Rathmann, Ken-Paul Spl.	3:36:11	138.767
1961	A.J. Foyt Jr., Bowes Seal Fast Spl.	3:35:37	139.130
1962	Rodger Ward, Leader Card 500	3:33:50	140.293
1963	Parnelli Jones, Agajanian Willard Spl.	3:29:35	143.137
1964	A.J. Foyt Jr., Sheraton-Thompson Spl.	3:23:35	147.350
1965	Jim Clark, Lotus Powered by Ford	3:19:05	150.686
1966	Graham Hill, American Red Ball Spl.	3:27:52	144.317
1967	A.J. Foyt Jr., Sheraton-Thompson Spl.	3:18:24	151.207
1968	Bobby Unser, Rislone Spl.	3:16:13	152.882
1969	Mario Andretti, STP Oil Treatment Spl.	3:11:14	156.867
1970	Al Unser, Johnny Lightning 500 Spl.	3:12:37	155.749
1971	Al Unser, Johnny Lightning Spl.	3:10:11	157.735
1972	Mark Donohue, Sunoco McLaren	3:04:05	162.962
1973	Gordon Johncock, STP Oil Filter Spl.	2:05:26	159.036
1974	Johnny Rutherford, McLaren	3:09:10	158.589
1975	Bobby Unser, Jorgensen Eagle	2:54:55	149.213
1976	Johnny Rutherford, Hy-Gain McLaren	1:42:52	148.725
1977	A.J. Foyt Jr., Gilmore Racing Team	3:05:57	161.331
1978	Al Unser, First National City	3:05:54	161.363
1979	Rick Mears, The Gould Charge	3:08:47	158.899
1980	Johnny Rutherford, Pennzoil Chaparral	3:29:59	142.862
1981	Bobby Unser, Norton Sprint Penske	3:35:47	139.029
1982	Gordon Johncock, STP Oil Spl. Wildcat	3:05:09	162.029

L.4 Cigarette Tar and Nicotine Data

This file contains information about several brands of cigarettes and the amount of tar and nicotine that they deliver. The measurements were taken from the cigarette packages as of April 1, 1978. The type classifications are as follows:

R	-	regular size	KS	-	king size	PR	-	premium size
P	-	plain	F	-	filter	C	-	cork tip
M	-	menthol						

The length measurements are in millimeters (mm), and the following diagram illustrates their meaning.

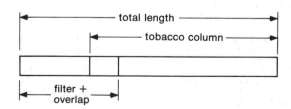

The tar and nicotine measurements are in milligrams (mg). The cigarettes were smoked to a butt length of either 30mm or (filter + overlap)+3mm, whichever is larger. These data were collected by Labstat Incorporated, Kitchener Ontario and are reprinted here with their permission.

Brand Name	Type			Dry Tar	Nic	Filter+ Overlap	Tobacco Column	Total Length
'Alpine	' 'KS'	'F'	'M'	17.	1.3	24	64	84
'Belmont Mild	' 'KS'	'F'	' '	11.	.9	30	64	84
'Belmont Mild	' 'R '	'F'	' '	7.	.6	23	52	72
'Belmont Mild	' 'KS'	'F'	'M'	13.	1.1	30	63	83
'Belvedere	' 'KS'	'F'	' '	27.	1.3	21	67	84
'Belvedere	' 'R '	'F'	' '	15.	1.1	17	59	72
'Belvedere	' 'KS'	'F'	'M'	17.	1.3	21	67	84
'Belvedere E.M.	' 'KS'	'F'	' '	11.	1.0	30	59	84
'Belvedere E.M.	' 'R '	'F'	' '	10.	.8	17	59	72
'Benson & Hedges	' 'PR'	'F'	' '	15.	1.1	30	74	99
'Benson & Hedges	' 'PR'	'F'	'M'	15.	1.1	30	74	99
'Black Cat	' 'R '	'P'	' '	18.	1.0	0	72	72
'Black Cat Cork	' 'C '	'P'	' '	18.	1.1	12	72	72
'Black Cat	' 'R '	'F'	' '	14.	.9	19	57	72
'Number 7	' 'KS'	'F'	' '	17.	1.1	21	67	84
'British Consols	' 'R '	'F'	' '	18.	1.3	18	59	72
'British Consols	' 'R '	'P'	' '	19.	1.2	0	71	71
'Buckingham	' 'KS'	'P'	' '	17.	1.0	0	84	84
'Buckingham	' 'R '	'P'	' '	17.	.9	0	72	72
'Cameo	' 'KS'	'F'	'M'	18.	1.2	20	66	83
'Cameo E.M.	' 'KS'	'F'	'M'	12.	.8	24	64	84
'Cavalier	' 'KS'	'F'	' '	18.	1.3	21	63	84
'Contessa Slims	' 'KS'	'F'	' '	13.	.8	24	63	83
'Craven A	' 'KS'	'F'	' '	15.	1.0	21	67	83
'Craven A	' 'R '	'F'	' '	8.	.5	19	57	73
'Craven A E.M.	' 'KS'	'F'	' '	5.	.4	30	64	84
'Craven A E.M.	' 'R '	'F'	' '	5.	.4	22	51	71
'Craven M	' 'KS'	'F'	'M'	11.	.8	21	66	83
'Du Maurier	' 'KS'	'F'	' '	18.	1.2	21	67	84
'Du Maurier	' 'KS'	'F'	'M'	13.	.8	21	67	84
'Du Maurier	' 'R '	'F'	' '	14.	.9	18	58	72
'Du Maurier	' 'KS'	'F'	' '	13.	.9	24	64	84
'Du Maurier S.M.	' 'PR'	'F'	' '	14.	1.0	24	79	99
'Dudes	' 'KS'	'F'	' '	19.	1.3	21	67	84
'Du Mont Select	' 'KS'	'F'	' '	9.	.6	25	64	84
'Dunhill	' 'KS'	'F'	' '	18.	1.2	21	62	83
'Embassy	' 'KS'	'F'	' '	18.	1.2	21	66	83
'Embassy	' 'R '	'F'	' '	16.	1.1	18	57	71
'Export	' 'R '	'F'	' '	19.	1.2	0	77	77
'Export A	' 'KS'	'F'	' '	19.	1.3	21	67	84
'Export A	' 'R '	'F'	' '	18.	1.2	18	57	72
'Export A L.	' 'KS'	'F'	' '	14.	1.0	25	63	84
'Export A L.	' 'R '	'F'	' '	14.	1.0	19	56	71
'Gauloises	' 'R '	'F'	' '	13.	.9	15	59	70
'Gauloises	' 'R '	'P'	' '	18.	1.2	0	70	70
'Gitaues	' 'R '	'F'	' '	12.	.8	15	59	70
'Gitanes	' 'R '	'P'	' '	19.5	1.2	0	70	70
'Goldcrest	' 'PR'	'F'	' '	15.	1.1	25	80	100
'John Player Spec.	' 'KS'	'F'	' '	16.	1.2	21	67	84
'Kool	' 'KS'	'F'	'M'	14.	.9	24	64	84
'MacDonald	' 'KS'	'F'	'M'	16.	1.1	21	67	84
'MacDonald	' 'R '	'F'	'M'	15.	1.0	18	57	72
'Mark Ten	' 'KS'	'F'	' '	17.	1.2	21	66	83
'Mark Ten	' 'KS'	'F'	'M'	17.	1.3	21	67	83
'Mark Ten	' 'R '	'F'	' '	16.	1.2	17	58	71
'Mark Ten	' 'KS'	'P'	' '	18.	1.3	0	84	84
'Mark Ten	' 'R '	'P'	' '	15.	1.0	0	72	72
'Matinee E. M.	' 'KS'	'F'	' '	4.	.4	30	64	84
'Matinee	' 'KS'	'F'	' '	12.	.8	21	64	83
'Matinee	' 'R '	'F'	' '	8.	.5	19	57	72
'Matinee S.F.	' 'KS'	'F'	' '	10.	.7	30	59	84
'Matinee S.F.	' 'PR'	'F'	' '	11.	.8	31	69	99
'Maverick	' 'KS'	'F'	' '	17.	1.3	21	66	83
'Medallion	' 'KS'	'F'	' '	1.	.1	30	64	84
'Millbank	' 'KS'	'F'	' '	19.	1.3	21	64	84
'Montclair	' 'KS'	'F'	' '	18.	1.3	21	66	83

'Pall Mall	'	'KS'	'P'	'	'	17.	1.0	0	83	83
'Peter Jackson	'	'KS'	'F'	'	'	18.	1.2	21	66	83
'Peter Jackson E. L.'	'R '	'F'	'	'	7.	.7	24	51	71
'Peter Stuyvesant	'	'KS'	'F'	'	'	18.	1.2	21	67	84
'Peter Stuyvesant	'	'PR'	'F'	'	'	16.	1.1	21	79	99
'Peter Stuyvesant	'	'PR'	'F'	'M'	16.	1.1	21	80	100
'Perillys	'	'KS'	'F'	'	'	16.	1.1	21	68	84
'Phillip Morris	'	'R '	'P'	'	'	16.	.9	0	69	69
'Plus	'	'PR'	'F'	'	'	19.	1.6	35	84	119
'Players	'	'KS'	'F'	'	'	18.	1.2	21	67	84
'Players	'	'R '	'F'	'	'	18.	1.2	18	58	72
'Players L.	'	'KS'	'F'	'	'	11.	1.1	20	67	83
'Players L.	'	'R '	'F'	'	'	14.	.9	18	58	72
'Players Navy	'	'R '	'F'	'	'	19.	1.3	18	56	72
'Players Navy	'	'R '	'P'	'	'	18.	1.1	0	72	72
'Players	'	'R '	'P'	'	'	19.	1.2	0	72	72
'Rothmans	'	'KS'	'F'	'	'	17.	1.1	21	68	84
'Rothmans	'	'KS'	'F'	'	'	12.	.9	24	63	83
'Rothmans S.	'	'R '	'F'	'	'	12.	.9	19	57	72
'Sportsman	'	'KS'	'F'	'	'	18.	1.2	21	66	83
'Sportsman	'	'R '	'F'	'	'	14.	.9	19	57	72
'Sportsman	'	'R '	'P'	'	'	18.	1.0	0	72	72
'Sweet Caporal	'	'KS'	'F'	'	'	18.	1.2	21	66	83
'Sweet Caporal	'	'R '	'F'	'	'	14.	.9	18	58	72
'Sweet Caporal	'	'R '	'P'	'	'	19.	1.1	0	72	72
'Tabac Leger	'	'KS'	'F'	'	'	14.	.8	21	67	83
'Tabac Leger	'	'R '	'F'	'	'	12.	.8	17	59	72
'Turret	'	'KS'	'F'	'	'	18.	1.2	24	64	84
'Turret	'	'R '	'F'	'	'	14.	1.0	18	58	72
'Vantage	'	'KS'	'F'	'	'	11.	.8	29	58	83
'Vantage	'	'R '	'F'	'	'	11.	.8	25	51	71
'Viceroy	'	'KS'	'F'	'	'	15.	.9	24	64	84
'Viscount	'	'R '	'F'	'	'	4.	.3	25	52	72
'Viscount	'	'KS'	'F'	'M'	5.	.4	30	64	84
'Viscount #1	'	'KS'	'F'	'	'	1.	.1	30	63	83
'Viscount #1	'	'R '	'F'	'	'	1.	.1	25	52	72
'Winston	'	'KS'	'F'	'	'	16.	1.1	25	63	84

L.5   National Hockey League Statistics

This section contains three data files for the National Hockey League. The first file contains the final league standings for the 1980–1981 season. The second file contains the player performance, while the third file lists the performance of goalies in the league.

a) Final League Standings   The final standings table contains the team name, their playing conference and division, the number of games they played, their win-loss-tie record, the total number of goals the team scored, the number of goals scored against the team, and the number of points the team earned. The column and symbols in the table have the following meanings.

```
C - conference: W - Wales, C - Campbell
D - division:   A - Adams, N - Norris,
                P - Patrick, S - Smythe
GP  - games played
W   - number of wins
L   - number of losses
T   - number of ties
GF  - number of goals scored for this team
GA  - number of goals scored against this team
Pts - number of points
```

Team Name	CD	GP	W	L	T	GF	GA	Pts
Buffalo	WA	80	39	20	21	327	250	99
Boston	WA	80	37	30	13	316	272	87
Minnesota	WA	80	35	28	17	291	263	87
Quebec	WA	80	30	32	18	314	318	78
Toronto	WA	80	28	37	15	322	367	71
Montreal	WN	80	45	22	13	332	232	103
Los Angeles	WN	80	43	24	13	337	290	99
Pittsburgh	WN	80	30	37	13	302	345	73
Hartford	WN	80	21	41	18	292	372	60
Detroit	WN	80	19	43	18	252	339	56
NY Islanders	CP	80	48	18	14	355	260	110
Philadelphia	CP	80	41	24	15	313	249	97
Calgary	CP	80	39	27	14	329	298	92
NY Rangers	CP	80	30	36	14	312	317	74
Washington	CP	80	26	36	18	286	317	70
St. Louis	CS	80	45	18	17	352	281	107
Chicago	CS	80	31	33	16	304	315	78
Vancouver	CS	80	28	32	20	289	301	76
Edmonton	CS	80	29	35	16	328	327	74
Colorado	CS	80	22	45	12	258	344	57
Winnipeg	CS	80	9	57	14	246	400	32

b) Player Performance and Team Data for 1980/81   The player performance statistics given below list the players name, their team, their position, the number of games played, goals and assists scored. The total number of points and number of penalty minutes are also given. The last three columns give the number of powerplay, of short-handed, and game winning goals scored. The following legend describes the column titles and symbols in the table.

```
P - position played
    W    - wing position
    C    - center position
    D    - defense position
    G    - goalie
GP  - games played
G   - goals scored
A   - assists scored
TP  - points scored
PM  - penalties in minutes
PP  - powerplay goals scored
SH  - short-handed goals scored
GW  - game winning goals scored
```

Player Name	Team Name	P	GP	G	A	Pts	PM	PP	SH	GW
Middleton, Rick	Boston	W	80	44	59	103	16	16	4	7
McNab, Peter	Boston	C	80	37	46	83	24	16	0	4
Park, Brad	Boston	D	78	14	52	66	111	10	0	2
Cashman, Wayne	Boston	W	77	25	35	60	80	7	0	2
Bourque, Ray	Boston	D	67	27	29	56	96	9	1	6
Kasper, Steve	Boston	W	76	21	35	56	94	5	0	1

O'Connell, Mike	Boston	D	82	15	38	53	74	3	2	0
Foster, Dwight	Boston	C	77	24	28	52	62	3	3	5
O'Reilly, Terry	Boston	W	77	8	35	43	223	0	0	0
Jonathan, Stan	Boston	W	74	14	24	38	192	0	0	2
Ratelle, Jean	Boston	C	47	11	26	37	16	4	0	2
Redmond, Dick	Boston	D	78	15	20	35	60	6	2	0
Marcotte, Don	Boston	W	72	20	13	33	32	4	1	2
McCrimmon, Brad	Boston	D	78	11	18	29	148	1	0	1
Crowder, Keith	Boston	W	47	13	12	25	172	1	0	1
Gillis, Mike	Boston	W	68	13	11	24	69	1	0	2
Milbury, Mike	Boston	D	77	0	18	18	222	0	0	0
Lalonde, Bobby	Boston	C	62	4	12	16	31	0	1	0
Morrison, Doug	Boston	W	18	7	3	10	13	2	0	0
MacTavish, Craig	Boston	C	24	3	5	8	13	0	0	0
Gare, Danny	Buffalo	W	73	46	39	85	109	15	0	7
Savard, Andre	Buffalo	W	79	31	43	74	63	2	2	4
McKegney, Tony	Buffalo	W	80	37	32	69	24	9	0	4
Van Boxmeer, J.	Buffalo	D	80	18	51	69	69	6	1	2
Smith, Derek	Buffalo	C	69	21	43	64	12	11	0	2
Ramsay, Craig	Buffalo	W	80	24	35	59	12	1	1	3
Perreault, Gil	Buffalo	C	56	20	39	59	56	5	0	3
Seiling, Ric	Buffalo	W	74	30	27	57	80	2	1	4
Dunn, Richie	Buffalo	D	79	7	42	49	34	4	0	1
Haworth, Alan	Buffalo	C	49	16	20	36	34	4	0	1
Schoenfeld, Jim	Buffalo	D	71	8	25	33	110	3	0	0
Ruff, Lindy	Buffalo	D	65	8	18	26	121	1	0	2
Hajt, Bill	Buffalo	D	68	2	19	21	42	0	0	0
Hamel, Gilles	Buffalo	W	51	10	9	19	53	2	0	0
Ramsey, Mike	Buffalo	D	72	3	14	17	56	0	0	1
McClanahan, Rob	Buffalo	W	53	3	12	15	38	1	0	1
Sauve, Jean	Buffalo	C	20	5	9	14	12	3	0	0
Playfair, Larry	Buffalo	D	75	3	9	12	169	0	0	1
Patrick, Stephen	Buffalo	W	30	1	7	8	25	0	0	0
Nilsson, Kent	Calgary	C	80	49	82	131	26	20	0	8
Chouinard, Guy	Calgary	C	52	31	52	83	24	10	0	1
Plett, Willi	Calgary	W	78	38	30	68	237	8	0	4
Reinhart, Paul	Calgary	D	74	18	49	67	52	10	0	0
Vail, Eric	Calgary	W	64	28	36	64	23	12	0	6
MacMillan, Bob	Calgary	W	77	28	35	63	47	2	4	2
Lever, Don	Calgary	W	62	26	31	57	56	4	1	4
Hislop, Jamie	Calgary	W	79	25	31	56	26	5	0	1
Rautakallio, P.	Calgary	D	76	11	45	56	64	3	0	1
Peplinski, Jim	Calgary	C	80	13	25	38	108	1	0	2
Lavallee, Kevin	Calgary	W	76	15	20	35	16	3	0	2
Clement, Bill	Calgary	C	78	12	20	32	33	1	2	2
Houston, Ken	Calgary	W	42	15	15	30	93	4	0	4
Russell, Phil	Calgary	D	80	6	23	29	104	1	1	1
Labraaten, Dan	Calgary	W	71	12	15	27	25	1	0	0
Murdoch, Bob	Calgary	D	74	3	19	22	54	0	0	0
Marsh, Brad	Calgary	D	80	1	12	13	87	0	0	0
Wilson, Bert	Calgary	W	50	5	7	12	94	0	0	1
McKendry, Alex	Calgary	W	36	3	6	9	19	0	0	0
Cyr, Dennis	Calgary	W	10	1	4	5	0	0	0	0
Holt, Randy	Calgary	D	48	0	5	5	165	0	0	0
Lysiak, Tom	Chicago	C	72	21	55	76	20	5	2	3
Savard, Denis	Chicago	C	76	28	47	75	47	4	0	3
Sutter, Darryl	Chicago	W	76	40	22	62	86	14	0	4
Murray, Bob	Chicago	D	77	13	47	60	93	5	0	1
Kerr, Reg	Chicago	W	70	30	29	59	56	5	0	4
Higgins, Tim	Chicago	W	78	24	35	59	86	1	0	1
Ruskowski, Terry	Chicago	C	72	8	51	59	225	2	0	2
Wilson, Doug	Chicago	D	76	12	39	53	80	3	0	1
Sharpley, Glen	Chicago	W	63	22	28	50	28	10	0	0
Brown, Keith	Chicago	D	80	9	34	43	80	0	1	1
Bulley, Ted	Chicago	W	68	18	16	34	95	3	0	2
Mulvey, Grant	Chicago	W	48	18	14	32	81	6	1	4
Secord, Al	Chicago	W	59	13	12	25	187	3	0	2
Marsh, Peter	Chicago	W	53	10	13	23	21	3	0	0
Preston, Rich	Chicago	W	47	7	14	21	24	3	0	1

Name	Team	Pos	GP	G	A	Pts	PIM			
Fox, Greg	Chicago	D	75	3	16	19	112	0	0	0
Zaharko, Miles	Chicago	D	42	3	12	15	30	0	0	1
Marks, John	Chicago	W	69	8	6	14	26	1	1	0
Hutchison, Dave	Chicago	D	59	2	9	11	124	0	0	0
Paterson, Rick	Chicago	C	49	8	2	10	18	1	2	1
Robidoux, Flo	Chicago	C	39	6	2	8	75	1	0	0
McDonald, Lanny	Colorado	W	80	35	46	81	56	11	0	2
Malinowski, M.	Colorado	C	69	25	37	62	61	4	0	1
Ramage, Rob	Colorado	D	79	20	42	62	193	12	1	3
Tambellini, Steve	Colorado	C	74	25	29	54	19	4	0	5
Beblois, Lucien	Colorado	W	74	26	16	42	78	9	1	2
Gagne, Paul	Colorado	W	61	25	17	42	12	9	0	2
McKechnie, Walt	Colorado	C	53	15	23	38	18	2	2	2
Vautour, Yvon	Colorado	W	74	15	19	34	140	3	0	0
Quenneville, Joel	Colorado	D	71	10	24	34	86	3	0	1
Pierce, Randy	Colorado	W	55	9	21	30	52	3	0	3
Norwich, Craig	Colorado	D	34	7	23	30	24	4	0	1
Delorme, Ron	Colorado	W	65	11	16	27	70	3	0	0
Cooper, Ed	Colorado	W	47	7	7	14	46	1	0	2
Miller, Bob	Colorado	W	52	9	4	13	34	2	1	1
Berry, Doug	Colorado	C	46	3	10	13	8	0	1	0
Valiquette, Jack	Colorado	C	25	3	9	12	7	0	0	0
Smith, Barry	Colorado	C	62	4	4	8	4	0	0	0
Kitchen, Mike	Colorado	D	75	1	7	8	100	0	0	0
Hughes, Jack	Colorado	D	38	2	5	7	91	1	0	0
Johansen, Trevor	Colorado	D	35	0	7	7	18	0	0	0
Crawford, Bobby	Colorado	W	15	1	3	4	6	0	0	0
Sheehan, Bobby	Colorado	C	41	1	3	4	10	0	0	0
Attwell, Bob	Colorado	W	15	0	4	4	0	0	0	0
Auge, Les	Colorado	D	6	0	3	3	4	0	0	0
Baker, Bill	Colorado	D	24	0	3	3	44	0	0	0
Dillon, Gary	Colorado	C	13	1	1	2	29	0	0	0
Giallonardo, M.	Colorado	D	15	0	2	2	4	0	0	0
Harper, Terry	Colorado	D	15	0	2	2	8	0	0	0
McCourt, Dale	Detroit	C	80	30	56	86	50	11	2	2
O'Grodnick, John	Detroit	W	80	35	35	70	14	9	2	2
Foligno, Mike	Detroit	W	80	28	35	63	210	3	0	5
Larson, Reed	Detroit	D	78	27	31	58	153	8	0	0
Huber, Willie	Detroit	D	80	15	34	49	130	3	0	0
Nedomansky, V.	Detroit	C	74	12	20	32	30	6	0	0
Kirton, Mark	Detroit	C	61	18	13	31	24	6	1	3
McAdam, Gary	Detroit	W	74	8	23	31	57	1	0	0
Lyle, George	Detroit	W	31	10	14	24	28	3	0	0
Woods, Paul	Detroit	W	67	8	16	24	45	1	1	1
Peterson, Brent	Detroit	C	53	6	18	24	24	1	0	1
Korn, Jim	Detroit	D	62	5	15	20	246	1	1	1
Smith, Brad	Detroit	W	65	12	6	18	158	1	0	1
Hicks, Glen	Detroit	W	58	5	10	15	84	1	0	0
Barrett, John	Detroit	D	56	3	10	13	60	0	0	1
Hamel, Jean	Detroit	D	68	5	7	12	57	0	0	0
Vasko, Rick	Detroit	D	20	3	7	10	20	1	0	0
Blaisdell, Mike	Detroit	W	32	3	6	9	10	0	0	0
Miller, Perry	Detroit	D	64	1	8	9	70	0	0	0
Ingarfield, Earl	Detroit	C	38	4	4	8	22	0	0	0
Paterson, Joe	Detroit	W	38	2	5	7	53	0	0	0
Gretzky, Wayne	Edmonton	C	80	55	109	164	28	15	4	3
Kurri, Jari	Edmonton	W	75	32	43	75	40	9	0	1
Messier, Mark	Edmonton	C	72	23	40	63	102	4	0	1
Callighen, Brett	Edmonton	W	55	25	35	60	32	6	0	1
Anderson, Glenn	Edmonton	W	58	30	23	53	24	10	3	5
Hagman, Matti	Edmonton	C	75	20	33	53	16	2	0	0
Siltanen, Risto	Edmonton	D	79	17	36	53	54	7	1	3
Lowe, Kevin	Edmonton	D	79	10	24	34	94	4	0	2
Weir, Stan	Edmonton	C	70	12	20	32	40	1	0	2
Coffey, Paul	Edmonton	D	74	9	23	32	130	2	0	0
Fogolin, Lee	Edmonton	D	80	13	17	30	137	0	4	1
Hunter, Dave	Edmonton	W	78	12	16	28	98	0	0	3
Hicks, Doug	Edmonton	D	59	5	16	21	76	1	1	0
Unger, Garry	Edmonton	C	71	10	10	20	46	1	0	0

Name	Team	Pos	GP	G	A	Pts	PIM			
Semenko, Dave	Edmonton	W	58	11	8	19	80	4	0	2
Murdoch, Don	Edmonton	W	40	10	9	19	18	4	0	2
Hughes, Pat	Edmonton	W	60	10	9	19	161	0	0	2
Lariviere, Gary	Edmonton	D	65	3	15	18	56	1	0	0
Lumley, Dave	Edmonton	W	53	7	9	16	74	0	0	1
Brackenbury, C.	Edmonton	W	58	2	7	9	153	0	0	0
Huddy, Charles	Edmonton	D	12	2	5	7	6	1	0	0
Ashby, Don	Edmonton	C	6	2	3	5	2	1	0	1
Driscoll, Peter	Edmonton	W	21	2	3	5	43	1	0	0
Mio, Ed	Edmonton	G	43	0	5	5	6	0	0	0
Hughes, John	Edmonton	D	18	0	3	3	30	0	0	0
Roulston, Tom	Edmonton	C	11	1	1	2	2	0	0	0
Rogers, Mike	Hartford	C	80	40	65	105	32	10	4	1
Boutette, Pat	Hartford	W	80	28	52	80	160	8	2	3
Stoughton, B.	Hartford	W	71	43	30	73	56	10	2	6
Howe, Mark	Hartford	D	63	19	46	65	54	7	2	3
Sims, Al	Hartford	D	80	16	36	52	68	5	0	1
Keon, Dave	Hartford	C	80	13	34	47	26	2	0	1
Miller, Warren	Hartford	W	77	22	22	44	37	3	3	1
Rowe, Tom	Hartford	W	74	13	28	41	190	1	0	1
Fidler, Mike	Hartford	W	58	14	21	35	10	2	0	0
Nachbaur, Don	Hartford	C	77	16	17	33	139	2	0	1
Debol, Dave	Hartford	C	44	14	12	26	0	2	0	0
Douglas, Jordy	Hartford	W	55	13	9	22	29	3	0	1
Meagher, Rick	Hartford	W	27	7	10	17	19	0	0	0
Abrahamsson, T.	Hartford	D	32	6	11	17	16	4	0	1
Neufeld, Ray	Hartford	W	52	5	10	15	44	0	0	0
Johnston, Bernie	Hartford	C	25	4	11	15	8	0	0	0
Barnes, Norm	Hartford	D	76	1	13	14	100	0	0	0
Volcan, Mickey	Hartford	D	49	2	11	13	26	0	0	0
Brubaker, Jeff	Hartford	W	43	5	3	89	93	0	0	0
Galarneau, Michel	Hartford	C	30	2	6	8	9	0	0	1
Smith, Stuart	Hartford	D	38	1	7	8	55	0	0	0
Lupien, Gilles	Hartford	D	51	2	5	7	73	0	0	0
McIlhargey, Jack	Hartford	D	51	1	6	7	164	0	0	0
Dionne, Marcel	Los Angeles	C	80	58	77	135	70	23	4	9
Taylor, Dave	Los Angeles	W	72	47	65	112	130	13	0	3
Simmer, Charlie	Los Angeles	W	65	56	49	105	62	23	0	9
Murphy, Larry	Los Angeles	D	80	16	60	76	79	5	1	1
Korab, Jerry	Los Angeles	D	78	9	43	52	139	3	0	2
Harris, Bill	Los Angeles	W	80	20	29	49	36	1	4	1
Fox, Jim	Los Angeles	W	71	18	24	42	8	2	0	2
Jensen, Steve	Los Angeles	W	74	19	19	38	88	5	1	4
Murphy, Mike	Los Angeles	W	68	16	22	38	54	2	1	1
Terrion, Greg	Los Angeles	C	73	12	25	37	99	2	0	2
Luce, Don	Los Angeles	C	71	16	13	29	21	0	4	2
Bonar, Dan	Los Angeles	C	71	11	15	26	57	3	1	3
Hopkins, Dean	Los Angeles	W	67	8	18	26	118	2	0	1
Hardy, Mark	Los Angeles	D	77	5	20	25	77	3	0	1
Martin, Rick	Los Angeles	W	24	8	15	23	20	2	0	1
Wells, Jay	Los Angeles	D	72	5	13	18	155	0	0	1
St. Laurent, A.	Los Angeles	C	22	10	6	16	63	0	0	2
Goldup, Glenn	Los Angeles	W	49	6	9	15	35	0	0	0
Lewis, Dave	Los Angeles	D	67	1	13	14	98	0	0	0
Kelly, Jean Paul	Los Angeles	W	19	3	6	9	8	0	0	0
Chartraw, Rick	Los Angeles	D	35	1	7	8	32	0	0	1
Palmer, Rob	Los Angeles	D	13	0	4	4	13	0	0	0
Smith, Bobby	Minnesota	C	78	29	64	93	71	13	0	7
Young, Tim	Minnesota	C	74	25	41	66	40	10	0	4
MacAdam, Al	Minnesota	W	78	21	39	60	94	6	0	7
Payne, Steve	Minnesota	W	76	20	28	58	88	11	0	2
Roberts, Gordie	Minnesota	D	77	8	42	50	175	4	0	0
McCarthy, Tom	Minnesota	W	62	23	25	48	62	4	0	2
Hartsburg, Craig	Minnesota	D	74	13	30	43	124	8	0	2
Andersson, K.E.	Minnesota	W	77	17	24	41	22	1	4	2
Christoff, Steve	Minnesota	W	56	26	13	39	58	9	0	2
Eaves, Mike	Minnesota	C	48	10	24	34	18	1	1	1
Ciccarelli, Dino	Minnesota	W	32	18	12	30	29	8	0	0
Giles, Curt	Minnesota	D	67	5	22	27	56	1	0	1

Name	Team	Pos							
Smith, Greg	Minnesota	D	74	5	21	26	128	1	0	1
Maxwell, Brad	Minnesota	D	27	3	13	16	98	3	0	1
Polich, Mike	Minnesota	C	74	8	5	13	19	0	1	0
Barrett, Fred	Minnesota	D	62	4	8	12	72	0	0	1
Sargent, Gary	Minnesota	D	23	4	7	11	36	2	0	0
Younghans, Tom	Minnesota	W	74	4	6	10	79	1	1	2
Shmyr, Paul	Minnesota	D	61	1	9	10	79	0	0	0
Carlson, Jack	Minnesota	W	43	7	2	9	108	0	0	0
Palmer, Brad	Minnesota	W	23	4	4	8	22	0	0	0
Solheim, Ken	Minnesota	W	10	4	1	5	0	0	0	0
Shutt, Steve	Montreal	W	77	35	38	73	51	7	0	3
Napier, Mark	Montreal	W	79	35	36	71	24	5	0	6
Lafleur, Guy	Montreal	W	51	27	43	70	29	7	0	7
Tremblay, Mario	Montreal	W	77	25	38	63	123	4	1	4
Houle, Rejean	Montreal	W	77	27	31	58	83	6	1	3
Lambert, Yvon	Montreal	W	73	22	32	54	39	4	0	3
Larouche, Pierre	Montreal	C	61	25	28	53	28	4	0	2
Robinson, Larry	Montreal	D	65	12	38	50	37	7	0	2
Gainey, Bob	Montreal	W	78	23	24	47	36	5	3	3
Langway, Rod	Montreal	D	80	11	34	45	120	5	1	2
Mondou, Pierre	Montreal	C	57	17	24	41	16	5	0	2
Acton, Keith	Montreal	C	61	15	24	39	74	3	0	2
Jarvis, Doug	Montreal	C	80	16	22	38	34	0	2	1
Risebrough, Doug	Montreal	C	48	13	21	34	93	1	0	1
Picard, Robert	Montreal	D	67	8	21	29	74	3	0	0
Engblom, Brian	Montreal	D	80	3	25	28	96	1	0	0
Gingras, Gaston	Montreal	D	55	5	16	21	22	3	0	1
Savard, Serge	Montreal	D	77	4	13	17	30	0	0	1
Wickenheiser, D.	Montreal	C	41	7	8	15	20	2	0	0
Nilan, Chris	Montreal	W	57	7	6	15	262	0	0	1
Lapointe, Guy	Montreal	D	33	1	9	10	79	1	0	1
Herron, Denis	Montreal	G	25	0	2	2	0	0	0	0
Charbonneau, Guy	Montreal	W	2	0	1	1	0	0	0	0
Joly, Yvan	Montreal	W	1	0	0	0	0	0	0	0
Orleski, Dave	Montreal	W	1	0	0	0	0	0	0	0
Sevigny, Richard	Montreal	G	33	0	0	0	30	0	0	0
Bossy, Mike	Islanders	W	79	68	51	119	32	28	2	10
Trottier, Bryan	Islanders	C	73	31	72	103	74	9	2	5
Gillies, Clark	Islanders	W	80	33	45	78	99	9	0	3
Bourne, Bob	Islanders	W	78	35	41	76	62	9	7	5
Potvin, Denis	Islanders	D	74	20	56	76	104	9	0	4
Kallur, Anders	Islanders	W	78	36	28	64	32	7	6	4
Persson, Stefan	Islanders	D	80	9	52	61	82	6	0	2
Goring, Butch	Islanders	C	78	23	37	60	0	4	1	1
Tonelli, John	Islanders	W	70	20	32	52	57	2	0	3
McEwen, Mike	Islanders	D	78	11	38	49	94	5	0	1
Nystrom, Bob	Islanders	W	79	14	30	44	145	3	0	0
Merrick, Wayne	Islanders	C	71	16	15	31	30	1	0	1
Howatt, Garry	Islanders	W	70	4	15	19	174	0	0	0
Sutter, Duane	Islanders	W	23	7	11	18	26	1	0	1
Langevin, Dave	Islanders	D	75	1	16	17	122	0	0	0
Morrow, Ken	Islanders	D	80	2	11	13	20	0	0	0
Lorimer, Bob	Islanders	D	73	1	12	13	77	0	0	0
Lane, Gord	Islanders	D	60	3	9	12	124	0	1	1
Marini, Hector	Islanders	W	14	4	7	11	39	1	0	0
Carroll, Bill	Islanders	C	18	4	4	8	6	0	0	1
Potvin, Jean	Islanders	D	18	2	3	5	25	2	0	1
Sutter, Brent	Islanders	C	3	2	2	4	0	0	0	1
Henning, Lorne	Islanders	C	9	1	2	3	24	0	0	0
Hedberg, Anders	Rangers	W	80	30	40	70	52	7	1	3
Johnstone, Ed	Rangers	W	80	30	38	68	100	4	3	5
Greschner, Ron	Rangers	D	74	27	41	68	112	6	0	1
Allison, Mike	Rangers	C	75	26	38	64	83	4	0	2
Vickers, Steve	Rangers	W	73	19	39	58	40	5	1	3
Maloney, Don	Rangers	W	61	29	23	52	99	7	5	9
Maloney, Dave	Rangers	D	79	11	36	47	132	3	0	1
Nilsson, Ulf	Rangers	C	51	14	25	39	42	1	0	3
Duguay, Ron	Rangers	C	50	17	21	38	83	5	1	0
Beck, Berry	Rangers	D	75	11	23	34	231	6	1	0

Talafous, Dean	Rangers	W	50	13	17	30	28	1	2	0
Laidlaw, Tom	Rangers	D	80	6	23	29	100	1	0	0
Tkaczuk, Walter	Rangers	C	43	6	22	28	28	1	0	0
Silk, Dave	Rangers	W	59	14	12	26	58	2	0	1
Gillis, Jere	Rangers	W	46	10	14	24	8	1	0	1
Nethery, Lance	Rangers	C	33	11	12	23	12	2	0	0
Vadnais, Carol	Rangers	D	74	3	20	23	91	1	0	0
Esposito, Phil	Rangers	C	41	7	13	20	20	3	0	0
Hospodar, Ed	Rangers	D	61	5	14	19	214	0	0	0
Fotiu, Nick	Rangers	W	69	9	9	18	170	1	0	0
Kotsopoulos, C.	Rangers	D	54	4	12	16	153	0	0	0
Barber, Bill	Philadelphia	W	80	43	42	85	69	16	2	2
MacLeish, Rick	Philadelphia	C	78	38	36	74	25	14	0	3
Leach, Reggie	Philadelphia	W	79	34	36	70	59	15	1	1
Propp, Brian	Philadelphia	W	79	26	40	66	110	6	0	5
Clarke, Bobby	Philadelphia	C	80	19	46	65	140	5	1	2
Wilson, Behn	Philadelphia	D	77	16	47	63	237	2	2	2
Holmgren, Paul	Philadelphia	W	77	22	37	59	306	3	0	2
Bridgman, Mel	Philadelphia	C	77	14	37	51	195	1	0	3
Linseman, Ken	Philadelphia	C	51	17	30	47	150	1	1	1
Kerr, Tim	Philadelphia	C	68	22	23	45	84	6	0	7
Gorence, Tom	Philadelphia	W	79	24	18	42	46	0	3	6
Dailey, Bob	Philadelphia	D	53	7	27	34	141	1	0	0
Hill, Al	Philadelphia	W	57	10	15	25	45	0	0	2
Murray, Terry	Philadelphia	D	71	1	17	18	53	0	0	0
Morrison, Gary	Philadelphia	W	33	1	13	14	68	0	0	1
Eriksson, Thomas	Philadelphia	D	24	1	10	11	14	1	0	0
Flockhart, Ron	Philadelphia	C	14	3	7	10	11	0	0	0
Wesley, Blake	Philadelphia	D	50	3	7	10	107	2	0	1
Cochrane, Glen	Philadelphia	D	31	1	8	9	219	0	0	1
Preston, Yves	Philadelphia	W	19	4	2	6	4	1	0	1
Busniuk, Mike	Philadelphia	D	72	1	5	6	204	0	0	0
Watson, Jim	Philadelphia	D	18	2	2	4	6	1	0	0
Bailey, Reid	Philadelphia	D	17	1	3	4	55	0	0	0
Adams, Greg	Philadelphia	W	6	3	0	3	8	0	0	0
Bathe, Frank	Philadelphia	D	44	0	3	3	175	0	0	0
St. Croix, Rick	Philadelphia	G	27	0	1	1	0	0	0	0
Peeters, Pete	Philadelphia	G	40	0	1	1	8	0	0	0
Evans, Paul	Philadelphia	C	1	0	0	0	2	0	0	0
Kehoe, Rick	Pittsburgh	W	80	55	33	88	6	20	0	5
Carlyle, Randy	Pittsburgh	D	76	16	67	83	136	7	1	1
Gardner, Paul	Pittsburgh	C	62	34	40	74	59	18	0	1
Lee, Peter	Pittsburgh	W	80	30	34	64	86	4	1	4
Schutt, Rod	Pittsburgh	W	80	25	35	60	55	11	0	5
Faubert, Mario	Pittsburgh	D	72	8	44	52	118	3	0	1
Malone, Greg	Pittsburgh	C	62	21	29	50	68	5	0	2
Lonsberry, Ross	Pittsburgh	W	80	17	33	50	76	7	1	2
Ferguson, George	Pittsburgh	C	79	25	18	43	42	7	3	1
Price, Pat	Pittsburgh	D	72	8	34	42	226	0	0	0
Thompson, Errol	Pittsburgh	W	73	20	20	40	64	5	0	3
Stackhouse, Ron	Pittsburgh	D	74	6	29	35	86	2	0	1
Johnson, Mark	Pittsburgh	C	73	10	23	33	50	0	0	1
Sheppard, Gregg	Pittsburgh	C	47	11	17	28	49	3	0	1
Baxter, Paul	Pittsburgh	D	51	5	14	19	204	1	0	0
Anderson, Russ	Pittsburgh	D	34	3	14	17	112	1	0	1
Libett, Nick	Pittsburgh	W	44	6	6	12	4	1	0	1
Kindrachuk, O.	Pittsburgh	C	13	3	9	12	34	1	0	0
Chorney, Marc	Pittsburgh	D	8	1	6	7	14	0	0	0
Hamilton, Jim	Pittsburgh	W	20	1	6	7	18	0	0	0
Bullard, Mike	Pittsburgh	C	15	1	2	3	19	0	0	0
Burrows, Dave	Pittsburgh	D	59	0	2	2	30	0	0	0
Millen, Greg	Pittsburgh	G	63	0	2	2	6	0	0	0
Rissling, Gary	Pittsburgh	W	26	1	0	1	143	0	0	0
Wolf, Bennett	Pittsburgh	D	24	0	1	1	94	0	0	0
Stastny, Peter	Quebec	C	77	39	70	109	37	11	2	4
Richard, Jacques	Quebec	W	78	52	51	103	39	16	0	5
Stastny, Anton	Quebec	W	80	39	46	85	12	12	0	4
Ftorek, Robbie	Quebec	C	78	24	49	73	104	8	0	3
Goulet, Michel	Quebec	W	76	32	39	71	45	3	2	3

Hunter, Dale	Quebec	C	80	19	44	63	226	2	0	2
Tardif, Marc	Quebec	W	83	23	31	54	35	11	0	3
Lacroix, Pierre	Quebec	D	61	5	33	38	54	4	0	0
Cote, Alain	Quebec	W	51	8	18	26	64	1	2	2
Marois, Mario	Quebec	D	69	5	21	26	181	1	0	0
Pichette, Dave	Quebec	D	46	4	16	20	62	2	0	0
Hoganson, Dale	Quebec	D	61	3	14	17	32	1	0	0
Weir, Wally	Quebec	W	54	6	8	14	77	0	0	0
Dupont, Andre	Quebec	D	63	5	8	13	93	1	1	0
Rochefort, N.	Quebec	D	56	3	8	11	51	0	0	0
Leduc, Richard	Quebec	C	22	3	7	10	6	0	0	0
Bernier, Serge	Quebec	C	46	2	8	10	18	1	0	0
Wensink, John	Quebec	W	53	6	3	9	124	0	0	1
Paddock, John	Quebec	W	32	2	5	7	25	0	0	0
Clackson, Kim	Quebec	D	61	0	5	5	204	0	0	0
Federko, Bernie	St. Louis	C	78	31	73	104	47	9	2	4
Babych, Wayne	St. Louis	W	78	54	42	96	93	14	0	7
Dunlop, Blake	St. Louis	C	80	20	67	87	40	6	0	2
Petterson, J.	St. Louis	W	62	37	36	73	24	8	0	5
Sutter, Brian	St. Louis	W	78	35	34	69	232	17	0	4
Zuke, Mike	St. Louis	C	74	24	44	68	57	10	1	1
Turnbull, Perry	St. Louis	W	75	34	22	56	209	5	0	5
Currie, Tony	St. Louis	W	61	23	32	55	38	2	0	4
Chapman, Blair	St. Louis	W	55	20	26	46	41	5	0	3
Patey, Larry	St. Louis	C	80	22	23	45	107	0	8	3
Lapointe, Rick	St. Louis	D	80	8	25	33	124	0	0	3
Micheletti, Joe	St. Louis	D	63	4	27	31	53	3	0	1
Brownschidle, J.	St. Louis	D	71	5	23	28	12	3	1	1
Crombeen, Mike	St. Louis	W	66	9	14	23	58	0	1	1
Stewart, Bill	St. Louis	D	60	2	21	23	114	0	0	0
Kea, Ed	St. Louis	D	74	3	18	21	60	0	0	0
Klassen, Ralph	St. Louis	W	66	6	12	18	23	0	1	0
Hart, Gerry	St. Louis	D	69	4	11	15	142	0	0	0
Maxwell, Bryan	St. Louis	D	40	3	10	13	137	0	0	0
Monahan, H.	St. Louis	W	25	4	2	6	4	0	2	0
Staniowski, Ed	St. Louis	G	19	0	2	2	0	0	0	0
Heinz, Rick	St. Louis	G	4	0	1	1	0	0	0	0
Lamby, Dick	St. Louis	D	1	0	0	0	0	0	0	0
Paiement, Wilf	Toronto	W	77	40	57	97	145	13	3	2
Sittler, Darryl	Toronto	C	80	43	53	96	77	14	2	2
Derlago, Bill	Toronto	C	80	35	39	74	26	6	0	3
Turnbull, Ian	Toronto	D	80	19	47	66	104	8	0	1
Salming, Borje	Toronto	D	72	5	61	66	154	1	1	1
Vaive, Rick	Toronto	W	75	33	29	62	229	8	2	1
Hickey, Pat	Toronto	W	72	16	33	49	49	5	0	1
Anderson, John	Toronto	W	75	17	26	43	31	2	0	1
Maloney, Dan	Toronto	W	65	20	21	41	183	13	0	2
Martin, Terry	Toronto	W	69	23	14	37	32	1	0	4
Boschman, Laurie	Toronto	C	53	14	19	33	178	3	0	4
Robert, Rene	Toronto	W	42	14	18	32	38	5	0	1
Saganiuk, Rocky	Toronto	W	71	12	18	30	52	2	0	3
Sedlbauer, Ron	Toronto	W	60	22	7	29	26	8	0	2
Boudreau, Bruce	Toronto	C	39	10	14	24	18	0	0	0
Zanussi, Ron	Toronto	W	53	9	11	20	25	0	0	0
Farrish, Dave	Toronto	D	74	2	18	20	90	1	0	0
Duris, Vitezslav	Toronto	D	57	1	12	13	50	0	0	0
Melrose, Barry	Toronto	D	75	3	6	9	206	0	1	0
Marshall, Paul	Toronto	W	26	3	2	5	6	1	0	0
Ellis, Ron	Toronto	W	27	2	3	5	2	0	0	0
Shand, David	Toronto	D	47	0	4	4	60	0	0	0
Gavin, Stewart	Toronto	W	14	1	2	3	13	0	0	0
Hotham, Greg	Toronto	D	11	1	1	2	11	0	0	0
Kaszycki, Mike	Toronto	C	6	0	2	2	2	0	0	0
Davis, Kim	Toronto	C	10	1	0	1	8	0	0	0
McCreary, Bill	Toronto	W	12	1	0	1	4	0	0	0
Gradin, Thomas	Vancouver	C	79	21	48	69	34	4	0	1
Smyl, Stan	Vancouver	W	80	25	38	63	171	6	1	2
Brasar, Per Olov	Vancouver	C	80	22	41	63	8	3	0	1
Williams, Dave	Vancouver	W	77	35	27	62	333	11	1	4

Schmautz, Bobby	Vancouver	W	73	27	34	61	137	9	0	3
Boldirev, Ivan	Vancouver	C	72	26	33	59	34	9	0	3
MacDonald, B.J.	Vancouver	W	62	24	33	57	37	7	0	3
Rota, Darcy	Vancouver	W	80	25	31	56	124	7	0	5
McCarthy, Kevin	Vancouver	D	80	16	37	53	85	4	1	1
Fraser, Curt	Vancouver	W	77	25	24	49	118	7	0	2
Ashton, Brent	Vancouver	W	77	18	11	29	57	0	0	0
Lanz, Rick	Vancouver	D	76	7	22	29	40	3	0	1
Butler, Jerry	Vancouver	W	80	11	15	26	60	0	2	2
Minor, Gerry	Vancouver	C	74	10	14	24	108	1	6	0
Lindgren, Lars	Vancouver	D	52	4	18	22	32	1	0	0
Halward, Doug	Vancouver	D	58	4	16	20	100	1	0	0
Snepsts, Harold	Vancouver	D	76	3	16	19	212	0	0	1
Kearns, Dennis	Vancouver	D	46	1	14	15	28	0	0	0
Manno, Bob	Vancouver	D	20	0	11	11	30	0	0	0
Campbell, Colin	Vancouver	D	42	2	7	9	75	0	0	0
Christie, Mike	Vancouver	D	9	1	1	2	0	0	0	0
Lupel, Gary	Vancouver	C	7	0	2	2	2	0	0	0
Blight, Rick	Vancouver	W	3	1	0	1	4	0	0	0
Bromley, Gary	Vancouver	G	20	0	1	1	0	0	0	0
Primeau, Kevin	Vancouver	W	2	0	0	0	4	0	0	0
Logan, Dave	Vancouver	D	7	0	0	0	13	0	0	0
Oddleifson, C.	Vancouver	C	8	0	0	0	6	0	0	0
Maruk, Dennis	Washington	C	80	50	47	97	87	16	2	5
Gartner, Mike	Washington	W	80	48	46	94	100	13	0	3
Walter, Ryan	Washington	C	80	24	45	69	150	4	0	1
Kelly, Bob	Washington	W	80	26	36	62	157	8	0	4
Pronovost, Jean	Washington	W	80	22	36	58	61	6	1	4
Gustafsson, B.	Washington	W	72	21	34	55	26	4	2	1
Ververgaert, D.	Washington	W	79	14	27	41	40	2	0	2
Green, Rick	Washington	D	65	8	23	31	91	2	0	1
Veitch, Darren	Washington	D	59	4	21	25	46	1	0	1
Hangsleben, Al	Washington	D	76	5	19	24	198	0	0	0
Tookey, Tim	Washington	W	29	10	13	23	18	6	0	1
Jarvis, Wes	Washington	C	55	9	14	23	30	0	1	0
Mulvey, Paul	Washington	W	55	7	14	21	166	1	0	0
Currie, Glen	Washington	C	40	5	13	18	16	2	1	0
Charron, Guy	Washington	C	47	5	13	18	2	2	1	0
Ribble, Pat	Washington	D	67	3	15	18	103	3	0	1
Edberg, Rolf	Washington	W	45	8	8	16	6	0	0	0
Walker, Howard	Washington	D	64	2	10	12	100	2	0	0
Smith, Rick	Washington	D	51	5	6	11	42	2	0	2
Bouchard, Pierre	Washington	D	50	3	7	10	28	0	0	0
Palmateer, Mike	Washington	G	49	0	8	8	17	0	0	0
McTaggart, Jim	Washington	D	52	1	6	7	185	0	0	0
Labre, Yvon	Washington	D	25	2	4	6	100	0	0	0
Lofthouse, Mark	Washington	W	3	1	1	2	4	0	0	0
Rausse, Errol	Washington	W	5	1	1	2	0	0	0	0
Theberge, Greg	Washington	D	1	1	0	1	0	0	0	0
Henderson, Archie	Washington	W	7	1	0	1	28	0	0	0
Lowdermilk, D.	Washington	D	2	0	1	1	2	0	0	0
Parro, Dave	Washington	G	18	0	1	1	2	0	0	0
Johnston, John	Washington	D	2	0	0	0	9	0	0	0
Christian, D.	Winnipeg	C	80	28	43	71	22	9	1	0
Lukowich, M.	Winnipeg	W	80	33	34	67	90	9	2	2
Dupont, N.	Winnipeg	W	80	27	26	53	8	8	0	1
Wilson, Ron	Winnipeg	C	77	18	33	51	55	4	1	0
Geoffrion, D.	Winnipeg	W	70	20	26	46	82	3	0	0
Babych, Dave	Winnipeg	D	69	6	38	44	90	3	0	0
Lindstrom, Willie	Winnipeg	W	72	22	13	35	45	6	0	1
Dudley, Rick	Winnipeg	W	60	15	18	33	30	2	0	0
Trimper, Tim	Winnipeg	W	56	15	14	29	28	1	0	1
Bowness, Rick	Winnipeg	W	45	8	17	25	45	0	0	1
Mantha, Moe	Winnipeg	D	58	2	23	25	35	1	0	0
Lecuyer, Doug	Winnipeg	C	59	6	17	23	107	0	0	1
Long, Barry	Winnipeg	D	65	6	17	23	42	0	0	0
Sullivan, Peter	Winnipeg	C	47	4	19	23	20	2	0	0
Manery, Kris	Winnipeg	W	47	13	9	22	24	4	1	0
Spring, Don	Winnipeg	D	80	1	10	19	18	0	0	0

Smail, Doug	Winnipeg	W	30	10	8	18	45	1	3	1
Steen, Anders	Winnipeg	C	42	5	11	16	22	3	0	1
Mann, Jimmy	Winnipeg	W	37	3	3	6	105	0	0	0
Plantery, Mark	Winnipeg	D	25	1	5	6	14	0	0	0
Legge, Barry	Winnipeg	D	38	0	6	6	69	0	0	0
Campbell, Scott	Winnipeg	D	14	1	4	5	55	0	0	0
Markell, John	Winnipeg	W	14	1	3	4	15	1	0	0
Mulhern, Richard	Winnipeg	D	19	0	4	4	14	0	0	0
Eaves, Murray	Winnipeg	C	12	1	2	3	5	1	0	0
Cameron, Al	Winnipeg	D	29	1	2	3	21	0	0	0
Beadle, Sandy	Winnipeg	W	6	1	0	1	2	0	0	0
Hoyda, Dave	Winnipeg	W	9	1	0	1	7	0	0	0
Cory, Ross	Winnipeg	D	5	0	1	1	9	0	0	0
Chartier, Dave	Winnipeg	C	1	0	0	0	0	0	0	0
Whelton, Bill	Winnipeg	D	2	0	0	0	0	0	0	0

c) Goaltender Statistics for 1980/1981   The third data file contains information for the goalies in the NHL during the 1980/1981 season.   The following legend decribes the meaning of each column title.

```
GP - games played
Mins - minutes played
GA - goals scored against
EN - empty net goals
SO - shutout games
Avg. - goals against average (GA / (Mins/60))
W - games won
L - games lost
T - games tied
```

Player	Team	GP	Mins	GA	EN	SO	Avg.	W	L	T
Wamsley, Rick	Montreal	5	253	8	0	1	1.90	3	0	1
Sevigny, Richard	Montreal	33	1777	71	0	2	2.40	20	4	3
Larocque, Michel	Montreal	28	1623	82	2	1	3.03	16	9	3
Herron, Denis	Montreal	25	1147	67	2	1	3.50	6	9	6
St. Croix, Rick	Philadelphia	27	1567	65	2	2	2.49	13	7	6
Peeters, Pete	Philadelphia	40	2333	115	5	2	2.96	22	12	5
Myre, Phil	Philadelphia	16	900	61	1	0	4.07	6	5	4
Edwards, Don	Buffalo	45	2700	133	4	3	2.96	23	10	12
Sauve, Bob	Buffalo	35	2100	111	2	2	3.17	16	10	9
Resch, Glenn	Islanders	32	1817	93	2	3	3.07	18	7	5
Melanson, Roland	Islanders	11	620	32	0	0	3.10	8	1	1
Smith, Billy	Islanders	41	2363	129	4	2	3.28	22	10	8
Beaupre, Don	Minnesota	44	2585	139	4	0	3.20	18	14	11
Meloche, Gilles	Minnesota	38	2215	120	1	2	3.25	17	14	6
Baron, Marco	Boston	10	507	24	1	0	2.84	3	4	1
Vachon, Rogie	Boston	53	3021	168	0	1	3.34	25	19	6
Craig, Jim	Boston	23	1272	78	1	0	3.68	9	7	6
Heinz, Rick	St. Louis	4	220	8	0	0	2.18	2	1	1
Liut, Mike	St. Louis	61	3570	199	2	1	3.34	33	14	13
Staniowski, Ed	St. Louis	19	1010	72	0	0	4.28	10	3	3
Lessard, Mario	Los Angeles	64	3746	203	3	2	3.25	35	18	11
Rutherford, Jim	Los Angeles	3	180	10	0	0	3.33	3	0	0
Grahame, Ron	Los Angeles	6	360	28	0	0	4.67	3	2	1
Keans, Doug	Los Angeles	9	454	37	1	0	4.89	2	3	1
Pageau, Paul	Los Angeles	1	60	8	0	0	8.00	0	1	0
Lemelin, Rejean	Calgary	29	1629	80	2	2	3.24	14	6	7
Riggin, Pat	Calgary	42	2411	154	3	0	3.83	21	16	4
Bouchard, Dan	Calgary	14	760	51	0	0	4.03	4	5	3
Brodeur, Richard	Vancouver	52	3024	177	2	0	3.51	17	18	16
Bromley, Gary	Vancouver	20	978	62	0	0	3.80	6	6	4
Hanlon, Glen	Vancouver	17	798	59	1	1	4.44	5	8	0
Esposito, Tony	Chicago	66	3935	246	5	0	3.75	29	23	14
Bannerman, Murray	Chicago	15	865	62	2	0	4.30	2	10	2
Weeks, Steve	Rangers	1	60	2	0	0	2.00	0	1	0

Thomas, Wayne	Rangers	10	600	34	2	0	3.40	3	6	1
Baker, Steve	Rangers	21	1260	73	2	2	3.48	10	6	5
Soetaert, Doug	Rangers	39	2320	152	2	0	3.93	16	16	7
Davidson, John	Rangers	10	560	48	2	0	5.14	1	7	1
Inness, Gary	Washington	3	180	9	1	0	3.00	0	1	2
Parro, Dave	Washington	18	811	49	2	1	3.63	4	7	2
Palmateer, Mike	Washington	49	2679	173	5	2	3.87	18	19	9
Stephenson, Wayne	Washington	20	1010	66	0	1	3.92	4	7	5
Boutin, Rollie	Washington	2	120	11	1	0	5.50	0	2	0
Bouchard, Daniel	Quebec	29	1740	92	1	2	3.17	19	5	5
Plasse, Michel	Quebec	33	1933	118	2	0	3.66	10	14	9
Dion, Michel	Quebec	12	688	61	3	0	5.32	0	8	3
Grahame, Ron	Quebec	8	439	40	1	0	5.47	1	5	1
Edwards, Gary	Edmonton	15	729	44	0	0	3.62	5	3	4
Moog, Andy	Edmonton	7	313	20	0	0	3.83	3	3	0
Mio, Ed	Edmonton	43	2393	155	4	0	3.89	16	15	9
Low, Ron	Edmonton	24	1260	93	2	0	4.43	5	13	3
Lopresti, Pete	Edmonton	2	105	8	1	0	4.57	0	1	0
Legris, Claude	Detroit	3	63	4	0	0	3.81	0	1	0
Gilbert, Gilles	Detroit	48	2618	175	5	0	4.01	11	24	9
Rutherford, Jim	Detroit	10	600	43	0	0	4.30	2	6	2
Lozinski, Larry	Detroit	30	1459	105	0	0	4.32	6	11	7
Jensen, Al	Detroit	1	60	7	0	0	7.00	0	1	0
Myre, Paul	Colorado	10	580	33	0	0	3.41	3	6	1
Resch, Glenn	Colorado	8	449	28	0	0	3.74	2	4	2
Astrom, Hardy	Colorado	30	1642	103	3	0	3.76	6	15	6
Smith, Al	Colorado	37	1909	151	4	0	4.75	9	18	4
Kaarela, Jari	Colorado	5	220	22	0	0	6.00	2	2	0
Ricci, Nick	Pittsburgh	9	540	35	1	0	3.89	4	5	0
Millen, Greg	Pittsburgh	63	3721	258	6	0	4.16	25	27	10
Holland, Robbie	Pittsburgh	10	539	45	0	0	5.01	1	5	3
Crha, Jiri	Toronto	54	3112	211	4	0	4.07	20	20	11
Rutherford, Jim	Toronto	18	961	82	2	0	5.12	4	10	2
Larocque, Michel	Toronto	8	40	40	0	0	5.22	3	3	2
Ridley, Curt	Toronto	3	124	12	0	0	5.81	1	1	0
Tremblay, Vicent	Toronto	3	143	16	0	0	6.71	0	3	0
Veisor, Mike	Hartford	29	1588	118	3	1	4.46	6	13	6
Garrett, John	Hartford	54	3152	241	3	0	4.59	15	27	12
Holland, Ken	Hartford	1	60	7	0	0	7.00	0	1	0
Mattsson, Markus	Winnipeg	31	1707	128	5	1	4.50	3	21	4
Hamel, Pierre	Winnipeg	29	1623	128	2	0	4.73	3	20	4
Dion, Michel	Winnipeg	14	757	61	1	0	4.83	3	6	3
Middlebrook, L.	Winnipeg	14	653	65	0	0	5.97	0	9	3
Loustel, Ron	Winnipeg	1	60	10	0	0	10.00	0	1	0

M
Areas Under the Standard Normal Curve

The following table gives the percentage area under the standard normal (z) curve between 0 and z as indicated in the diagram. Since the curve is symmetric, the area for a given value of z also applies for $-z$. The values given in the table are rounded to the number of digits shown.

Figure M.1 Standard normal (z) curve showing area given by table.

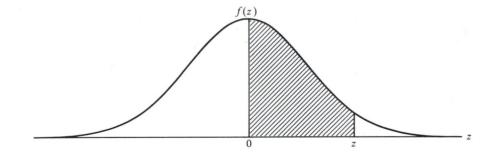

Figure M.2   Table of the area under the standard normal curve.

z	.00	.01	.02	.03	.04	.05	.06	.07	.08	.09
0.0	.0000	.0040	.0080	.0120	.0160	.0199	.0239	.0279	.0319	.0359
0.1	.0398	.0438	.0478	.0517	.0557	.0596	.0636	.0675	.0714	.0753
0.2	.0793	.0832	.0871	.0910	.0948	.0987	.1026	.1064	.1103	.1141
0.3	.1179	.1217	.1255	.1293	.1331	.1368	.1406	.1443	.1480	.1517
0.4	.1554	.1591	.1628	.1664	.1700	.1736	.1772	.1808	.1844	.1879
0.5	.1915	.1950	.1985	.2019	.2054	.2088	.2123	.2157	.2190	.2224
0.6	.2257	.2291	.2324	.2357	.2389	.2422	.2454	.2486	.2518	.2549
0.7	.2580	.2612	.2642	.2673	.2704	.2734	.2764	.2794	.2823	.2852
0.8	.2881	.2910	.2939	.2967	.2995	.3023	.3051	.3078	.3106	.3133
0.9	.3159	.3186	.3112	.3238	.3264	.3289	.3315	.3340	.3365	.3389
1.0	.3413	.3438	.3461	.3485	.3508	.3531	.3554	.3577	.3599	.3621
1.1	.3643	.3665	.3686	.3708	.3729	.3749	.3770	.3790	.3810	.3830
1.2	.3849	.3869	.3888	.3907	.3925	.3944	.3962	.3980	.3997	.4015
1.3	.4032	.4049	.4066	.4082	.4099	.4115	.4131	.4147	.4162	.4177
1.4	.4192	.4207	.4222	.4236	.4251	.4265	.4279	.4292	.4306	.4319
1.5	.4332	.4345	.4357	.4370	.4382	.4394	.4406	.4418	.4429	.4441
1.6	.4452	.4463	.4474	.4484	.4495	.4505	.4515	.4525	.4535	.4545
1.7	.4554	.4564	.4573	.4582	.4591	.4599	.4608	.4616	.4625	.4633
1.8	.4641	.4649	.4656	.4664	.4671	.4678	.4686	.4693	.4699	.4706
1.9	.4713	.4719	.4726	.4732	.4738	.4744	.4750	.4756	.4761	.4767
2.0	.4772	.4778	.4783	.4788	.4793	.4798	.4803	.4808	.4812	.4817
2.1	.4821	.4826	.4830	.4834	.4838	.4842	.4846	.4850	.4854	.4857
2.2	.4861	.4864	.4868	.4871	.4875	.4878	.4881	.4884	.4887	.4890
2.3	.4893	.4896	.4898	.4901	.4904	.4906	.4909	.4911	.4913	.4916
2.4	.4918	.4920	.4922	.4925	.4927	.4929	.4931	.4932	.4934	.4936
2.5	.4938	.4940	.4941	.4943	.4945	.4946	.4948	.4949	.4951	.4952
2.6	.4953	.4955	.4956	.4957	.4959	.4960	.4961	.4962	.4963	.4964
2.7	.4965	.4966	.4967	.4968	.4969	.4970	.4971	.4972	.4973	.4974
2.8	.4974	.4975	.4976	.4977	.4977	.4978	.4979	.4979	.4980	.4981
2.9	.4981	.4982	.4982	.4983	.4984	.4984	.4985	.4985	.4986	.4986
3.0	.49865	.4987	.4987	.4988	.4988	.4989	.4989	.4989	.4990	.4990
3.1	.49903	.4991	.4991	.4991	.4992	.4992	.4992	.4992	.4993	.4993
3.2	.4993129	.4993	.4994	.4994	.4994	.4994	.4994	.4995	.4995	.4995
3.3	.4995166	.4995	.4995	.4996	.4996	.4996	.4996	.4996	.4996	.4997
3.4	.4996631	.4997	.4997	.4997	.4997	.4997	.4997	.4997	.4998	.4998
3.5	.4997674	.4998	.4998	.4998	.4998	.4998	.4998	.4998	.4998	.4998
3.6	.4998409	.4998	.4999	.4999	.4999	.4999	.4999	.4999	.4999	.4999
3.7	.4998922	.4999	.4999	.4999	.4999	.4999	.4999	.4999	.4999	.4999
3.8	.4999277	.4999	.4999	.4999	.4999	.4999	.4999	.5000	.5000	.5000
3.9	.4999519	.5000	.5000	.5000	.5000	.5000	.5000	.5000	.5000	.5000
4.0	.4999683									
4.5	.4999966									
5.0	.4999997133									

N
Built-in FORTRAN/77 Functions

This appendix describes the built-in or intrinsic functions which are part of the FORTRAN/77 compiler. These functions are supplied automatically by the compiler whenever a program references them. The following notation is used in the tables to describe the type of the function arguments and the type of the function itself:

> i4 - an INTEGER*4 expression (full-word integer)
> r4 - a REAL*4 expression (single-precision real)
> r8 - a REAL*8 expression (double-precision real)
> c8 - a COMPLEX*8 expression (single-precision complex)
> ch - a CHARACTER
> ch* - a CHARACTER string
> l - a LOGICAL value

For some compilers it is also possible to use half-word integers and extended-precision real and complex (INTEGER*2, REAL*16, COMPLEX*16, COMPLEX*32) in which case special prefixes to the function name are used. In the definition of the function the following notation is used:

> a - argument (used when only one argument eists)
> a_1 - argument number 1
> a_2 - argument number 2
> . . . - many arguments

If no argument is specified, the function is called generic and will accept any appropriate argument type.

Purpose	*Function name and type of arguments*	*Definition*	*Result*
Absolute value	ABS	$\lvert a \rvert$	
	IABS(i4)		i4
	ABS(r4)		r4
	DABS(r8)		r8
	CABS(c8)	$\sqrt{a^2 + b^2}$ for $a + bi$	r4
Truncation	INT	sign of a times largest integer $\leq \lvert a \rvert$	i4
	INT(r4)		i4
	AINT(r4)		r4
	DINT(r8)		r8
	IDINT(r8)		i4
Nearest whole number	ANINT	int($a + .5$) if $a > 0$ int($a - .5$) if $a < 0$	
	ANINT(r4)		r4
	DNINT(r8)		r8
Nearest INTEGER	NINT	int($a + .5$) if $a > 0$ int($a - .5$) if $a < 0$	
	NINT(r4)		i4
	IDNINT(r8)		i4
Modular arithmetic	MOD	$a_1(\mathrm{mod}\, a_2) = a_1 - a_2 \times \mathrm{int}(a_1/a_2)$	
	MOD(i4,i4)		i4
	AMOD(r4,r4)		r4
	DMOD(r8,r8)		r8
Largest value	MAX	$\max(a_1, a_2, \ldots)$	
	MAX0(i4,i4,...)		i4
	MAX1(r4,r4,...)		i4
	AMAX0(i4,i4,...)		r4
	AMAX1(r4,r4,...)		r4
	DMAX1(r8,r8,...)		r8
Smallest value	MIN	$\min(a_1, a_2, \ldots)$	
	MIN0(i4,i4,...)		i4
	MIN1(r4,r4,...)		i4
	AMIN0(i4,i4,...)		r4
	AMIN1(r4,r4,...)		r4
	DMIN1(r8,r8,...)		r8
Square root	SQRT	$\sqrt{a}$	
	SQRT(r4)		r8
	DSQRT(r8)		r8
	CSQRT(c8)		c8

Purpose	Function name and type of arguments	Definition	Result
Type conversion	INT	Convert to INTEGER	i4
	IFIX(r4)		i4
	REAL	Convert to REAL	r4
	FLOAT(i4)		r4
	DFLOAT(i4)		r8
	SNGL(r8)	Truncate REAL*8 to REAL*4	r4
	DBLE	Convert to REAL*8	r8
	CMPLX	Convert two values to COMPLEX	c8
	AIMAG(c8)	Obtain imaginary part of COMPLEX value	r4
	ICHAR(ch)	Convert CHARACTER to INTEGER	i4
	CHAR(i4)	Convert INTEGER to CHARACTER	ch
Complex conjucate	CONJG(c8)	$(x, -y)$ for $a = (x,y)$	c8
Transfer of sign	SIGN	Sign of a_2 times $\lvert a_1 \rvert$	
	ISIGN(i4,i4)	$\text{sign}(a_2) = \begin{cases} +1, & a_2 \geq 0 \\ -1, & a_2 < 0 \end{cases}$	i4
	SIGN(r4,r4)		r4r8
	DSIGN(r8,r8)		
Positive difference	DIM	$a_1 - \min(a_1, a_2)$	
	IDIM(i4,i4)		i4
	DIM(r4,r4)		r4
	DDIM(r8,r8)		r8
Exponential	EXP	e^a where $e \simeq 2.718282$	
	EXP(r4)		r4
	DEXP(r8)		r8
	CEXP(c8)		c8
Natural logarithm	LOG	$\log_e a$	
	ALOG(r4)		r4
	DLOG(r8)		r8
	CLOG(c8)		c8
Common logarithm	LOG10	$\log_{10} a$	
	ALOG10(r4)		r4
	DLOG10(r8)		r8
Sine	SIN	sine a (a must be in radians)	
	SIN(r4)		r4
	DSIN(r8)		r8
	CSIN(c8)		c8
Cosine	COS	cosine a (a must be in radians)	
	COS(r4)		r4
	DCOS(r8)		r8
	CCOS(c8)		c8

Purpose	Function name and type of arguments	Definition	Result
Tangent	TAN	tangent a (a must be in radians)	
	TAN(r4)		r4
	DTAN(r8)		r8
Arcsine	ASIN	$x = $ arcsine a ($-\pi/2 \leq x \leq +\pi/2$)	
	ASIN(r4)		r4
	DASIN(r8)		r8
Arccosine	ACOS	$x = $ arccosine a ($0 \leq x \leq \pi$)	
	ACOS(r4)		r4
	DACOS(r8)		r8
Arctangent	ATAN	$x = $ arctangent a $(-\pi/2 \leq x \leq +\pi/2)$	
	ATAN(r4)		r4
	DATAN(r8)		r8
	ATAN2	$x = $ arctangent$(a1/a2)$ $(-\pi \leq x \leq +\pi)$	
	ATAN2(r4,r4)		r4
	DATAN2(r8,r8)		r8
Hyperbolic sine	SINH	sinh a	
	SINH(r4)		r4
	DSINH(r8)		r8
Hyperbolic cosine	COSH	cosh a	
	COSH(r4)		r4
	DCOSH(r8)		r8
Hyperbolic tangent	TANH	tanh a	
	TANH(r4)		r4
	DTANH(r8)		r8
Length	LEN(ch*)	length of CHARACTER entity	i4
Index	INDEX(ch*,ch*)	location of ch*$_2$ in ch*$_1$	i4
Lexical comparison	LGE(ch*,ch*)	lexically greater than or equal	l
	LGT(ch*,ch*)	lexically greater than	l
	LLE(ch*,ch*)	lexically less than or equal	l
	LLT(ch*,ch*)	lexically less than	l

Index

2's complement notation, 590
A-mask, 597
abs, 25
ABS, 136
absolute value, 25, 136, 365
absolute value function, 101
acceleration, 440, 441
action sequence, 8, 14, 21, 28, 54, 211
actuarial mathematics, 349
adapative quadrature, 192
Aho, A.V. 266, 293, 342
algorithm
  area finding, Ch. 8. *See also* area finding.
  complexity, 251
  correctness, 87, 92, 97
  Dekker, 173
  design, 288, 419, 508, Ch. 4, Ch. 10. *See also*
    design.
  development, 3, 4, 74, 83, 199
  efficiency. *See* efficiency.
  Gaussian Elimination, 413
  modules, 103
  order of, 252, 254
  searching, Ch. 13. *See also* searching.
  simulation, Ch. 16–17. *See also* simulation.
  sorting, Ch. 13. *See also* sorting.
  termination, 11, 506, 512
  testing, 12, 16, 31, 32, 45, 77, 88, 90, 97, 114,
    118, 243, 290, 344
  zero finding, Ch. 7. *See also* zero finding.
alphabetical order, 303, 304
and, 20, 57, 505
AND, 57, 87, 522, 572

Anscombe, F.J. 386
Apple computer, 49
aprime, 104, 212
APRIME, 109
area between two curves problem, 223–231
area finding, 181, 223, 238, Ch. 8
  Adaptive Quadrature, 192
  error estimation, 187, 189
  exact solution, 227
  rectangle rule, 182
  Simpson's Rule, 188–192
  trapezoidal rule, 184–188
areas
  approximation of, Ch. 8
argument lists, 99, 286
arithmetic
  pseudocode, 9–10, 504
  INTEGER, 52, 68–70, 82, 570
  REAL, 52, 82, 579
  DOUBLE PRECISION, 555, App. I
  COMPLEX, 547, App. J
  FORTRAN/**77**, 51–53
arithmetic evaluation, 10, 51, 504
arithmetic expressions, 9–10, 504, 509, 521–522, 530
arithmetic operators, 10, 51
arithmetic parentheses, 10, 51
arithmetic priority, 51, 530
arithmetic mean, 363, 365
arithmetic operations, 256, 300
arithmetic IF, 531
arrays, 271, 272, 489, 504, 532–537, Ch. 12
  CHARACTER, 620
  FORTRAN/**77**, 269–273, 283–287
  in modules, 286

arrays (*continued*)
　in subprograms, 286
　input of, 272, 280, 282
　multidimensional, 279, 283, 504, 532–537
　name of, 272, 280
　one-dimensional, 272–279
　output of, 273, 280
　pseudocode, 272–275, 279–283
　subscript, 272, 280, 283, 286, 504, 532
　two-dimensional, 279–287
　use in algorithms, Ch. 12–15
arrival, 481
arrival time, 464, 482
ascending order, 34, 305, 311, 344, 347, 364
ASCII, 591
assertions, 88
ASSIGN, 537
assigned GOTO, 538
assignment, 7, 42
　BASIC, 39
　CHARACTER, 622–623
　COMPLEX, 650–651
　DOUBLE PRECISION, 640–641
　FORTRAN/77, 51, 82, 512, 539
　INTEGER, 82
　LOGICAL, 633–634
　PASCAL, 41
　pseudocode, 10, 505
　REAL, 82
average, 274, 282, 348, 363, 365, 370, 377, 387, 389,
　482, 485, 489, 493
average temperature problem, 274–279
Babbage, Charles, 1
back-substitution, 408, 409, 422. *See also* linear
　equations.
backsolve, 408–409
BACKSPACE, 540
backtracking, 200, 208, 227, 485
Balintfy, J.L. 493
Barrodale, I. 173, 193, 419
base conversion, 587–589
BASIC, 37–38, 61
bimodal, 364
binary, 305-309
BINARY, 310
binary operator, 20, 24, 505
binary representation, 587
binary search, 159, 304, 305, 311, 321, 344, 345
birth and death process, 444
bisect, 163–164
BISECT, 165
bisection, 159–166, 225, 238–240, 306, 441
Bjorck, A. 419
block, 40
BLOCK DATA, 540
BN-code, 598
boolean. *See* flags, logical.
Boswell, F.D. 61
bouncing ball problem, 428, 440–443
Braun, M. 462

Brown, A.R. 214
BSOLVE, 410
bubble, 315–318
bubble sort, 315–318, 332
buffer, 610
bugs, 47. *See also* errors.
built-in functions, 67, 70, 133, App. N
bull-hiker pursuit problem, 432–439
Burdick, D.S. 493
byte, 589
BZ-code, 598
call, 99
CALL, 99, 527, 542
Campbell, S.K. 350, 386
carriage control, 610
cashier's problem, 74–81, 205–206
ceiling, 25
Celsius, 8, 11, 15, 31, 38, 54
change of state, 428, 429, 435, 436, 440, 444, 446,
　449, 452, 456, 463, 472, 483
character, 140, 341, 361, App. G
CHARACTER, 542–543, App. G
character strings, 341, App. G
character encoding problem, 625–629
Chu, K. 493
classification
　class frequency, 350, 353, 356
　class ranges, 387
　class width, 351, 353, 359, 387, 469
　classes, 350, 469
　histogram, 353–361
classify, 351–353
CLOSE, 543
CLSIFY, 354
COBOL, 37
cofactor, 255, 257
collating sequence, 591
column-major order, 281, 283
comfortable temperature problem, 17–19, 54–55, 60
comments, 203, 506
　BASIC, 39
　FORTRAN, 41, 523, 544
　pseudocode, 12, 506, 523
　PASCAL, 39
COMMON, 241–242, 544
compilation, 42
compile-time errors, 45, 61, 91, 295
compile-time initialization, 546–547, 621
compiler, 42
COMPLEX, 547, App. J
complex function tabulation problem, 653–655
complex roots, 209
complexity, Ch. 11
　algorithm, 251
　order of, 252
　time, 252–253
　of sorting algorithms, 336
composite number, 82, 94
compound condition, 305
compound sort key, 337–342

compound Simpson's Rule, 188
computed GOTO, 547–548
computer memory, 303
condition, 14, 19, 20, 56, 57, 87, 504, 507, 508, 514.
    See also logical expressions.
condition, 14, 20, 87
congruential methods, 465
constants
    FORTRAN/77, 48, 520, 548
    pseudocode, 9, 503
Conte, S.D. 193
continuation indicator, 41, 68
CONTINUE, 59, 526, 549
continuous function, 126, 177
continuous models, 427
control structure, 26–29, 55, 58–59, 200, 217
control variable, 14, 33, 204
converting 7 temperatures problem, 15–18
correctness, 87, 92, 97, 200
correlation, 376, 378, 389, 466
D-mask, 599
Dahl, O.J. 214
Dahlquist, G. 419
DATA, 549
data
    datafiles, App. L
    in FORTRAN/77, 51–53, 70–74
    in pseudocode, 15–17
data validation problem, 625–626
data structures, 271, 293
Deboor, C. 193
debugging, 47, 91
DEC. *See* VAX.
declarations
    arrays, 275, 285, 286
    functions, 67, 108, App. N
    subroutines, 105
    variables, 42, 50, 68, 104, 106
decomposition
    initial , 200, 203
    iterative , 202, 205, 207
    sequence , 202–203
definite integral, 181
Dekker's algorithm, 173
depth gauge problem, 231–237, 248
derivative, 168, 171, 300
Descartes Rule of Signs, 300
descriptive statistics, 349
design, Ch. 9
    algorithm, Ch. 4, Ch. 9, Ch. 10
    module, 211
    top-down, 199–201
deterministic model, 428
deterministic simulation, 493, Ch. 16
deviation, 365, 377
diagonal, 298, 301, 408, 411, 413
difference curve, 224
difference function, 227, 233
differential equation, 445
Dijkstra, E.W. 214

DIMENSION, 551
dimensioning, 275, 285, 551
direct access input/output, 566–569
Dirksen, P.H. 61
discrete distribution, 479
discrete models, 427
DISECT, 644
disk files, 303
distribution, 469
distribution function, 464
distributions
    discrete, 479
    exponential, 478–479
    frequency, 350, 378
    normal (Gaussian), 372–374, 388, 477, 489
    Poisson, 479, 489
    uniform, 465, 475–477, 482–483
divide by zero, 43, 47, 91, 134, 206, 413
divide and conquer, 199
division of integers, 69
DO
    statement, 59, 525, 551–553
    loop, 59, 277, 525
    implied loop, 273, 277, 286, 576, 578
documentation, 12, 39, 41, 203
DOUBLE PRECISION, 554, App. I
DSIMP, 647
Dyck, V.A. 61
dynamics simulation, 440
E-mask, 599
E-notation, 48, 71
EBCDIC, 591
echo printing, 71, 282
ecology, fundamental equation, 445
efficiency, 156, 161, 169, 212, 234, 251, 254, 259,
    261, 262, 265, 304, 311, 317, 421
    of algorithms, Ch. 11
    bubble sort, 317
    insertion sort, 321
    Quicksort, 333, 346
    searching, 344
    sorting, 346–347
Ehle, B.L. 173, 193, 419
Ehrenberg, A.S.C. 386
elimination, 422
ELSEIF, 54, 554
end module, 99
END, 42, 59, 555
ENDFILE, 555
ENDIF, 54. *See also* IF-THEN and
    IF-THEN-ELSE.
END=, 568
end-of-data, 72, 207, 290
end-of-file, 23, 26, 72, 75
ENTRY, 556
EQ, 57, 87, 522, 580
EQUIVALENCE, 557
EQV, 87, 572
Eratosthenes, 296
errors, 44
    compile time, 44–47

errors (*continued*)
  divide by zero, 413
  estimation in area finding, 187–192
  execution time, 44–47, 295
  in zero-finding algorithms, 161, 164, 226
  messages, 44–47, 91, 226
  off-by-one, 89
  out-of-range, 352
  round-off, 130, 134, 135, 191–192
ERR=, 567, 569
Euclidean Algorithm, 121
exchange, 113, 315, 317, 332, 344
exchange sort, 315
execution phase, 42
execution-time errors, 45, 61, 91, 295, 352
EXPON, 479
exponent, 48, 591
exponent notation, 9, 48
exponential distribution, 478–479
exponentiation, 51
export
  arguments, 99
  list, 101
  parameters, 163, 304, 315, 319, 325, 352
exports, 99, 116
expressions
  arithmetic, 9–10, 51–52, 504, 521–522, 530
  character, 622–623
  logical, 14, 56, 572, 633–634
  relational, 14, 56, 579, 633–634
extended precision. *See* DOUBLE PRECISION.
EXTERNAL, 166, 561
F-mask, 601
factorial, 35, 122
factors, 94, 257
Fahrenheit, 8, 11, 15, 31, 38
Fahrenheit to Celsius temperature conversion
    problem, 8–14
false, 14, 20, 504, 514, 515
FALSE, 57, 85–87
Fibonacci, 31, 120, 216
fields, 71, 597
field count, 613
field width, 597
file structures, 271
flags, 83, 207, 226, 317, 352, 413
FLOAT, 82, 685
floating-point number. *See* REAL.
floor, 25
flowchart, 4, 28, 32, 33, 511, App. B
fmodule, 101, 103, 108, 509
for, 22–23, 59, 273, 305, 317, 507
  simulation of **while–do**, 22, 23
  translation to FORTRAN/77, 59, 525
force, 296, 440
FORMAT, 562, App. F
format codes, 596
format masks, 596
formatted output, App. F
FORTRAN, 41, App. C, App. D

FORTRAN/77
  arrays, 283
  multidimensional arrays, 283
Forsythe, G.E. 173, 193, 244, 420, 466, 467, 493
free body diagram, 440
Freeman, P. 214, 244
frequency, 304
  class, 350, 352
  count, 352
  curve, 359, 364
  distribution, 350, 372
  polygon, 359, 389
  table, 351, 353, 356, 359, 387
frequency classification/histogram problem,
    361–362
frequency table module, 351
frequency tables, 385
friendly number, 95, 220
FUNCTION, 103, 107, 528, 563, 582
functions
  absolute value, 101
  built-in, 67, 70, 133, App. N
  characteristics of, Ch. 6
  continuous, 126
  intrinsic. *See* built-in.
  modules, 101, 240, 508
  plotting of, 137–144
  rational, 134–136
  tabulation of, 127–137
  transcendental, 132–134
  zero of, Ch. 7
function tabulation problems, 127–137
fundamental equation of ecology, 445
G-mask, 602
gas station problems, 482–493
gauss, 415
GAUSS, 416
Gaussian distribution, 372, 477
Gaussian elimination, 411, 413, 422
  linear equations, 406–419
  module, 415
  subroutine, 416
  pivoting strategy, 413–414
  row operations, 413
  use of, 417–419
GCD, 95, 121, 215, 299
GE, 57, 87, 522, 580
general simulation model, 474
geometric mean, 364
get, 7, 15, 40, 41, 272, 506, 513
GOTO
  assigned, 538
  computed, 547
  simple, 54, 59, 525, 564
Graham, J.W. 61
graphs
  construction of, 137–144
gravity, 440, 441, 460, 461
greatest common divisor, 95, 121, 215, 299
greedy fox problem, 449–455

Gregorian calendar, 93
group counts, 613
group factor, 613
grouped data, 350
growth rate, 444, 446, 449, 462
GT, 57, 87, 522, 580
H-code, 603
harmonic mean, 364
hexadecimal, 588–590
HISTGM, 360
histogram, 353, 355, 359, 387, 389, 469
Hoare, C.A.R. 214, 321
Hollerith, Herman, 2
Honeywell, 49, 190, 467, 588
Hopcroft, J.E. 266, 293
Horner's Rule, 131, 300
Horowitz, E. 293
Hughes, J.K. 214
Hull, C.H. 385, 386
Huskey, H.D. 4
Huskey, V.R. 4
hyperbola, 125
hypotenuse, 221, 264
I-mask, 604
I.M.S.L. 244
IBM, 43–53, 70, 130, 367, 588, 589
IF
    arithmetic, 531
    block, 54, 524, 541
    logical, 573
IF-THEN, 58, 524, 541
if–then, 21, 508, 515
IF-THEN-ELSE, 58, 524, 541
if–then–else, 7, 18, 20, 54, 508, 515
IFIX, 82, 685
implementation efficiency, 412
IMPLICIT, 565
implied loop, 273, 277, 281, 286, 576, 578
import arguments, 99, 102
import parameter, 101, 163, 288, 315, 319, 325, 352,
    356
imports, 98
imports, 99, 116
indentation, 40
Indianapolis 500 problem, 23–25
inductive statistics, 349
infinite loops, 14, 89
initial approximations, 226
initial decomposition, 202, 203, 207, 215, 225, 233,
    238, 274, 281, 307, 312, 319, 325, 352, 429,
    435, 441, 456, 474, 482
initial market shares problem, 417–419
initial state, 428, 435, 440, 483
initialization
    compile-time, 546–547
inner product, 296
input
    pseudocode, 17, 273, 281, 506
    FORTRAN/77, 41, 52, 277, 285–286, 523–524,
    566–569, 577–579

input techniques, 70
INQUIRE, 569
insert, 319–322
insertion sort, 319–322
int, 25
INTEGER, 50, 68, 275, 570
integers
    constant, 48–49
    conversion from real, 69, 76, 82
    division of, 52, 69
    formats, App. F
    INTEGER type, 50, 68, App. D
    variables, 50, 68, App. D
integral
    application of, 181
    approximation. *See* area finding.
    definition of, 181–182
integration algorithms
    error estimation, 187–188, 191–192
    round-off error, 191–192
    Simpsons's Rule, 188–192
    trapezoidal rule, 184–188
intellectually manageable, 199
interactive computing, 38, 70, 77–81
interchange, 113, 317
interpreter, 39
INTRINSIC, 572
investment simulation problem, 429–432, 471–474
invoking modules, 102
iteration, 12, 74, 239
iterative decomposition, 202, 204, 205, 207, 212,
    214, 215, 233
Jacquard loom, 2
Julian date, 150
Kalbfleisch, J.G. 386
Kelly, J.R. 214
keys
    searching, 304–310
    sorting, 339–340
keyword, 42
Klecka, W.R. 385, 386
Knuth, D.E. 493
L-mask, 605
language standards, 48
languages
    BASIC, 37–38
    COBOL, 37
    FORTRAN, 41
    machine, 41, 42
    PASCAL, 37, 39–41
    PL/1, 37
    programming, 4, 38–42
    SPSS, 385
Laplace's equation, 423
Latin square, 301
Lawson, J.D. 61
LCM, 95, 215
LE, 57, 87, 522, 580
least common multiple, 95, 215
least squares approximation, 381–384

Leavenworth, K. 244
Leibniz, Gottfried Wilhelm, 1
line number, 43
linear, 304–305
linear equations, 35, 118, 384, 391, 397
   Gaussian elimination, 411–419
   solving triangular systems of, 407–409
linear insertion sort. *See* insertion sort.
linear regression, 376, 380–385
linear search, 304–305, 311, 320, 321, 343, 345
local variables, 100
LOGICAL, 85–87, 574, App. H
logical
   56–57, 85–87, 574, App. H
   expressions, 14, 56, 572, 633
   flag. 83. *See also* flags.
   operators, 14, 57, 87, 504, 632
   LOGICAL type, 85–87, 574, 631
   IF, 573
   variables, 83, 85–87, 574, 631
loop control mechanism, 204
loop termination, 89
looping mechanism, 75
loops
   control mechanism, 75, 205
   infinite, 14, 89
   structure, 286
   termination, 73, 75, 82, 240
LT, 57, 87, 522, 580
machine language, 41–42
machine readable, 43
magnetic tape, 303
main module, 98
Malcolm, M.A. 173, 193, 244, 420, 493
manual verification, 45, 87
mathematical models, 125, 271, Ch. 16, Ch. 17
matmpy, 403
MATMPY, 403
matrix, 301, 391–406
   as a transformation, 392, 400
   matrix-vector multiplication, 392–400
   multiplication of, 400–406
   singularity of, 413
matvec, 393–394
MATVEC, 395
maximum, 34, 126, 145, 148, 214, 289, 350, 385,
   482, 485
McGown, C.L. 214
McPhee, K.I. 61
mean, 363
   arithmetic, 363, 368–372, 385–388, 478, 489
   geometric, 364
   harmonic, 364
mean deviation, 365
mean value theorem, 182
measures of central tendency, 363
measures of dispersion, 365
median, 364, 365, 385, 387
Meyers, G.J. 244
Michton, J.I. 214

microFORTRAN, 61
microBASIC, 61
minimum, 34, 126, 145, 214, 289, 350, 385
minimum/maximum problem, 288
minmax, 288–290
MINMAX, 291
mixed congruential method, 465, 467
mixing data types, 69–70, 82
MOD, 69, 684
mode, 363–365, 385
models
   deterministic, Ch. 16
   mathematical. *See* mathematical models.
   probabilistic, Ch. 17
   simulation, Ch. 16–17
modularity, Ch. 5
modules, Ch. 5
   advantages of, 97, 117
   argument lists, 99–103, 286–293
   arrays in, 286–293
   calling of, 99, 102
   decomposition into, 98, 211
   design considerations for, 97–98, 211
   imports and exports, 99–103, 286
   interfaces of, 97, 99, 163, 212, 225, 245, 288, 315,
      352, 356, 387, 393
   parameters of, 99, 102, 286, 288
   pseudocode, 99, 102. *See also* modules
      (pseudocode).
   recursion, 325
   testing of, 114
modules (pseudocode)
   aprime, 104, 212
   backsolve, 408–409
   binary, 305–310, 345
   bisect, 163–164
   bubble, 315–318
   classify, 351–353, 356
   gauss, 411–415
   histogram, 356–359
   insert, 319–322
   linear, 304–307
   matmpy, 401–403
   matvec, 393–394
   minmax, 288–290, 313, 350
   partition, 331–334
   primetest, 100–101
   quicksort, 321–329
   select, 311–315
   sort2, 113, 317
   sort3, 114
   tankvol, 240–241
Moler, C.B. 173, 193, 244, 420, 493
money changing problem, 26–27, 67–73, 88
Monte Carlo, 463
multidimensional arrays, 279–283, 532–537
multimodal, 365
multiple precision arithmetic, 300. *See also* DOUBLE
   PRECISION.
multiple-pump gas station problem, 489–494

National Hockey League. *See* NHL.
Naylor, T.H. 493
NE, 57, 87, 522, 580
negative correlation, 376, 377
NEQV, 87, 572
NEWTON, 172
Newton's Method, 64, 171–175, 300
NHL
    goalie statistics, 348
    player data, 370
    player scoring statistics problem, 371–372
    player standings problem, 342
    player statistics, 347
    team statistics, 347
nicotine measurements, 279
Nie, N.H. 385, 386
Noble, B. 420
NORMAL, 478
normal, 372, 388
normal distribution, 372, 374, 388, 477, 489
normalized data, 299
not, 20, 57, 505
NOT, 57, 87, 522, 572
number of comparisons. *See* efficiency.
numbers
    composite, 82, 94
    Fibonacci, 31, 120, 216
    floating point. *See* real.
    friendly, 95, 220
    integer. *See* integers.
    line, 43
    perfect, 95, 214
    prime, 82, 94, 203
    pseudo random, 464
    real. *See* real.
    statement, 43
numerical integration, 223, 233, 249, 373, 388
octal representation, 588, 590
one-dimensional array, 271, 272, 283
OPEN, 574
operators
    arithmetic, 10, 51, 530
    binary, 20, 24, 505, 530
    logical, 14, 19, 56–57, 87, 504, 632
    priority, 20, 51, 57, 87, 504, 530
    relational, 14, 56–57, 505, 579, 633
    unary, 20, 24, 505, 530
optimizations, 259, 265
or, 20, 57, 505
OR, 57, 87, 522, 572
order of complexity, 252–254
output
    arrays, 273, 285–286
    formatting, 53, 71, App. F
    headings, 16, 67, 71, 286
    messages, 10–11, 18
    pseudocode, 10, 273, 280, 506
    FORTRAN/77, 42, 53, 71, 273, 285–286, 524, 566–569, 576
    techniques, 70

overflow, 134
P-mask, 606
panels, 189, 227, 234
parabola, 227, 249
PARAMETER, 575
parameters. *See* modules.
parentheses, 10, 87
partition, 322
PARTIT, 335–336
partition, 331–334
PASCAL, 37, 39–41
Pascal, Blaise, 1
PAUSE, 576
perfect number, 95, 214
pivot, 322, 331, 413
pivoting strategy, 323, 345
planimeters, 182
PLOT, 140, 660–664
plotting, 137–144, App. K
plotting a cubic polynomial problem, 138–140
plotting a line and polynomial problem, 141–142
PL/1, 37
pointers, 307
points on the Cartesian plane problem, 635–638
POISSN, 480
Poisson distribution, 479, 489
polynomials, Ch. 6, 300, 384
    evaluation by Horner's rule, 131
    plotting, 137–144
    tabulation, 125–131
population dynamics, 444–455
population growth problem, 444–446
population growth with competition problem, 446–455
portable, 130
prey-predator, 446–455
prime factors, 220
prime number, 82, 94, 203, 211, 253, 296, 343
prime number classification problem, 82–86, 100–110, 203–205, 259–261
prime pairs problem, 110–112
PRIMET, 107
primetest, 100–101
PRINT, 53, 71, 277, 285, 524, 576, App. F
printer listing, 43
priority. *See* operators, priority.
probabilistic investment problem, 471–474
probabilistic simulation, Ch. 17
problem analysis, 3, 203, 206, 211, 231, 238
problem definition, 3
problem solving, 2–4
problems
    area between two curves, 223–231
    area finding, Ch. 8
    average temperature, 274–279
    bouncing ball, 440–443
    bull-hiker pursuit, 432–439
    cashier's, 74–81, 205–206
    character encoding, 625–629
    comfortable temperature, 17–19, 54–55, 60
    complex function tabulation, 653–655

problems (*continued*)
  data validation, 625–626
  depth gauge, 231–237
  frequency classification/histogram, 361–362
  function tabulation, 127–137
  greedy fox, 449–455
  Indianapolis 500, 23–25
  initial market shares, 417–419
  investment simulation, 429–432, 471–474
  linear equations, 406–419
  matrix multiplication, 401–406
  minimum/maximum, 288–293
  money changing, 26–27, 67–73
  multiple-pump gas station, 489–494
  NHL player scoring statistics, 371–372
  NHL player standings, 339–342
  plotting functions, 138–144
  points on a Cartesian plane, 635–638
  population growth, 444
  population growth with competition, 445–448
  prime number classification, 82–86, 100–110,
    203–205, 259–261
  prime pairs, 110–112
  probabilistic investment, 471–474
  Pythagorean triples, 261–264
  quadratic equation, 206–210
  rabbit/fox, 446–451
  rainfall analysis, 281–289
  scatter plot, 382–384
  searching, 304–311
  single die, 472, 474–477
  single-pump gas station, 482–488
  sorting, 311–342
  temperature conversion, 8, 11–13, 15–16, 22, 38
  three bakery, 397–400
  three number ordering, 112–116
  twin primes, 211–213
  two bakery, 392–397
  volume gauge, 237–243
  zero finding, Ch. 7
PROGRAM, 577
program
  correctness, 91
  debugging, 47, 91
  libraries, 243
  readability, 39, 111
  style, 48, 71
  testing, 91–92
programming languages, 48. *See also* languages.
  definition, 4
prompting, 71
pseudo-random numbers, 464
pseudocode, 4, 7, 503
  arrays. *See* arrays.
  assignments. *See* assignment.
  basic actions, 4
  built-in functions, 26
  comments, 12, 506
  constants, 9, 503
  data list, 17
  expressions, 504

pseudocode (*continued*)
  modules, 98, 508. *See also* modules.
  operators. *See* operators.
  translation to FORTRAN/77, 41–42, App. C
punched card, 1, 42
pursuit problems, 432–439
put, 7, 10, 40, 41, 273, 507, 513
Pythagorean Identity, 221
Pythagorean relation, 434
Pythagorean triples problem, 261–264
quadratic equation, 5, 151, 206–210, 252
quadratic equation problem, 206–210
queues, 481–494
QUICK, 330
Quicksort, 321–336
quicksort, 321–329
quotient, 25, 67, 69, 76
quotient, 25
rabbit/fox problem, 446–455
Rabinowitz, P. 173
rainfall analysis problem, 281, 289
Ralston, A. 173
RAND Corporation, 464, 493
RANDOM, 467
random numbers
  generator, 465–467
  subprogram for, 467
  tables of, 464
range of data, 350, 365, 385
rational function tabulation, 134–137
rational functions, 134
raw data, 350, 373
READ, 52, 277, 285, 523, 577, App. F
REAL, 50, 68, 579
real
  constants, 48–49
  conversion with integers, 82
  formats, App. F
  REAL type, 48, 579
  variables, 48
rectangle rule, 182–184
recursion, 325, 346
refinement
  step-wise, Ch. 9. *See also* step-wise refinement.
regression, 376, 380–385
regula falsi, 167
relational operators, 14, 56, 504
reliability, 92
rem, 25
repetition, 12, 22–23, 58–59
reproducibility, 464, 468
residuals, 381
RETURN, 105, 108, 580
REWIND, 580
Roberts, F.D.K. 173, 193, 419
roots. *See* zero finding.
Rosen, S. 4
round-off error, 130, 135, 190, 380. *See also* errors.
row-major order, 280–282
S-code, 607

Sahni, S. 293
sample, 349
Sampson, W.A. 214
scaling, 356
scatter plot, 376–385
searching, Ch. 13
    binary, 305–309
    efficiency, 305, 311
    key, 304
    linear, 304–305
secant method, 172. *See also* zero finding.
seed, 465, 489, 493
select, 311–315
selection sort, 344. *See also* sorting.
semantic rules, 48
sentinel. *See* flags.
sequence decomposition, 202, 203, 214, 225, 274,
        281, 352
series, 63, 120, 121, 146
server, 481
service time, 464, 482, 484, 489
SETPLT, 139, 657, 659
Shannon, R.E. 493
Sieve of Eratosthenes, 296
significant digits, 91
SIMP, 189
Simpson's Rule, 188–192, 227, 234
simulation, 427, Ch. 16–17
    deterministic, Ch. 16
    models, 427
    of dynamics, 440–443
    of investments, 429–432, 471–474
    of populations, 444–455
    of pursuits, 432–439
    parameters, 429, 432, 435, 446, 471, 472, 475,
        483, 489
    probabilistic, Ch. 17
simulation algorithm
    general structure, 428
single die problem, 472, 474–477
single species population, 444–446
single-pump gas station problem, 482–488
singular matrix, 413, 417
Smith, J.A. 61
smodule, 99–100, 509
solution of equations, 428
Sorenson, P.G. 293
sort2, 113
sort3, 114
sorting, 34, 119, 303, Ch. 13
    applications, 336–342
    bubble sort, 315–318
    comparison of methods, 336–337
    compound sort keys, 338–342
    efficiency, 315, 318, 322, 336
    exchange sort, 315–318
    external, 303
    field, 337
    insertion sort, 319–322
    internal, 303
    pointer sort, 337–338

sorting (*continued*)
    Quicksort, 321–336
    records, 337
    selection sort, 311–315
space requirements, 251
Spiegal, M.R. 386
SPSS, 385
sqrt, 25
Squires, E. 5
standard deviation, 366–370, 373–375, 385, 478, 489
standard FORTRAN, 37, 41, 529
standard statistical measures, 385
standardized normal distribution, 374
state variables, 427–430, 433, 436, 440, 446, 456,
        483–485
statement number, 41, 59
statement ordering, 583
statistics, Ch. 14
STATS1, 369
STATS2, 370
Steffensen's method, 178
step-wise refinement, 199, 254, 261
    backtracking, 208
    correctness, 200
    expansion, 200
    iterative decomposition. *See* iterative
        decomposition.
    labeling scheme, 201
    modularity in, 210
    sequence decomposition. *See* sequence
        decomposition.
stochastic model, 463, 477
stop, 7, 11, 42, 506, 512
STOP, 42, 59, 523, 583
STOPNT, 139, 658, 660
storage efficiency, 251
storage media, 303
storage techniques, 271
strings. *See* character strings.
student data, 389
Sturge's formula, 351
style, 12, 40, 54, 58
style output, 71
subproblems, 75, 199
subprograms (FORTRAN/77)
    APRIME, 109
    BINARY, 310
    BISECT, 165, 227, 242
    BSOLVE, 410
    CLSIFY, 354
    DISECT, 644
    DSIMP, 647
    EXPON, 479
    GAUSS, 416
    HISTGM, 360
    MATMPY, 403
    MATVEC, 395
    MINMAX, 292
    NEWTON, 172
    NORMAL, 478
    PARTIT, 335–336

subprograms (FORTRAN/77) (*continued*)
PLOT, 140, 660–664
POISSN, 480
PRIMET, 107
PTRBUB, 340
QUICK, 330
RANDOM, 467
SECANT, 170
SETPLT, 139, 657, 659
SIMP, 189, 227, 236, 242
SORT2, 115
SORT3, 115
STATS1, 369
STATS2, 370
STOPNT, 139–140, 658, 660
SUBROUTINE, 103, 104, 527, 584
subroutine modules, 98–101
subroutines, 98–101
subscript range, 275, 285
subscripts, 272, 275, 280
symbolic constants. *See* PARAMETER.
T-code, 607
tabulating a complex function problem, 652
tank, 241
tankvol, 240
temperature conversion, 8, 11–13, 15–16, 22, 38
temperature conversion table problem, 11
temporary variables, 113
testing, 97, 114, 118, 169, 290, 295, 344, 452
text editing, 42
textbook data, 378, 383, 385
three bakery problem, 397–400
three number ordering problem, 112–116
time complexity, 254
time requirements, 251
tolerance, 158–166, 169–172, 226, 231
top-down design, 199. *See also* step-wise refinement.
tracing, 91
transcendental function tabulation problem, 132–134
transcendental functions, 132
transformation, 392, 400, 404
translation, 4, 38
Trapezoidal Rule, 184–188
Tremblay, J.P. 293
triangular systems of equations, 407–409
true, 14, 20, 504, 514, 515
TRUE, 57, 85–87
twin primes, 96, 119, 211, 215
twin primes problem, 211–213
two bakery problem, 392–397
two-dimensional arrays, 279–287

types
CHARACTER, 341, 371, 542–543, App. G
COMPLEX, 547, App. J
DOUBLE PRECISION, 554, App. I
INTEGER, 50, 68, 275, 570
LOGICAL, 85–87, 574, App. H
REAL, 50, 68, 579
Ullman, J.D. 266, 293
unary operators, 20, 24, 505
unconditional branch. *See* GOTO.
undefined, 304
undefined variables, 9, 47, 91, 92, 503
ungrouped data, 350
uniform distribution, 465, 482
uniform variate, 475, 477, 483
Van Tassel, D. 266
variables
declaration of, 40, 67, 68
in pseudocode, 9, 503
in FORTRAN/77, 48, 520–521, 585–586
state. *See* simulation.
undefined. *See* undefined variables.
variance, 368, 380, 385, 387
VAX, 43–53, 70, 130
vector, 296, 391
velocity, 296, 440, 441
volume gauge problem, 237–243
Weide, B. 266
Welch, J.W. 61
well-defined, 97
while–do, 7, 12, 14, 272, 317, 507, 514
simulation of, 22–23, 58–59
Wilkes, M.V. 5
Wirth, N. 37, 214, 293
worst case complexity, 253, 259
WRITE, 586, App. F
X-code, 608
z-score, 375–378, 389
zero finding, Ch. 7
automatic search, 155
bisection, 159–166
graphical, 152–154
Newton's Method, 171–173
regula-falsi, 167
secant, 168–171
systematic refinement, 155–159
zeros of functions, 126, 127, 142, 145, 151, 223, 224
/-code, 608
'-code, 609
:-code, 609